Working and Poor

Working and Poor

How Economic and Policy Changes
Are Affecting Low-Wage Workers

Rebecca M. Blank, Sheldon H. Danziger, and Robert F. Schoeni, Editors

The National Poverty Center Series on Poverty and Public Policy

Russell Sage Foundation ◇ New York

Library of Congress Cataloging-in-Publication Data

Blank, Rebecca M.
   Working and poor : how economic and policy changes are affecting low-wage workers / Rebecca Blank, Sheldon Danziger, and Robert Schoeni.
       p. cm.
   Includes bibliographical references and index.
   ISBN-10: 0-87154-075-4
   ISBN-13: 978-0-87154-075-1
   1. Unskilled labor—Supply and demand—United States.   2. Labor market—United States.   3. Unemployment—United States.   4. Poverty—United States.   5. Temporary employment—United States.   I. Danziger, Sheldon.   II. Schoeni, Robert.   III. Title.
HD5724.B543   2006
331.7'980973—dc22   2006018385

Text design by Suzanne Nichols.

RUSSELL SAGE FOUNDATION
112 East 64th Street, New York, New York 10021
10 9 8 7 6 5 4 3 2 1

Contents

Contributors

REBECCA M. BLANK is codirector of the National Poverty Center and Joan and Sanford Weill Dean of Public Policy at the Gerald R. Ford School of Public Policy, Henry Carter Adams Collegiate Professor of Public Policy, and professor of economics at the University of Michigan.

SHELDON H. DANZIGER is Henry J. Meyer Distinguished University Professor of Public Policy and codirector of the National Poverty Center at the Gerald R. Ford School of Public Policy at the University of Michigan.

ROBERT F. SCHOENI is research associate professor at the Institute for Social Research and associate professor of economics and public policy at the University of Michigan.

DAVID AUTOR is associate professor of economics at the Massachusetts Institute of Technology and a faculty research fellow at the National Bureau of Economic Research.

GEORGE J. BORJAS is Robert W. Scrivner Professor of Economics and Social Policy at the John F. Kennedy School of Government at Harvard University and research associate at the National Bureau of Economic Research.

MARIA CANCIAN is professor of public affairs and social work, and director of the Institute for Research on Poverty at the University of Wisconsin–Madison.

DAVID CARD is professor of economics at the University of California at Berkeley and research associate at the National Bureau of Economic Research.

KERWIN KOFI CHARLES is a professor in the Harris School of Public Policy at the University of Chicago.

JOHN DINARDO is professor of economics and professor in the Gerald R. Ford School of Public Policy at the University of Michigan and research associate at the National Bureau of Economic Research.

ROBERT W. FAIRLIE is associate professor of economics at the University of California at Santa Cruz.

ERIC FRENCH is a senior economist in the Research Department at the Federal Reserve Bank of Chicago.

STEVEN J. HAIDER is associate professor of economics at Michigan State University.

ROBERT E. HALL is the Robert and Carole McNeil Professor of Economics and Senior Fellow at the Hoover Institution at Stanford University and director of the Research Program on Economic Fluctuations and Growth of the National Bureau of Economic Research.

KEVIN A. HASSETT is resident scholar and director of economic policy studies at the American Enterprise Institute for Public Policy Research.

SUSAN HOUSEMAN is senior economist at the W. E. Upjohn Institute for Employment Research.

PHILLIP B. LEVINE is William R. Kenan Jr. Professor in the Department of Economics at Wellesley College.

HELEN LEVY is research assistant professor at the Institute for Social Research and assistant research scientist at the School of Public Health at the University of Michigan.

REBECCA A. LONDON is associate director of research at the John W. Gardner Center for Youth and Their Communities at Stanford University.

BHASHKAR MAZUMDER is a senior economist at the Federal Reserve Bank of Chicago and executive director of the Chicago Census Research Data Center.

KATHLEEN MCGARRY is professor of economics at the University of California, Los Angeles, and research associate at the National Bureau of Economic Research.

THERESE J. MCGUIRE is professor and chair of the Management and Strategy Department in the Kellogg School of Management and faculty fellow at the Institute for Policy Research at Northwestern University.

DAVID F. MERRIMAN is professor of economics at Loyola University, Chicago.

DANIEL R. MEYER is professor and director of the School of Social Work at the University of Wisconsin–Madison.

ANNE MOORE is a Ph.D. candidate in the Department of Economics at the University of California at Berkeley.

HEIDI SHIERHOLZ is assistant professor of economics at the University of Toronto.

MELVIN STEPHENS JR. is Raymond John Wean Foundation Career Development Associate Professor of Economics at the H. John Heinz III School of Public Policy and Management at Carnegie Mellon University.

CHRISTOPHER TABER is professor in the Department of Economics and faculty fellow at the Institute for Policy Research at Northwestern University.

Introduction

Work and Poverty During the Past Quarter-Century

Rebecca M. Blank, Sheldon H. Danziger, and Robert F. Schoeni

Fluctuations in the economy have a strong effect on the extent of poverty and well-being among low-income families.[1] Reduced economic demand during recessions can significantly increase the unemployment rate, as was the case in the early 1980s. A sustained economic expansion can substantially reduce the unemployment rate and contribute to increased experience on the job and in wage growth, as occurred in the late 1990s. The employment of less-skilled workers has tended to fluctuate more across the business cycle than the employment of other workers.

Longer-run developments in the economy, such as labor-saving technological changes, the globalization of the economy, declines in the degree of unionization, and the changing skill mix of the labor force, also affect the economic well-being of less-skilled workers independent of the business cycle. For example, over the last quarter-century, the wage rates of high school graduates and high school dropouts have fallen dramatically relative to those of college graduates. And wage growth for all workers has been slow in this quarter-century relative to the experience of the quarter-century following the end of World War II.

Improvements in employment opportunities and wage rates are important to low-income families because less-skilled workers have more cyclical employment opportunities and their income fluctuates more with the economic cycle (Borjas, this volume). In 2004, 61 percent of families with income below the poverty line contained at least one worker; 28 percent contained at least one full-time, year-round worker (U.S. Department of Commerce 2005b).

Several chapters in this volume analyze the ways in which the business cycle and long-run changes in the economic environment since the late 1970s have affected the employment and earnings opportunities for less-skilled workers. Other chapters focus on the demographic composition and material well-being of low-income families; still others evaluate the effectiveness of federal and state social policies and the federal and state tax systems and how they interact with the economy over the long run and over the course of the business cycle. One key question connects the chapters in this volume: how have economic changes and the economic cycle affected the well-being of less-skilled workers and low-income families over the last quarter-century?

An examination of changes in employment, earnings, and income among less-skilled workers and low-income families reveals that other trends have been as important as—and in some cases more important than—those directly related to economic conditions. Thus, a second question arises: how have long-term changes in the demographic composition of the population, changes in work participation patterns and family behaviors, and changes in policy and program rules interacted with economic changes to affect the well-being of less-skilled workers and low-income families?

The volume documents the variety of changes that affected less-skilled workers and their families from 1979 through 2004. This quarter-century is important for several reasons. First, macroeconomic changes over this period were striking, including strong expansions in the late 1980s and 1990s. The economy experienced the longest historical period of sustained economic growth from the end of the recession in March 1991 through the start of the next recession in March 2001; economic growth was particularly strong in the last half of the 1990s.

Three recessions also occurred in the past quarter-century, with one long period of economic contraction in the early 1980s (actually two back-to-back recessions, January to July 1980 and July 1981 to November 1982) and two shorter and milder recessions in the early 1990s (July 1990 to March 1991) and the early 2000s (March to November 2001), both of which were followed by several years of sluggish growth. These cyclical changes provide an opportunity for several of the contributors to evaluate how economic cycles affected the labor market outcomes of less-skilled workers.

Second, other important economic changes over the past twenty-five years have interacted with the macroeconomy. Most notable is the dramatic increase in wage and family income inequality that was particularly pronounced in the 1980s. Closely related are the substantial growth in world trade and the widespread adoption of new labor-saving computer and information technologies by both businesses and consumers. At the same time, high rates of immigration (especially among Hispanics), declines in the percentage of persons living in married-couple families, and dramatic increases in women's labor market involvement have changed the face of the American workforce. These trends have had particularly large effects on the employment and earnings of less-skilled workers.

Third, important policy changes over the past quarter-century have interacted with economic, demographic, and behavioral changes. Most notable are the welfare reforms of the mid-1990s, which ended the entitlement to cash assistance and required low-skilled single mothers to seek and maintain employment. Over the entire period the inflation-adjusted minimum wage has fallen and risen and then fallen again. Other programs that assist low-income working families have provided increasing assistance to a greater percentage of poor families. These include several large expansions in the Earned Income Tax Credit (EITC), which provides subsidies through the tax system to workers in low-income families with children. Other changes include increased provision of public medical insurance, especially for children in low-income families; increased efforts to establish paternity for nonmarital births and to collect child support from absent fathers; and increased public spending to subsidize the child care expenses of low-income families. These changes have fostered the development of a "work support" public assistance system in which more assistance is given to low-income families with workers and less to those without a wage earner (Blank 2002; Ellwood 2000).

The effect on poor families of these numerous policy changes is particularly salient for the period during and after the 2001 recession, the first since many of the work-focused policies were implemented in the 1990s. The chapters in this volume seek to understand how poor families have fared now that they have less access to cash assistance than in earlier periods and how well policies focused on supporting low-wage workers (rather than providing cash assistance) have performed in a slower-growth economy.

WHO ARE THE WORKING POOR?

The initial chapters in this volume focus primarily on less-skilled workers; later chapters also focus on poor or low-income families, regardless of whether the household head is a worker. In all of these chapters, the authors are looking at persons (or household heads) between the ages of eighteen and fifty-four; this volume does not examine issues related to retirement or aging. In this introduction, we provide background by reviewing the economic trends for eighteen- to fifty-four-year-olds, and we also look at those whose family income is below 200 percent of the official poverty line, one measure of the low-income population.

Established in 1964 and updated each year only to account for inflation (Citro and Michael 1995), the federal poverty line is a somewhat arbitrary concept. It provides an inflation-constant benchmark against which to compare family incomes over time.

Table I.1 provides a snapshot of eighteen- to fifty-four-year-old individuals whose family income was below 200 percent of the poverty line for the years 1979, 1989, 1999, and 2003. In 2003, 200 percent of the poverty line was $37,320 for a married couple with two children, $29,648 for a single parent with two children, and $19,146 for a single nonelderly individual. The last row indicates that, in each of the years shown, about one-quarter of adults in this age group lived in families with incomes below these levels. Thus, this table can also be interpreted as showing the characteristics of those persons in the bottom quarter of the individual income distribution. In 2003 about 41 percent of prime-age adults in low-income families lived in married-couple families; another 20 percent were in single-parent families; about 38 percent were single persons without children. Among these poor and near-poor individuals, 63.8 percent worked at a median hourly wage of $7.29; their median family income was $14,706.

TABLE I.1 / Characteristics of Individuals Age Eighteen to Fifty-Four with Family
Income Less Than 200 Percent of the U.S. Poverty Line, 1979 to 2003

	1979	1989	1999	2003
Share employed (at any point in previous year)	0.682	0.684	0.668	0.638
Median hourly wage	$6.38	$6.25	$6.83	$7.29
Median family income	$14,499	$14,093	$14,681	$14,706
Family composition (share)				
Married couple	0.569	0.493	0.428	0.414
Single parent	0.186	0.201	0.216	0.201
Other single male	0.111	0.149	0.161	0.177
Other single female	0.134	0.157	0.195	0.208
Race-ethnicity (share)				
Black non-Hispanic	0.206	0.205	0.201	0.187
Hispanic	0.101	0.154	0.224	0.256
White and other non-Hispanic	0.693	0.641	0.575	0.556
Education level (share)				
Less than high school	0.397	0.334	0.295	0.280
High school degree	0.344	0.385	0.374	0.370
Some college	0.186	0.200	0.247	0.253
BA degree or more	0.073	0.082	0.084	0.097
Share of individuals aged 18 to 54 who live in families with income below 200 percent of U.S. poverty line	0.25	0.26	0.26	0.26

Source: Authors' tabulations from Current Population Survey's March Supplement data.
Note: Wage and income numbers inflation-adjusted to 2000 dollars.

Table I.1 documents the changing demographic composition of low-income
persons. Since 1979, these adults have become less likely to live in married-
couple families (a decline from 57 to 41 percent) and are much more likely to be
single males (11 to 18 percent) or single females (13 to 21 percent). Extensive
immigration over this quarter-century has increased the share of low-income
adults who are Hispanic from 10 to 26 percent. Low-income individuals have
become somewhat more educated over time, mirroring overall trends in the population—the share with less than a high school degree declined from 40 to 28
percent, while the share with more than a high school degree rose from 26 to 35
percent.

The share who are employed declined slightly, from 68.2 percent in 1979 to
63.8 percent in 2003. Among low-income workers, the median hourly wage increased over the past twenty-five years by only 14 percent (from $6.38 in 1979 to
$7.29 in 2003), and their median family income was virtually constant ($14,500
in 1979; $14,700 in 2003).

Some prime-age individuals who live in families with incomes below 200 percent of the poverty line are not the focus of much policy concern because they may have higher earnings opportunities but choose not to pursue them. Examples include students who are temporarily poor and working part-time while attending college or graduate school or individuals who have voluntarily chosen to work few hours. Many of the individuals included in table I.1, however, live in families with children, and many are involuntarily unemployed or are working at low wage rates. Their low incomes are largely due to economic constraints that limit their employment opportunities and/or wage rates.

Because the chapters in this volume focus on those with limited long-term earnings opportunities, they analyze the prospects, not of individuals who happen to be poor in a given year, but of less-skilled individuals—those with the most constrained labor market options. Throughout the volume, "less-skilled" is defined as those who are high school dropouts or who have only a high school degree.

TRENDS IN THE ECONOMY, 1979 TO 2004

This volume discusses both long-run economic trends over the past quarter-century and cyclical changes associated with recessions and recoveries. Figure I.1 shows two key economic indicators for each year between 1979 and 2004: real (that is, inflation-adjusted) gross domestic product (GDP) per capita, a commonly used indicator of the overall wealth of the economy; and the annual unemployment rate for all persons over sixteen years of age. The shaded areas indicate the four recessionary periods during this quarter-century.

Real GDP per capita rose by 59 percent between 1979 and 2004. While the average annual rate of growth in GDP per capita was 1.7 percent between 1979 and 1995, it was 2.9 percent between 1995 and 2000. This latter period was particularly prosperous: the rapid GDP growth was accompanied by the first sustained real wage increases for less-skilled workers since the early 1970s.

The unemployment rate is an indicator of cyclical changes: it rises during recessions and falls during economic recoveries. Unemployment rates are a particularly important labor market indicator for less-skilled workers. The most sustained rise in unemployment occurred between 1979 and 1982, when the rate rose from 5.8 to 9.7 percent. While the recessions of 1990 to 1991 and of 2001 were milder (and shorter), economic growth also did not rebound as quickly; the years immediately following these recessions (1992 to 1994 and 2002 to 2004) were therefore periods of slow expansion. The unemployment rate was below 5 percent in only five of the twenty-six years shown in the figure—each year from 1997 through 2001.

Figure I.1 tells a generally positive story about the economy over the quarter-century. After the recession of the early 1980s, economic growth was substantial. The two recessions were relatively mild, and unemployment rates for the 1995 to 2004 decade were always below 6 percent, in contrast to 1980 to 1986, a period when the rate each year exceeded 7 percent.

FIGURE I.1 / Per Capita Gross Domestic Product and Unemployment Rates

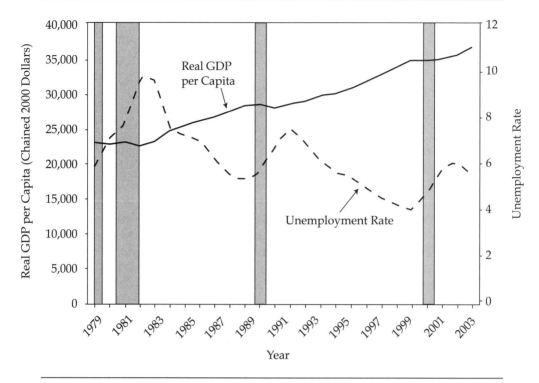

Source: U.S. Department of Commerce, Bureau of Economic Analysis (www.bea.gov), U.S. Department of Labor, Bureau of Labor Statistics (www.bls.gov), and National Bureau of Economic Research, "Business Cycle Expansions and Contractions" (http://www.nber.org/cycles.html/). *Note:* Shaded portions indicate periods of recession.

Unfortunately, less-skilled workers have not gained as much from these overall economic trends as we might expect. With lower unemployment rates since the mid-1990s, jobs have been more available for those who actively search for work. However, wages among less-skilled workers declined for much of the past quarter-century, rising only during the rapid expansion of the late 1990s.

Figure I.2 displays real (inflation-adjusted) hourly wage rates from 1979 to 2004 among male and female workers between the ages of eighteen and fifty-four. The solid line shows median wages among those without a high school degree, the dashed line shows median wages among those with only a high school degree, and the dotted line shows wages among those with more than a high school degree. (These three educational categories are used by all the contributors to this volume.)

Figure I.2 shows the much-discussed rise in between-group wage inequality of the past twenty-five years, with wages rising throughout the period for the

FIGURE I.2 / Median Real Hourly Wages for Workers Age Eighteen to Fifty-Four

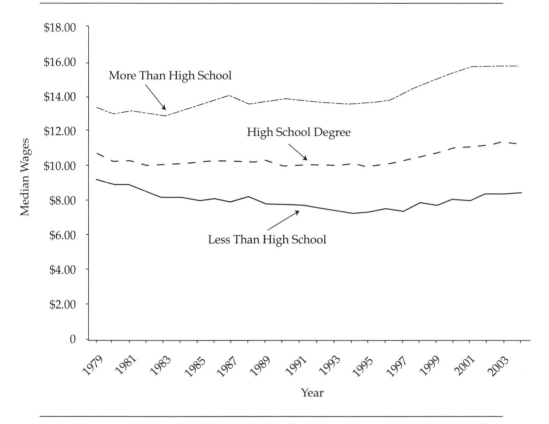

Source: Authors' tabulations from the Current Population Survey outgoing rotation group data.

more-skilled groups. Among workers who are high school dropouts, wages fell in most years between 1979 and 1994, rose from 1995 to 2000, and edged up only slowly after 2000. In 2004 real wages were 9 percent below their 1979 levels for dropouts ($8.35 versus $9.14) and 5 percent higher ($11.18 versus $10.62) for workers who graduated from high school. Among workers with more than a high school degree, wages were about 19 percent higher at the end of the quarter-century ($15.77 versus $13.28).

These trends in median wage rates by educational attainment hide substantial heterogeneity within the low-wage and low-skilled workforce. As chapter 1 discusses in detail, wages among less-skilled women have risen somewhat, even while wages have been falling among less-skilled men. Wage declines among African American men have been greater than among white men, primarily because a larger percentage of African Americans are in the low-skilled category. For instance, among high school dropouts, the wages of black and white men have fallen at about the same rate. Wages of Hispanic dropouts have fallen faster

FIGURE I.3 / Real Hourly Wages at Various Points of the Wage Distribution

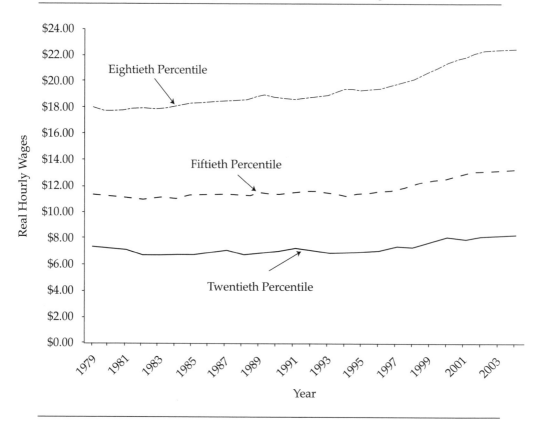

Source: Authors' tabulations from the Current Population Survey outgoing rotation group data.

than among other racial-ethnic groups within this skill category, largely owing to low-skilled immigration over the time period.

The change in the share of workers in different skill groups over time has also affected wage rates. In particular, if high school dropouts become increasingly less skilled as their population share declines, this might lead to declining wages. Figure I.3 avoids this problem by focusing on wage rates at a specific percentile in the distribution rather than on wages by skill level. The three lines show real wages at the twentieth percentile (that is, one-fifth of all workers in each year earn less than this wage level), at the median, and at the eightieth percentile (four-fifths of all workers in each year earn less than this wage). Wages fell at the twentieth percentile of workers from 1979 to 1984, remained flat until the mid-1990s, then rose through 2004. In 2004 wages at the twentieth percentile were at $8.11, about 11 percent above the $7.32 1979 level. This suggests that selectivity is partly responsible for declining wages among the less-skilled. Wages at the median rose by 18 percent and by 26 percent at the eightieth per-

FIGURE I.4 / Employment-to-Population Ratios by Skill Level and Gender, 1979 to 2004

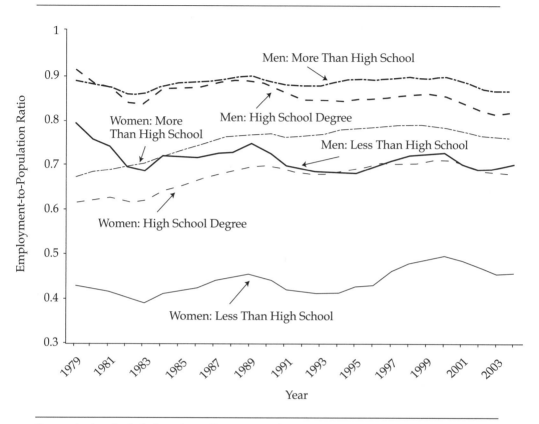

Source: Authors' tabulations from Current Population Survey outgoing rotation group data, 1979 to 2004. Based on all noninstitutionalized civilian adults age eighteen to fifty-four.

centile, showing widening wage inequality across the distribution of all prime-age workers.

Wages are one factor for evaluating the well-being of less-skilled workers, but employment rates are also important. Figure I.4 plots the employment-to-population ratios among men and women between the ages of eighteen and fifty-four by education level. Employment-to-population ratios declined among high school dropouts between 1979 and 1984 and then were largely flat; this ratio declined more steadily among high school graduates. Overall, the employment-to-population ratio among the less-skilled population (including both of these groups) declined slowly over time, from 86 percent in 1979 to 78 percent in 2004. This decline would be even larger if our data included incarcerated men, whose population share has been increasing but who are excluded from the data used here. Among men with more than a high school degree, there was little change:

88 percent worked in 1979, and 86 percent worked in 2004. Employment choices are affected by wages, of course, and declining real wages among less-educated men have contributed to their declining employment rates (Juhn 1992).

Among women, employment-to-population ratios have risen for each education category. Among all women, this ratio increased from 59 to 70 percent between 1979 and 2004. In 1979 the ratio for all women was twenty-eight points less than that for all men (59 versus 87 percent); by 2004 the gender gap in employment had fallen to twelve points (70 versus 82 percent). Employment among less-skilled women rose particularly fast in the mid-1990s, at about the time that EITC expansions and work-oriented welfare reform were being implemented (Blank 2002).

The net effect of these long-run trends in wages and employment is a decline in earnings among all less-skilled men, who have seen both their wages and their employment-to-population shares decline somewhat. This occurred most rapidly in the 1979 to 1984 period; there was some recovery in the expansion of the 1990s, but the long-term trend in earnings for less-skilled men has been downward. Among women, earnings have not declined, and among some groups—especially single mothers—they have risen substantially. This increase is attributable primarily to substantially increased employment. Female wages have declined only slightly among dropouts and have risen among high school graduates.

Overall economic well-being is determined not just by the labor market income of individuals but also by the ways in which individuals come together in families and share their resources and by income sources other than earnings. Figure I.5 shows the evolution of poverty rates for all persons over the past twenty-five years. The figure shows the percentage of the population below the official government poverty rate (the solid line), and the percentage below 200 percent of the official government poverty rate (the dotted line), our measure of those who are poor and near-poor. An alternative poverty definition based on a broader income definition (the dashed line) was calculated by the Census Bureau for the 1980 to 2003 period. Rather than comparing a family's cash income with the official poverty line, this alternative measures disposable income, taking account of sources that are not included in the official measure, such as taxes paid, tax credits received, and noncash public assistance transfers.

All three measures show that the poverty rate is affected by the macroeconomy. During recessions, poverty increases; as the economy expands, poverty falls. The strong economic expansion of the 1990s brought poverty rates to their lowest levels in many years. In 2004, 12.7 percent of all persons were poor, and 31.2 percent were below twice the poverty line. The quarter-century trend is disappointing, however, given the GDP growth shown in figure I.1. Official poverty rates in 2004 were slightly above their 1979 levels, and at about the same level as they were in the late 1960s. The alternative definition shows a pattern similar to the official definition: the rate was 10.1 percent in 1980, reached a maximum of 12.7 percent after the recession of the early 1980s, and was 9.7 percent in 2003.

In short, substantial growth in aggregate income over this quarter-century did

FIGURE I.5 / Official and Alternative Poverty Measures, 1979 to 2004

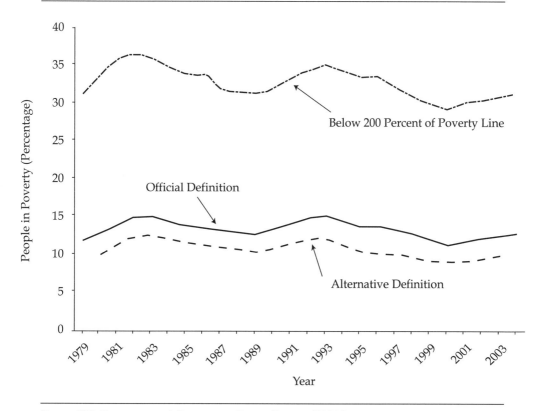

Source: U.S. Department of Commerce, Census Bureau (2005a).
Notes: The official definition is the share of persons whose cash income is below the official federal poverty line. The alternative definition uses disposable income rather than cash income and takes account of taxes and noncash transfers (from U.S. Bureau of the Census 2005a, table B-1, definition 14).

not produce equivalent income increases among those at the bottom of the income distribution—in part because declining real wages among less-educated workers prevented them from fully sharing in the rising prosperity. But the failure of poverty to fall is also due to changes in the demographic composition of the population, changes in living arrangements, and declines in receipts of cash transfers, such as welfare and unemployment compensation. The increases in both the (disproportionately low-income) immigrant population and in single-parent families have kept poverty rates higher than they would have been in the absence of these changes. Increasing work by women in married-couple families has kept poverty rates from rising even further.

In analyzing the factors behind the changing well-being of families at the bottom of the income distribution—particularly less-skilled workers and poor and near-poor persons who rely on labor market income—the chapters in this volume address a number of questions.

WHAT IS CHANGING IN THE LABOR MARKET FOR LOW-SKILLED WORKERS, AND WHY?

The volume opens with two chapters that describe changes in the low-skilled labor market. The first focuses on differences between men and women, the second on differences between the native-born and immigrants from varying race and ethnic groups. In their investigation of differences in the trends in employment and wages among less-skilled men and women, Rebecca Blank and Heidi Shierholz show in chapter 1 that less-skilled women have improved their labor market position—their labor force participation has increased and their wages have remained flat or risen—while less-skilled men have worked less and earned less.

Less-skilled women have lost ground, however, relative to more-skilled women. Blank and Shierholz examine how changes in levels of experience and education, as well as changes in marriage and fertility patterns, affect these results. They conclude that less-skilled women have found an "intermediate" place in the labor market. These women have higher real wages and higher employment rates today than a quarter-century ago, but their wage rates have fallen relative to those of women with higher education. The labor force participation and wages of all women are less affected today by marital status or family composition than they were a quarter-century ago. These changes have reduced the gender gap in wages for workers at all skill levels.

In chapter 2, George Borjas analyzes differences between immigrant and native workers classified by race and ethnicity and documents dramatic changes in the racial-ethnic composition of less-skilled workers, emphasizing growth in the representation of Hispanic workers in this population. Declining relative wages for less-skilled Hispanics hide a great deal of variation among Hispanic workers and largely reflect a substantial increase in the share of specific Hispanic subpopulations. At least half of the native-immigrant wage gap can be explained by differences in observable characteristics. Wage trends among less-skilled minority workers are particularly sensitive to business cycle fluctuations and are also influenced by continuing immigration. Although past studies have found limited effects of immigration on wages, Borjas argues that a superior approach shows bigger effects, and he estimates that the large immigration between 1980 and 2000 reduced the wages of the typical high school dropout by 11 percent in the short run.

HOW DO ECONOMIC TRENDS AFFECT LESS-SKILLED WORKERS?

Chapters 3 through 5 focus on how economic changes over the past twenty-five years have affected the less-skilled workforce. In chapter 3, Robert Hall uses a macroeconomic framework to describe aggregate economic trends and economic cycles in the past quarter-century. He compares the economic expansions of the 1980s and the 1990s and shows that these were very different decades in the way that aggregate growth affected less-skilled workers. The 1990s expansion was particularly strong: extensive capital deepening led to wage increases that exceeded the increase in the price of goods and services. The demand for workers at all skill levels grew in the 1990s, unlike the 1980s, when demand increases were concentrated among the more-skilled. The recession of 2001 was an unusual one that had an equal effect on less- and more-skilled workers, largely owing to the industries that were most affected by this economic downturn. Hall speculates that rises in productivity in the early 2000s may suggest further wage growth in the near future.

A primary reason often given for declining wages among less-skilled workers is skill-biased technological change—that is, changes due to computerization or other changes in employment practices that displace less-skilled workers and advantage more-skilled workers. In chapter 4, David Card and John DiNardo critically review the literature that tries to link technological change and widening wage inequality. They cite a variety of inconsistencies in this literature. For instance, there appears to be little link between the speed with which new technologies were adopted across countries and the growth in wage inequality within those countries. They conclude that technological changes probably account for a portion of the growing disadvantage of less-skilled workers within the U.S. wage distribution, but that the evidence on the causal nature of this link remains tenuous. They call for a more multicausal model of the forces driving increased inequality and argue that we cannot assume that the ongoing adoption of new technologies will necessarily disadvantage less-skilled workers.

A key question for low-skilled workers is the extent to which their wages rise with labor market experience. In chapter 5, Eric French, Bhashkar Mazumder, and Christopher Taber explore how wage growth varies across the economic cycle. Experience accumulation leads to growing wages, but the return to experience can vary significantly with the economic cycle. Wage growth is procyclical, that is, wages grow faster when unemployment rates are low. The procyclical effect appears to be quite similar across different skill groups and for men and women.

Experience accumulation is much more important for wage growth among new labor market entrants at all levels of education than are improvements in the job match resulting from a job change. These results suggest that it does not matter a great deal whether workers enter the labor market in good or bad economic times, so long as they persist in employment and acquire additional experience.

HOW DO MACROECONOMIC CHANGES INFLUENCE WELL-BEING MEASURES BEYOND INCOME?

While substantial research attention has been devoted to measuring the impact of macroeconomic changes on wages and employment, there are many other aspects of family well-being that might be affected by fluctuations in the economy. Chapters 6 through 8 examine the relationships between macroeconomic changes and consumption, resource sharing, and living arrangements.

In chapter 6, Kerwin Charles and Melvin Stephens investigate the extent to which economic cycles result in cyclical changes in consumption. Although figure I.5 shows that poverty rates fluctuate with the business cycle, standard economic theory assumes that families smooth expenditures over time to deal with short-run changes in income; by implication, then, personal consumption should show less dramatic short-run changes over the business cycle. Charles and Stephens find that consumption in middle- and higher-income families varies less than income with the business cycle, as the theory predicts, but that consumption in lower-income families does decline in recessions. Low-income families are less able to smooth their consumption during downturns, probably because they have few liquid assets; their reductions in consumption are driven largely by cuts in spending on entertainment and personal care.

Labor market earnings and government transfers are the most important sources of income for many families, but transfers of cash and other resources from relatives and friends can also affect measured poverty. In chapter 7, Steven Haider and Kathleen McGarry examine some of the ways in which family members help each other, especially in low-income families. Using the limited data that are available to examine financial transfers, they conclude that private transfers of cash are important for many less-educated individuals and that family financial assistance has become more common over the last twenty-five years. More importantly, coresidence and the potential of income sharing within a household appear to have increased substantially. More research and better-quality data on the ways in which family members and friends help each other, whether through money, shared housing, or time spent providing assistance, will be important to furthering our understanding of how families weather financial shocks.

During the past two decades there has been a large rise in the share of children living in single-parent families. In chapter 8, Rebecca London and Robert Fairlie investigate the impact of the economy and other factors on the composition of the households in which children live, using both cross-sectional and longitudinal analyses to examine changes in living arrangements for children. The data do not tell a simple story. The cross-sectional analyses indicate that recessions increase the odds of children living in single-parent households, perhaps because job loss or economic hardship leads their parents to split up. At the same time, the longitudinal analyses indicate that poor economic conditions cause some families to co-reside. For example, children in single-parent families move into alternative arrangements such as parental cohabitation or living with other relatives.

HOW DO POLICY CHANGES INTERACT WITH THE ECONOMY AND ECONOMIC WELL-BEING?

Chapters 9 through 14 focus on specific policy areas and discuss the interactions between policy design and policy effects and the economic environment. Chapters 9 and 10 focus on tax policies, while the remaining chapters focus on how low-income workers and families are affected by temporary agency employment, the child support system, unemployment insurance, and health insurance.

In chapter 9, Kevin Hassett and Anne Moore examine changes in federal, state, and local tax policies over the past twenty-five years and find that total direct taxes paid by low-income families with children have declined significantly, particularly since the late 1990s. Low-income adults without children have not benefited from these changes; their tax burdens have been constant over the last quarter-century. Federal income taxes for families with children have declined because of the refundable child tax credit (instituted in 2001), several expansions of the Earned Income Tax Credit, and lower marginal tax rates. At the same time, state sales tax collections have increased and payroll taxes and property taxes have stayed relatively constant. For example, for a family of three with a single parent earning $14,000 in 2004, the tax system provided a net subsidy to work of $2,613 because the EITC exceeded the sum of all taxes paid.

Hassett and Moore also find that the ratio of taxes other than income taxes (state sales taxes, local property taxes) to total taxes for low-income families has increased sharply over time. For a married couple with two children and an annual income of about $27,000, the share of non-income taxes rose from 23 percent of taxes paid in 1979 to 65 percent in 2004.

In chapter 10, Therese McGuire and David Merriman analyze how states have coped with recessions and the variations in their expenditures on public assistance programs over the cycle. Comparing state revenue and expenditure changes during the 2001 recession with the downturns of the early 1990s and the early 1980s, they pay particular attention to whether states cut social spending during the economic slowdown of the early 2000s. They find that state spending on cash welfare is countercyclical—it increases when unemployment rises—and that this effect was stronger in the most recent slowdown than earlier. Hence, states do not seem to have reduced their willingness to fund welfare programs since the 1996 federal welfare reform. Of course, spending on cash welfare has declined dramatically, so there was less to be gained from cuts in benefits by 2001 than in earlier recessions. Medicaid spending for low-income families has increased dramatically as a share of the state budget, and it also increased in the economic slowdown of the early 2000s. In short, there is no evidence that states used the recent recession as an excuse to cut public assistance programs.

In chapter 11, David Autor and Susan Houseman evaluate the increased use of temporary agencies to place welfare recipients in jobs. This practice has sparked debate about whether temporary jobs help the poor transition into stable employment and out of poverty or whether they place workers in dead-end jobs and provide little work experience that is of any value. Autor and Houseman studied welfare recipients in a city that assigned them to various service providers based only on their residential location. Because some providers relied heavily on temporary agencies and others rarely used them, this "natural experiment" allowed the authors to ask whether temporary agency placements helped participants achieve earnings sufficient to leave welfare and escape poverty, relative to the outcomes for those placed in nontemporary (direct-hire) jobs or those who received no job placement. They find that placing a participant in either a temporary or direct-hire job improved her chances of leaving welfare and escaping poverty in the short term. Over a one- or two-year time horizon, however, a participant with a temporary job placement was no better off—and was possibly worse off—than would have been the case with no such job placement.

As the proportion of children living with both parents has fallen and as public support for sole-parent families has been reduced, child support has become a more important income source for single-parent families. In chapter 12, Maria Cancian and Daniel Meyer describe the child support system and consider the relationship between economic conditions, child support, and poverty. Child support is an unreliable income source for poor single-mother families, in part because the children's fathers typically have limited economic resources. For example, in 2001 only about half of poor single mothers had a child support order. However, child support can be an important part of poor single mothers' income packages; among those who received any support in a year, the average amount received was $3,200. Nonpoor custodial mothers are more likely to have an order and to receive higher payments, but many of them also receive either no child support or less than they are owed.

Enhanced child support enforcement and other policy changes have contributed to increased collections, but the system faces difficult trade-offs. Because most child support orders are fixed at the time they are issued, the obligation is more financially burdensome for nonresident parents who experience earnings losses and less burdensome for those whose earnings increase. Stable child support orders and payments could provide insurance against cyclical variations in the resident parent's earnings; however, this would lead to fluctuations in the income of the nonresident parent.

In chapter 13, Phillip Levine describes how the unemployment insurance (UI) program raises taxes from employers and provides benefits to unemployed workers. Because low-wage jobs tend to provide less stable employment than other jobs, the availability of UI for less-skilled workers who are unemployed is quite important for their economic well-being. However, because UI is an insurance system, benefits are not paid out according to need but according to the loss incurred. Eligibility rules make it more difficult for those with the greatest need to qualify for benefits. Workers cannot have left a job voluntarily, and they must have had a sufficient work history prior to the job loss—typically measured as minimum earnings requirements—to qualify for benefits. Lower-wage workers and those who have difficulty maintaining steady employment because of lack of skills have a tougher time satisfying these requirements. Over the last quarter-century, UI receipt has fallen among high school dropouts relative to more-educated workers. In 2003 only 20 percent of unemployed high school dropouts and 35 percent of unemployed workers with more education received benefits.

Health insurance has become an increasingly important—and expensive—commodity. It accounts for a substantial portion of total compensation costs for employers, and government expenditures on health care continue to grow. Yet, during the record-setting expansion of the economy in the 1990s, when wages for most workers rose, health insurance coverage actually fell. In chapter 14, Helen Levy documents the facts and examines competing hypotheses about why coverage has changed.

Levy finds that employment and earnings gains contributed to increased private coverage for both men and women, and for both low-skilled and high-skilled workers. For low-skilled men and high-skilled women, who do not rely heavily on public coverage, employment and earnings gains led to modest declines in public coverage that were much smaller than the increases in private coverage. But for groups who rely heavily on public insurance, most notably low-skilled women, the reduction in public coverage was even larger than the gains in private coverage. While improvement in employment outcomes for low-skilled women during this period can account for a substantial share of the loss in public coverage, it cannot explain why health insurance coverage declined. In speculating as to why this was the case, Levy considers welfare reform as one possible factor.

WHAT IS TO BE DONE ABOUT THE CHALLENGES FACING LESS-SKILLED WORKERS AND THEIR FAMILIES?

Four primary lessons emerge from these chapters that lead us to identify several policy options that we think provide the most promise for improving the well-being of less-skilled workers and low-income families.

First, a growing economy is a prerequisite for improvement in the well-being of low-wage workers and low-income families. Economic growth in the late 1990s, which led to higher wage rates and increased employment, was particularly beneficial for less-skilled workers. When the unemployment rate fell below 5 percent, large numbers of less-skilled individuals entered the labor market and accumulated valuable work experience, particularly single mothers who entered the labor force in response to welfare reform and expansions in the EITC.

At the same time, because recessions (at least since 1982) have been relatively mild, business cycle fluctuations have had less impact than long-term labor market changes on the economic well-being of less-skilled workers. These changes, including labor-saving technological changes, declining unionization rates, and globalization, have reduced the relative demand for less-skilled workers and contributed to falling real wages among less-skilled men and to lower relative wages among less-skilled women. Declining real wages have contributed to declining labor force participation among less-skilled men as well. Because workers at the bottom of the distribution have not shared proportionally in the economic growth of the last quarter-century, earnings inequality has increased among both male and female workers.

Economic changes affect other aspects of well-being as well. Relative to nonpoor families, during recessions poor families are at higher risk of reduced consumption, disrupted living arrangements, lowered child support income, limited access to employer-provided health insurance, and reduced access to unemployment insurance.

Second, the past decade has been a period of unusual economic patterns, making it difficult to forecast both economic prospects for the near future and economic challenges for the working poor. We believe it is unlikely that we will see a repeat of the unusually robust and sustained economic growth of the 1990s, but we would probably have made this pessimistic forecast in the early 1990s as well. Certainly, such a period of sustained growth would be ideal for raising wages and increasing job advancement options for less-skilled workers. The eight-month recession of 2001 was also unusual in that it had a smaller negative impact on less-skilled workers than other recent recessions. In particular, the effects on less-skilled women were mild, largely because the industries most affected by the economic slowdown (especially manufacturing) were not significant employers of low-skilled women.

Although the decline in wages among less-skilled men was reversed for several years in the late 1990s and their wages have been stagnant since, it is difficult to forecast how economic changes will affect their wage rates over the next several years. We are still uncertain about the importance of various factors in causing these prior economic shifts against the less-skilled. Yet it seems safe to say that even a decade hence the absolute wage levels of less-skilled male workers are not likely to be much higher than they were in the early 1970s. And there is little reason to think that very much of the dramatic increase in earnings inequality of the last quarter-century will be reversed.

It is also difficult to predict how government policies might change in the future and how participation in current government transfer programs will evolve. The fact that cash welfare caseloads did not increase substantially during the recent recession indicates that the reforms of the 1990s fundamentally altered the relationship between macroeconomic growth and welfare participation. At the same time, the recession was modest; a more severe downturn might lead to a more substantial rise in the cash welfare rolls.

Third, the evolution of federal and state social welfare programs and tax policies over the past quarter-century has had significant effects on the well-being of less-skilled workers and low-income families. Federal income tax policies have been a particularly important source of income for families with children given the growth in the refundable EITC. However, there were relative increases in state and local taxes on low-wage workers, and most childless low-wage workers pay the same percentage of their income in taxes now as they did in the late 1970s.

Welfare policy reforms and a host of related changes in public assistance programs have pushed more less-skilled women into work and raised the importance of earnings to their overall economic well-being. Medicaid and the State Child Health Insurance Program (SCHIP) cover an increasing share of poor people, particularly low-income children, but a smaller share of unemployed workers receive UI.

Immigration policy has allowed large increases in legal immigration over the past twenty-five years; most observers believe that illegal immigration has also increased. As a result, there has been very rapid growth in the share of all less-skilled workers who are immigrants. Undocumented immigrants are likely to avoid interaction with the government and therefore rarely participate in programs designed to alleviate poverty. The access of legal immigrants to social assistance programs has also been constrained over the past decade. As a result, government policies and programs may have become less effective in dealing with poverty because an increasing share of the poor do not receive assistance from these programs.

Fourth, as these chapters demonstrate, attitudes and learned behavior have probably been as important as economic and policy changes in their effects on everything from debt burdens to marital and fertility choices to income-sharing across families. For instance, an individual's willingness to participate in the public assistance system is clearly shaped by more than economic opportunity, as indicated by the ongoing (and in some cases rising) nonparticipation in public assistance among some eligible families. Seemingly large rates of nonparticipation among potentially eligible persons in cash welfare and unemployment insurance are interpreted quite differently by different observers. Some perceive a failure in program implementation: some low-income individuals who would gain economically from receiving public assistance are not being served. Others believe, however, that nonparticipants want to be independent of government assistance as they look for their next job or that they prefer to rely on assistance from family or partners.

The issues raised in this volume lead naturally to a discussion of policy options. The welfare reform debates of the mid-1990s reflected the public's preference for shifting resources from the nonworking to the working poor. The expansions in the EITC and increased state and federal spending on child care for the working poor also reflected this concern. Yet there remain a very large number of working-poor and near-poor families who receive no assistance or too little assistance. We believe that helping these families work more, even while also supplementing their earnings, is good public policy. No benefit accrues to either worker productivity or child development when unstable jobs and unemployment lead to eviction, family disruption, or loss of health insurance.

The specific policy proposals discussed in various chapters in this volume include the role of minimum wages and changes in child support benefits, unemployment insurance, tax policies, and health insurance. Our own priorities for enhancing the economic well-being of low-income workers include:

- A minimum wage that would be increased and indexed to inflation to maintain its real value over time. We tentatively suggest that the minimum wage be somewhere around 40 percent of the average wage, which was its historical level over much of the quarter-century following World War II.

- A further expansion of the State Child Health Insurance Program to cover not only low-income children but also their parents.

- An expanded Earned Income Tax Credit for low-income, childless adults whose tax burdens have not been reduced over the past quarter-century, as well as a higher EITC schedule for families headed by married couples to reduce marriage disincentives within the EITC.
- Changes in the child support system that would provide some minimum public benefit for low-income custodial parents who have child support orders but who receive little or no child support.
- Changes in the structure of the unemployment insurance program so that a larger percentage of low-income workers, including part-time workers, would be eligible for benefits.

Public discussions of poverty and government assistance in the United States have always emphasized the value of work and the importance of personal responsibility. Millions of low-income workers take these values seriously and try hard to find and keep jobs that will raise the economic well-being of their families. Yet the economic changes discussed in this volume demonstrate that many workers cannot rely on their earnings alone if they are to achieve economic self-sufficiency. These policies would encourage low-income workers to work more, while at the same time supplementing their earnings and raising the economic well-being of their families.

NOTE

1. Thanks are due to James Sallee for excellent data assistance and to two anonymous referees for comments on a previous version of this introduction. This project was funded by grants from the Office of the Assistant Secretary for Planning and Evaluation in the U.S. Department of Health and Human Services, and the Charles Stewart Mott Foundation.

REFERENCES

Blank, Rebecca M. 2002.. "Evaluating Welfare Reform in the United States." *Journal of Economic Literature* 40(4): 1105–66.

Citro, Constance F., and Robert T. Michael, eds. 1995. *Measuring Poverty: A New Approach.* Washington, D.C.: National Academy Press.

Ellwood, David T. 2000. "Antipoverty Policy for Families in the Next Century: From Welfare to Work—and Worries." *Journal of Economic Perspectives* 14(1): 187–98.

Juhn, Chinhui. 1992. "The Decline in Male Labor Market Participation: The Role of Declining Market Opportunities." *Quarterly Journal of Economics* 107(1): 79–121.

U.S. Department of Commerce. Bureau of the Census. 2005a. *Alternative Poverty Estimates in the United States* 2003. P60–227. Washington: U.S. Bureau of the Census.

———. 2005b. *Annual Demographic Survey: March Supplement.* Washington: U.S. Bureau of the Census. Available at: http://pubdb3.census.gov/macro/032005/pov/new06_000.htm.

Part I

What Is Changing in the Labor Market for Low-Skilled Workers, and Why?

Chapter 1

Exploring Gender Differences in Employment and Wage Trends Among Less-Skilled Workers

Rebecca M. Blank and Heidi Shierholz

A s many of the chapters in this volume emphasize, labor force participation and real wage rates among less-skilled men have fallen since the late 1970s.[1] A substantial literature has investigated the declining returns to less-skilled jobs and the growing wage inequality between more- and less-skilled workers in the U.S. labor market (Autor and Katz 1999; Autor, Katz, and Kearney 2004). Most of this literature, however, has focused on men. The research on the effects of welfare reform has recognized growing labor force participation among less-skilled women, but rarely does it directly compare the very different trends among less-skilled men and women. In contrast to their male counterparts, real wages among less-skilled women have not fallen, and their labor force participation has in fact risen.

This chapter investigates trends in labor market outcomes for both male and female workers of different skill levels over the past twenty-five years. We look at gender differences by skill level in labor force participation and wages, exploring why less-skilled women have done better than less-skilled men in recent decades, even while losing ground relative to more-skilled women. This chapter also provides background information for the rest of this volume, showing the comparative trends among more- and less-skilled workers, by gender, since the late 1970s.

The differential trends in labor market outcomes by skill and gender raise a number of questions. To what extent do these trends reflect differences in the human capital characteristics that men and women bring into the labor market? For instance, as we shall see, full-time work experience has risen among women and fallen among men, and education levels have risen faster among women than among men. Alternatively, these trends may reflect differences in the jobs held by men and women or changes in how men's and women's skills are valued. For instance, if discrimination against women has fallen in the past three decades, women may have gained ground in the labor market relative to men.

There is a large literature on trends in male-female wage differences among all workers (Altonji and Blank 1999; Bayard et al. 2003; Blau and Kahn, forthcoming), but it gives little attention to gender differences by skill level (for an exception, see Blau and Kahn 1997 or Blau 1998). Furthermore, there is very little literature on differential trends in labor force participation between women and men. Two recent papers address this topic (Blau and Kahn 2005; Mulligan and Rubinstein 2005), but again, they do not look at differences across skill groups. This chapter explores these gender- and skill-related trends in a relatively simple way, identifying areas where more statistically and theoretically complex analyses might add to our ability to better understand these changes.

TRENDS IN LABOR MARKET OUTCOMES BY SKILL LEVEL AND GENDER

In this section, we examine long-term trends in four key labor market outcomes: trends in labor force participation rates, unemployment rates, wage rates, and the overall responsiveness of labor market outcomes to economic cycles.[2] In each case, we present these trends over the past twenty-five years by gender and skill level. Throughout this chapter, we focus on men and women between the ages of eighteen and fifty-four. We define "less-skilled" as those whose highest educational credential is a high school degree or less, and we compare them to the "more-skilled," defined as those who have post–high school training. When discussing the less-skilled, we frequently distinguish between those with a high school degree and high school dropouts. We analyze data from 1979 through 2004. The data in this section are based on tabulations from the Current Population Survey outgoing rotation groups (ORG) data, which provide large annual samples.[3]

Labor Force Participation

Figure 1.1 plots labor force participation rates, the share of all adults who are either working or looking for work, for men (darker lines) and women (lighter lines) by skill level. Labor force participation among those with less than a high school degree is shown by the solid lines, among those with a high school degree by the long dashed lines, and among those with more than a high school degree by the short dashed lines.

The most visible feature of figure 1.1 is the narrowing over time of the male and female labor force participation gap. This trend is strongest among more-skilled men and women (the lines with short dashes), where the gender difference in labor market participation narrows from twenty-one percentage points

FIGURE 1.1 / Labor Force Participation by Skill Level and Gender, 1979 to 2004

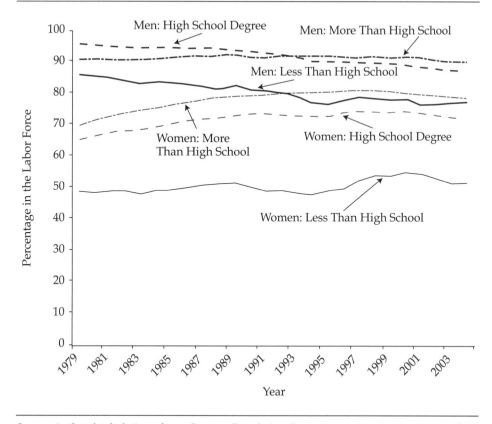

Source: Authors' tabulations from Current Population Survey outgoing rotation group data, 1979 to 2004.
Note: Based on all noninstitutionalized civilian adults age eighteen to fifty-four.

in 1979 (91 percent for men and 70 percent for women) to eleven points in 2004 (90 percent for men and 79 percent for women). The declining gap is almost entirely due to substantial increases in labor market involvement among more-skilled women. Among less-skilled groups, the gender gap is larger and narrows at a somewhat slower rate. The gap fell from thirty-seven points in 1979 to twenty-four points in 2004 among high school dropouts, primarily because male labor force involvement fell and female labor force involvement rose.

We do not show the results separately by race or ethnicity, but the equivalent graph using data only among Hispanics shows very similar trends. Among African Americans, labor force participation has converged more within each skill group than it has among whites. Among those with less than a high school degree, the decline in black male labor force participation is especially dramatic:

FIGURE 1.2 / Unemployment Rates by Skill Level and Gender, 1979 to 2004

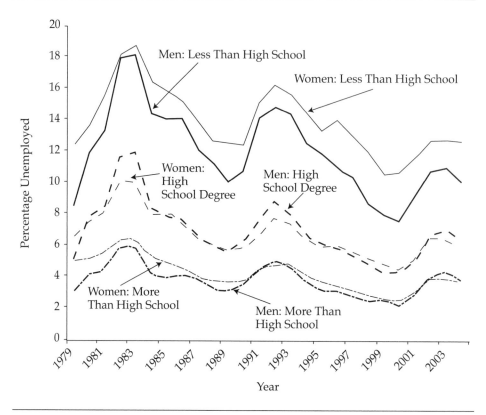

Source: Authors' tabulations from Current Population Survey outgoing rotation group data, 1979 to 2004.
Note: Based on all noninstitutionalized civilian labor force participants age eighteen to fifty-four.

there is only a five-point gap between black men and women who were high school dropouts in 2004.

Unemployment Rates

The unemployment rate shows the share of all labor market participants who are seeking jobs but have not found one. Figure 1.2 plots comparisons in unemployment rates between men and women by skill level. Equivalent graphs that look only at blacks or Hispanics show very similar results.

Among the more-skilled (short dashed lines), women's unemployment rates have converged with men's. In 1979 these rates were 5.0 percent and 3.2 percent for women and men, respectively; by 2004, they were 3.8 percent and 3.9 percent. Among those with a high school degree (long dashed lines), women were below or at the male unemployment rate throughout the period. Among high school dropouts (solid lines), women's unemployment rates have been consistently higher than men's, and they are somewhat less cyclical. There was a slight widening in the gender unemployment gap among this least-skilled group during the 1990s. We suspect that this reflects the increased labor force participation among less-skilled women in the mid-1990s; with welfare reform, many low-skilled women with limited experience began to search for work.

Hourly Wages

Figure 1.3 plots median real hourly wages over time within each gender and skill group.[4] In 1979 hourly wages among all female skill groups were lower than hourly wages among all male skill groups; one consequence was that women with more than a high school education earned less than male high school dropouts ($10.62 versus $10.94). More-skilled men and women both showed substantial increases in earnings between 1979 and 2004, with slight convergence over time. Male earnings among the more-skilled increased by 12 percent, from $15.94 to $17.83, while equivalent women's earnings increased by 31 percent, from $10.62 to $13.91. The increase in wages among these more highly skilled workers was particularly dramatic since this group has been a rapidly growing share of the population over time.[5]

Less-skilled men—both high school graduates and high school dropouts—showed real wage declines from 1979 through the mid-1990s. Their wages rose after 1995 but remained below where they were at the start of the period. In 2004 male high school dropouts earned $9.27 per week, 15 percent below the 1979 level; high school graduates earned $12.80, 6 percent less than in 1979. In comparison, less-skilled women showed rising wages over this period: high school dropouts earned $7.08 in 1979 and $7.42 in 2004; high school graduates earned $8.50 in 1979 and $9.95 in 2004. The combination of declines in male wages and increases in female wages leads to a narrowing of gender wage differences among the less-skilled. The female-male ratio in 2004 was 0.80 for high school dropouts, 0.78 for high school graduates, and 0.78 for those with more education.

Equivalent graphs of hourly wages among only black or Hispanic workers show remarkably similar trends for less-skilled workers. Among the more-skilled, the black and Hispanic male-female gender wage gap has narrowed much more than among whites, largely because more-skilled men's wages in these groups have not risen as consistently as they have among more-skilled white males. Rising wages among more-skilled black and Hispanic women have thus helped them catch up faster.

Changing relative wages between men and women have been linked with the trends toward rising inequality across skill groups. Francine Blau and Lawrence Kahn (1997) argue that widening wage inequality pulled less-skilled women's

FIGURE 1.3 / Real Median Hourly Wage Rates by Skill Level and Gender, 1979 to 2004

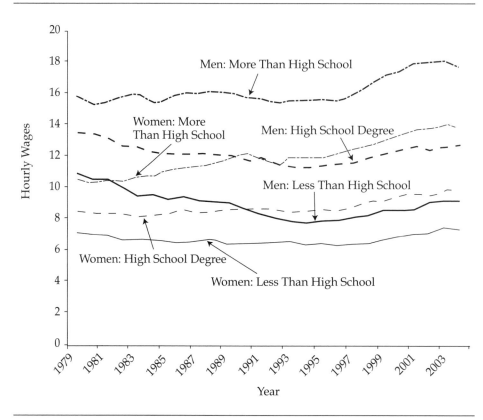

Source: Authors' tabulations from Current Population Survey outgoing rotation group data, 1979 to 2004.
Note: Based on all noninstitutionalized civilian workers age eighteen to fifty-four.

wages down in the 1980s, but that this was more than offset by improvements in women's experience and in their occupational placement. Finis Welch (2000) suggests that men's widening wage inequality is causally linked with the declining gender gap in wages, since the technological shifts that caused losses to less-skilled men also brought relative gains to women. Nicole Fortin and Thomas Lemieux (2000) also present evidence consistent with this story.

Cyclicality

Finally, we look at the effect of cyclicality on male and female workers by skill level. Previous work suggests that men's and women's labor market responsive-

TABLE 1.1 / Responsiveness of Labor Market Outcomes to Unemployment Changes, by Gender and Skill Level

Skill Level	Fraction of Weeks Worked		Real Log Hourly Wages		Real Log Annual Earnings	
	Men	Women	Men	Women	Men	Women
Less than high school	−0.007*	−0.006*	−0.003	−0.004	−0.026*	−0.019*
	(0.001)	(0.001)	(0.002)	(0.003)	(0.003)	(0.005)
High school degree	−0.012*	−0.009*	−0.005*	0.001	−0.027*	−0.014*
	(0.001)	(0.001)	(0.001)	(0.001)	(0.002)	(0.002)
More than high school	−0.006*	−0.005*	−0.004*	0.000	−0.019*	−0.013*
	(0.000)	(0.001)	(0.001)	(0.001)	(0.002)	(0.002)
All	−0.009*	−0.008*	−0.002*	0.001)	−0.021*	−0.014*
	(0.000)	(0.000)	(0.001)	(0.001)	(0.001)	(0.001)

Source: Authors' calculations.
Notes: Each number shows the coefficient on the state unemployment rate from a regression based on pooled CPS samples for this group from 1979 through 2003. State and year fixed effects are included. Other variables included in the regression are years of education; potential experience and potential experience squared; dummy variables to indicate race, Hispanic ethnicity, and location in an SMSA; dummy variables to indicate whether an individual is married or a single mother (women only); number of children, number of preschoolers, and number of infants. The wage regressions also include a control for part-time work.
*Significant at 5 percent level or higher.

ness to unemployment is generally similar, although less-skilled workers experience greater cyclicality than more-skilled workers (Hoynes 2000).

Table 1.1 shows the effect of changes in unemployment rates on men's and women's labor market outcomes, using pooled data from 1979 to 2003. The three dependent variables used in the analysis are the fraction of weeks worked in a year, log hourly wages, and log annual earnings. Within each gender and skill group, the table reports the coefficient on state unemployment rates in a regression that also includes state and year fixed effects, as well other variables identified at the bottom of the table.

The first two columns in table 1.1 show the effect of a one-percentage-point increase in the state unemployment rate on the fraction of weeks worked in a year. In general, the fraction of weeks women work is only slightly less responsive to the economic cycle than the fraction men work. For instance, among all adults, a 1.0-point rise in unemployment leads to a 0.9-point drop in the fraction of weeks worked among men and a 0.8-point drop among women. For both men and women, the fraction of weeks worked is most cyclical among those with only a high school degree; a 1.0-point rise in unemployment leads to a 1.2-point drop in the fraction of weeks worked among men and a 0.9-point drop among women.

Not surprisingly, hourly wages display much less cyclicality (middle two columns of table 1.1). Women show no evidence of significant wage changes over the cycle. Among men, wages are somewhat cyclical: a one-percentage-point increase in the state unemployment rate reduces male hourly wages by 0.2 percent. Annual earnings, on the other hand, display considerable cyclicality (last two columns of table 1.1). The cyclicality in annual earnings is more pronounced for the less-skilled than for the more-skilled and more pronounced for men than for women. For men with less than a high school education, a one-percentage-point increase in the state unemployment rate reduces annual earnings by 2.6 percent, whereas the reduction is 1.9 percent for equivalent women. Our analysis implies that the increase in unemployment during the recession of the early 2000s (from 4.0 percent in 2000 to 6.0 percent in 2003) should have caused a 3.8 percent decline in real annual earnings for low-skilled women and a 5.2 percent decline in real annual earnings for low-skilled men.

Although not shown in the table, for both men and women, cyclicality is much more pronounced for blacks and Hispanics than for whites. For example, while a 1.0 percent increase in the state unemployment rate reduces the real annual earnings of white females by 1.1 percent, it reduces the annual earnings of Hispanic females by 1.7 percent and of black females by 2.0 percent. (For men, those numbers are 1.7 percent, 2.9 percent, and 3.7 percent, respectively.)

The bottom line of this review of labor market trends is that less-skilled women have fared better than have less-skilled men. The labor force participation of less-skilled women has risen while it has fallen among equivalent men. Relative male-female unemployment rates have not changed much. Less-skilled women's wages have risen relative to their male peers, so that the female-male wage gap is about 50 percent lower than it was a quarter-century earlier. Less-skilled women are also less disadvantaged by economic cycles than are less-skilled men. While more-skilled women have done even better, making greater gains in labor force participation and wages, so have more-skilled men, and these gains may reflect the overall growth in the labor market returns to skill. The remainder of this chapter investigates why less-skilled women did better than their male counterparts.

POSSIBLE EXPLANATIONS FOR CHANGING GENDER DIFFERENTIALS

Although there are many possible reasons for the substantial narrowing in gender differences in labor market outcomes, in this section we focus particularly on changes in experience and education, the two human capital attributes most often discussed among labor economists who study wage determination. We describe the significant relative shifts over time in education and experience between men and women and briefly mention a variety of other factors that could also be accounting for gender shifts in the labor market. The discussion in this section provides background for the regressions in the following section.

Changes in Experience

Past labor market experience is a key determinant of current labor market outcomes. During the prime working years, persons with more experience tend to earn more and are more likely to be in the labor market than those with less experience. Historically, women's worse labor market outcomes have been partly ascribable to their lower levels of labor market experience, due to the greater time they spend in home production rather than market production, especially when they have small children. Over the last quarter-century, however, increases in women's labor force involvement have led to greater accumulated labor market experience. Blau and Kahn (1997) suggest that a major reason why women did better than men in the 1980s is that their growing labor market experience offset some of the changes in the wage structure that worked increasingly against low-wage workers.

To investigate changes in experience, we turn to the Panel Study of Income Dynamics (PSID), which contains longitudinal data on a national sample of the population over the past three decades. The PSID data, unlike the CPS data, provide information on actual accumulated labor market experience.[6] Figure 1.4 shows the age-experience profile for less-skilled workers, plotting the relationship between age and accumulated full-time labor market experience separately for men and women in both 1979 and 2000.

In 1979 less-skilled women's full-time work experience increased about four months with each year of age between ages eighteen and fifty-four, whereas in 2000 full-time experience increased by about six months with each year of age. For less-skilled men, the story is reversed. In 1979 their full-time experience increased by eleven months with each year of age, whereas in 2000 it increased by only nine months. Thus, as figure 1.4 demonstrates, between 1979 and 2000 there was a substantial narrowing of the gender gap in full-time experience among the less-skilled. There is a similar pattern of narrowing experience differentials among the more-skilled over this time period.

In addition to considerable changes in experience levels, the relationship between experience and labor market outcomes might have also changed. Historically, even at equivalent levels of labor market experience, women were less likely to work and earned less than men. These lower returns to experience may reflect different preferences that led women to select jobs that offered lower returns but other benefits (such as flexible scheduling), or it may be due to discrimination against women that devalued their experience.

Figure 1.5 investigates the relationship between accumulated experience and labor market participation among less-skilled women and men in 1979 and 2000, providing an "experience-participation" curve. At every level of experience in

FIGURE 1.4 / Years of Full-Time Work Experience by Age and Gender, 1979 and 2000, Less-Skilled Workers Only

Source: Authors' tabulations from Panel Study of Income Dynamics, survey years 1980 and 2001.
Note: Based on all noninstitutionalized civilian adults age eighteen to fifty-four with a high school degree or less.

1979, less-skilled women worked at significantly lower rates than men, but less-skilled women's propensity to work rose at every level of experience between 1979 and 2000. In contrast, men's propensity to work fell at every level of experience between 1979 and 2000.

By 2000, women with low levels of accumulated experience still tended to work less than men with low levels of accumulated experience. For example, among women with four to five years of experience, the participation rate was 58 percent; for men with four to five years, it was 79 percent. However, labor market participation among women who were more attached to the labor market (those with fifteen years of experience or more) was identical to that of their male counterparts by 2000. The labor force participation rate among women with sixteen to twenty-five years of experience was 87 percent; for equivalent men, it was 88 percent. Figure 1.4 suggests that women's labor force participation rose because their accumulated experience levels grew over the past several decades;

FIGURE 1.5 / Labor Force Participation by Years of Full-Time Work Experience and by Gender, 1979 and 2000, Less-Skilled Workers Only

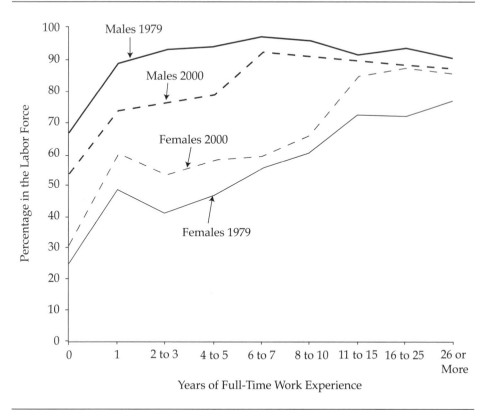

Source: Authors' tabulations from Panel Study of Income Dynamics, survey years 1980 and 2001.

Note: Based on all noninstitutionalized civilian adults age eighteen to fifty-four with a high school degree or less.

figure 1.5 suggests that women's labor force participation also rose because women's likelihood of working in 2000 was higher at every level of experience than it was in 1979.

Figure 1.6 shows the "experience-wage" curve, plotting accumulated experience against current wages for less-skilled workers. Women's wage-experience profile was similar in 2000 and 1979 for women with ten years of experience or less, but wages were higher among women with greater accumulated experience in 2000. In 2000 a less-skilled woman with sixteen to twenty-five years of experience earned a median wage of $13.07 per hour; in 1979 she earned only $9.99. Among less-skilled men, wages were lower at every experience level in 2000 compared to 1979, although their experience-wage curve remains above women's. Figure 1.6 suggests that women's relative wages rose not only because of

FIGURE 1.6 / Median Hourly Wages by Years of Full-Time Work Experience and by
Gender, 1979 and 2000, Less-Skilled Workers Only

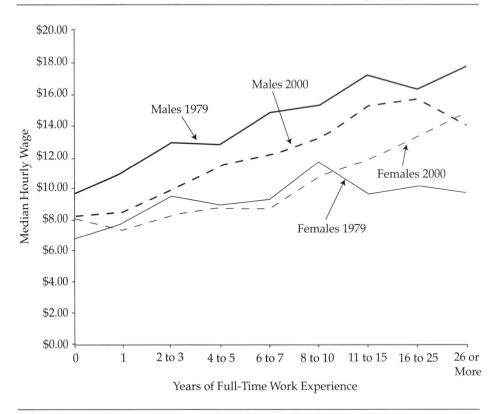

Source: Authors' tabulations from Panel Study of Income Dynamics, survey years 1980 and
2001.
Note: Based on all noninstitutionalized civilian adults age eighteen to fifty-four with a high
school degree or less. Inflation-adjusted to 2000 dollars.

greater accumulated experience but also because the relative returns to experience rose among women with high levels of work experience.

Changes in Education

The substantial increases in educational attainment over the last quarter-century
suggest that less-skilled workers have become more negatively selected within
the ability distribution in the population. If women's educational levels have
changed at a different rate than men's, this could lead to differential labor market
outcomes.

FIGURE 1.7 / Education Selectivity by Skill Level and Gender, 1979 to 2004

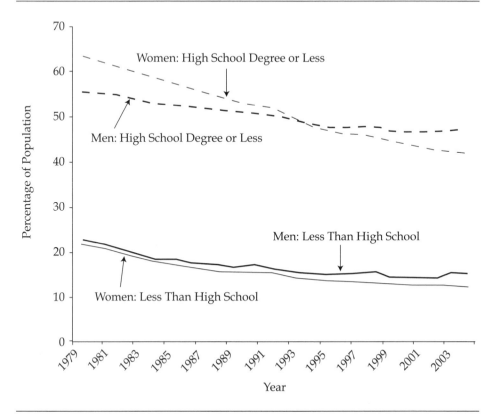

Source: Authors' tabulations from Current Population Survey outgoing rotation group data, 1979 to 2004.
Note: Based on all noninstitutionalized civilian adults age eighteen to fifty-four.

Figure 1.7 plots educational attainment levels for men and women. The lower (solid) lines show the share of high school dropouts in the total population by gender. These two lines lie almost on top of each other, suggesting that this group has shrunk as rapidly among men as among women over time. By 2004 only 12 percent of women and 15 percent of men between the ages of eighteen and fifty-four were high school dropouts. The top (dashed) lines show the less-skilled share of the total population—those with no more than a high school degree—by gender. Women were more likely to be less-skilled than men in 1979 (63 percent versus 56 percent), but they increased their education levels at a somewhat higher rate, so that they were less likely to be in this category by 2004 (42 percent versus 47 percent). Figure 1.7 suggests that there have been substantial changes in the selectivity of both men and women into the more- and less-skilled categories in our data. The more rapid decline in the share of less-skilled women suggests, however, that their (negative) selectivity should have been greater, a change that would drive women's wages down at a faster rate, all else being equal. Selectivity cannot explain less-skilled women's improving labor market outcomes relative to men.

Historically, men and women with equivalent levels of education have worked different amounts over their lifetimes. This gendered relationship between education and labor market involvement might be shifting for reasons such as changes in expectations about market work careers among women, changes in the returns to work, or declining employer discrimination. As we see later, there are substantial gender and skill differences in the wage returns to education. Declining gender discrimination might lead to relative female wage gains even when wages among the less-skilled are falling. Blau and Kahn (1997) provide evidence consistent with this over the 1980s.

We plot the relationship between education levels and labor force participation rates in 1979 and 2000 in figure 1.8.[7] The figure shows labor force participation rising with years of education among both men and women. For example, in 2000 the rate for women with ten years of education was 57 percent, whereas it was 83 percent for women with sixteen years or more. In 2000 women at all education levels worked more than in 1979, while less-skilled men worked less, narrowing the gender gap. Figure 1.8 implies that increases in education increase women's labor force participation both because more education leads to higher levels of market work and because work at every level of education has risen.

Figure 1.9 shows the relationship between education levels and median hourly wages. For both men and women, wages rise little at low levels of education, but faster as education increases. As expected, women with equivalent levels of education have lower wages. Among female workers who are high school dropouts, the education-wage relationship changed little over this period, but wages have risen among women with high school degrees or more. In short, we find the same pattern in figure 1.9 as elsewhere: rising education levels lead to rising wages, but even if education levels had not risen, women would be earning more at most levels of education.

Changes in the Industrial Distribution of Jobs

Men and women have always worked in very different industries and occupations, and these differences are greater among less-skilled workers. Figure 1.10 demonstrates the differences in the distribution of jobs by industry among less-skilled men and women in 2002. Men were far more likely than women to be working in agriculture, fisheries, mining, or construction (54 percent versus 7 percent) or manufacturing industries (39 percent versus 27 percent), while women were more likely to be employed in personal services (17 percent versus 4 percent) or professional service industries (48 percent versus 9 percent). A long literature has investigated the effects of differences in both industry and occupation on wages. For example, Kimberly Bayard and her colleagues (2003) find that

FIGURE 1.8 / Labor Force Participation by Years of Education and Gender, 1979 and 2000

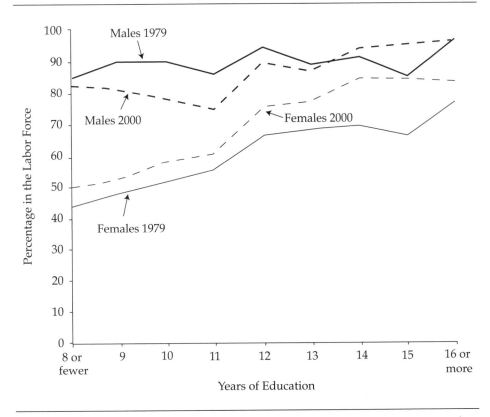

Source: Authors' tabulations from the Current Population Survey outgoing rotation group data, 1979 and 2000.
Note: Based on all noninstitutionalized civilian adults age eighteen to fifty-four.

occupational and industrial placement in the labor market explains about half of the gender wage gap.

Gender differences across the distribution of industries have changed little over the past twenty-five years. A standard index of industry segregation among less-skilled men and women was at 0.365 in 1983 and 0.390 in 2002.[8] This index also shows little change among more-skilled workers. Similarly, an occupation segregation index for less-skilled men and women was 0.482 in 1983 and 0.486 in 2002. This index falls significantly, however, among more-educated workers.

Thus, gender segregation by occupation and industry has been largely invariant among less-skilled workers and can do little to explain differential gender trends in outcomes. It is worth noting that industry location does have real effects on cyclical trends in the labor market. Between 1999 (a business cycle peak)

FIGURE 1.9 / Median Hourly Wages by Years of Education and Gender, 1979 and 2000

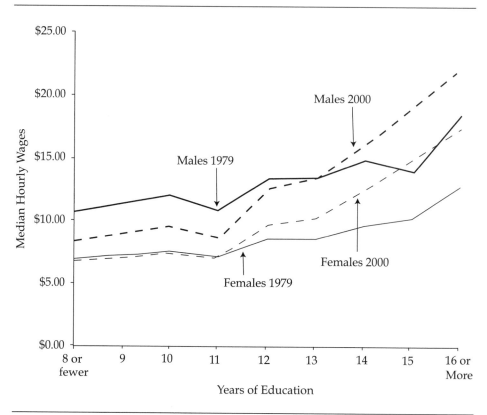

Source: Authors' tabulations from the Current Population Survey outgoing rotation group data, 1979 and 2000.
Note: Based on all noninstitutionalized civilian workers age eighteen to fifty-four. Inflation-adjusted to 2000 dollars.

and 2002 (a year of sluggish economic growth), less-skilled men's unemployment rates rose from 4.9 percent to 7.4 percent, while less-skilled women's rates rose less, from 5.5 percent to 7.3 percent. All else being equal, had women worked in the same industries as men, women's unemployment would have been higher in 1999, at 6.0 percent, and would have risen to 8.8 percent.[9]

Fertility and Marriage Changes

Because women on average put much more time into child care and child-rearing than men, changes in household composition and fertility are more likely to influence women's labor market involvement than men's. Even among men,

FIGURE 1.10 / Industry Location Among Less-Skilled Workers, by Gender, 2002

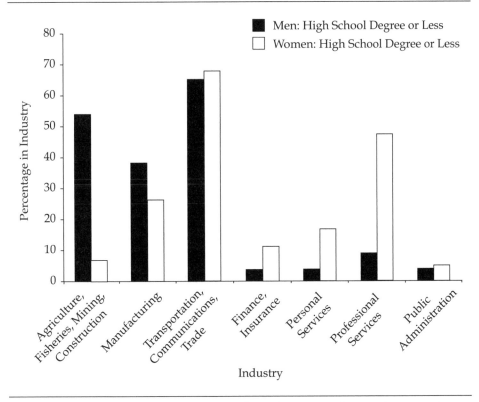

Source: Authors' tabulations from Current Population Survey outgoing rotation group data.
Note: Based on all noninstitutionalized civilian workers age eighteen to fifty-four.

however, research indicates that marriage influences labor market outcomes (Hellerstein and Neumark, forthcoming). Over the past twenty-five years, there has been only a small increase in less-skilled women's propensity to stay single and childless, but their likelihood of being an unmarried mother has increased by ten percentage points, from 12 to 22 percent. Their likelihood of being married has declined by thirteen percentage points, from 68 to 55 percent, and the number of children in families has decreased.

The expected impact of changes in childbearing and marriage on women's labor market choices is unclear. On the one hand, women tend to work less when they have greater child care responsibilities and substitute home production for market production. On the other hand, women's income needs rise with children, particularly if there are no earnings from a spouse or partner. As noted earlier, labor market outcomes and household composition are linked for women, so these household changes (especially declines in family size) may lead to wage changes. It is also worth noting that childbearing and marriage may both be endogenous to labor market outcomes.

Other Possible Causes of Changing Gender Differentials

Other less easily measured factors can also influence differential gender trends in wages and labor force participation. First, changes in the legal landscape and in public awareness of gender-based discrimination are likely to have made employers more open to hiring women, although this may have affected more-skilled women more than less-skilled women if a main effect of discrimination had been to close off high-wage, high-status jobs to women (Blau and Kahn, forthcoming). Changes in social norms and expectations about work among women with children have also changed over this time.

Second, changes in male incarceration rates may have influenced observed labor market outcomes among men. Since the 1970s, Congress and state legislatures have passed a variety of tougher sentencing policies that have led to an unprecedented rise in incarceration rates among younger men, particularly younger minority men.[10] Between 1979 and 2003, the male incarceration rate rose from 254 males in prison per 100,000 males in the population to 846 per 100,000. Less-skilled men were disproportionately affected by these changes. Steven Raphael (2005) indicates that the net effect of these changes is to reduce labor force participation among the non-incarcerated in the most affected groups.

Third, as George Borjas (this volume) indicates, growing immigrant shares can also influence male-female labor market outcomes. Between 1980 and 2003, the foreign-born population in the United States increased from 6.2 to 11.7 percent, reflecting high rates of immigration. Immigrants may have different labor force participation patterns by gender; most noticeably, immigrant families often have lower female labor force participation, both because these families tend to have more children to care for and because of differences in cultural norms about working wives.

Fourth, U.S. policy changes have influenced women's work choices. During the 1990s, the United States made major efforts to move welfare recipients (typically less-skilled single mothers) into work. Single mothers' labor force participation rates rose faster than those of less-skilled childless or married women between 1989 and 1999. A number of studies indicate that these labor force changes were at least partially due to welfare reforms (Blank 2002), which could have led to less-skilled women's labor market participation increasing faster than men's. If more women entered the labor market and displaced men, this could have depressed male labor force participation. Rebecca Blank and Jonah Gelbach (2006) find no evidence of any impact of the 1990s increases in female labor force participation and associated changes in welfare programs on work behavior among low-skilled men.[11]

Other policies also increased work incentives among the less-skilled, most notably increases in the Earned Income Tax Credit, which provided growing incentives for labor market entry among nonworking household heads with children (primarily single mothers). The evidence suggests that the positive labor supply effects of the EITC were greater for single mothers than for married men. On the other hand, the EITC appears to have discouraged work among married women, so that the net effect on gender-specific labor market trends is unclear (Hoffman and Seidman 2003).

Although we believe that these other causal factors may be important in explaining gender differences in labor market outcomes, we have limited data on them. Policy changes vary only at the state level or the national level. Lacking individual-level data on incarceration or immigration (before the early 1990s) in the CPS data, we can only measure these variables at the state level. State-level variables are poorly identified in cross-sectional data, and (for reasons described later) we focus on cross-sectional estimates from 1979 and 2004. Given this, we opt to include state fixed effects in our regressions and to allow these fixed effects to absorb the impact of demographic and policy differences across states that are not explicitly measured in our regressions.

ESTIMATING LABOR FORCE PARTICIPATION AND WAGES

Based on the discussion in the previous section about the factors that might be affecting labor market outcomes among men and women, this section presents multivariate estimates of the determinants of two key labor market variables: labor force participation and wage rates. Although many others have estimated such regressions, this analysis compares changes in the determinants of labor supply and wages over a twenty-five-year period, updating estimates such as those by Blau and Kahn (forthcoming), which go only through the 1990s. It focuses on differences in the determinants of labor market outcomes among different skill groups, rather than looking at aggregate results for men and women. It directly compares the determinants of wages and labor force participation. Although our estimation approach is quite simple, these results allow us to compare changes across both of these labor market outcomes over time and among groups.

We estimate the determinants of labor force participation separately by gender and skill level in both 1979 and 2003. The four groups we focus on in each year are less-skilled men (those with a high school education or less), more-skilled men (those with more than a high school education), less-skilled women, and more-skilled women. The data come from the CPS Annual Demographic Survey (March supplement), in 1980 and 2004, which provides information on work and earnings in the previous year. We include all persons between the ages of eighteen and fifty-four. Labor market participation is a binary variable, equal to one if an individual reports working one thousand hours or more in the previous year. Imposing the one-thousand-hour restriction primarily gets rid of occasional and nonattached workers. Of those omitted by this restriction, over 75 percent identify their primary activity as going to school, taking care of the home or family (rather than working), or being retired, or they identify themselves as ill or disabled. This restriction also gets rid of most outliers in hourly wages, which we calculate by dividing annual earnings by total annual hours (weeks worked times usual hours per week worked).

We focus on cross-sectional regressions in these two years rather than utilizing stacked CPS cross-sections from all the years. Stacked data would provide better identification of a variety of coefficients (such as policy effects that change over time). Unfortunately, there are two selectivity issues changing over time that we do not know how to deal with effectively using stacked cross-sections. On the one hand, we believe that selectivity into the labor force has changed over time (among both men and women). On the other hand, selectivity into our skill groups has changed over time as well (see figure 1.7). Because we are unable to deal adequately with these selectivity issues, we elect to estimate reduced-form regressions from the beginning and ending years of the period. We note that solving this dual-selectivity problem and estimating changing labor market outcomes over time are important topics for future research. Alternatively, we could utilize longitudinal data (such as the PSID). Unfortunately, this would provide much smaller sample sizes, particularly given the separate skill and gender samples that we need.

We use a linear probability model to estimate labor force participation in a specific year (1979 or 2003) as follows:

$$LFP_i = \beta_0 + X_i\beta_1 + Y_i\beta_2 + Z_s\beta_3 + \mu_i \tag{1.1}$$

where i indexes individuals in a particular gender, skill, or year sample. X is a vector of person-specific variables that affect both wages and labor force participation, and β_1 is the associated vector of coefficients. X includes years of education, potential experience (defined as age-education-5), race, and ethnicity. In the wage equation that follows, X also includes a control for part-time work. To allow for nonlinearity in returns to education for low-skilled workers, we also include a dummy variable to indicate whether the person holds a high school degree.

Y is a vector of family-specific variables, with the associated coefficient vector β_2. Although we believe that these variables should primarily affect labor force participation decisions, there is evidence that marital status and children can affect wage outcomes as well. Y includes marital status, number of children, number of children under age six, number of infants, and whether the person is a single mother (for women only). Z is a vector of location-specific variables, with the associated coefficient vector β_3. Z includes a set of state dummy variables that control for state fixed effects. Because we are estimating equation 1.1 separately in each year, these fixed effects control for any differences in the state environment, including differences in unemployment rates, unionization, welfare benefit levels and other welfare policy differences, state incarceration rates and policies, and other variables. Z also contains a dummy variable indicating whether an individual lives within a standard metropolitan statistical area (SMSA), providing a control for urban location.

We also estimate a wage equation for each gender, skill, and year group:

$$\text{Ln(wage)}_i = \alpha_0 + X_i\alpha_1 + Y_i\alpha_2 + Z_s\alpha_3 + \varepsilon_i \qquad (1.2)$$

where the dependent variable is the natural logarithm of real hourly wages and other variables are defined as before.

We do not do selectivity corrections on our wage estimates, that is, we do not take account of who is working or not working in estimating wages. Instead, our wage regressions can be viewed as reduced-form regressions. The coefficients not only show the effects of these variables on wage determination but also reflect the impact of these variables on who chooses to work (and hence, who has reported wages). We report the reduced form rather than the selectivity-corrected estimates for several reasons. First, because we are estimating these regressions separately by skill level, we suspect that the biggest selectivity effect over time is due to changes in who is in each skill grouping (see figure 1.7). There is no obvious way to control separately for this type of selectivity, and we suspect that skill selectivity is tangled with factors (such as family composition) that are typically used to identify selection into the labor force.

Second, we estimated a large number of standard selectivity-corrected wage regressions in preliminary work, and we found that the wage coefficients (particularly the education coefficients) were extremely sensitive to how we identified the selectivity effect. This reinforces our concern that selectivity into these skill groupings is influencing the results and that we cannot interpret the selectivity coefficient in the standard manner (that is, as representing selectivity into the labor force only). Given these concerns, we prefer to report the descriptive reduced-form wage regressions in this chapter. By controlling for family composition variables (the Y vector) in the wage regression, we hope that we have absorbed at least some of the labor force participation selectivity effects (as well as some of the skill group selectivity) with these variables, but we recognize that our coefficients on the X vector are likely to be affected as well. We emphasize that this means the coefficients on the wage regression cannot be interpreted as the direct effect of these variables on wage determination alone.

We do not include dummy variables for industry and occupation. We prefer to think of industry and occupation selection as a joint outcome with wages, rather than including them as controls in a wage regression. For instance, if labor market discrimination against women in manufacturing forces them into service occupations, then including these variables "overexplains" gender wage differentials by ascribing to occupational choice what should be ascribed to discrimination. As we noted earlier, these variables change little over time and are not likely to explain a great deal of the change in male-female wages, which is the focus of our concern.[12]

Table 1.2 shows the results from eight regressions estimating the determinants of labor force participation for men and women by skill level in 1979 and 2003.

TABLE 1.2 / Determinants of Labor Force Participation by Gender and Year

	1979				2003			
	Men		Women		Men		Women	
	High School or Less	More Than High School	High School or Less	More Than High School	High School or Less	More Than High School	High School or Less	More Than High School
Years of education	0.013** (0.002)	0.008** (0.002)	0.018** (0.002)	0.037** (0.003)	-0.002 (0.002)	0.019** (0.002)	0.012** (0.003)	0.027** (0.002)
High school degree (1 = yes)	0.038** (0.010)		0.107** (0.010)		0.126** (0.012)		0.158** (0.012)	
Potential experience	0.008** (0.001)	0.034** (0.002)	0.009** (0.001)	0.023** (0.002)	0.015** (0.001)	0.028** (0.001)	0.014** (0.001)	0.018** (0.001)
Potential experience squared	-0.023** (0.003)	-0.091** (0.004)	-0.021** (0.003)	-0.066** (0.005)	-0.041** (0.003)	-0.074** (0.004)	-0.026** (0.004)	-0.040** (0.004)
Race (1 = black)	-0.030 (0.011)	-0.033* (0.016)	-0.026* (0.011)	0.057** (0.017)	-0.097** (0.012)	-0.036** (0.011)	-0.014 (0.012)	0.043** (0.010)
Ethnicity (1 = Hispanic)	0.043** (0.011)	-0.014 (0.018)	0.013 (0.011)	0.014 (0.021)	0.087** (0.010)	0.033** (0.011)	0.000 (0.011)	0.026* (0.011)

Marital status (1 = married)	0.151**	0.141**	-0.148**	-0.087**	0.145**	0.126**	-0.023	-0.019
	(0.008)	(0.010)	(0.010)	(0.013)	(0.008)	(0.007)	(0.012)	(0.010)
Household status (1 = single mother)			-0.002	0.111**			0.086**	0.112**
			(0.012)	(0.019)			(0.013)	(0.011)
Number of children	-0.007**	-0.009**	-0.015**	-0.024**	0.008**	0.003	0.000	-0.009**
	(0.002)	(0.002)	(0.002)	(0.003)	(0.002)	(0.002)	(0.003)	(0.002)
Number of preschoolers	0.015**	0.018**	-0.020**	-0.051**	0.000	0.001	-0.029**	-0.038**
	(0.004)	(0.005)	(0.005)	(0.008)	(0.006)	(0.004)	(0.006)	(0.005)
Number of infants	-0.005	0.004	-0.034**	0.005	0.008	0.013*	-0.040**	0.005
	(0.007)	(0.007)	(0.007)	(0.012)	(0.009)	(0.007)	(0.009)	(0.008)
Observations	25,047	17,373	30,660	15,708	23,188	28,174	23,375	33,301

Source: Authors' calculations.

Note: All regressions include controls for location (SMSA) and state fixed effects. Potential experience is defined as age-education-5; the coefficient on potential experience squared is multiplied by 100. Number of children is the total number of children in the family less than age eighteen; number of preschoolers is the total less than age six; and number of infants is the total less than age two. Standard errors in parentheses.

*Significant at 5 percent level or higher.
**Significant at 1 percent level or higher.

The coefficients in the first row show that each additional year of education has a positive and significant effect on labor force participation, as expected (except in 2003 among less-skilled men without high school degrees). This education effect is stronger among less-skilled women than less-skilled men, consistent with the data in figure 1.8. Over time, the impact of a year of education on labor force participation declines among both male and female high school dropouts, but the returns to a high school degree rise. In 2003 a male (female) worker with a high school degree had a 12.4 (17.0) percent higher probability of being in the labor force than a high school dropout with eleven years of education.

Experience has a positive effect on labor force participation among all groups, and this effect grows over time except among more-skilled men. In 2003 increasing potential experience from five to ten years raised the likelihood of labor market involvement by 5 percent for a female high school graduate and by 4 percent for an equivalent man.

The effect of race on labor market involvement is relatively constant over time, except among less-skilled black men, who were far less likely to work in 2003 than in 1979. By 2003, a less-skilled black man was 10 percent less likely to work than an equivalent white man. All else being equal, race and Hispanic ethnicity have no differential effect on labor force participation among less-skilled women. Hispanic ethnicity was associated with higher levels of work among all other groups in 2003.

Not surprisingly, family characteristics have a different effect on less-skilled women's labor force participation than on men's. As others have noted, marriage has a positive effect on men's labor market involvement and a negative effect on women's, although our estimates indicate that this effect has virtually disappeared over time among women. In contrast, single-parenting has a positive effect on labor supply among more-skilled women (true in both years). Less-skilled single mothers were no more likely to work than equivalent unmarried childless women (the omitted category) in 1979, but by 2003 their labor force participation was higher. We might interpret this change as the result of policy efforts to increase labor supply among welfare recipients.

In general, we expect that having more children, especially more young children, will decrease the likelihood of labor force involvement among women.[13] The number-of-preschoolers variable indicates whether there is any differential effect of preschoolers, after controlling for the total number of children. The number-of-infants variable indicates whether there is a differential effect of infants, after controlling for the number of preschoolers. By 2003, among less-skilled women, the number of children over the age of five was unrelated to labor force participation, while the negative effect of children under age five was somewhat larger than in 1979. More-skilled women's labor market choices have become less affected by the number and ages of children over time.

Table 1.3 presents the coefficients on the wage equations by year and gender, using a specification similar to that in table 1.2. Because the dependent variable is log wages, we can interpret the coefficients in table 1.3 as the percentage effect on wages of a one-unit change in the independent variable. Higher education levels lead to higher wages, as expected. Among both male and female high school dropouts, the returns to each year of education have fallen slightly, from 3.6 percent to 2.6 percent per year of education for women, and from 4.7 percent to 3.6 percent per year of education for men. The wage returns to a high school degree have increased. Among men, the additional gain in wages from a high school degree rose from 9.3 percent in 1979 to 16.1 percent in 2003. Among women, the gain from finishing high school went from 10.5 percent to 18.0 percent in 2003. The returns to additional years of education have risen among more-skilled men and women as well. This finding is consistent with other evidence on the changing returns to education across skill groups.

In contrast, the wage returns to experience have remained relatively constant over time for all groups shown in table 1.3. The combined coefficients on potential experience and its square indicate that an increase in potential experience from five to ten years increased wages by 11 percent among women and 12 percent among men in 2003. We worry that our coefficients on experience are hard to interpret since we can only measure potential experience in the CPS rather than actual years of work experience. To check this, we have estimated equivalent regressions using a measure of actual experience, with PSID data from 1980 and 2001. Somewhat surprisingly, the experience variables in the PSID estimates are quite close to those in the CPS estimates. For instance, in the 2001 PSID the returns to experience for the less-skilled are estimated at 5.8 percent for men and 3.4 percent for women. These compare to 2003 estimates in table 1.3 of 3.2 percent and 2.9 percent. Among more-skilled workers, the returns to experience are 4.7 percent (CPS) versus 4.8 percent (PSID) among men and 4.3 percent (CPS) and 4.6 percent (PSID) among women. These comparisons reassure us that our potential experience estimates from the CPS are not too unreliable. Because of the much larger CPS sample sizes, we prefer to utilize this dataset.

Workers who are black or of Hispanic origin earn lower wages than white workers, all else being equal. For instance, in 2003 less-skilled black workers, both male and female, earned about 14 percent less than equivalent white workers. More-skilled black men earned 17 percent less and more-skilled black women earned 6 percent less than equivalent white workers. The negative impact of Hispanic ethnicity on wages was even greater in 2003, with less-skilled Hispanic men earning 30 percent less and less-skilled Hispanic women earning 21 percent less. Of course, this may reflect discrimination in the labor market against workers of color, or it may reflect differential skill levels that are not well measured in the other variables. For instance, black or Hispanic workers may have attended worse schools, or Hispanic workers may have more limited English skills. As expected, part-time work also results in lower wages. For less-skilled male workers, the negative wage effects of part-time work appear to have grown over time.

Finally, at the bottom of table 1.3 we show the effect of a variety of family and children variables on wages. As discussed, because we believe that the coefficients on these variables reflect selectivity into work as well as any direct effect of the variables on wages, we do not want to interpret the coefficients too

TABLE 1.3 / Determinants of Log Wages by Gender and Year

| | 1979 | | | | 2003 | | | |
| | Men | | Women | | Men | | Women | |
	High School or Less	More Than High School	High School or Less	More Than High School	High School or Less	More Than High School	High School or Less	More Than High School
Years of education	0.047** (0.005)	0.056** (0.003)	0.036** (0.007)	0.090** (0.004)	0.036** (0.004)	0.109** (0.003)	0.026** (0.007)	0.115** (0.003)
High school degree (1 = yes)	0.093** (0.017)		0.105** (0.022)		0.161** (0.019)		0.180** (0.023)	
Potential Experience	0.037** (0.002)	0.048** (0.002)	0.027** (0.002)	0.041** (0.003)	0.032** (0.002)	0.047** (0.002)	0.029** (0.003)	0.043** (0.002)
Potential experience squared	-0.058** (0.005)	-0.092** (0.007)	-0.050** (0.005)	-0.099** (0.009)	-0.049** (0.005)	-0.091** (0.006)	-0.049** (0.006)	-0.088** (0.006)
Race (1 = black)	-0.194** (0.017)	-0.098** (0.024)	-0.079** (0.016)	0.021 (0.022)	-0.136** (0.019)	-0.167** (0.019)	-0.137** (0.018)	-0.060** (0.015)
Ethnicity (1 = Hispanic)	-0.144** (0.018)	-0.088** (0.024)	-0.059** (0.019)	-0.027 (0.025)	-0.176** (0.017)	-0.221** (0.021)	-0.176** (0.019)	-0.110** (0.018)

Part-time worker (1 = part-time)	-0.159** (0.044)	-0.217** (0.040)	-0.201** (0.016)	-0.175** (0.025)	-0.300** (0.041)	-0.329** (0.039)	-0.210** (0.019)	-0.165** (0.016)
Marital status (1 = married)	0.229** (0.014)	0.177** (0.016)	0.029* (0.014)	0.033 (0.017)	0.172** (0.014)	0.198** (0.013)	0.095** (0.019)	0.131** (0.016)
Household status (1 = single mother)			0.041* (0.018)	0.073** (0.026)			0.072** (0.021)	0.052** (0.018)
Number of children	0.004 (0.003)	0.013** (0.004)	-0.018** (0.004)	-0.039** (0.007)	0.009* (0.004)	0.006 (0.003)	-0.011* (0.005)	-0.015** (0.004)
Number of preschoolers	-0.005 (0.008)	-0.017 (0.009)	0.008 (0.009)	0.032* (0.014)	0.003 (0.009)	0.030** (0.008)	0.001 (0.011)	0.029** (0.009)
Number of infants	0.005 (0.012)	0.029* (0.013)	0.024* (0.012)	0.040* (0.019)	-0.011 (0.014)	-0.020 (0.012)	0.025 (0.017)	0.011 (0.013)
Observations	19,441	13,674	14,028	8,767	17,014	22,616	12,848	21,726

Source: Authors' calculations.

Note: All regressions include controls for location (SMSA) and state fixed effects. Potential experience is defined as age-education-5; the coefficient on potential experience squared is multiplied by 100. Number of children is the total number of children in the family less than age eighteen; number of preschoolers is the total less than age six; and number of infants is the total less than age two. Wages are inflation-adjusted to 2000 dollars using the GDP Personal Consumption Expenditure deflator.

Standard errors in parentheses.

*Significant at 5 percent level or higher.
**Significant at 1 percent level or higher.

strongly. Some of these variables may have a direct effect on wages; for instance, the literature suggests that married workers have higher productivity (Hellerstein and Neumark, forthcoming). Consistent with this literature, we find that marriage has a positive correlation with the wages of all groups in both years, although the effects are bigger among men.

Other variables (such as the children variables) may reflect the selection of who works. For instance, if women with more children generally prefer not to work, it may be only low-income mothers with larger families who can't afford to stay home who remain in the workforce. This would result in a negative coefficient on the number of children. Alternatively, if infant and preschool care is expensive, only higher-wage women may be able to afford to pay for child care and work. This would result in a positive coefficient on the preschooler and infant variables. As we expect, the presence of children in the household has bigger and more significant effects on women's wages than on men's, almost surely reflecting both which women go to work and the types of jobs they take.

Two broad generalizations from tables 1.2 and 1.3 should be noted. First, the determinants of labor force participation and wages differ substantially by gender, and these differences have changed over time. Second, the determinants of labor force participation and wages differ substantially by skill group, and these differences have also changed over time. Because it is hard to interpret the overall effects of these changes by looking at the estimates in tables 1.2 and 1.3, we turn in the next section to a decomposition that summarizes these results.

WHAT HAS CAUSED CHANGES IN RELATIVE WAGES AMONG LESS-SKILLED WOMEN?

In this final section, we use the estimates from tables 1.2 and 1.3 to calculate how changing factors are influencing relative labor force and wage changes among less-skilled women. We utilize a simple decomposition that characterizes the change in wages (or labor force participation) between two periods as

$$\Delta (\text{lnwage}) = (\Delta X)\, \hat{a}_1 + (\Delta \hat{a})\, X_2, \tag{1.3}$$

where Δ indicates the change between period 1 (1979) and period 2 (2003) in the means of the indicated variable, X_t is a vector of the means of all variables in the regression in period t, and $\hat{a}_t$ is the vector of estimated coefficients on each variable in period t. Comparing the results from this decomposition between less-skilled men and women and between less-skilled women and more-skilled women gives us a sense of the different changes that are occurring in the labor market over time.[14]

Table 1.4 shows the results from these decompositions for changes in labor force participation rates. The first two rows show the level values of labor force participation for each group in 2003 and 1979, and the third row shows the change over time. The next four rows decompose this total change into the

TABLE 1.4 / Comparative Sources of Change in Labor Force Participation

	Low-Skilled Women Versus Low-Skilled Men			Low-Skilled Women Versus More-Skilled Women		
	Women	Men	Difference	Less-Skilled	More-Skilled	Difference
2003 level	54.7	71.4	−16.7	54.7	65.8	−11.1
1979 level	46.4	77.9	−31.5	46.4	55.8	−9.4
Total change	8.3	−6.5	14.8	8.3	10.0	−1.7
Change due to						
Education	−2.0	−10.2	8.2	−2.0	−15.4	13.4
Potential experience	8.2	5.2	3.0	8.2	3.0	5.2
Family composition	13.9	−1.0	14.9	13.9	9.3	4.6
Other variables	−11.8	−0.5	−11.3	−11.8	13.1	−24.9
Change due to mean changes only						
Education	0.8	0.7	0.1	0.8	−0.4	1.2
Potential experience	1.0	1.0	0.0	1.0	2.5	−1.5
Family composition	1.7	−3.1	4.8	1.7	1.5	0.2
Other variables	0.0	1.4	−1.4	0.0	0.3	−0.3
Change due to coefficient changes only						
Education	−2.8	−11.0	8.2	−2.8	−15.0	12.2
Potential experience	7.1	4.3	2.8	7.1	0.5	6.6
Family composition	12.2	2.1	10.1	12.2	7.8	4.4
Other variables	−11.7	−1.9	−9.8	−11.7	12.8	−24.5

Source: Authors' calculations.
Note: Based on the estimated regressions shown in table 1.2.

change due to education variables, experience variables, family composition variables (including marital status and children), and all other variables (including the race, ethnicity, SMSA, and state fixed effects). By including the state fixed effects (the equivalent of fifty state constants) in the "other variables" category, we subsume into this category any unexplained effects that are part of the constant, including shifts in discrimination. Below this, we decompose these factors into the amount due to changes in the means of the explanatory variables and to changes in the coefficients over time. The first three columns compare less-skilled women and men; the last three columns compare less-skilled and more-skilled women.

Look first at labor force participation changes over time among less-skilled women, the first column on the left-hand side of table 1.4. The 8.3-percentage-point increase in labor force participation rates among less-skilled women is being driven by changes in the effects of experience and family composition. These factors driving up labor force participation are offset somewhat by changes in education and in other variables that would have reduced labor force participation. The next several rows indicate that almost none of the change in women's labor force participation is due to changes in the mean levels of the Xs; virtually all of it is due to changes in the coefficients, where the declining effect of education on labor supply for less-skilled women is more than offset by the growing positive effect of experience and family composition. (More accurately, the negative effects of family composition on women's labor force participation are becoming smaller over time.)

In contrast, the 6.5-point decline in labor force participation among low-skilled men (column 2) is dominated by substantial declines in the coefficients on education that are only somewhat offset by the growing positive effect of experience on labor force participation. The declining effect of education on less-skilled men's labor force participation—the 11.0-point change in the coefficient on education—is driving much of the decline in male labor force participation.

As column 3 indicates, the gap in male-female labor force participation falls by almost fifteen percentage points, mostly because of shifts in the relative returns on education, experience, and family variables that favored low-skilled women. These positive factors for relative female labor supply were at least partially offset by a shift in the other variables that has favored low-skilled men over women.

The three columns on the right-hand side of table 1.4 compare labor force participation changes among less-skilled women and more-skilled women. Labor force participation rates have grown a little more slowly among the less-skilled (by 8.3 points versus 10.0 points among the more-skilled), widening the gap between these groups by 1.7 percentage points. The effect of education on labor supply has declined markedly among more-skilled women, because the coefficient on education has fallen sharply. Essentially, most of these women now work, so the slope of labor supply by years of education has become flatter. This effect is more than offset by increasing positive effects on labor supply from all other variables. Most notably, the changing effect of family composition has driven up labor supply among both less- and more-skilled women. The "other" variables (race-ethnicity effects, SMSA location, and unexplained state-specific constants) shifted in ways that enhanced the labor force participation of more-skilled women while reducing the labor force participation of less-skilled women.

It is striking that so little of the change in labor force participation is due to actual changes in education or experience; instead, these changes are largely driven by changing coefficients. (Of course, the use of potential experience rather than actual experience understates the actual gain in years of labor market experience among women.) This conclusion about the importance of the coefficients is stronger than in previous work by Blau and Kahn, who find that both changes in the Xs and changes in coefficients are affecting the male-female wage gap. In part, this reflects the fact that we separate our sample by skill level; each skill

TABLE 1.5 / Comparative Sources of Change in Log Wages

	Low-Skilled Women Versus Low-Skilled Men			Low-Skilled Women Versus More-Skilled Women		
	Women	Men	Difference	Less-Skilled	More-Skilled	Difference
2003 level	2.300	2.517	−0.217	2.300	2.726	−0.426
1979 level	2.166	2.582	−0.416	2.166	2.430	−0.264
Total change	0.134	−0.065	0.199	0.134	0.296	−0.162
Change due to						
Education	−0.042	−0.065	0.023	−0.042	0.348	−0.390
Potential experience	0.086	−0.017	0.103	0.086	0.132	−0.046
Family composition	0.055	−0.060	0.115	0.055	0.089	−0.034
Other variables	0.036	0.077	−0.041	0.036	−0.273	0.309
Change due to means changes only						
Education	0.009	0.015	−0.006	0.009	−0.021	0.030
Potential experience	0.039	0.030	0.009	0.039	0.083	−0.044
Family composition	0.001	−0.031	0.032	0.001	0.008	−0.007
Other variables	−0.028	−0.034	0.006	−0.028	−0.016	−0.012
Change due to coefficients changes only						
Education	−0.051	−0.081	0.030	−0.051	0.369	−0.420
Potential experience	0.046	−0.047	0.093	0.046	0.049	−0.003
Family composition	0.054	−0.029	0.083	0.054	0.081	−0.027
Other variables	0.064	0.111	−0.047	0.064	−0.257	0.321

Source: Authors' calculations.
Note: Based on the estimated regressions shown in table 1.3.

group has smaller average changes in education and experience than does the total sample across all skill groups.

The strong effects of changing coefficients can reflect changing demand for different types of work as well as changes in labor market discrimination. Relative to less-skilled men, the returns to less-skilled women's characteristics improved more (experience and family composition) or deteriorated less (education). Relative to more-skilled women, the returns to some characteristics improved more (experience and family composition) or deteriorated less (education), while race-ethnicity and unexplained factors greatly advantaged more-skilled women's labor force participation.

Table 1.5 decomposes real wage changes in a similar way and has a similar organization. We can read changes in log wages as (approximately) equal to percentage changes, so the left two columns suggest that less-skilled women's wages rose 13.4 percent while men's fell 6.5 percent between 1979 and 2003, leading to a 19.9 percent narrowing in the male-female wage gap for less-skilled workers. In contrast, more-skilled women's wages (column 5) rose 29.6 percent, so the wage gap between more-skilled and less-skilled women rose by 16.2 percent.

As with labor force participation, almost all of the change in less-skilled women's wages was due to changes in the coefficients rather than changes in the means of the explanatory variables. Returns to education fell among less-skilled women (by 5.1 points), while their returns to experience rose (4.6 points). Less-skilled men showed falling returns to both education and experience over this time period. Family composition changes enhanced women's wages while they reduced men's wages. Hence, the overall reduction of 19 percent in the wage gap between less-skilled men and women is largely explained by shifts in the impact of education, experience, and family composition on wages that favored less-skilled women over less-skilled men.

Comparing more- and less-skilled women gives a very different story. Unlike the less-skilled, more-skilled women saw strong increases in the wage returns to education, so the overall effect of education on more-skilled women's wages is strongly positive, while it is negative for the less-skilled.[15] Both more- and less-skilled women experienced increases in returns to experience as well as positive shifts in the effect of family variables on wages. More-skilled women also had greater gains in potential experience levels than did less-skilled women. The gains from these changes were partially offset by changes in the other variables that reduced wages somewhat among more-skilled females.

The message from tables 1.4 and 1.5 is that the characteristics of low-skilled women are not changing much relative to those of low-skilled men or more-skilled women (although the women are gaining experience and the men are not). Instead, the primary factors driving differential wage and labor force participation changes among these groups are differential changes in the coefficients that link worker characteristics to labor market involvement and wages. The impact of education on labor force participation and wages among less-skilled men and women has deteriorated, but it has deteriorated more for men. The returns to experience (as a driver for both wages and labor force participation) have grown for all women. The effect of family characteristics on labor market and wage behavior among less-skilled women has changed in ways that increase their work and their wages, an effect that is also evident among more-skilled women. These changing coefficients can be the result of changes in labor market demand and employer behavior as well as changes in women's behavior over the past twenty-five years. This chapter cannot pinpoint the reasons behind these shifts, but it does indicate that it is the *translations* between personal characteristics and labor market outcomes that are shifting differentially across groups.

CONCLUSIONS

This chapter has investigated why less-skilled women have done relatively better than their less-skilled male counterparts over the last several decades, even while they have lost ground relative to more-skilled women. While education levels have grown among less-skilled women over this period, they have grown almost as fast among less-skilled men. Accumulated labor market experience has grown among both more- and less-skilled women, although it has grown faster among the more-skilled. In the end, however, changes in the levels of these characteristics are not the dominant force behind different labor market trends among these groups. Instead, there have been large changes in the *relationship* between worker characteristics and labor market outcomes. On the one hand, less-skilled women experienced declining returns to education while the wage returns to education grew among more-skilled women, consistent with widening wage inequality between skill groups. There has been a growing positive effect of experience on labor market participation and on wages among women at all skill levels, while the effect of experience on wages among less-skilled men has declined. Furthermore, shifts in the effect of family composition on less-skilled women's labor supply have increased women's relative labor force participation, and these effects were greater among the less-skilled than the more-skilled.

Less-skilled women have thus found themselves in an "intermediate" place in the labor market. They have experienced deteriorating returns to education, but they have benefited from a growing positive impact of accumulated experience on labor market outcomes that has offset some of the declining educational effects. This has worked to close the gender gap in wages among less-skilled workers. In contrast, less-skilled women's labor market outcomes have improved at a much slower rate than those of more-skilled women, who benefited from improvements in the returns to both experience and education. While more-skilled women are doing well, they continue to lag behind more-skilled men, whose wages rose equally fast.

It would be useful to understand the shifts discussed here more fully. Why are the labor market returns to women's accumulated experience rising? To what extent does the shifting relationship between children, marriage, and women's work reflect changes in institutional structure, such as the growing availability of child care? Nailing down causal interpretations will require more careful empirical work that accounts for changing selectivity effects and looks at changes between cohorts over time rather than pooling the entire adult-age distribution.

Although less-skilled women have done better than less-skilled men in the labor market in the recent past, it is not clear that this pattern will continue. As the determinants of women's and men's labor market outcomes converge, this may be bad news for less-skilled women, who could find themselves more subject to the negative trends that have disadvantaged less-skilled men for the past twenty-five years. Policies that subsidize work among the less-skilled, such as the EITC, child care, or health care subsidies, will be of ongoing importance to encourage labor market participation and reward work among low-wage and low-skilled workers.

NOTES

1. Thanks are due to Ari Kushner and Emily Beam for excellent research assistance and to James Sallee for his help with construction of the data.
2. We focus on labor force participation (working or actively looking for work) as opposed to employment because we think it is a better measure of labor force involvement. In table 1.1, when we analyze cyclical patterns, we switch to employment (fraction of weeks worked) because that variable is more commonly used to measure cyclicality.
3. The number of observations in a year ranges from 189,066 to 259,279.
4. Adjusted to 2000 dollars with the GDP Personal Consumption Expenditures deflator.
5. The most dramatic growth in wages occurs among the college-educated over this time period. There is more rapid convergence in male-female wages among this group as well.
6. PSID data from the survey years 1980 and 2001 were used for this analysis. The sample was restricted to "heads" and "wives" age eighteen to fifty-four and was weighted using individual weights. Actual experience was obtained primarily from retrospective variables in which respondents were asked the number of years they had worked full-time since they were eighteen. Missing data were filled in by calculating years of work based on annual surveys.
7. Figures 1.8 and 1.9 are based on data from the Current Population Survey ORGs, which provide large samples. We utilize 2000 as the end comparison date to make these figures comparable with the PSID data utilized in figures 1.5 and 1.6. Using 2004 data for figures 1.8 and 1.9 would not affect the results.
8. This index indicates the share of women (or men) who would have to change industry in order for men and women to have equal industry distributions. Industry and occupational codings change every ten years, and it is difficult to recode across these breakpoints. We have translated the industry coding used from 1983 to 1992 to the coding used from 1993 to 2002, using crosswalk information provided by the U.S. Census Bureau.
9. This simulation assigns women's actual unemployment rate within an industry but weights women's employment across industries using men's industry share.
10. This legislation includes mandatory minimum drug sentencing laws, "three strikes" or habitual offender laws, and truth-in-sentencing laws that restrict the possibility of early release.
11. Chinhui Juhn and Dae Il Kim (1999) look at the broader question of whether rising female labor supply has depressed male wages and find little evidence for such an effect.
12. We estimated equivalent wage regressions including controls for occupation and

industry. The results are generally consistent with those in table 1.3, but they show smaller returns to education and smaller race and ethnicity effects.

13. Surprisingly, we know of almost no research that investigates the effects of family composition on male labor supply, although we find significant effects in table 1.2. Within a very particular family composition experiment, Joshua Angrist and William Evans (1998) indicate that number of children has little effect on fathers' labor supply.

14. Others (for example, Blau and Kahn 1997, 2005) have done more complex decompositions.

15. The mean education level among more-skilled women declined between 1979 and 2003. A growing group of women have moved into the more-skilled group—that is, those with more than a high school degree. Since most of this movement is occurring at the margin, it means that overall years of education among this group decreased slightly.

REFERENCES

Altonji, Joseph G., and Rebecca M. Blank. 1999. "Race and Gender in the Labor Market." In *Handbook of Labor Economics*, vol. 3C, edited by Orley C. Ashenfelter and David Card. Amsterdam: Elsevier.

Angrist, Joshua D., and William N. Evans. 1998. "Children and Their Parents' Labor Supply: Evidence from Exogenous Variation in Family Size." *American Economic Review* 88(3): 450–77.

Autor, David H., and Lawrence F. Katz. 1999. "Changes in the Wage Structure and Earnings Inequality." In *Handbook of Labor Economics*, vol. 3A, edited by Orley C. Ashenfelter and David Card. Amsterdam: Elsevier.

Autor, David H., Lawrence F. Katz, and Melissa S. Kearney. 2004. "Trends in U.S. Wage Inequality: Reassessing the Revisionists." Working paper 11627. Cambridge, Mass.: National Bureau of Economic Research.

Bayard, Kimberly, Judith Hellerstein, David Neumark, and Kenneth Troske. 2003. "New Evidence on Sex Segregation and Sex Differences in Wages from Matched Employee-Employer Data." *Journal of Labor Economics* 21(4): 887–922.

Blank, Rebecca M. 2002. "Evaluating Welfare Reform in the U.S." *Journal of Economic Literature* 40(4): 451–68.

Blank, Rebecca M., and Jonah Gelbach. 2006. "Are Less-Educated Women Crowding Less-Educated Men Out of the Labor Market?" In *Black Males Left Behind*, edited by Ron Mincy. Washington, D.C.: Urban Institute.

Blau, Francine D. 1998. "Trends in the Well-Being of American Women, 1970–1995." *Journal of Economic Literature* 36(1): 112–65.

Blau, Francine D., and Lawrence M. Kahn. 1997. "Swimming Upstream: Trends in the Gender Wage Differential in the 1980s." *Journal of Labor Economics* 15(1, pt. 1): 1–42.

———. 2005. "Changes in the Labor Supply Behavior of Married Women: 1980–2000." Working paper 11230. Cambridge, Mass.: National Bureau of Economic Research.

———. Forthcoming. "The U.S. Gender Pay Gap in the 1990s: Slowing Convergence." *Industrial and Labor Relations Review*.

Fortin, Nicole M., and Thomas Lemieux. 2000. "Are Women's Wage Gains Men's Losses? A Distributional Test." *American Economic Review* 90(2): 456–60.

Hellerstein, Judith K., and David Neumark. Forthcoming. "Production Function and Wage Equation Estimation with Heterogeneous Labor: Evidence from a New Matched Employer-Employee Dataset." In *Hard-to-Measure Goods and Services: Essays in Honor of Zvi Griliches*, edited by Ernst R. Berndt and Charles M. Hulten. Chicago: University of Chicago Press.

Hoffman, Saul D., and Laurence S. Seidman. 2003. *Helping Working Families: The Earned Income Tax Credit*. Kalamazoo, Mich.: W. E. Upjohn Institute for Employment Research.

Hoynes, Hilary W. 2000. "The Employment, Earnings, and Income of Less-Skilled Workers over the Business Cycle." In *Finding Jobs: Work and Welfare Reform*, edited by David Card and Rebecca M. Blank. New York: Russell Sage Foundation.

Juhn, Chinhui, and Dae Il Kim. 1999. "The Effects of Rising Female Labor Supply on Male Wages." *Journal of Labor Economics* 17(1): 23–48.

Mulligan, Casey B., and Yona Rubinstein. 2005. "Selection, Investment, and Women's Relative Wages Since 1975." Working paper 11159. Cambridge, Mass.: National Bureau of Economic Research.

Raphael, Steven. 2005. "The Socioeconomic Status of Black Males: The Increasing Importance of Incarceration." In *Poverty, the Distribution of Income, and Public Policy*, edited by Alan Auerbach, David Card, and John Quigley. New York: Russell Sage Foundation.

Welch, Finis. 2000. "Growth in Women's Relative Wages and in Inequality Among Men: One Phenomenon or Two?" *American Economic Review* 90(2): 444–49.

Chapter 2

Wage Trends Among
Disadvantaged Minorities

George J. Borjas

The resurgence of large-scale immigration in recent decades fundamentally altered the racial and ethnic composition of the disadvantaged population in the United States.[1] In 1960, 21.3 percent of working men in the bottom 20 percent of the wage distribution were African American and only 3.6 percent were foreign-born. By 2000, the black share in this low-wage workforce had fallen to 13.1 percent, but the immigrant share had risen to 17.4 percent.

It is well known that the "new immigration" contains a very large number of low-skilled workers (Borjas 1999). In fact, the data reveal that, at least through the mid-1990s, each successive wave of post-1960 immigrants entered the United States with less earnings potential than the preceding wave. The sizable increase in the size of the immigrant influx—as well as the changing demographic and skill characteristics of the immigrants—can be attributed not only to an increase in illegal immigration (it is estimated that at least 10 million illegal immigrants resided in the country by 2005) but also to changes in legal immigration policy that emphasize family reunification rather than the skills of potential migrants in the awarding of entry visas. Inevitably, the changes in immigration policy and the lax border enforcement changed the ethnic and racial mix of the disadvantaged population. Moreover, these changes are likely to continue, since the pace of modern immigration has not yet abated.

This chapter documents and explores some of the implications of these shifts in the demographic composition of the disadvantaged workforce. In particular, the study analyzes wage trends among disadvantaged minorities and examines a number of factors that are likely to influence these trends. The study uses data drawn from the 1980 to 2000 Integrated Public Use Microdata Samples (IPUMS) of the U.S. decennial census. Not surprisingly, the data indicate that the racial-ethnic composition of the disadvantaged population changed dramatically in the past two decades, becoming heavily Hispanic and also increasing in the representation of Asian immigrants. It seems therefore that our traditional stereotypes about the racial composition of the disadvantaged workforce—based on the racial demographics that characterized the country's population prior to the resurgence of large-scale immigration—are due for a major overhaul.

The chapter identifies and measures the importance of three factors that play important roles in determining wage trends among disadvantaged minorities: (1) the changing composition of particular ethnic groups in terms of both immigration status and national origin; (2) the "excess sensitivity" shown by low-skilled minorities, and particularly low-skilled immigrants, to business cycle fluctuations; and (3) the continuing entry of large numbers of low-skilled immigrants who compete directly in the labor market with the preexisting disadvantaged workforce.

THE DATA

The empirical analysis uses data drawn from the IPUMS files of the U.S. census between 1980 and 2000. These data comprise a 5 percent random sample of the population. The entire available sample in each census is used in the empirical analysis.

The study focuses on four racial-ethnic groups: whites, blacks, Hispanics, and Asians.[2] The classification of workers into these groups uses the information provided by both the race and Hispanic-origin variables in each census. In particular, the Hispanic-origin variable gives the worker's self-identification of Hispanic status (and also provides information on the type of Hispanic ancestry). I use this variable to assign workers into the Hispanic category. I then use the race variable to classify workers who report that they are *not* of Hispanic origin into the other categories. By construction, therefore, the groups of white, black, and Asian workers are composed entirely of persons who are not of Hispanic origin. I further classify workers in each of the four racial-ethnic groups by immigration status. A person is defined as an immigrant if he or she was born abroad and is either a noncitizen or a naturalized citizen; all other persons are classified as natives.

It is important to emphasize that the census data contain both legal immigrants and the many illegal immigrants who answered the census questionnaire and that the number of illegal immigrants enumerated by the census increased rapidly between 1990 and 2000. The number of foreign-born persons residing illegally in the United States was estimated to be 3.5 million in 1990 and 7 million in 2000 (U.S. Immigration and Naturalization Service 2003).[3] Because the census data do not provide any information on the visa status of foreign-born persons, it is not possible (without making many heroic assumptions) to ascertain the trends in the skill level of the illegal immigrant population or to determine precisely where these immigrants fall in the skill or wage distribution. Nevertheless, because illegal immigrants now make up at least one-quarter of the foreign-born population enumerated in the census, it is likely the case that many of the trends in the disadvantaged population discussed in this chapter are greatly influenced by the growth of illegal immigration.

In each census, the study is restricted to persons age eighteen to fifty-four who work in the civilian sector, are not enrolled in school, and do not reside in group quarters.[4] Whenever appropriate, the sampling weights reported in the 1990 and 2000 IPUMS data are used in the calculations.

Table 2.1 begins the descriptive analysis by documenting the changing size of the various racial-ethnic groups between 1980 and 2000. The first three columns of the table report the fraction of the workforce in each census year (and by gender) that can be classified into the various groups. The data document the well-known increase in the relative size of the minority nonblack workforce and the corresponding decline in the size of the white workforce. In 1980, 83.0 percent of working men were white. By 2000, this group accounted for only 71.8 percent of the workforce. Note that the decline in the white male workforce was not accompanied by an increase in the relative number of African American working men. The share of the black workforce, in fact, remained stable at around 9 percent. The fraction of the workforce composed of men of Hispanic origin, however, rose markedly, from 6.2 to 13.0 percent, while the fraction composed of men of Asian ancestry rose from 1.5 to 3.7 percent.

The remaining rows of table 2.1 document the extent to which these demographic changes can be attributed to immigration. It is clear, for instance, that the immigration of white workers did not increase very much (at least in proportionate terms) between 1980 and 2000. White immigrants made up 2.5 percent of the workforce in 1980 and 2.6 percent of the workforce in 2000. Similarly, the immigration of black men, though it increased rapidly during this period, was still only a very small component of total immigration. As a result, only 0.3 percent of the workforce were black immigrants in 1980, and that proportion rose to only 0.8 percent in 2000. Immigration, however, played *the* central role in the growth of the Hispanic and Asian workforce: the immigrant share of the workforce more than tripled for each of these groups. The share of Hispanic immigrants rose from 2.5 percent in 1980 to 7.9 percent in 2000, while the share of Asian immigrants rose from 1.0 to 3.1 percent.

Although these aggregate statistics show interesting and relevant trends, they also mask a great deal of the increased clustering of some racial-ethnic groups, particularly Hispanic immigrants, into certain segments of the skill distribution. The remaining columns of table 2.1 illustrate this clustering effect by reporting the racial-ethnic distribution of workers within a particular education group (for each census year and gender). I use three educational attainment groups to simplify the presentation: workers who were high school dropouts (less than twelve years of schooling), workers who were high school graduates (exactly twelve years of schooling), and workers who had more than a high school education (more than twelve years of schooling).

Consider initially the trend in the representation of Hispanic workers in each of the three skill categories. In 1980, 13.8 percent of workers who were high school dropouts were Hispanic (7.0 percent were Hispanic natives, and the re-

TABLE 2.1 / Distribution of Ethnicity Within Education Groups (Percentage Belonging to Classification)

Group	All Workers			High School Dropouts			High School Graduates			More Than High School		
	1980	1990	2000	1980	1990	2000	1980	1990	2000	1980	1990	2000
Male												
White	83.0%	79.0%	71.8%	70.4%	58.6%	41.7%	85.2%	78.8%	71.0%	88.0%	84.6%	79.0%
Native	80.4	76.6	69.2	67.2	56.0	39.9	83.3	77.0	69.1	85.0	81.7	75.8
Immigrant	2.5	2.5	2.6	3.2	2.6	1.9	1.9	1.8	1.9	3.0	2.9	3.2
Black	8.7	9.1	9.1	13.9	12.1	8.8	8.7	11.1	11.8	5.7	6.8	7.6
Native	8.4	8.5	8.3	13.4	11.3	8.0	8.4	10.6	11.0	5.4	6.3	6.8
Immigrant	0.3	0.6	0.8	0.4	0.8	0.8	0.3	0.6	0.8	0.3	0.5	0.8
Hispanic	6.2	8.6	13.0	13.8	26.3	44.2	4.6	7.6	12.5	3.4	4.7	6.5
Native	3.7	4.2	5.1	7.0	7.8	8.4	3.3	4.6	6.0	2.3	3.0	3.8
Immigrant	2.5	4.4	7.9	6.8	18.5	35.8	1.3	3.0	6.5	1.2	1.7	2.7
Asian	1.5	2.6	3.7	0.9	2.0	2.9	0.9	1.6	2.2	2.4	3.4	4.8
Native	0.5	0.6	0.6	0.2	0.2	0.2	0.4	0.4	0.4	0.7	0.8	0.9
Immigrant	1.0	2.0	3.1	0.7	1.7	2.7	0.4	1.2	1.8	1.7	2.7	3.9
Female												
White	80.7	77.8	71.3	67.3	57.9	41.3	83.5	78.3	69.5	84.0	81.3	76.4
Native	78.0	75.6	69.0	63.5	55.1	39.3	81.2	76.2	67.6	81.2	79.0	73.8
Immigrant	2.7	2.3	2.3	3.8	2.8	1.9	2.3	2.0	1.9	2.7	2.4	2.5
Black	11.2	11.5	12.3	16.9	14.9	14.1	10.3	12.5	14.6	9.5	10.2	10.8
Native	10.8	10.9	11.4	16.3	14.0	12.9	10.0	11.9	13.6	9.2	9.7	10.0
Immigrant	0.4	0.6	0.9	0.7	0.9	1.2	0.4	0.6	1.0	0.3	0.5	0.8
Hispanic	5.6	7.1	10.4	12.9	22.5	37.0	4.4	6.6	10.9	3.3	4.6	6.4
Native	3.5	4.1	5.3	6.7	7.9	9.7	3.3	4.4	6.2	2.2	3.1	4.2
Immigrant	2.0	3.1	5.1	6.2	14.7	27.4	1.1	2.2	4.7	1.1	1.4	2.2
Asian	1.7	2.8	3.8	1.8	3.4	4.9	1.1	1.8	2.5	2.7	3.3	4.4
Native	0.6	0.6	0.7	0.2	0.2	0.2	0.5	0.4	0.4	0.9	0.8	0.9
Immigrant	1.2	2.2	3.2	1.5	3.2	4.6	0.7	1.4	2.2	1.8	2.5	3.5

Source: Author's compilations.

Notes: For each column (by gender), the information reported for white, black, Hispanic, and Asian groups (or the more detailed information provided by immigration status) would add up to 100 percent if the comparable information for the residual group of "other ethnicity" were also reported.

maining 6.8 percent were Hispanic immigrants). By 2000, 44.2 percent of workers who were high school dropouts were of Hispanic origin (8.4 percent were Hispanic natives, and 35.8 percent were Hispanic immigrants). Therefore, over a remarkable twenty-year period, the low-skilled workforce—at least as defined by very low levels of educational attainment—became almost majority-Hispanic. In contrast, Hispanic workers were a much less important part of the high-skilled workforce. In 1980, 3.4 percent of workers with at least a high school education were Hispanic; by 2000, 6.5 percent were Hispanic.

In contrast to the increased clustering of Hispanics at the low end of the skill distribution, the growth of the Asian workforce has been distributed more evenly across the distribution—even though, as with Hispanics, immigration accounts for much of the growth in the number of Asian workers. In 1980 Asians were 0.9 percent of high school dropouts (0.2 percent were native-born Asians, and the remaining 0.7 percent were Asian immigrants). By 2000, Asians were 2.9 percent of high school dropouts (0.2 percent were native Asians, and 2.7 percent were Asian immigrants). Similarly, in 1980 Asians made up 2.4 percent of the high-skilled group (0.7 were Asian natives, and 1.7 percent were Asian immigrants). By 2000, Asians were 4.8 percent of the high-skilled group (0.9 percent were Asian natives, and 3.9 percent were Asian immigrants).

Partly because of the rapid increase in the educational attainment of the black native workforce (O'Neill 1990), the fraction of high school dropouts who were black natives declined markedly between 1980 and 2000 while the fraction of high-skilled workers who were blacks rose significantly. In 1980, for instance, 13.9 percent of high school dropouts were black; by 2000, only 8.8 percent were black. In contrast, 4.7 percent of the high-skilled workforce in 1980 was black, and this statistic increased to 7.6 percent by 2000. The fraction of high school dropouts who were white also dropped (at an even more precipitous rate) for similar reasons, from 70.4 to 41.7 percent between 1980 and 2000.

As implied by the trends in the educational attainment of black and white workers, there may be some confusion in the interpretation of the statistics reported in table 2.1: the increasing representation of some minority groups in the low-skilled category may be driven, not by an increase in the number of low-skilled minorities, but by the remarkable drop in the number of low-skilled white and black natives. Table 2.2 looks at the same census data from a different angle so as to address this potential problem more directly. In particular, it reports the distribution of educational attainment within a particular racial-ethnic group. This different perspective on the data can therefore isolate the trends in educational attainment within particular minority groups. The table clearly documents that the decreasing representation of black and white natives in the low-skilled workforce is partly attributable to the fact that there are many fewer black and white natives who are high school dropouts. In 1980, for example, 18.7 percent of white native men and 35.7 percent of black native men were high school dropouts. By 2000, these statistics had declined by around two-thirds, to 6.9 and 11.6 percent, respectively.

The table also documents, however, that the fraction of Hispanics (and Asians)

TABLE 2.2 / Distribution of Educational Attainment Within Racial-Ethnic Groups,
1980 to 2000

	High School Dropouts			High School Graduates			More Than High School		
Group	1980	1990	2000	1980	1990	2000	1980	1990	2000
Men									
White	18.9%	10.0%	7.0%	40.3%	35.2%	33.2%	40.8%	54.8%	60.0%
Native	18.7	9.9	6.9	40.7	35.5	33.5	40.7	54.6	59.6
Immigrant	27.3	14.1	8.5	28.8	25.8	24.6	43.9	60.1	66.9
Black	35.5	18.0	11.6	39.4	43.4	43.3	25.1	38.6	45.2
Native	35.7	18.0	11.6	39.5	44.1	44.2	24.8	37.9	44.3
Immigrant	30.2	17.8	11.6	36.7	34.0	33.9	33.2	48.2	54.5
Hispanic	49.7	41.2	40.7	29.0	31.1	32.2	21.3	27.8	27.1
Native	41.7	25.1	19.8	35.0	38.9	39.7	23.3	36.0	40.5
Immigrant	61.8	56.5	54.2	20.0	23.6	27.5	18.3	20.0	18.4
Asian	13.4	10.2	9.4	23.3	21.9	19.5	63.3	67.9	71.1
Native	9.9	5.0	3.8	34.8	26.8	19.7	55.3	68.1	76.5
Immigrant	15.2	11.7	10.6	17.6	20.5	19.4	67.2	67.8	70.0
Women									
White	15.1	7.5	4.8	48.7	37.5	30.7	36.2	55.1	64.5
Native	14.8	7.3	4.7	49.0	37.6	39.8	36.2	55.1	64.4
Immigrant	25.3	12.3	7.0	40.0	33.4	26.2	34.7	54.4	66.8
Black	27.3	12.9	9.6	43.2	40.4	37.5	29.5	46.7	52.9
Native	27.2	12.8	9.4	43.3	40.5	37.8	29.5	46.7	52.8
Immigrant	29.1	15.1	11.1	42.7	38.4	34.7	28.3	46.5	54.2
Hispanic	42.0	31.7	29.7	37.2	34.5	33.1	20.8	33.8	37.2
Native	34.4	19.5	15.2	43.9	40.0	36.8	21.7	40.5	48.0
Immigrant	55.3	48.0	44.9	25.6	27.2	29.2	19.2	24.8	25.9
Asian	17.9	12.3	10.6	29.8	24.6	20.9	52.4	63.2	68.5
Native	7.8	3.6	3.0	38.3	25.6	17.4	53.9	70.8	79.6
Immigrant	22.3	14.8	12.2	26.0	24.2	21.6	52.7	61.0	66.2

Source: Author's compilation.
Note: For a given census year, the rows in this table add up to 100 percent (except for rounding
error).

who were high school dropouts also dropped over the twenty-year period, but
the rate of decline was far slower than that observed among white and black
workers. In 1980, for instance, 49.7 percent of Hispanic men and 13.4 percent of
Asian men were high school dropouts; by 2000, these statistics had fallen only
to 40.7 and 9.4 percent, respectively. The differential rates of decline in the high
school dropout workforce among the various ethnic groups implies that a randomly chosen high school dropout was far more likely to be Hispanic in 2000
than in 1980.

Of course, educational attainment is not the only factor that determines income disadvantage for a particular worker or minority group. It is of interest, there-fore, to examine whether alternative definitions of skill groups also reveal a fun-damental shift in the racial-ethnic mix of the disadvantaged population. To de-termine the sensitivity of the evidence, I examined the log wage distribution by census year and gender and calculated the racial-ethnic composition of workers who were in the bottom 20 percent of the wage distribution, the fraction who lay between the twentieth and fortieth percentile of the wage distribution, and the fraction who were above the fortieth percentile.[5]

Table 2.3 replicates the exercise first summarized in table 2.1, but uses the placement in the wage distribution, rather than educational attainment, to define the skill groups. It turns out that the qualitative nature of the evidence is very similar in the two tables. There has been a precipitous drop in the relative num-ber of white workers who place in the bottom quintile of the wage distribution. In 1980, 72.2 percent of the working men in the bottom quintile were white; by 2000, only 55.4 percent were white. There has also been a modest decline in the representation of blacks in this low-skilled group, from 15.1 to 13.5 percent. In contrast, the fraction of the workers at the bottom of the wage distribution who were Hispanic rose from 10.2 to 24.6 percent, with much of the increase attribut-able to immigration (4.6 percent of the workers in the bottom quintile were His-panic immigrants in 1980, as compared to 16.9 percent in 2000). There was also a rise in the Asian share in the bottom quintile (again due to immigration), from 1.5 percent in 1980 to 3.4 percent in 2000.

The descriptive evidence presented in this section, therefore, suggests a re-markable change in the racial-ethnic mix of the disadvantaged workforce over the past two decades. As recently as 1980, blacks made up 15.1 percent of low-wage workers (as defined by the bottom 20 percent of the skill distribution), Hispanics were 10.2 percent, and Asians 1.5 percent. By 2000, blacks made up 13.5 percent, Hispanics 24.6 percent, and Asians 3.4 percent. The economic and social implications of this change in the racial-ethnic composition of the disad-vantaged workforce are not yet fully understood or appreciated, but the "new look" of this workforce is likely to play an important part in the inevitable social policy debates for decades to come.

TRENDS IN RELATIVE WAGES: COMPOSITION EFFECTS

I now use the decennial census data to document trends in the relative wages of the various racial-ethnic groups between 1980 and 2000 and to highlight how within-group changes in the demographic composition of the racial-ethnic classi-fication can play an important role in determining the aggregate trend. The top panel of table 2.4 reports the unadjusted log weekly wage differential between the various racial-ethnic groups—blacks, Hispanics, and Asians—and a baseline group consisting of white native workers. The unadjusted wage differentials are calculated separately in each census and by gender.[6] The data indicate that the

TABLE 2.3 / Distribution of Ethnicity Within Skill Groups, by Placement in the Wage Distribution, 1980 to 2000

Group	Below Twentieth Percentile			Twentieth to Fortieth Percentile			Above Fortieth Percentile		
	1980	1990	2000	1980	1990	2000	1980	1990	2000
Male									
White	72.2%	65.8%	55.4%	79.6%	74.6%	66.0%	87.7%	84.9%	79.4%
Native	70.3	64.3	53.6	77.3	72.7	64.0	84.8	82.0	76.2
Immigrant	1.9	1.5	1.8	2.3	1.9	2.0	3.0	3.0	3.1
Black	15.1	14.9	13.5	10.4	11.0	11.2	6.0	6.4	7.0
Native	14.6	14.2	12.5	9.9	10.3	10.2	5.8	5.9	6.3
Immigrant	0.5	0.7	1.0	0.4	0.8	1.0	0.2	0.5	0.7
Hispanic	10.2	15.6	24.6	7.9	11.0	17.0	4.3	5.5	7.8
Native	5.5	6.2	7.7	4.6	5.0	6.1	2.8	3.2	3.9
Immigrant	4.6	9.4	16.9	3.3	5.9	10.9	1.5	2.3	3.9
Asian	1.5	2.5	3.4	1.4	2.5	3.3	1.5	2.6	3.9
Native	0.4	0.5	0.5	0.4	0.5	0.5	0.5	0.7	0.7
Immigrant	1.0	2.0	2.9	1.0	2.0	2.8	1.0	2.0	3.2
Female									
White	81.9	77.1	67.5	79.2	75.3	66.6	80.9	79.0	74.1
Native	79.3	75.3	65.6	76.6	73.3	64.5	78.1	76.5	71.6
Immigrant	2.6	1.8	2.0	2.6	2.1	2.0	2.8	2.5	2.5
Black	10.6	11.6	12.4	11.6	12.0	13.4	11.3	11.4	11.8
Native	10.3	11.3	11.7	11.2	11.4	12.5	10.9	10.6	10.8
Immigrant	0.3	0.4	0.7	0.4	0.6	0.9	0.5	0.7	1.0
Hispanic	5.6	8.5	14.5	7.0	9.3	14.3	5.1	5.9	7.7
Native	3.7	4.5	6.2	4.1	4.6	6.3	3.3	3.7	4.7
Immigrant	1.9	4.0	8.3	2.9	4.7	8.0	1.8	2.2	3.0
Asian	1.2	1.8	2.9	1.5	2.5	3.2	2.1	3.2	4.3
Native	0.3	0.3	0.4	0.4	0.4	0.4	0.7	0.8	0.8
Immigrant	0.9	1.5	2.5	1.1	2.1	2.8	1.4	2.4	3.5

Source: Author's compilation.
Notes: The information reported for white, black, Hispanic, and Asian groups in each column (or the more detailed information provided by immigration status) would add up to 100 percent if the comparable information for the residual group of "other ethnicity" were also reported.

unadjusted black-white log wage gap for working men was constant over the past twenty years, hovering at around -.35 throughout the period. The data also show a stable wage gap between Asian and white workers—at zero! The table clearly shows, however, that the relative wage of Hispanics fell substantially during the period. The log wage gap between Hispanic and white men stood at -.30 in 1980 and dropped to -.45 in 2000.

TABLE 2.4 / Log Wage Differentials, Relative to White Natives, 1980 to 2000

Specification or Group	Male			Female		
	1980	1990	2000	1980	1990	2000
Unadjusted wage gap						
White immigrant	.108	.182	.159	.050	.113	.095
Black	−.345	−.374	−.353	.026	−.023	−.065
Native	−.347	−.385	−.365	.023	−.033	−.075
Immigrant	−.295	−.224	−.227	.108	.158	.063
Hispanic	−.300	−.395	−.451	−.054	−.140	−.237
Native	−.263	−.303	−.335	−.051	−.088	−.141
Immigrant	−.355	−.482	−.525	−.058	−.210	−.337
Asian	−.002	−.003	.003	.184	.191	.152
Native	.003	.023	.025	.226	.271	.260
Immigrant	−.004	−.011	−.001	.166	.168	.129
Adjusted wage gap						
White immigrant	.032	.002	−.018	.060	.004	−.049
Black	−.242	−.262	−.242	.051	.026	.026
Native	−.244	−.266	−.244	.048	.019	.020
Immigrant	−.235	−.259	−.276	.142	.115	.021
Hispanic	−.152	−.159	−.170	.011	−.025	−.045
Native	−.146	−.139	−.140	.008	−.007	−.011
Immigrant	−.183	−.232	−.249	.034	−.071	−.154
Asian	−.086	−.123	−.103	.092	.059	.061
Native	−.066	−.069	−.053	.125	.103	.122
Immigrant	−.121	−.186	−.172	.094	−.043	−.021
High school dropouts						
White immigrant	.142	.339	.241	.133	.285	.211
Black	−.272	−.222	−.237	−.004	.023	.022
Native	−.275	−.231	−.255	−.010	.007	.005
Immigrant	−.198	−.081	−.051	.146	.268	.204
Hispanic	−.208	−.188	−.156	.021	.036	.016
Native	−.169	−.137	−.157	−.001	.022	.015
Immigrant	−.248	−.209	−.156	.045	.044	.017
Asian	−.169	−.127	−.091	.111	.194	.153
Native	−.018	−.124	−.148	.127	.124	.208
Immigrant	−.217	−.127	−.086	.109	.199	.151

Source: Author's compilation.
Notes: The explanatory variables of the regression model used to estimate the coefficients reported in the middle panel include dummy variables indicating the worker's educational attainment (whether the worker has less than twelve years of school, exactly twelve years, twelve to fifteen years, or at least sixteen years); a third-order polynomial in the worker's age; a vector of variables indicating the number of years the immigrant has resided in the United States; and a vector of fixed effects indicating the worker's state of residence. The adjusted differences between immigrant groups and natives in the middle panel refer to wage gaps experienced by immigrants who have been in the country ten to fifteen years. Although the standard errors of the coefficients are not reported, the sample size of the regressions ensures that practically all of the coefficients are statistically significant (at conventional levels).

It turns out that this decline in the relative wage of the "typical" Hispanic worker is quite misleading, for it is distorted by the increasing number of Hispanic immigrants and their worsening economic outcomes. For each of the racial-ethnic groups, table 2.4 also reports the log weekly wage of both native and immigrant workers (relative to the log wage of white natives). Even though the unadjusted Hispanic-white wage gap fell by 0.15 log points between 1980 and 2000, the decline among native-born Hispanic men was only 0.07 log points. In contrast, the unadjusted log wage gap between Hispanic immigrants and white natives dropped from -0.36 to -0.53, a 0.17-log-point drop. Not only do Hispanic immigrants earn substantially less than white natives, but the relative economic status of Hispanic immigrants within the Hispanic population worsened dramatically in the twenty-year period. As a result, much of the drop in the economic status of the "typical" Hispanic in the United States can be explained by a composition effect created by an immigration-induced demographic shift in this population. In other words, much of the decline in the relative wage of Hispanics can be attributed to: (1) the increasing number of Hispanic immigrants in the workforce (the immigrant share among Hispanic men increased from 40 percent to over 60 percent between 1980 and 2000); (2) the lower wage of Hispanic immigrants relative to Hispanic natives; and (3) the worsening economic outcomes experienced by Hispanic immigrants during the period.

The middle panel of table 2.4 illustrates the extent to which differences in socioeconomic characteristics generate some of the observed wage differentials among racial-ethnic groups. In particular, I estimated the following regression model separately by census year and gender:

$$\log w_{ijt} = X_{ijt}\beta_t + \gamma_t R_{it} + v_{jt} + \varepsilon_{ijt}, \tag{2.1}$$

where w_{ijt} gives the weekly wage of worker i at time t; X_{ijt} is a vector of socioeconomic characteristics; R_{it} is a vector of dummy variables indicating the racial-ethnic classification of the worker; and v_{jt} represents a vector of fixed effects indicating the worker's state of residence. The vector X includes dummy variables indicating the worker's educational attainment; a third-order polynomial in the worker's age; and a vector of variables indicating the number of years the immigrant has resided in the United States.[7] I estimated two alternative specifications of the model. The first defines the vector R_{ijt} simply in terms of the four racial-ethnic groups: white, black, Hispanic, and Asian. The second expands the vector R_{ijt} by including variables that identify whether the worker in a particular ethnic group is native- or foreign-born (for example, black natives, black immigrants). As before, all of the wage differentials are reported relative to white natives. Finally, the wage differentials estimated for immigrants refer to the wage gaps between immigrants who have been in the United States between ten and fifteen years (roughly the "typical" group in the foreign-born population) and white natives.

The middle panel of table 2.4 reports the adjusted wage differentials. The comparison of these adjusted wage gaps with the unadjusted differences reported in the top panel yields a number of interesting findings. First, the unexplained wage gap between black and white natives was stable over the 1980 to 2000 period, hovering around -.24 log points. Equally interesting, it is evident that differences in educational attainment, age, and state of residence explain only about one-third of the unadjusted wage gap for black natives (see also Altonji and Blank 1999).

The regression results for Hispanics are quite different. The adjusted log wage gap hovers around -.16 for Hispanics and -.14 for Hispanic natives, and it increases from -.18 to -.25 for Hispanic immigrants. By 2000, the adjusted log wage gap between Hispanics and white natives was substantially smaller than the unadjusted log wage gap (-0.17 versus -0.45). In other words, the relatively small set of socioeconomic variables introduced in the regression model accounts for over 60 percent of the wage gap between the two groups. The explanatory power of these variables is large even for Hispanic immigrants, where the adjusted wage gap in 2000 is -0.25 and the unadjusted wage gap is -.53. In short, differences in socioeconomic characteristics (and, as I will show, particularly differences in educational attainment) explain between half and two-thirds of the Hispanic-native wage gap (see Trejo 1997).

There are also dramatic differences between adjusted and unadjusted wage differentials for Asian working men. As noted earlier, the unadjusted wage gaps are numerically indistinguishable from zero. The adjusted wage gaps, however, are negative and numerically large, particularly for Asian immigrants. In other words, Asian natives (and particularly Asian immigrants) earn substantially less than similarly skilled white natives. In 2000, for example, even though the typical Asian immigrant earned about the same as the typical white native, the log wage gap was -.17 after controlling for differences in socioeconomic characteristics.

The presentation of the regression results in the middle panel of table 2.4 does not isolate *which* socioeconomic characteristics are most responsible for generating the observed wage gaps. It turns out, however, that much of the difference between the top and middle panels of the table reflects the differences in educational attainment among the groups. To illustrate this fact, the bottom panel of the table pursues a different approach to controlling for differences in socioeconomic characteristics. Instead of using a regression model, this panel simply reports the log wage gap between immigrants and natives who are high school dropouts. The evidence tends to be quite similar to that obtained from the regression model in equation 1.1. Once the analysis controls for educational attainment, the log wage gap between Hispanics and white native workers narrows substantially, while the log wage gap between Asian and white natives increases substantially. For example, in 2000 the unadjusted wage gap between Hispanic and white men was -.45, while the wage gap between Hispanic and white men who were high school dropouts was only -.16. Controlling for differences in educational attainment therefore narrows the wage gap between the two groups substantially.

The data show that the dramatic increase in Hispanic immigration explains much of the relative decline in the economic status of the "typical" Hispanic in the United States. There is, in fact, an additional compositional effect at work *within* the Hispanic population. The Hispanic workforce comprises four disparate groups that share the same language but differ substantially in other cultural and economic traits: Mexicans, Puerto Ricans, Cubans, and "other" Hispanics.[8] As documented in the top panel of table 2.5, the demographic and economic content of the label "Hispanic" has changed over time. In particular, there has been a dramatic increase in the fraction of the Hispanic population who are Mexican immigrants. In 1980 only 23.4 percent of Hispanics were Mexican immigrants; this proportion had increased to 40.4 percent by 2000. The only other Hispanic group that increased its representation substantially was the "other Hispanic immigrant" group, composed mainly of workers born in Central and South America. These immigrants made up 10.6 percent of Hispanics in 1980, but 17.7 percent by 2000.

The increasing demographic importance of these two groups is significant because they happen to be the *least-skilled* groups within the Hispanic workforce. As the middle panel of table 2.5 shows, 62.2 percent of Mexican immigrants and 41.4 percent of "other Hispanic immigrants" were high school dropouts in 2000. In contrast, only 20.4 percent of native-born workers of Mexican ancestry, 21.9 percent of Puerto Rican natives, and 17.5 percent of Cuban immigrants were high school dropouts.

The changing definition of who is represented by the "typical" Hispanic suggests that the aggregate trend in the relative wage for either Hispanic natives or Hispanic immigrants is itself not very meaningful, since the trend could be capturing the changing national-origin mix of the Hispanic population. To illustrate, the bottom panel of table 2.5 reports the unadjusted log wage gap between the various Hispanic subgroups and white (non-Hispanic) natives. These data suggest that there has been a sizable decline in the relative wage of both Mexican natives and Mexican immigrants, although the decline is steeper for Mexican immigrants. Between 1980 and 2000, the relative wage of Mexican immigrants fell from -.44 to -.58 log points. This decline is important because Mexican immigrants make up an increasingly larger part of the Hispanic workforce and happen to be the least economically successful subgroup among Hispanics.[9]

Note that the decline observed among Mexican immigrants stands in sharp contrast with the relatively stable wage disadvantage experienced by Puerto Ricans—they earned 34.9 percent less than white natives in 1980, and 31.6 percent less in 2000—and with the more modest decline observed among Cuban immigrants, from a -15.0 percent wage advantage in 1980 to a -21.9 percent wage disadvantage in 2000. The only other group of Hispanics that experienced a substantial decline in the relative wage is the fast-growing group of "other Hispanic immigrants," whose relative wage fell from -26.5 percent in 1980 to -44.3 percent in 2000. This decline may itself have been caused by compositional changes in the national-origin mix of this group, since the immigrants in 1980 may well have originated in a different set of countries than those in 2000.

The descriptive analysis reported in this section yields an important lesson: it is very difficult to generalize about or correctly interpret aggregate trends in the

TABLE 2.5 / Size and Characteristics of Hispanic Groups

	Male			Female		
	1980	1990	2000	1980	1990	2000
Hispanics who are:						
Mexican	61.4%	63.0%	62.3%	57.3%	57.7%	54.7%
Native	38.0	30.9	21.9	40.4	36.0	27.8
Immigrant	23.4	32.1	40.4	16.8	21.7	27.1
Puerto Rican	11.6	10.3	8.0	10.9	11.6	10.7
Cuban	5.9	4.8	3.4	7.1	5.4	3.8
Native	0.5	0.8	0.8	0.6	1.1	1.0
Immigrant	5.4	4.0	2.6	6.5	4.4	2.8
Other Hispanic	21.1	21.9	26.2	24.8	25.2	30.9
Native	10.5	6.9	8.5	12.0	8.7	12.1
Immigrant	10.6	15.0	17.7	12.8	16.6	18.8
Hispanics who are high school dropouts:						
Mexican	55.7	47.6	47.5	47.7	36.8	35.8
Native	43.0	25.2	20.4	37.4	20.7	15.7
Immigrant	76.4	69.3	62.2	72.3	63.5	56.3
Puerto Rican	52.8	32.0	21.9	38.9	22.0	16.6
Cuban	34.6	23.0	15.1	31.5	17.5	10.1
Native	21.0	11.9	7.7	18.4	7.2	5.3
Immigrant	36.0	25.2	17.5	32.7	20.0	12.0
Other Hispanic	34.6	30.9	33.6	33.4	27.6	25.8
Native	26.6	16.4	17.4	21.8	13.1	13.7
Immigrant	42.6	37.5	41.4	44.3	35.1	33.6
Log wage gap relative to white natives:						
Mexican	−0.330	−0.458	−0.502	−0.095	−0.206	−0.291
Native	−0.261	−0.332	−0.356	−0.072	−0.135	−0.167
Immigrant	−0.442	−0.579	−0.582	−0.126	−0.322	−0.419
Puerto Rican	−0.349	−0.273	−0.316	0.007	0.003	−0.092
Cuban	−0.156	−0.152	−0.191	0.046	0.087	0.034
Native	−0.210	−0.180	−0.101	0.099	0.125	0.148
Immigrant	−0.150	−0.146	−0.219	0.041	0.078	−0.010
Other Hispanic	−0.224	−0.323	−0.405	−0.014	−0.106	−0.224
Native	−0.182	−0.232	−0.325	−0.006	−0.038	−0.151
Immigrant	−0.265	−0.366	−0.443	−0.021	−0.141	−0.270

Source: Author's compilation.
Notes: The classification into the various Hispanic groups uses the self-identification provided by the Hispanic-origin variable in the census.

economic status of the Hispanic (and, to a lesser extent, Asian) workforce in the United States. The difficulties arise because Hispanic immigrants are becoming an ever-larger part of the Hispanic population, and Hispanic immigrants tend to earn less than Hispanic natives. Second, the national-origin groups that make up the Hispanic population have dramatically different economic experiences, and part of the decline in the economic status of the "typical" Hispanic can be attributed to the increasing representation in this population of two low-wage groups: Mexicans and the "other Hispanic immigrants." Obviously, many other factors besides composition effects are likely to influence wage trends among disadvantaged minorities. The remainder of this chapter examines two factors suggested by previous research: business cycle fluctuations and the labor market consequences of continued immigration.

THE CYCLICAL SENSITIVITY OF EMPLOYMENT OUTCOMES

Although previous studies have documented the sensitivity of black wages and employment to the business cycle (Blank 1989; Lundberg 1985), relatively few studies have measured the cyclicality of the employment outcomes of other minority groups. To determine the business cycle sensitivity of employment and wages for the various racial-ethnic groups, I pooled the 1980 to 2000 censuses and estimated the following regression model separately within each of the four main racial-ethnic groups:

$$Y_{ijt} = X_{ijt}\beta + \gamma I_{it} + \delta_0 U_{jt} + \delta_1 (U_{it} \times I_{it}) + v_j + \pi_t + \varepsilon, \qquad (2.2)$$

where Y_{ijt} is a socioeconomic outcome for person i, residing in state j, in year t; X_{ijt} is a vector of background characteristics; I_{it} is a dummy variable indicating whether person i is an immigrant; U_{jt} is the unemployment rate in state j at time t; v_j is a vector of state-of-residence fixed effects; and π_t is a vector of period fixed effects. The vector X includes dummy variables indicating the worker's educational attainment and a third-order polynomial in the worker's age. The coefficient vector (δ_0, δ_1) gives the parameters that measure the sensitivity of employment outcome Y to business cycle fluctuations. The coefficient δ_0 gives the business cycle effect for native workers, and δ_1 gives the differential effect between immigrants and natives. Note that the regression controls for both period and state-of-residence fixed effects, so that the identification of cyclical sensitivity depends solely on within-state variation in the unemployment rate.

The analysis uses three alternative dependent variables: the proportion of weeks worked in the year prior to the census (this variable is defined for both workers and nonworkers so that it ranges from zero to one); the log weekly wage (calculated only in the sample of workers); and log annual earnings (again calculated only in the sample of workers).

The top panel of table 2.6 reports the vector (δ_0, δ_1) for the various specifica-

TABLE 2.6 / Sensitivity of Labor Market Outcomes to Aggregate Unemployment Fluctuations

| | Dependent Variable | | | | | |
| | Fraction of Time Worked | | Log Weekly Earnings | | Log Annual Earnings | |
Group	U_{jt}	$I_{ijt} \times U_{jt}$	U_{jt}	$I_{ijt} \times U_{jt}$	U_{jt}	$I_{ijt} \times U_{jt}$
Men						
White	−0.006	0.006	−0.026	−0.014	−0.033	−0.008
	(0.000)	(0.001)	(0.001)	(0.001)	(0.001)	(0.001)
Black	−0.015	0.003	−0.023	−0.020	−0.039	−0.023
	(0.001)	(0.002)	(0.001)	(0.003)	(0.002)	(0.004)
Hispanic	−0.013	0.008	−0.034	−0.010	−0.050	−0.005
	(0.001)	(0.001)	(0.001)	(0.002)	(0.002)	(0.002)
Asian	0.001	−0.006	−0.009	−0.028	−0.008	−0.036
	(0.001)	(0.002)	(0.003)	(0.003)	(0.004)	(0.004)
Male high school dropouts						
White	−0.012	−0.001	−0.034	−0.026	−0.049	−0.024
	(0.001)	(0.002)	(0.001)	(0.003)	(0.001)	(0.003)
Black	−0.020	−0.014	−0.026	−0.026	−0.046	−0.043
	(0.001)	(0.004)	(0.003)	(0.007)	(0.004)	(0.010)
Hispanic	−0.014	0.004	−0.025	−0.014	−0.046	−0.011
	(0.002)	(0.001)	(0.002)	(0.002)	(0.003)	(0.003)
Asian	0.031	−0.037	0.003	−0.051	−0.026	−0.079
	(0.006)	(0.006)	(0.011)	(0.011)	(0.013)	(0.014)
Women						
White	−0.007	0.011	−0.022	0.004	−0.026	0.015
	(0.000)	(0.001)	(0.001)	(0.001)	(0.001)	(0.002)
Black	−0.017	0.024	−0.023	−0.008	−0.033	−0.038
	(0.001)	(0.002)	(0.001)	(0.003)	(0.002)	(0.022)
Hispanic	−0.013	0.021	−0.033	0.001	−0.038	0.007
	(0.001)	(0.001)	(0.002)	(0.002)	(0.002)	(0.003)
Asian	−0.002	−0.006	−0.012	−0.009	−0.009	−0.023
	(0.002)	(0.002)	(0.003)	(0.004)	(0.004)	(0.005)
Female high school dropouts						
White	−0.010	−0.002	−0.028	−0.014	−0.036	−0.008
	(0.001)	(0.002)	(0.001)	(0.003)	(0.002)	(0.005)
Black	−0.018	0.028	−0.026	−0.009	−0.039	−0.014
	(0.001)	(0.004)	(0.003)	(0.008)	(0.004)	(0.011)
Hispanic	−0.018	0.025	−0.033	−0.003	−0.034	−0.006
	(0.001)	(0.002)	(0.003)	(0.003)	(0.004)	(0.005)
Asian	0.002	−0.013	−0.011	−0.016	0.005	−0.041
	(0.007)	(0.007)	(0.012)	(0.012)	(0.016)	(0.016)

Source: Author's compilation.

Notes: Standard errors are reported in parentheses. The variable U_{jt} gives the unemployment rate in state j at time t; I_{ijt} is a dummy variable indicating whether worker i is an immigrant. The regression also includes dummy variables indicating the worker's educational attainment (whether the worker has less than twelve years of school, exactly twelve years, twelve to fifteen years, or at least sixteen years); a third-order polynomial in the worker's age; and a vector of fixed effects indicating the worker's state of residence.

tions of the regression model estimated in the sample of male workers. Consider initially the regression model estimated for white workers, the largest race group. Not surprisingly, the evidence shows that both employment and wages among white natives are sensitive to fluctuations in state-level economic conditions. The data also indicate significant differences in business cycle sensitivity between immigrants and natives. Consider the regression where the dependent variable is the fraction of weeks worked. The coefficient for native workers is -.006 and highly significant. This coefficient implies that a two-percentage-point rise in the unemployment rate (say from 4 to 6 percent) lowers the fraction of weeks worked by about 1.2 percentage points.

Note, however, that the coefficient of the interaction variable between the unemployment rate and immigration status is positive and significant, and of a magnitude that is exactly equal to that of the main effect on white natives. In other words, there is little evidence that the employment of white immigrants is very sensitive to the business cycle. This result is quite interesting and raises a number of questions that deserve further study. It is well known, for instance, that immigrants tend to have larger labor force participation rates than natives; this is not surprising as long as immigration is motivated mainly by a desire to maximize income. What is surprising, however, is that this type of selection seems to make immigrant employment rates less sensitive to fluctuations in the aggregate economy.

The first row of the second panel in table 2.6 replicates the regression analysis in the disadvantaged sample of white male high school dropouts. The comparison of the regression coefficients in this panel with those reported in the top panel suggests that the employment propensities of low-skilled white natives are more cyclically sensitive. The estimated coefficient is -.012, implying that a two-percentage-point rise in the state unemployment rate lowers the probability of employment during the year by 2.4 percent. Interestingly, the positive coefficient of the immigration-unemployment interaction variable obtained in the entire sample of white natives disappears. Instead, the coefficient now becomes slightly negative (but statistically insignificant). Both native- and foreign-born low-skilled white workers therefore exhibit greater sensitivity to business cycle fluctuations than white workers with higher levels of skills.

The remaining rows of the table replicate the analysis for the other ethnic groups. Among native workers, the evidence suggests that the employment propensities of black and Hispanic men—particularly low-skilled blacks and low-skilled Hispanics—exhibit the most cyclical sensitivity. Among high school dropouts, for example, the regression results imply that a two-percentage-point rise in the unemployment rate reduces the probability of native black employment by four percentage points, and that of Hispanics by 2.8 percentage points. The coefficient of the interaction variable between immigration and unemployment is positive (though numerically small) for low-skilled Hispanic immigrants, suggesting that employment propensities for the largest immigrant group remain sensitive to the business cycle (though the employment of low-skilled Hispanic immigrants is less cyclically sensitive than the employment of low-skilled Hispanic natives).

The other columns of table 2.6 show the cyclical sensitivity of wages, as measured either by the log weekly wage or by log annual income. The regression results indicate that the coefficients of both the unemployment rate and the interaction variable are systematically negative. In general, real wages fall as the unemployment rate rises, and the decline in the real wage is larger for immigrant workers. There is little evidence, however, to suggest that the wages of disadvantaged minorities exhibit greater cyclical sensitivity than those of other workers. Nevertheless, the cyclical effects for low-skilled minorities are sizable. In the sample of low-skilled Hispanic workers, for instance, the regression coefficients imply that a two-percentage-point rise in the unemployment rate reduces the annual earnings of low-skilled Hispanic natives by about 9.2 percent, and that of low-skilled Hispanic immigrants by 11.4 percent.

The bottom two panels of the table replicate the regression analysis using the sample of working women. Although different factors tend to influence labor force participation decisions for men and women, the cyclical sensitivity of female employment propensities roughly mirrors those found among men. The coefficients suggest that native employment propensities are more cyclically sensitive than those of immigrants. Similarly, the earnings of native women fall significantly during recessions, while the earnings of immigrant women are at least as cyclically sensitive as those of native women.

THE LABOR MARKET IMPACT OF IMMIGRATION

Finally, I consider a factor that may play a very large role in determining wage trends among disadvantaged minority workers: the continuing entry into the labor market of large numbers of low-skilled immigrants. Economic theory implies that immigration should lower the wage of competing workers and increase the wage of complementary workers. An immigrant influx of low-skilled workers should reduce the economic opportunities for low-skilled workers, who now face stiffer competition in the labor market. At the same time, high-skilled natives may gain substantially. They pay less for the services that low-skilled immigrants provide, and natives who hire these immigrants can now specialize in producing the goods and services that better suit their skills.

Because of the policy significance associated with determining the impact of immigration on the labor market opportunities of native workers, a large literature has attempted to measure this impact (see, for example, Altonji and Card 1991; Card 1990; Grossman 1982). The starting point for much of this literature is the fact that immigrants in the United States cluster in a small number of geographic areas. In 2000, for example, 38.4 percent of immigrants lived in four metropolitan areas (New York, Los Angeles, Chicago, and San Francisco), but only 12.2 percent of natives lived in the four metropolitan areas with the largest native-born populations (New York, Chicago, Los Angeles, and Philadelphia).

Practically all empirical studies in the academic literature exploit this geographic clustering to construct a methodological exercise that purports to measure the labor market impact of immigration. The typical study defines a metropolitan area as the labor market that is penetrated by immigrants. The study then goes on to calculate a cross-city correlation measuring the relation between the native wage in a locality and the relative number of immigrants in that locality. A negative correlation, indicating that native wages are lower in markets with many immigrants, would suggest that immigrants worsen the employment opportunities of competing native workers.

Although there is a great deal of dispersion in the findings reported in the literature, the estimated cross-city correlations tend to cluster around zero, helping to create the conventional wisdom that immigrants have little impact on the labor market opportunities of native workers, perhaps because "immigrants do jobs that natives do not want to do." It would seem, therefore, that a fundamental implication of the standard textbook model of the labor market—that an increase in supply lowers wages—is soundly rejected by the data.

Recent research, however, raises two questions about the validity of interpreting near-zero cross-city correlations as evidence that immigration has no labor market impact. First, immigrants may not be randomly distributed across labor markets. If immigrants cluster in cities with thriving economies (and high wages), there would be a built-in positive correlation between immigration and wages. Second, natives may respond to the wage impact of immigration by moving their labor or capital to other cities. For example, native-owned firms see that cities in southern California flooded by low-skilled immigrants pay lower wages to laborers. Employers who hire laborers will want to relocate to those cities. Similarly, laborers living in California may decide to move elsewhere. These flows of labor and capital tend to equalize economic conditions across localities. As a result, intercity comparisons of native wage rates may not be very revealing: capital flows and native migration diffuse the impact of immigration across the national economy.

Because local labor markets adjust to immigration, some recent studies have begun to emphasize that the labor market impact of immigration may be measurable only at the *national* level (Borjas, Freeman, and Katz 1997). The empirical analysis reported in this section reestimates a labor demand model I developed (Borjas 2003) to measure the impact of immigration on the wages of competing workers in the national labor market. This approach defines national skill groups in terms of educational attainment and work experience. As in Borjas (2003), male workers are classified here into four distinct education groups: workers who were high school dropouts, high school graduates, workers who had some college, and college graduates. Work experience is defined as the number of years elapsed since the person completed school. The analysis is restricted to workers with one to forty years of experience. Workers are then grouped into eight different experience groups: those with one to five years of experience, those with six to ten years, eleven to fifteen years, and so on. There are therefore a total of thirty-two skill groups in the labor market (four education and eight experience groups).

To measure the effects of immigration on the wage structure, it is important to note that the influx of immigrants into a particular skill group is likely to affect not only the earnings of workers in that skill group but the earnings of workers in other skill groups as well. For example, the large immigrant influx of high school dropouts may well have a beneficial effect on the earnings of native college graduates.

The problem with estimating these "cross-effects" is that there are over five hundred cross-effects that need to be estimated across the thirty-two skill groups in the analysis. As a result, any study of these cross-effects must narrow the scope of the problem by relying on a specific model derived from economic theory. The typical approach used in the labor demand literature (see, for example, Hamermesh 1993) specifies a production function that delineates how various types of labor and capital interact in the production process and estimates the implied parameters by assuming that workers are paid the value of their contribution to the firm's revenue (a standard result in competitive labor markets).

The appendix to this chapter describes the technical model I used to estimate both the own-effects and cross-effects of immigration on wages. In general terms, the model assumes that the economywide production function can be represented in terms of a three-level CES technology, a specification that aggregates across different levels of work experience and education groups in order to form the national workforce (Borjas 2003, 1359–68). In this framework, similarly educated workers with different levels of work experience are aggregated to form the effective supply of an education group, and workers across education groups are then aggregated to form the national workforce.

The assumption that the aggregate economy can be represented in terms of a three-level CES production function greatly reduces the number of parameters that need to be estimated. In particular, there are now three different responses of interest: how immigration in a particular skill group (say high school graduates with twenty years of experience) affects the earnings of native high school graduates with twenty years of experience; how these immigrants affect the wages of younger and older high school graduates; and how these immigrants affect the wages of workers in different education groups.

Using the estimated elasticities of substitution, I conducted two separate simulations to illustrate how the earnings opportunities of workers changed as a result of the immigrant influx into the United States between 1980 and 2000. The first simulation is a "short-run" simulation, which essentially holds the capital stock fixed. (In other words, the other factors of production have not been adjusted to account for the additional labor.) Over time, the capital stock clearly adjusts to the immigrant supply shift—as firms make additional investments to incorporate the additional workers. These adjustments in the capital stock continue until the rate of return to capital returns to its pre-immigration equilibrium level. The "long-run" simulation assumes that the capital stock adjusts completely to the immigrant supply shift.

The top panel of table 2.7 summarizes the short-run simulation results for the various racial-ethnic groups analyzed in this chapter. The first column reveals a great deal of variation in the measured impact of immigration across racial-ethnic groups. In the short run, the 1980 to 2000 immigrant influx lowered the wage of the typical working man by about 3.4 percent. The adverse impact of immigration, however, was larger for blacks (4.1 percent), and it was particularly large for Hispanics (5.2 percent). The data also reveal that there was a great deal of variability *within* the Hispanic population: immigration had a very large adverse effect on Mexicans and Puerto Ricans (about 5.5 percent) and a smaller effect on Cubans (3.7 percent). The next two columns of the table estimate the impact of immigration separately for native- and foreign-born workers. These calculations reveal that the preexisting immigrant stock was more adversely affected by continuing immigration, and that Hispanic immigrants (particularly Mexican immigrants) tended to suffer the largest wage losses. In particular, the 1980 to 2000 immigrant influx lowered the wage of the pre-1980 Mexican immigrant stock by 7.2 percent.

The bottom panel of table 2.7 reports the results obtained from the long-run simulation. Because the theoretical exercise assumes that the U.S. economy can be represented by a production function that has constant returns to scales, the long-run effect of immigration on the aggregate wage must be zero. Nevertheless, immigration still has significant adverse effects on both absolute and relative wages for some racial-ethnic groups. Even in the long run, after all of the potential adjustments to capital have taken place, the 1980 to 2000 immigrant influx generated a 1.8 percent wage reduction for the typical Hispanic working man, a 2.0 percent wage reduction for the typical Puerto Rican, and a 3.8 percent reduction for the typical Mexican immigrant.

The remaining columns of table 2.7 show that the adverse impacts of immigration were even larger when the simulation considers only the subsample of low-skilled workers (those who were high school dropouts). The 1980 to 2000 immigrant influx reduced the wage of low-educated native workers by 7.0 percent in the short run and by 3.6 percent in the long run. Of course, immigration also has had beneficial wage impacts on some groups in the long run (since the average wage effect must be zero). Nevertheless, table 2.7 shows that the predicted positive effects (mainly for workers in the middle of the educational attainment distribution) tended to be relatively small. In short, the large-scale immigration of low-skilled workers is an important determinant of wages among low-skilled minorities.

Finally, it is worth emphasizing that the simulations obviously rely on the estimated values of the elasticities of substitution among the various factors of production. As a result, it is important to ascertain the sensitivity of the predicted wage effects to alternative assumptions about the elasticities. I conducted alternative simulations (not shown) that shifted the estimated elasticities of substitution among education groups or among experience groups by one standard error

TABLE 2.7 / Predicted Percentage Wage Impact of the 1980 to 2000 Immigrant Influx

	All Education Groups			High School Dropouts		High School Graduates		Some College		College Graduates	
	All Workers	Natives	Immigrants	Natives	Immigrants	Natives	Immigrants	Natives	Immigrants	Natives	Immigrants
Short run											
All men	-3.4	-3.3	-4.6	-7.0	-7.9	-1.8	-1.8	-2.0	-2.1	-3.3	-3.4
White	-3.2	-3.2	-3.6	-6.8	-6.8	-1.8	-1.8	-2.0	-2.1	-3.3	-3.4
Black	-4.1	-4.1	-4.2	-7.3	-8.0	-1.9	-2.0	-2.0	-2.1	-3.2	-3.3
Asian	-3.4	-2.7	-3.7	-6.3	-7.7	-1.7	-2.0	-2.0	-2.1	-3.2	-3.4
Hispanic	-5.2	-4.6	-6.1	-7.7	-8.4	-1.9	-1.9	-1.9	-2.0	-3.2	-3.4
Mexican	-5.6	-4.6	-7.2	-7.6	-8.7	-1.9	-1.9	-1.9	-1.9	-3.2	-3.2
Puerto Rican	-5.4	-5.4	—	-8.2	—	-2.0	—	-1.9	—	-3.1	—
Cuban	-3.7	-3.3	-3.7	-6.8	-6.1	-1.8	-1.7	-1.8	-2.1	-3.1	-3.4
Other Hispanic	-4.4	-3.6	-5.1	-7.3	-8.6	-1.9	-2.0	-2.0	-2.1	-3.2	-3.4
Long run											
All men	0.0	0.1	-1.2	-3.6	-4.5	1.6	1.5	1.4	1.3	0.1	-0.0
White	0.2	0.2	-0.2	-3.4	-3.4	1.6	1.6	1.4	1.3	0.1	-0.0
Black	-0.7	-0.7	-0.8	-3.9	-4.6	1.4	1.4	1.4	1.3	0.2	0.1
Asian	0.0	0.7	-0.3	-2.9	-4.3	1.7	1.4	1.4	1.3	0.3	-0.0
Hispanic	-1.8	-1.2	-2.7	-4.3	-5.0	1.5	1.5	1.5	1.3	0.2	0.0
Mexican	-2.2	-1.3	-3.8	-4.2	-5.3	1.5	1.5	1.5	1.5	0.2	0.2
Puerto Rican	-2.1	-2.0	—	-4.8	—	-1.4	—	-1.5	—	-0.3	—
Cuban	-0.3	0.1	-0.3	-3.4	-2.7	1.6	1.7	1.6	1.3	0.3	-0.0
Other Hispanic	-1.0	-0.2	-1.7	-3.9	-5.2	1.5	1.4	1.4	1.3	0.2	-0.0

Source: Author's compilation.
Notes: The simulation models in equations 2.7 and 2.8 generate wage effects for specific education-experience cells. The short-run simulation holds the capital stock fixed; the long-run simulation holds the rental price of capital fixed. I used the size of the workforce in 1980 in each of the cells to calculate the weighted aggregates reported in this table. The predicted percentage changes refer to the product of the predicted log wage change times 100.

from the estimated value.[10] It turns out that the predicted wage effects do not change the thrust of the results summarized in table 2.7. Suppose, for instance, that both elasticities of substitution are one standard error below the values implied by the estimation of the labor demand model. The short-run simulation then suggests that the 1980 to 2000 immigrant influx reduced the wage of the typical high school dropout by 10.9 percent, the wage of the typical Hispanic by 6.7 percent, and the wage of the typical low-skilled Mexican worker by 12.4 percent. In contrast, suppose the elasticities of substitution are one standard error larger than the regression estimates. The wage of the average high school dropout falls by 3.3 percent, the wage of the typical Hispanic by 3.7 percent, and the wage of the typical low-skilled Mexican worker by 4.0 percent.

CONCLUSIONS

This chapter examined the changing racial-ethnic composition and economic status of the low-skilled workforce in the United States. The analysis uses data drawn from the 1980 to 2000 decennial censuses. The data clearly indicate that the racial-ethnic composition of the disadvantaged population has changed dramatically in the past two decades, becoming much more heavily Hispanic and taking on an increasing representation of Asians. A major revision of our traditional stereotypes about the racial-ethnic composition of the disadvantaged population in the United States is clearly required.

The empirical analysis indicated that aggregate trends in the relative wage of the "typical" Hispanic and Asian worker in the U.S. workforce mask a great deal of variation that arises because of the changing composition of these populations. The declining relative wage of the typical Hispanic, for instance, is in large part due to the disproportionate increase in the number of low-wage immigrants in this population. The analysis also indicated that wage trends for low-skilled minorities (particularly low-skilled immigrant men) are particularly sensitive to business cycle fluctuations and to the labor market impact of the continuing immigrant influx, which has a sizable adverse effect on the wages of low-skilled workers in the United States.

The increasing presence of immigrants in the disadvantaged population raises a number of policy questions that are sure to generate substantial debate in the future. Perhaps the most important of these questions concerns the rate of economic mobility between the immigrant generation and their children and grandchildren. It is unclear whether the historical path of social mobility exhibited by past immigrant waves (like those that arrived in the early 1900s) serves as a model for the current influx of immigrants. Today's low-skilled immigrants, after all, are entering a labor market that seems increasingly predisposed to reward high skills and that is also adjusting to the rapidly decreasing importance of the manufacturing sector. Moreover, current immigrants enter a cultural and social milieu that often denigrates the process of cultural assimilation and instead encourages the preservation of cultural differences. This expectation stands in sharp contrast to the "melting pot" ideology that earlier immigrant waves encountered. It will be of great interest—and of fundamental social importance—to witness the mobility experienced by the children and grandchildren of today's immigrants.

APPENDIX

Suppose the aggregate production function for the national economy at time t is:

$$Q_t = [\lambda_{Kt} K_t^v + \lambda_{Lt} L_t^v]^{1/v}, \tag{2A.1}$$

where Q is output, K is capital, L denotes the aggregate labor input, and $v = 1 - 1/\sigma_{KL}$, with σ_{KL} being the elasticity of substitution between capital and labor $(-\infty < v \leq 1)$. The vector λ gives technology parameters that shift the production frontier, with $\lambda_{Kt} + \lambda_{Lt} = 1$. The aggregate labor input L_t incorporates the contributions of workers who differ in both education and experience. Let:

$$L_t = \left[\sum_i \theta_{it} L_{it}^\rho \right]^{1/\rho}, \tag{2A.2}$$

where L_{it} gives the number of workers with education i at time t, and $\rho = 1 - 1/\sigma_E$, with σ_E being the elasticity of substitution across these education aggregates $(-\infty < \rho \leq 1)$. The θ_{it} give time-variant technology parameters that shift the relative productivity of education groups, with $\Sigma_i \theta_{it} = 1$. Finally, the supply of workers in each education group is itself given by an aggregation of the contribution of similarly educated workers with different experience. In particular,

$$L_{it} = \left[\sum_j \alpha_{ij} L_{ijt}^\eta \right]^{1/\eta}, \tag{2A.3}$$

where L_{ijt} gives the number of workers in education group i and experience group j at time t (given by the sum of N_{ijt} native and M_{ijt} immigrant workers); and $\eta = 1 - 1/\sigma_X$, with σ_X being the elasticity of substitution across experience classes within an education group $(-\infty < \eta \leq 1)$. Equation 2A.3 assumes that the technology coefficients α_{ij} are constant over time, with $\Sigma_j \alpha_{ij} = 1$.

Borjas (2003) shows that the elasticities σ_X and σ_E can be estimated by regressing the log wage of particular education-experience groups on the log of the size of the workforce in the various cells and instrumenting the supply variable by the size of the immigrant workforce in the skill cell. More precisely, the model generates two estimating equations. The first regresses the log wage of a skill group (defined by education and experience) on various fixed effects and on the log of the size of the workforce in that group. This regression identifies σ_X. The second aggregates the data to the education-group level and regresses the log wage of an education group on vectors of fixed effects and on the log of the size of the workforce in the education group. This regression identifies σ_E.

Borjas (2003) analyzes the earnings of workers in the wage-and-salary sector using data from the census and the Current Population Surveys and estimated $\sigma_X = 3.5$ and $\sigma_E = 1.3$. The results summarized in this chapter are based on a reestimation of the econometric framework that uses data from the 1960 to 2000 IPUMS and that includes both wage-and-salary and self-employed workers. In addition, the reestimation incorporates the most recent findings on the trends in relative demand for various skill groups. In particular, Lawrence Katz and Kevin Murphy (1992) documented that the secular trend in relative demand shifts for high-skilled workers in a CES framework could be approximated by linear trends specific to each education group. This approximation became an important identification restriction for the estimation of the elasticity of substitution across education groups in Card and Lemieux (2001) and Borjas (2003). More recently, David Autor, Lawrence Katz, and Melissa Kearney (2004) have documented that the growth rate in the relative demand for skilled workers slowed in the 1990s. In particular, they find a 20 percent decline in the secular growth rate of demand for skilled workers during the 1990s as compared to the growth rate prior to the 1990s. To capture this break in the secular trend, I included education-specific splines in the marginal productivity equation that identifies σ_E (instead of simple linear trends). For each education group, this variable is defined by a linear trend that increases at the rate of one per year between 1960 and 1990. The trend variable then increases at a rate of 0.8 per year between 1990 and 2000.

The coefficient that represents the parameter $(1/\sigma_X)$ was estimated to be .332, with a standard error of .129, while the coefficient that represents the parameter $(1/\sigma_E)$ was estimated to be .413, with a standard error of .312. The implied elasticities are $\sigma_X = 3.01$ and $\sigma_E = 2.42$. Because the empirical implementation of the three-level CES technology described here does not use any data on the aggregate capital stock, σ_{KL} cannot be directly estimated. However, Daniel Hamermesh (1993, 92) concludes that the aggregate U.S. economy can be reasonably described by a Cobb-Douglas production function, suggesting that σ_{KL} equals one.

The factor price elasticity giving the impact on the wage of factor y of an increase in the supply of factor z is defined by:

$$\varepsilon_{yz} = \frac{d \log w_y}{d \log L_z}, \tag{2A.4}$$

It is easy to show that the factor price elasticities depend on the income shares accruing to the various factors and on the three elasticities of substitution that lie at the core of the three-level CES framework. The marginal productivity condition for the typical worker in education group s and experience group x can be written as $w_{sx} = D(K, L)$, where L is a vector indicating the number of workers in each education-experience group. Suppose initially that the capital stock is constant, so that capital does not adjust at all to the immigrant influx. The *short-run* impact of immigration on the log wage of group (s, x) is then given by:

$$\Delta \log w_{sx} = \sum_i \sum_j \varepsilon_{sx,ij} \, m_{ij}, \qquad (2A.5)$$

where m_{ij} gives the percentage change in labor supply due to immigration in skill cell (i, j).

Of course, over time the capital stock adjusts as investors take advantage of the immigrant-induced, higher-than-normal rental rate of capital. If the capital stock adjusted completely to the immigrant influx, the rental rate of capital would return to its preexisting equilibrium level. It can be shown that this alternative counterfactual implies that the *long-run* impact of immigration on the log wage of group (s, x) is given by:

$$\Delta \log w_{sx} = s_K \, \tilde{K} + \sum_i \sum_j \varepsilon_{sx,ij} \, m_{ij}, \qquad (2A.6)$$

where s_K is capital's share of income (assumed to be 0.3), and $\tilde{K}$ is the percentage change in the capital stock induced by immigration. The derivation of equation 2A.8 uses the assumption that $\sigma_{KL} = 1$. It can be shown that the optimal change in the capital stock, $\tilde{K}$, can be represented as a weighted average of the immigrant supply shocks in the various skill groups, where the weights are the shares of income accruing to the various education-experience cells.[11] It is worth noting that equation 2A.6 differs from equation 2A.5 only by a constant, $s_k\tilde{K}$. Put differently, full capital adjustment mutes the absolute wage impact of immigration but leaves the relative wage effects unchanged.

The simulation requires a measure of the immigrant supply shock for each skill group. Because the size of the native labor force in each skill group is shifting over time, I define m_{ij} as:

$$m_{ij} = \frac{M_{ij,2000} - M_{ij,1980}}{0.5(N_{ij,1980} + N_{ij,2000}) + M_{ij,1980}}, \qquad (2A.7)$$

so that the baseline population used to calculate the percentage increase in labor supply averages out the size of the native workforce in the skill cell and treats the preexisting immigrant population as part of the "native" stock.

Note that equations 2A.5 and 2A.6 generate a vector of statistics giving the wage impact of immigration for each education-experience group. This impact is obviously the same for all workers who have the same educational attainment and experience, regardless of the racial-ethnic background of the workers. The results reported in table 2.7 are obtained by averaging the measured impact of immigration across all workers within a particular racial-ethnic group. It is worth noting that the natural weighting variable implied by the theoretical framework is the share of income accruing to each education-experience cell. Using this weight to calculate the weighted average must imply that the long-run aggregate wage change in equation 2A.6 must be zero because the production function assumes constant returns to scales. This weighting, however, may have little policy relevance if we wish to estimate the mean impact of immigration on the earnings of a subpopulation that has a large number of low-skilled workers. For example, many blacks are high school dropouts and earn relatively little. They would then contribute little to the calculation of the mean wage effect, even though many blacks would be disproportionately affected by immigration. The simulations presented in table 2.7 use the 1980 size of the workforce to aggregate the predictions in equations 2A.5 and 2A.6, but calibrate the calculations so that the average wage impact for the total sample (all workers across all education groups) is the mean wage change predicted by the simulation that uses income shares as the weights.

NOTES

1. I am grateful to Steven Raphael and Rebecca Blank for providing many useful comments on an earlier draft.
2. A small group of persons cannot be classified into any of these four racial-ethnic categories. In 1990 only 0.7 percent of the workforce was in this residual category. By 2000, however, residual workers had grown to 2.3 percent of the workforce, probably because of the redesign of the 2000 census race question. The economic outcomes experienced by the residual group of "other" workers are ignored in the discussion that follows.
3. The size of the illegal immigrant population has been rising at an even faster pace since 2000. Jeffrey Passel (2005) estimates that 10.3 million illegal immigrants resided in the United States in March 2004.
4. The wage measure is based on a worker's total income earned from both salaried work and self-employment. Workers who have outlying wage observations are deleted from the analysis. I calculated a wage rate for each worker by taking the ratio of annual earnings to the product of weeks worked and hours worked weekly, and I restricted the sample in each census to workers whose calculated hourly wage rate lies between $1 and $250 (in 1999 dollars).
5. Because the wage distributions of male and female workers are studied separately, the cutoff points differ greatly between the two groups. In 2000 the twentieth percentile cutoff points for men and women were 5.715 and 5.206, respectively. Similarly, the fortieth percentile cutoff points for the two groups were 6.127 and 5.657.
6. To conserve space, the discussion focuses on the trends in the relative wage of working men. The trends in the relative wage of working women are, of course, affected by differential trends in labor force participation rates and by the self-selection that marks the labor force participation decision. It should be noted, however, that the trends observed among working women often mirror those observed among working men.
7. The vector of variables representing the worker's educational attainment includes dummy variables indicating whether the worker has less than twelve years of school,

exactly twelve years, twelve to fifteen years, or at least sixteen years. The vector of variables representing the number of years the immigrant has lived in the United States includes dummy variables indicating whether the foreign-born worker has lived in the country less than five years, five to ten years, ten to fifteen years, fifteen to twenty years, twenty to thirty years, and over forty years. These dummy variables are set to zero for native-born workers.

8. Workers in the "other" Hispanic category originated mainly in Central and South American countries. The Puerto Rican category is defined only for natives because persons born in Puerto Rico, like persons of Puerto Rican ancestry born in the United States, are American citizens.

9. Lawrence Katz and I (Borjas and Katz 2005) have analyzed the trends in the relative skills and wages of Mexican immigrants in the United States throughout the twentieth century. Most of the very large wage disadvantage experienced by Mexican immigrants can be attributed to their very low levels of educational attainment.

10. The regression estimates of the elasticities of substitution are $\sigma_X = 3.0$ and $\sigma_E = 2.4$. The sensitivity analysis assumes that $\sigma_X = 2.2$ or 4.9, and that $\sigma_E = 1.2$ or 62.5. These additional simulations maintain the assumption that the elasticity of substitution between labor and capital equals one.

11. To simplify notation, let n be the subscript indicating the education-experience skill group ($n = 1, \ldots, 32$). The immigrant-induced change in the capital stock

$$\tilde{K} = \sum_n s_n m_n / s_L,$$

where s_L is labor's share of income.

REFERENCES

Altonji, Joseph G., and Rebecca M. Blank. 1999. "Race and Gender in the Labor Market." In *Handbook of Labor Economics*, vol. 3C, edited by Orley Ashenfelter and David Card. Amsterdam: Elsevier.

Altonji, Joseph G., and David Card. 1991. "The Effects of Immigration on the Labor Market Outcomes of Less-Skilled Natives." In *Immigration, Trade, and the Labor Market*, edited by John M. Abowd and Richard B. Freeman. Chicago: University of Chicago Press.

Autor, David H., Lawrence F. Katz, and Melissa S. Kearney. 2004. "Trends in U.S. Wage Inequality: Reassessing the Revisionists." Working paper 11627. Cambridge, Mass.: National Bureau of Economic Research.

Blank, Rebecca M. 1989. "Disaggregating the Effect of the Business Cycle on the Distribution of Income." *Economica* 56(2): 141–63.

Borjas, George J. 2003. "The Labor Demand Curve *Is* Downward Sloping: Reexamining the Impact of Immigration on the Labor Market." *Quarterly Journal of Economics* 118(4): 1335–74.

Borjas, George J., Richard B. Freeman, and Lawrence F. Katz. 1997. "How Much Do Immigration and Trade Affect Labor Market Outcomes?" *Brookings Papers on Economic Activity* (1): 1–67.

Borjas, George J., and Lawrence F. Katz. 2005. "The Evolution of the Mexican-Born Workforce in the United States." Working paper 11281. Cambridge, Mass.: National Bureau of Economic Research.

Card, David. 1990. "The Impact of the Mariel Boatlift on the Miami Labor Market." *Industrial and Labor Relations Review* 43(2): 245–57.

Card, David, and Thomas Lemieux. 2001. "Can Falling Supply Explain the Rising Return to College for Younger Men? A Cohort-Based Analysis." *Quarterly Journal of Economics* 116(2): 705–46.

Grossman, Jean Baldwin. 1982. "The Substitutability of Natives and Immigrants in Production." *Review of Economics and Statistics* 54(4): 596–603.

Hamermesh, Daniel. 1993. *Labor Demand*. Princeton, N.J.: Princeton University Press.

Katz, Lawrence F., and Kevin M. Murphy. 1992. "Changes in the Wage Structure, 1963–1987: Supply and Demand Factors." *Quarterly Journal of Economics* 107(1): 35–78.

Lundberg, Shelly. 1985. "The Added Worker Effect." *Journal of Labor Economics* 3(1): 11–37.

O'Neill, June. 1990. "The Role of Human Capital in Earnings Differences Between Black and White Men." *Journal of Economic Perspectives* 4(4): 25–45.

Passel, Jeffrey. 2005. "Unauthorized Migrants: Numbers and Characteristics." Washington, D.C.: Pew Hispanic Center.

Trejo, Stephen J. 1997. "Why Do Mexican-Americans Earn Low Wages?" *Journal of Political Economy* 105(6): 1235–68.

U.S. Immigration and Naturalization Service. 2003. "Estimates of the Unauthorized Immigrant Population Residing in the United States: 1990 to 2000." Washington: Office of Policy and Planning.

Part II

How Do Economic Trends Affect Less-Skilled Workers?

Chapter 3

The Macroeconomy and Determinants of the Earnings of Less-Skilled Workers

Robert E. Hall

Poverty is a condition with multiple causes, but every analysis agrees on the importance of the earnings of less-skilled workers.[1] Macroeconomic—that is, economywide—influences determine average earnings. This chapter looks at data from the U.S. economy through the lens of macroeconomics. Some of the key questions I consider are: How much have wages in general risen over the past fifty years in terms of the value of what workers produce and what workers consume? How has productivity growth and rising stocks of plant and equipment contributed to wage growth in general? How have wages of workers at the bottom of the skill distribution (those who did not finish high school), in the middle (high school graduates with no college), and at the top (college graduates) changed over time? What has happened to the demand for workers in these skill groups? What has happened to the fraction of Americans living in poverty as wages have risen? What happens to workers in the various skill groups when employment falls sharply in a recession?

I break down the macroeconomic determinants of earnings into those that affect all workers and those that operate differently by education group. Economic analysis points to two fundamental factors that affect average wage growth—productivity growth and capital deepening, that is, the accumulation of additional plant and equipment per worker. Both have been important over the past fifty years. Productivity growth in the 1990s was lower than in almost any other period, but capital deepening added to wage growth and wages significantly outperformed the neoclassical benchmark, so total wage growth was impressive.

The American economy has been quite successful in raising the wages of its workers measured in terms of the products that the country produces. For two reasons, it has been less successful in raising wages in terms of what people consume. First, the United States is a major producer of capital goods, especially computers and software, and rapid productivity growth in this area has driven down the prices of these products, which families consume in only small amounts. The services that account for a large part of consumption have become relatively more expensive. Second, the United States has suffered a long decline in its terms of trade with the rest of the world, partly resulting from increases in the price of oil. People consume imported products that have become gradually more expensive in relation to domestically produced products. The 1990s saw some relief from this trend, but it was substantial in the 1980s and resumed after 2000.

The real earnings of the least-skilled workers—here taken to be those who did not finish high school—rose by about 1.5 percent per year in the boom years of 1992 to 2000, after stagnating in the previous boom of 1982 to 1990. In addition to the factors that caused earnings in general to rise, this group enjoyed an unusual increase in demand associated with the expansion of industries, such as construction and auto repair, that hire large proportions of the least-educated. And the number of people in the United States who had not graduated from high school fell by 1.3 percent per year.

Stagnant earnings of low-skilled workers coincided with increases in the incidence of poverty in the 1980s, while improvements in their earnings in the 1990s coincided with modest declines in the incidence of poverty. A long-term trend toward higher educational attainment contributed to improvements in the distribution of income at all times. Nonetheless, poverty was just as frequent in 2003 as it was in 1975. Factors that may account for the difference are outside the province of macroeconomics; they include increases in the dispersion of earnings within skill groups and the growing tendency for individuals to live by themselves, sacrificing the economies of living in larger households.

The business cycle is an important and enduring feature of the macroeconomy. Measured in terms of output, the cycle comprises a sharp and brief contraction followed by a long period of expansion. Usually output growth is highest just after the contraction, as the economy rebounds from the shock that caused the recession in the first place. Over U.S. history, recessions have occurred about twice a decade, but the frequency has been once a decade over the past thirty years. In the labor market, employment falls and unemployment rises during a contraction. In the past two recessions, 1990 to 1991 and 2001, employment growth lagged behind output growth in the first two years of the recovery. The labor market remained soft for several years following these recessions. Although recessions do not have strong effects on wages earned per hour of work, they have sharp downward effects on earnings, because employment falls and the hours of work of the employed also fall. Recessions have uneven effects across the economy—employment falls sharply in manufacturing, especially in capital goods, autos, and other durables. In past recessions, employment fell in construction as well, but the recession of 2001 was unique in avoiding this consequence. The industries that contract in recessions generally employ lower-skilled workers, so recessions result in rising poverty. Because the 2001 recession did not include a contraction of construction employment and because construction is particularly intensive in its use of low-skilled workers, the recession did not have as large an adverse effect on poverty as did earlier recessions.

This chapter does not attempt to survey the research by microeconomic specialists on related topics. The other chapters in this volume, especially those by David Card and John DiNardo and by Rebecca Blank, provide many references. I concentrate here on earnings before income taxes and transfers. The effects of changes in tax rates, changes in the Earned Income Tax Credit (EITC), and welfare reform are beyond my scope.

PRODUCT WAGES

I start this section by describing a simple model of production and wages that sees wide use in economics as a benchmark. Because the model bears the name "neoclassical," I refer to calculations from the model as the "neoclassical benchmark." The neoclassical economy has competitive labor and product markets and a simple technology. I explain later how departures from these and other properties may explain the actual performance of wages.

Robert Solow (1956) developed the neoclassical model in the form I use here. The economy has a single production function,

$$Y_t = A_t F(L_t, K_t). \tag{3.1}$$

Here A_t is an index of total factor productivity. The index can be calculated from data on output, Y_t, labor, L_t, and capital, K_t, according to a robust procedure from Solow (1957). When productivity enters in the form shown in this equation—multiplying the total contribution of all of the factors of production—it is said to be "Hicks-neutral."

If firms hire in a competitive labor market at wage w_t and sell their output in a competitive product market at price p_t, then they adjust their capital-labor ratio to satisfy

$$\frac{w_t}{p_t} = A_t \frac{\partial F(L_t, K_t)}{\partial L}. \tag{3.2}$$

This equation states the equality of the wage and the marginal product of labor. The left side is the *product wage*, the ratio of the wage paid to the price received. It differs from the *real wage*, which is the wage received by workers divided by the cost of living. The product wage includes capital goods, such as computers and software, whose prices have declined relative to consumption goods prices. Further, workers consume imported goods and the United States produces exported goods, so changes in the relative price of imports to exports cause the product wage to move differently from the real wage. The relative price is called the *terms of trade*. A conspicuous manifestation of this phenomenon in the United

States is the decline in real wages when oil prices rise. In principle, oil prices have no direct effect on the product wage. Many other factors, including the declining relative price of capital goods (a major component of U.S. exports), have contributed to the worsening of the terms of trade since the mid-1980s.

In the special case of Cobb-Douglas technology, the production function is

$$Y_t = A_t L_t^\alpha K_t^{1-\alpha}, \tag{3.3}$$

where α is the elasticity of output with respect to labor input, assumed to be a constant. The marginal product of labor is

$$A_t \frac{\partial F(L_t, K_t)}{\partial L} = A_t \alpha \left(\frac{K_t}{L_t} \right)^{1-\alpha}. \tag{3.4}$$

In this case, the product wage is

$$\frac{w_t}{p_t} = A_t \alpha \left(\frac{K_t}{L_t} \right)^{1-\alpha}. \tag{3.5}$$

This equation shows that the product wage has only two determinants—productivity A_t and the capital-labor ratio K_t/L_t.

If the measured real wage departs from this simple relation, the cause is some combination of the following factors:

- Markets are not competitive, so changes in market power result in changes in the product wage.
- Technical change is not Hicks-neutral but is biased toward capital or labor.
- The elasticity, α, is not a constant.
- The elasticity of substitution is not one, as in Cobb-Douglas, but is greater than or less than one.
- There are errors in the data.

With respect to the first entry in the list, I should say some more about how I am using the term "competition." If competition in product markets is limited, firms are charging prices that exceed marginal cost—market power boosts the price above the perfectly competitive level. Higher product prices result in lower product or real wages—purchasing power that would flow to workers in a competitive economy is diverted to the owners of firms with market power. I am distinguishing product-market competition from another type of competition, in the context of the global economy, where foreign producers may shift the terms of trade adversely, resulting in a decline in the real wage. I take account of this type of competition through the calculation of real wages, which includes the terms-of-trade effect.

FIGURE 3.1 / Product Wage and Determinants, 1948 to 2003

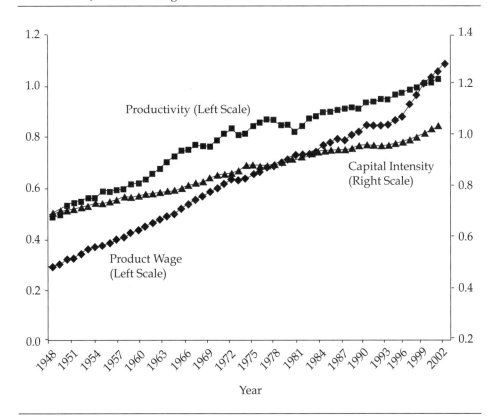

Sources: Author's compilation. Productivity: From Bureau of Labor Statistics, "Multifactor Productivity," http://www.bls.gov/mfp/home.htm. Capital intensity: Capital services index from above source divided by labor hours, same source. Product wage: Hourly compensation from BLS, "Productivity and Costs," http://www.bls.gov/lpc/home.htm, divided by GDP deflator, same source.

The measure of wages I study here and throughout the chapter is comprehensive—it counts all of the economic value that a worker receives from an employer. In particular, wages include the value of fringe benefits. Discussions of wages that omit fringes are seriously misleading, because fringes—mainly the value of retirement benefits and health insurance—grow at variable rates but usually faster than cash wages.

Figure 3.1 shows the hourly product wage for all private workers in the U.S. economy, as calculated by the Bureau of Labor Statistics, with adjustments for the age, education, and sex composition of employed workers. The nominal wage is divided by the price index for GDP. The product wage has risen consistently over the past sixty years—the only important interruption occurred in the early 1990s.

FIGURE 3.2 / Product Wage as Ratio to Neoclassical Benchmark

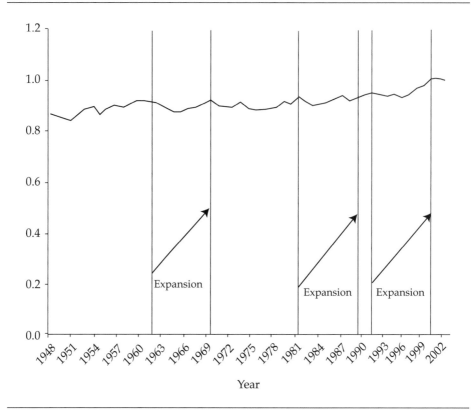

Source: Author's compilation.
Notes: Product wage from figure 3.1. Benchmark: Productivity from figure 3.1 divided by capital intensity raised to the power 0.3 (corresponding to $\alpha = 0.7$).

Figure 3.1 shows that both productivity and capital deepening have been sources of product wage growth over the period. I should note that capital deepening is not really an independent factor in the longer run. An economy cannot continue raising its capital-labor ratio unless productivity increases provide the necessary resources. But in the shorter run, productivity and capital deepening can move separately.

Productivity growth is not much associated with booms and recessions. In particular, productivity did not grow rapidly during the great boom of the 1990s. On the other hand, capital deepening tends to occur in the later periods of booms. Capital itself rises rapidly throughout a boom, but in the earlier phase, employment also rises rapidly, so the capital-labor ratio does not grow rapidly. After employment growth slows, investment continues and the capital-labor ratio grows more rapidly than average.

Figure 3.2 shows the product wage as a ratio to the neoclassical benchmark of

TABLE 3.1 / Annual Percentage Growth of Product Wage and Components of Benchmark

	Product Wage	Productivity	Capital Deepening	Benchmark	Wage Growth Relative to Benchmark
1948 to 2002	2.4	1.4	0.8	2.2	0.3
1962 to 1970	2.9	1.9	0.9	2.8	0.1
1982 to 1990	1.6	1.4	0.3	1.7	−0.1
1992 to 2000	2.2	0.9	0.5	1.5	0.7

Source: Author's compilation.
Notes: Product wage, productivity, and capital deepening are percentage growth rates for the data from figure 3.1. Benchmark and wage divided by benchmark are from figure 3.2.

equation 3.5. I calculate the neoclassical benchmark as the ratio of productivity from figure 3.1 to the capital intensity raised to the power 0.3, corresponding to $\alpha = 0.7$. If the wage tracked the benchmark perfectly, the figure would show a horizontal line at one. In fact, the line rises gradually over time, at about one-quarter of a percent per year. By the list I gave earlier, this means that market power has fallen slightly, that technical change is biased toward labor, that the elasticity of substitution is greater than one, or that there is a growing overstatement of the wage from mismeasurement. The only implausible member of this group is cumulative mismeasurement. Many observers believe that the U.S. economy is becoming more competitive. Estimates of the elasticity of substitution generally find values below one. But the magnitude of the trend in the discrepancy between the product wage and the benchmark is so small that it should not interfere with the analysis in this chapter.

The upward arrows in the figure mark the three great expansions of the second half of the twentieth century, 1962 to 1970, 1982 to 1990, and 1992 to 2000. In these expansions, the wage-benchmark ratio declined in the early years and rose in the later years. This behavior is consistent with models of lags in wage adjustment. In the expansion of the 1980s, the rise toward the end was small. The difference turns out to be critical for the experiences of all skill levels of workers—the 1980s were a disappointing period for wages, while the 1960s and 1990s saw substantial increases.

Table 3.1 summarizes the data on the product wage and the benchmark for the entire period and for the three major booms. All of the figures are average annual percentage growth rates. The product wage rose between 2 and 3 percent per year in all of the periods except the boom of the 1980s, when it grew 1.6 percent per year. Productivity rose about 1.4 percent per year on the average over the whole period, with the most rapid growth in the 1960s and the slowest in the 1990s. (Productivity has grown rapidly in the current decade—not shown separately in the table.) Capital deepening ran at 0.75 percent per year for the whole period and ranged from 0.31 percent in the 1980s to 0.93 percent per year in the 1960s. Finally, wages beat the benchmark over the entire period and in the booms of the 1960s and 1990s and fell short by a slim margin in the 1980s. The 1990s were the standout among the three booms in terms of wage increases above the benchmark.

Note that the variations of wage growth around the benchmark are relatively small, both in absolute terms and in relation to the general amount of noise in the data. The unusual performance of the 1990s is far from statistically significant. Nonetheless, the cumulative extra wage growth of about 5 percent over the eight years of the 1990s boom is important for the topic of this chapter, because it was present in the wages of low- as well as high-skilled workers.

What are the lessons from the behavior of the product wage over the past fifty years? The product wage is the purchasing power of the wage in terms of the products that the United States makes. I find that it behaved much as the neoclassical model predicts. Wage growth depends primarily on productivity growth and secondarily on capital deepening. Because of rapid productivity growth and capital deepening, the product wage grew rapidly for the first half of the fifty-year period. The second half was more disappointing in both respects. The 1990s were a period of moderate productivity growth but fairly rapid product wage growth, because wages outperformed the neoclassical benchmark. The acceleration of productivity growth (not capital deepening) in recent years may raise the growth of the product wage during the current decade.

REAL WAGES

Now I turn to the real wage, the purchasing power that workers enjoy from their earnings. I have already mentioned that the real wage differs from the product wage because it focuses on the products that workers consume rather than the ones they produce. Going from the product wage to the real wage requires removing capital goods and exports and bringing imports into the picture. The real wage is not so much a measure of the performance of the U.S. economy as of the world economy. If an imported product such as oil becomes more expensive in the world market, the purchasing power of U.S. workers declines even though their productivity is not affected.

Real wages measure the claim over consumption goods that workers receive from their work. Measurement of real wages requires the economist to take a stand on some controversial issues. In principle, the real wage needs to take account of all of the ways that taxes reduce the actual amount of consumption that earnings can support. Taxes include excise, sales, and property taxes imposed on goods and services, payroll taxes, and income taxes. Further, programs, such as the Earned Income Tax Credit (EITC), that subsidize wages ought to be treated as factors that increase the real wage by extending purchasing power from earnings.

The situation is even more complicated for taxes that are directly related to

FIGURE 3.3 / Ratio of Prices, Private GDP to Consumption Goods and Services

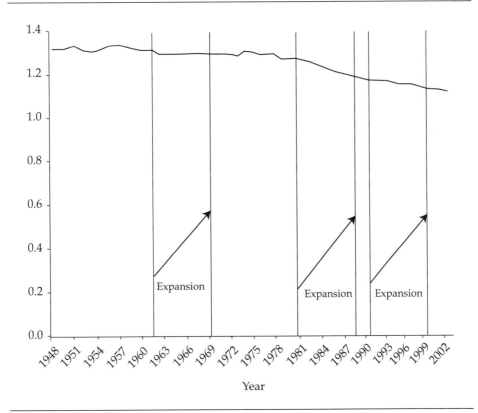

Source: Author's compilation.
Notes: Consumer price deflator from National Income and Products Accounts (NIPA), table 1.1.4, http://www.bea.gov/bea/dn/nipaweb/. Table.asp?Selected = N; GDP deflator from figure 3.1.

programs that provide the taxpayer direct value. The leading example is the payroll tax for Social Security. Many workers receive Social Security benefits worth more than their payroll tax payments—this is most likely for low-wage workers whose benefits are in the progressive part of the benefit formula.

Untangling the tax factors that belong in a fully accurate measure of the real wage is beyond the scope of this chapter. I consider only the important difference between the product and the real wage that arises from capital goods, exports, and imports. This difference can be measured by the ratio of the price of GDP to the price of consumption goods. Figure 3.3 shows the data. The decline in the second half of the period indicates a time when the real wage was not rising as fast as the product wage. Although rising energy prices are one factor, by far the biggest is the rise in the price of consumption goods and services relative to the

TABLE 3.2 / Annual Average Percentage Growth in Real Wages

Period	Product Wage	GDP Price	Consumption Price	Difference in Price Change	Real Wage
1948 to 2002	2.4	3.2	3.5	0.3	2.1
1962 to 1970	2.9	2.6	2.7	0.1	2.8
1982 to 1990	1.6	2.8	3.7	0.9	0.7
1992 to 2000	2.2	1.5	1.9	0.4	1.8

Source: Author's compilation.
Notes: Product wage and GDP price from figure 3.1. Consumption price from figure 3.3. Real wage is product wage multiplied by the ratio of the GDP deflator to the consumption deflator.

price of investment goods. This rise became important in the 1980s, when computers and software became a substantial share of total investment. The terms-of-trade effect cut real wage growth by 0.309 percent per year for the whole period, by 0.10 in the 1960s boom, by 0.88 percent in the 1980s boom, and by 0.42 percent in the 1990s boom. These figures are shown in table 3.2 in the column headed "Difference in Price Change." Again, the effect of the adjustment is to enlarge the difference between the 1980s and the 1990s.

Table 3.2 shows real wage growth for the entire period from 1948 through 2002 and for the three major booms. Real wages grew the most in the 1960s, when the product wage grew rapidly from productivity growth and capital deepening and the terms-of-trade effect was essentially neutral. Real wages grew the least in the 1980s, when productivity grew a bit below average, capital deepening was minimal, and the terms of trade shifted quite adversely. In these episodes, wage movements relative to the benchmark were not an important factor. In the 1990s, productivity growth was at its lowest level, but capital deepening was greater, the terms of trade did not shift as adversely, and the product wage rose relative to the benchmark. As a result, the real wage rose by a full percentage point more per year in the 1990s than in the 1980s. Real wage growth was only a bit below average in the boom of the 1990s, despite poor productivity growth.

The examination of real wages shows that the product wage—earnings stated in terms of what workers produce—gives too optimistic a picture of the benefits that workers receive from the growth of the economy. The U.S. economy specializes in making products such as computers and other capital goods that are becoming cheaper, while the nation imports products such as oil that are becoming more expensive. The real wage gives a more realistic view of what workers actually gain in economic terms from their work. Real wage growth was rapid until the 1970s, slowed down abruptly in the 1970s and 1980s, and then resumed in the 1990s. Although rising oil prices in 2004 and 2005 inevitably cut into real wage growth, the effect has been small as of this writing—from the first quarter of 2004 through the second quarter of 2005, the prices of goods consumed, including oil, rose only about three-quarters of a percentage point more than the prices of goods produced.

WAGES BY EDUCATION GROUP

The rest of the chapter studies wages and earnings by education group. Poverty is concentrated in the lowest-skilled group, those who have not graduated from high school. It is useful to compare the wages of the least-skilled to those in other skill groups. I consider three other groups—high school graduates, those who started college but did not receive a BA, and college graduates. My investigation starts by building measures of wages for the four groups that are reasonably comprehensive—they include the value of fringe benefits. As in the case of overall wages, the measures can be stated as product wages or as real wages. I compare product wages to a neoclassical benchmark. While overall wages track the benchmark reasonably well, wages by education group diverge conspicuously—wage growth among the least-educated has fallen far short of the benchmark. The actual real earnings of the most-educated, college graduates, rose rapidly. Real earnings of the least-educated fell during the 1980s but grew reasonably rapidly in the 1990s. For an extended review of these wage changes and the related literature, see Autor and Katz (1999).

To understand the differences in the experiences of the least-skilled in the two decades, I examine measures of the demand and supply for the four education groups. Demand rose rapidly for the two top groups. Demand fell sharply during the 1980s for the least-educated group but rose during the 1990s—hence the improvement in earnings. Some industries that employ significant fractions of the least-educated, notably construction, grew during the 1990s after shrinking during the 1980s. On the supply side, I find that the least-educated were helped by declining supply. This earnings decline from shrinking supply might have been somewhat offset by the tendency for the remaining less-educated population to be drawn from further down the skill distribution. The growth of real earnings for this group in the 1990s was the result of growing demand and shrinking supply.

In this investigation, I make use of a consistent tabulation of the March Current Population Survey on annual earnings by education group, 1975 through 2002. The CPS reports earnings in the sense of the amount reported on a worker's W-2 form. The concept of earnings appropriate for the analysis in this chapter includes not only cash earnings in the W-2 sense but also fringe benefits provided in kind, which are omitted from W-2s. The National Income and Products Accounts (NIPAs) make a serious attempt to include fringes in reported compensation, based on data provided by employers to the Internal Revenue Service (IRS) and on other information. I am not aware of any other comprehensive measure of the value of fringe benefits. The ratio of NIPA compensation to CPS compensation measures the extent of the extra element in compensation across all workers. It is not possible to break it down by education group. However, there are reasons to believe that the ratio is not too different by education or earnings level. The biggest single element is the employer's contribution to Social Security, a fixed ratio up to the cutoff. With respect to other elements, some factors point to an increasing ratio of total compensation to CPS compensation—such as the fact that more education-intensive industries tend to have higher fringes—while others point in the opposite direction—such as the fact that non-discrimination laws require employers, in some cases, to offer the same benefits packages to high- and low-wage workers.

To scale up to a more complete concept of earnings, I multiply all of the figures by the ratio of total compensation in the NIPAs (tables 6.2B and 6.2C) to the total reported for the CPS. This ratio was 1.13 in 1975, rose to 1.20 in 1992, and then declined back to 1.13 in 2002. Without this adjustment, the performance of earnings in the 1990s would appear to be even more favorable but would fail to agree with the highly reliable figures from the NIPAs.

The Cobb-Douglas benchmark model I discussed earlier extends easily to an economy with several kinds of labor. Let L_t be a particular category of labor, such as the lowest skill group. Let X_t be another input, such as another skill group. The production function becomes

$$Y_t = A_t L_t^\alpha X_t^\beta K_t^{1-\alpha-\beta},$$

(3.6)

where now α is the elasticity of output with respect to unskilled labor input. The profit-maximizing condition becomes

$$\frac{w_t}{p_t} = A_t \alpha L_t^{\alpha-1} X_t^\beta K_t^{1-\alpha-\beta}.$$

(3.7)

Substitute in the expression for output, Y_t, to get

$$\frac{w_t}{p_t} = \alpha \frac{Y_t}{L_t}.$$

(3.8)

The product wage depends only on the output-labor ratio. Output stands in for both productivity and the capital stock in the earlier equation.

Figure 3.4 displays the ratio of the left side of equation 3.8 to the right side, stated as an index. This index is the ratio of the product wage to the prediction for the product wage given the level of output and the volume of employment for each of the four education categories. I measure the product wage as the average earnings of people with earnings, from the CPS, to the consumption deflator from the NIPA.

Figure 3.4 illustrates a point that has received enormous attention in recent years—the wages of less-skilled workers have grown far less than predicted by the Cobb-Douglas benchmark and the wages of the more-skilled have grown correspondingly faster. Often this finding is formulated in terms of skill-biased technical change. That is, one explanation is that technical progress does not take

FIGURE 3.4 / Ratio of Product Wage to Cobb-Douglas Benchmark

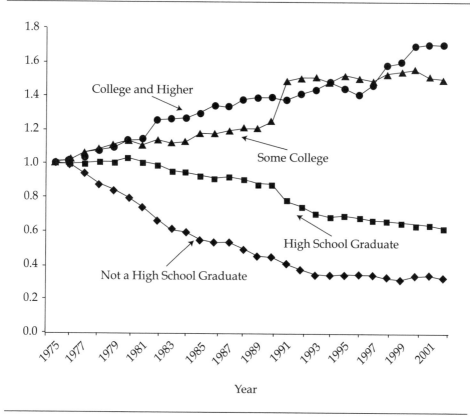

Source: Author's compilation.
Notes: Output is real GDP, NIPA, table 1.1.3. Employment is number of workers with earnings, CPS, http://www.census.gov/population/socdemo/education/tabA-3.xls. Nominal wage rate is average earnings per worker, same source. Adjustment for compensation is not included in the CPS: ratio of compensation in NIPA, table 6.2, to total compensation from the CPS (source above). Deflated by GDP deflator, NIPA, table 1.1.4.

the form in equation 3.8, where a single index amplifies the productivity of all inputs jointly, but rather each input is amplified by its own productivity index.

I turn now to data on real earnings. I study real earnings per person. Changes in this measure occur because of changes in wages, changes in labor force participation, and changes in annual hours of work per worker. The CPS reports total earnings for an education group and the number of people with any earnings.

Figure 3.5 shows the results of these calculations, presented as annual real earnings per person for each of the four education groups. The figure documents a familiar story—starting in the 1980s, the earnings of people with higher education have grown much faster than the earnings of those with a high school education or less. The figure also shows that earnings per person reached a low

FIGURE 3.5 / Real Annual Earnings per Person by Education, 1975 to 2002

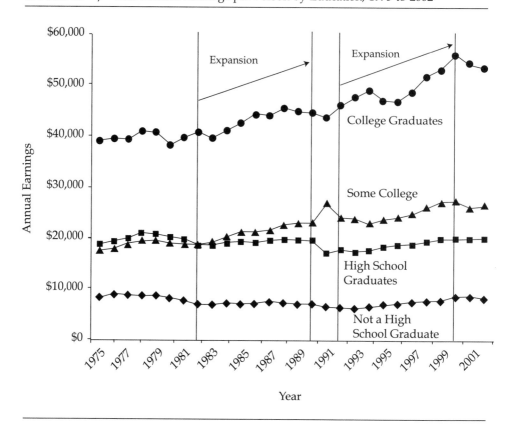

Source: Author's compilation.
Notes: Number of people with earnings, CPS (source above) multiplied by average earnings from figure 3.4, divided by estimated population in the education group. Population twenty-five and older from the CPS (source above), table A-2. I approximated the distribution of the population age sixteen to twenty-four by tabulating the distribution from the raw data for the March 2003 CPS (using the Census Bureau's Data Ferrett program) and applying the distribution to the number of people age sixteen to twenty-four obtained from U.S. Census Bureau, *Historical Statistics of the United States*, table HS-3. This source gives the population age fifteen to twenty-four, so I approximated the population as 90 percent of the reported number. Adjusted as in figure 3.4 for compensation omitted from the CPS. Deflated by the consumption deflator.

point for the two less-skilled groups around 1990. Earnings in these groups rose during the 1990s, though not as fast as for those with higher education.

Growth in earnings per person decomposes into growth in earnings per worker and growth in workers per person, that is, in employment rates. Figure 3.6 shows employment rates measured as the fraction of the population with any earnings at all during the year. The only group with important systematic varia-

FIGURE 3.6 / Employment Rates by Education

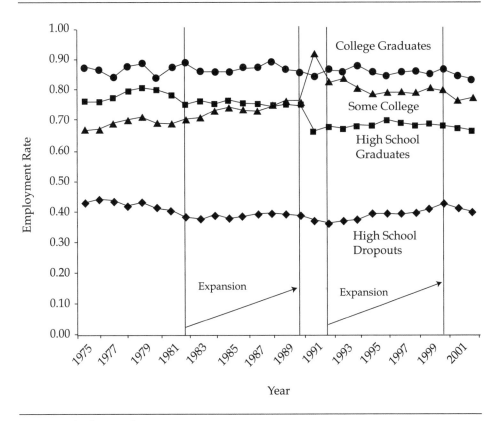

Source: Author's compilation.
Note: Ratio of number of people with earnings to total population in education group, using sources as in figure 3.5.

tions in employment rates is high school dropouts. Their employment rate rose by almost 2 percent per year in the boom of the 1990s, after having been essentially constant in the boom of the 1980s. A further decomposition by sex would show some disparity.

The other element of the decomposition is real earnings per worker. Table 3.3 shows the CPS data for this measure. Real earnings rose faster in the 1990s than in the 1980s in every education group. The difference is around 1 percent per year—enough to cumulate to more than 8 percent over the length of the boom. Notice that the improvement is the same as shown in table 3.2 for the real wage averaged across education groups. The factors that accounted for favorable wage growth in general—notably the unexplained growth of wages relative to the neoclassical benchmark—operated roughly uniformly across education groups.

TABLE 3.3 / Annual Percentage Growth in Real Earnings per Year, by Education, Expansions of 1982 to 1990 and 1992 to 2000

	Not a High School Graduate	High School Graduate	Some College	College Graduate
1982 to 1990	−0.1	0.6	1.6	1.6
1992 to 2000	1.5	1.4	1.9	2.6
Improvement	1.6	0.7	0.3	1.0

Source: Author's compilation.
Note: From figure 3.5.

The largest improvement in wage growth was for dropouts and the smallest for those with some college but no degree.

DEMAND BY EDUCATION GROUP

In this section, I discuss an index of the demand for workers in the education groups considered in the previous section. The index is simply total real spending by employers for the workers in the education group. If the elasticity of demand for an education group is one, then the product of the wage and the level of employment is a given amount, independent of the position of labor supply. Further, if labor supply is inelastic, then the number of people in the education group is a measure of supply. Thus, the total earnings of an age group in a year provide a reasonable index of demand in that year, and the number of people measure supply. These are useful measures even if the two elasticity assumptions—one for demand and zero for supply—are not strictly true.

Figure 3.7 shows indexes of total real earnings of the four education groups for the period 1975 through 2002, from the CPS, adjusted to NIPA totals, as described earlier. Rapid increases in demand for the more-skilled workers with at least some college is the most conspicuous feature of the figure. In the lowest skill group, demand fell substantially to a trough in 1993 and has risen since then. This increase in demand was responsible for the favorable performance of earnings per worker in the 1990s. Though the 1990s were famous for the growth of education-intensive industries, such as finance and high-tech, other industries offering opportunities for those with little education also grew. The most important was construction. High school graduates enjoyed modest increases in demand except for a decline following the recession that began in 1990. Table 3.4 summarizes the data for the two long expansions of the 1980s and 1990s.

Some have argued that demand for less-skilled workers fell because the industries that hire these workers have shrunk. Figure 3.8 shows the absence of such a tendency. It is a scatter plot across industries of intensity of low-skilled workers (the fraction of the wage bill earned by dropouts) on the horizontal axis and the

FIGURE 3.7 / Indexes of Labor Demand by Education Group

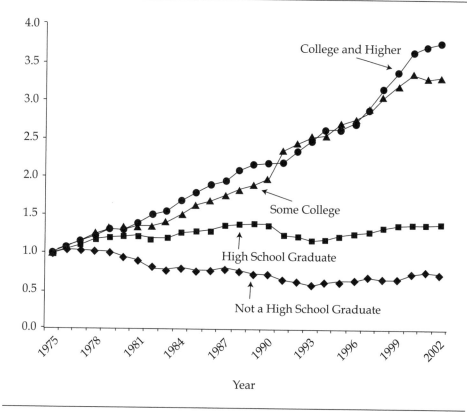

Source: Author's compilation.
Note: Total earnings from figure 3.5, deflated by the GDP deflator.

TABLE 3.4 / Annual Growth Rates of Labor Demand by Education Groups

	Not a High School Graduate	High School Graduate	Some College	College Graduate
1982 to 1990	−1.4	2.0	4.7	4.8
1992 to 2000	2.1	1.5	3.9	5.6

Source: Author's compilation.
Note: From figure 3.7.

FIGURE 3.8 / Low-Skill Share and Low-Skill Growth by Industry, 1992 to 2000

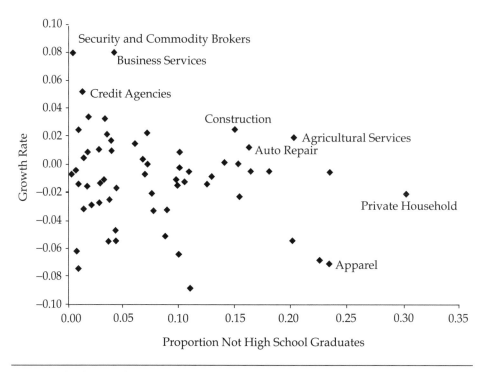

Source: Author's compilation.
Notes: For each industry reported in the NIPA earnings data, table 6.2, the horizontal axis measures the proportion of earnings paid to workers with less than a high school education, obtained from the 2000 census using the DataFerrett, and the vertical axis is compensation in 2000 divided by compensation in 1992, deflated by the consumption deflator.

annual growth rate of demand for low-skilled workers on the vertical axis. There is essentially no correlation between intensity and growth. A few of the industries are identified. Some correspond to general impressions about the changes in the economy over the 1990s: financial services grew rapidly and employ essentially no low-skilled workers; apparel shrank rapidly and is highly intensive in low skills; construction, agricultural services, and auto repair are low-skill-intensive industries that grew during the 1990s.

SUPPLY BY EDUCATION GROUP

The other part of the story of the labor market is supply changes in the education groups. Figure 3.9 shows indexes of the number of people age sixteen and older in each education group since 1948. The less-than-high-school group was roughly constant until the mid-1960s and then began to fall continuously

FIGURE 3.9 / Indexes of the Number of People Age Sixteen and Older, by Education Group, 1948 to 2000

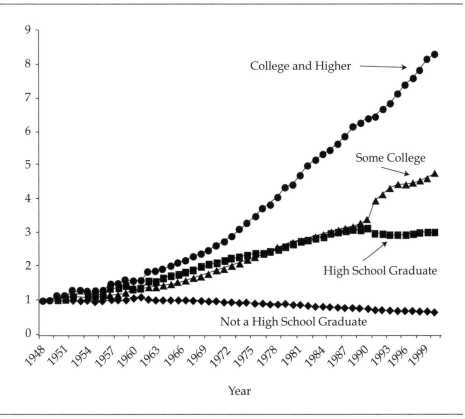

Source: Author's compilation.
Note: Data from figure 3.5.

through the present. The declining size of this population is a key factor in the reduction in poverty over the past forty years. The number of people who graduated from high school but did not go to college at all grew continuously until 1992 and then fell and leveled off. The discontinuous change in the high-school-only group is matched by complementary change in the some-college group, which rose dramatically in the early 1990s. Finally, the number of people with at least a college education rose exponentially throughout the period.

Table 3.5 shows the annual growth rates of the population age sixteen and over by education, for the whole period and for the three major expansions. The dropout population fell in all expansions, especially in the 1980s and 1990s. The 1990s were exceptional for the low growth of the high-school-only population, which grew rapidly in earlier years. The two college-and-higher groups grew rapidly in all years.

TABLE 3.5 / Annual Growth Rates of Population Sixteen and Older

	Not a High School Graduate	High School Graduate	Some College	College Graduate
1948 to 2003	−0.7	2.0	2.9	4.0
1962 to 1970	−0.3	3.5	3.2	3.7
1982 to 1990	−1.5	1.4	2.2	3.7
1992 to 2000	−1.3	0.1	2.4	3.2

Source: Author's compilation.
Note: Data from figure 3.5.

POVERTY AND EARNINGS

As I noted at the beginning of this chapter, the level of earnings of the least-skilled workers is a central determinant of the incidence of poverty. Discussions of poverty often focus on the fraction of people whose family incomes fall below the official poverty threshold. In this section, I make some observations about the complex relation between earnings and poverty.

Figure 3.5 showed that real earnings of the less-skilled population have been roughly stable for the past twenty-five years. Figure 3.9 documented the dramatic reduction in the fraction of the population with less than a high school education. From these figures, we might reasonably infer that the fraction of people in poverty declined over the period. In fact, as table 3.6 shows, poverty rates rose during the 1970s and 1980s and declined in the 1990s, going back to the same levels as in 1975. Progress from improved education did not result in any corresponding overall decline in the incidence of poverty. Rising real earnings in the 1990s were part of the reason that the poverty rate declined in that decade.

A comprehensive reconciliation of these divergent trends is beyond the scope of this chapter. The measurement of poverty involves many contentious issues, including the treatment of in-kind and monetary transfers (see Citro and Michael 1995). I mention here only two of the factors that appear to be important. First, the distribution of earnings within each education group is highly dispersed. As usual in data on individuals, within-group dispersion exceeds cross-group dispersion. Increasing dispersion of earnings is probably a factor in the failure of the poverty rate to decline.

Second, the poverty rate is based on family income for people who live in families. The definition of poverty presumes high returns to scale in family operation. For example, in 2003 the poverty threshold for a single adult under age sixty-five was $9,573, while the threshold for a couple was $12,321. A couple with an income of $16,000 is well above the threshold, but if they decide to live separately and divide their income equally, both will be in poverty with incomes of $8,000. The definition incorporates such high returns to scale because it is

TABLE 3.6 / Poverty Rates (Percentages)

Year	People in Poverty	People in Families in Poverty
1975	12.3%	10.9%
1990	13.5	12.0
2003	12.5	10.8

Source: Author's compilation.
Notes: Data from census poverty data, table 2, "Poverty Status of People by Family Relation-ship, Race, and Hispanic Origin, 1959 to 2003," http://www.census.gov/hhes/poverty/hist-pov/hstpov2.html.

based not on consideration of the economies from all sources of living together, but only on preparing and consuming food. Even at the conceptual level, the poverty measure does not consider preferences about living arrangements.

The high level of returns to scale built into the poverty definition has had a large effect on the measured incidence of poverty because of an important trend away from cohabitation. In 1960 the United States had 3.4 people per household. This figure fell to 3.0 in 1975 and to 2.6 in 2003.

Because households do enjoy returns to scale, measures of poverty should consider this issue. Americans have spent a good part of the benefit of rising real earnings on the establishment of additional households. Older people are less likely to live with their offspring. The fraction of the population living with spouses has declined. The current official definition of poverty makes a large deduction on account of the proliferation of households without considering the benefits that people may achieve by living separately.

RECESSIONS

Every five or ten years, the economy sinks into a recession. Employment falls, unemployment rises, and the labor market enters a period of slack that may last several years after the end of the contraction itself. The most recent recession ran from early to late 2001, but the unemployment rate even at the time of writing in late 2005 is still well above its pre-recession level. How do recessions affect earnings in general and the earnings of the least-skilled in particular?

Recessions tend to undo some of the gains of the preceding expansions. Table 3.7 presents the data on real earnings per person from figure 3.4 as percentage changes from the peak year to the second year following the peak. (In the case of 2000, the business cycle peak occurred in early 2001, but with annual data it is appropriate to treat 2000 as the peak, since the economy declined substantially during 2001.)

Recessions are times of shrinking earnings per person, mainly because of higher unemployment. In the two earlier recessions, the least-skilled suffered large reductions in earnings, while those with at least some college had increases

TABLE 3.7 / Two-Year Changes in Real Earnings per Person in Three Recessions

	Not a High School Graduate	High School Graduate	Some College	College Graduate
1981 to 1983	−11.6	−5.6	−0.2	−0.2
1990 to 1992	−9.6	−9.4	4.0	3.4
2000 to 2002	−4.5	−0.2	−4.0	−4.7

Source: Author's compilation.
Note: Data from figure 3.5.

or only small decreases. The most recent recession looks quite different. All skill groups had declines—only the high-school-graduate group avoided substantial earnings losses. But the least-skilled, dropout group had about the same earnings reductions as those with at least some college. The reason is the unusual industry composition of the most recent contraction. Construction, an industry with substantial employment of the least-educated workers and normally a major victim of recessions, enjoyed employment increases.

CONCLUSIONS

One of the important determinants of poverty is the earnings of low-skilled workers. I have examined both the overall behavior of real earnings and the behavior of the earnings of people who did not finish high school. In the 1990s, overall earnings rose slightly less in relation to the prices of private goods and services produced in the United States than they did for the past fifty years, but the rise was well above what occurred in the boom of the 1980s. Productivity growth was unusually low in the 1990s, below even the 1980s, but capital deepening made an important contribution to wage growth. In addition, wages grew spontaneously by about six-tenths of a percent per year over the simple neoclassical benchmark set by productivity growth and capital deepening. The extra wage growth has a number of plausible explanations, such as improving competition in product markets. Thus, one of the reasons that the 1990s were a relatively good period for the unskilled was the reasonably high rate of growth of wages in relation to the prices of goods and services produced in the United States.

I have not tried in this chapter to translate wages paid into some kind of bottom line of wages received after taxes and other costs, such as fringe benefits, that employers pay but workers do not receive in cash, and after taxes and other working costs paid by workers themselves. The only adjustment I have explored is for the terms of trade—that is, for the fact that workers spend their wages in part on products imported from the rest of the world. This adjustment is slightly negative for the 1990s, but not nearly as negative as it was in the 1980s. Real wages in the sense of compensation divided by the cost of living rose by about 1.8 percent per year in the 1990s, below the fifty-two-year average of 2.1 percent but above the rise of 0.7 percent per year in the 1980s.

The 1990s were also a good period for the earnings of unskilled workers. Real earnings rose by 1.5 percent per year for those who did not finish high school, a bit better than the 1.4 percent for those who graduated but did not continue. By contrast, real earnings in the lowest education group fell during the 1980s. The least-educated enjoyed an acceleration of wage growth of 1.6 percent per year in the 1990s over the 1980s.

To understand the favorable experience of the least-skilled in the 1990s, I studied demand and supply. Real compensation paid to a group of workers serves as an index of demand. The results for the lowest-skilled group showed an annual growth rate of 3.5 percent in the 1990s, compared to 1.8 percent in the 1980s. Demand growth in the 1990s was about equal for all four education groups. Although some industries that employ large proportions of the least-educated workers—such as apparel—declined in the 1990s, others—such as construction and auto repair—expanded.

The declining supply of unskilled workers also contributed to their favorable experience. The number of people age sixteen and older with less than a high school education fell at a rate of 1.3 percent per year in the 1990s. The number of people who finished high school but did not continue to college—which had grown rapidly from 1948 until 1992—hardly grew at all during the period 1992 to 2000.

The favorable performance of low-skilled wages in the 1990s contributed to a moderate decline during the decade in the incidence of officially measured poverty. But this improvement only brought poverty back to the level of 1975. The fraction of the U.S. population living at the low standard of the poverty threshold has not declined despite stable earnings per person among the least-skilled and a declining fraction of the population in the lowest skill category. Increases in within-category dispersion of earnings and the strong trend toward living in smaller households, with the resulting sacrifice of economies of scale, are two influences among those that account for the differences in the two measures of performance—earnings of the least-skilled per person and the incidence of poverty.

What is the outlook for earnings growth among the least-skilled and the resulting amelioration of poverty in the current decade? As I have stressed throughout the chapter, rising productivity is the primary driving force of rising real wages. Productivity has grown rapidly so far in the decade, and the outlook for further growth is favorable, though it will probably not occur at the same high rate seen from 2000 to 2004. Some of the forces that helped the low-skilled over the past ten years, notably the rapid growth of construction employment, are unlikely to continue. The end of the housing bubble forecasted by every real estate expert will bear negatively on the less-educated workforce of that industry. There is every reason to expect the continuation of the forces that have delivered rapid real earnings growth to the more-educated as the United States continues to delegate the physical production of goods to other countries and to specialize in administration, research, and other function that call for a college education. All workers are at risk for downward pressure on real earnings from higher energy prices, though the magnitude of this effect so far, with oil prices more than doubling, has been tiny.

NOTE

1. This research is part of the Program on Economic Fluctuations and Growth of the National Bureau of Economic Research. A complete spreadsheet with all data, showing the details of all calculations, is available at stanford.edu/~rehall.

REFERENCES

Autor, David H., and Lawrence F. Katz. 1999. "Changes in the Wage Structure and Earnings Inequality." In *Handbook of Labor Economics*, vol. 3A, edited by Orley C. Ashenfelter and David Card. Amsterdam: North-Holland.

Citro, Constance F., and Robert T. Michael. 1995. *Measuring Poverty: A New Approach.* Washington, D.C.: National Academy Press.

Solow, Robert M. 1956. "A Contribution to the Theory of Economic Growth." *Quarterly Journal of Economics* 70: 65–94.

———. 1957. "Technical Change and the Aggregate Production Function." *Review of Economics and Statistics* 39: 312–20.

Chapter 4

The Impact of Technological Change on Low-Wage Workers: A Review

David Card and John DiNardo

T he relationship between technological change and the earnings of less-skilled workers is one of the oldest issues in economics (Berg 1984).[1] Renewed interest in the link was spawned by labor market trends in the 1980s, including the decline in real wages for younger and less-educated workers and the sharp increase in the wage gap between college- and high school–educated workers. At the same time, the introduction of the microcomputer was hailed as a revolutionary event that promised to change the nature of work. Two prominent studies written at the close of the decade (Bound and Johnson 1992; Katz and Murphy 1992) argued that the falling fortunes of less-skilled workers were caused by adverse demand shocks, specifically "skill-biased" technological changes induced by the new computer technology. A vast subsequent literature has tended to confirm this basic view.[2] By now it is widely accepted that technological changes have hurt, and will continue to hurt, the labor market prospects for less-skilled workers in the United States and other advanced countries. The technological change hypothesis, in turn, has provided a powerful intellectual foundation for a laissez-faire approach to policies for aiding less-skilled workers.

In this chapter, we present a critical review of the literature linking technological change to the structure of wages in the U.S. economy. We argue that the evidence for the technological change hypothesis is weaker than many observers have recognized. From a research design perspective, we identify two key concerns. First, many studies reason backward from an effect (recent changes in the time-series behavior of wage inequality) to a single or small number of "causes." A typical study does not ask: what is the evidence that some intervention (which reliably leads to technological "progress") has had an effect on wage inequality? Rather, most have adopted a forensic approach, asking: *why* has wage inequality increased? In a world where there are many potential causes, some of which interact with other causes and some of which are unknown (or ignored), a forensic approach can only eliminate candidate explanations. Even when such an analysis has ruled out all but one of the enumerated hypotheses, the analysis provides at best only limited support for the remaining explanation, since others could be constructed to explain the same set of facts.

A second fundamental problem is that demand shocks are inherently unobservable. Shifts in demand can only be measured within a specific structural model of supply and demand. Consequently, to an extent that seems to have been underappreciated, much of the evidence in favor of (or against) the technology hypothesis is *model-dependent*. Different analysts, often using the same data, have reached different conclusions because they have worked with different structural models. Given the model-dependent nature of the evidence, a convincing case for the technological change hypothesis requires an evaluation of the maintained structural model. In reality, these models are oversimplified and often make other predictions that are inconsistent with key facts. Many of the structural models used in the technological change literature completely ignore the supply side of the labor market, and nearly all abstract from factors like discrimination and frictional imperfections that may have an impact on low-skilled workers. Reliance on simple structural models to infer the effects of technological change has led analysts to downplay or ignore important changes that might otherwise be interpreted as evidence against the technological change explanation, such as the dramatic rise in female relative wages or the near-constancy of the wage gap between high school dropouts and those with a high school degree.

More generally, we believe that analysts interested in understanding the effects of technology on less-skilled workers could usefully adopt an expanded paradigm that explicitly incorporates supply-side considerations as well as imperfections like discrimination, search frictions, and incomplete information. Indeed, in the broader labor economics literature, these factors are often invoked to explain phenomena that have an important influence on the structure of wages, such as industry differentials, firm-size differentials, and the effects of job tenure. A more comprehensive approach seems especially important because low-wage workers tend to have many disadvantages: they are younger, less educated, less healthy, and more likely to be minority and/or female; they live in worse neighborhoods, have few family or friends with good jobs, work in low-wage industries and in smaller firms, and have limited job tenure. Although factors beyond simple supply and demand are an important feature of the labor economics literature, they seem to have been pushed into the background by a focus on the technological change hypothesis.

Maybe it is not surprising then that the technology and wages literature has put little emphasis on the search for specific policy remedies that could be used to improve the prospects for less-skilled workers—apart from the need for low-wage workers to upgrade their skills. A "tax on computers" is never seriously discussed as a policy remedy for the problems caused by technology shocks (Johnson 1997). Indeed, the class of models used in the technological change literature would seem to point to policies like lowering minimum wages and welfare payments as "natural" responses to adverse relative demand shocks, although such policies are rarely evaluated in this literature. It therefore seems particularly important to understand the limitations of these models and the robustness of any conclusions about the role of technological change in determining recent trends in the labor market prospects for less-skilled workers.

APPROACHES TO MEASURING THE EFFECTS OF TECHNOLOGY

It is helpful to distinguish between two broad classes of approaches that labor economists have used to measure the impacts of skill-biased technological change (SBTC) on the relative earnings of less-skilled workers. In both cases, the focus of the existing literature has been on measuring the effects of exogenous technological changes.[3] One approach, which we call the "model-specific" approach, defines SBTC as that part of the variation in relative employment and wages that is left unexplained after accounting for observable changes in the supply or demand for different groups of workers (see, for example, Bound and Johnson 1992; Card and Lemieux 2001; Juhn, Murphy, and Pierce 1993; Katz and Murphy 1992; Levy and Murnane 1992). This approach has two key features that have made it attractive to many analysts. First, it can explain enormous quantities of labor market data from long time periods with very few parameters. Second (and related), this approach leads to a substantial reduction in the set of "facts" to be explained. For example, in some studies the entire wage structure of the economy at a point in time is summarized by a single number representing the mean wage gap between men with a college degree and those with a high school degree. However, as David Autor and Lawrence Katz (2000, 1516) have observed, a serious limitation of this approach is that "strong assumptions about functional forms and substitution possibilities between different types or groups of workers must be imposed to make this approach feasible." As we explain later, a less transparent but equally serious limitation is that the set of "facts" one chooses to consider are themselves model-dependent, sometimes in non-obvious ways.

A second approach to assessing the importance of technological changes is to correlate observed measures of technology with changes in wage structure. Although this approach has sometimes been combined with the model-specific approach, in principle it is more closely related to traditional notions of research design. Within the limits of the "experiments" nature has provided, we can ask how observed measures of technology are related to relative wages.

Alan Krueger (1993) provides the best-known and most influential example of this approach. He estimated the wage premium for employees who use a computer on the job and used the resulting estimates to infer the effect of the spread of computers on the return to education. A substantial literature, which we will not review, has followed this approach and confirmed that computer users earn higher wages in many different settings. Apart from the problems associated with the nonrandom incidence of computer use, the key limitation of this approach is that its relation to the debate on the role of SBTC is unclear. As Autor and Katz (2000, 1533) explain: "The existence of a positive computer wage differential is neither a necessary nor a sufficient condition for the diffusion of computers to have induced a shift in the relative demand for more-skilled workers and to have affected the wage structure."[4]

A variant of the direct approach to measuring the impact of technological change is the case study approach. In a later section, we discuss several prominent case studies that have documented the changes in employment and wages following the adoption of a new technology at a single firm or a small group of firms. These studies are helpful in assessing the magnitude of the relative demand shifts associated with the adoption of a specific technology at a specific set of employers. Nevertheless, they are not as useful in quantifying the overall trend in the demand for less-skilled workers. Thus, case studies have mainly served to complement the model-based approaches taken by most previous researchers.

Model-Based Evidence on the Role of Technology

We begin by reviewing the basic framework underlying the model-based approach to measuring the impact of technology. In practice, this approach proceeds in two steps. In the first step, the labor force is partitioned into a number of discrete skill groups, and data on mean wages and employment for each group are collected from the Current Population Survey (CPS) or other data sources at several different points in time. These cell means become the "facts" that have to be explained. Next, changes over time in these means are related to each other in a simple supply-and-demand framework. In the absence of technological change, the model is assumed to be able to fully explain the observed changes in the wages and employment of the different skill groups (that is, yield an R-squared statistic close to one). The presence of technological change is inferred by a failure of the model to rationalize the comovements of wages and employment for different groups over the sample period.

It has long been recognized that the choices made by the researcher in both steps have important consequences for the resulting estimates of technological change. For example, in the first stage of their investigation, John Bound and George Johnson (1992) partition the labor force into groups defined by experience, education, and gender. This division is tied to their model-based assumption that men and women with the same education and experience are imperfect substitutes in production. Since the number of women working in each education and experience group rose relative to the number of men, and the relative wages of women also increased, Bound and Johnson infer that technological changes led to a positive relative demand shock for female labor in the 1980s.[5]

Although researchers may agree that the decision to model male and female labor markets separately is natural and appropriate, it is important to recognize that this decision has a powerful impact on the facts to be explained. When men and women are treated separately, the 1980s emerges as a decade of rapidly rising individual wage inequality (Autor and Katz 2000; Autor, Katz, and Kearney 2004; Bound and Johnson 1992; Card and DiNardo 2002; DiNardo, Fortin, and Lemieux 1996; Katz and Murphy 1992; Levy and Murnane 1992). When they are taken together, however, the overall rise in wage inequality during the decade is quite modest. Indeed, as shown by David Lee (1999), after taking account of changes in the minimum wage, there is almost no change in wage inequality in the pooled distribution of men's and women's wages over the 1980s. Moreover, the decision to view men and women as separate factors of production means that any spillover effects between the gender groups are either ignored or pushed very far into the background.

A similar relationship between the facts to be explained and the choice of model emerges in the recent literature on the evolution of the college–high school wage gap. To understand this point, consider the model developed in Card and Lemieux (2001), which includes as a special case the benchmark specification of Freeman (1976) and Katz and Murphy (1992). In this model, aggregate output y is produced through a CES production function that combines high school-equivalent labor at time t (H_t) with college-equivalent labor (C_t):

$$y_t = (\theta_{ht}H_t^\rho + \theta_{ct}C_t^\rho)^{\left(\frac{1}{\rho}\right)} \tag{4.1}$$

Here the θ parameters measure the efficiency of technology in period t. The key parameter in the model is $\rho = 1 - 1/\sigma_E$, where σ_E is the elasticity of substitution between the two education groups.

Unlike Freeman (1976) and Katz and Murphy (1992), Card and Lemieux (2001) explicitly allow imperfect substitution between workers with similar schooling but different ages (or different levels of potential labor market experience). This is accomplished by letting both high school–equivalent labor and college-equivalent labor be CES subaggregates of labor of different age groups.[6] Specifically, Card and Lemieux assume that

$$H_t = \left[\sum_j (\alpha_j H_{jt}^\eta)\right]^{\frac{1}{\eta}} \tag{4.2}$$

$$C_t = \left[\sum_j (\beta_j C_{jt}^\eta)\right]^{\frac{1}{\eta}} \tag{4.3}$$

where α_j and β_j are relative efficiency parameters that are assumed to be fixed over time, and $\eta = 1 - 1/\sigma_A$, where σ_A is the elasticity of substitution between different age groups with the same education.

Assuming full employment, and that the relative wages of different skill groups are proportional to their relative productivity, we can derive the following convenient expression for the log relative wage gap between college-educated and high school–educated workers in age group j in year t:

$$\log\left(\frac{w^c_{jt}}{w^h_{jt}}\right) = \log\left(\frac{\theta_{ct}}{\theta_{ht}}\right) + \log\left(\frac{\beta_j}{\alpha_j}\right) + \frac{1}{\sigma_E}\log\left(\frac{C_t}{H_t}\right) - \left(\frac{1}{\sigma_A}\right)\left[\log\left(\frac{C_{jt}}{H_{jt}}\right) - \left(\frac{C_t}{H_t}\right)\right] + e_{jt} \quad (4.4)$$

where e_{jt} represents sampling variation and any other unmeasured determinants of relative wages.

Assuming that the relative numbers of workers with a college or high school education in a cohort do not change once the cohort enters the labor market, the ratio C_{jt}/H_{jt} is fixed for a given cohort. Thus, equation 4.4 partitions the college–high school wage gap for different age groups in different years into four components:

1. A time effect: $\log(\theta_{ct}/\theta_{ht}) - (1/\sigma_E - 1/\sigma_A)\log(C_t/H_t)$
2. An age effect: $\log(\beta_j/\alpha_j)$
3. A cohort effect: $(1/\sigma_A)[\log(C_{jt}/H_{jt})]$
4. A residual component: e_{jt}

In this framework, technologically induced relative demand shocks are identified as the component of the trend in the college–high school wage gap that remains once the effects of aggregate supply have been factored out.[7]

Although this model represents only a small departure from the benchmark specification used by Richard Freeman (1976) and by Lawrence Katz and Kevin Murphy (1992), the introduction of imperfect substitutability between different age groups with the same education has a potentially important effect on the facts to be explained. The benchmark model assumes that $1/\sigma_A = 0$, implying that the cohort effects are ignorable. The benchmark model therefore asserts that the facts to be explained are merely a function of the regression coefficients on a set of dummies that can be depicted as:

$$\log \omega_{a,s,t} = f(\text{Age} \otimes \text{Education} \otimes \text{Year}) \quad (4.5)$$

Where $\log \omega_{a,s,t}$ is the mean log wage of a worker in age group a, schooling level s in year t. Such a framework is at the heart of the facts helpfully laid out in Levy and Murnane (1992).

The model in Card and Lemieux (2001), by contrast, can be depicted as:

$$\log \omega_{a,s,t,c} = f(\text{Age} \otimes \text{Education} \otimes \text{Year} \otimes \text{Cohort}) \quad (4.6)$$

From the textbook omitted-variables analysis, the set of facts generated from equation 4.5 will be the same as the facts generated by equation 4.6 only if these cohort effects are orthogonal to the age, education, and year effects. It is widely recognized, however, that this is not the case, especially with changes in cohort size induced by the postwar "baby boom." For example, in their review of the standard earnings regressions, James Heckman, Lance Lochner, and Petra Todd (2003, n.p.) find "important differences between cohort based and cross-sectional estimates of the rate of return to schooling" and observe that "in the recent period of rapid technological progress, widely used cross-sectional applications of the Mincer model produced dramatically biased estimates of cohort returns to schooling."

This sensitivity of structural models is not an argument against the use of such structural models. Indeed, one surprise in Card and Lemieux (2001) is how *well* such a simple model can rationalize a large number of wage differentials for the United States, Britain, and Canada over many years, once proper consideration is given to the role of cohort-specific supplies of college-educated labor. As a matter of research design, however, we believe that a structural approach is better suited to testing hypotheses about the effect of *observed* factors (such as cohort-specific supply effects) than as a method for identifying the effects of technological change, since ultimately any misspecification or error feeds into the residual and becomes part of the estimate of technological change.

CONSTANT OR ACCELERATING TECHNOLOGY? Whatever the choice of model, the effect of technology is pinned down by imposing a specific time pattern for technology, usually by restricting the time-series pattern of the relative technology term in equation 4.4, $\log(\theta_{ct}/\theta_{ht})$. Two different assumptions are common in the literature. The first is that the relative technology effect follows a linear time trend, $\log(\theta_{ct}/\theta_{ht}) = \delta t$, with $\delta > 0$ under the assumption that technological changes are skill-biased. An alternative assumption—sometimes called the "accelerationist" hypothesis—asserts that there was a trend break in the pace of technological change at some time during the 1980s (say, coincident with the introduction of the personal computer), implying $\log(\theta_{ct}/\theta_{ht}) = (\delta + D\gamma)t$, where D is a dummy indicating the postbreak period, and γ is a parameter reflecting the faster pace of technological innovation in the later period.

The two alternative specifications have different implications for the role of exogenous technology in affecting the wage structure. The "constant trend" version suggests that although technology plays a role in determining relative wages, there is nothing particularly remarkable about the new technologies that developed in the 1980s and 1990s. Rather, these technologies should be interpreted as part of a steady stream of innovations over the recent past. The accelerationist view, by contrast, suggests that the pace of technological progress was faster in the 1980s and 1990s than in previous decades and that recent inventions such as the microcomputer and the Internet represent a quantum break from the past. Unfortunately, in the absence of direct measurement of technological change, or even of an exact date for the timing of any acceleration, it has proven difficult to distinguish between these alternative specifications (see Borjas and Ramey 1995).

TABLE 4.1 / College–High School Wage Differentials by Age and Year

	Age Range						
	26 to 30	31 to 35	36 to 40	41 to 45	46 to 50	51 to 55	56 to 60
United States							
1959	0.136	0.268	0.333	0.349	0.364	0.379	0.362
	(0.007)	(0.007)	(0.008)	(0.011)	(0.013)	(0.016)	(0.021)
1969 to 1971	0.193	0.272	0.353	0.382	0.360	0.378	0.371
	(0.013)	(0.015)	(0.015)	(0.016)	(0.018)	(0.022)	(0.028)
1974 to 1976	0.099	0.225	0.310	0.355	0.366	0.369	0.363
	(0.012)	(0.014)	(0.017)	(0.018)	(0.019)	(0.020)	(0.028)
1979 to 1981	0.111	0.180	0.265	0.281	0.336	0.349	0.355
	(0.011)	(0.012)	(0.015)	(0.017)	(0.017)	(0.018)	(0.021)
1984 to 1986	0.275	0.315	0.324	0.378	0.402	0.433	0.401
	(0.012)	(0.012)	(0.014)	(0.017)	(0.020)	(0.021)	(0.025)
1989 to 1991	0.331	0.410	0.392	0.395	0.381	0.357	0.461
	(0.012)	(0.013)	(0.014)	(0.015)	(0.018)	(0.022)	(0.025)
1994 to 1996	0.346	0.479	0.482	0.443	0.407	0.384	0.421
	(0.014)	(0.014)	(0.015)	(0.017)	(0.017)	(0.023)	(0.030)
United Kingdom							
1974 to 1977	0.172	0.323	0.267	0.338	0.340	0.371	0.455
	(0.026)	(0.034)	(0.046)	(0.049)	(0.057)	(0.059)	(0.086)
1978 to 1982	0.103	0.173	0.267	0.278	0.259	0.325	0.331
	(0.020)	(0.022)	(0.034)	(0.032)	(0.040)	(0.047)	(0.056)
1983 to 1987	0.193	0.154	0.300	0.234	0.292	0.330	0.420
	(0.022)	(0.025)	(0.029)	(0.039)	(0.048)	(0.054)	(0.064)
1988 to 1992	0.272	0.304	0.306	0.284	0.292	0.392	0.393
	(0.025)	(0.029)	(0.031)	(0.035)	(0.047)	(0.049)	(0.075)
1993 to 1996	0.306	0.369	0.352	0.318	0.325	0.285	0.337
	(0.032)	(0.032)	(0.037)	(0.038)	(0.046)	(0.066)	(0.095)

THE FACTS WHEN WORKERS OF DIFFERENT AGES ARE IMPERFECT SUB-
STITUTES   Table 4.1, taken from Card and Lemieux (2001), presents estimates
of the log wage gap between college- and high school–educated workers in different age groups and in different time periods for the United States, Canada,
and Britain. The three countries share many similarities, including relatively similar education systems and relatively low rates of institutional intervention in the
wage determination process. Moreover, employers in all three economies have
adopted computers and other advanced technologies at about the same pace.
Contrary to the impression conveyed by much of the recent literature, however,
the data in table 1 do not seem to show evidence of a ubiquitous increase in the
returns to skill since 1980, even in these three countries. Figure 4.1 plots an ad-
mittedly selective subset of the college–high school wage gaps by age and country that underscore this point.[8]

TABLE 4.1 / (*Continued*)

	Age Range						
	26 to 30	31 to 35	36 to 40	41 to 45	46 to 50	51 to 55	56 to 60
Canada							
1980	0.095	0.182	0.256	0.297	0.291	0.393	0.366
	(0.012)	(0.014)	(0.017)	(0.024)	(0.028)	(0.031)	(0.035)
1985	0.115	0.214	0.279	0.263	0.327	0.356	0.433
	(0.014)	(0.014)	(0.015)	(0.018)	(0.026)	(0.030)	(0.035)
1990	0.146	0.253	0.263	0.279	0.297	0.337	0.349
	(0.011)	(0.011)	(0.012)	(0.013)	(0.018)	(0.023)	(0.031)
1995	0.151	0.304	0.299	0.271	0.297	0.285	0.320
	(0.012)	(0.012)	(0.013)	(0.014)	(0.015)	(0.020)	(0.034)

Source: Card and Lemieux (2001), table 1.
Notes: Standard errors are in parentheses. The elements of the table are as follows:
United States: The table entries are estimates of the difference in mean log weekly earnings between full-time individuals with sixteen and twelve years of education in the indicated years and age range. Samples contain a rolling age group. For example, the twenty-six- to thirty-year-old group in the 1979 to 1981 sample includes individuals age twenty-five to twenty-nine in 1979, twenty-six to thirty in 1980, and twenty-seven to thirty-one in 1981.
United Kingdom: The table entries are estimates of the difference in mean log weekly wage between U.K. men with a university education or more versus those with only A-level or O-level qualifications. Samples contain a rolling age group. For example, the twenty-six to thirty-year-old group in the 1978 to 1982 sample includes individuals age twenty-four to twenty-eight in 1978, twenty-five to twenty-nine in 1979, twenty-six to thirty in 1980, twenty-seven to thirty-one in 1981, and twenty-eight to thirty-two in 1982.
Canada: The table entries are estimates of the difference in mean log weekly earnings between full-time Canadian men with a bachelor's degree (but no postgraduate degree) versus those with only a high school degree.

A close examination of the wage differentials in table 4.1 suggests some amendments to the "facts" for which technological change has been proposed as an explanation:

1. *The increase in the college–high school wage differential is not ubiquitous across countries and age groups.* In Britain, a model-based technology story needs to explain why there was a (sometimes substantial) *drop* in the college–high school wage premium for men over the age of forty over the period 1974 to 1996. For men age fifty-six to sixty, for example, the college–high school differential fell from 0.455 to 0.337. For men age forty to forty-five, the differential in the gap fell from 0.338 to 0.318. Such facts are not impossible to explain with an important role for skill-biased technological change; some caution is suggested, however, in assuming that an increased college–high school gap is a ubiquitous feature of economies that have seen important changes in technology. In Canada the story is similar, with the college–high

FIGURE 4.1 / Selected College High School Gaps by Age and Country

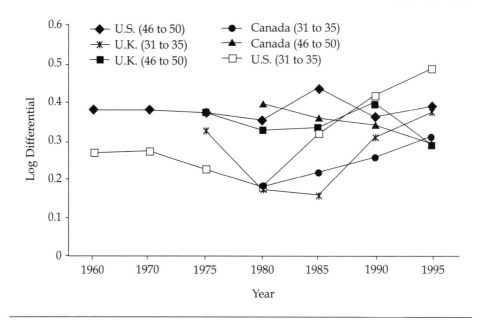

Source: Authors' compilation.

school wage differential for men age forty-one to forty-five, fifty-one to fifty-five, and fifty-six to sixty falling over the period 1980 to 1995.

2. *The increase in the college–high school wage differential is concentrated among younger workers in the United States, Britain, and Canada.* Here the increase in the college–high school wage differential has been quite striking. It appears that estimates of the trend in the "overall" college–high school wage gap have been driven by increases in the gap for younger workers.

3. *Even in the United States, the patterns for workers over the age of thirty-five do not seem to show continuous rises in wage differentials over the 1980s and 1990s.* A general description of the patterns for U.S. workers in table 4.1 is that college–high school wage gaps were roughly constant during the 1960s, fell during the 1970s, rose sharply in the mid-1980s, and then grew more modestly or not at all afterward. The fact that much of the change in college–high school wage gaps has affected younger workers and had comparatively little effect on older workers argues against viewing these developments as consistent with a ubiquitous increase in the relative wage of college graduates.

As noted in Card and DiNardo (2002), from the vantage point of the late 1980s, the rapid increase in the overall college–high school wage differential in the early 1980s did seem anomalous given the constant or falling differentials over the previous decades and the rather large increases in the supply of college-educated workers. Indeed, from that vantage point, the supply-and-demand-plus-technology framework strongly suggested a further rapid expansion of college–high school wage differentials in the 1990s. For instance, in one particularly clear discussion about the implications of a broad class of supply-and-demand models, Bound and Johnson (1992, 389) noted:

> It is interesting to speculate about what the results imply about the course of relative wages in the future. Given a continuation of the increase in the relative demand for highly educated labor, wage differentials by education are likely to continue to increase unless there is a sharp rise in college attendance and completion rates. Such an increase does not appear to be likely in the near future . . . in the absence of drastic changes in educational policy at all levels.

Although this seems to be the right prediction given the basic model, it was not borne out by subsequent events. Indeed, many measures of inequality were fairly stable, or increased only modestly, over the 1990s.[9] Obviously, the slowdown can be rationalized by assuming that there was a deceleration in the pace of technological change relative to the 1980s or that other factors emerged to obscure the underlying trend in technology.

WHAT ABOUT THE BOTTOM OF THE EDUCATION DISTRIBUTION? Much of the inequality literature has focused on interpreting trends in the wage differential between college and high school workers. In part, this reflects the influence of Richard Freeman (1976), who first proposed a supply-and-demand framework for analyzing trends in the college wage premium. In part, it also reflects the legacy of Jacob Mincer (1974), who specified a linear relationship between log earnings and years of schooling. According to Mincer's specification, the wage gap between college and high school workers is proportional to other education-related wage gaps in the labor market, so there is no loss in generality in focusing on the college premium. During the 1980s and 1990s, however, the relationship between earnings and years of schooling became more convex. In addition, analysts have begun to make a distinction between inequality trends among higher-wage workers and trends for lower-wage workers. In particular, Autor, Katz, and Kearney (2004) have emphasized the divergence in trends in inequality for the "upper half" of the wage distribution (between the median and ninetieth percentile of wages) and the "lower half" (between the median and tenth percentile).

Surprisingly, the technology and wage inequality literature has paid little or no attention to the relative wages of people with less than a high school education. Nevertheless, in thinking about the implications of technological change for less-skilled workers, it seems particularly important to understand the trends for people with below-average levels of education. Based on trends in the college–high school wage premium, we might have expected that the wage gap between high school dropouts and those with a high school diploma would have also

FIGURE 4.2 / The High School–Dropout Gap and the Returns to School

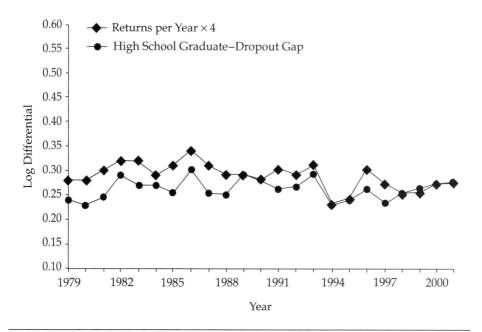

Source: Authors' compilation.

risen during the 1980s and 1990s. Figure 4.2, however, tells a different story. The figure plots two measures: the mean log wage differential between high school graduates and dropouts, and the average return per year of schooling among those with twelve or fewer years of schooling, multiplied by four.[10] Since 1979, the wage premium for high school graduates relative to dropouts has fluctuated in the range of 25 to 30 percent, with a modest rise in the early 1980s and more or less steady declines since then. By contrast, the similarly measured college–high school gap was 50 percent higher in 2000 than in 1979.

The framework of equation 4.4 suggests that it is important to control for differences in the relative supply of high school versus dropout labor in order to interpret the trend in the relative wage differential. Using data on education shares in the 1980 and 2000 censuses reported in Card (2005), we estimate that the log relative supply of high school labor relative to dropout labor increased by about as much as the log relative supply of college labor relative to high school labor. Arguably, then, in the presence of uniformly skill-biased technical change, the high school–dropout wage premium should have risen by about as much as the college–high school premium. The remarkable stability of the high school–dropout premium provides further evidence against the ubiquitous technical change hypothesis.

IMPLICITLY MODEL-BASED EVIDENCE: RESIDUAL INEQUALITY Since Juhn, Murphy, and Pierce (1993), it has become standard practice to decompose wage inequality into two components—one that relates to observed measures of skill, such as age and education, and a second that relates to unobserved skills. Empirically, unobserved skill is defined as the difference between the observed wage and the part of wages that can be predicted by observed skill factors, that is, as the residual component of earnings. Special emphasis is often given to an analysis of time-series trends in the variance of the residuals from a standard human wage equation (so-called "within inequality"). For example, Frank Levy and Richard Murnane (1992) studied trends in residual wage inequality for U.S. workers in the 1970s and 1980s, Claudia Goldin and Robert Margo (1992) used similar methods to study changes in inequality before 1940, Stephen Machin (1996) applied a parallel analysis to recent trends in Britain, and Peter Gottschalk and Timothy Smeeding (1997) studied trends for a large set of countries.

Although inspired by the formal model of wage determination developed by Juhn, Murphy, and Pierce (1993), most of the literature has treated the analysis of residual wage inequality as an accounting exercise rather than as a model-dependent procedure, and most research has treated the measured trend in residual inequality as one of the important "facts to be explained."[11] As Maarten Goos and Alan Manning (2003) have observed, "A small industry has been established based on the premise that wage inequality has risen very markedly among 'identical' workers and has been building theoretical explanations of this 'fact.'"

As in the case of education-related wage differentials, we believe that casual readers of the technology literature may have missed two important points. First, there has not been a ubiquitous rise in residual wage inequality across all skill groups and in all developed economies (for a helpful review, see Gottschalk and Smeeding 1997). Second, as has been clearly demonstrated by Lemieux (2004), estimating the trend in residual wage inequality is not a "model-free " exercise. Rather, the trend depends critically on a number of choices, including the choice of dataset to measure wages and the specific procedure adopted to adjust for the changing skill characteristics of the labor force.

To understand the analysis in Lemieux (2004), it is helpful to begin with an overview of the standard procedure for measuring trends in residual wage inequality. Although the exact implementation varies somewhat, a simple representation of current practice is to begin with a simple wage equation:

$$\log \omega_{it} = \alpha_t + X_{it}\beta_t + \varepsilon_{it} \tag{4.7}$$

where ω_{it} represents the wage of individual i observed in period t, α_t is a constant, X includes a vector of standard human capital variables (Mincer 1974) such as education, age, or gender, and β_t is a coefficient vector. The covariates are taken as measures of skill. Standard practice treats the residual from equation 4.7 as the product of a one-dimensional measure of the unobservable ability of individual i and a time-varying "price" of skill:

$$e_{it} = p_t a_i, \tag{4.8}$$

although it should be noted that when the dependent variable is the logarithm of wages, this naming convention may be confusing.

For a single time period, a convenient measure of the importance of unobservable skill in explaining wage inequality is $\sigma^2(1 - R^2)$, where σ^2 is the variance in log wages and R^2 is the usual measure of the proportion of variance in wages that is explained by the observed skill variables (X). Equation 4.8 implies that the variance of unobserved wage inequality in period t is $p^2_t \mathrm{Var}(a_i)$, where $\mathrm{Var}(a_i)$ denotes the cross-sectional variance of the unobserved ability component. Assuming that the distribution of unobserved ability is a constant over time, a rising value of the residual variance $\sigma^2(1 - R^2)$ implies that there has been a rise in the return to unobserved ability.

An obvious limitation of this framework is that any conclusion about the trend in residual wage inequality is likely to depend on the observable skill components that are included as controls. Using data for Britain, for example, Goos and Manning (2003) find that including a longer list of job quality characteristics has an important impact on the facts about residual inequality. Indeed, once they control for job conditions, they find that the previously documented rise in residual inequality in Britain disappears. Their finding also raises an interesting question: should residual wage inequality be defined after controlling for both supply- and demand-side characteristics, or only the former?

Although deciding which controls to include in the wage equation is probably of first-order importance, we assume that such a problem does not exist and instead examine the inherent difficulties with such analyses even if the models are correctly specified.[12]

To explain the problem with much of current practice, it is helpful to take a special case with a single binary covariate. Accordingly, restrict the wage equation to:

$$\log \omega_{it} = \alpha_t + \beta_t C_{it} + \varepsilon_{it} \tag{4.9}$$

Where $C_{it} = 1$ if worker i at time t has a college degree, and zero if not (that is, for high school–educated workers). Let C_t represent the fraction of workers with a college degree in year t. Then,

$$\mathrm{Var}(\varepsilon_{i,t}) = (1 - \bar{C}_t)\mathrm{Var}(\varepsilon_{i,t} \mid C = 0) + \bar{C}_t \mathrm{Var}(\varepsilon_{it} \mid C = 1)$$

This simple decomposition illustrates that the residual variance of wages at any point in time is a weighted average of the residual variances within skill groups. Over time, two things can happen: the fraction of workers in different skill groups can change, and the residual variance of wages within any given group can change. If the error component in wages is heteroskedastic, then a shift in the skill composition of the labor force can lead to a change in the overall residual variance, even when there is no change in dispersion within skill groups.

Unfortunately, the assumption of homoskedasticity in wage regressions is decisively rejected for the United States for data as far back as 1940 (for helpful reviews, see Lemieux 2005a; Heckman et al. 2003). Moreover, a large and well-established theoretical literature argues that heteroskedasticity should be a pervasive feature in wage regressions. In the standard human capital framework (Mincer 1974), for example, residual variance first falls with experience and then rises after the "overtaking point" of about ten years.[13] Similarly, Gary Becker's (1975) well-known model of comparative advantage in schooling choice leads to the prediction that the residual variance in wages will be higher for better-educated workers (Mincer 1997).[14]

To illustrate the implications of heteroskedasticity for interpretations of residual inequality, imagine that in both education groups the residual wage component can be decomposed into the product of a return and an unobserved ability and that the return to unobserved ability p_t is the same in both groups. Then the overall variance in residual inequality can be written as:

$$\text{Var}(\varepsilon_{it}) = p_t^2[\text{Var}(\alpha_i \mid C = 0) + \bar{C}_t\{\text{Var}(\alpha_i \mid C = 1)) - \text{Var}(\alpha_i \mid C = 0)\}]$$

Assuming that $\text{Var}(a_i \mid C = 1)) > \text{Var}(a_i \mid C = 0)$, this implies that a rise in the fraction of the labor force with a college degree will lead to an increase in overall residual inequality even when p_t is constant.

What is required to make a valid inference about the trend in the return to unobserved ability becomes clear from writing down the ratio of the residual variance at two points in time.

$$\frac{\text{Var}(\varepsilon_{i,t+1})}{\text{Var}(\varepsilon_{it})} = \frac{p_{t+1}^2[\text{Var}(a_i \mid C = 0, t+1) + \bar{C}_{t+1}\{\text{Var}(a_i \mid C = 1, t+1) - \text{Var}(a_i \mid C = 0, t+1)\}]}{p_t^2[\text{Var}(a_i \mid C = 0, t) + \bar{C}_t\{\text{Var}(a_i \mid C = 1, t) - \text{Var}(a_i \mid C = 0, t)\}]}$$

Lemieux's (2004) observation is that even if the distributions of unobserved ability are constant within education groups over time, the ratio is an admixture of the changes in the price of skill p_{t+1}/p_t and a "composition effect"—changes in the "weights" C_t over time. His solution to the problem is to keep the weights fixed at either the base period or the end period. Remarkably, when he does so, the puzzle posed by Levy and Murnane (1992) nearly disappears—composition-adjusted residual inequality is stable in the 1970s, shows a modest rise in the early 1980s, and is constant or even falling after the mid-1980s, much like the time trend in the college–high school differential.[15]

Although this approach is a natural one, one might be uncomfortable with the assumption that the conditional variance in unobserved skill within cells remains constant. Unfortunately, there is no way to pin down both the change in the price of unobserved skill and the variance in unobserved ability simultaneously. Moreover, as both Lemieux (2004) and Autor, Katz, and Kearney (2004) observe, the time-series path of residual inequality is somewhat sensitive to the choice of datasets and the use of end-of-period versus beginning-of-period weights to standardize the distribution of observed skills. For example, the trend in residual inequality is bigger in the March CPS (where wages are typically computed by dividing annual earnings by annual hours) than in the CPS outgoing rotation group (ORG) files (where hourly wage rates are reported directly by a majority of workers and estimated from weekly or monthly earnings and hours for others). Lemieux (2004) argues that at least some of the faster rise in the March CPS is attributable to increasing measurement error. This argument is downplayed by Autor, Katz, and Kearney (2004), who nevertheless acknowledge that most of the rise in residual wage inequality in the late 1980s and 1990s is explained by rising dispersion in the upper half of the residual distribution. To the extent that one's focus is on workers in the lower half of the distribution, this would seem to suggest that technology-induced increases in the return to unobserved skills are not particularly important.

Given the critical model-dependence of any decomposition of residual wage inequality and the large number of alternative explanations for movements in within-cell inequality (including measurement error and choice of job characteristics), we are not sanguine about the potential for such an analysis to reveal very much about the returns to unobserved ability in the economy or to inform policymakers about the importance or unimportance of technological explanations for the wage outcomes of workers at the bottom of the U.S. labor market.

Case Study Evidence on the Role of Technology

Some of the most compelling evidence for the role of technology in the employment prospects of traditionally low-wage workers comes in the form of case studies. The approaches taken are too varied to summarize; most of them involve a detailed evaluation of the changes in employment, wages, skill requirements, and conditions of work at a single firm or group of firms following the adoption of a new production technology. Interestingly, there is a long history of case studies that focus on the effects of technology on the structure of wages and employment. In response to concerns about "automation" in the mid-1950s, for example, the U.S. Bureau of Labor Statistics (BLS) commissioned a set of plant-level case studies in industries such as petroleum refining and electronics (Mark 1987). An underlying motivation for the case study literature is the age-old concern that modern technology will make certain types of workers "redundant."[16]

If there is a common theme from the case study literature, it is that improvements in technology do not lead to long-term unemployment. Both the BLS case studies of the mid-1950s and those conducted by the same agency in the mid-1980s predicted that employment growth would keep up with increases in the working-age population, regardless of new technology. Clearly, these predictions have been borne out. The BLS did observe that new technologies introduced in the mid-1980s seemed to lower the demand for specific types of skills—manual dexterity, physical strength for materials handling, and traditional craftsmanship (Mark 1987)—although other technologies appeared to have led to an *increase* in the demand for low-skilled labor, including relatively unskilled clerical work.

CASE STUDIES OF SBTC   Some of the more recent case study literature has concerned itself specifically with the SBTC hypothesis (for a particularly careful review of a number of recent case studies, see Handel 2003). A prominent example is the study by Roberto Fernandez (2001), which utilizes longitudinal data on employment and wages from a unionized food-processing plant from before and after the introduction of new machinery in the late 1980s. Fernandez specifically argues that his case study provides a "natural experiment" that opens up the "black box" of new technology:

> While all previous empirical studies of the phenomenon infer an exogenous demand-side shift in the labor market, the workers at this company experienced such a shift in a dramatic way. As such, this study provides an exceptionally clean setting in which to observe the key processes alleged to be operating in the skill-biased technological change account of growing wage inequality. Since this company endeavored to keep all its workers through the change in technology this study also avoids the main threat to validity in extant skill-bias studies, that is, the problem of self-selection of people into jobs for which their skills complement the technology. Past studies have run the risk of attributing observed wage changes to the use of the technology rather than to the individual factors that led the person to the job in the first place. (Fernandez 2001)

With some qualifications, Ferndandez views the results of his study as consistent with a role for SBTC in increasing wage inequality. Although average real wages were relatively constant, wage dispersion increased at the firm—in large part because three additional (and highly paid) maintenance electricians were hired.[17] Interestingly, despite the substantial change in technology, and apart from electricians, the change in inequality was *lower* within the firm than in the local market for similar workers. In particular, wages for the least-skilled workers at the firm fell less quickly than wages for similar workers in the local labor market. Fernandez also documents an increase in skill requirements at the firm, although this increase was typically "absorbed" by the workers and led to no increase in the typical amount of time it took to be trained.

Fernandez is quite clear in defining the counterfactual for his study as the changes that might have occurred at the plant in the absence of the technological change. Despite this clarity, we are sympathetic with the argument made by Michael Handel (2003) that it remains unclear whether the evidence points toward SBTC as an important causal factor in explaining wage changes. One particular source of ambiguity is the role of the latest (post-1981) technologies in the changes made at the plant. First, the single plant research design is silent on the issue of whether the technological changes experienced at the plant were typical of the changes experienced at other plants in the industry, or whether they represented an "upper bound." Second, plant-level case studies do not really tell us whether the employment changes observed at the plant are large enough to have an impact on the overall labor market. Put differently, even if we adopt the view that such change is pervasive and of recent origin, it would seem to require a great deal more data than are available to assess the importance of such change for the trends in the aggregate wage structure.

A related concern with a firm-level case study, underscored by case study research, is the potential selectivity of the firms that actually implement new technology. Marc Maurice, François Sellier, and Jean-Jacques Silvestre (1984), for example, put a great deal of emphasis on the question of why firms adopt the technology they do. In their comparison of petrochemical plants in Germany and France, these researchers observe that although the menu of technological opportunities was the same for the French and German companies, and they were producing identical commodities, firms in the two countries had very different patterns of wage inequality. Although it is impossible to do justice here to their argument, suffice to say that they view the difference as partially attributable to differences in the structure of educational and skill inequality in the two countries generated by different historical traditions about investments in schooling and job-specific skills.

Another compelling case study that supports a role for SBTC in the evolution of the structure of wages is Autor, Levy, and Murnane (2002), a study that carefully describes the changes that occurred at "Cabot Bank" following the introduction of "check imaging" and optical character recognition (OCR) equipment that photographed and read the amounts on checks written by the bank's customers. One feature that makes this case study particularly interesting is that "the technology and the organization of work had been remarkably stable before the changes . . . studied" (Autor et al. 2002). Using an interpretative framework developed elsewhere (Autor, Levy, and Murnane 2003), these authors document that the changes were skill-biased, and specifically that "the introduction of image processing and OCR software led to the replacement of high school graduates by computers in the deposit processing department, thereby increasing the share of bank employees who had more formal education."

Like Fernandez's study, this study adds to our understanding of how specific technological innovations lead to shifts in firm-level demand for different skill groups. Nevertheless, and also as in Fernandez's study, the interpretation of the timing of the investment by Cabot Bank is unclear. On the one hand, Cabot Bank implemented the new technologies in the mid-1990s, about a decade after the most important rises in wage inequality in the overall labor market. On the other hand, OCR technology and the mechanical processing of checks are relatively old technologies (see Schantz 1982). Indeed, Autor, Levy, and Murnane (2002) remark on Bank of America's introduction of magnetic ink character recognition as an early example of "computers substituting for human labor input." Thus, it is difficult to tell whether the new technology at Cabot Bank was part of a continuing stream of innovations in the banking industry that had been occurring for several decades or a quantum leap forward that led to an acceleration in the trend in relative demand for different types of workers. When Bank of America launched ERMA (electronic recording machine—accounting), a press release noted that the new technology would allow nine bookkeepers to do the work of fifty (Fisher and McKenney 1993).

THE LIMITS OF THE CASE STUDY EVIDENCE   We have not enumerated many of the traditional critiques of case study evidence, in part because they are so well understood. A core criticism is that a case study approach is often silent about causes.[18] On the other hand, a weakness of the traditional labor economics focus on causality is that even when we have reliable estimates of the causal effect of a particular policy, we may have little understanding of why or how the policy works. In this light, a useful feature of case studies is that they can provide insights into the mechanisms that actually relate technological choices to relative demand shifts.

A second core concern about case studies is generalizability. There is no denying that workers in most industries perform different tasks than they did fifty or even twenty years ago—in many cases because the technologies they use today did not exist in the past. Nevertheless, as Eileen Appelbaum, Annette Bernhardt, and Richard Murnane (2003) argue, the effects of new technology are context-specific and highly dependent on factors like managerial discretion and product market competition. Consequently, they conclude, "technology has had quite different effects on the tasks that workers perform and the skills required; in a surprising number of cases, there is little effect at all." In view of this conclusion, the evidence from individual case studies has to be interpreted carefully and balanced against other quantitative evidence on general trends in the market as a whole.

A final concern is that although recent case studies like Fernandez (2001) and Autor, Levy, and Murnane (2002) provide compelling examples of the impacts of recent technological changes, there is no way to contrast these examples to the changes that were happening in earlier decades. Goldin (1998) provides evidence suggesting that the process of skill-biased technological change dates back to at least the early part of the twentieth century. In light of that evidence, a persuasive case for the unusual role of skill-biased technology in the 1980s and 1990s would seem to require a careful comparison of the impacts of new technology before 1980 to the impacts in recent decades.

TRADE *VERSUS* TECHNOLOGY, TRADE *AND* TECHNOLOGY, OR SOMETHING ELSE?

So far we have focused our discussion on the potential effects of technological change on the labor market prospects for low-skilled workers. The leading alternative explanation for rising wage inequality and the fall in the real wages of low-skilled workers in the 1980s is trade. Although a comprehensive review of trade theories is beyond the scope of this essay, some remarks on the interactions between trade and technology explanations are in order. In particular, these theories highlight the challenges when facts are heavily "model-dependent."

In common with technological explanations, the timing of changes in trade flows is not easy to reconcile with a large role for trade in explaining rising wage inequality. Although imports grew rapidly over the past decade, the big reduction in the absolute and relative wages of low-skilled workers occurred in the 1980s, during a period of only modest expansion of trade.[19] Imports from India and China, which now attract widespread attention from academics and policy analysts, were at relatively low levels in the 1980s. Indeed, throughout the 1980s imports from Japan were routinely cited as a leading source of concern for U.S. policymakers (see, for example, Lincoln 1990; Lawrence 1993; Krugman 1991). As with technology, it is important to resist the temptation to explain trends in the 1980s with factors that did not emerge until the 1990s.

Although there is a substantial literature on the possible effects of trade on the absolute or relative wages of low-skilled workers in the United States, a cursory reading of the literature shows a remarkable level of *disagreement* over the actual impacts of trade. Bound and Johnson (1992), Borjas, Freeman, and Katz (1992), Krugman (1993, 2000), and Lawrence and Slaughter (1993) argue that the quantitative impacts of trade are small. Other researchers, including Wood (1995), Borjas and Ramey (1995), Feenstra and Hanson (1996), and Leamer (1998), have argued that the impacts are potentially larger.

As emphasized by Paul Krugman (2000), a key reason for the disagreement is the absence of a credible and "model-free" research design for evaluating the impact of expanding imports. In the absence of such a research design, there are significant disagreements between researchers over the correct model of world trade (Leamer 1998), the correct model of industry competition in developed economies (Borjas and Ramey 1995; Neary 2002), the correct model of the sources of expanding imports (for a clear statement of some of the alternatives, see Krugman 2000), and the correct model of intermediate versus finished goods imports (Feenstra and Hanson 1996). Most of the existing studies are accounting exercises that use a particular model to derive the fraction of the trend in the absolute or relative wages of low-skilled U.S. workers that can be explained by expanding trade *under the assumptions of the model* and that ignore other potential explanations for the same facts.

Our reading of the literature is that trade-based explanations for rising wage inequality rely on "model-based evidence" to an even greater extent than technological explanations. Not surprisingly, then, it is unclear whether the central question—is it trade or technology?—can be resolved. What constitutes "evidence" on the role of technology under the assumptions of the highly simplified models used in the literature on SBTC is inadmissible as evidence when viewed through the lens of trade-theoretic models.

To illustrate, consider the "model-specific" approach to assessing the role of technology that we discussed earlier. In this approach, SBTC is defined as that part of the variation in relative wages left unexplained by changes in relative employment in a (country-specific) supply-and-demand model. Most of the existing studies of the effect of trade are based on variants of the Hecksher-Olin (HO) framework. According to this model, trade in goods or services provides a powerful force that tends to equalize the wages of different skill groups across different countries. In its purest form, the HO model implies that the wage structure in any one country is *independent* of the relative supplies of different types of labor in that country. If one adopts the pure form of the HO model, however, the entire exercise of inferring technological change from the part of the covariation in relative wages and relative employment that cannot be explained by a (country-specific) demand-supply model is nonsensical. Put a different way, systematic variation between relative wages and relative employment within a country is a requirement for the usual SBTC explanation of widening wage inequality, but constitutes evidence against the underlying modeling framework used by many trade economists.

Although the HO framework presents a logical challenge to the existing literature on technological change and wage inequality, it is widely perceived as a failure in describing patterns of intercountry trade (for a recent evaluation, see Neary 2002). Even within the United States, the HO model's key prediction—that differences in the relative supply of different skill groups will be absorbed by shifts in industry composition—is not very helpful in describing differences across local labor markets. As documented in Lewis (2003), Card and Lewis (2005), and Card (2005), for example, intercity differences in the relative supply of education groups are only weakly related to differences in the relative size of industries that use high- or low-skilled workers more or less intensively. Despite the absence of a correlation between the relative wages of less-educated workers and their relative supply (a pattern that is consistent with the HO framework), differences in the relative supply of low-education labor are mainly absorbed by within-industry changes in dropout intensity.[20] This underscores a fundamental problem in evaluating trade-theoretic explanations for the fall in the labor market prospects of low-skilled workers. If the basic predictions of the model are rejected within the United States, it may be inappropriate to put a lot of weight on model-based empirical exercises that assume these predictions are true across countries.

CONCLUSIONS

Since the late 1980s, a consensus has emerged that the decline in real wages for low-skilled workers in the early 1980s and the subsequent slow recovery of these wage levels are explained by skill-biased technological change. In this chapter, we have argued that the evidence underlying this consensus is remarkably frail. Much of the evidence takes the form of "proof by residual." After accounting for changes in relative supply and (in some cases) making a modest list of other factors, proponents of this consensus note that the decline in the relative wages of low-skilled labor remains unexplained. Skill-biased technological change is then left as the only plausible explanation for the facts. Given the state of knowledge about how labor markets work, we find this line of argument unconvincing. Moreover, the evidence that emerges from such an exercise is highly model-specific. Depending on how the data for different groups are organized, the degree of substitution that is allowed between workers of different genders or ages, and the list of other job characteristics that are included in the decomposition, the results can suggest that rising inequality was either a ubiquitous phenomenon affecting virtually all workers over the past three decades or a trend that mainly affected young workers in the early 1980s.

Although it seems quite possible that exogenous changes in technology are important factors in the evolution of wage inequality and the trend in wages for low-skilled workers, our judgment is that the evidence that has been assembled so far falls well short of the standard that labor economists have established in other areas. Moreover, despite an enormous effort involving multiple datasets and sophisticated analysis techniques, the literature has turned up surprisingly few insights into appropriate policy responses. Even if we could agree that technological change has accounted for the relatively slow growth in real living standards for low-skilled workers in the United States over the past thirty years, eliminating technology is hardly a meaningful option.

Given the innumerable ways in which the poor are disadvantaged in the United States, it seems that a continuing narrow focus on the role of technological change is misplaced and that researchers interested in policy options for improving the fortunes of less-skilled workers should look elsewhere. This would appear to be the case whether one sees the future as a glass that is "half empty," with "technology tilt[ing] the playing field against less-educated workers" (Levy and Murnane 2004) or "half full," in the sense articulated by Murphy and Welch (2001) that "increase[s] in the disparity in incomes between those with more skills and those with less skills . . . represents a significant opportunity . . . to expand our nation's investments in skills and reap historically high rates of returns on those investments."

NOTES

1. We would like to thank Joseph Altonji and the editors for helpful comments.
2. See, for example, the useful spring 1997 symposium in the *Journal of Economic Perspectives*. See especially Gottschalk (1997), Johnson (1997), and Topel (1997). In that same symposium, Nicole Fortin and Thomas Lemieux (1997) take a different tack and focus on "institutional" explanations.
3. Such a focus may be overly restrictive. In Beaudry and Green (2003, 2005), for example, the choice of technology is endogenous and responds to other shocks in the labor market, most notably changes in the relative supply of skilled labor and the price of capital. Ethan Lewis (2003) uses "immigration shocks" to evaluate their effects on technology *choices*. Outside of the field of labor economics there is a stronger focus on this sort of endogenous technological change. David Noble (1984), for exam-

ple, provides a historian's perspective on technological adoption in the United States, while Jan Berting (1993) presents a sociological perspective on endogenous technology. Judith Sutz (2003) discusses the diffusion of new technology as a possible mechanism to reduce inequality in developing countries.

4. Autor and Katz (2000) provide the example of a fall in the price of computing leading to an increase in demand for highly educated (skilled) workers. They also consider the case where competition in the labor market requires that across firms equally skilled workers are paid the the same wage. In that case, the typical cross-sectional regression used to assess the computer wage differential (with sufficient controls for "skill") would exhibit no premium.

5. They clearly acknowledge that there are other possible explanations for this fact.

6. Imperfect substitution between age groups can be introduced in a number of different ways. Paul Beaudry and David Green (2000), for example, use a specification that implies that there are cohort-specific age-earnings profiles for different education classes.

7. The aggregate supply effect is $(1/\sigma_E - 1/\sigma_A)\log (C_t/H_t)$.

8. The lack of ubiquity in rising education-related wage gaps across OECD countries has been noted by others. Stephen Nickell and Brian Bell (1996, 302–303) assemble data for a sample of eight OECD countries from 1971 to 1993 and observe that "the key facts are that in Britain and the United States there has been a large fall in the relative wages of the unskilled from 1980 onward and that falls of this magnitude are not apparent in any other country." Like Nickell and Bell, David Card, Francis Kramarz, and Thomas Lemieux (1999) observe that the lack of movement in the skill differential in most of the OECD countries *cannot* be easily explained by a systematic increase in the unemployment rates of the unskilled in those same countries.

9. See, for example, Mishel, Bernstein, and Boushey (2002). One potentially important issue that we ignore in our discussion is the overhaul of the CPS in the mid-1990s. For a description of the changes and their effects on measurement, see Polivka (1996), Polivka and Rothgeb (1993), and Cohany, Polivka, and Rothgreb (1994). There seems to be evidence that the redesign affected the *level* of wages, but it is not clear what effect (if any) it had on measures of inequality. For different viewpoints, see Bernstein and Mishel (1997) and Lerman (1997).

10. These wage gaps refer to the hourly earnings of men age eighteen to sixty-four in the 1980 to 2002 March CPS and are estimated from models that include controls for a cubic in potential experience and dummies for black race and Hispanic ethnicity.

11. Indeed, Levy and Murnane (1992) argue that the upward trend in residual wage inequality is the single most important unresolved puzzle in the wage inequality literature.

12. Note that changes in survey instruments and processing procedures are likely to lead to changes in residual inequality that have no economic content. For example, over the past twenty years, the fraction of people with allocated earnings information in the CPS has risen significantly.

13. This phenomenon arises because different individuals invest in on-the-job training at different rates in Mincer's model.

14. Many other theoretical channels would be expected to generate higher residual variance in wages for older and better-educated workers, including on-the-job learning and differences in school quality.
15. Lemieux's (2004) analysis also helps to resolve another problem, which is how to reconcile the apparently steady rise in returns to unobserved ability with falling and rising returns to education over the 1970 to 2000 period. For further discussion of this problem, see Acemoglu (2002).
16. Manning (2004) refers to this as the fear of a "science fiction" technology and notes that such concerns ignore the insights of a supply-and-demand framework.
17. This hiring pattern is not unexpected. Joan Woodward (1965) describes case studies from the late 1950s that illustrate the complementarity between highly skilled maintenance workers and more advanced machinery.
18. See Shadish, Cook, and Campbell (2002, 500–501) for a discussion of what they label "intensive qualitative case studies." They conclude that "case studies are very relevant when causation is at most a minor issue."
19. Imports as a fraction of GDP were 6.4 percent in 1979, 7.8 percent in 1985, 8.5 percent in 1990, 10.6 percent in 1995, 15.0 percent in 2000, and 15.9 percent in the last quarter of 2004 (Council of Economic Advisers 2005, table B-2).
20. Much of the focus in the trade and wages literature is on the impacts of trade on U.S. workers, but similar problems arise when we consider the impact of trade with the United States on Canadian labor markets. Lemieux (2005b) tries to assess a weak version of "factor price equalization" following the passage of the North American Free Trade Act (NAFTA) and finds that "there has been, if anything, a divergence between the wage structures in Canada and the U.S. over the last 20 years. In many cases, however, Canada-U.S. differences . . . are not large relative to regional [Canadian] differences in the wage structure."

REFERENCES

Acemoglu, Daron. 2002. "Technical Change, Inequality, and the Labor Market." *Journal of Economic Literature* 40(March): 7–72.

Appelbaum, Eileen, Annette D. Bernhardt, and Richard J. Murnane, eds. 2003. *Low-Wage America: How Employers Are Reshaping Opportunity in the Workplace*. New York: Russell Sage Foundation.

Autor, David, and Lawrence Katz. 2000. "Changes in the Wage Structure and Earnings Inequality." In *Handbooks in Economics*, vol. 3, *Handbook of Labor Economics*, edited by Orley Ashenfelter and David Card. Amsterdam: North-Holland.

Autor, David H., Lawrence F. Katz, and Melissa S. Kearney. 2004. "Trends in U.S. Wage Inequality: Reassessing the Revisionists." Working paper 11627. Cambridge, Mass.: National Bureau of Economic Research.

Autor, David H., Frank Levy, and Richard J. Murnane. 2002. "Upstairs, Downstairs: Computer Skills on Two Floors of a Large Bank." *Industrial and Labor Relations Review* 55(3, April): 432–47.

———. 2003. "The Skill Content of Recent Technological Change: An Empirical Explora-tion." *Quarterly Journal of Economics* 118(4, November): 1279–1334.

Beaudry, Paul, and David A. Green. 2000. "Cohort Patterns in Canadian Earnings: Assess-ing the Role of Skill Premia in Inequality Trends." *Canadian Journal of Economics* 33(4, November): 907.

———. 2003. "Wages and Employment in the United States and Germany: What Explains the Differences?" *American Economic Review* 93(3, June): 573–602.

———. 2005. "Changes in U.S. Wages, 1976–2000: Ongoing Skill Bias or Major Technolog-ical Change?" *Journal of Labor Economics* 23(3): 491–526.

Becker, Gary S. 1975. "Woytinsky Lecture, University of Michigan, 1967." In *Human Capi-tal*, 2nd ed. Cambridge, Mass.: National Bureau of Economic Research.

Berg, Maxine. 1984. *The Machinery Question and the Making of Political Economy, 1815–1848*. Cambridge: Cambridge University Press.

Bernstein, Jared, and Lawrence Mishel. 1997. "Has Wage Inequality Stopped Growing?" *Monthly Labor Review* 120(12, December): 3–16.

Berting, Jan. 1993. "Technological Impacts on Human Rights: Models of Development, Science and Technology, and Human Rights." In *The Impact of Technology on Human Rights: Global Case Studies*, edited by C. G. Weeramantry. Tokyo: United Nations Uni-versity.

Borjas, George, Richard Freeman, and Lawrence Katz. 1992. "On the Labor Market Effects of Immigration and Trade." In *Immigration and the Workforce*, edited by George Borjas and Richard Freeman. Chicago: University of Chicago Press, 1992.

Borjas, George J., and Valerie A. Ramey. 1995. "Foreign Competition, Market Power, and Wage Inequality." *Quarterly Journal of Economics* 110(4, November): 1075–1110.

Bound, John, and George Johnson. 1992. "Changes in the Structure of Wages in the 1980s: An Evaluation of Alternative Explanations." *American Economic Review* 82(June): 371–92.

Card, David. 2005. "Is the New Immigration So Bad?" Unpublished paper. Berkeley: Uni-versity of California, Center for Labor Economics (January).

Card, David, and John DiNardo. 2002. "Skill-Biased Technological Change and Rising Wage Inequality: Some Problems and Puzzles." Working paper 8769. Cambridge, Mass.: National Bureau of Economic Research (February).

Card, David, Francis Kramarz, and Thomas Lemieux. 1999. "Changes in the Relative Structure of Wages and Employment: A Comparison of the United States, Canada, and France." *Canadian Journal of Economics* 32(4, August): 843–77.

Card, David, and Thomas Lemieux. 2001. "Can Falling Supply Explain the Rising Return to College for Younger Men? A Cohort-Based Analysis." *Quarterly Journal of Economics* 116(2, May): 705–46.

Card, David, and Ethan Lewis. 2005. "The Diffusion of Mexican Immigrants in the 1990s: Patterns and Impacts." Unpublished paper. Berkeley: University of California, Center for Labor Economics (January).

Cohany, Sharon R., Anne E. Polivka, and Jennifer M. Rothgreb. 1994. "Revisions in the Current Population Survey Effective January 2004." CPS technical documentation CPS-94, attachment 5. Washington: U.S. Bureau of the Census.

Council of Economic Advisers. 2005. *Economic Report of the President*.

DiNardo, John, Nicole Fortin, and Thomas Lemieux. 1996. "Labor Market Institutions and the Distribution of Wages, 1973–1993: A Semiparametric Approach." *Econometrica* 64(5, September): 1001–45.

Feenstra, Robert C., and Gordon Hanson. 1996. "Foreign Investment, Outsourcing, and Relative Wages." In *The Political Economy of Trade Policy: Essays in Honor of Jagdish Bhagwati*, edited by Robert C. Feenstra, Gene M. Grossman, and Douglas A. Irwin. Cambridge, Mass.: MIT Press.

Fernandez, Roberto M. 2001. "Skill-Biased Technological Change and Wage Inequality: Evidence from a Plant Retooling." *American Journal of Sociology* 107(2, September): 273–320.

Fisher, Amy Weaver, and James L. McKenney. 1993. "The Development of the ERMA Banking System: Lessons from History." *IEEE Annals of the History of Computing* 15(1): 44–56.

Fortin, Nicole M., and Thomas Lemieux. 1997. "Institutional Changes and Rising Inequality: Is There a Linkage?" *Journal of Economic Perspectives* 11(2, Spring): 75–96.

Freeman, Richard B. 1976. *The Overeducated American*. San Diego: Academic Press.

Goldin, Claudia Dale. 1998. "The Origins of Technology-Skill Complementarity." *Quarterly Journal of Economics* 113(3, August): 693–732.

Goldin, Claudia, and Robert Margo. 1992. "The Great Compression: The Wage Structure in the United States at Midcentury." *Quarterly Journal of Economics* 107(1, February): 1–34.

Goos, Maarten, and Alan Manning. 2003. "Lousy and Lovely Jobs: The Rising Polarization of Work in Britain." CEP working paper 604. London: London School of Economics (December).

Gottschalk, Peter. 1997. "Inequality, Income Growth, and Mobility: The Basic Facts." *Journal of Economic Perspectives* 11(2, Spring): 21–40.

Gottschalk, Peter, and Timothy M. Smeeding. 1997. "Cross-National Comparisons of Earnings and Income Inequality." *Journal of Economic Literature* 35(2, June): 663–87.

Handel, Michael J. 2003. "Implications of Information Technology for Employment, Skills, and Wages: A Review of Recent Research." Final Report P10168. Arlington, Va.: SRI International (July).

Heckman, James J., Lance J. Lochner, and Petra E. Todd. 2003. "Fifty Years of Mincer Earnings Regressions." Working paper 9732. Cambridge, Mass.: National Bureau of Economic Research (May).

Johnson, George. 1997. "Changes in Earnings Inequality: The Role of Demand Shifts." *Journal of Economic Perspectives* 11(2, Spring): 41–54.

Juhn, Chinhui, Kevin M. Murphy, and Brooks Pierce. 1993. "Wage Inequality and the Rise in the Returns to Skill." *Journal of Political Economy* 101(3, June): 410–42.

Katz, Lawrence, and Kevin Murphy. 1992. "Changes in Relative Wages, 1963–1987: Supply and Demand Factors." *Quarterly Journal of Economics* 107(1, February): 35–78.

Krueger, Alan. 1993. "How Computers Have Changed the Wage Structure: Evidence from Microdata, 1984–1989." *Quarterly Review of Economics* 108(February): 33–60.

Krugman, Paul R. 1991. *Trade with Japan: Has the Door Opened Wider?* Chicago: University of Chicago Press.

———. 1993. "International Trade and American Wages in the 1980s: Giant Sucking

Sound or Small Hickup?" *Brookings Papers on Economic Activity: Microeconomics*: 161–210.

———. 2000. "Technology, Trade, and Factor Prices." *Journal of International Economics* 50(1, February): 51–71.

Lawrence, Robert Z. 1993. "Japan's Different Trade Regime: An Analysis with Particular Reference to Keiretsu." *Journal of Economic Perspectives* 7(Spring): 3–19.

Lawrence, Robert Z., and Matthew J. Slaughter. 1993. "International Trade and American Wages in the 1980s: Giant Sucking Sound or Small Hickup?" *Brookings Papers on Economic Activity: Microeconomics*: 161–210.

Leamer, Edward J. 1998. "In Search of Stoper Samuelson Linkages Between International Trade and Lower Wages." In *Imports, Exports, and the American Worker*, edited by Susan M. Collins. Washington, D.C.: Brookings Institution Press.

Lee, David S. 1999. "Wage Inequality in the United States During the 1980s: Rising Dispersion or Falling Minimum Wage?" *Quarterly Journal of Economics* 114(3, August): 977–1023.

Lemieux, Thomas. 2004. "Increasing Residual Wage Inequality: Composition Effects, Noisy Data, or Rising Demand for Skills?" Unpublished paper. Vancouver: University of British Columbia (May).

———. 2005a. "The Mincer Equation Thirty Years After *Schooling, Experience, and Earnings*." In *Jacob Mincer: A Pioneer of Modern Labor Economics*, edited by S. Grossbard-Shechtman. Heidelberg: Springer-Verlag.

———. 2005b. "Trade Liberalization and the Labor Market." In *Social and Labor Market Aspects of North American Linkages*, edited by Thomas Lemieux and Richard G. Harris. Calgary: University of Calgary Press.

Lerman, Robert I. 1997. "Reassessing Trends in U.S. Earnings Inequality." *Monthly Labor Review* 120(12, December): 17–25.

Levy, Frank, and Richard Murnane. 1992. "U.S. Earnings Levels and Earnings Inequality: A Review of Recent Trends and Proposed Explanations." *Journal of Economic Literature* 30(September): 1331–81.

———. 2004. *The New Division of Labor: How Computers Are Creating the Next Job Market*. Princeton, N.J.: Princeton University Press.

Lewis, Ethan. 2003. "Local, Open Economies Within the U.S.: How Do Industries Respond to Immigration?" Working paper 04–1. Philadelphia: Federal Reserve Bank of Philadelphia (December 3).

———. 2004. "How Did the Miami Labor Market Absorb the Mariel Immigrants?" Working paper 04–3. Philadelphia: Federal Reserve Bank of Philadelphia(January 12).

Lincoln, Edward. 1990. *Japan's Unequal Trade*. Washington, D.C.: Brookings Institution Press.

Machin, Stephen. 1996. "Wage Inequality in the U.K." *Oxford Review of Economic Policy* 12(1): 47–64.

Manning, Alan. 2004. "We Can Work It Out: The Impact of Technological Change on the Demand for Low-Skill Workers." *Scottish Journal of Political Economy* 51(5, November): 581–608.

Mark, Jerome A. 1987. "Technological Change and Employment: Some Results from BLS Research." *Monthly Labor Review* 110(4, April): 26–29.

Maurice, Marc, François Sellier, and Jean-Jacques Silvestre. 1984. "The Search for a Societal Effect in the Production of Company Hierarchy: A Comparison of France and Germany." In *Internal Labor Markets*, edited by Paul Osterman. Cambridge, Mass.: MIT Press.

Mincer, Jacob. 1974. *Schooling, Experience, and Earnings*. New York: National Bureau of Economic Research.

———. 1997. "Changes in Wage Inequality, 1970–1990." *Research in Labor Economics* 16: 1–18.

Mishel, Lawrence, Jared Bernstein, and Heather Boushey. 2002. *The State of Working America: 2002–2003*. Ithaca, N.Y.: ILR Press.

Murphy, Kevin, and Finis Welch. 2001. "Wage Differentials in the 1990s: Is the Glass Half-Full or Half-Empty?" In *The Causes and Consequences of Increasing Inequality*, vol. 2 of *Bush School Series in the Economics of Public Policy*, edited by Finis Welch. College Station, Tex., and Chicago: Texas A&M University and University of Chicago Press.

Neary, J. Peter. 2002. "Competition, Trade, and Wages." In *Trade, Investment, Migration, and Labor Market Adjustment*, edited by David Greenaway, Richard Upward, and Katharine Wakelin. Basingstoke, U.K.: International Economic Association and Palgrave Macmillan.

Nickell, Stephen, and Brian Bell. 1996. "Changes in the Distribution of Wages and Unemployment in OECD Countries." *American Economic Review* 86(2, May): 302–8.

Noble, David. 1984. *Forces of Production: A Social History of Industrial Automation*. New York: Alfred A. Knopf.

Polivka, Anne E. 1996. "Data Watch: The Redesigned Current Population Survey." *Journal of Economic Perspectives* 10(3, Summer): 169–80.

Polivka, Anne E., and Jennifer Rothgreb. 1993. "Overhauling the Current Population Survey: Redesigning the Questionnaire." *Monthly Labor Review* (September): 10–28.

Schantz, Herbert F. 1982. *The History of OCR: Optical Character Recognition*. Manchester Center, Vt.: Recognition Technologies Users Association.

Shadish, William R., Thomas D. Cook, and Donald T. Campbell. 2002. *Experimental and Quasi-Experimental Designs for Generalized Causal Inference*. Boston: Houghton Mifflin.

Sutz, Judith. 2003. "Inequality and University Research Agendas in Latin America." *Science, Technology, and Human Values* 28(1): 52–68.

Topel, Robert. 1997. "Factor Proportions and Relative Wages: The Supply-Side Determinants of Wage Inequality." *Journal of Economic Perspectives* 11(2, Spring): 55–74.

Wood, Adrian. 1995. "How Trade Hurt Unskilled Workers." *Journal of Economic Perspectives* 9: 57–64.

Woodward, Joan. 1965. *Industrial Organization: Theory and Practice*. London: Oxford University Press.

Chapter 5

The Changing Pattern of Wage Growth
for Low-Skilled Workers

Eric French, Bhashkar Mazumder, and Christopher Taber

O ne of the fundamental facts in labor economics is that, on average, wages tend to rise rapidly early in a worker's career.[1] Since wage growth during the early stages of one's career provides a potential pathway out of poverty, it is important to understand what causes this wage progression and how it is affected by changes in the overall economy. In this chapter, we focus on the key components that determine an individual's early career wage growth and how these factors have changed for less-skilled workers over the last twenty years. In particular, we examine the relative importance of accumulating work experience as compared to the quality of job matches in influencing wage growth over this time period.

The importance of experience accumulation on wage growth is a particularly relevant concern for policymakers in light of the reforms to the tax and welfare systems that have taken place since the early 1990s. The expansion of the Earned Income Tax Credit (EITC) and the Personal Responsibility and Work Opportunity Reconciliation Act (PRWORA) were specifically designed to encourage low-skilled individuals to enter the workforce. Perhaps as a result of these policies, the labor force participation rates of men and women with low levels of schooling did in fact increase during the 1990s. However, entry-level wages for low-skilled workers are low and have been stagnant over the last twenty-five years.[2] This calls into question whether these programs can really do much to alleviate poverty.

Although starting wages of low-skilled workers are low, they may increase with experience. Therefore, the success of tax and welfare reforms in reducing poverty rests critically upon the extent to which experience accumulation increases the wages of low-skilled individuals. To highlight the importance of experience accumulation, consider figure 5.1, which shows the extent to which wages increase with age.[3] Between ages eighteen and twenty-eight, wages grow

FIGURE 5.1 / Log Wage Profile for Men with No College

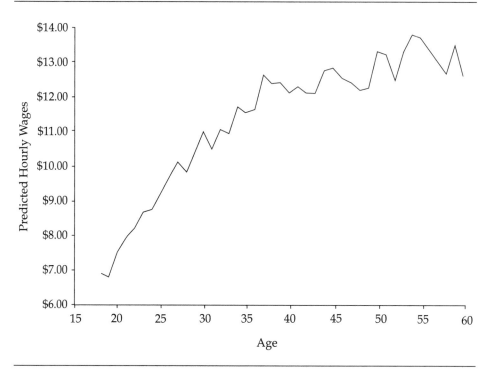

Source: SIPP and authors' calculations.

by about 45 percent, from $6.90 to $10.00 per hour, for men with no college. For a single earner in a four-person household working forty hours per week, fifty weeks per year, such a wage gain would actually move the family out of poverty. Clearly, labor force experience has the potential to raise wages substantially.

However, labor market experience is not the only potentially important source of wage growth for younger workers. Robert Topel and Michael Ward (1992) show that for workers who entered the labor market in the late 1950s, earnings gains at job switches accounted for about one-third of early career earnings growth. Arguably, the earnings increases associated with job switches reflect improvements in the quality of job matches over an individual's career. Concerns about job match quality might be especially important for low-skilled workers, because they have less stable employment patterns. As a result, some observers have expressed concern that difficulties in holding jobs and in moving to better ones (Holzer and LaLonde 2000) retards wage growth for low-skilled workers.

We would expect the job match process to change over the business cycle in ways that would lead this component of wage growth to be highly cyclical. First, it is likely to be much easier to find a good job during a boom than during a recession. Second, since layoffs are typically associated with wage declines, we would expect the higher rate of layoffs during recessions to depress wage

FIGURE 5.2 / Wage Growth, 1980 to 2004, CPS, by Education Group

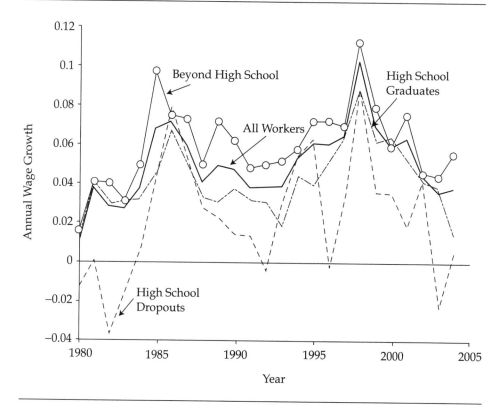

Source: CPS and authors' calculations.

growth. This suggests that an analysis of the changing pattern of wage growth should disentangle the importance of finding a good job, or *matching*, from the importance of work experience in determining wage growth.

Despite the centrality of early career wage *growth* to labor economics, it is surprising how little we know about the factors that determine wage growth, their cyclical properties, and how they have changed over time.[4] The primary purpose of this chapter is to document how wage growth has changed over the last twenty years for low-skilled workers and to understand which components have driven these changes. To motivate our analysis we present some basic facts concerning early career wage growth for low-skilled workers. Figure 5.2 plots hourly wage growth for workers age eighteen to twenty-eight who did not attend college using the matched Current Population Survey (CPS) outgoing rotation group data.[5] This group, which contains both men and women, acts as our primary reference group throughout our analysis. The data show that young workers' wages increase about 4.5 percent per year, on average. Figure 5.2 also makes clear that wage growth varies considerably over time and may be related to the business cycle. Wage growth was about 3 percent per year during 1980 to 1983, 1990 to 1994, and 2002 to 2004, the years when unemployment rates were high and rising. In contrast, wage growth averaged 6 percent during 1984 to 1987 and 1995 to 2001, the years when unemployment was low and falling.[6]

For our main analysis, we use data from the Survey of Income and Program Participation (SIPP) covering the years 1984 to 2003. The key advantage of the SIPP is that it allows us to track the same individuals over several years, thereby making it possible to estimate the rate of job transitions, as well as the wage gains associated with those transitions.

Our empirical strategy is as follows. We first assume that wage changes for continuously employed workers reflect returns to experience. For workers who switch jobs, wage changes result from both experience accumulation and changes in the quality of the job match. Using these assumptions, we estimate a baseline model that decomposes wage growth over this period into changes that arise from experience accumulation, the returns to experience, the rate of job matching, and the returns to match quality. As our second specification, we augment the baseline model to also include a common time effect that affects all individuals' wages, regardless of experience or match quality. We then decompose the residual wage growth (net of this common component) into the key factors of interest. We identify the common effect using wage levels for new labor market entries. The results from both decompositions allow us to better understand the extent to which the temporal pattern of wage growth is driven by changes in experience accumulation and matching.

Our main finding is that wage growth has varied considerably over the last twenty years. We find that the vast majority of the variation in wage growth is due to variability in the return to experience over time.[7] Although the return to experience seems to change from year to year, there is no strong evidence of a secular trend. On average over this time period, an additional year of experience increases wages about 4 percent, but this gain varies from as much as 6 percent to as little as 2 percent. In contrast, essentially none of the changing pattern of wage growth can be attributed to changes in experience accumulation, job-to-job finding rates, or layoff rates. Although these variables have the expected cyclical relationships, the overall magnitude of their contributions to changes in wage growth is extremely small. Therefore, we find that the return to experience is much more important than job matching for explaining the variability in early career wage growth. We know of no other work that has examined this question.

The extent to which the wage growth pattern varies with the business cycle depends crucially on our specification. In our base model (which does not account for common time effects), we find that the return to experience is strongly procyclical. In our second model (which does account for common time effects), we find that the cyclicality of returns to experience results fully from the wage-level effects. That is, after we account for the common time effect, we find no remaining relationship between the returns to experience and the business cycle. We are unaware of any previous work that documents how the determinants of wage growth vary over the business cycle, let alone how they vary for any particular subgroup of the population.

We also estimate the model separately by skill groups and gender. While our estimates by subgroup are noisy, we find that average returns to experience and matching, as well as their cyclical and secular patterns, do not vary systematically by education or gender. Thus, we see no evidence that increasing differences in the return to experience and job matching across skill groups play an important role in explaining rising wage inequality.

Our results suggest that policymakers should not be overly concerned that workers who enter the labor market during a recession will receive less wage growth over their first ten years than workers who enter during a boom. The recent efforts of policymakers to promote working among young, low-skilled workers may therefore not be misplaced. Furthermore, we find that, for an average worker, experience accumulation is much more important than job matching in determining early career wage growth. Nonetheless, policies that deliver especially high-quality job matches may also be desirable.

RELATED WORK

Although we are unaware of any previous study that has analyzed the changing pattern of life-cycle wage growth and its determinants, our research does intersect with a wide range of studies on related topics. There is a long literature in labor economics that has studied the age-earnings profile, beginning with Jacob Mincer (1962) and Yoram Ben Porath (1967). These studies have shown that earnings increase rapidly early in the life cycle (between ages eighteen and twenty-eight) as workers invest in their human capital by gaining experience on the job (for a more recent version of this basic model, see Heckman, Lochner, and Taber 1998). In other words, they are more productive because they have more skills, and they are compensated accordingly.

A second literature has emphasized the importance of job matching in explaining life-cycle wage growth. Workers are able to find better matches for their skills over time. For example, since searching for a job is time-consuming, an individual straight out of school may not wait until she finds the best match for her skills but instead may take a job she can find quickly. Over time, however, she may find better matches for her skills. A substantial literature has arisen that examines the effects of job mobility (or job stability) on earnings using either regression analysis or structural modeling (see, for example, Antel 1991; Farber 1994; Flinn 1986; Klerman and Karoly 1994; Loprest 1992; Mincer and Jovanovic 1981; Topel and Ward 1992; Wolpin 1992). Theresa Devine and Nicholas Kiefer (1991) and Kenneth Wolpin (1995) provide surveys of different aspects of these literatures. These papers show that turnover is an important engine for wage growth.

Another strand of the literature has focused specifically on wage growth among low-wage workers. Fredrik Andersson, Harry Holzer, and Julia Lane (2005) make use of a unique matched worker-firm dataset to study job mobility for this particular group. They provide a very detailed analysis of worker mobility and wage progression that demonstrates, among other things, the importance of turnover as a component of wage growth.

A number of papers have studied the relationship between the determinants of life-cycle wage growth and skill levels. Focusing on younger workers, Tricia Gladden and Christopher Taber (2000, 2004) compare the wage growth of medium-skilled workers with the wage growth of low-skilled workers and find that they are similar. Helen Connolly and Peter Gottschalk (2000) look across all age groups of workers and find that more-educated people receive higher returns to both tenure and experience. Since these papers use somewhat different concepts and different comparison groups, they are not directly comparable.

Another related literature has examined how labor market transitions have changed over the business cycle. In a well-known study, Steven Davis, John Haltiwanger, and Scott Schuh (1996) use plant-level data and find that job destruction is strongly countercyclical in the manufacturing sector. In contrast, Eva Nagypal (2004) and Robert Shimer (2005) utilize individual-level data on workers in all sectors of the economy and find that job separation rates are not countercyclical.[8] These authors also document that job-finding rates and job-to-job transitions are highly procyclical.

There is an extremely large literature on the cyclicality of aggregate wage *levels*. Katherine Abraham and John Haltiwanger (1995) provide a nice summary of the literature and conclude that aggregate wages are slightly procyclical but have become more so in recent years. They also suggest that wages are procyclical at the individual level, but that aggregate wages can mask this fact, owing to composition effects. This is because low-wage workers, whose employment patterns are more procyclical, constitute a larger fraction of the labor force in booms than in busts. This selection effect lowers average wages in booms.

A few papers have studied the effects of economic conditions early in one's career on earnings later in life. Paul Beaudry and John DiNardo (1991) are not interested in wage growth per se, but rather in contracting over the business cycle. They show that the lowest unemployment rate during an individual's tenure at a firm is a strong predictor of current wages. David Neumark (2002) examines the effects of job turnover on future wages. In doing so, he uses local labor market conditions when an individual is young as an instrument for turnover. He finds that job stability at a young age leads to higher earnings at an older age. Phil Oreopolous, Till von Wachter, and Andrew Heisz (2006) find that there are large initial earnings losses from graduating from college during a recession that dissipate after about eight to ten years. They find evidence of heterogeneous effects—for example, relatively lower-skilled college graduates suffer larger and more permanent earnings losses.

THE METHODOLOGY

In this section, we present our framework for modeling wage growth. Since previous research has shown that experience accumulation and job transitions are associated with wage growth, we model both labor market transitions and wage dynamics. We assume that time is discrete and denoted by t, which in practice will be monthly. Let j_{it} denote the job held by individual i at time t. To keep the notation simple we denote nonemployment with a zero, so that $j_{it} = 0$ means that individual i was not working at time t. Therefore, for individuals who are working at time $t - 1$ (that is, $j_{it-1} \neq 0$), there are three possible labor market transitions: stay on the same job, become nonemployed, or switch to a new job. We write these three transition probabilities respectively as:

$$\Pr(j_{it} = j_{it-1} \mid j_{it-1} \neq 0)$$
$$\Pr(j_{it} = 0 \mid j_{it-1} \neq 0)$$
$$\Pr(j_{it} \neq j_{it-1}, j_{it} \neq 0 \mid j_{it-1} \neq 0) \tag{5.1}$$

Clearly these must sum to one.

Individuals who are not employed at time $t - 1$ start a new job with probability $\Pr(j_{it} \neq 0 \mid j_{it-1} = 0)$ and fail to start a new job with probability $\Pr(j_{it} = 0 \mid j_{it-1} = 0)$. Again, these two probabilities must sum to one.

Our primary focus is the relationship between labor market transitions and wage dynamics. Let ω_{it} denote the wage of individual i at time t. A key feature of our data (which we discuss in the data section) is that we do not use wages from every month. As a result, the number of months between wage observations varies across observations. With this in mind, define the ℓth period difference operator as Δ_ℓ, for example, $\Delta_\ell \omega_{it} = \omega_{it} - \omega_{it-\ell}$. We consider two different empirical specifications for wage changes. In our first approach, we assume that the structural (true) model[9] of wages is:

$$\Delta_\ell \omega_{it} = \beta_t \Delta_\ell A_{it} + \Delta_\ell \eta_{ij_{it}} + \Delta_\ell \varepsilon_{it}, \tag{5.2}$$

where A_{it} represents actual experience (and thus $\Delta_\ell A_{it}$ is the amount of accumulated work experience between time periods $t - \ell$ and t), $\eta_{ij_{it}}$ is a match-specific component between individual i and job j_{it}, and ε_{it} represents an error term that is orthogonal to the other components of the model. We assume that the quality of a match does not change unless an individual changes jobs so that for job stayers $\Delta_\ell \eta_{ij_{it}} = 0$ by assumption. We are also ignoring any effect from job tenure so that $\Delta_\ell \eta_{ij_{it}}$ may also include any effects from the loss of job tenure. Note that we assume that wage growth is linear in experience, which is a reasonable approximation given that we analyze only young workers.

In our second specification, we allow for a common wage-level effect on all individuals' wages regardless of their experience or the quality of their job match. To motivate this specification, suppose that wages are determined by the pricing equation $\omega_{it} = R_t H_{it}$, where R_t is the rental rate of human capital at time t, and H_{it} is the amount of human capital for individual i at time t. Taking logs, we define $\alpha_t = log(R_t)$, which we refer to as the common time effect. We assume that $\Delta_\ell \log(H_{it}) = \gamma_t \Delta_\ell A_{it} + \Delta_\ell \eta_{ij_{it}} + \Delta_\ell \varepsilon_{it}$ and redefine ω_{it} to be the log wage so that

$$\Delta_\ell \omega_{it} = \Delta_\ell \alpha_t + \gamma_t \Delta_\ell A_{it} + \Delta_\ell \eta_{ij_{it}} + \Delta_\ell \varepsilon_{it}. \tag{5.3}$$

In this framework, fluctuations in wage changes may be due to one of several factors. First, it may be that $\Delta_t \alpha_t$ changes over time, affecting everyone's wage, regardless of human capital level. For example, in Robert Hall's model (this volume), $\Delta_t \alpha_t$ represents the growth rate of technological improvements or growth in the amount of capital used by each worker. Macroeconomists typically focus on α_t as the *sole* factor in explaining wage fluctuations (see, for example, Abraham and Haltiwanger 1995). This is a reasonable first approximation since for much of U.S. history wage gains were shared by all skill groups. However, as Robert Hall points out, his model fails to account for many recent changes in the distribution of wages, such as the well-documented increase in wage dispersion. Moreover, as we pointed out earlier, there is ample evidence that other factors influence wage growth as well. These other factors are the focus of the chapter.

A second explanation for shifts in wage growth is that the return to experience may change over time (that is to say, through β_t in equation 5.2 or γ_t in equation 5.3). This might be the case if the rate at which individuals learn on the job varies over time, for example.[10] A third possibility is that changes in the amount of experience accumulation (that is to say, $\Delta_t A_i$) may result in changing wage growth. We generally would expect this component to be procyclical because during recessions individuals who are unemployed are not gaining work experience. Thus, we would expect this effect to lead overall wage growth to be higher during a boom.

A fourth factor in explaining variation in wage growth is changes in the quality of job matches over time (that is to say, $E(\Delta_t \eta_{ijt})$). We examine this empirically by looking at both job-switchers who go directly from one job to another as well as job-switchers who experience an intervening spell of unemployment. Direct job switches lead to changes in wage growth either because the rate of job switching changes or because the wage gains associated with each switch change. As Robert Shimer (2005) and Eva Nagypal (2004) point out, job-to-job switching is procyclical. Given that wages tend to rise with job-to-job transitions, increased job-to-job transitions will raise wages even if the average wage gain associated with these job changes does not change over time. Of course, it could also be the case that the average wage gain associated with job switching (the average change in the value of η_{ijt} given a job change) has changed over time. Similarly, job changes involving an unemployment spell are likely to lead to negative wage growth either because those transitions (which typically involve wage losses) are countercyclical or because the amount of the wage loss is countercyclical.

When confronted with estimating equations 5.2 or 5.3, several identification issues arise. First, as with all wage regressions, there is a selection issue because wage growth is observed only for workers who are employed in both periods. We assume that sample selection is based on an individual fixed effect, which is differenced out, but that there is no selection on $\Delta_t \varepsilon_{it}$. That is, we allow individuals with permanently low productivity to have different participation rates than those with permanently high productivity. However, we do not allow short-term wage fluctuations from changes in ε_{it} to affect the decision to work.

A second problem lies in estimating the returns to experience (β_t in equation 5.2 or γ_t in equation 5.3). For many reasons we would expect job matches (η_{ij_t}) to be correlated with experience (A_{it}). For example, a worker who has been unemployed for an extended period of time may become less choosy about jobs and may accept a worse match. This is problematic because it is very difficult to measure match quality.[11] As a result, running a regression of wage growth on the change in experience without including match quality does not yield a consistent estimate of the returns to experience. Instead, we use an alternative approach in which we utilize only the sample of workers who do not switch jobs (stayers) so that $\Delta_\ell \eta_{ij_t} = 0$. Under the model in equation 5.2, we can write

$$E\left(\frac{\Delta_\ell \omega_{it}}{\Delta_\ell A_{it}} \middle| \Delta_\ell j_{it} = 0\right) = E\left(\frac{\beta_t \Delta_\ell A_{it} + \Delta_\ell \varepsilon_{it}}{\Delta_\ell A_{it}} \middle| \Delta_\ell j_{it} = 0\right) = \beta_t \qquad (5.4)$$

where

$$E\left(\frac{\Delta_\ell \varepsilon_{it}}{\Delta_\ell A_{it}} \middle| \Delta_\ell j_{it} = 0\right) = 0$$

by assumption. Thus, in principle, we can estimate β_t consistently by simply taking the sample mean of $\frac{\Delta_\ell \omega_{it}}{\Delta_\ell A_{it}}$ for stayers in each month. Since the sample sizes are too small to estimate this parameter month by month, we smooth across months using kernel regression.

Separately identifying the change in the common time effect ($\Delta_t \alpha_t$) from the return to experience (γ_t) in the model in equation 5.3 is not straightforward. The problem is that for continuously employed workers, if we measure wage changes over a fixed time period, say four months, there is no variation across this group in the amount of experience accumulated ($\Delta_t \alpha_{it}$). As a result, it is impossible to identify separately these two components using wage changes on stayers, as we did in equation 5.4.[12] One approach would be to use movers with spells of nonemployment to try to identify these parameters separately. However, as we pointed out previously, the change in experience is likely to be correlated with the change in match quality, which we are unable to measure very well. Therefore, to obtain consistent estimates of the parameters of the model, we take an alternative approach. First, we estimate α_t, the common time component to wages, using the wages of new labor market entrants because they all have zero experience. Assuming that the quality of new workers, θ_i (θ_i is discussed more formally in note 9), and the quality of new matches does not change over time, changes in the wages of new entrants change only because of changes in α_t. That is, we assume that we can write expected wages of new entrants as

$$E[\omega_{it} \mid A_{it} = 0] = \alpha_t + E[\theta_i + \eta_{ij_t} + \varepsilon_{it} \mid A_{it} = 0]$$
$$= \alpha_t + \text{a constant.}$$

Because wages of new entrants are equal to α_t (plus a constant that can be differenced away), changes in average wages of entrants yield consistent estimates of $\Delta_t \alpha_t$. We use monthly data to estimate α_t and smooth as above with kernel regression. For this estimation procedure, we use the larger CPS sample rather than the SIPP in order to obtain more precise estimates.

In the second stage, now that we have estimated α_t, we use a strategy for estimating γ_t that is analogous to the model in equation 5.3:

$$E\left(\frac{\Delta_\ell \omega_{it} - \Delta_\ell \hat{\alpha}_t}{\Delta_\ell A_{it}} \middle| \Delta_\ell j_{it} = 0\right) = E\left(\frac{\gamma_t \Delta_\ell A_{it} + \Delta_\ell \varepsilon_{it}}{\Delta_\ell A_{it}} \middle| \Delta_\ell j_{it} = 0\right) = \gamma_t. \tag{5.5}$$

Here we take the sample mean of

$$\frac{\Delta_\ell \omega_{it} - \Delta_\ell \hat{\alpha}_t}{\Delta_\ell A_{it}}$$

smoothing with kernel regression. Compared to our estimation of the first model, which does not account for a possible common time effect, we have simply taken our estimates of wage growth and first subtracted out our estimates of changes in the common component of wages before applying our statistical procedure.

We should point out some problems that arise with our approach to estimating α_t. The fundamental problem is that the value of the unobserved components of workers' wages $(\theta_i + \eta_{ijt} + \varepsilon_{it})$ may change across new entrant cohorts for one of several reasons. For example, it could be that the average individual fixed effect (θ_i) changes from cohort to cohort because of changes in the quality of education. A second, and probably more serious, issue is sample selection bias. To be included in our sample, an eighteen-year-old had to be working and not in school. However, there have been both secular and cyclical changes in labor force participation rates and college attendance rates of young individuals. Most notably, labor force participation rates for eighteen-year-olds were falling over our sample period.

Since we do not believe that it is possible to perfectly separate changes in the common aggregate component from the returns to experience, we present results using models both with and without our estimates of α_t and allow readers to choose their preferred specification. We can interpret the estimates without α_t as incorporating both time and experience effects. The results with α_t try to separate these two processes, although this separation is not as clean as we might like. We show below that many of our main results are qualitatively unaffected by the assumptions used to obtain $\Delta_t \alpha_t$. However, we find one very important difference: experience growth is strongly procyclical in the first specification, but this procyclicality disappears when we control for $\Delta_t \alpha_t$.

Our next goal is to summarize the importance of changes in job matches on wage growth. Since it is very difficult to measure changes in match quality $(\Delta_\ell \eta_{ijt})$, as we pointed out earlier, we simply estimate the expected wage gains for two types of switchers: job-to-job switchers and job-to-nonemployment-to-job switchers. For brevity, we describe our methodological approach for our second model in which we do not include α_t. Define $N_{it\ell}$ to be an indicator of whether person i experienced a nonemployment spell between periods $t - \ell$ and t. For a job-to-nonemployment-to-job switcher, the average wage gain at switching is

$$E(\Delta_\ell \eta_{it_{it}} \mid j_{it} \neq j_{it-\ell}, N_{it\ell} = 1) = E(\Delta_\ell \omega_{it} - \hat{\gamma}_t \Delta_\ell A_{it} \mid j_{it} \neq j_{it-\ell}, N_{it\ell} = 1), \qquad (5.6)$$

where the expectation is over all possible durations of nonemployment. We estimate this just by taking the sample mean of $(\Delta_\ell \omega_{it} - \hat{\gamma}_t \Delta_\ell A_{it})$ for job to-nonemployment-to-job switchers in each month (using kernels to smooth). Basically, we take wage growth in each period for this sample and subtract out our estimates of the change in the common time component (estimated earlier) and also subtract out the change in wages due to experience. Similarly, we can identify the average wage gain at switching for job-to-job switchers using

$$E(\Delta_\ell \eta_{ij_{it}} \mid j_{it} \neq j_{it-1}, N_{it\ell} = 0) = E(\Delta_\ell \omega_{it} - \hat{\gamma}_t \Delta_\ell A_{it} \mid j_{it} \neq j_{it-\ell}, N_{it\ell} = 0). \qquad (5.7)$$

In words, this is the average wage gain that occurs at job-to-job switches. We estimate this in a manner analogous to the job-to-nonemployment-to-job switchers.

Given our estimates of the various sources of wage growth, our next goal is to decompose overall wage growth into its various components using Oaxaca-style decomposition. We describe the decomposition for the first model in which we do not incorporate α_t. The extension to the model including α_t is straightforward in that we just perform the same decomposition of wage growth net of changes in aggregate wage levels (that is, we decompose $E(\Delta_1 \log(H_{it})) = E(\Delta_1 \omega_{it} - \Delta_1 \alpha_t)$ rather than $E[\Delta_1 \omega_{it}]$). One issue that arises in this type of decomposition is the definition of wage growth among workers who are not working. To keep the model as simple as possible, for workers who are not working we define their implicit wage (or match component) as their wage (or match component) on their previous job. Thus, wage growth is zero by definition for a nonemployed worker, but nonzero when he or she starts a new job. We also note that wage growth at time t is well defined only for individuals who worked at some point prior to t. We leave this conditioning implicit, since every expectation we write below conditions on individuals who worked at some point prior to time t. Under this normalization, we can write:

$$E(\Delta_1 \omega_{it}) = \beta_t E(\Delta_1 A_{it}) + E(\Delta_1 \eta_{ij_{it}} \mid j_{it} \neq 0, j_{it-1} = 0) \Pr(j_{it} \neq 0, j_{it-1} = 0)$$
$$+ E(\Delta_1 \eta_{ij_{it}} \mid j_{it} \neq j_{it-1}, j_{it-1} \neq 0) \Pr(j_{it} \neq j_{it-1}, j_{it-1} \neq 0)$$

The first component is the wage growth due to experience gained on the job, the second represents the change (probably negative) associated with job-to-nonemployment-to-job changes, and the third represents the wage gains that occur at job-to-job transitions. Since our SIPP panels are relatively short (two to four years), and since durations of nonemployment can sometimes be very long, we estimate the three transition rates described in equation 5.1 and use these to simulate the probability of a job-to-nonemployment-to-job transition.[13]

It is easiest to explain the decomposition if we stack the parameters and write it in vector notation:

$$
G_t = \begin{bmatrix} \beta_t \\ E(\Delta_1 \eta_{ij_t} \mid j_{it} \neq 0, j_{it-1} = 0) \\ E(\Delta_1 \eta_{ij_t} \mid j_{it} \neq j_{it-1}, j_{it-1} \neq 0) \end{bmatrix}, X_t = \begin{bmatrix} E(\Delta_1 A_{it}) \\ \Pr(j_{it} \neq 0, j_{it-1} = 0) \\ \Pr(j_{it} \neq j_{it-1}, j_{it-1} \neq 0) \end{bmatrix} \tag{5.8}
$$

We denote the mean of parameters over years as

$$
\bar{X} \equiv \frac{1}{T} \sum_{t=1}^{T} X_t.
$$

The advantage of this additional notation is that it allows us to express the decomposition in the following way:

$$
\begin{aligned}
E(\Delta_1 \omega_{it}) &= G_t' X_t \\
&= G_t' \bar{X} + G_t'(X_t - \bar{X}).
\end{aligned} \tag{5.9}
$$

The first part of this decomposition, $G_t' \bar{X}$, reflects how much of the wage change can be explained purely by changes in the coefficients over time. The remaining component contains the amount left that is due to labor market transitions changing over time.

We decompose the result even further. In each year the value of $G_t' \bar{X}$ is a sum of three separate components (associated with change in experience, number of job-to-job transitions, and number of job-to-nonemployment-to job transitions). We present each of these three components later in the chapter.

We estimate the regressions above and perform the decompositions above allowing the coefficients to vary over time and across various demographic groups.

This decomposition should be interpreted as descriptive. Separating the returns to tenure from the returns to experience and dealing with the many sample selection problems inherent with turnover and labor supply among low-wage workers is beyond the scope of this work. Our results should be interpreted as a statistical decomposition of the observed wage growth in the data rather than as causal effects.

THE DATA

For our main analysis, we use pooled data from the Census Bureau's Survey of Income and Program Participation. The SIPP surveys are a series of two- to four-year panels that began in 1984. The SIPP panels from 1984 through 1993 consist of a national sample of around twenty thousand households. The 1996 and 2001 SIPP panels include close to forty thousand households. Combining all of the SIPP panels, we have information on all years from 1984 to 2003 except for 2000. The SIPP interviews households every four months and collects detailed labor market information on all individuals in the household over the previous four months. Each interview is referred to as a wave. A key aspect of the SIPP for our analysis is that the survey identifies up to two different employers for each individual in each wave and these job identifiers are consistent across waves.[14] As a result, we are able to identify cases by month of individuals transitioning from nonemployment into work, going from work into nonemployment, staying in the same job, or switching employers.[15]

The SIPP also provides direct data on hourly wages for workers who are paid by the hour. For salaried workers, we calculate hourly wages for each employer by dividing monthly earnings by usual hours per week worked times weeks worked in the month.[16] This allows us to calculate the wage changes associated with labor market transitions. Hourly wages are deflated to 2003 dollars using the monthly CPI price index, and we drop individuals whose hourly wages are ever below $1.00. Since the focus of our analysis is on wage growth early in the career, we confine our sample to individuals between the ages of eighteen and twenty-eight who were never enrolled in school during the time they were in the SIPP. We divide the sample into three educational groups: those who have not completed high school (dropouts), high school graduates with no college, and those with some college or more. Our main sample includes over 900,000 person-month observations. It is worth noting that the time-series patterns of unemployment and annual wage growth in the SIPP closely track those found in the CPS.

The fact that the SIPP collects new data every four months is clearly advantageous compared to annual surveys that suffer from greater recall bias. On the other hand, it is well known that for many variables respondents do not accurately report changes that occur each month. Instead, changes tend to be clumped at the seam between the last month of a previous interview and the first month of the next interview. Because of this "seam bias," we use only one wage observation on each interview wave for workers who are continuously employed with the same firm. Thus, for workers who stay on the same job, we construct our wage change measure as $\omega_{it} - \omega_{it-\ell}$ where ℓ is four (months). We then use the number of weeks worked in the interval as our measure of $[A_{it} - A_{it-\ell}]$.

When a person worked on two different jobs between interviews, we record two wages for that wave and use both in constructing our wage differential. So, for example, suppose a worker was interviewed in April (call this $t = 4$). In July they switched to a new job and then were interviewed again in August. We would gather two wages from the August interview: the wage during the last month (June) on the old job and the wage from the current job (in August). We would then have obtained two wage changes in this wave for the person. First we would take their wage from the last month working at their old job (June, which corresponds to $t = 6$) and subtract the wage from the previous wave,

$\omega_{i6} - \omega_{i4}$. The person would be recorded as a stayer in this case because they had not yet switched employers. For the second wage observation, we would use the wage from the interview month (August) and subtract the previous wage (June) to form $\omega_{i8} - \omega_{i6}$. This observation would correspond to a job-to-job transition, since the person was working a different job in August than in June and was continuously employed. As a result, job-changers are overrepresented in our sample of wage changes. However, this does not bias our results, since we condition on job changing in the empirical work. Note that given the manner in which the data are constructed, we never observe more than one job change in a period in which we obtain wage differentials.

THE RESULTS

Earlier in the chapter, we showed that the wages of low-skilled young workers grow about 4.5 percent per year. Using estimates from our two models of wage growth, this section presents evidence on the sources of that wage growth.

Returns to Experience Accumulation and Job Changes

First, we present parameter estimates from equation 5.2, which does not include the common time effect α_t. The parameters represent the returns to experience (that is, the average wage change associated with an extra year of work for stayers), the returns to job-to-job switches (that is, the average wage change associated with a job switch), and the returns to job changes with an intervening nonemployment spell. These are graphed in the top panel of figure 5.3 for the combined group consisting of high school graduates and dropouts. The returns to experience, β_t, depicted with a solid line, vary considerably over this period but average about 4 percent. The other two lines, representing the wage gains associated with job-to-job transitions (dashed line) and job-to-nonemployment-to-job transitions (dash-dot lines), also vary over time. On average, wages rise about 3 percent during job-to-job switches and decline about 3 percent during job switches with an intervening nonemployment spell.

These results are similar in magnitude to those found by Helen Connolly and Peter Gottschalk (2000), who include older workers and also use the SIPP pooling data over the 1986 to 1993 period. For example, for workers with a high school education or less, they find that wage gains at job-to-job changes are around 3.5 percent and that wage losses are just under 3 percent for job-to-nonemployment-to-job transitions. Our estimates of the wage losses associated with job-to-nonemployment-to-job transitions are smaller than Henry Farber's (2005) estimates of the wage losses associated with job loss using the Displaced Workers Survey, but show similar time trends. Farber finds that earnings losses of displaced workers (including forgone earnings growth from not having a job) declined from 13

FIGURE 5.3 / Coefficients Over Time (G_t), Ages Eighteen to Twenty-Eight, No College

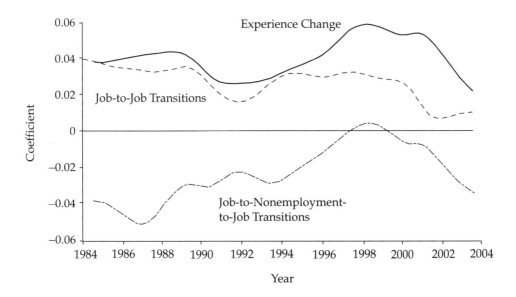

Without Common Time Effect (α_t)

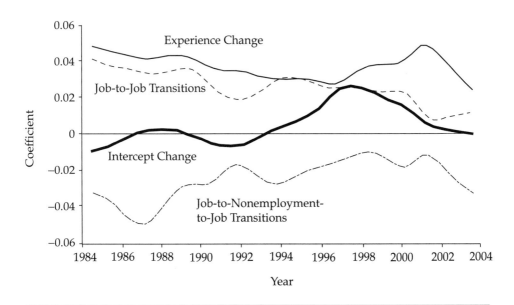

With Common Time Effect (α_t)

Source: SIPP and authors' calculations.

TABLE 5.1 / Tests of the Constancy of Parameter Estimates and Transition Rates

	p-Values on Parameters from Wage Growth Model		
	Coefficient on Experience	Coefficient on Job-to-Job Transitions	Coefficient on Job-to-Nonemployment-to-Job Transitions
Model without α	0.003	0.035	0.227
Model with α	0.000	0.005	0.052

	p-Values on Labor Market Transition Rates		
	Job-to-Job	Job-to-Nonemployment	Nonemployment-to-Job
	0.0000	0.0000	0.0000

Source: SIPP and authors' calculations.
Note: Table entries show the probability values for the null hypothesis of parameter constancy over time against the alternative of time-varying parameters.

percent in the 1980s to 10 percent in the early 1990s to 8 percent in the late 1990s, then increased to 17 percent in the early 2000s.[17]

In the bottom panel of figure 5.3, we present results that account for changes in the common time effect on wage levels using the model described in equation 5.3. The bottom panel of figure 5.3 is analogous to the top except that we also include our estimate of $\Delta_1 \alpha_t$ (that is, the change in the common time effect, at an annualized rate) as the bold line. Clearly, including α_t does make some difference in the results, although the overall patterns do not differ dramatically. For example, the returns to experience continue to show considerable variation over time. However, we can see that the pattern of the returns to experience is distinctly less procyclical in the bottom panel than in the top. Most notably, a dip in the returns to experience in 1992 just after the 1990 to 1991 recession is clearly visible in the top pattern but disappears in the bottom.

In the first two rows of table 5.1, we formally test whether the time patterns apparent in the figures are statistically significant by performing Wald tests for whether the parameter values are constant across all months of the data.[18] The columns refer to the parameter being tested, and the rows refer to whether the model contains the common time effect. The table entries show the p-values from the Wald tests. Whether or not we include the common time effect, we strongly reject the null hypothesis that the return to experience is constant over time. We also reject the null that the return to job-to-job switches is constant over time. However, despite the notable movements shown in figure 5.3, we actually do not reject that the job-to-nonemployment-to-job return is constant, although the p-value in the second model is 0.0518, which is very close to a marginal rejection of constancy.

In table 5.2, we test the cyclicality of the parameter values by taking each of the time series of monthly estimates and regressing them on a constant, a time

TABLE 5.2 / Tests of the Cyclicality of Parameter Estimates and Transition Rates

	Regression of Parameters from Wage Growth Model on Unemployment Rate		
	Coefficient on Experience	Change in Wage at Job-to-Job Transitions	Change in Wage at Job-to-Nonemployment-to-Job Transitions
Model without α	−0.0113	−0.0051	−0.0055
	(0.0033)*	(0.0055)	(0.0069)
Model with α	−0.0003	−0.0053	−0.0018
	(0.0079)	(0.0055)	(0.0061)

	Regression of Job Transition Probabilities on Unemployment Rate		
	Job-to-Job	Job-to-Nonemployment	Nonemployment-to-Job
	−0.0024	0.0015	−0.0064
	(0.0006)*	(0.0006)*	(0.0015)*

Source: SIPP and authors' calculations.
Notes: Table entries show the results of regressions on the monthly unemployment rate. Newey-West standard errors are in parentheses.
*Statistically significant at the 5 percent level.

trend, and the monthly unemployment rate. The entries in the table show the coefficient on the unemployment rate and the standard error from the regression. In our model without the common time effect, we find that the return to experience is highly procyclical. A 1 percent increase in the unemployment rate is associated with a 1 percent annual decline in the return to experience. This result is highly significant. The coefficients on job-to-job and job-to-nonemployment-to-job rates are both procyclical: a 1 percent increase in the unemployment rate is associated with a 0.5 percent decline in wage growth for both job-to-job and job-to-nonemployment-to-job switchers. However, the procyclical patterns for job-switchers are not statistically significant.

When we include the common time effect, which is strongly cyclical, we find that even the return to experience is not cyclical. This is not purely due to an increase in standard errors. The point estimate on cyclicality for the returns to schooling in table 5.2 falls from -0.0113 to -0.0003 after we control for $\Delta_t \alpha_t$. The results strongly suggest that the pro-cyclicality of β_t was due to the procyclicality associated with the common component to wage levels rather than in the returns to experience. Interpreting this in terms of the economics framework in the methodological section, this suggests that the human capital rental rate appears to be procyclical, while the human capital production function is not. Interpreted in this way, this result seems quite reasonable: the demand for human capital rises during a boom owing to increased productivity. This suggests that this component is actually a transitory component of wage levels rather than permanent wage growth. We view this as an important finding. Because of the problems with this specification discussed earlier, results from this specification should be taken with some caution. However, the fact that including this variable in the regression makes such a difference suggests that at the very least it is not simply noise.

In figure 5.4, we show the parameter estimates when we estimate the model separately by education groups. Figure 5.5 shows parameter estimates for men and women. Both figures refer to results from the first model without α_t (that is to say, equation 5.2). The top left panels of figures 5.4 and 5.5 show the estimated return to experience. Although there is a lot of variability in these series, both across time and across demographic groups, there is no strong secular change in the return to experience. Looking at the top left panel of figure 5.4, the trends in return to experience appear to differ by education groups, with larger trends for the more-educated. We examined this more in-depth. While the point estimates do suggest stronger trends for the more-educated, the standard errors are large enough that we cannot say much about this trend with confidence. Furthermore, for all demographic groups (except college), the return to experience is about 4 percent. In other words, an additional year of experience, holding all else constant, increases wages by about 4 percent. The return to experience for college graduates is about 5 percent. The top right and bottom left panels of figures 5.4 and 5.5 also show the average wage change associated with a job-to-job change and a job-to-nonemployment-to-job change, respectively.

The most dramatic difference across groups is that the coefficients for dropouts are particularly procyclical—both the return to experience and the return to job-to-nonemployment-to-job changes appear to be more procyclical than for other groups.

When we account for the common time effect α_t, results are very similar to the results in figures 5.4 and 5.5, so we do not present those results. Accounting for α_t slightly reduces the estimated return to experience for high school graduates and dropouts (although it is still estimated at over 3 percent for both groups). Also, the estimated fall in the return to experience for college graduates and high school graduates largely vanishes. As in figure 5.3, the return to experience appears to be less procyclical after accounting for the common time effect, although owing to the noisier results, the pattern is less transparent.

To summarize, all three of the returns to labor market transitions vary considerably over time, and all exhibit some procyclicality. However, only the return to experience is related to the business cycle in a statistically significant fashion. Once we control for the common time effect, however, the return to experience is no longer procyclical.

Patterns in Labor Market Transitions

In the previous section, we examined how the *returns* to labor market transitions changed over time and examined the cyclical properties of our parameter estimates. However, wage growth can also vary over time because of changes in the

FIGURE 5.4 / Coefficients Over Time (G_t), by Education Group

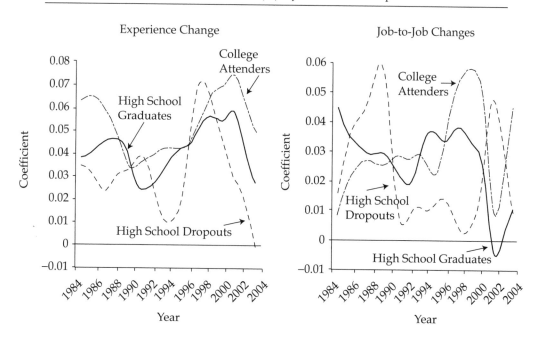

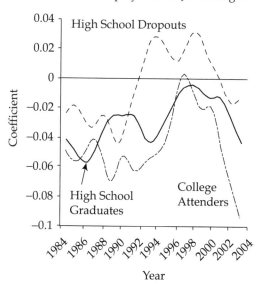

Source: SIPP and authors' calculations.

FIGURE 5.5 / Coefficients Over Time (G_t), by Gender

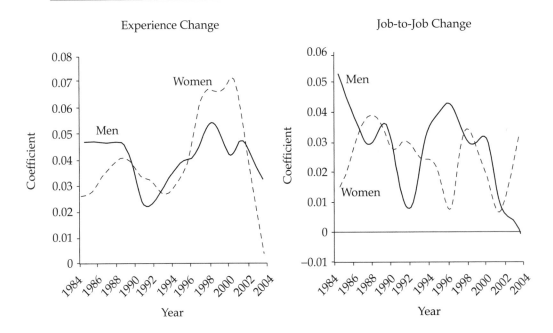

Source: SIPP and authors' calculations.

rates of these transitions irrespective of their returns. For example, more people are working and accumulating experience during booms. With that goal in mind, we now document trends in labor market transitions over the last twenty years. Recall that we examine three types of labor market transitions in our model: staying at the same job, making job-to-job transitions, and making job-to-nonemployment-to-job transitions. Also recall that because the SIPP panels are short, we cannot directly observe all job-to-nonemployment-to-job transitions, since we do not know whether individuals moving from nonemployment to employment were ever previously employed. Therefore, to measure these transition rates with our SIPP data, we estimate the three transition probabilities described earlier: employment to nonemployment, nonemployment to employment, and job to job. We then use these transition probabilities to simulate the labor market transitions for our model. Clearly, the job-to-job transition rate is directly related to the probability of a job-to-job switch. However, the job-to-nonemployment-to-job switches depend on two transition probabilities, the transition into nonemployment and then the subsequent transition to employment. Experience accumulation also depends on both the job-to-nonemployment rate and the nonemployment-to-employment rate.

We calculate the underlying transition rates that determine our labor market transitions annually for the combined group of dropouts and high school graduates. These are shown in figure 5.6. The patterns show considerable variability over time. These movements are strongly statistically significant, as can be seen in the bottom row of table 5.1, where we show that we strongly reject that the transition rates are constant over time. In the bottom row of table 5.2, we also find that these rates are all closely related to the business cycle (in the direction that we would expect). As we mentioned earlier, this is also consistent with the findings of Eva Nagypal (2004) and Robert Shimer (2005).

We present the transition rates by education group in figure 5.7 and by gender in figure 5.8. The results are fairly similar across groups, with a few notable exceptions. Nonemployment-to-employment transition rates are higher for men and for more-educated workers. Employment-to-nonemployment transition rates are lower for men and for more-educated workers. Therefore, the higher employment rates of men and the educated are the result of both higher nonemployment-to-employment transition rates and lower employment-to-nonemployment transition rates. Furthermore, nonemployment-to-employment transitions for less-educated workers are more procyclical than for more-educated workers. Another notable difference is a much stronger decline in job-to-job transitions for high school dropouts than for the other education groups.

Although all three transition rates appear to be trending downward somewhat, all three are highly cyclical, as we would expect. The job-to-job rate and the nonemployment-to-job rate are highly procyclical, while the job-to-nonemployment rate is countercyclical.

We use the estimated transition rates and the simulation model to calculate the probability that someone is employed, making a job-to-job change, or a job-to-nonemployment-to-job change, for each month during our sample period. For

FIGURE 5.6 / Transition Probabilities, Eighteen- to Twenty-Eight-Year-Olds, No College

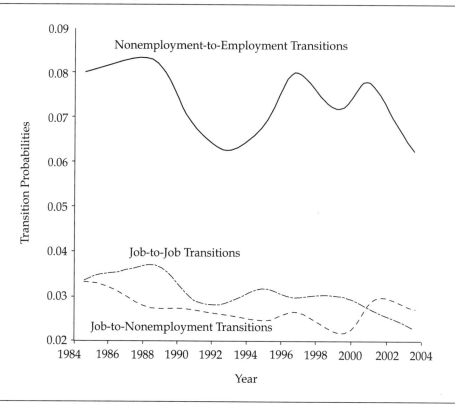

Source: SIPP and authors' calculations.

the most part, results from the model are unsurprising, so we do not show graphs of the results. The employment rate, which we use for measuring the amount of accumulated experience, is procyclical. For our base sample of high school graduates and dropouts, the employment rate rises from 69 percent in 1984 to 73 percent in 1989, declines to 69 percent in 1993, rises to 75 percent in 1999, then declines back to 70 percent in 2003. These participation rates line up closely with values from the CPS.[19] The job-to-nonemployment-to-job rate is slightly procyclical, falling from 2.1 percent per month in the mid-1980s to 1.5 percent in 1992, rising to 1.7 percent in 1996, falling to 1.5 percent in 1999, then rising to 1.7 percent in 2003. Recall that the job-to-nonemployment-to-job rate is a function of the job-to-nonemployment rate (which is countercyclical) and the nonemployment-to-job rate (which is procyclical), so the resulting series is some-what acyclical. Lastly, the simulated job-to-job transition rate, unsurprisingly, looks like the estimated job-to-job transition rate.

FIGURE 5.7 / Transition Probabilities, by Education Group

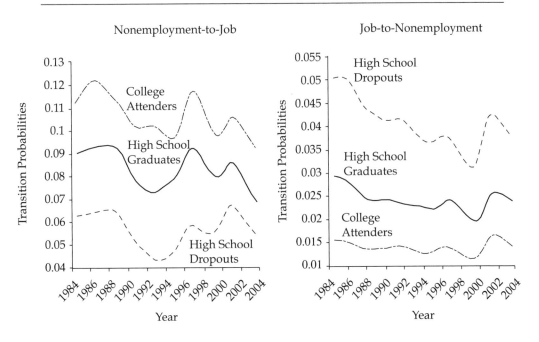

Nonemployment-to-Job

Job-to-Nonemployment

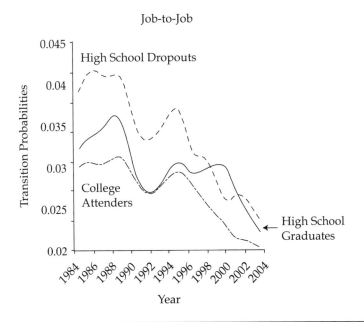

Job-to-Job

Source: SIPP and authors' calculations.

FIGURE 5.8 / Transition Probabilities, by Gender

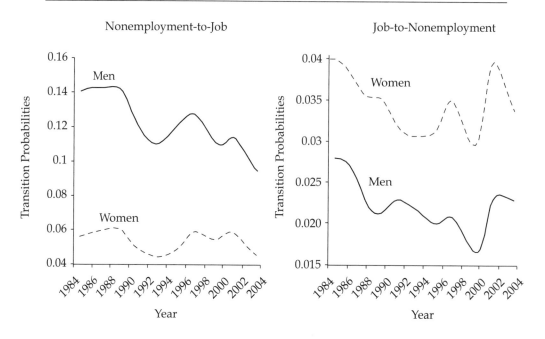

Nonemployment-to-Job

Job-to-Nonemployment

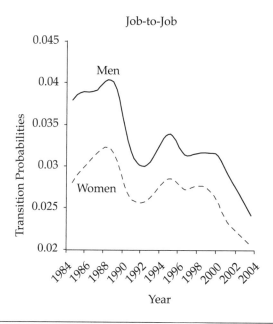

Job-to-Job

Source: SIPP and authors' calculations.

Decomposing Changes in Wage Growth over Time

Thus far, we have shown that there have been substantial changes over time in labor market transition rates and in the wage changes associated with these transitions. In this section, we decompose overall wage growth into its various components using the Oaxaca decomposition approach described in equation 5.9. This method basically attempts to ask the following question: what would the time series of wage growth look like if we simply held the transition rates constant at their average value over the whole time period so that all wage growth was only due to the changing returns? The result of this experiment would give us a sense of how much of the observed pattern of wage growth was due to changes in transition rates versus changes in returns.

In figure 5.9, we graph the results of the decomposition described in equation 5.9, converting our monthly estimates into annual units. The top panel presents the decomposition of the change in wage growth over time ($E[\Delta_1\omega_{it}]$), while the bottom panel presents the decomposition of wage changes net of the common time component ($E[\Delta_1\omega_{it} - \Delta_1\alpha_t]$). In both panels, the solid line represents the overall predicted wage growth ($G'_t X_t$). The dashed line presents the component that only allows the coefficients (returns) to change $G'_t \bar{X}$, while the dotted line presents the remainder term ($G'_t(X_t - \bar{X})$). Clearly, the dashed line explains virtually all of the change in the life-cycle wage growth. This result is also robust across subgroups (not shown). In short, changes in the coefficients explain almost all of the variability in wages, and changes in the transition rates explain essentially none of it.

Another perhaps surprising aspect of this is that we do not find that trends in the amount of labor force experience (due to labor supply) are important. We looked at this more closely for both men and women. For this sample, there is essentially no trend in labor force experience for either of these groups.

We find this result extremely surprising. As expected, experience and job-to-job transitions are associated with wage gains, while nonemployment spells are associated with wage losses. Also, as expected, job-to-job and job-finding rates are highly procyclical, while job-to-nonemployment rates are countercyclical. However, the magnitude of these effects in explaining the variation in overall wage growth is minuscule, as is clearly evident in figure 5.9.

We next decompose the dashed line in figure 5.9 ($G'_t\bar{X}$) into its various parts: a component related to the return to experience, a component related to job-to-job switches, and a component related to job-to-nonemployment-to-job switches. We show this for both of our wage growth models in the two panels in figure 5.10. The solid line in each panel reproduces the value of $G'_t\bar{X}$ from figure 5.9. We then present the three different components that contribute to it. Very clearly, the coefficient on experience is chiefly responsible for the main result. In short, the great majority of the variability in wage growth over time comes from one source: variability in the returns to experience.

Another interesting finding is also apparent in figure 5.10. Although the level

FIGURE 5.9   /   Predicted Wage, Decomposed into Subcomponents

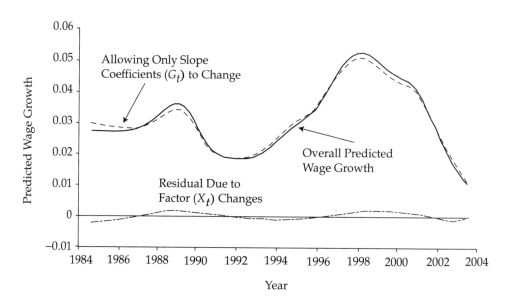

Without Common Time Effect (α_t)

Allowing Only Slope
Coefficients (G_t) to Change

Overall Predicted
Wage Growth

Residual Due to
Factor (X_t) Changes

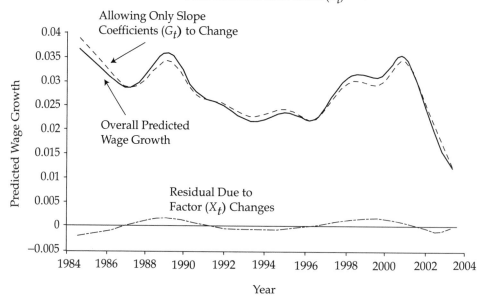

With Common Time Effect (α_t)

Allowing Only Slope
Coefficients (G_t) to Change

Overall Predicted
Wage Growth

Residual Due to
Factor (X_t) Changes

Source: SIPP and authors' calculations.

FIGURE 5.10 / Decomposition of Wage Growth: Coefficients

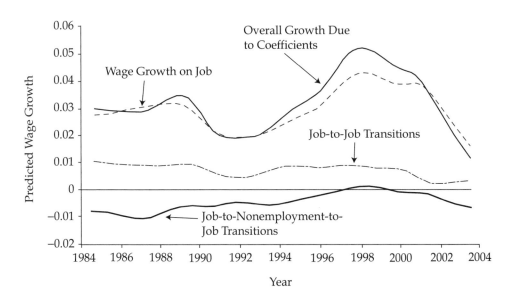

Without Common Time Effect (α_t)

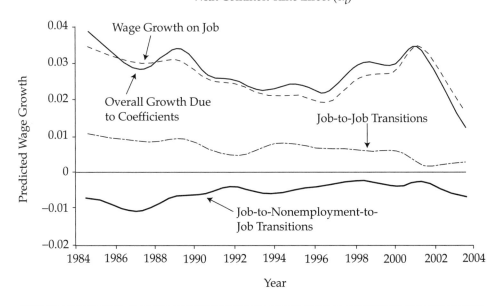

With Common Time Effect (α_t)

Source: SIPP and authors' calculations.

of wage growth is entirely accounted for by the return to experience, job-to-job transitions lead to positive effects while job-to-nonemployment-to-job transitions lead to negative effects, and these two roughly offset each other. In most years wage growth associated with job changes accounts for less than 10 percent of wage growth. Thus, we find that job changes are less important for understanding early career wage growth than does Topel and Ward (1992), who find that 30 percent of early career wage growth occurs at job-to-job transitions. Gadi Barlevy (2005) finds that job-to-job transitions are more important for wage growth than they are in our findings, but that they are less important for wage growth than in Topel and Ward's findings. Further research is necessary to better understand whether differences in results are attributable to differences in data (ours are more recent and for less-educated workers) or differences in methodology.

Ideally, we would like to understand why the return to experience has changed over time, but unfortunately we see no obvious explanation. We leave further exploration of this result to future research.

CONCLUSIONS

This chapter has analyzed the changing patterns of early career wage growth for less-skilled workers over the last twenty years. We find that wage progression has varied considerably over this period. Wage growth for young individuals averaged about 4.5 percent over this period, ranging from as high as 6 percent to as low as 3 percent.

We developed a model of wage changes in order to identify the key determinants of life-cycle wage growth for younger workers and the impact of these factors on the changing pattern of wage growth. In our first specification, in which we did not attempt to account for the common time effect on wages shared by all workers, we find that the returns to experience are highly variable and procyclical. In our second specification, which incorporates a common time effect, we find no relationship between the return to experience and the business cycle. Instead, we find that most of the procyclicality of wage growth comes from the common time effect. Nevertheless, even in this second model the returns to experience still exhibit a fair degree of variation over time.

Because our strategy for identifying the common time effect is problematic, we cannot be sure whether it is the common time effect or the return to experience that causes the procyclicality of wages during our sample period. To the extent that it is the common time effect that is responsible for the procyclicality in wages, the results are straightforward to interpret. Improvements in technology and increases in the amount of capital per worker imply that the productivity of all workers increases, regardless of experience level. This makes it a good time to hire, even if the wages of workers are being bid up. Thus, the wages of continuing workers rises.

We then examined the wage gains associated with different labor market transitions in order to identify the relative importance of wage growth on the job (which we interpret as the return to experience plus, potentially, a common time component) and wage growth when moving across jobs (which we interpret as the change in job match quality). Surprisingly, we find that virtually all of the change in wage growth over time is accounted for by wage growth on the job. Although we do find that experience accumulation and job changes are related to the business cycle, the magnitude of the contributions to overall wage growth from these sources is negligible.

Although there is variability in the return to experience, it has averaged a healthy 4 percent over our sample period and, generally speaking, does not vary much by gender or education level. The fact that the returns to experience have moved in ways unrelated to the business cycle is an interesting finding that deserves more attention. We have no obvious explanation for this result and thus are hesitant to make policy prescriptions based on this finding. Future research both to confirm our results and to delve deeper into this issue is clearly needed.

Taken as a whole, our results suggest that the business cycle plays a surprisingly small role in life-cycle wage growth and that policymakers should not be overly concerned that workers who enter the labor market during recessions will suffer slower wage growth over their careers. Although it is true that workers who are in the labor market during a downturn will experience longer unemployment spells and fewer job-to-job transitions, this will have relatively little effect on wage growth over the first ten years of their careers. Overall, our results suggest that experience accumulation may be an important pathway out of poverty and thus that attempts by policymakers to encourage work do not seem to be misplaced. In contrast, we do not find job switching to be an important explanation for early career wage growth, at least on average. Nonetheless, policies that produce particularly high-quality matches may still be desirable.

NOTES

1. We thank Dan Aaronson for his help with the CPS data and Phil Doctor for excellent research assistance. We thank the editors, Peter Gottschalk, and two anonymous referees for comments.
2. For example, wages of high school dropouts age eighteen to twenty-eight fell from about $12.00 an hour in 1979 (in 2004 dollars) to under $10.00 an hour in 2004.
3. We constructed this profile using the 1996 Survey of Income and Program Participation (SIPP) panel. We regressed log wages on age dummies and calendar year dummies for high school graduate and high school dropout men. We then presented the predicted value from this regression in 1996 looking across ages. The profile should therefore be interpreted as the wages of individuals of different ages in a single year.
4. It is important to distinguish our discussion of *changes* in wages for individuals from the extensive literature on the cyclicality of aggregate wage *levels*.
5. Specifically, we estimate the percentage increase in the hourly wage for individuals who were working in the survey wave and were also working in the previous outgoing rotation group twelve months prior.

6. Note that sample members in figure 5.2 age one year between the two time periods in which we observe them. In other words, we are measuring wage growth between ages eighteen and nineteen, between nineteen and twenty, and so on, for the same people between adjacent years. Furthermore, figure 5.1 shows that wages increase rapidly with age. So although there has been little aggregate change in wage levels for low-skilled workers over this time period, the wages of continuously employed young workers grow as they age.

7. In the augmented model that accounts for the common component to wages, we find that this component explains a large portion of wage growth. This is not surprising given previous work on the changing wage structure and the variation in wages across the business cycle. Nonetheless, wage growth *net* of this component is virtually entirely explained by changes in the return to experience.

8. Robert Shimer (2005) claims that the differences come from two sources. First, Davis, Haltiwanger, and Schuh (1996) use manufacturing-sector data, which may not be representative of the economy as a whole. Second, they use plant-level data instead of individual-level data. A plant can destroy jobs by merely not hiring new workers. If firms quit hiring new workers during a recession, jobs will be destroyed as workers quit (although the job separation rate may not necessarily rise), but the hiring rate will fall. Therefore, a countercyclical job destruction rate is consistent with an acyclical job separation rate.

9. Equation 5.2 can be derived from the following model of wage levels:

$$\omega_{it} = \theta_i + \sum_{s=0}^{t} \beta_s (A_{is} - A_{is-1}) + \eta_{ij_{it}} + \varepsilon_{it}$$

Where θ_i is an individual specific fixed effect that is potentially correlated with experience A_{is} and match quality $\eta_{ij_{it}}$. First differencing this equation and assuming that β_s changes slowly enough that $\beta_t \approx \beta_{t-t}$ yields equation 5.2.

10. In a standard human capital model, we would expect the returns to experience to be countercyclical, since the cost of investing in human capital is lower during a recession.

11. For an attempt to measure the distribution of $\eta_{ij_{it}}$, see Gladden and Taber (2006).

12. This is essentially an example of the fundamental problem of separating time, age, and cohort effects. For stayers, age, time, and experience are perfectly collinear.

13. For details on the simulation, see the working paper version of this study available at www.faculty.econ.northwestern.edu/faculty/taber.

14. In the CPS, job-to-job transitions can only be identified beginning in 1994 (Fallick and Fleischman 2001).

15. For the 1996 and 2001 SIPPs, job changes are only identified across waves.

16. The fact that some months contain five weeks rather than four sometimes leads to spurious wage changes within a wave. For these cases, we use 4.3 weeks rather than the actual weeks to calculate the wage. In the 1996 and 2001 SIPP panels, we do not know weeks worked in a month by employer. Adjusting the pre-1996 SIPP data to correspond to this measure of weeks has almost no effect on our results.

17. We should point out that Farber (2005) estimates the earnings loss associated with

being a displaced worker, whereas our measure is the wage loss for job-to-nonem-ployment-to-job transitions. The associated job loss may be voluntary, or the job loss may be for cause. Furthermore, we measure wages, whereas Farber measures earnings. Lastly, we measure wage losses for a younger group of workers who have not had time to find good matches and have not had time to gain firm-specific human capital. Nevertheless, we both find that earnings losses associated with job loss diminished in size during the 1990s.

18. Our use of a kernel smoother to present the results in the figures can make parameter estimates appear more stable over time than they actually are. We are using a two-stage procedure to estimate the mean wage changes for movers, and thus the calculation of standard errors is not straightforward, since we must correct for the first-stage estimation of β_t. We allow for this estimation error by treating the full model as one large Generalized Method of Moments (GMM) system and then performing Wald tests for the constancy of parameter values across all months.

19. Employment rates in the CPS tend to be about 2 percent lower than in our simulated data in every year. However, this difference does not change over time, so both series show almost identical cyclical fluctuations.

REFERENCES

Abraham, Katherine, and John Haltiwanger. 1995. "Real Wages and the Business Cycle." *Journal of Economic Literature* 33: 215–64.

Andersson, Fredrik, Harry Holzer, and Julia Lane. 2005. *Moving Up or Moving On*. New York: Russell Sage Foundation.

Antel, John. 1991. "The Wage Effects of Voluntary Labor Mobility With and Without Intervening Nonemployment." *Industrial and Labor Relations Review* 44: 299–306.

Barlevy, Gadi. 2005. "Estimating Models of On-the-Job Search Using Record Statistics." Unpublished paper. Federal Reserve Bank of Chicago.

Beaudry, Paul, and John DiNardo. 1991. "The Effect of Implicit Contracts on the Movement of Wages over the Business Cycle: Evidence from Micro Data." *Journal of Political Economy* 99(4): 665–88.

Ben Porath, Yoram. 1967. "The Production of Human Capital and the Life Cycle of Earnings." *Journal of Political Economy* 75(4, pt. 1): 352–65.

Connolly, Helen, and Peter Gottschalk. 2000. "Returns to Tenure and Experience Revisited: Do Less-Educated Workers Gain Less from Work Experience?" Unpublished paper. Chestnut Hill, Mass.: Boston College.

Davis, Steven, John Haltiwanger, and Scott Schuh. 1996. *Job Creation and Destruction*. Cambridge, Mass.: MIT Press.

Devine, Theresa, and Nicholas Kiefer. 1991. *Empirical Labor Economics*. Oxford: Oxford University Press.

Fallick, Bruce, and Charles Fleischman. 2001. "Employer-to-Employer Flows in the U.S. Labor Market: The Complete Picture of Gross Worker Flows." Unpublished paper. Board of Governors of the Federal Reserve System.

Farber, Henry. 1994. "The Analysis of Interfirm Worker Mobility." *Journal of Labor Economics* 12: 554–93.

———. 2005. "What Do We Know About Job Loss in the United States? Evidence from the Displaced Workers Survey, 1984–2004." *Economic Perspectives* (2nd quarter): 13–28.

Flinn, Christopher. 1986. "Wages and Job Mobility of Young Workers." *Journal of Political Economy* 94: S88–110.

Gladden, Tricia, and Christopher Taber. 2000. "Wage Progression Among Low-Skilled Workers." In *Finding Jobs: Work and Welfare Reform*, edited by David Card and Rebecca Blank. New York: Russell Sage Foundation.

———. 2004. "The Relationship Between Wage Levels and Wage Growth." Unpublished paper. Evanston, Ill.: Northwestern University.

———. 2006. "Turnover and Wage Growth in the Transition from School to Work." Unpublished paper. Evanston, Ill.: Northwestern University.

Heckman, James, Lance Lochner, and Christopher Taber. 1998. "Explaining Rising Wage Inequality: Explorations with a Dynamic General Equilibrium Model of Labor Earnings with Heterogeneous Agents." *Review of Economic Dynamics* 1(1): 1–58.

Holzer, Harry, and Robert LaLonde. 2000. "Job Change and Job Stability Among Less-Skilled Young Workers." In *Finding Jobs: Work and Welfare Reform*, edited by David Card and Rebecca Blank. New York: Russell Sage Foundation.

Klerman, Jacob, and Lynn Karoly. 1994. "Young Men and the Transition to Stable Employment." *Monthly Labor Review* 117(8): 31–48.

Loprest, Pamela. 1992. "Gender Differences in Wage Growth and Job Mobility." *American Economic Review* 82(2): 526–32.

Mincer, Jacob. 1962. "On-the-Job Training: Costs, Returns, and Some Implications." *Journal of Political Economy* 70(supp., no. 5, pt. 2): 50–79.

Mincer, Jacob, and Boyan Jovanovic. 1981. "Labor Mobility and Wages." In *Studies in Labor Markets*, edited by Sherwin Rosen. Chicago: Chicago University Press.

Nagypal, Eva. 2004. "Worker Reallocation over the Business Cycle: The Importance of Job-to-Job Transitions." Working paper. Evanston, Ill.: Northwestern University.

Neumark, David. 2002. "Youth Labor Markets in the U.S.: Shopping Around Versus Staying Put." *Review of Economics and Statistics* 84(3): 462–82.

Oreopolous, Phil, Till von Wachter, and Andrew Heisz. 2006. "The Short- and Long-Term Career Effects of Graduating in a Recession: Hysteresis and Heterogeneity in the Market for College Graduates." Unpublished paper. New York: Columbia University.

Shimer, Robert. 2005. "The Cyclicality of Hires, Separations, and Job-to-Job Transitions." Unpublished paper. Chicago: University of Chicago.

Topel, Robert, and Michael Ward. 1992. "Job Mobility and the Careers of Young Men." *Quarterly Journal of Economics* 108: 439–79.

Wolpin, Kenneth. 1992. "The Determinants of Black-White Differences in Early Employment Careers: Search, Layoffs, Quits, and Endogenous Wage Growth." *Journal of Political Economy* 100: 535–60.

———. 1995. "Empirical Methods in the Study of Labor Force Dynamics." In *Foundations of Pure and Applied Economics*. London: Hardwood Academic Publishers.

Part III

How Do Macroeconomic Changes Influence Well-Being Measures Beyond Income?

Chapter 6

The Level and Composition of Consumption over the Business Cycle: The Role of "Quasi-Fixed" Expenditures

Kerwin Kofi Charles and Melvin Stephens Jr.

The years from 1988 to 2000 spanned large changes in the macroeconomy. There was a sharp economic downturn in the early 1990s, a long and robust expansion in the mid to later parts of the decade, and an economic slowdown at decade's end.[1] How did these macroeconomic fluctuations affect the well-being of American families? Were the effects similar across households at different positions in the income distribution, or were households with low or modest income affected disproportionately? In this chapter, we investigate how recent macroeconomic changes and the changes in income and unemployment associated with them affected the *level* and *composition* of households' consumption, paying particular attention to the differential changes across the income distribution.

Although the overwhelming majority of the literature studying household economic well-being has focused on income, wages, or earnings as the outcomes of interest, many recent authors, studying a variety of research questions, have focused on household consumption—usually measured by *expenditures* devoted to a given bundle of consumption items (Cutler and Katz 1991; Krueger and Perri 2002). Among the things that recommend this focus on consumption is its connection to economic theory, which usually models utility not as a direct function of their income but rather as a function of the consumption and leisure that income finances.

Ever since the seminal work of Milton Friedman (1957), Albert Ando and Franco Modigliani (1963), and Modigliani and Richard Brumberg (1954), economists have argued that consumption in every period is determined by consumers' "permanent income." The life-cycle–permanent-income hypothesis posits that a rational consumer solves the dynamic consumption problem by "smoothing" consumption across periods. That is, he saves when income is high by consuming less than his income, and he either borrows against future income or uses previously acquired savings when income is low. These actions ensure that the marginal (expected) utility of consumption is equalized across periods and that consumption is unaffected by period-to-period transitory variation in income.[2]

But this hypothesis's prediction of consumption smoothing across periods and states of the world depends crucially on whether particular textbook assumptions are satisfied. For example, the real-world phenomena of uncertainty and risk aversion can significantly weaken this sharp prediction. An even more important real-world departure from what is usually explicitly assumed in the standard model is that capital markets are not perfect. Because consumers might not be able to borrow against their future income when their current income is low, imperfect capital markets might cause the level of consumption to change with current changes in economic fortunes, relative to the presumed smooth life-cycle path.

Current consumption and current income may be linked for another reason that has been much less emphasized in the literature: the ease with which expenditure outlays devoted to different consumption items can be adjusted. Indeed, in the short run, expenditures on particular classes of consumption items are effectively *fixed*—or at least are inflexible to the extent that they cannot be adjusted downwards without incurring some substantially penalty. To see how this fact, especially in an environment with imperfect capital markets, might cause income shocks to alter the composition if not the level of consumption suboptimally, consider the following scenario.

Suppose that individuals live for two periods, and that in each period they consume two goods—say, "trips to the movies" and "housing." These goods are financed out of income flows received in the two periods. The life-cycle–permanent-income hypothesis says that utility-maximizing agents should equalize the (expected) marginal utility of a particular consumption good *over* time and across goods at *any given* time. We have already discussed how negative shocks to income may cause total consumption to be suboptimally adjusted downward if capital markets are imperfect. Notice that because it is generally very difficult to lower housing payments, these reductions in total consumption expenditure should come disproportionately out of the easy-to-adjust item of movie attendance. As a result, adverse income shocks might cause the marginal utility of movie attendance to be suboptimally high relative to that of housing. In general, if capital markets are not perfect, and if items in the consumption bundle are relatively *inflexible, regular,* and *unavoidable,* the consumption of other, more flexible aspects of consumption is forced to be lower than the consumer would optimally prefer. In this chapter, we refer to these difficult-to-adjust or -avoid types of expenditures as quasi-fixed expenditure (QFE).[3]

The preceding discussion forms the foundation of the empirical work in this chapter. Like the other authors in this volume, we are interested in the effect of the business cycle changes during the 1990s on the well-being of U.S. households, especially on those of lower income. Our organizing assumptions are: (1) that capital markets are less than perfect, especially for low-income households; and (2) that an important part of a household's expenditure outlays are QFEs, in the sense already described.[4] Given these assumptions, we expect recent macro-economic changes to have generated several effects, and we formally test for those changes in the data.

First, contrary to the basic life-cycle–permanent-income hypothesis, changes in the macroeconomy and the income changes associated with them should have changed the *level* of households' consumption (as measured by their expenditures). Second, business cycle changes should have changed the *composition* of consumption bundles, with the largest changes occurring for low-income families. Specifically, we expect that the share of households' total expenditure outlays devoted to quasi-fixed consumption items should have risen in bad times and (perhaps) fallen in good, with these effects most pronounced for those at the bottom of the income distribution. A corollary is that the share of household expenditure devoted to easily adjustable nondurable consumption should have moved procyclically, especially for the low-income. Third, since households are most likely to make short-term credit adjustments by using instruments like store or commercial credit cards, we expect relatively larger percentage changes in total noncollateralized debt during bad periods for the less-constrained high-income than we do among lower-income families. The chapter finds very strong support for the first two propositions. Curiously, the evidence about debt holdings is much less convincing.

THE DATA

Consumer Expenditure Survey Overview

This study uses data from the Consumer Expenditure Survey (CEX) Interview Survey (U.S. Department of Labor, various years). The CEX is an ongoing, rotating, panel dataset in which consumer units (CUs), or households, are interviewed up to five times, at intervals of three months between interviews. In any given calendar quarter, approximately five thousand CUs are interviewed, with some beginning their participation in the survey and others completing their fifth (and final) interview. The initial interview collects household demographic information, which is updated during subsequent interviews to reflect any changes in household composition. The second through fifth interviews collect CU expenditure information for the three calendar months immediately preceding the interview.

The CEX also collects information regarding labor force activities and government transfer receipt for each CU member age fourteen and older. Labor force information includes data on earned income, annual works worked, and usual weekly hours. Data on transfer program participation and benefit amounts include Social Security, supplemental security income (SSI), and unemployment insurance (UI). Income and benefit amounts correspond to the twelve months prior to the interview date. Following the advice of the Bureau of Labor Statistics (BLS) staff, federal, state, and FICA (Social Security) taxes for each CU are calculated by using the TAXSIM program of the National Bureau of Economic Research (NBER) (Feenberg and Coutts 1993). All dollar figures are deflated to the January 2000 CPI-U using information on the interview month and year.

Unfortunately, because labor force and transfer receipt information is collected only during the second and fifth interviews, changes in labor force and transfer payment outcomes can only be ascertained between these interviews. It is difficult to interpret these changes in the data because the questions put to respondents concern the preceding twelve months, while there are only nine months between these two surveys. A further limitation is that rather than asking a labor force participation question similar to those found in other studies, such as whether the respondent is disabled, retired, or unemployed, labor force status information is acquired only for those who did not work *at all* during that past twelve months. These issues greatly complicate any examination of the relationship between changes in expenditures and changes in labor force and/or transfer payment outcomes *within* households. As such, we limit our analysis here to examining differences *across* households by focusing only on the data reported by households in their second interviews. Although limiting the sample to just one interview per CU results in a large loss of expenditure data, we are greatly limited by the fact that the labor market and transfer information is not collected as frequently as the expenditure data.[5]

Expenditure Information in the CEX

The primary data collection undertaken in the CEX involves expenditures on a wide variety of items. The CEX Interview Survey collects information on all expenditures except housekeeping supplies, personal care products, and nonprescription drugs. However, since these items make up a fairly small share of total expenditures, the BLS believes that the Interview Survey captures up to 95 percent of total expenditures.[6] For this study, total expenditures consist of two parts: outlays on what we term "quasi-fixed" expenditures, and all other expenditures. The CEX's Monthly Expenditure Files (MTAB) contain information on all new spending.[7] Thus, since loan payments represent payments on previously purchased items rather than new spending, no information on loan payments is contained in the MTAB files. Loan payments on mortgages or on vehicles—two of the main components of "quasi-fixed" expenditures—are not to be found in these files and are calculated from another source, which we describe later. On the other hand, some of the expenditures in the MTAB do represent outlays on QFEs. Vehicle lease payments, rent for homes and apartments, and insurance payments are the main examples of this sort. To compute total nonfixed payments, we sum all quarterly expenditures on the MTAB files and then subtract out the measures we characterize as quasi-fixed.[8]

The CEX collects a wide array of information concerning payments we characterize as quasi-fixed outlays. Housing expenditures represent our main example of expenditures that cannot be easily adjusted. For homeowning households, a large number of questions are asked pertaining to the financing of the home. For each house owned by the CU, detailed information is collected for each mortgage that the household holds and is made available on the public use files beginning in 1988. The survey measures the amount of the monthly payment for each mortgage. Since 1991, the CEX has also collected information on regular payments for home equity loans and payments on home equity lines of credit. For all these loan types, information on property taxes, property insurance, and mortgage guarantee insurance is also collected. Since these housing expenses are difficult to adjust, we include them in our measure of quasi-fixed housing payments. Finally, the CEX also collects information on rent payments for CUs renting their residence.

Expenditures on vehicles are the second class of QFE. The CEX includes information for all vehicles, including cars, trucks, motorcycles, and boats. Data about each vehicle include information on the vehicle model, the purchase date, and, if one exists, the vehicle loan or lease. Most important for our study, the regular payment amount for each loan and lease is collected.

In the empirical work, our main measure of quasi-fixed expenditures combines payments on residences (mortgages, home equity loans and lines of credit, rent, property taxes, and homeowner fees) and payments on vehicles (vehicle loan and lease payments). Some other forms of expenditures, such as utility payments and insurance payments, might be considered "quasi-fixed," but we study expenditures on this category of outlays separately, for reasons discussed later. Total expenditures are, of course, the sum of the particular quasi-fixed and all other expenditure outlays coded in the CEX.[9]

The third outcome discussed earlier is a measure of a household's noncollateralized debt. This is the debt that a household holds on things like department store or bank credit cards. We treat these obligations as a separate item for a couple of reasons. On the one hand, these obligations may be too large to be completely ignored, and they may also be the major mechanism by which a household might adjust its consumption on other items. On the other hand, even if a household runs up substantial credit card debt, its outlays on that debt can be quite minimal. We thus use a measure of noncollateralized debt that measures not how much people pay to service this type of debt each year but rather how much they report owing on this type of debt as of the interview month.[10]

Some consumer units were deleted because of missing data. The primary reason for deleting CUs is incomplete income data (20 percent of the sample). This designation by the BLS is based in general on the reporting of values for major sources of income such as wages and salaries, self-employment income, and Social Security income. These households are not used because the BLS sets all income data to zero (even for categories in which data are reported) for this set of CUs. In addition, we exclude households with missing or top-coded data for home or vehicle loan information or for rental payments.[11]

TABLE 6.1 / Summary Statistics of Key Outcome Variables Across All Households, 1988 to 2000

	Quarterly Total Expenditures	QFE1: Quarterly Quasi-fixed Expenditures: (payments on home, vehicles)	QFE2: Quarterly Quasi-fixed Expenditures: (home, vehicles, insurance)	Debt Owed
Mean	8,243	2,142	2,612	2,633
Standard deviation	(7,236)	(2,776)	(2,942)	(11,953)
Tenth percentile	2,428	125	439	0
Median	6,398	1,580	1,985	140
Ninetieth percentile	15,752	4,717	5,456	7,246

Source: Authors' compilation. Data from the Consumer Expenditure Survey, 1988 to 2000.

Basic Summary Statistics

Table 6.1 presents the summary statistics for the three main outcomes variables, over all households and for the years 1988 to 2000. As mentioned earlier, all dollar figures are in January 2000 dollars. Over the thirteen years studied, quarterly household total expenditures averaged $8,243. The standard deviation around this expenditure was quite large, at $7,236. The last three entries in the column show the tenth, median, and ninetieth percentiles of the total expenditure distribution. These numbers show that the distribution of total expenditures was quite uneven: half of all households had quarterly expenditures of $6,400 or less, while households in the top 10 percent of expenditures spent more than $15,700 a quarter.

The second column shows the means for the main measure of QFE used in this chapter. This index is the sum of all payments on home and vehicle payments. Expenditures devoted to the items averaged $2,142 a quarter across all households and years, with a standard deviation that was larger than this mean at $2,776. If anything, the distribution for QFE is even more skewed than for total expenditures, with the tenth, median, and ninetieth percentiles being $125, $1,580, and $4,717, respectively. Occasionally, we use another measure of QFE: the sum of home and vehicle payments and payments made to insurance. Like home and vehicle payments, insurance payments are a commitment generally made prior to the current period and are difficult to adjust by varying use. Utility payments might also have a quasi-fixed character, but we look at results for this outcome separately. The table indicates that quarterly outlays to the alternative quasi-fixed items of home, vehicles, and insurance payments averaged $2,600 a quarter across all households and years, on average. Adding insurance payments does little to change the uneven nature of the QFE distribution: the tenth, me-

FIGURE 6.1 / Mean Across Households' Quarterly Income, Quarterly Total
Expenditures, QFE1 (Home, Vehicles), QFE2 (Home, Vehicles,
Insurance, Utilities), and Noncollaterized Debt Owed, 1988 to 2000

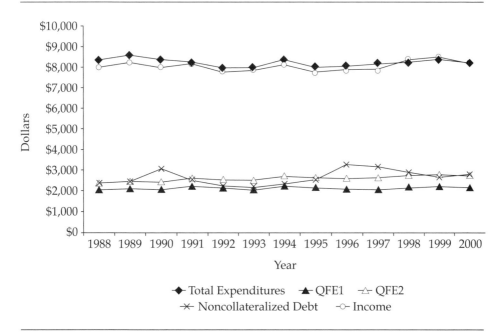

Source: Authors' compilation.

dian, and ninetieth percentiles of the distribution are $439, $1,985, and $5,456,
respectively.

The final column in the table shows that the noncollateralized debt held as of
the interview month by households across all the years studied was $2,633. The
standard deviation is more than four times the mean, at $11,953. As the remain-
der of the table illustrates, the distribution of credit card and store card debt (the
principal components of noncollateralized debt) over the period studied was
very much right-skewed: high-debt households held dramatically more debt
than did other households.

Figure 6.1 presents the average in each year of quarterly after-tax income,
quarterly total expenditure, the two quasi-fixed expenditures measures, and noncollateralized debt owed. The figure shows that across all years studied, average
total expenditure and average quarterly income across all households closely
track each other, with reported expenditures slightly exceeding income in most
years.[12] The income numbers are of special interest, since it is presumably
changes in this variable over the course of the business cycle that gives rise to
the behavioral responses of interest. There is some evidence of average income
tracking the business cycle, but the pattern in these average numbers is certainly
not striking.

Figure 6.1 shows that average total expenditures across all households averaged slightly above $8,000 in 2000 dollars. From a high of just under $8,600 in 1989, average total expenditures declined slightly to a low of $8,000 in 1993 and were relatively constant at about $250 higher over the succeeding years. The figure shows that quasi-fixed expenditures were quite constant, on average, over the years studied. Quarterly outlays on payments related to households' homes and cars were around $2,000 in each year studied. When insurance payments are added to the measure of QFE, average payments to this type of expenditure were about $400 and quite flat over time.

The patterns for average total noncollateralized debt owed show much greater variation over time. In particular, outstanding debt rises somewhat before 1990, up to a maximum of around $3,000. Over the first three years of the 1990s, debt owed fell by close to $1,000. Average outstanding debt then rose by about $1,000 over the next several years, reaching the late 1980s levels by 1996. In the final four years studied, outstanding debt again declined, although in these years the average decline was only about half as large as that during the early 1990s.

Somewhat surprisingly, we find that both income and total expenditures, while exhibiting cyclical fluctuations, do not show any evidence of an upward trend over this period. The lack of an increase in the CEX expenditure data during the 1990s while the personal consumption expenditures component of the National Income and Products Accounts (NIPA) increased has been noted by other researchers (Attanasio, Battistin, and Ichimura 2004). For our main empirical investigation, we are primarily interested in the variation in expenditure and income over the business cycle, specifically the degree to which these measures vary with state-level employment fluctuations. As such, the decline in these measures in the early 1990s and the subsequent increases in the latter part of the decade suggest that there is indeed interesting variation over the business cycle to examine, the lack of an upward trend notwithstanding.

CLASSIFYING HOUSEHOLDS BY INCOME POSITION

We are interested in the effect of macroeconomic changes on the consumption patterns of households at different positions in the income distribution. Ideally, we would like to sort households by their levels of permanent income and assess how macroeconomic variation differentially affects them. Because we do not observe permanent income, our strategy is to sort households by their position in the CEX national income distribution. One consequence of this choice is that households are stratified by their position in the distribution of a variable that is itself determined by business cycle changes. We doubt that this is a serious problem since, as we discuss later, the variation in the regression analysis is within-state, idiosyncratic variation; such variation is unlikely to affect appreciably how a household compares to all households in the country. Nevertheless, to raise confidence that our results do indeed reflect differences across persons with different levels of lifetime resources, we also present results in which households

FIGURE 6.2 / Annual After-Tax Household Income, by Year and Income Quartile

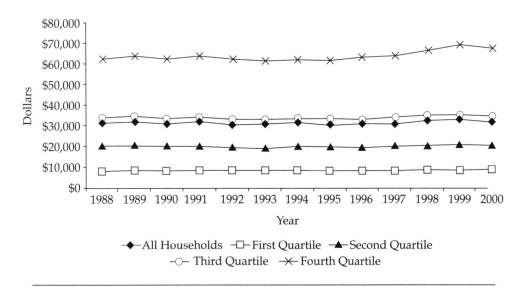

Source: Authors' compilation.

are distinguished by the education of the household head, the race of the household, and whether or not the household is headed by a single mother.

Figure 6.2 shows the after-tax mean of annual household income across all the households used in the analysis, by income quartile. On average, household income was just above $30,000 in each year. Average incomes for the households in the bottom three quartiles of the national income distribution exhibit very little variation over time. In each year, after-tax incomes for these three groups diverge by between $1,000 and $1,200, with the incomes for the lowest quartile averaging slightly less than $9,000. The figure reflects the skewness of the overall after-tax income distribution: households in the highest quartile of the income distribution have incomes that are, on average, double those of households in the third quartile.

As mentioned, we also discuss results in which groups are distinguished along other dimensions that are likely to be correlated with their levels of lifetime resources. Figure 6.3 shows mean after-tax income for subgroups in the different categories whose permanent incomes we would expect to be relatively low. The figure plots average after-tax income for African Americans, single mothers, and high school dropouts. For ease of comparability, we have kept the scale of the graphs in figures 6.2 and 6.3 the same so that the reader can readily compare incomes for these groups to the overall income distribution. Figure 6.3 shows that all of these groups have incomes below the mean for all households, with the possible exception of single mothers. Since the very low-educated, racial minorities and single mothers are precisely the persons whose permanent income

FIGURE 6.3 / Annual After-Tax Household Income for Selected Groups, by Year and Group

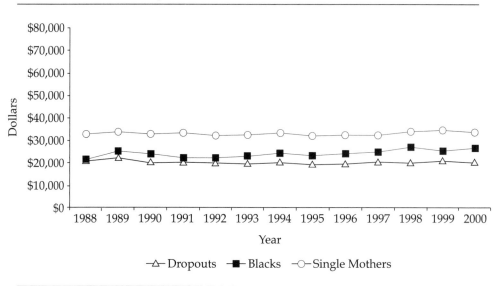

Source: Authors' compilation.

we expect to be especially low, these results further justify our focus on a household's quartile position in the national income distribution as the measure of lifetime or permanent income. As noted, we also present results in which the focus is on variation by household race, family type, and schooling.

Next, we briefly show how the key outcomes of interest in this chapter changed over time for different sorts of households. Figures 6.3 through 6.6 summarize changes in the four measures for persons at different positions in the income distribution. Figure 6.4 shows that such changes to total expenditure as occurred over the years seem to have been driven by changes in the expenditure outlays of households in the highest quartile of the income distribution. For example, in 1990 total quarterly expenditures for this group of households were just over $14,800. During the first three years of the 1990s, expenditures fell for this group by almost $1,500 a quarter. In the mid-1990s, expenditures rose again, then declined and stabilized at close to the levels observed in the late 1980s. By contrast, for the lowest-income American households, total expenditures were almost perfectly flat at $4,000 through all of the years.

Figures 6.5 and 6.6 show changes in average QFE outlays over the business cycle for households at different points in the income distribution. The figures show that, apart from a decline for the highest-income households between 1992 and 1993, these outlays were relatively flat over time for each type of household, and from year to year, in much the same manner for each group.

The patterns for noncollateralized outstanding debt depicted in figure 6.7

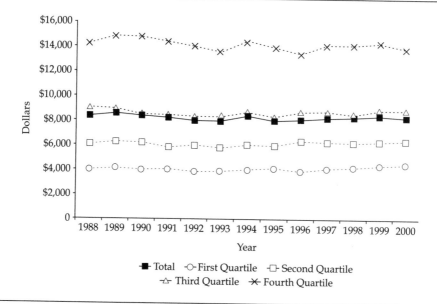

FIGURE 6.4   /   Total Expenditure over the Business Cycle, by Income Quartile

Source: Authors' compilation.

FIGURE 6.5   /   Average Household Expenditures on Home and Vehicle Payments, by Year and Income Quartile, 1988 to 2000

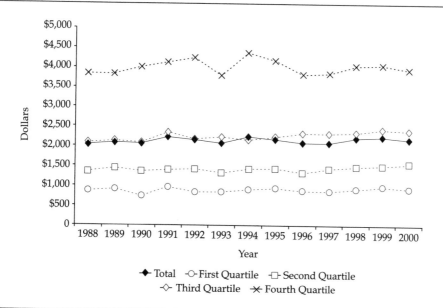

Source: Authors' compilation.

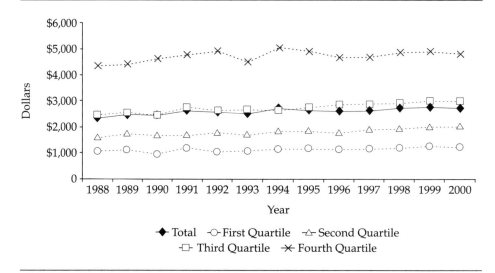

FIGURE 6.6 / Average Expenditures on Home, Vehicle, and Insurance Payments, by Year and Income Quintile, 1988 to 2000

Source: Authors' compilation.

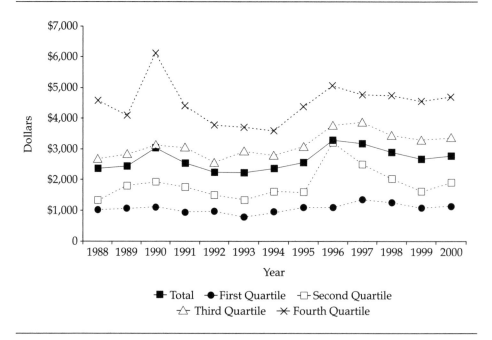

FIGURE 6.7 / Total Noncollateralized Outstanding Debt, by Year and Income Quartile

Source: Authors' compilation.

show that most of the changes in the mean over time were driven by changes in the highest-income households. In particular, the strong U-shaped pattern in average debt holdings over the recession of the early 1990s and the recovery later in the decade was due almost exclusively to changes in the debt holdings of the high-income. For those at the bottom of the income distribution, debt holding seemed to change only very modestly over the years studied.

These figures hint at a very modest procyclical dimension to total expenditures, and a weaker one for quasi-fixed expenditures. It must be emphasized that these aggregate patterns are merely suggestive. Changes in the various outcomes are not purged of any secular effects that might be coincidentally correlated with business cycle changes and driving the relationships indicated. For example, a national expansion in credit that happened to coincide with national economic downturns would exaggerate the apparent extent to which households used credit when times were bad. Nor do these results control for systematic sources of variation for each of the outcomes, such as the effect of life-cycle considerations. Finally, these aggregate patterns do not account for regional variation, such as that due to differences in economic fluctuations across industries. The causal relationship of interest would seem to be the relationship between the economic conditions in a state on the consumption expenditure and debt-holding patterns of the people who live there. In the next section, we use regression analysis to study the connection between local (state-level) economic conditions and the level and composition of consumption within the state. Apart from state-level controls, our regression specifications also control for age of household and other systematic effects.

REGRESSION ESTIMATES OF EFFECT OF UNEMPLOYMENT VARIATION AND CHANGES IN LEVEL AND COMPOSITION OF EXPENDITURES

In this section, we formally assess how recent macroeconomic changes affected the level and composition of consumption expenditures and debt using a series of regressions. Two questions are of interest to us: Do expenditures on quasi-fixed expenditure outlays "crowd out" other forms of expenditure during bad economic times? And how do the various effects differ for households at different positions in the income distribution?

Framework

We estimate regressions of the form:

$$y_{it} = \theta_s + \theta_t + \beta_1 X_{it} + \beta_2 U_{st} + \beta_3 IQ_i + \beta_4 (U_{st} \times IQ_i) + \varepsilon_{it} \tag{6.1}$$

In equation 6.1, y_{it} is either total expenditure, total debt owed, or share or fraction of total spending devoted to particular expenditure items. The variables θ_s and θ_t are vectors of state and time fixed effects. The vector X_{it} contains controls like the age of household, household size, race, and family structure. U_{st} measures the unemployment rate in the state at time t. IQ_i is an indicator variable denoting the household's position in the income distribution. We mainly measure that position by an indicator denoting the income quartile to which the household belongs, but we also discuss results where income position is measured by the education of the household head, the race of the household, and whether it is headed by a single mother.

Because they contain state fixed effects, the regressions in equation 6.1 measure how, for households in a given state, higher unemployment in that state in a particular year, relative to the state's time mean, affects expenditure and debt holdings. The inclusion of the time fixed effects ensures that the estimates are purged of the possible contamination that affects all groups equally and is attributable to unobserved secular trends. Because there might also be secular effects specific to particular groups, such as the very low-income or those with low levels of schooling, we also add group-specific trends to the various regressions.

We are chiefly interested in three sets of coefficients from the regressions: β_2 through β_4. The coefficient β_2 measures how the particular outcome variable changes, on average, across all households with changes in the business cycle. β_3 measures systematic differences across income groups in expenditure and debt holding for the different income and education groups. The β_4 on the interaction term measures whether macroeconomic changes produce different effects on expenditures and debt holdings for the various income groups. If a particular income (or education, race, or family structure) group's response to macroeconomic changes is the same as that of the excluded groups (those with the lowest income or lowest education), the estimated coefficient for the particular interaction term is zero.

In some regressions, we focus on the various "ratio measures"—specifically, the share of a household's total expenditure that goes to a particular type of expenditure. Since we also separately study results for total expenditure, it is straightforward in most cases to combine these results to determine how the level of expenditure on a particular item is affected over the business cycle. For example, if total expenditure for particular groups remains constant during booms, but the share of expenditure devoted to item x rises, then it follows that total spending on good x goes up. We focus on these ratios because they directly address the issue of the composition of expenditure over the business cycle (one of our chief interests).

Measuring Consumption

In our estimation of equation 6.1, we use two measures of quasi-fixed expenditures. The first combines payments on residences (mortgages, home equity loans

FIGURE 6.8 / Share of Total Expenditure Devoted to Quasi-fixed Expenditures
and All Nondurable Expenditures over the Life Cycle Under
Alternative Definitions: Regression-Adjusted for State and Year Effects

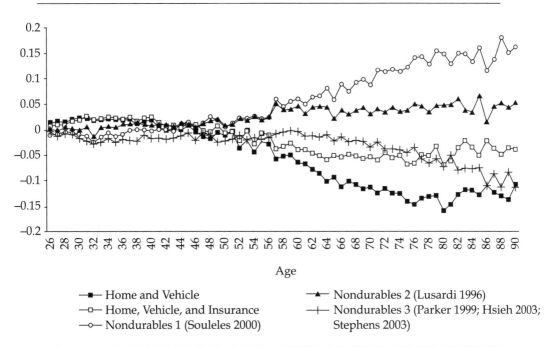

Age

—■— Home and Vehicle   —▲— Nondurables 2 (Lusardi 1996)
—□— Home, Vehicle, and Insurance   —+— Nondurables 3 (Parker 1999; Hsieh 2003;
—○— Nondurables 1 (Souleles 2000)   Stephens 2003)

Source: Authors' compilation.

and lines of credit, rent, property taxes, and homeowner fees) and payments on
vehicles (vehicle loan and lease payments). The other adds insurance payments
to this measure.

One difficulty we confront is how to measure aspects of consumption that are
not the QFEs. The convention in the previous work on consumption has been to
lump various "nondurable" consumption items into a single category. However,
there has been considerable variation in the particular items that scholars choose
to include in their measures. To help determine which variant, if any, of the
different measures that have appeared in the literature we should use in our
analysis, we decided on the simple strategy of examining what the alternative
measures that have appeared in the literature say about life-cycle consumption
patterns. If the picture one gets about life-cycle consumption differs markedly
from one measure to the next, then it would seem appropriate to not rely on the
choice of any of these measures in our analysis but instead to focus on the specific items that make up the composite nondurable measure.

Figure 6.8 plots the coefficients from a series of regressions in which the spending measure is regressed on a full vector of dummy variables for age and on

state and time fixed effects. The plotted effects show how expenditure changes over the life cycle, relative to the excluded age (twenty-five), netting out the effect of national variation and the effect of anything systematic about the state in which the household member happens to be located. If over the life cycle expenditure on nondurables remained the same, all of the plotted age effects would be zero.

Nicholas Souleles (2000) uses a nondurable expenditure measure consisting of outlays on food, alcohol, tobacco and smoking supplies, utilities, personal care, household operations (personal services and other household expenses), public transportation, gas and motor oil, apparel, health expenditures, education, and reading materials. Annamaria Lusardi (1996) uses a measure of nondurable expenditure called "strictly nondurable consumption," which is the same as the Souleles measure except that it subtracts off education, health, apparel, and reading material. Lusardi's measure attempts to capture expenditures that are truly nondurable over a quarterly interval. Jonathan Parker (1999), Chang-Tai Hsieh (2003), and Melvin Stephens (2003) all study how predictable changes in income affect consumption behavior. These papers measure nondurable expenditures as the sum of food, alcohol, textiles, small appliances, miscellaneous equipment, apparel, entertainment, personal care, reading, tobacco or smoking, public transportation, and gas and motor oil. Their nondurable measure does not include health, education, or utilities, as do the Souleles and Lusardi measures, but does include entertainment, unlike those other measures.

Figure 6.8 shows the differences over the life cycle in the fraction of outlays devoted to nondurable consumption, as captured by these three measures. The figure shows that the Lusardi measure's share of total expenditure is the same as the Souleles measure's share until age fifty-five. Thereafter, its share of total expenditure is basically flat, while that of the Souleles measure rises dramatically. The measure used by Parker, Hsieh, and Stephens exhibits a very different pattern from either of the other two measures. In particular, the share of expenditure devoted to this nondurable measure consistently falls below age-twenty-five levels once a household reaches age sixty, then falls further in each successive year.

What accounts for the difference across the various measures? In figure 6.9, we present results similar to those in figure 6.8, but for specific expenditure items. The figure presents results for health expenditures, food, utilities, and outlays on entertainment and personal care. We have drawn the graphs in figures 6.8 and 6.9 on the same scale. From a comparison of the figures, it is clear that increased health spending accounts for the difference between the Souleles and Lusardi nondurable measures. The pattern for utilities also explains, in turn, why the Parker-Hsieh-Stephens measure diverges from the Lusardi measure.

Rather than use an aggregate nondurable measure in the following analysis, we study particular consumption items separately. The results reported in this section suggest that the obvious individual measures to focus on are health, food, entertainment and personal care, and utilities. Looking at each of these items

FIGURE 6.9 / Share of Total Expenditures Devoted to Consumption Categories over the Life Cycle: Regression-Adjusted for State and Time Effects

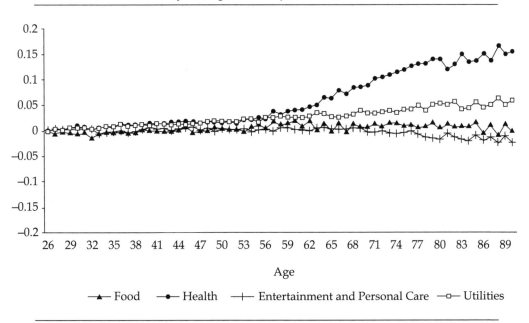

Source: Authors' compilation.

separately obviates the need to choose between the different nondurable measures that have appeared in the literature and also allows us to characterize more precisely the dimensions along which households adjust the composition of their expenditures as macroeconomic conditions change.

THE RESULTS

Table 6.2 investigates how business cycle fluctuations affect households' after-tax income. The first column of the table presents the relationship between state unemployment and income in a regression with state and time fixed effects. The point estimate implies that a one-percentage-point increase in a state's unemployment rate lowers after-tax income by about $390, averaged across all households. In the specifications in the second and third columns, the coefficient on the unemployment rate measures how business cycle changes affect the expenditures of the excluded group—households with the lowest income or schooling.[13] These regressions—and all others like them to follow—also control for household age, race, marital status, household size, and differential time period effects for the specific group being investigated.[14] The coefficients on the interaction

TABLE 6.2 / Effect of Local Unemployment on Change in Quarterly After-Tax Income

	(1)	(2)	(3)
Unemployment rate	−393.68	−458.98	−233.80
	(213.81)	(101.10)**	(94.58)*
Unemployment rate × Inc_Q2		58.77	
		(70.28)	
Unemployment rate × Inc_Q3		287.95	
		(77.13)**	
Unemployment rate × Inc_Q4		740.59	
		(265.25)**	
Unemployment rate × HS			−91.47
			(106.93)
Unemployment rate × SomeColl			161.26
			(117.48)
Unemployment rate × CollPlus			245.70
			(191.51)
Household income quartile			
Inc_Q2		11,112.81	10,769.14
		(460.15)**	(109.19)**
Inc_Q3		22,583.24	23,941.94
		(610.36)**	(167.76)**
Inc_ Q4		47,848.26	52,716.47
		(1,795.02)**	(572.54)**
Head's education			
High school (HS)		589.98	1,007.29
		(154.22)**	(703.66)
Some college (SomeColl)		1,498.80	0.0000
		(178.66)**	(0.0000)
College plus (CollPlus)		5,776.79	3,863.95
		(293.51)**	(1,318.07)**
Additional controls			
State and year fixed effects	Yes	Yes	Yes
Demographic variables	No	Yes	Yes
Income group time trends	No	Yes	No
Education group time trends	No	No	Yes
Observations	45,563	45,242	45,242
R-squared	0.02	0.75	0.75

Source: Authors' compilation.
Notes: The standard errors (in parentheses) allow for arbitrary correlation between observations from the same state over time. Demographic variables include age of the household head, family size, race of the household head, and marital status.
*Significant at 5 percent; **significant at 1 percent.

terms measure how much higher or lower the response for the indicated group is relative to that of the lowest income-education households. The coefficient on the unemployment rate measures the impact of unemployment on the lowest income-education group.

These results show that increases in unemployment lower the incomes of households in the lowest income quartiles by relatively large and strongly statistically significant amounts, while affecting the incomes of those with higher levels of income and schooling only modestly, if at all. For example, the results in column 2 suggest that each one-percentage-point change in unemployment lowers after-tax income in the lowest income quartile by about $450 and lowers incomes in the third quartile by only half this amount.

We estimated regressions like those shown in the last column of table 6.2, but with households distinguished by race and single-mother status. Consistent with our expectations, we find that unemployment lowers income for blacks and for single mothers, relative to other groups. For tables 6.3, 6.5, 6.6, and 6.7, we also estimate versions of the models with household position denoted by race, single-head status, and education. To avoid clutter we show none of these tables but do discuss the various results. The relevant tables are available from the authors upon request.

The results in table 6.3 show how macroeconomic changes affect total expenditure. The first column in the table shows that a one-percentage-point increase in unemployment lowers total expenditure by a modest $116 across all households. The results in the second column show that each one-percentage-point increase in unemployment lowers total expenditures for the lowest income quartile by a statistically significant $170. The point estimates imply that a 1.9-percentage-point increase in the unemployment rate, such as the increase that occurred nationally between 1990 and 1992, lowered total expenditures of the lowest-income households by about $324. This represents an 8 percent reduction relative to mean expenditures for this group of about $4,000 in a given year. The other point estimates in the second column suggest that there is effectively no change in total expenditures over the business cycle for households other than those at the bottom of the income distribution. The results in the third column, in which the unemployment rate is interacted with the household's education rather than with its income position, are broadly consistent with these results.

When we estimate a version of the regressions in the last column of table 6.3, distinguishing households by race and marital status, we find that unemployment has the same effect on total expenditure for all races, but that single mothers sharply lower total expenditures when unemployment rises. Given the earlier results for income, which showed that both racial minorities and single mothers experience disproportionately large income losses when unemployment increases, the fact that the two groups respond so differently with respect to total expenditure is surprising.

The next set of regression results measures how the composition of expenditures varies over the business cycle. In these regressions, the outcomes are the

TABLE 6.3 / Effect of Local Unemployment on Household Total Expenditure

	(1)	(2)	(3)
Unemployment rate	−116.32	−170.82	−226.17
	(78.57)	(65.17)*	(103.69)*
Unemployment rate × Inc_Q2		−59.62	
		(54.36)	
Unemployment rate × Inc_Q3		133.99	
		(59.20)*	
Unemployment rate × Inc_Q4		245.99	
		(161.00)	
Unemployment rate × HS			66.68
			(103.42)
Unemployment rate × SomeColl			216.19
			(146.38)
Unemployment rate × CollPlus			270.40
			(119.22)*
Household income quartile			
Inc_Q2		1,369.29	943.10
		(412.73)**	(70.56)**
Inc_Q3		2,362.15	2,514.43
		(454.93)**	(131.59)**
Inc_ Q4		5,765.89	6,884.21
		(1,005.77)**	(252.26)**
Head's education			
High school (HS)		774.57	673.51
		(96.25)**	(665.51)
Some college (SomeColl)		1,711.74	0.0000
		(144.06)**	(0.0000)
College plus (CollPlus)		2,962.50	2,093.64
		(134.40)**	(751.28)**
Additional controls			
State and year fixed effects	Yes	Yes	Yes
Demographic variables	Yes	Yes	Yes
Income group time trends	No	Yes	No
Education group time trends	No	No	Yes
Observations	45,563	45,242	45,242
R-squared	0.02	0.31	0.31

Source: Authors' compilation.
Notes: The standard errors (in parentheses) allow for arbitrary correlation between observations from the same state over time. Demographic variables include age of the household head, family size, race of the household head, and marital status.
*Significant at 5 percent; **significant at 1 percent.

TABLE 6.4 / Share of Total Expenditures Devoted to Various Items, 1988 to 2000, by Income Quartile

	Home and Vehicle	Home, Vehicle, and Insurance	Food	Health	Entertainment and Personal Care	Utilities
Mean	0.26	0.32	0.19	0.07	0.08	0.10
(Standard deviation)	(0.17)	(0.17)	(0.11)	(0.10)	(0.07)	(0.07)
Income quartile 1						
Mean	0.22	0.29	0.23	0.08	0.08	0.13
(Standard deviation)	(0.18)	(0.18)	(0.13)	(0.11)	(0.07)	(0.10)
Income quartile 2						
Mean	0.24	0.32	0.20	0.08	0.08	0.11
(Standard deviation)	(0.17)	(0.17)	(0.10)	(0.12)	(0.06)	(0.07)
Income quartile 3						
Mean	0.27	0.34	0.18	0.06	0.08	0.09
(Standard deviation)	(0.15)	(0.15)	(0.09)	(0.08)	(0.07)	(0.05)
Income quartile 4						
Mean	0.30	0.35	0.15	0.05	0.09	0.07
(Standard deviation)	(0.15)	(0.15)	(0.08)	(0.06)	(0.07)	(0.04)

Source: Authors' compilation.
Note: Data from the Consumer Expenditure Survey 1988 to 2000.

share of household expenditure devoted to each of the indicated expenditure items. Before presenting these results, table 6.4 presents the means for these share variables over the years studied for all households and by household income quartile. The table shows that for all households, expenditures on the quasi-fixed categories of home and vehicle payments represent about one-quarter of all expenditures across households, with the share rising slightly the higher the household's income. When QFEs include insurance payments, the share is about five to seven percentage points higher for every group. Outlays on food amount to about one-fifth of the expenditures of the average household. Unlike QFE outlays, the importance of this item in the expenditure set, following the familiar Engel's Law, falls slightly as income rises. Utilities exhibit a pattern similar to that found for food expenditures. For all households, expenditures on health and outlays on entertainment and personal care each constitute about 8 percent of expenditures.

Table 6.5 presents results for the effect of local unemployment changes on the fraction of expenditures devoted to home and vehicle payments. It has been our argument throughout that because these quasi-fixed expenditures are difficult to adjust in the short run, they constitute a larger share of total expenditures in bad

TABLE 6.5 / Effect of Local Unemployment Variation on Fraction of Total
Expenditures Devoted to Quasi-fixed Expenditures of Home
and Vehicle Payments

	(1)	(2)	(3)
Unemployment rate	0.0031	0.0083	0.0093
	(0.0015)*	(0.0030)**	(0.0031)**
Unemployment rate × Inc_Q2		−0.0076	
		(0.0030)*	
Unemployment rate × Inc_Q3		−0.0068	
		(0.0032)*	
Unemployment rate × Inc_Q4		−0.0061	
		(0.0030)*	
Unemployment rate × HS			−0.0054
			(0.0030)
Unemployment rate × SomeColl			−0.0091
			(0.0046)
Unemployment rate × CollPlus			−0.0089
			(0.0045)
Household income quartile			
Inc_Q2		0.0416	0.0052
		(0.0154)*	(0.0032)
Inc_Q3		0.0276	0.0132
		(0.0194)	(0.0057)*
Inc_ Q4		0.0498	0.0265
		(0.0173)**	(0.0057)**
Head's education			
High school (HS)		−0.0050	0.0235
		(0.0025)	(0.0194)
Some college (SomeColl)		−0.0070	0.0000
		(0.0049)	(0.0000)
College plus (CollPlus)		0.0003	0.0464
		(0.0047)	(0.0257)
		(0.0098)**	
Additional controls			
State and year fixed effects	Yes	Yes	Yes
Demographic variables	Yes	Yes	Yes
Income group time trends	No	Yes	No
Education group time trends	No	No	Yes
Observations	45,563	45,243	45,243
R-squared	0.04	0.15	0.15

Source: Authors' compilation.
Notes: The standard errors (in parentheses) allow for arbitrary correlation between observations
from the same state over time. Demographic variables include age of the household head,
family size, race of the household head, and marital status.
*Significant at 5 percent; **significant at 1 percent.

times, and a smaller share if households are forced to vary total expenditures over the business cycle. Are the results consistent with this reasoning? In the first column of table 6.5, the estimated point estimate, which represents the mean across all households, is indeed positive and statistically significant.

In the second and third columns, the interaction terms assess how this effect varies across households defined by income quartile and schooling. Now the coefficient on the unemployment variable measures the effect for the lowest-income households. The point estimate is positive and strongly statistically significant. It suggests that a two-percentage-point increase in the unemployment rate increases the fraction of expenditures going to home and car payments by about 0.016. This represents about an 8 percent increase in the share of expenditures going to these quasi-fixed outlays for this group of households. The positive estimated interaction terms in the column imply that the effects for other income quartiles are smaller by statistically significant amounts from what occurs for the lowest income quartile. Indeed, since the total effect for any of these other groups is the sum of the point estimate of the unemployment variable and the relevant interaction term, the results indicate that for households other than the lowest-income the share of total expenditures going to home and vehicle payments changes very little over the business cycle. The final column in the table tells a virtually identical story to that in column 2: changes in the business cycle affect the share of resources devoted to quasi-fixed payments, but only for households at the bottom of the income distribution.[15]

As with the earlier analysis, we also estimate regressions in which households are distinguished by race and single-mother status. Consistent with the notion that the lowest-income households spend larger fractions of their budgets on housing and vehicle payments in bad economic times, we find strong effects for single mothers. However, as with the results for total expenditure, we again find the somewhat surprising result that racial minorities are no more likely to see the share of their expenses going to these two main quasi-fixed expenditures rise with increases in unemployment, even though income is falling for this group. It is worth noting, though, that the point estimates on the two race variables are twice the size of the main effect. It may be that the lack of power precludes any significant conclusions in these data.

The results show that for some households quasi-fixed expenditures rise as a share of total expenditure outlays when the economy does poorly and rise when it does well. What types of expenditure are "crowded out" or increased from those households' consumption bundles as a result? Table 6.6 examines the share of total expenditures going to the four largest items in households' nondurable expenditures: food (both eaten at home and away), health, entertainment and personal care, and utilities. The table presents results only for the main regressions in which the unemployment rate is interacted with household income quartile.

The results in table 6.6 show that for health and utility expenditures, business cycle variation produces no changes in the fraction going to consumption for any type of family. For higher-income households, these results are not too sur-

TABLE 6.6 / Effect of Local Unemployment Variation on Fraction of Total Expenditure Going to Food, Health, Entertainment, and Utilities

	Food	Health	Entertainment and Personal Care	Utilities
Unemployment rate	−0.0007	−0.0020	−0.0024	−0.0022
	(0.0018)	(0.0013)	(0.0007)**	(0.0018)
Unemployment rate × Inc_Q2	0.0023	−0.0012	0.0032	0.0027
	(0.0015)	(0.0012)	(0.0011)**	(0.0017)
Unemployment rate × Inc_Q3	−0.0018	0.0023	0.0034	0.0030
	(0.0018)	(0.0011)*	(0.0009)**	(0.0021)
Unemployment rate × Inc_Q4	−0.0038	0.0041	0.0031	0.0035
	(0.0021)	(0.0012)**	(0.0007)**	(0.0025)
Household income quartile				
Inc_Q2	−0.0547	0.0062	−0.0080	−0.0312
	(0.0115)**	(0.0087)	(0.0070)	(0.0103)**
Inc_Q3	−0.0455	−0.0202	−0.0063	−0.0448
	(0.0145)**	(0.0054)**	(0.0067)	(0.0119)**
Inc_ Q4	−0.0560	−0.0336	−0.0028	−0.0573
	(0.0147)**	(0.0061)**	(0.0061)	(0.0140)**
Additional controls				
State and year fixed effects	Yes	Yes	Yes	Yes
Demographic variables	Yes	Yes	Yes	Yes
Income group time trends	Yes	Yes	Yes	Yes
Observations	45,242	45,242	45,242	45,242
R-squared	0.14	0.23	0.03	0.21

Source: Authors' compilation.
Notes: The standard errors (in parentheses) allow for arbitrary correlation between observations from the same state over time. Demographic variables include age of the household head, family size, race of the household head, marital status, and household head education group variables.
*Significant at 5 percent; **significant at 1 percent.

prising, since we could find no reductions in total expenditures for them and virtually no changes in the fraction they allocated to outlays on quasi-fixed expenses. It is reassuring, however, to observe that the adjustments the lowest-income households make to their consumption expenditures do not come out of these immensely important items. Nor do the lowest-income families adjust by altering their food consumption over the business cycle.

Table 6.6 shows dramatically that it is on expenditures devoted to entertainment and personal care where the lowest-income families make adjustments over the business cycle. The strongly statistically significant estimate in the first line implies that households at the bottom of the income distribution lower the share of their outlays going to things like movie and concert tickets, haircuts, televisions, radios, and sound equipment in bad times, and increase them in good times, by about -0.002 for each one-percentage-point increase in the state's unemployment rate. The other entries in the column show that the share devoted to entertainment and personal consumption by higher-income households over the business cycle is different in a strongly significant way to that for the lowest-income. In particular, the results indicate that for every type of household except those in the bottom income quartile, entertainment's share as a fraction of total expenditure outlays does not change at all as the business cycle changes.

In other analyses, we find results that should be very familiar by now. Specifically, we find that the results for other low-income groups closely match income quartile results, except for the results for racial minorities. Thus, for entertainment and personal care, the only category for which we find any evidence of compositional change over the business cycle, single mothers lower expenditures devoted to this item in bad times. There is no such effect for racial minority groups, despite the fact that their income losses during recessions are about the same size as those for single mothers.

Our results thus far have shown that both the level and composition of expenditure of the lowest-income households appear to have been affected by the macroeconomic changes of the past decade and a half. When the economy is bad and income falls, their total expenditures fall and the share of resources they devote to quasi-fixed payments, such as home and vehicle payments, rise. Further, the results suggest that low-income households make these adjustments to the composition of their expenditure outlays principally by lowering their expenditure on entertainment and personal care rather than things like health, utilities, or food.

What accounts for these different patterns across groups? One obvious possible answer might be that the lowest-income households are more credit-constrained than other income groups. Thus, rather than using credit to smooth consumption and keep the composition of consumption the same over the business cycle, they are forced to make the adjustments described here. In the final table in the chapter, table 6.7, we examine how total noncollateralized debt owed varies over the business cycle for different groups.

On the whole, the results for debt owed are not precisely estimated. Nonetheless, the point estimates do offer some suggestive evidence that might partly explain our results, which indicate that, consistent with our expectation, lower-income groups do not increase their debt holdings over the business cycle and might actually lower debt slightly. By contrast, there is weak evidence that higher-income households slightly increase debt in bad times—precisely what the standard model would predict for non-credit-constrained households. One interesting additional result is for blacks, for whom we find slight increases in debt in bad times, unlike single mothers, whose debt holding appears to fall slightly. This differential response with respect to debt holdings might explain

TABLE 6.7 / Effect of Local Unemployment on Total Non-Collateralized Debt Owed

	(1)	(2)	(3)
Unemployment rate	−27.26	−89.78	−161.45
	(59.42)	(91.61)	(123.86)
Unemployment rate × Inc_Q2		1.35	
		(82.03)	
Unemployment rate × Inc_Q3		−13.33	
		(96.69)	
Unemployment rate × Inc_Q4		252.54	
		(134.41)	
Unemployment rate × HS			154.37
			(113.87)
Unemployment rate × SomeColl			195.20
			(122.59)
Unemployment rate × CollPlus			181.33
			(165.01)
Household income quartile			
Inc_Q2		71.68	266.19
		(591.58)	(100.22)*
Inc_Q3		985.82	1,068.45
		(607.38)	(126.80)**
Inc_ Q4		1,023.12	1,851.83
		(727.07)	(227.67)**
Head's education			
High school (HS)		134.96	−829.01
		(112.14)	(685.28)
Some college (SomeColl)		810.37	0.0000
		(184.47)**	(0.0000)
College plus (CollPlus)		1,414.56	388.04
		(192.73)**	(849.34)
Additional controls			
State and year fixed effects	Yes	Yes	Yes
Demographic variables	Yes	Yes	Yes
Income group time trends	No	Yes	Yes
Observations	45,563	45,242	45,242
R-squared	0.00	0.04	0.04

Source: Authors' compilation.
Notes: The standard errors (in parentheses) allow for arbitrary correlation between observations from the same state over time. Demographic variables include age of the household head, family size, race of the household head, marital status, and household head education group variables.
*Significant at 5 percent; **significant at 1 percent.

why blacks are the only low-income group for which we find changes in neither the level nor composition of consumption expenditure over the business cycle.

CONCLUSIONS

In this chapter, we have argued that because of the credit market and other imperfections, transitory variations in income such as those arising from business cycle fluctuations may cause consumption behavior to depart from the textbook standard. In particular, in bad economic times such imperfections might cause affected households to lower total expenditure and to increase the share of their overall consumption devoted to expenditure items, such as car and vehicle payments, that are difficult to adjust without a cost.

Our main results distinguish households by their position in the national income distribution. We also discuss results where households are denoted instead by their race and single-mother status. Using a series of regressions in which we exploit state-specific variation over time, we find that local variation in unemployment is generally associated with reductions in after-tax income for the lowest-income groups. We find much smaller or nonexistent reductions for subgroups with higher permanent income. Our results indicate that most lower-income groups lower total expenditure when state unemployment is high. There are no reductions for households higher up in the income distribution.

Changes in the composition of expenditure outlays are also concentrated among lower-income groups—to the extent that they exist at all. We find that when state unemployment rises, most lower-income groups raise the fraction of their expenditure outlays devoted to what we term quasi-fixed expenditure. Interestingly, we find that the only specific nondurable consumption items on which these groups lower expenditure are in the category of entertainment and personal care. Important expenditures such as food and health do not appear to be affected. These results hold up for lower-income groups, with the interesting exception of racial minorities. Despite the fact that their income falls when state unemployment rises, we find little evidence that they alter either their total consumption or their outlay on particular items over the business cycle. What accounts for these patterns is somewhat of a puzzle, and in fact they may be an artifact of sampling variability, considering the very small sample sizes for racial minorities.

An interesting area for future work would be to combine other forms of household adjustment to business cycle shocks with the consumption expenditure adjustments that are our focus here. For example, whether a family changes its living arrangements as the business cycle changes—an issue studied in this volume by London and Fairlie—might differ across various lower-income subgroups. Adjustments of this form might have important implications for how outlays on quasi-fixed expenditures affect the level and composition of overall consumption over the business cycle. Combining all the components of adjustment in one analysis would be an interesting effort for future work.

NOTES

1. According to the National Bureau of Economic Research, the business cycle peaked in July 1990, hit a trough in March 1991, and did not reach another peak until March 2001. See http://www.nber.org/cycles.html/.

2. Although this smoothing behavior is typically ascribed only to nondurable consumption, the theoretical result also extends to durable goods (Mankiw 1982). Moreover, households not only act to smooth their *stocks* of durable goods but also smooth their durable good *expenditures*.

3. Martin Browning and Thomas Crossley (2004) present a model in which credit-constrained households have differential responses to income shocks across goods with differing degrees of durability. In their framework, a credit-constrained household that suffers a small negative transitory income shock will cut back primarily on durable expenditures but very little on nondurable expenditures. Intuitively, since households derive utility from their stocks of durable goods, which are in part carried over from the previous period, these relatively larger changes in durable expenditures do not correspond to nearly as dramatic changes in utility (see also the empirical results in Dynarski and Gruber 1997). Browning and Crossley note that if durable purchases are irreversible, then large negative income shocks will lead to large changes in nondurable consumption, since households will be unable to lower their accumulated durable stocks to help smooth nondurable consumption. Analogously for the current chapter, we can view QEFs as durable goods with a positive irreversibility constraint that leads households to undergo larger changes in nondurable consumption than they would in the absence of the constraint.

4. Tullio Jappelli (1990) finds that roughly 20 percent of U.S. households are credit-constrained.

5. Given our emphasis on quasi-fixed expenditures, of which housing expenditures are a major component, the ability to examine changes in these payments would be useful. For households that take out a new mortgage, purchase a new vehicle, or pay off an existing loan, we can track these changes in the CEX. However, since the CEX tracks *residences*, not individual households, we cannot follow changes from being a renter to becoming a homeowner and vice versa. A similar scheme of sampling residences is used by the Current Population Survey.

6. See U.S. Department of Labor (various years) for more details. The codebook for the Interview Survey notes that 5 to 15 percent of total expenditures is accounted for by the categories not collected by the Interview Survey.

7. The MTAB files include information on the month of expenditure. Some expenditures in these files do not perfectly align with the three-month reference period prior to the interview month. Following previous studies, expenditures are allocated to the appropriate reference period. In addition, pension contributions and cash contributions are not included in our analysis.

8. Specifically, rent payments, vehicle lease payments, property taxes, homeowner fees (such as condominium fees), the interest portion of payments on home and vehicle loans, and payments on homeowner's, renter's, and vehicle insurance plans are con-

sidered fixed payments that appear in the MTAB files. In some of our analysis, we also consider utility payments to be fixed payments.

9. In the previous literature, total expenditures are defined as the sum of expenditures on the MTAB files with some exceptions such as pension and cash contributions (Parker 1999; Souleles 1999). Our definitions include these expenditures as well as the fixed housing and vehicle payments that do not appear in the MTAB files but are found elsewhere in the CEX data.

10. The fifth interview of the CEX contains information on the total amount of finance charges and late fees paid in the last year. However, information on monthly payment amounts on noncollateralized debt is not available.

11. This last restriction affects 5 percent of the observations.

12. CEX income is an annual income measure. We divide this computed annual number by four for presentation in this figure 6.1.

13. The CEX includes a variable for the household's place in the income distribution for households that are deemed complete income reporters. Indicators for income quartile are created from this variable. The four education categories are high school dropout, high school graduate, some college, and college graduate.

14. For example, when the unemployment rate is interacted with each of the quartile indicators, the specification includes differential time period effects for each quartile to capture any differential national trends across the income quartiles.

15. We estimate but do not present the results measuring QFE as home and vehicle payments plus payments on insurance and/or utility payments. The results are similar to those shown in table 6.5.

REFERENCES

Ando, Albert, and Franco Modigliani. 1963. "The Life-Cycle Hypothesis of Saving: Aggregate Implications and Tests." *American Economic Review* 53(1): 55–84.

Attanasio, Orazio P., Erich Battistin, and Hidehiko Ichimura. 2004. "What Really Happened to Consumption Inequality in the U.S.?" Working paper 10338. Cambridge, Mass.: National Bureau of Economic Research.

Browning, Martin, and Thomas F. Crossley. 2004. "Shocks, Stocks, and Socks: Smoothing Consumption over a Temporary Income Loss." Working paper 2004–05. Copenhagen: University of Copenhagen, Center for Applied Microeconometrics.

Cutler, David, and Lawrence Katz. 1991. "Macroeconomic Performance and the Disadvantaged." *Brookings Papers on Economic Activity* 2: 1–74.

Dynarski, Susan, and Jonathan Gruber. 1997. "Can Families Smooth Variable Earnings?" *Brookings Papers on Economic Activity* 1: 229–303.

Feenberg, Daniel and Elisabeth Coutts. 1993. "An Introduction to the TAXSIM Model." *Journal of Policy Analysis and Management* 12(1): 189–94.

Friedman, Milton. 1957. *A Theory of the Consumption Function.* Princeton, N.J.: Princeton University Press.

Hsieh, Chang-Tai. 2003. "Do Consumers React to Anticipated Income Changes? Evidence from the Alaska Permanent Fund." *American Economic Review* 93(1): 297–405.

Jappelli, Tullio. 1990. "Who Is Credit-Constrained in the U.S. Economy?" *Quarterly Journal of Economics* 105(1): 219–34.

Krueger, Dirk, and Fabrizio Perri. 2002. "Does Income Inequality Lead to Consumption Inequality? Evidence and Theory." Working paper 9202. Cambridge, Mass.: National Bureau of Economic Research.

Lusardi, Annamaria. 1996. "Permanent Income, Current Income, and Consumption: Evidence from Two Panel Datasets." *Journal of Business and Economic Statistics* 14(1): 81–90.

Mankiw, N. Gregory. 1982. "Hall's Consumption Hypothesis and Durable Goods." *Journal of Monetary Economics* 10(3): 417–25.

Modigliani, Franco, and Richard H. Brumberg. 1954. "Utility Analysis and the Consumption Function: An Interpretation of Cross-Section Data." In *Post-Keynesian Economics*, edited by Kenneth K. Kurihara. New Brunswick, N.J.: Rutgers University Press.

Parker, Jonathan A. 1999. "The Reaction of Household Consumption to Predictable Changes in Social Security Taxes." *American Economic Review* 89(4): 959–73.

Souleles, Nicholas S. 1999. "The Response of Household Consumption to Income Tax Refunds." *American Economic Review* 89(4): 947–59.

———. 2000. "College Tuition and Household Savings and Consumption." *Journal of Public Economics* 77(2): 185–207.

Stephens, Melvin, Jr. 2003. "The Consumption Response to Predictable Changes in Discretionary Income: Evidence from the Repayment of Vehicle Loans." Working paper 9976. Cambridge, Mass.: National Bureau of Economic Research.

U.S. Department of Labor. Various years. Consumer Expenditure Survey, Interview Survey[Computer file]. ICPSR version. Washington: U.S. Department of Labor, Bureau of Labor Statistics [producer]. Ann Arbor, Mich.: Inter-university Consortium for Political and Social Research [distributor].

Chapter 7

Recent Trends in Resource Sharing Among the Poor

Steven J. Haider and Kathleen McGarry

During the 1990s, the U.S. economy experienced sustained economic growth with low levels of unemployment and high levels of wage growth accruing across the skill distribution.[1] Along with this robust economic performance, there were substantial changes in economic and social policies: the minimum wage was raised for the first time in fifteen years, the Earned Income Tax Credit (EITC) was expanded, and cash welfare assistance was changed from an entitlement to a temporary assistance program that imposes strict work requirements and lifetime limits on benefits.

Many of these changes would be expected to have had large effects on the incomes of the poor, and consequently there has been a spate of research assessing how the low-income population has fared. Some of these studies have focused on specific changes—such as changes in the wage distribution (Autor, Katz, and Kearney 2004), the Earned Income Tax Credit (Meyer and Rosenbaum 2001), and cash welfare assistance (for a useful review, see Blank 2002), while others have examined the overall changes in the incomes of the poor (Blank and Schoeni 2003).

One source of income that has received comparably little attention is income from private transfers. Private transfers can come from relatives, friends, or non-spousal partners and can consist of cash or noncash transfers or shared living arrangements.[2] We refer to this broad definition of private transfers as "resource sharing." Shared resources could be especially important for low-income individuals who may not qualify for benefits from social insurance programs such as unemployment insurance or workers' compensation, both of which require some degree of previous attachment to the labor force. Moreover, the recent changes in public assistance programs, including time limits on benefit receipt and work requirements, will result in a reduction in assistance for some. Absent these formal sources of support, low-income individuals may turn to family or friends. Recent research has indeed provided some evidence that resource sharing is an important component of income for individuals leaving the welfare rolls (Danziger et al. 2002; Moffitt and Winder 2005).

In this chapter, we consider the importance of resource sharing to the financial well-being of low-income households and changes in this importance over time. We begin in the next section with a broad discussion of resource sharing, drawing on several existing literatures. We consider both the potential motivation for sharing and the different modes through which such sharing can occur. Because this volume focuses on the low-income population, we pay specific attention to the interaction between private transfers and government assistance programs.

We then undertake an empirical analysis of resource sharing. Following many of the other chapters in this volume, we use data from the 1980 to 2003 Current Population Surveys (CPS). Our analysis yields several important findings. First, although much of the economics literature has focused on cash transfers, shared living arrangements provide an alternative mode of resource sharing that is quite common and potentially significant among the low-income population. Second, although they are difficult to measure, private cash transfers from outside the household appear to be an important source of income for recipients; they are more common when the economy is weak and often made to individuals enrolled in school. Third, the importance of these private cash transfers and income from unrelated household members rose beyond that predicted by macroeconomic and demographic changes, suggesting that factors such as changes in public programs—for example, Temporary Assistance for Needy Families (TANF) and the EITC—could also be important determinants of sharing behavior.

Overall, our analysis, like those on which it builds, is limited by the available data. We conclude by discussing these limitations, offering suggestions for future research, and reviewing the implications of our findings for public policy.

THE RELATED LITERATURE

The recent literature on the well-being of the low-income population has focused on the importance of labor market opportunities and public transfer programs. However, both the robustness of the labor market faced by less-skilled workers and the regulations governing the receipt of public assistance are beyond the control of these individuals. When faced with a reduction in income, an individual may look for assistance from private sources, such as family and friends. Despite the potential importance of private transfers, relatively little research has focused on such assistance. In this section, we draw on a diverse set of literatures to consider the potential importance of private transfers and to lay the groundwork for our empirical analyses.

We take a broad view of private transfers, including both cash and noncash transfers and shared living arrangements. Measurement of these transfers is not always straightforward. For example, embedded in the value of shared living arrangements is the direct transfer of such tangible items as food, shelter, and household goods, as well as less readily measurable assistance implicit in the returns to scale in household production.[3] We use the term "transfers" to refer to direct assistance provided through cash or noncash transfers or through shared residence, and we reserve the more general concept of "resource sharing" to indicate both these direct transfers and the indirect gains obtained through coresidence. In many cases, we observe only the income of each individual and not how resources are actually shared among coresident individuals. When discussing the phenomenon of coresident individuals combining their incomes, we use the term "income pooling." We note also that the focus of this chapter is on *voluntary* resource sharing. We refer the reader to the chapter by Maria Cancian and Daniel Meyer (this volume) for a discussion of legally mandated transfers such as alimony and child support.

Motives for Resource Sharing

A family can provide assistance to one of its members out of concern for the well-being of the (potential) recipient (Barro 1974; Becker 1974) or as part of a quid pro quo arrangement (Bernheim, Schleifer, and Summers 1985).[4] These competing explanations, the former an altruistic motivation and the latter based on exchange, have generated a sizable volume of research, much of which attempts to discern the motive that is most consistent with the data.[5] Despite these efforts, a consensus has yet to be reached, and recent work suggests that each model may play an important role (Light and McGarry 2004). The existing literature has generally found, however, that transfers are strongly compensatory, with both the probability of a transfer and the amount higher for lower-income recipients (Cox 1987; Altonji, Hayashi, and Kotlikoff 1997; McGarry and Schoeni 1995, 1997).[6] Furthermore, the probability of making a transfer and the amount transferred are positively related to the donor's income. These findings suggest that we would observe changes in the pattern of resource sharing in response to changes in the income of either party and to changes in the economic environment more generally.

When family or friends provide assistance in response to declines in the income of the recipient, they could be providing a form of insurance to each other, akin to that provided by formal private insurance markets or by publicly provided social insurance. This notion has been developed in several papers. For example, Laurence Kotlikoff and Avia Spivak (1981) present a model in which families provide insurance (annuities) for their elderly members to protect against the possibility of "living too long" and exhausting their assets. Similarly, Donald Cox (1990) and Cox and Tullio Jappelli (1990) model the potential for familial transfers to alleviate liquidity constraints. Social insurance programs such as unemployment insurance, Social Security, and workers' compensation can provide substantial protection against negative shocks to income (see, for example, Gruber 1997; Dynarski and Gruber 1997). However, because these programs typically require some previous attachment to the labor force, many of the lowest-income individuals may not qualify for benefits. For this population, then, families could play a particularly important role.[7]

Modes and Magnitudes of Resource Sharing

Although economists often focus on cash transfers, resource sharing can occur through other modes as well, such as the transfer of goods, time help, or a reduction in expenses through shared living arrangements. The optimal choice of mode is determined by the characteristics of the donor and the recipient, such as their financial resources, their preferences, and the opportunity cost of their time. For example, a retired parent facing a low opportunity cost of her time may choose to assist her daughter by providing child care to her grandchild, whereas a fully employed parent might choose to make cash transfers to pay for child care. These sorts of trade-offs between time and financial assistance have been documented in several empirical studies (see Couch, Daly, and Wolf 1999). Despite the potential for transfers of various types to substitute for one another, research has tended to focus on each mode in isolation (for an important exception to this practice, see Mark Rosenzweig and Kenneth Wolpin 1993, 1994).

Studies examining cash transfers have found that they are relatively common (Altonji, Hayashi, and Kotlikoff 1997, 2000; McGarry and Schoeni 1995, 1997). These studies estimate that 20 to 30 percent of parents make inter vivos transfers to their adult children, with positive transfer amounts averaging $2,000 to $3,000 a year. In addition, substantial amounts are transferred as bequests (see, for example, Gale and Scholz 1994).

Ethnographic evidence also points to the importance of private transfers. In a compelling descriptive study of the resources of low-income households, Kathryn Edin and Laura Lein (1997, 150–51) report that approximately 80 percent of the single mothers in their study received transfers from private sources and that these transfers accounted for 20 percent of household resources. Twenty-five percent of their respondents also reported "doubling up" with friends or relatives to reduce living expenses (54, 115). Similarly, Carol Stack (1974) highlights the importance of a network of family and friends in a low-income black community. However, these studies do not analyze how resource sharing responds to changes in the economic and policy environment, and because these studies are not based on randomly selected samples from well-defined populations, it is impossible to generalize the findings to larger populations.

Of the studies that have attempted to measure noncash transfers, attention has been primarily limited to the transfer of time. These studies have found that the provision of home health care is a common type of time transfer, with over one-third of such assistance flowing from adult children to their elderly parents (U.S. Department of Health and Human Services 1998). Kathleen McGarry and Robert Schoeni (1995) find that, among individuals in their fifties who are providing care to elderly parents, the average amount provided was over seven hundred hours a year. At a wage rate of $18.00 an hour (MetLife Mature Market Institute

2004), these services are comparable to cash transfers of at least $12,000 a year. When help with tasks other than personal care items is included in the measure of time help, the fraction providing assistance rises substantially (Altonji et al. 2000). The family also figures prominently in the care of children. When the child's mother is employed and not the primary caregiver, nearly 40 percent of the time the primary caregiver is a relative (Blau and Currie 2004).

Another potential mode of transfer is the provision of coresidence. This form of assistance is perhaps the most difficult to evaluate. Not only is it difficult to measure accurately the multitude of direct subsidies that are provided through food, shelter, and time help, but monetary values must also be assigned to the returns to scale implicit in such arrangements and the potential costs associated with the loss of privacy.[8] Empirical analyses of shared living arrangements have again focused largely on the behavior of the elderly (Korbin 1976; Pampel 1983; Michael, Fuchs, and Scott 1980), though some work examines the behavior of young adults (Whittington and Peters 1996).

In many datasets, including the one we use in our empirical analysis, income is collected for each household member but no information is collected on how income is shared. Thomas DeLeire and Ariel Kalil (2005) show that expenditures on child-specific consumption items differ markedly between cohabiting and married couples, with cohabiting couples spending less on children. This finding suggests that income is not simply pooled at the household level, but rather that household structure matters. Even more striking, a growing branch of the literature has focused on income pooling among spouses. Important early work by Duncan Thomas (1990) and by Shelly Lundberg, Robert Pollak, and Terence Wales (1997) finds that expenditure patterns differ significantly depending on which spouse controls the resources, with mothers devoting a larger share of spending to children. Thus, not only is the assumption of equal sharing likely to be invalid in the case of coresidency, but it is unlikely even to hold between spouses. These findings have important implications for our empirical analysis.

Resource Sharing and the Policy and Economic Environment

As we have noted, decisions to share resources within and between households are likely to be influenced by the existing policy and economic environments. In fact, the structure of many government assistance programs explicitly defines the economic unit in which resource sharing is expected to occur. As with much in our society, these assumptions have changed repeatedly over time, reflecting shifts in attitudes regarding public and private roles in meeting economic needs. For example, the former state-run Old-Age Assistance (OAA) programs often included "relative responsibility" clauses that obligated children to provide financial support to their elderly parents (Epler 1954). Failure to support needy parents could result in court action and denial of public assistance to the parent. These requirements were abolished in 1974 when the Supplemental Security Income (SSI) program replaced OAA. Similarly, Aid to Families with Dependent Children (AFDC) initially targeted only unmarried mothers and their children; the presence of *any* adult male in the household was held to be sufficient grounds for the denial of benefits, presumably under the assumption that his resources were available to the children. Supreme Court decisions eventually invalidated this practice (Patterson 2000, 173–74), and by the 1980s and 1990s states generally ignored the resources of nonparents (Moffitt, Reville, and Winkler 1998).[9] Under the Temporary Assistance for Needy Families (TANF) regulations applicable today, some states have returned to stricter requirements regarding the inclusion of resources from other household members—for example, requiring that a minor mother live with a parent or guardian and including a portion of that person's income when determining benefits (for a more complete description of TANF regulations across states, see Rowe and Russell 2004).

Even at a specified time, there is variation across assistance programs in the definition of the economic unit. For example, the Food Stamp Program (FSP) has consistently used a broad definition, including all individuals in a household who purchase or prepare food together, regardless of their relationship (Haider, Jacknowitz, and Schoeni 2003). In contrast, cash welfare assistance (TANF) generally only includes the income of a child's parent and direct cash assistance from others when computing benefits.

Several studies have examined the extent to which private cash transfers respond to public assistance programs.[10] In an early empirical study, Robert Lampman and Timothy Smeeding (1983) discuss the potential for government transfers to "crowd out" or replace private cash assistance and provide suggestive evidence of such a trade-off. More recent studies have confirmed the relationship, finding that private cash transfers decline in response to increased public assistance, although the overall responses are very small (Cox and Jakubson 1995; Schoeni 1997, 2002; Rosenzweig and Wolpin 1993, 1994).

Similar analyses of the relationships between the policy and economic environments and the choice of living arrangements have been undertaken. With respect to the living arrangements of the elderly, several studies have concluded that the dramatic improvement in the financial situation of older persons evident over much of the last century has led to a sharp decline in the probability of coresidency (Michael et al. 1980; Schwartz, Danziger, and Smolensky 1984). Using expansions of Social Security, OAA programs, and SSI to identify the relationship between income and living arrangements, several studies have subsequently confirmed the important interactions between public and private transfers (Costa 1999; McGarry and Schoeni 2000; Engelhardt, Gruber, and Perry 2002). Studies of the living arrangement choices of younger populations have demonstrated that they too respond to the structure of cash assistance programs (Rosenzweig and Wolpin 1993, 1994; Bitler, Gelbach, and Hoynes 2004).

In comparison to even this somewhat limited body of research assessing the interaction between public and private transfers, the relationship between macroeconomic conditions and private transfers has received relatively little attention. Many of the general principles, however, should be the same. To the extent that an improving economy leads to an improvement in the economic status of recipients, we would expect fewer transfers. However, because broad-based economic changes could affect the resources of donors as well as recipients, both the supply and demand for transfers will change and the net effect may be ambiguous.

RECENT TRENDS IN INCOME SHARING

The recent literature has tended to focus either on transfers from outside the household, referred to as *inter*household transfers, or on income pooling within the household, referred to as *intra*household transfers. In our empirical work, we examine the relevance of both modes of resource sharing and focus on how these patterns have changed in response to changes in the macroeconomic environment.

Data and Definitions

Our data are drawn from the Current Population Surveys (CPS) for the years 1980 to 2004. We use the March supplements for each year, at which time information is obtained about income in the preceding year. We thus refer to our data as pertaining to the years 1979 through 2003. The CPS provides detailed information on income components and household living arrangements for a large, nationally representative sample. With these data, we can identify both cash transfers from outside the household and the *potential* for income pooling within the household. A detailed household roster allows us to distinguish various types of living arrangements, including whether the other individuals in the household are relatives, nonrelatives, or, in the later years of our data, cohabiting partners.[11]

Our definitions of income sharing are straightforward. For interhousehold income sharing, we use the CPS question that specifically asks about "regular financial assistance from friends or relatives not living in this household." This question necessarily limits our focus to cash transfers, although in-kind transfers such as help with child care are likely to be important. In addition, the phrase "regular financial assistance" presumably further limits the type of income transfers that are reported. Respondents must use their judgment regarding what qualifies as "regular," and transfers that are made to offset temporary income shortfalls may be excluded. Such concerns are corroborated by past research that suggests the CPS-type question dramatically underestimates the amount of private transfers actually received.[12]

With regard to intrahousehold income sharing, the detailed information on the components of income contained in the CPS allows us to measure the income of various household members separately. The ability to define the relationship between household members is central to our analysis, and the definitions we use are largely determined by the structure of the CPS. We define the "nuclear family" as an individual or a married couple living with any unmarried and childless children. This nuclear family is part of a potentially larger household, defined as all individuals occupying an independent housing unit, such as a house or apartment. Other household members are classified as relatives if they are related by blood or marriage to any member of the nuclear family; if not, other household members are referred to as nonrelatives. Based on these definitions, unmarried, cohabiting partners are *not* considered part of the same nuclear family, but rather are defined as living in unrelated families.

There are three important considerations that should be noted when examining within-household income sharing. First, we do not know the extent to which total household income is indeed shared by household members; we can therefore speak only to the *potential* for income sharing. Second, along with the potential for pooling cash resources, these shared living arrangements involve some degree of pooling of noncash resources, such as time spent engaged in household chores or child care; these we are also unable to measure. Third, there is an implicit gain in resources from the returns to scale in household production, such as the sharing of housing and utility costs and quantity discounts on food. Although these factors are important to understanding the transfers embedded in coresidency, we largely ignore them in our empirical analysis, owing to data constraints.

Our analysis is based on women age eighteen to fifty-four.[13] For these individuals, we examine the incomes of all members of their nuclear family and the incomes of others in the household; income accruing to these "other" household members is further broken down by relationship to our sample person (that is, income from related persons, from unrelated persons, and, in the years for which it is possible, from cohabiting partners). Within these categories, we classify income into four sources: earnings, means-tested public transfers, private financial transfers, and other income. To highlight the patterns of resource sharing for the low-income population, we divide our sample of individuals into three groups based on schooling level: less than high school, a high school degree, and schooling beyond high school. Our discussion focuses primarily on the less-than-high-school group and uses the more-schooled for comparisons. We apply sample weights throughout our analysis.[14]

Income Sharing in 2003

In the top panel of table 7.1, we examine the sources of income for our sample of women. Unsurprisingly, we find extremely large differences in mean nuclear family income by schooling level, as well as differences in the components of income. Nuclear family income for low-schooled women averages $35,248, while those in our highest education group report an average nuclear family income of $77,756. Labor earnings are a less important source of this income for the less-skilled women than for the more-skilled women, while income from means-

TABLE 7.1   /   Income by Source, Family Unit, and Education, 2003

	Less Than High School	High School Degree	More Than High School
All women			
Observations	7,007	16,926	32,821
Mean nuclear family income	$35,248	$51,034	$77,756
Nuclear family income by source[a]			
Earnings	78.6%	85.1%	87.4%
Private financial transfers	0.5	0.5	0.9
Means-tested transfers[b]	8.2	3.0	1.0
Other[c]	12.7	11.4	10.7
Mean household income	$42,089	$57,906	$83,900
Household income by source			
Nuclear family income	84.6%	89.0%	92.1%
Related family income	5.8	3.6	1.8
Cohabiting family income	4.9	4.3	2.7
Nonrelated family income	4.6	3.1	3.3
Single mothers			
Observations	1,034	1,976	2,981
Mean nuclear family income	$31,568	$32,339	$54,126
Nuclear family income by source[a]			
Earnings	73.1%	79.0%	80.4%
Private financial transfers	0.3	0.7	0.4
Means-tested transfers[b]	11.7	6.0	2.5
Other[c]	15.0	14.3	16.6
Mean household income	$41,145	$46,179	$64,974
Household income by source			
Nuclear family income	77.2%	76.8%	85.3%
Related family income	13.0	12.7	9.0
Cohabiting family income	6.4	7.4	3.8
Nonrelated family income	3.3	3.1	1.9

Source: Authors' calculations based on Current Population Survey, March supplement.
[a]These tabulations are the mean across families of the fraction of income by source; nuclear families with zero total income are excluded.
[b]Means-tested transfers include income from the TANF program and the SSI program.
[c]Other income includes transfers from the unemployment insurance, disability insurance, and workers' compensation programs, alimony and child support, asset income, retirement benefits, and other miscellaneous income.

tested transfer programs is a more important source of income for them. The mean fraction of nuclear family income from earnings is 78.6 percent for the less-educated women, compared to 85.1 percent for women with a high school diploma and 87.4 percent for women with more than a high school education. In contrast, means-tested transfers account for 8.2, 3.0, and 1.0 percent of income, respectively.

Looking at the results reported in the table, private financial transfers appear to be fairly unimportant, accounting on average for less than 1 percent of nuclear family income for all educational groups. However, as discussed earlier, previous studies have concluded that CPS-type questions dramatically underestimate the amount of private transfers actually received. Although we cannot demonstrate it with these data, we expect that private transfers are substantially more important than they appear to be based on this evidence.

The top panel of table 7.1 also presents information on the source of total household income for women in our sample. Unsurprisingly, total household income increases with schooling level, ranging from $42,089 for the least-educated group to $83,900 for the most-educated group. However, the *fraction* of total income attributable to household members outside of the nuclear family is much more important for the less-schooled group. For example, among women without a high school diploma, 85 percent of household income accrues to the nuclear family, 6 percent to related household members, and 5 percent to both cohabiting partners and unrelated individuals. For women with more than a high school diploma, the figures are 92 percent to the nuclear family, 2 percent to related household members, and 3 percent to both cohabitors and unrelated individuals. These results suggest that the least-educated women could be relying more on resources stemming from shared living arrangements than are women with more education. Moreover, among the least-educated, transfers arising from shared residence are potentially much more important than transfers from outside the household. Rosenzweig and Wolpin (1994) draw a similar conclusion using National Longitudinal Survey of Youth (NLSY) data.

Although our focus is on all women, we present a similar set of tabulations for single women with a child under eighteen years old in the lower panel of table 7.1. The same general patterns emerge: nuclear family income and household income increase with education, the relative importance of different income sources is comparable, and the scope for resource sharing from within the household appears to be much greater than the measured private financial transfers reported by a nuclear family. Perhaps the most notable difference between the two panels is that, for less-educated single mothers, the role of related family income in the household is greater than for the general population of less-educated women. For example, related family income makes up 6 percent of household income for all less-educated women, but 13 percent of household income for less-educated single mothers. However, given the similarity in overall patterns, we focus the rest of our analysis on all women.

In table 7.2, we focus on the importance of resource sharing by examining the

TABLE 7.2 / Transfers by Source and Education, 2003

	Private Financial Transfers			Non-nuclear Family Income		
	Less Than High School (1)	High School Degree (2)	More Than High School (3)	Less Than High School (4)	High School Degree (5)	More Than High School (6)
Proportion receiving any transfers	0.011	0.013	0.022	0.236	0.190	0.146
Transfer amount among recipients						
Observations	64	196	583	1,643	3,224	4,425
Twenty-fifth percentile	$960	$900	$2,000	$12,156	$14,400	$16,014
Median	2,000	2,000	4,500	21,800	26,000	30,200
Seventy-fifth percentile	7,920	5,000	9,000	37,400	45,676	51,696
Mean	6,574	5,182	7,621	28,987	36,258	42,116
Standard error of mean	1,388	685	409	707	779	692
Characteristics of recipients						
Observations	64	196	583	1,643	3,224	4,425
Nuclear family income	$24,683	$26,072	$31,318	$17,169	$26,619	$37,105
Household income	26,615	30,285	41,542	46,156	62,877	79,221
Age	34.5	31.3	28.9	31.9	33.3	32.2
Proportion married	0.200	0.266	0.212	0.232	0.193	0.139
Proportion with children	0.493	0.460	0.280	0.486	0.420	0.284
Proportion in school	0.105	0.126	0.379	0.095	0.047	0.173
Characteristics of nonrecipients						
Observations	6,943	16,730	32,238	5,364	13,702	28,396
Nuclear family income	$35,362	$51,369	$78,817	$40,833	$56,743	$84,699
Household income	42,257	58,277	84,868	40,833	56,743	84,699
Age	33.8	37.1	36.8	34.3	37.9	37.4
Proportion married	0.472	0.571	0.580	0.542	0.654	0.646
Proportion with children	0.624	0.539	0.508	0.664	0.566	0.541
Proportion in school	0.126	0.039	0.094	0.135	0.038	0.087

Source: Authors' calculations based on Current Population Survey, March supplement.

distributions of these private financial transfers and non-nuclear family income more generally. The table also highlights some of the more interesting differences in demographic characteristics for the recipients and nonrecipients of each form of transfer (or potential transfer). Despite the probable underreporting of the receipt of private cash transfers, columns 1 through 3 demonstrate that, when the private transfers are reported, the amounts are large. The mean amount of private transfers for the least-schooled is $6,574, and one-quarter of the recipients reported transfers of over $7,900. Because the mean nuclear family income among women in the lowest education group is just $24,683, the average cash transfer was nearly one-third of average income. Average transfer amounts are similarly large for the other education groups, with the women in the high school diploma group receiving an average of $5,182 and women with more than a high school diploma receiving $7,621. However, because nuclear family income is substantially higher for these more highly educated women, cash transfers are less important relative to total income.

In comparing those who receive cash transfers with those who do not among the least-educated women, transfer recipients have lower nuclear family incomes on average than nonrecipients and are less likely to be married, to have children, or to be in school. The patterns are similar for the two other educational groups, with the notable exception of the relationship between transfer receipt and school attendance. In each of the more highly educated groups, transfer recipients are substantially more likely to be attending school than their nontransfer counterparts. This difference in school enrollment suggests that the transfers reported in the CPS for those with a high school diploma could represent familial financial assistance in financing a college education.

In columns 4 through 6 of table 7.2, we similarly examine non-nuclear family income. The probability of having non-nuclear family income is much higher than it is for receiving private financial transfers, ranging from 24 percent for women in the lowest educational group to 15 percent for women in the highest. Moreover, conditional on having some non-nuclear family income, the amount of such income is *larger* than mean nuclear family income, a result that holds for all educational groups. The existence of non-nuclear family income is concentrated among those who are relatively young, less likely to be married, and less likely to have children. Again, among those with at least a high school education, those who have some non-nuclear family income are more likely to be enrolled in school. Overall, the recipient-nonrecipient comparisons for non-nuclear family income are similar to those for private financial transfers, consistent with the notion that private financial transfers and coresidency are different modes of the same economic process of income sharing.

Trends in Income Sharing

In figure 7.1, we show the trends from 1979 to 2003 in the importance of various components of household income for each of our schooling categories. The

FIGURE 7.1 / Components of Total Household Income

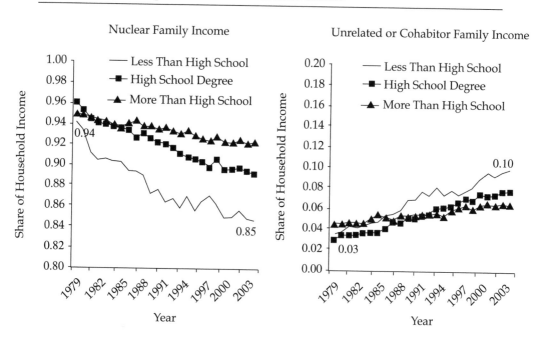

Nuclear Family Income

Unrelated or Cohabitor Family Income

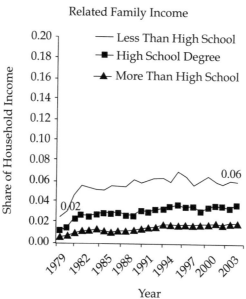

Related Family Income

Source: Authors' calculations based on Current Population Survey, March supplement.

height of each line depicts the sample average of the fraction of total household income coming from each of three underlying components: nuclear family income, related family income, and family income from unrelated or cohabiting members of the household. The first panel demonstrates a clear decline over time in the relative importance of nuclear family income. This decline is particularly dramatic for the less-educated women, falling from approximately 94 percent of total household income in 1979 to 85 percent in 2003. As the next two panels demonstrate, this decline was offset by an increase in the fraction of income coming from unrelated or cohabiting individuals (a seven-percentage-point increase) and a somewhat smaller increase in the fraction of household income from related family members (a four-percentage-point increase).

There are two potential sources for the substantial decline in the fraction of total income attributable to individuals in the nuclear family: changes in the composition of household living arrangements and changes in the importance of nuclear family income *within* living arrangement type. As an example of the first source, suppose that disadvantaged women begin to live with other individuals who are not their spouses. To the extent that these other individuals have income, then these women experience a decline in the amount of total income attributable to the nuclear family. Alternatively, even in households whose composition remains unchanged, the income received by the members of the nuclear family could decline relative to that received by other household members or relative to income coming from individuals outside the home. It is important to note that, despite any underreporting of income or cash transfers due to the wording of the survey question, we have no reason to believe that such misreporting changes over time. Thus, it is likely that the reported trends accurately reflect changes over time in the importance of various income components.

In figure 7.2, we decompose the total change in the fraction of household income coming from the nuclear family into the portion attributable to each of these sources, and we do so separately for each of our three schooling groups.[15] We consider four mutually exclusive and exhaustive living arrangement groups: married women; unmarried women who live with only nuclear family members; unmarried women who live with at least some related family members but not any unrelated individuals; and unmarried women who live with any unrelated individuals, regardless of whether there are other relatives in the household. The top panel presents the results for the years 1979 to 2003. The first bar in each set shows the total decline, and the next two bars illustrate the portion due to a change in living arrangements and the portion due to a change in income shares within living arrangement. The height of each bar depicts the percentage *decline*. For those in the less-than-high-school category, the total change in the fraction of household income attributable to nuclear family income is a reduction of 9.5 percentage points. Of this decline, about three-quarters (7.0 percentage points) is attributable to changes in living arrangements and the remaining one-quarter (2.5 percentage points) is attributable to changes in income fractions within living arrangement types. For the more-schooled groups, the decline in nuclear family income is less (6.9 percentage points for women with a high school diploma and

FIGURE 7.2 / Decomposition of Decline in Nuclear Family Income, 1979 to 2003 and 1994 to 2003

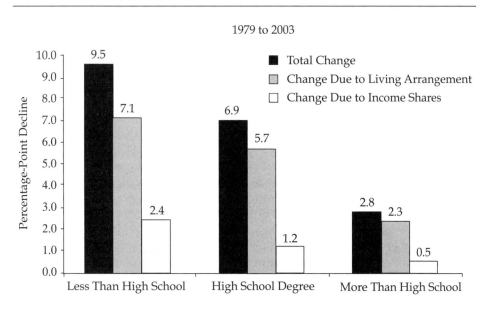

1979 to 2003

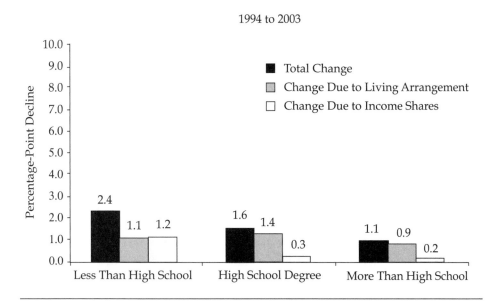

1994 to 2003

Source: Authors' calculations based on Current Population Survey, March supplement.

2.8 percentage points for women with more than a high school diploma), but the relative importance of the two sources of change is similar.

Using this decomposition technique, we can also examine which types of living arrangements rose in prominence and which declined. The details of this decomposition are presented in Haider and McGarry (2005). We find that the 75 percent of the decline in the importance of nuclear family income that was due to changing living arrangements arose primarily from a reduction in the proportion of women living in married households and an increase in the proportion in each of our three unmarried groups. Among these unmarried groups, the increase in women living with unrelated individuals (possibly cohabiting partners) was twice as important as the increases in the two other unmarried groups.

These results demonstrate an important increase in the number of women living with unrelated individuals. One potential explanation for this increase is a movement from marriage to cohabitation, because, as we noted earlier, spouses are defined as part of the same nuclear family while cohabiting partners are not. Such a movement would thus shift income from the nuclear family to an unrelated family member. To examine this possibility we repeat our analysis for the period 1994 to 2003, the years when the CPS distinguished cohabiting partners from other unrelated individuals. These results are presented in the lower panel of figure 7.2. The overall change in the importance of nuclear family income for the least-schooled category over this shorter time period is a decline of 2.4 percent, somewhat smaller than would be expected if the change over the longer time period were distributed evenly. Furthermore, the source of the change is divided about equally between changes in living arrangements and changes in the distribution of income within household types (-1.1 and -1.2 percent, respectively). When we disaggregate these results further to examine the role of specific types of living arrangements (not shown), we find that all of the decline due to changing living arrangements is attributable to increased cohabitation.

We now turn to a detailed examination of the components of nuclear family income. We examine four nuclear family income sources: earnings; means-tested transfers; private financial transfers, including child support and alimony; and other income, such as asset income, retirement benefits, workers' compensation, and unemployment insurance. Figure 7.3 graphs the respective fractions of household income from these sources over our sample period.

For women in the lowest educational category, there was a fairly consistent decline in the importance of earnings throughout the 1980s and early 1990s. However, beginning in 1994, there was a sharp reversal of this trend: the portion of family income coming from earnings increased substantially. This reversal was probably related to the strong economic growth during this period and changes in welfare policy (Schoeni and Blank 2000; Klerman and Haider 2004). The pattern for means-tested public transfers mirrors that for earnings: this source of income increased during the 1980s and early 1990s and then fell dramatically.

Although it is difficult to discern in the figure, there is a notable increase in income coming from private financial transfers, child support, and alimony, par-

FIGURE 7.3 / Components of Nuclear Family Income

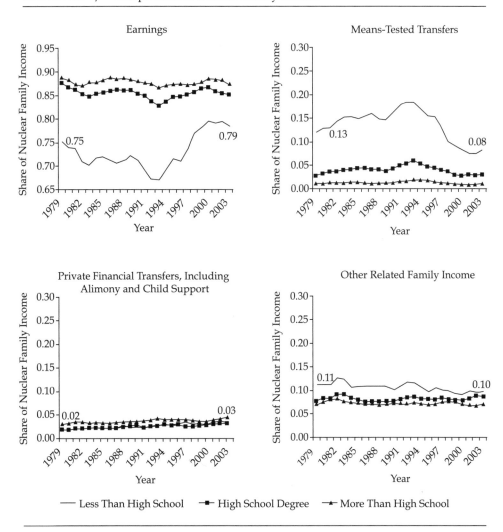

Source: Authors' calculations based on Current Population Survey, March supplement.

ticularly toward the end of this period.[16] The change is small in an absolute sense, increasing from two to three percentage points of family income, but large in percentage terms, increasing by 50 percent. This trend toward private transfers could be a response to the decline in public support, as well as to the increased efforts to establish paternity and collect child support (Cancian and Meyer, this volume). Also of interest is the relatively high and consistent level of related family income, which remained fixed at approximately 10 percent throughout the period for the least-educated women.

TABLE 7.3 / OLS Model for Fraction of Household Income by Source

	Nuclear Family Income Sources				Non-nuclear Family Income Sources	
Regressor	Earnings	Private Transfers	Means-Tested Transfers	Other Income	Related Individuals	Unrelated Individuals
Unemployment rate	−0.522 (0.044)**	0.024 (0.008)**	0.186 (0.022)**	0.320 (0.030)**	0.009 (0.020)	−0.017 (0.027)
Mean of the dependent variable	77.99	0.42	3.22	9.59	2.77	6.01
R-squared	0.200	0.010	0.110	0.040	0.040	0.160

Source: Authors' calculations based on Current Population Survey, March supplement.
Note: The estimates for these tables are based on equation 7.1. The regressions are based on a sample of 736,024 observations.
*p < .05, **p < .01

Assessing Macroeconomic Effects

To assess the relationship between the economy and the relative importance of the various sources of income net of other household characteristics, we turn to a regression analysis. For this exercise, we divide household income into six categories, four of which pertain to the income of the nuclear family (earnings, means-tested public transfers, private transfers, and other income) and two of which pertain to income accruing to non-nuclear members (related family income and the income of unrelated or cohabiting household members). We then construct six different dependent variables, Y_{it}, to be the percentage of total household income coming from each of these sources and regress these dependent variables on a measure of macroeconomic performance and other standard controls.[17] Specifically, we estimate the regression equation

$$Y_{it} = \beta_0 + \beta_1 U_{it} + \beta_2 X_{it} + \alpha_s + \gamma_t + \varepsilon_{it} \qquad (7.1)$$

We use annual state unemployment rates U_{it} as our proxy for the macroeconomic conditions. As other controls X_{it}, we include our three schooling levels, race-ethnicity, age, marital status, whether the woman is enrolled in school, and the presence of children in the nuclear family. State fixed effects α_s are included to control for persistent differences across states in policies and the economic environment. We use year fixed effects γ_t to capture other nationwide changes over time, such as changes in public assistance programs, the Earned Income Tax Credit (EITC), and social norms. We use data from 1987 through 2003 that yields approximately three-quarters of a million observations. In table 7.3, we present only the results for our key coefficient U_{it}; see Haider and McGarry (2005) for complete regression results.

Unsurprisingly, we find that higher unemployment rates are associated with a reduced percentage of household income from nuclear family earnings and an increased fraction from means-tested public transfers. These effects, although statistically strong, are not economically large. An increase in the unemployment rate of one percentage point is associated with a decline of half a percentage point in the fraction of income coming from the labor earnings of nuclear family members. This is equivalent to a decline of just 0.6 percent (0.522 percent/77.99 percent). The increase in the probability of means-tested transfers associated with a one-percentage-point increase in the unemployment rate is even smaller in percentage-point terms (0.2), but because such transfers are less common than labor earnings, the percentage effects are large, corresponding to a 5.8 percent increase in the fraction of income from means-tested public transfers (0.186 percent/3.22 percent). Private transfers also increase significantly with the unemployment rate by a similar 5.7 percent (an increase of 0.024 percentage points). Thus, even though private transfers are relatively rare, they may play an important role in smoothing the consumption of low-income families over the business cycle. However, we find no significant relationship between the unemployment rate and income from either category of non-nuclear family members.

Our regression methodology also allows us to examine yearly trends in the importance of income sources, net of the business cycle and the other factors that are controlled for in the regressions. These trends are simply the coefficients on the dummy variables denoting each year of our sample. In figure 7.4, we plot the values of these coefficients for each of the six regressions. Many of the same patterns we have already identified are apparent. Perhaps most importantly, there is a strong secular increase in earnings from unrelated and cohabiting individuals: this increase reaches almost three percentage points by the end of our sample period. There is also a steady increase in the fraction of household income from related family members. Finally, the decline and then increase in the importance of nuclear family earnings, with an opposite pattern for means-tested transfers, is also apparent in these estimated effects.

Poverty Rates and Income Sharing

The results presented thus far indicate that private cash transfers and transfers through shared living arrangements can be important sources of support for the low-income population. In this section, we address the potential for these transfers to mitigate economic hardship. To do so, we examine the effect of various transfers and income pooling arrangements on poverty rates. The basis for our analysis is the official poverty measure defined by the U.S. Census Bureau, but we explore alternative definitions of income and the relevant economic unit.[18]

In table 7.4, we tabulate the poverty rate for seven different definitions of the appropriate economic unit and income measure. In the first row of the table, the

FIGURE 7.4 / Regression-Adjusted Trends in the Fraction of Household Income, by Source for All Women

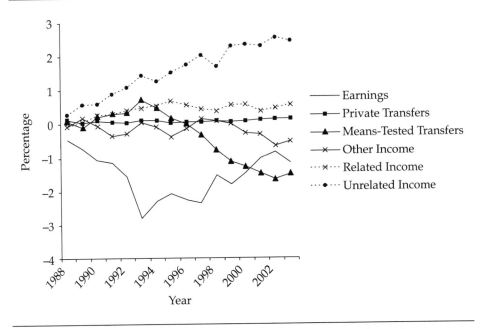

Source: Authors' calculations based on Current Population Survey, March supplement.
Note: The estimates for these figures are based on equation 7.1.

TABLE 7.4 / Poverty Rate by Alternative Definitions of Economic Unit and Income, 2003

Economic Unit and Income Measure	Less Than High School	High School Degree	More Than High School
Nuclear family, excluding public and private transfers	35.6%	16.6%	8.7%
Nuclear family, excluding private transfers	33.9	15.7	8.4
Nuclear family	33.8	15.6	7.8
Nuclear and related family (official rate)	31.4	14.1	7.1
Nuclear and cohabitor family	31.0	13.8	7.0
Nuclear family, related family, and cohabitor family	28.6	12.4	6.3
Entire household	26.4	11.3	5.4

Source: Authors' calculations based on Current Population Survey, March supplement.

economic unit is defined as the nuclear family and income as total nuclear family income, exclusive of all means-tested transfers and all private cash transfers. For the lowest-schooled in our sample, the poverty rate based on this definition is 35.6 percent. The next row adds public transfers to the definition of income but continues to exclude private cash transfers. Here the poverty rate for the least-educated group falls to 33.9 percent. Adding private transfers (row 3) has little effect on poverty: the rate is reduced to 33.8 percent. In the next row, we expand the economic unit to include all related family members in the household and increase income and the needs standard accordingly. This poverty measure, which corresponds to the official census definition, is 31.4 percent. This decline in the poverty rate indicates that related persons bring more than enough income into the household to cover their needs (as defined by the increment in the poverty threshold).

In row 5, we define the economic unit as the nuclear family with just cohabiting partners. It might be that such an economic unit better corresponds to actual income pooling arrangements than does the official poverty measure. Although the poverty rate falls substantially compared to the poverty rate based on the nuclear family alone, it is quite similar to that calculated for the related family in row 4 (the official poverty measure). When we expand the economic unit to include both related family members and cohabiting partners (row 6), the poverty rate declines even further, to 28.6 percent. The final row (row 7) incorporates all persons in the household, and the poverty rate drops to 26.4 percent for the least-schooled and 5.9 percent for those with the most schooling. Thus, the "choice" to live with others *may* improve economic well-being substantially. In total, the poverty rate declines by over 20 percent when the relevant unit is expanded from the nuclear family with all public and private transfers included in income (row 3) to the extended household.

We note, however, that these broader definitions assume that household income is shared in the same way among members of the economic unit, regardless of their relationships. Such an assumption is almost certainly not valid.

CONCLUSIONS

There are many dimensions in which individuals can adjust their behavior in response to economic change. They may increase or decrease their employment levels, retrain for new jobs, alter their reliance on public assistance programs, and give or receive private support from family and friends. Despite the central role played by the family in current policy discussions, surprisingly little research has examined the role of the family in protecting against negative economic shocks. To begin to fill this void, we have provided a synthesis of several related literatures on private transfers and then presented new empirical evidence on the importance of these transfers and how they vary with the economic and policy environment.

The theoretical literature contains several well-developed models of resource sharing between and within households that provide important insights into possible motives. Moreover, the empirical literature demonstrates clearly that individuals make substantial transfers and employ numerous modes of resource sharing. Recent work suggests that the probability and amount of cash transfers depend on the resources of both the potential donors and recipients and on the availability of public assistance programs. However, few studies have examined multiple modes of assistance simultaneously, how transfers vary over time, or how transfers respond to the economic environment more generally. Our empirical work begins to fill these gaps.

We find that transfers provide an important source of support for low-income individuals and that coresidency is particularly important. In addition, our results indicate that, while transfers respond significantly to macroeconomic conditions, there has also been a steady increase in shared living arrangements that is unexplained by macroeconomic and demographic changes. We hypothesize that these changes may be due to changes in attitudes and social norms.

As in past studies, our investigation of cash transfers is limited by the data. Interhousehold cash transfers appear to be poorly measured in the CPS, and it is thus impossible to assess accurately their true significance. However, we do find that, when such transfers are reported, the amounts are large relative to the nontransfer incomes of the recipients. More recent surveys, such as the Health and Retirement Study, employ more detailed questions on transfers than have been asked in the past and will provide the opportunity to reexamine this issue in the future. We note also that the phenomenon of income sharing within households is poorly understood. Although economists have developed elegant household bargaining models that predict that the income of household members is unlikely to be pooled completely, an understanding of exactly how income is shared awaits additional empirical analyses. Importantly, our results suggest that the *potential* for improvement in financial status from income pooling is large.

Finally, one of the more important avenues for additional research is an examination of the choice of living arrangements. Decisions about coresidence depend on the living arrangement options available to an individual, the availability of other forms of public and private support, household production processes, and the relative value of privacy. Because such decisionmaking can be complicated, a rigorous investigation of coresidency requires sophisticated modeling and extremely detailed data. Although difficult, an understanding of the decision to live with others and the transfers embedded in such arrangements is crucial for an understanding of the resources available to the low-income population.

Despite the limitations of our study, our results suggest at least two important lessons for public policy. First, when interpreting the effects of economic or policy changes, the potential for changes in private support must be considered. For example, studies that find only small effects of welfare reform on income may miss the importance of income provided by family and friends and thus the burdens imposed on nonwelfare recipients. Second, poverty measurement and the functioning of public assistance programs depend critically on the definition of the economic unit. Any definition makes implicit assumptions about how resources are shared among family and household members, yet there is relatively little empirical evidence to justify the choice of one definition over another. This lack of evidence again highlights the importance of additional research on private transfers and the responsiveness of these transfers to changes in both public assistance programs and the economy.

NOTES

1. We are grateful for useful advice from Rebecca Blank, Sheldon Danziger, Jonathan Gruber, Robert Schoeni, and participants at the "Working and Poor" project conferences in Ann Arbor, Michigan, and Washington, D.C. Both authors gratefully acknowledge financial support—Haider from the National Institute for Child Health and Development (R03 HD42084–01) and McGarry from the National Institute on Aging (R29 AG14110–05).

2. Although assistance from charitable institutions may be an important source of support for some low-income families, we do not address it here.

3. For example, the fixed cost of telephone service is the same regardless of how many individuals share an apartment.

4. Although we are equally interested in sharing among related and unrelated persons and examine both in our empirical analysis, we follow the existing literature and couch our conceptual discussion in terms of sharing among extended family members.

5. See Cox (1987) for a clear description of these alternative models of altruism and exchange and a formal test of the validity of the altruism model.

6. This result is consistent with an altruistic model wherein the donor is seeking to increase the consumption of a less well-off recipient but is also consistent with an exchange regime in which the transfer represents payment for a service, behavior, or previous assistance provided by the recipient.

7. The notion of families or communities providing insurance against consumption shortfalls has been emphasized in the context of developing countries, where formal insurance markets are less prevalent. Robert Townsend (1995) provides a good discussion of some of the relevant literature.

8. Although we do not attempt to quantify them here, the returns to scale can be considerable. For example, in determining the appropriate poverty thresholds, the U.S. Census Bureau assumes that two individuals need only 28 percent more income than a single individual to obtain the same standard of living. See Citro and Michael (1995) for a detailed discussion of the returns to scale in the poverty measure. These financial gains may be offset, at least in part, by the utility loss associated with less privacy. Magnuson and Smeeding (2005, 19), in a study of low-income new mothers, conclude, "In this case and others we encountered, the decision to live with relatives was determined more [by] necessity than by choice."

9. States have differed in their treatment of nonparental income (Hutchens, Jakubson, and Schwartz 1989). In terms of benefit calculation, the Supreme Court decision barred the assumption that all income of the nonparent adult benefited the child.

However, some states inquired specifically about direct cash transfers to the child and included this amount in the benefit calculation.

10. Theoretically, the specific relationship depends on the underlying motive for transfers. The predictions are the most clearly defined when altruism is the primary motivation. In this case, as the income of a recipient rises, the marginal utility of a dollar transferred to her is reduced and the marginal utilities of the donor and recipient (appropriately weighted) are equalized with fewer transfers. With an exchange motivation, the exact relationship depends on the relative elasticities for the supply and demand of the exchanged goods.

11. Information about cohabiting partners is collected from 1994 through the end of our sample period. Although nuclear family relationships are clearly delineated for everyone in the CPS, non-nuclear relatives and cohabiting partners are identified only for the household "reference person," who is defined as the person who "owns or rents" the unit (Current Population Survey 2002).

12. In 1988 the Panel Study of Income Dynamics (PSID) included a question about private transfers that is fairly similar to the CPS question and an alternatively worded question that asked about transfers more fully. McGarry and Schoeni (1995) show that the alternative wording increased the prevalence of reported transfers from 4.9 to 20 percent for the same respondents. This result suggests that interhousehold transfers in the CPS may be substantially more common than our data indicate.

13. The patterns we report here for women are fairly similar to those observed for men. Owing to space constraints, we do not report the results for men.

14. We make two adjustments to these income data. First, we recode negative earnings and negative income to be zero, viewing a loss in these dimensions as a reduction in wealth. Second, we drop from the analysis all households that report zero total income. The results are not sensitive to these decisions.

15. The decomposition is implemented as follows. Let θ_t be the population ratio of nuclear family income to household income at time t. Let θ_t^j be the equivalent ratio for each subgroup j at time t, and let π_t^j be the proportion of the population in each subgroup. For the simple case with just two subgroups, a and b, θ_t can be written as a weighted average of the income ratio for each subgroup, $\theta_t = \pi_t^a \theta_t^a + \pi_t^b \theta_t^b$. Then the change in the relative importance of nuclear family income between time t and s can be expressed as:

$$\theta_t - \theta_s = (\pi_t^a + \pi_s^a)\theta_s^a + (\pi_t^b - \pi_s^b)\theta_s^b + (\theta_t^a - \theta_s^a)\pi_t^a + (\theta_t^b - \theta_s^b)\pi_t^b$$

where the first two terms reflect the effect of shifts in the proportion of the population in groups a and b, holding relative income constant at the initial period s level, and where the second two terms reflect the change due to changes in the relative importance of nuclear family income, holding the proportion of the population in each group constant at the final period t level.

16. We combine these sources because they were not separately identified until 1987.

17. Because the dependent variables sum to 100 across income sources for each individual, the coefficients on any particular regressor must sum to zero across income sources. The individual coefficients should be interpreted as the relative cyclicality of each of the underlying sources.

18. The census definition of poverty is based on a comparison of the income of the economic unit (defined as all related members of a household) to an income threshold specific to the size of the unit. This measure provides a convenient metric for judging well-being that is widely cited and easily calculated for economic units of various sizes and different income measures. However, this measure is not without its critics. See Citro and Michael (1995) for a discussion of its weakness and some suggested modifications.

REFERENCES

Altonji, Joseph, Fumio Hayashi, and Laurence Kotlikoff. 1997. "Parental Altruism and Inter Vivos Transfers: Theory and Evidence." *Journal of Political Economy* 105(6): 1121–66.

——. 2000. "The Effects of Earnings and Wealth on Time and Money Transfers Between Parents and Children." In *Sharing the Wealth: Demographic Change and Economic Transfers Between Generations,* edited by Andrew Masson and Georges Tapinos. Oxford: Oxford University Press.

Autor, David H., Lawrence F. Katz, and Melissa S. Kearney. 2004. "Trends in U.S. Wage Inequality: Reassessing the Revisionists." Working paper 11627. Cambridge, Mass.: National Bureau of Economic Research.

Barro, Robert. 1974. "Are Government Bonds Net Wealth?" *Journal of Political Economy* 82(6): 1095–1117.

Becker, Gary. 1974. "A Theory of Social Interactions." *Journal of Political Economy* 82(6): 1063–93.

Bernheim, B. Douglas, Andrei Shleifer, and Lawrence Summers. 1985. "The Strategic Bequest Motive." *Journal of Political Economy* 93(6): 1045–76.

Bitler, Marianne P., Jonah Gelbach, and Hilary Hoynes. 2004. "Welfare Reform and Children's Living Arrangements." Working paper WR-111. Santa Monica, Calif.: RAND Corporation.

Blank, Rebecca. 2002. "Evaluating Welfare Reform in the United States." *Journal of Economic Literature* 40(4): 1105–66.

Blank, Rebecca, and Robert Schoeni. 2003. "Changes in the Distribution of Children's Family Income over the 1990s." *American Economic Review: Papers and Proceedings* 93(2): 304–8.

Blau, David, and Janet Currie. 2004. "Preschool, Day Care, and Afterschool Care: Who's Minding the Kids?" Working paper 10670. Cambridge, Mass.: National Bureau of Economic Research.

Citro, Constance F., and Robert T. Michael. 1995. *Measuring Poverty: A New Approach.* Washington, D.C.: National Research Council and National Academy Press.

Costa, Dora. 1999. "A Home of Her Own." *Journal of Public Economics* 72(1): 39–59.

Couch, Kenneth, Mary Daly, and Douglas Wolf. 1999. "Time? Money? Both? The Allocation of Resources to Older Parents." *Demography* 36(2): 219–32.

Cox, Donald. 1987. "Motives for Private Income Transfers." *Journal of Political Economy* 95(3): 508–46.

————. 1990. "Intergenerational Transfers and Liquidity Constraints." *Quarterly Journal of Economics* 105(1): 187–217.

Cox, Donald, and George Jakubson. 1995. "The Connection Between Public Transfers and Private Interfamily Transfers." *Journal of Public Economics* 57(1): 129–67.

Cox, Donald, and Tullio Jappelli. 1990. "Credit Rationing and Private Transfers: Evidence from Survey Data." *Review of Economics and Statistics* 72(3): 445–54.

Current Population Survey. 2002. "Current Population Survey: Design and Methodology." Technical paper 63RV. Washington: U.S. Department of Labor, Bureau of Labor Statistics.

Danziger, Sheldon, Colleen Heflin, Mary Corcoran, Elizabeth Oltmans, and Hui-Chen Wang. 2002. "Does It Pay to Move from Welfare to Work?" *Journal of Policy Analysis and Management* 21(Fall): 671–92.

DeLeire, Thomas, and Ariel Kalil. 2005. "How Do Cohabiting Couples with Children Spend Their Money?" *Journal of Marriage and Family* 67: 285–94.

Dynarski, Susan, and Jonathan Gruber. 1997. "Can Families Smooth Variable Earnings?" *Brookings Papers on Economic Activity* 1997(1): 229–303.

Edin, Kathryn, and Laura Lein. 1997. *Making Ends Meet.* New York: Russell Sage Foundation.

Engelhardt, Gary, Jonathan Gruber, and Cynthia Perry. 2002. "Social Security and Elderly Living Arrangements." Working paper 8911. Cambridge, Mass. : National Bureau of Economic Research.

Epler, Elizabeth. 1954. "Old-Age Assistance: Plan Provisions on Children's Responsibility for Parents." *Social Security Bulletin* (April): 3–12.

Gale, William, and John Karl Scholz. 1994. "Intergenerational Transfers and the Accumulation of Wealth." *Journal of Economic Perspectives* 8(4): 145–60.

Gruber, Jonathan. 1997. "The Consumption Smoothing Benefits of Unemployment Insurance." *American Economic Review* 87(1): 192–205.

Haider, Steven J., Alison Jacknowitz, and Robert F. Schoeni. 2003. "Food Stamps and the Elderly: Why Is Participation So Low?" *Journal of Human Resources* 38(S): 1080–1111.

Haider, Steven J., and Kathleen McGarry. 2005. "Recent Trends in Resource Sharing Among the Poor." Working paper 11612. Cambridge, Mass.: National Bureau of Economic Research.

Hutchens, Robert, George Jakubson, and Saul Schwartz. 1989. "AFDC and the Formation of Subfamilies." *Journal of Human Resources* 24(4): 599–628.

Klerman, Jacob, and Steven J. Haider. 2004. "A Stock-Flow Analysis of the Welfare Caseload." *Journal of Human Resources* 39(4): 865–86.

Korbin, Frances. 1976. "The Fall in Household Size and the Rise of the Primary Individual." *Demography* 13: 127–38.

Kotlikoff, Laurence, and Avia Spivak. 1981. "The Family as an Incomplete Annuities Market." *Journal of Political Economy* 89(2): 372–91.

Lampman, Robert, and Timothy Smeeding. 1983. "Interfamily Transfers as Alternatives to Government Transfers to Persons." *Review of Income and Wealth* 29 (1): 45–66.

Light, Audrey, and Kathleen McGarry. 2004. "Why Parents Play Favorites: Explanations for Unequal Bequests." *American Economic Review* 39(4): 624–48.

Lundberg, Shelly, Robert Pollak, and Terence Wales. 1997. "Do Husbands and Wives Pool

Their Resources? Evidence from the United Kingdom Child Benefit." *Journal of Human Resources* 32(3): 463–80.

Magnuson, Katherine, and Timothy Smeeding. 2005. "Earnings, Transfers, and Living Arrangements in Low-Income Families: Who Pays the Bills?" Paper presented to the National Poverty Center conference "Mixed Methods Research on Economic Conditions, Public Policy, and Family and Child Well-being." Ann Arbor, Mich. (June 22–28, 2005).

McGarry, Kathleen, and Robert Schoeni. 1995. "Transfer Behavior in the Health and Retirement Study: Measurement and the Redistribution of Resources Within the Family." *Journal of Human Resources* 30(S): 184–226.

———. 1997."Transfer Behavior Within the Family: Results from the Asset and Health Dynamics Study." *Journals of Gerontology* 52B: 82–92.

———. 2000. "Social Security, Economic Growth, and the Rise of Independence of Elderly Widows in the 20th Century." *Demography* 37(2): 221–36.

MetLife Mature Market Institute. 2004. *Market Survey of Nursing Home and Home Health Care Costs*. Westport, Conn. : MetLife Mature Market Institute.

Meyer, Bruce, and Dan Rosenbaum. 2001. "Welfare, the Earned Income Tax Credit, and the Labor Supply of Single Mothers." *Quarterly Journal of Economics* 116(3): 1063–1114.

Michael, Robert, Victor Fuchs, and Sharon Scott. 1980. "Changes in the Propensity to Live Alone: 1950–1976." *Demography* 17(1): 39–53.

Moffitt, Robert, Robert Reville, and Anne Winkler. 1998. "Beyond Single Mothers: Cohabitation and Marriage in the AFDC Program." *Demography* 35(3): 259–78.

Moffitt, Robert, and Katie Winder. 2005. "Does It Pay to Move from Welfare to Work? A Comment on Danziger, Heflin, Corcoran, Oltmans, and Wang." *Journal of Policy Analysis and Management* 24(2): 399–409.

Pampel, Fred. 1983. "Changes in the Propensity to Live Alone: Evidence from Consecutive Cross-sectional Surveys, 1960–1976." *Demography* 20(4): 433–48.

Patterson, James T. 2000. *America's Struggle Against Poverty in the Twentieth Century*. Cambridge, Mass.: Harvard University Press.

Rosenzweig, Mark, and Kenneth Wolpin. 1993. "Intergenerational Support and the Life-Cycle Incomes of Young Men and Their Parents: Human Capital Investments, Coresidence, and Intergenerational Financial Transfers." *Journal of Labor Economics* 11(1): 84–112.

———. 1994. "Parental and Public Transfers to Young Women and Their Children." *American Economic Review* 84(5): 1195–1212.

Rowe, Gretchen, and Victoria Russell. 2004. "The Welfare Rules Databook: State Policies as of July 2002." Discussion paper 04–06. Washington, D.C.: Urban Institute.

Schoeni, Robert. 1997. "Does Aid to Families with Dependent Children Displace Familial Assistance?" Unpublished paper. Ann Arbor: University of Michigan.

———. 2002. "Does Unemployment Insurance Displace Familial Assistance?" *Public Choice* 110(1–2): 99–119.

Schoeni, Robert, and Rebecca Blank. 2000. "What Has Welfare Reform Accomplished? Impacts on Welfare Participation, Employment, Income, Poverty, and Family Structure." Unpublished paper. Ann Arbor: University of Michigan.

Schwartz, Saul, Sheldon Danziger, and Eugene Smolensky. 1984. "The Choice of Living Arrangements Among the Aged." In *Retirement and Economic Behavior*, edited by Henry Aaron and Gary Burtless. Washington, D.C.: Brookings Institution.

Stack, Carol. 1974. *All Our Kin: Strategies for Survival in a Black Community*. New York: Harper & Row.

Thomas, Duncan. 1990. "Intrahousehold Resource Allocation: An Inferential Approach." *Journal of Human Resources* 25(4): 635–64.

Townsend, Robert. 1995. "Consumption Insurance: An Evaluation of Risk-Bearing Systems in Low-Income Economies." *Journal of Economic Perspectives* 9(3): 83–102.

U.S. Department of Health and Human Services. 1998. *Informal Caregiving: Compassion in Action*. Washington: U.S. Department of Health and Human Services, Office of the Assistant Secretary for Planning and Evaluation.

Whittington, Leslie, and Elizabeth Peters. 1996. "Economic Incentives for Financial and Residential Independence." *Demography* 33(1): 82–97.

Chapter 8

Economic Conditions and Children's Living Arrangements

Rebecca A. London and Robert W. Fairlie

Household and family living arrangements have become increasingly visible in public policy discussions, especially with the passage of the landmark Personal Responsibility and Work Opportunity Reconciliation Act of 1996 (PRWORA).[1] The legislation—a response to a trend of rising rates of childbirth outside of marriage—emphasizes the reinforcement of marriage as the preferred arrangement for families with children. PRWORA also attempts to influence children's living arrangements in another way—by mandating multigenerational households for teen parents who have not completed high school. Although the population of teen parents receiving welfare is small, the focus on their living arrangements signals policymakers' interest in shaping living arrangements beyond marriage.

The law's primary focus on marriage was partly motivated by the disconcerting finding that children who grow up with a single parent fare worse later in life than those growing up with married parents (McLanahan and Sandefur 1994). Even after controlling for income and other intervening factors, children living with single parents have worse educational and family formation outcomes than those living with two parents or with stepparents. Children of divorced parents similarly fare worse than those in intact families on these and other measures (Amato 2000; Seltzer 1994).

Demographic shifts in living arrangements have led to fewer children living with married parents over time. For instance, between 1985 and 2000, children became less likely to live with married parents and more likely to live instead with a single mother, particularly one who cohabited with an unmarried partner (who might or might not be the child's biological father) (Dupree and Primus 2001). These trends were especially strong for poor children. A similar trend occurred for adult living arrangements, which showed increases in cohabitation over this same time period (Bumpass and Lu 2000; London 1998).

The shifts in societal and personal beliefs regarding marriage, divorce, and cohabitation that have occurred since the 1960s are a prime reason for demographic trends away from marriage. Less traditional views have taken root, and as a result the stigma associated with divorce and cohabitation has decreased over time. In particular, sexual intimacy, childbearing, and child rearing have become increasingly acceptable outside of marriage (Thornton and Young-DeMarco 2001).

Another documented reason for shifts in family living arrangements is the imposition of welfare waiver programs in the 1990s, culminating in 1996 with PRWORA (Acs and Nelson 2004; Bitler, Gelbach, and Hoynes 2006; Schoeni and Blank 2000). In general, findings from these studies indicate that welfare reforms have had results consistent with the goal of increasing two-parent or married families, at least for some subgroups. The effects are mostly small, owing in part to the short time period in which these reforms were implemented.

Fluctuations in the economy represent a third and unexplored potential cause of movements in the distribution of living arrangements over time. There are several reasons to expect economic conditions to affect the distribution of living arrangements. First, the financial pressure placed on families by economic recessions might lead to doubling up through marriage, cohabitation, or living with other unrelated or related adults or families. At the same time, there may be an offsetting effect: job loss may create financial hardship, resulting in increased rates of marital dissolution. Assuming that parents tend to prefer living independently over living in shared nonmarital arrangements, one would expect economic expansions to lead to more independent arrangements. Finally, economic conditions may affect the attractiveness of potential partners. Previous research finds evidence that men's economic status affects union formation for both African Americans and whites (for a review, see Fein et al. 2003).

In this chapter, we explore the role that economic conditions play in determining the distribution of children's living arrangements. We use data from the 1979 to 2004 annual demographic files of the Current Population Survey (CPS) and the 1986 to 2001 panels of the Survey of Income and Program Participation (SIPP). The long time period and large sample sizes of the CPS allow us to examine the relationship between economic conditions and living arrangements over the past twenty-five years and for several subgroups of children. The SIPP's longitudinal panels allow us to examine the effects of economic conditions on transitions into and out of living arrangements. This is critical to the analysis because economic conditions may have larger or at least different effects on flows into and out of living arrangements compared to the stock of living arrangements.

PREVIOUS STUDIES

The literature on family living arrangements has focused on two broad questions. First, what are the consequences for children of living in different or changing household structures? And second, what demographic trends and policy changes have affected the distribution of living arrangements over time? We focus on the second question in the empirical analysis, but briefly review the literatures on both questions to provide context and motivation.

A large body of research provides evidence that the composition of children's households affects their outcomes later in life and that childhood living arrangements can thus provide important information about young adult and adult economic and family circumstances. In their 1994 book, Sara McLanahan and Gary Sandefur demonstrate that children who grow up with a single parent fare worse than their counterparts who grow up with married parents. In particular, children of single parents have lower educational achievement, higher rates of teen birth (women), and higher rates of adult idleness (men). Furthermore, children of single or divorced parents are more likely than those in married-parent families to leave home at an early age (Cherlin, Kiernan, and Chase-Lansdale 1995); to have intercourse at an earlier age (Kiernan and Hobcraft 1997); to have a nonmarital teen birth (Cherlin, Kiernan, and Chase-Lansdale 1995); to form adult unions with lower rates of success (Teachman 2004); and to have other behavioral problems and health vulnerabilities (Dawson 1991).

Single-parent families are complex, and not all such living arrangements are associated with similarly negative outcomes for children. For instance, Thomas DeLeire and Ariel Kalil (2002) show that children who live in multigenerational families with a single parent and at least one grandparent have developmental outcomes that are on par with those for children from married-couple families. With young parents in particular, multigenerational families can provide positive parenting support (Chase-Lansdale, Brooks-Gunn, and Zamsky 1994). Children living in a stepfamily with a divorced parent who has remarried tend to fare at least as bad as those with an unmarried single parent (McLanahan and Sandefur 1994). Over the past two decades children have become increasingly likely to live with a parent and an unmarried cohabitor. Cohabitation is a less stable arrangement than marriage, and as a result children living in cohabiting families are more likely to experience family instability (Bumpass and Lu 2000), which in itself can be damaging to their outcomes.

Children in single-parent families and stepfamilies are nearly twice as likely to experience a childhood move as children with married parents (Astone and McLanahan 1994). This mobility is a key contributor to the lower educational attainment for children in non-intact families (Astone and McLanahan 1994; Crowder and Teachman 2004). Higher rates of transition in childhood living arrangement are also associated with increased risk of early premarital intercourse (Albrecht and Teachman 2003). Children who move may be adversely affected because they are likely to have weaker connections to their community, including their peers and neighbors, and therefore less social capital than children who do not move (McLanahan and Sandefur 1994).

In short, previous research offers substantial evidence that children's living arrangements are important determinants of future outcomes. These findings provide a motivation for the second strand of literature, which focuses on identifying the determinants of living arrangements. Studies have examined a number of determinants but generally focus on the role of welfare benefits and reforms on family or child living arrangements. The most recent papers examine the effects on living arrangements of the 1990s welfare waivers and the implementation in the late 1990s of Temporary Assistance for Needy Families (TANF). These studies rely on state differences in the timing and type of pre-PRWORA welfare waivers and TANF policies to identify their effects. For instance, Marianne Bitler, Jonah Gelbach, and Hilary Hoynes (2006) find that welfare reforms over the 1990s shifted the distribution of living arrangements for specific subgroups, sometimes in unexpected ways. African American children living in households where the head has no more than a high school diploma are more likely to live without their parents as a result of reforms. Latino children are more likely to live with married parents. Corroborating these findings, Peter Brandon and Gene Fischer (2001) find that children living in states with lower welfare benefits have higher rates of separation from their parents.

Two types of reforms are primarily responsible for the observed shifts in living arrangement distributions: increased child support enforcement (Acs and Nelson 2004; Jagannathan 2004) and family caps (Acs and Nelson 2004).[2] Both serve to increase the percentage of children living with two parents (married or not). Robert Schoeni and Rebecca Blank (2000) also find that pre-PRWORA waivers led to small increases in marriage, with commensurately small decreases in female headship, particularly among lesser-educated women. In contrast, John Fitzgerald and David Ribar (2004) find little evidence that waivers affected female headship decisions. Other recent work shows that welfare waivers and TANF have slowed entry into marriage but also reduced divorce (Bitler et al. 2004).

Random assignment evaluations of welfare waivers have also examined the effects of reforms on marriage, with mixed and modest results (Fein et al. 2002). Reanalysis of four states' experimental data shows some evidence that where economic impacts of welfare reforms were greatest, demographic effects—including marriage, cohabitation, and living with others—were also larger (Fein, London, and Mauldon 2005).

The majority of these studies have controlled for economic conditions in their analyses, but they typically cover just the time period in which welfare waivers and TANF were implemented. This period may not be long enough to understand how changes in the business cycle affect child living arrangements. There has been some recent attention to the effects of the economy on family living arrangements, and evidence suggests that the economy may indeed play a role in living arrangement decisionmaking. Daniel Lichter, Diane McLaughlin, and David Ribar (2002) find that the retreat from marriage was not counteracted by the economic expansion of the 1990s, although the expansion did serve to slow the decline that might otherwise have occurred. Rebecca London (2000a) and Anne Winkler (1992) demonstrate that housing costs are important factors in single parents' living arrangement decisions at a point in time. Studies also indicate that state welfare benefit levels affect single parents' living arrangements (Folk 1996; London 2000a; Winkler 1992).

Although the literature on children's living arrangements has yet to establish a link between economic conditions and household composition for children, there is an established literature that documents the effects of financial stress on marriage outcomes. Rand Conger and his colleagues (1990) demonstrate that economic pressure affects how married couples interact with each other, and in particular that it leads to more hostile interactions. These hostilities can result in divorce, and a number of studies have demonstrated this effect. In a review of this literature, Lynn White and Stacy Rogers (2000) find consistent evidence that, among married couples, a spell of unemployment for the husband doubles the rate of divorce. Income loss is particularly troubling for African American families, whose divorce response to this loss is two to three times larger than whites' (Yeung and Hofferth 1998). There is mixed evidence on the effects of wives' unemployment on marital stability (White and Rogers 2000). Some studies indicate that higher earnings among women lead to stability in the marriage, but others find that higher wages and rates of employment lead to an increased probability of divorce. Generally, the literature finds that economic factors play a larger role in the marital instability of African Americans than that of whites.

DATA AND LIVING ARRANGEMENT DEFINITIONS

We use data from two sources in this chapter: the 1979 to 2004 annual demographic files of the Current Population Survey and the 1986 to 2001 panels of the Survey of Income and Program Participation. The SIPP data cover most years between 1986 and 2002, but even with overlapping panels, they omit 1989, 1995, and 1999 to 2000. Both sources of data span a long time frame, offering information about periods of low and high unemployment. Using the CPS, we examine the relationship between economic conditions and the distribution of children's living arrangements over a twenty-five-year period. We also explore the relationship using a more detailed set of living arrangements over the past fifteen years. Using panel data from the SIPP, we examine the effects of economic conditions on annual changes in children's living arrangement status over the past two decades.[3] We discuss each dataset and our living arrangement definitions in more detail in the next sections.

The Current Population Survey

The annual demographic file of the CPS is collected in March by the U.S. Bureau of the Census and the Bureau of Labor Statistics. It is representative of the entire U.S. population and contains responses for more than 130,000 people. The CPS collects information on every member of the household and catalogs the relationship of each of the members to the household head. By examining relationship codes and the characteristics of the household members, we are able to create a set of detailed living arrangements that capture whether children live with married parents or an unmarried parent and whether other adults are present in the household. Using this information for the entire 1979 to 2004 period, we examine three categories of living arrangements:

- Children living with married parents and no other adults in the household[4]
- Children living with an unmarried parent and no other adults in the household
- Children living in all other arrangements, including without any parents

Beginning in 1989, the CPS provides a more detailed set of household relationship codes that allow us to expand our living arrangement categories as follows:

- Children living with married parents and no other adults in the household
- Children living with an unmarried parent and no other adults in the household
- Children living with an unmarried parent and the parent's cohabitor, who may also be the child's parent or may have his or her own children in the household
- Children living with married or unmarried parents and one or more grandparents
- Children living with married or unmarried parents and other related or unrelated adults (who are not cohabitors or grandparents)
- Children living in households that do not contain a parent

It is important to note that prior to 1996 the CPS did not explicitly identify cohabitors. We rely on the methodology used in London (1998) to identify potential cohabitors. Specifically, people classified as cohabiting must be of the opposite sex, be unrelated and unmarried, and be within ten years of age of each other. The introduction of explicit codes for cohabitors in 1995 allows us to examine the efficacy of these assumptions. We find some overcounting of cohabitors in earlier years, but a smooth upward trend in the rate of children living with cohabitors that is consistent with the cohabitation trends identified in the literature during this time period. We include code-change dummy variables as appropriate in our regression specifications to capture the 1995 change. In addition, the 1994 redesign of the CPS changed many of the basic questions. We include a code-change dummy for that year as well.

We limit our sample to children who are not household heads, spouses, or cohabitors. We further limit our analysis to children age three to fifteen, for several reasons. First, it is possible that childbearing is associated with changes in economic conditions, and we want to ensure that we do not confound the effects of economic conditions on childbearing and living arrangements. Limiting the analysis to children over age two should reduce this problem. We limit the analysis to children under age sixteen because we do not want to include teen parents in our sample of children. Their living arrangement decisions are likely to be based on criteria that do not apply to the remainder of the sample. The children of teen parents are included in the sample. In addition, young people over age fifteen may decide to leave home for a variety of reasons that are related to their own personal preferences and hence not applicable to other children (for a review of the home-leaving literature, see Goldscheider 1997). We find similar results to those reported here when we include all children age zero to seventeen.

The Survey of Income and Program Participation

The SIPP was created jointly by the U.S. Department of Health and Human Services and the Bureau of the Census to be a major source of information on demographic and economic conditions in the United States. It is a longitudinal survey that interviews respondents every four months for a period of twenty-four to forty-eight months for the panels we use. During each interview, respondents are asked to recall their activities over the prior four months, resulting in monthly data. The earliest SIPP panel began in 1984, but we exclude the 1984 and 1985 panels because the relationship-to-head codes we use to create living arrangements are less detailed then than in the later years. We also exclude the 1989 panel because it does not cover a full year. With the 1986 to 2001 SIPP panels, we are able to create a more detailed set of living arrangement codes equivalent to the set of living arrangements defined in the CPS.

The SIPP follows original adult household members throughout each panel, even if they leave the household. Original child household members are followed only if they continue to live with an original sample adult. For example, if a child moves from a parent's household to a grandparent's household, the child is not reinterviewed until he or she returns to the parent's household. As a result, we cannot follow moves from parental to nonparental homes. We therefore omit children who live without their parents at any point in the panel months we examine. We instead concentrate on the vast majority of children who continue to live with at least one parent even when the composition of others in the household changes.

Starting in the 1996 panel, unmarried cohabitors are coded separately from other unrelated roommates, allowing a more precise identification of cohabiting parents. In the earlier panels, we considered anyone who was an unrelated roommate or cohabitor of the opposite sex and appropriate age group a cohabitor. Where appropriate, we include a code-change dummy to account for this change.

We concentrate on one-year transitions in living arrangements—for example, comparing each child's living arrangement in their wave 1–month 4 interview to their living arrangement in their wave 4–month 4 interview. Similarly, we compare living arrangements from the wave 4–month 4 interview to those in the wave 7–month 4 interview. In the 1996 panel, which has the longest time frame, we also compare their wave 7–month 4 interview living arrangements to their wave 10–month 4 living arrangements. We use the interview in month 4 of each wave to minimize recall bias. As with the CPS, we limit our child respondents to those who were between the ages of three and fifteen at the time of their first interview and are not household heads, spouses, or cohabitors. We also exclude children who live in states that are not uniquely identified by the SIPP.[5]

Measures of Economic Conditions and Welfare

We use state-level unemployment rates to measure the economic conditions in a particular year. In the CPS, we use the annual unemployment rate corresponding to the year prior to the March interview. In the SIPP, we use the seasonally adjusted monthly rate that corresponds to the month in question. We also create dummy variables indicating the presence of a welfare waiver in the state during the period of the interview and whether or not TANF had been implemented in the state.[6] These variables turn on and off during the period between 1992 and 1998; before 1992, there were no waivers, and after 1998 all states had implemented TANF. We also include the maximum state welfare benefit available to a family of three in each year, adjusted to 2004 dollars.

THE EMPIRICAL MODEL

To explore the effects of economic conditions on children's living arrangements we estimate several models of living arrangements. The probability of living in a particular arrangement can be expressed as:

$$L_{ist} = \beta X_{ist} + \delta U_{st} + \chi S_{st} + \gamma T_t + \alpha_s + \varepsilon_{ist}, \tag{8.1}$$

where L_{ist} is one of six potential living arrangements, X_{ist} are individual-level characteristics of the children, U_{st} is the state-level unemployment rate, S_{st} are state-level controls for maximum welfare benefits and waiver and TANF implementation, T is a time specification, α_s are state fixed effects, and ε is the error term.

In X_{ist}, we include only children's characteristics as control variables because of concerns about the endogeneity of the characteristics of adults in the household and children's living arrangements. In all models, we include the child's age, race and ethnicity, and sex and a measure of urbanicity—central-city status in the CPS and metropolitan-area status in the SIPP.

Children's living arrangements might respond to economic conditions in a variety of ways. For example, in periods of high unemployment when families may be feeling economic pressure, they may be more likely to double up with others (London 2000a). Families with one parent may opt to combine households with other family members or with a cohabitor in order to share expenses. At the same time, job loss and economic pressure can create marital problems, leading to marital breakup and resulting in fewer children living with married parents (Conger et al. 1990; Yeung and Hofferth 1998; White and Rogers 2000). Slack labor markets may also have an effect on the attractiveness of potential spouses by increasing unemployment and lowering wages. Hence, in relatively high unemployment periods, we might expect to see some offsetting trends. At the same time, we might find marital dissolution and worsening marriage markets, leading to increases in children living alone with one parent; we might also see increased doubling up, which would decrease the share of children living alone with one parent.

In the stock model that examines trends over time in living arrangements, we use CPS data to test how variation in unemployment rates across states and over time affects the distribution of living arrangements. We separately model the probability of each living arrangement using probit models. We are most interested in the magnitude of the estimated coefficient δ, which demonstrates the effect of unemployment rates on the probability of living in a particular arrangement.

The previous model captures the effects of economic conditions on the stock or net flows of living arrangements, but we might expect stronger effects on the flows into and out of living arrangements. For example, recessions may increase both flows into single-parent households through martial dissolution and flows out of single-parent households because of financial pressure. These dynamic effects might result in a small or nonexistent response of the stock measure to changes in the economy.

The probability of a child making a living arrangement transition over a one-year period can be expressed as:

$$LT_{ist} = \beta X_{ist} + \delta U_{st} + \chi S_{st} + \gamma T_t + \alpha_s + \varepsilon_{ist} \qquad (8.2)$$

We estimate probit models for the probability of transitioning into and out of each living arrangement over the course of one year. In both the stock and transition models, standard errors are corrected for serial correlation across states.

It is important to note that the distribution of family living arrangements changed tremendously over the time period we are examining. In the last two decades of the twentieth century, children became less likely to live with married parents and more likely to live with a single parent, particularly one who was cohabiting with an unrelated partner. It is likely that some portion of these trends is the result of changes in societal norms, including a less stigmatizing view of divorce and nonmarital cohabitation. It is important to ensure that our estimates of the effects of unemployment levels on living arrangements and living arrangement transitions are purged of these underlying trends. We therefore experiment with several specifications aimed at controlling for the underlying trends. We estimate models that include quadratic time trends, code-change

FIGURE 8.1 / Children Living with Married Parents

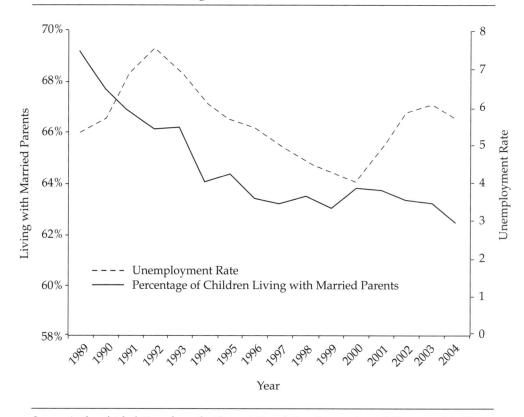

Source: Authors' tabulations from the Current Population Survey Annual Demographic files.

dummy variables (which refer to the timing of survey code changes in the data), and year fixed effects. As discussed in the next section, the results are qualitatively similar. We include year fixed effects as our preferred model throughout the chapter.

TRENDS IN LIVING ARRANGEMENTS AND LIVING ARRANGEMENT TRANSITIONS

Figures 8.1 through 8.3 compare children's living arrangements in the CPS with the national unemployment rate from 1989 to 2004. Over this time period, the decline in marriage is quite evident (figure 8.1) and does not appear to correspond strongly to fluctuations in the national unemployment rate. The decline in the percentage of children living with married parents (and no other adult) occurs during periods of both high and low unemployment, although the trend

FIGURE 8.2 / Children Living with a Single Parent

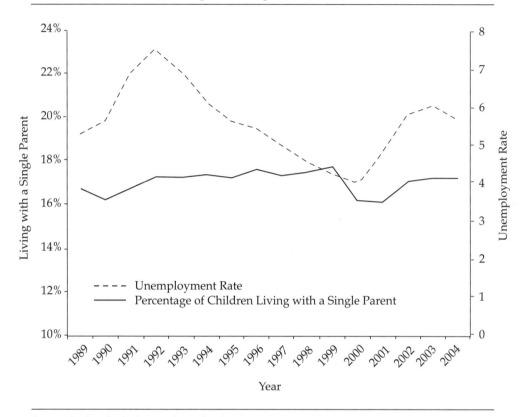

Source: Authors' tabulations from the Current Population Survey Annual Demographic file.

is somewhat flat in the late 1990s, when the national unemployment rate reached its low point.

The trend in the percentage of children living with a single parent (and no other adult) also does not appear to be strongly related to aggregate unemployment (figure 8.2); the trend remains largely flat throughout the period. However, between 2000 and 2004, changes in the percentage of children living with a single parent do follow a trend similar to the aggregate unemployment rate. There is a small decline in the percentage of children living with a single parent when unemployment was low and a slight rise in this percentage as unemployment rose. This relationship is not consistent with the prediction that single-parent families will respond to economic pressure by doubling up.

Figure 8.3 displays trends in the other four living arrangements we examine: children living with a parent and cohabitor, in multigenerational households, with others, or without parents. Note that between 1993 and 1995 two of the trends experience discontinuities, which are evident in the sudden rise in chil-

FIGURE 8.3 / Children Living in Other Arrangements

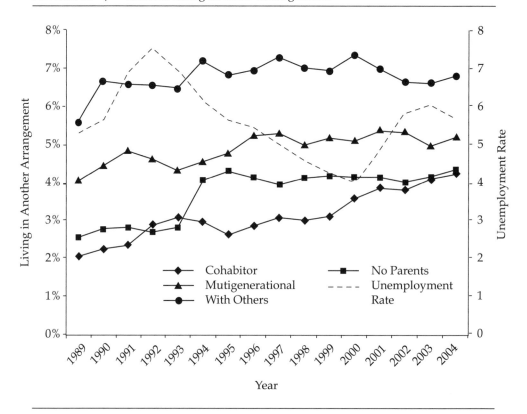

Source: Authors' tabulations from the Current Population Survey Annual Demographic files.

dren living without parents between 1993 and 1994 and in the dip in the percentage of children living with a single parent and cohabitor that occurs between 1994 and 1995. These are the result of changes in the CPS survey that occurred during the time period.

These discontinuities notwithstanding, we find increases in each of the three shared parental living arrangements over time and no change in the percentage of children living without parents. The percentage of children living with a cohabiting parent rose from 2 percent to over 4 percent between 1989 and 2004, and this trend does not appear to align with aggregate unemployment rates over the period. The percentage of children living in multigenerational households increased from 4 to 5.5 percent. In the early 1990s, there was some comovement between aggregate unemployment rates and the percentage of children living in this arrangement; in more recent years, however, this is not apparent. The percentage of children living in other parental arrangements or with roommates, aunts or uncles, or others increased and fell slightly during the time period, but overall it changed very little and appears to be unresponsive to aggregate unemployment.

Figures 8.1 through 8.3 illustrate the overall trends in living arrangements, which are likely to respond to differences in societal norms as well as to other factors, including economic conditions. Although dramatic changes occurred in the distribution of living arrangements over this time period, it is important to note that the vast majority of children continued to live with either married parents or a single parent and no other adults in the household. Between 1979 and 2004, the percentage of children living in parent-only households fell from 86 percent to 79 percent.

Thus far, the reported estimates only capture the relationship between national unemployment rates and living arrangements as they exist at a point in time. It is possible that even if economic fluctuations do not have a large effect on the overall distribution of living arrangements, they might have a large effect on the probability of moving into or out of specific living arrangements, perhaps owing to the counteracting influences that we hypothesized earlier. Figures 8.4 and 8.5 use data from the 1986 to 2001 SIPP panels to examine the probabilities of transitioning into and out of various living arrangements. Note that even with overlapping panels, the SIPP does not cover each year from 1986 to 2002. The dotted lines in the two figures connect points across years for which we are missing data.

Between 8 and 10 percent of children change living arrangements over a one-year period. There is some fluctuation in this overall transition rate, but not necessarily in concert with fluctuations in the aggregate unemployment rate. When we examine the types of transitions that occur, however, we find what appears to be some comovement with trends in economic conditions. Figure 8.4 graphs the trends in transition rates into and out of married-parent(-only) households. The transition rate into a married-parent living arrangement is defined for those not living in this arrangement in the base year. The discontinuities between 1994 and 1996 are probably the result of a code change in the 1996 SIPP that affects how cohabitors are identified. Because we are better able to identify children living with cohabitors in 1996, movement from this arrangement into marriage is adjusted upward for 1996 and beyond. Removing this discontinuity, the trend would show a constant decline over the 1995 to 1998 period.

Figure 8.4 demonstrates that in the raw data there appears to be comovement between the aggregate unemployment rate and both transitions into and out of marriage. If one visually shifts down the portion of the lines from 1996 forward to meet the earlier line, a steady decline in both transitions can be observed during the strong economic expansion of the late 1990s. An increase in transitions out of marriage can be observed when the aggregate unemployment rate begins to rise, but not for transitions into marriage that remain flat. Note that a transition out of marriage may not always signal a divorce or separation. Children moving from a household that includes their parents as the only adults into a household that has other related or unrelated adults in it are also coded as moving out of a married-parent household. In both cases, movement out of mar-

FIGURE 8.4 / Transitions into and out of Married-Parent Households
and Unemployment Rates

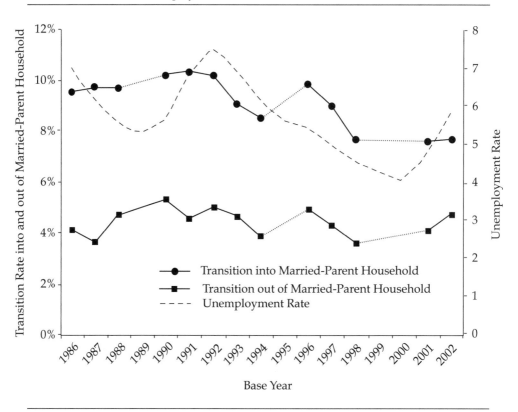

Source: Authors' tabulations from the Survey of Income and Program Participation.

riage is consistent with our theory, which predicts that higher unemployment will lead to marital strife and doubling up.

Figure 8.5 shows trends for transition rates into and out of single-parent households. This figure shows a clearer relationship between transitions out of single-parent households and unemployment. Ignoring the discontinuity in 1996 that results from the code change, the transition rates out of single-parent households appear to map closely to the national unemployment rate. This is consistent with our theory, which predicts that in times of greater economic pressure, single-parent households will be more likely to double up by getting married, cohabiting, or sharing housing with other relatives or nonrelatives. The converse does not appear to be true—transitions into single-parenthood do not fluctuate with the business cycle.

FIGURE 8.5   /   Transitions into and out of Single-Parent-Only Households
                  and Unemployment Rates

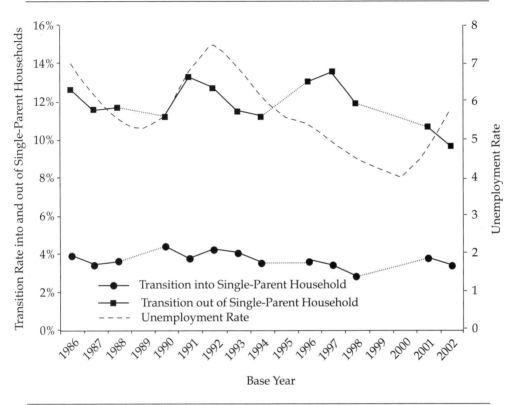

Source: Authors' tabulations from the Survey of Income and Program Participation.

THE EFFECTS OF ECONOMIC CONDITIONS ON CHILDREN'S LIVING ARRANGEMENTS

Although the comparisons of trends in economic conditions and living arrangements are suggestive of potential effects, we need to control for other factors, such as the demographic trend away from marriage and the major changes that occurred in welfare over the past decade and a half. As discussed previously, we experiment with three models to separate the demographic trend from the effects of unemployment and other factors. We also examine the relationship between living arrangements and more local measures of unemployment rates.

Table 8.1 presents the results of these three models for the more detailed living arrangements in the CPS. We report marginal effects and their standard errors for probit regressions that also include dummy variables for child sex, age, race,

TABLE 8.1 / Living Arrangement Probit Results, 1989 to 2004: March Current
Population Survey

	Married Parents	Single Parent	One Parent and Cohabitor	Multi-generational Household	Parent and Others	No Parents
Mean of dependent variable	0.6572	0.1781	0.0298	0.0359	0.0433	0.0653
Quadratic time trend						
Unemployment rate	−0.0035**	0.0038**	0.0005	−0.0006	−0.0001	−0.0004
	(0.0012)	(0.0012)	(0.0004)	(0.0006)	(0.0006)	(0.0004)
Quadratic time trend and code-change dummies (1994 and 1995)						
Unemployment rate	−0.0043**	0.0047**	−0.0002	−0.0007	0.0000	0.0002
	(0.0015)	(0.0012)	(0.0004)	(0.0006)	(0.0007)	(0.0005)
Year fixed effects						
Unemployment rate	−0.0035	0.0036*	−0.0004	0.0002	−0.0001	−0.0001
	(0.0019)	(0.0015)	(0.0005)	(0.0008)	(0.0009)	(0.0005)
Sample size	547,535	547,535	547,535	547,535	547,535	547,535

Source: Authors' tabulations from the Current Population Survey Annual Demographic files.
Notes: All specifications include dummy variables for sex, age, race, central-city status, welfare waiver and TANF implementation, state fixed effects, and the maximum welfare benefit level for a family of three. Marginal effects and robust standard errors are reported.
*p < .05, **p < .01

and central-city status and for welfare waivers and TANF implementation timing. All models also include the maximum welfare benefit for a family of three
in each state and year as well as state fixed effects. Standard errors are adjusted
for the presence of common random shocks at the state level to address concerns
regarding understated standard errors and serially correlated outcomes (see Bertrand, Duflo, and Mullainathan 2002; Kezdi 2002).

Estimates of the magnitude of the effects of unemployment rates on living
arrangements are not overly sensitive to how we specify time trends, but we do
find some variability in statistical significance. The first set of models reported
in the table includes a quadratic time trend. The advantage of the quadratic time
trend is that theoretically we expect societal preferences for living arrangements
to follow a relatively smooth adjustment process. The quadratic trend allows for
this sort of smooth change in norms and tastes for living arrangements over
time, capturing, for instance, the relatively steady growth in cohabitation that
occurred over our time period. In the second set of models, we add dummy
variables for coding changes in the CPS survey instrument for living arrangements. In the last row, we allow for the most flexibility in controlling for other

factors that change over time by including year fixed effects, which may be important if trends in norms and tastes for household and family structure are not entirely smooth. In particular, the change in welfare policy around 1996 might have led to a relatively quick change in tastes and norms that the quadratic time trend would not capture. However, year fixed effects might lead to an understatement of the effects of economic conditions on living arrangements because they also capture annual fluctuations in the macroeconomy.

Each model in table 8.1 shows that, as unemployment increases, there is an increase in the probability that a child will live with a single parent (with no other adults) and an almost equal-sized decrease in the probability that he or she will live with married parents (with no other adults). In the year-fixed-effect model (bottom row of table 8.1), the point estimate indicates that a one-percentage-point increase in the unemployment rate over the 1989 to 2004 period is associated with a 0.36-percentage-point increase in the probability of living with a single parent. A comparable increase in unemployment is associated with an offsetting 0.35-percentage-point decline in the probability of living with married parents (although the coefficient is not statistically significant at conventional levels). This effect is of the same magnitude that is seen in the model that includes a quadratic time trend and no code-change dummies, which is more precisely measured and thus has a statistically significant marginal effect. The specification that includes a quadratic time trend and the code-change dummies shows a larger negative and statistically significant effect on the probability of living with married parents (-0.43 percentage points) and a larger positive and statistically significant effect on the probability of living with a single parent (0.47 percentage points). We find no evidence in any of the models that the unemployment rate affects the probability that a child will live in an arrangement other than with a single parent or with married parents. For simplicity, in the remainder of this chapter we present only specifications that include year fixed effects. Although not shown, we generally find a stronger relationship between unemployment and living arrangements in additional specifications that include a quadratic time trend with the code-change dummies.

The regression results appear to identify a correlation between unemployment and the probability of living with a single parent (or, in some specifications, married parents) that the raw data (shown in figures 8.1 and 8.2) do not. This is because the national unemployment rate, shown in the figures, does not capture state-level variation in unemployment, which is driving the results of the regression. Models that include only the state unemployment rate as a regressor also show large and significant effects on some living arrangements.

Children of different races or ethnicities have very different living arrangement distributions. The means shown in table 8.2 indicate that over the 1989 to 2004 time period white children were substantially more likely than African American or Latino children to live with married parents. African American children were the most likely to live with a single parent or in a multigenerational family and had the highest rate of living without parents. Latino children were the most likely to live in other shared arrangements, including with other family

TABLE 8.2 / Living Arrangement Probit Results by Race, 1989 to 2004: March Current Population Survey

	Married Parents	Single Parent	One Parent and Cohabitor	Multi-generational Household	Parent and Others	No Parents
White (N = 361,700)						
Mean of dependent variable	0.7447	0.1320	0.0278	0.0298	0.0432	0.0220
Unemployment rate	−0.0039	0.0033*	−0.0007	0.0014	0.0003	−0.0005
	(0.0022)	(0.0015)	(0.0006)	(0.0009)	(0.0009)	(0.0005)
African American (N = 68,617)						
Mean of dependent variable	0.3317	0.3864	0.0362	0.0751	0.0819	0.0881
Unemployment rate	−0.0010	0.0020	0.0012	−0.0014	−0.0028	0.0022
	(0.0044)	(0.0054)	(0.0018)	(0.0021)	(0.0042)	(0.0025)
Latino (N = 88,911)						
Mean of dependent variable	0.5545	0.1761	0.0335	0.0583	0.1347	0.0422
Unemployment rate	−0.0037	0.0057*	−0.0013	−0.0013	−0.0013	0.0009
	(0.0050)	(0.0028)	(0.0020)	(0.0023)	(0.0040)	(0.0018)

Source: Authors' tabulations from the Current Population Survey Annual Demographic files.
Notes: All specifications include dummy variables for sex, age, central-city status, welfare waiver and TANF implementation, state fixed effects, year fixed effects, and the maximum welfare benefit level for a family of three. Marginal effects and robust standard errors are reported.
*p < .05; **p < .01

members or nonrelatives. Given these differences, we might also expect that the effect of economic conditions on living arrangements would differ by children's race or ethnicity. Indeed, the estimates reported in table 8.2 indicate different effects of unemployment on the distribution of living arrangements for white, African American, and Latino children.

The results for white and Latino children are similar to those for children as a whole: higher unemployment is associated with a higher probability of living with a single parent. The unemployment rate has no statistically significant effect on the probability of living in the other defined arrangements for these children. However, for whites, the negative effect of unemployment on living with married parents is even larger in absolute value than the effect on living with a single parent, and a comparably sized effect exists for Latinos as well. In models that include the quadratic time trend and code-change dummies (not shown), we find a negative and statistically significant effect of unemployment on living with married parents for whites. The unemployment rate has a smaller and sta-

TABLE 8.3 / Living Arrangement Probit Results, 1979 to 2004: March Current
Population Survey

	Married Parents	Single Parent	Other Arrangement
All children (N = 882,988)			
Mean of dependent variable	0.6609	0.1701	0.1691
Unemployment rate	−0.0012	0.0003	0.0005
	(0.0009)	(0.0008)	(0.0011)
White (N = 596,661)			
Mean of dependent variable	0.7548	0.1268	0.1184
Unemployment rate	0.0001	0.0004	−0.0006
	(0.0010)	(0.0007)	(0.0009)
African American (N = 111,192)			
Mean of dependent variable	0.3380	0.3665	0.2954
Unemployment rate	−0.0016	0.0014	0.0006
	(0.0024)	(0.0030)	(0.0024)
Latino (N = 133,087)			
Mean of dependent variable	0.5631	0.1770	0.2599
Unemployment rate	−0.0076*	0.0016	0.0062
	(0.0036)	(0.0025)	(0.0043)

Source: Authors' tabulations from the Current Population Survey Annual Demographic files.
Notes: All specifications include dummy variables for sex, age, central-city status, welfare waiver and TANF implementation, state fixed effects, year fixed effects, and the maximum welfare benefit level for a family of three. The first specification also includes controls for race. Marginal effects and robust standard errors are reported.
*p < .05; **p < .01

tistically insignificant effect on the probability that African American children will live with either a single parent or married parents.

An important finding from tables 8.1 and 8.2 is that the probability of living in any of the other arrangements—including cohabitation, which was the fastest-growing living arrangement over this time period—is not significantly related to changes in unemployment. The unemployment rate coefficients are statistically insignificant in the main specification (table 8.1) and in each of the specifications for racial groups (table 8.2).

We can use the CPS to examine the relationship between living arrangements and economic conditions over a longer time period that includes additional recessionary and growth periods. Estimates for probit regressions using data from 1979 to 2004 are reported in table 8.3. Prior to 1989, it is not possible to identify all six living arrangements, and thus we concentrate on the main two living arrangements—living with married parents and living with a single parent, grouping all other arrangements. In aggregate, we find results that are smaller than those for the period 1989 to 2004. For instance, over the longer period a one-percentage-point increase in the unemployment rate is associated with a 0.12-percentage-point decline in the probability of living with married parents (compared to the 0.35-percentage-point decline for the shorter time period). A comparable increase in unemployment is associated with a 0.03-percentage-point increase in the probability of living with a single parent, compared to 0.36 percentage points over the shorter time period. Similar differences can generally be seen across race and ethnicity groups. An exception occurs, however, for Latino children. The effect of a one-percentage-point increase in unemployment is a 0.76-percentage-point decline in marriage over the longer time period and a 0.37-percentage-point decline in the shorter time period. Although estimates for the longer time period are generally smaller and more likely to be statistically insignificant, they do not conflict with the shorter time frame results.

Not shown in tables 8.1 through 8.3 are estimates for the effects of welfare reform on the distribution of children's living arrangements. Included in all regressions are two welfare reform measures: a dummy variable indicating the timing of the implementation of a state welfare waiver and a dummy variable indicating the timing of TANF implementation. All waivers were implemented during the 1992 to 1996 period, and all TANF programs were implemented between 1996 and 1998. Given the truncated period in which these programs occurred and the long time period we examine, we find little consistent evidence that waiver programs and TANF affected children's living arrangements in either the 1979 to 2004 or the 1989 to 2004 period.[7]

THE EFFECTS OF ECONOMIC CONDITIONS ON TRANSITIONS IN CHILDREN'S LIVING ARRANGEMENTS

As noted previously, the static distribution of living arrangements may be less responsive to changes in economic conditions than the dynamic distributions of living arrangements. We now turn to estimating the relationship between unemployment and transitions into and out of living arrangements. Table 8.4 reports a five-by-five transition matrix of living arrangements in year 1 and living arrangements in year 2. Looking down the diagonal, one can observe that children living with married parents in year 1 are least likely to change living arrangements. Fewer than 5 percent are in another living arrangement one year later. Children living with a single parent and no other adults are the next least likely to change households, followed by those living in multigenerational households, children in cohabiting families, and children in all other arrangements.

The transition patterns are in line with other research indicating that when transitions occur, they are likely to progress toward independence (London 2000b). For example, much of the movement between family types is movement from arrangements in which parents live with other nonparental adults into arrangements where other adults are not present. The most likely transitions occur when cohabiting unions dissolve or result in marriage and when families in

TABLE 8.4 / Living Arrangement Transition Matrix, 1986 to 2002: Survey of Income and Program Participation

Year 1	Year 2					
	Married Parents Alone	Single Parent Alone	Cohabiting Single Parent	Multi-generational Household	Other Shared Household	N (Un-weighted)
Married parents alone	95.48%	2.68%	0.08%	0.43%	1.33%	108,085
Single parent alone	5.92	88.00	1.89	1.20	2.98	29,738
Cohabiting single parent	11.91	15.68	67.88	0.62	3.91	2,981
Multigenerational household	7.79	7.35	0.54	80.87	3.44	6,864
Other shared household	18.97	10.39	1.44	1.61	67.59	10,164

Source: Authors' tabulations from the Survey of Income and Program Participation.

shared housing arrangements begin to live without other adults present. Note that these transitions may entail either a move by the transitioning family or a move by another household member out of the residence.

To explore the effects of economic conditions on living arrangement transitions, we estimate probit regressions using the SIPP. Table 8.5 compares estimates from the CPS and SIPP using the stock living arrangement model (corresponding to year 1 for the SIPP). The SIPP control variables are largely the same except that the SIPP does not have a measure of central-city status; instead, we use a dummy variable indicating residence in a metropolitan area. Living arrangements are defined in the same way for both datasets, although we are unable to measure accurately transitions into and out of no-parent households in the SIPP, and therefore we exclude that arrangement. The main differences between the SIPP and CPS samples are their different coverage of years (1989 to 2004 in the CPS and 1986 to 2002 in the SIPP) and the exclusion of certain states that are not uniquely identified in the SIPP. Without unique identification, we cannot assign an appropriate unemployment rate. The CPS results in panel 1 are the same as those reported in the bottom row of table 8.1, with the distribution of living arrangements adjusted to reflect the presence of five rather than six categories. Panel 2 results are also from the CPS, but restricted to the SIPP time frame and states. Panel 3 shows results from the SIPP.

The estimates reported in table 8.5 indicate a difference in cohabitation rates between the datasets, which appear to result from the different sample definitions. The cohabitation rate we observe over the time period for children is lower in the SIPP than in the CPS, but also lower in the restricted CPS sample than in the full sample. In all cases, we are providing a rough estimate of cohabitation

TABLE 8.5 / Living Arrangement Probit Results: Comparison of SIPP and CPS

	Married Parents	Single Parent	One Parent and Cohabitor	Multi-generational Household	Parent and Others
CPS 1989 to 2004 (N = 547,535)					
Mean of dependent variable	0.6927	0.1906	0.0319	0.0384	0.0463
Unemployment rate	−0.0035	0.0036*	−0.0004	0.0002	−0.0001
	(0.0019)	(0.0015)	(0.0005)	(0.0008)	(0.0009)
CPS 1989 to 2002, states restricted to SIPP states (N = 410,722)					
Mean of dependent variable	0.6938	0.1915	0.0302	0.0378	0.0466
Unemployment rate	−0.0029	0.0033*	−0.0007	0.0002	−0.0001
	(0.0022)	(0.0016)	(0.0006)	(0.0009)	(0.0010)
SIPP 1986 to 2002 (N = 157,832)					
Mean of dependent variable	0.6927	0.1871	0.0180	0.0411	0.0612
Unemployment rate	−0.0017	0.0042	0.0004	−0.0028**	0.0001
	(0.0030)	(0.0025)	(0.0009)	(0.0010)	(0.0014)

Source: Authors' tabulations from the Current Population Survey Annual Demographic files and the Survey of Income and Program Participation.
Notes: All specifications include dummy variables for sex, age, race, central-city status, welfare waiver and TANF implementation, state fixed effects, year fixed effects, and the maximum welfare benefit level for a family of three. Marginal effects and robust standard errors are reported. The restricted CPS sample and the SIPP sample exclude Maine, North Dakota, South Dakota, Vermont, and Wyoming in all years, and also Alaska, Idaho, Iowa, and Montana prior to 1996. These states are not uniquely identified in the SIPP.
*p < .05; **p < .01

rates for the earlier years of the sample. The probability of living in either of the two main arrangements is equivalent.

A comparison of the effects of unemployment on living arrangements across the three samples generally reveals similar results. As discussed previously, in the unrestricted CPS model we find what appears to be a trade-off between married-parent arrangements and single-parent arrangements as unemployment increases, though the effects of unemployment on living with married parents is not statistically significant. In the SIPP, we find a smaller effect of increased unemployment on living with married parents and a larger effect on living with one parent, though neither is statistically significant. (The unemployment marginal effect in the single-parent regression would be significant at the 10 percent level.) Table 8.5 also reveals a counterintuitive result in the SIPP: there is a negative effect of unemployment on living in a multigenerational household. When we restrict the CPS sample to the SIPP states and years (middle panel), we find results that are somewhere between the unrestricted CPS and SIPP models. We find an insignificant effect of unemployment on living with married parents and a smaller significant positive effect on living with a single parent. We conclude that the differences between the CPS and SIPP in the stock models appear to be at least partially the result of unavoidable differences in sample definitions. Although the results are dissimilar in magnitude and significance, the SIPP and CPS stock model results tell largely the same story—when unemployment increases, there appears to be movement between children living with single and married parents.

Even if unemployment is unrelated to the stock measure of living with married parents in the SIPP, the trends displayed in figure 8.4 suggest that unemployment may play a role in determining transitions into and out of this arrangement. Table 8.6 examines the effects of unemployment rates on transitions into and out of the two most prevalent children's living arrangements: living with married parents and no other adults, and living with a single parent and no other adults.

Results for children of all racial and ethnic backgrounds, shown in the first panel, indicate that unemployment is positively related to the transition out of living with a single parent. A one-percentage-point increase in unemployment is associated with a 0.83-percentage-point increase in the transition rate out of single-parenthood. The unemployment rate, however, does not have an effect on transitions into single-parent households. We also do not find evidence of a statistically significant relationship between the unemployment rate and the probabilities of transitioning into and out of living with married parents.

The results for white children are comparable to those for children overall. Neither African American nor Latino children have statistically significant responses to unemployment fluctuations with transitions into or out of these living arrangements. However, the magnitude of the estimated effects of unemployment rates on transitions into living with married parents (for Latinos) and transitions out of living with single parents (for both groups) are large.

Transitions into and out of the other three living arrangements show different patterns (see table 8.7). The probability of transitioning into cohabitation, a multigenerational household, or another type of shared arrangement is very low, between 0.5 and 1 percent. The probability of transitioning out of these arrangements is far higher, ranging between 19 and 32 percent. Our results indicate that transitions into cohabitation and shared household arrangements (not including multigenerational households) are responsive to increases in unemployment. When unemployment increases by one percentage point, the probability of children transitioning into cohabitation increases by 0.06 percentage points, and the probability of transitioning into other shared arrangements increases by 0.16 percentage points. The point estimate in the transition-out-of-cohabitation regression implies that unemployment has a sizable, but statistically insignificant,

TABLE 8.6 / Living Arrangement Transition Probit Results, 1986 to 2002: Survey of Income and Program Participation

	Transition into Married- Parents Household	Transition out of Married- Parents Household	Transition into Single- Parent Household	Transition out of Single- Parent Household
All Children				
Mean of dependent variable	0.0912	0.0452	0.0378	0.1200
Unemployment rate	−0.0018	0.0008	−0.0001	0.0083**
	(0.0029)	(0.0014)	(0.0014)	(0.0030)
Sample size	49,747	108,085	128,094	29,738
White				
Mean of dependent variable	0.1113	0.0411	0.0334	0.1450
Unemployment rate	−0.0024	0.0010	0.0006	0.0106*
	(0.0045)	(0.0016)	(0.0014)	(0.0048)
Sample size	27,473	86,272	97,592	16,153
African American				
Mean of dependent variable	0.0452	0.0657	0.0698	0.0807
Unemployment rate	0.0002	−0.0074	−0.0082	0.0010
	(0.0038)	(0.0052)	(0.0045)	(0.0060)
Sample size	14,472	8,578	13,177	9,873
Latino				
Mean of dependent variable	0.1103	0.0610	0.0419	0.1176
Unemployment rate	−0.0119	0.0027	−0.0040	0.0082
	(0.0072)	(0.0078)	(0.0047)	(0.0129)
Sample size	5,150	8,365	10,841	2,674

Source: Authors' tabulations from the Survey of Income and Program Participation.
Notes: All specifications include dummy variables for sex, age, metropolitan status, welfare waiver and TANF implementation, state fixed effects, year fixed effects, and the maximum welfare benefit level for a family of three. Marginal effects and robust standard errors are reported.
*$p < .05$; **$p < .01$

effect on the probability. The point estimate implies that an increase in the unemployment rate of one percentage point leads to a reduced transition out of cohabitation of 1.3 percentage points. Both these sets of findings are consistent with theoretical predictions. When economic pressure mounts, families are more likely to double up, even if they do not change their marital status. Cohabitating parents may be less likely to marry or to separate when unemployment rates increase.

Table 8.7 also shows that increasing unemployment has an effect on children moving into shared arrangements that are not multigenerational, such as living with a sibling, friend, or same-sex cohabitor. An increase in unemployment of

TABLE 8.7 / Living Arrangement Transition Probit Results, 1986 to 2002: Survey of Income and Program Participation

	Transition into Arrangement	Transition out of Arrangement
Single parent and unmarried cohabitor		
Mean of dependent variable	0.0053	0.3212
Unemployment rate	0.0006*	−0.0132
	(0.0003)	(0.0251)
Sample size	154,851	2,981
Multigeneration Family (married or single)		
Mean of dependent variable	0.0066	0.1913
Unemployment rate	0.0002	−0.0079
	(0.0004)	(0.0094)
Sample size	150,968	6,864
Other shared arrangement (married or single)		
Mean of dependent variable	0.0180	0.3241
Unemployment rate	0.0016*	−0.0048
	(0.0008)	(0.0177)
Sample size	147,668	10,164

Source: Authors' tabulations from the Survey of Income and Program Participation.
Notes: All specifications include dummy variables for sex, age, race, metropolitan status, welfare waiver and TANF implementation, state fixed effects, year fixed effects, and the maximum welfare benefit level for a family of three. Marginal effects and robust standard errors are reported.
*$p < .05$; **$p < .01$

one percentage point is associated with a 1.6-percentage-point increase in living in other shared arrangements. As with cohabitation, the effect of increased unemployment on transitions out of this arrangement is negative and larger in absolute value, but statistically insignificant.

The results from the SIPP transitions analysis provide a different story than those from the CPS and SIPP stock analyses for living with a single parent. The stock models imply that the effect of increasing annual state unemployment rates is a small increase in the probability of living with a single parent. The transitions analysis indicates that increasing monthly unemployment rates are associated with movement out of single-parent homes and into shared arrangements, such as living with a cohabitor or with other friends or relatives. This latter finding is consistent with theories predicting that increased economic pressure (as approximated by an increase in unemployment) will lead families to double up in some way. We might expect that changes in economic conditions have a larger and more immediate effect on movements between living arrangements than on the overall distribution of living arrangements. In addition, because the stock level of any living arrangement is a complex relationship between entry and exit rates, it may be more meaningful to estimate transitions separately.

CONCLUSIONS

Previous research indicates that living arrangements and living arrangement transitions are important determinants of children's future well-being. The distribution of living arrangements has changed dramatically over the past twenty-five years, with children becoming increasingly likely to live with a single parent—particularly one who cohabits with an unmarried partner—and less likely to live with married parents. This chapter has examined the relationship between economic conditions and the distribution of children's living arrangements and transitions into and out of various arrangements.

Economic conditions are likely to influence children's living arrangements through three main avenues. First, economic pressure creates family stress, which can lead to marital dissolution. Second, economic pressure can create a need to double up with other adults in order to share household expenses. Doubling up can take a number of forms, including marriage, cohabitation, multigenerational households, and other shared arrangements. Finally, slack labor markets may reduce the attractiveness of potential spouses, leading to reduced entry into marriage.

Some of our results are consistent with these hypotheses. Using the CPS, we find that higher unemployment is associated with a higher probability that children will live in single-parent households (without other adults present). These findings may be consistent with the first hypothesis—that economic pressure leads to marital dissolution—if the increase in single-parenthood comes at the expense of children living with married parents, but that assumption is not borne out in all specifications. In the year-fixed-effects model, the effect of an increase in unemployment is a decrease in living with married parents of about the same magnitude as the increase in living with single parents, but the marginal effect on living with married parents is insignificant at conventional levels. This negative relationship between unemployment and the probability of living with married parents appears to be weakly consistent with the spousal attractiveness hypothesis, although the marginal effect is statistically significant only in the alternative specifications. The CPS findings do not appear to support the second hypothesis that increased unemployment leads families to double up.

To further examine the ways in which economic conditions affect children's living arrangements, we model the probability of transitions into and out of various living arrangements using data from the SIPP. We find that between 1986 and 2002 higher rates of unemployment are positively associated with transitions out of single-parent living arrangements. When we examine other living arrangements, we find that economic pressure is associated with an increased probability of entry into cohabitation and shared living arrangements, both of which are consistent with the doubling-up theory.

Both the SIPP and CPS stock models show, with varying levels of significance, a positive relationship between unemployment and living with single parents. This contrasts with the SIPP transition regression results, which provide evidence that higher unemployment is associated with movement out of single-parent households and into shared or cohabiting ones. Although an increased transition rate out of single-parent households and a constant transition rate into single-parent households are inconsistent with an increased level of living with single parents, the relationships between the effects on stocks and flow rates do not necessarily hold when examining estimates from multivariate regression models. Estimates of the effects of economic conditions on living arrangements from the transition models may be more reliable than those from the stock models because estimates from the stock models capture a complex combination of effects on both entry and exit rates. The transition models estimate these effects separately.

The association between higher unemployment rates and movement out of single-parent-only households is in line with our expectations. Recessions may create economic pressure that increases the likelihood of movement out of the most independent living arrangements and into shared arrangements. These movements may partly offset the potential income and consumption losses caused by recessions, but the instability associated with these changes may have large negative consequences for children's future outcomes.

NOTES

1. For guidance and valuable input on earlier drafts, we would like to thank Gregory Acs, Marianne Bitler, Rebecca Blank, Sheldon Danziger, Jonah Gelbach, Robert Schoeni, participants at the "Working and Poor" preconference in Ann Arbor, Michigan and at the final conference in Washington, D.C., and participants at the 2005 Population Association of America annual meeting. Oded Gurantz provided excellent research assistance.
2. Family cap policies remove the incremental welfare benefits associated with additional children for women who become pregnant while receiving aid.
3. We cannot use matched CPS data to examine living arrangement transitions because individuals and families who move are not followed in the CPS.
4. Adult children of the parents who live in the household are not considered other adults. If a child lives in a household with his or her parents and an adult sibling, that child is coded as living with married parents.
5. In the 1996 and 2001 panels, these states are Maine, North Dakota, South Dakota, Vermont, and Wyoming. Prior to 1996, Alaska, Idaho, Iowa, and Montana were also not uniquely identified.
6. These dummy variables are coded using information provided in U.S. Department of Health and Human Services (1999).
7. When we restrict our time frame and sample to those used by Bitler and her colleagues (2006), we obtain results that are highly comparable to theirs and that show

that for some groups of children welfare reforms affected the probability of living in certain arrangements.

REFERENCES

Acs, Gregory, and Sandi Nelson. 2004. "Changes in Living Arrangements During the Late 1990s: Do Welfare Policies Matter?" *Journal of Policy Analysis and Management* 23(2): 273–90.

Albrecht, Chris, and Jay D. Teachman. 2003. "Childhood Living Arrangements and the Risk of Premarital Intercourse." *Journal of Family Issues* 24(7): 867–94.

Amato, Paul R. 2000. "The Consequences of Divorce for Adults and Children." *Journal of Marriage and the Family* 62(4): 1269–87.

Astone, Nan Marie, and Sara S. McLanahan. 1994. "Family Structure, Residential Mobility, and School Dropout: A Research Note." *Demography* 31(4): 575–84.

Bertrand, Marianne, Esther Duflo, and Sendhil Mullainathan. 2002. "How Much Should We Trust Differences-in-Differences Estimates?" Working paper 8841. Cambridge, Mass.: National Bureau of Economic Research.

Bitler, Marianne, Jonah Gelbach, and Hilary Hoynes. 2006. "Welfare Reform and Children's Living Arrangements." *Journal of Human Resources* 41(1): 1–27.

Bitler, Marianne, Jonah Gelbach, Hilary Hoynes, and Madeline Zavodny. 2004. "The Impact of Welfare Reform on Marriage and Divorce." *Demography* 41(2): 213–36.

Brandon, Peter D., and Gene A. Fisher. 2001. "The Dissolution of Joint Living Arrangements Among Single Parents and Children: Does Welfare Make a Difference?" *Social Science Quarterly* 82(1): 1–19.

Bumpass, Larry, and Hsien-Hen Lu. 2000. "Trends in Cohabitation and Implications for Children's Family Contexts in the United States." *Population Studies* 54(1): 29–41.

Chase-Lansdale, P. Lindsay, Jeanne Brooks-Gunn, and Elise S. Zamsky. 1994. "Young African American Multigenerational Families in Poverty: Quality of Mothering and Grandmothering." *Child Development* 65: 373–93.

Cherlin, Andrew J., Kathleen E. Kiernan, and P. Lindsay Chase-Lansdale. 1995. "Parental Divorce in Childhood and Demographic Outcomes in Young Adulthood." *Demography* 32(3): 299–318.

Conger, Rand D., Glen H. Elder Jr., Frederick O. Lorenz, Katherine J. Conger, Ronald L. Simons, Les B. Whitbeck, Shirley Huck, and Janet N. Melby. 1990. "Linking Economic Hardship to Marital Quality and Instability." *Journal of Marriage and the Family* 52(3): 643–56.

Crowder, Kyle, and Jay Teachman. 2004. "Do Residential Conditions Explain the Relationship Between Living Arrangements and Adolescent Behavior?" *Journal of Marriage and the Family* 66(3): 721–38.

Dawson, Deborah A. 1991. "Family Structure and Children's Health and Well-being: Data from the 1988 National Health Interview Survey on Child Health." *Journal of Marriage and the Family* 53(3): 573–84.

DeLeire, Thomas, and Ariel Kalil. 2002. "Good Things Come in Threes: Single-Parent Multigenerational Structure and Adolescent Adjustment." *Demography* 39(2): 393–413.

Dupree, Allen, and Wendell Primus. 2001. "Declining Share of Children Lived with Single Mothers in the Late 1990s: Substantial Differences by Race and Income." Washington, D.C.: Center on Budget and Policy Priorities.

Fein, David J., Nancy R. Burstein, Greta G. Fein, and Laura D. Lindberg. 2003. *The Determinants of Marriage and Cohabitation Among Disadvantaged Americans: Research Findings and Needs*. Report prepared for the U.S. Department of Health and Human Services, Administration for Children and Families, Office of Planning Research and Evaluation. Cambridge, Mass.: Abt Associates.

Fein, David J., Laura D. Lindberg, Rebecca A. London, and Jane G. Mauldon. 2002. "Welfare Reform and Family Formation: Assessing the Effects." Research brief 1. Cambridge, Mass., and Berkeley: Abt Associates and University of California.

Fein, David J., Rebecca A. London, and Jane G. Mauldon. 2005. "Has Moving Welfare Recipients from Welfare to Work Influenced Their Demographic Behavior? A Nonexperimental Analysis of Experimental Data from Four States." Paper presented to the annual meeting of the Population Association of America. Philadelphia (March 31).

Fitzgerald, John M., and David C. Ribar. 2004. "Welfare Reform and Female Headship." *Demography* 41(2): 189–212.

Folk, Karen Fox. 1996. "Single-Parent Mothers in Various Living Arrangements: Differences in Economic, Time, and Social Resources." *Journal of Economics and Sociology* 53: 277–93.

Goldscheider, Frances. 1997. "Recent Changes in U.S. Young Adult Living Arrangements in Comparative Perspective." *Journal of Family Issues* 18(6): 708–25.

Jagannathan, Radha. 2004. "Children's Living Arrangements from a Social Policy Implementation Perspective." *Children and Youth Services Review* 26: 121–41.

Kezdi, Gabor. 2002. "Robust Standard Error Estimation in Fixed-Effects Panel Models." Unpublished paper. Ann Arbor: University of Michigan.

Kiernan, Kathleen E., and John Hobcraft. 1997. "Parental Divorce During Childhood: Age at First Intercourse, Partnership, and Parenthood." *Population Studies* 51(1): 41–55.

Lichter, Daniel, Diane K. McLaughlin, and David C. Ribar. 2002. "Economic Restructuring and the Retreat from Marriage." *Social Science Research* 31(2): 230–56.

London, Rebecca A. 1998. "Trends in Single Mothers' Living Arrangements from 1970 to 1995: Correcting the Current Population Survey." *Demography* 35(1): 125–31.

———. 2000a. "The Interaction Between Single Mothers' Living Arrangements and Welfare Participation." *Journal of Policy Analysis and Management* 19(1): 93–117.

———. 2000b. "The Dynamics of Single Mothers' Living Arrangements." *Population Research and Policy Review* 19: 73–96.

McLanahan, Sara, and Gary Sandefur. 1994. *Growing Up with a Single Parent: What Hurts, What Helps*. Cambridge, Mass.: Harvard University Press.

Schoeni, Robert F., and Rebecca M. Blank. 2000. "What Has Welfare Reform Accomplished? Impacts on Welfare Participation, Employment, Income, Poverty, and Family Structure." Unpublished paper. Ann Arbor: University of Michigan.

Seltzer, Judith. 1994. "The Consequences of Marital Dissolution for Children." *Annual Review of Sociology* 20: 235–66.

Teachman, Jay D. 2004. "The Childhood Living Arrangements of Children and the Characteristics of Their Marriages." *Journal of Family Issues* 25(1): 86–111.

Thornton, Arland, and Young-DeMarco, Linda. 2001. "Four Decades of Trends in Attitudes Toward Family Issues in the United States: The 1960s Through the 1990s." *Journal of Marriage and the Family* 63(4): 1009–37.

U.S. Department of Health and Human Services. 1999. *State Implementation of Major Changes to Welfare Policies, 1992–1998*. Washington: U.S. Government Printing Office.

White, Lynn, and Stacy J. Rogers. 2000. "Economic Circumstances and Family Outcomes: A Review of the 1990s." *Journal of Marriage and the Family* 62: 1035–51.

Winkler, Anne E. 1992. "The Impact of Housing Costs on the Living Arrangements of Single Mothers." *Journal of Urban Economics* 32(3): 388–403.

Yeung, W. Jean, and Sandra L. Hofferth. 1998. "Family Adaptations to Income and Job Loss in the United States." *Journal of Family and Economic Issues* 19(3): 255–83.

Part IV

How Do Policy Changes Interact with the
Economy and Economic Well-Being?

Chapter 9

How Do Tax Policies Affect Low-Income Workers?

Kevin A. Hassett and Anne Moore

The study of tax incidence under the U.S. tax system has a long and impressive history that has proceeded along many different complementary paths.[1] Arnold Harberger (1962) laid the groundwork for distributing the burden of taxes. Beginning with the pioneering work of Joseph Pechman and Benjamin Okner (1974), scholars have explored the impact of a wide array of taxes on the distribution of income. Theoretical work has subsequently incorporated distributive objectives into optimal tax design (see Auerbach 1985). Other work has explored the direct and indirect impacts of various tax reform proposals and also identified the effects that different tax reforms have on the distribution of income across income classes (see Burman and Saleem 2004; Carasso and Steuerle 2003; Devarajan, Fullerton, and Musgrave 1980; Gale and Orzag 2004).

Although the literature presents interesting snapshots of the impact of the U.S. tax system on low-income individuals, these snapshots are difficult to assemble into a complete view, something that was last done exhaustively in Pechman (1985). Ample data exist that document changes in federal tax policy over time, but information on state and local taxes, especially sales and property taxes, is less abundant (for recent studies of state taxes, see Center on Budget and Policy Priorities 2004; Institute on Taxation and Economic Policy 2003).

Income distribution issues not only are academically interesting but often are key factors in public policy debates. Proponents and opponents of a particular bill often emphasize the distributional characteristics of their proposal. For example, in the 2000 presidential election, George W. Bush presented evidence suggesting that his tax changes would significantly improve the welfare of low-income individuals. Others presented evidence to the contrary.

Inferences concerning distributional issues depend, of course, on the impact of specific bills on the entire income distribution. In this chapter, we abstract from this and focus our attention on low-income individuals. Specifically, we attempt to gather data on every tax payment made by typical families to government at all levels in the United States for the longest period that data will allow. We collect these observations into an aggregate payment that includes sales, excise, income, and property taxes—and even at times the lottery—and we explore the movements of this aggregate variable over time.[2] We document movements both in marginal and in average tax rates and payments over time.

To foreshadow our conclusions, we find that total direct taxes paid by low-income families have declined significantly and that they have dropped especially sharply since the late 1990s. This overall result reflects a number of different factors. Federal income taxes have declined sharply for families because of the refundable child tax credit (instituted in 2001 for taxpayers with fewer than three children), expansions of the Earned Income Tax Credit (EITC), and lower marginal tax rates. At the same time, state sales taxes paid have increased significantly, but not enough to offset the decline in federal taxes paid. Payroll taxes and property taxes have stayed relatively constant throughout the last several decades.

Together, these results lead to our second finding. Non-income taxes as a percentage of total taxes for low-income families have increased sharply over time. One possible explanation for this pattern may be that issues of fairness appear to have put significant downward political pressure on tax liabilities for low-income families where taxes whose incidence is readily observable are involved, but not taxes, such as sales taxes, with less obvious distributional effects. Another explanation is that states, which levy most of the non-income taxes, tend to be less redistributive than the federal government. Finally, while overall taxes paid have declined notably, the phase-out range of the EITC applies relatively high marginal tax rates to low-income families. Accordingly, average tax rates have declined, but in some income ranges marginal tax rates have done the opposite.

METHODS AND DATA

This chapter focuses on direct cash-flow measures of tax incidence. The actual incidence of any tax may differ from the incidence implied by direct payments. Numerous studies in public finance have modeled the incidence of many different taxes (see, for example, Fullerton, Shoven, and Whalley 1978). Such detailed analysis requires elaborate models and detailed estimates of elasticities and is beyond the scope of this chapter. Our objective is to exhaustively collect information on every tax payment made by typical low-income families and aggregate these into a single measure of taxes paid. We do not believe that these measures are accurate measures of the ultimate incidence of these taxes, although Shantayanan Devarajan, Don Fullerton, and Richard Musgrave (1980) find evidence supportive of the view that exercises such as these provide a reasonable estimate of the true underlying incidence of many taxes.

Sample Families

We perform our analysis for selected, hypothetical low-income families. These include a single mother with two children, a married couple with two children, and an unmarried adult with no children. We assume that the single mother earns $7.00 an hour and, working full-time, thus earns $14,000 a year, and that the husband of the married couple works full-time at a wage of $8.50 an hour, earning an annual income of $17,000. We further assume that the wife earns $5.15 an hour (the federal minimum wage since 1997) and makes $10,300 annually. The unmarried adult, like the husband of the married couple, has a wage rate of $8.50 an hour and makes $17,000 a year. All of these incomes are in 2004 dollars and are deflated using the personal consumption expenditures index from the National Income and Products Accounts (NIPA) for earlier years.

Marginal Federal and State Income Tax Rates

We estimate marginal and average federal and state income taxes for our hypothetical families. We perform the marginal income tax rate calculations using software we developed; this program adds $50 to the income of a representative individual and estimates the change in tax payment associated with that increase. The marginal tax rate calculations incorporate the negative marginal tax rate in the phase-in range of the EITC, the positive marginal tax rate in its phase-out range, and other tax variables. We then construct a "skyline" chart for the income ranges relevant to this study for each year from 1979 to 2004. To economize on space, we report complete skylines for 1980 and 2004.[3]

We also construct measures of taxes paid for these families over time. We use two complementary approaches. First, we use the National Bureau of Economic Research Tax Simulation Model (TAXSIM) to estimate the tax liability for a hypothetical family for each year from 1979 to 2004. Second, we construct an alternative measure of average tax paid from the Internal Revenue Service's Statistics of Income (SOI). We could not gather state income tax data from the SOI because most low-income families do not itemize deductions and hence do not report state income taxes on their federal returns. However, we can estimate the state income tax that they probably paid from the TAXSIM calculator.

Sales Taxes

A major contribution of this chapter is the incorporation of state sales taxes and state and local property taxes into the overall analysis of taxes paid by low-income families. Because our estimates required a number of difficult judgments and have little precedent to draw on, we outline our methodology in some detail.

We construct marginal sales tax rates for each year from 1979 until the present and apply them to estimates of consumption of taxable expenditures for low-income families. Average state sales tax rates at the national level were calculated for general sales, food, clothing, services, prescription drugs, medical services, and utilities by taking the average of the fifty-one-state (including the District of Columbia) sales tax rates weighted by state population.[4] Data for state tax rates and exemptions were gathered from the World Tax Database of the University of Michigan's Office of Tax Policy Research, the Commerce Clearing House *State Tax Reporters*, and state revenue departments.[5]

Finding historical local sales tax rates was difficult because local jurisdictions with taxing authority number in the thousands. Therefore, instead of trying to find the sales tax rates of each locality over the last twenty-five years, we estimated local tax rates using data from the Governments Division of the U.S. Bureau of the Census, following the methodology of Elaine Maag and Diane Rogers (2000).

The Census Bureau has gathered information on the total amount of tax receipts collected by the state government and local governments in each state and in the United States as a whole by year. For sales and use taxes, receipts are broken down into general sales taxes, utilities taxes, motor fuels taxes, and other specific goods and services sales taxes. To calculate the average local sales tax rate on general sales, food, clothing, services, medical services, and prescription drugs, we found the ratio of each state's local sales tax receipts to state sales tax receipts and increased the state tax rate by that amount.[6] Because local tax receipt data were missing for 2001, 2003, and 2004, we applied the previous year's percentage for those three years.

Because many states exempt utilities from taxation and yet contain local jurisdictions that tax them, we could not use this approach to calculate local utilities tax rates by state. Instead, we took the ratio of local utility taxes to state taxes for the entire United States and increased the average state utility tax rate by that amount. Since our ultimate goal is to calculate a nationwide average sales tax for the relevant measure of expenditure, this step should not significantly affect the accuracy of our results.

We then applied all these sales tax rates to each expenditure category for each household in the Consumer Expenditure Survey (CEX). To form our CEX dataset, we used the Consumer Expenditure Survey family-level extracts available at the NBER website, which has data on annual expenditures for consumer units beginning with the survey of the first quarter of 1980 and ending in the second quarter of 1998. Since these extracts are divided into separate datasets for each quarter when families began the survey, we combined the datasets with families who began the survey in the first and second quarters of one year with the third- and fourth-quarter datasets of the previous year to form each year's dataset. One drawback to using these data is that they end in 1998. Extending the NBER's CEX database beyond that time frame was beyond the scope of this chapter. By relating our CEX-based results to aggregates that are available after 1998, however, we are able to impute measures of sales taxes made up to 2004. Imputed values are delineated in our tables and charts, and the method is described in more detail later in the chapter.

To calculate sales taxes paid for each of the three hypothetical families, we selected the sixty families headed by nonelderly adults with the same family size (a one-, three-, and four-person household for the unmarried adult, single mother, and married couple, respectively) in each year with income (as calculated later in the chapter) nearest to the sample family's income—thirty had income above the sample family's income, and thirty had income below.[7] We added the single mother's federal tax refund to her $14,000 of real earnings; her total income thus varies by year. The married couple and the unmarried adult have positive tax liabilities from 1980 to 1998 and therefore have no income adjustment. We then averaged the sales taxes owed by these sixty families to calculate the sales taxes owed by the hypothetical families.[8]

Since households in the Consumer Expenditure Survey with low reported incomes may not actually be low-income, owing to underreporting of income, we used a different measure of household income than that reported in the CEX.[9] To estimate each household's income, we added its total outlays, taxes paid, and saving.

- *Total outlays* include current consumption (which includes sales and excise taxes), retirement and pension payments, charitable contributions, and alimony paid. It excludes the purchase price of financed vehicles and houses; instead, it includes principal payments and interest payments on vehicles and property.
- *Taxes paid* include federal and state income taxes, owned housing and personal property taxes, and nontaxes (car registration fees, driver's license fees), except that negative tax liabilities are not included.
- *Saving* includes the change in the value of savings accounts and checking accounts, the net value invested in a farm or business, and the change in the amount owed to creditors.

When matching sales tax data with the income tax data from other sources, we use this comprehensive income measure as income, rather than income as reported in the CEX.

To provide estimates for sales taxes outside of the CEX sample period, we estimated values for 1979 and for 1999 to 2004 by running a regression of sales taxes paid (calculated by the method just described) on sales tax receipts (from the NIPA tables) and the average sales tax rate. We used this regression to predict sales taxes for the missing years.

Gasoline Taxes

We calculated gasoline taxes paid differently than regular sales taxes, since most of the taxes levied on gasoline are excise taxes.[10] Gasoline excise taxes are imposed by federal and state governments, and some states also levy additional sales taxes on gasoline. We found estimates of the average tax on gasoline in cents per gallon from the American Petroleum Institute (API), whose estimates include both federal and state excise and sales taxes for each year. API does not include local taxes, so we used the census government finance data and the same methodology as with sales taxes to estimate average local tax rates.

Then, for each household, we estimated the number of gallons of gasoline purchased by dividing gasoline expenditures in the CEX by the average price of gas for each year, which we obtained from the American Automobile Association (AAA). We then applied the combined federal, state, and local tax rate to the number of gallons of gas purchased and predicted gas taxes paid for the missing years using the same regression method described earlier.

Property Tax

Property tax is one of the most important taxes paid by some low-income families, but it is difficult to estimate since the sample sizes in the CEX for low-income families are relatively small.

We examined two types of property tax: housing property tax and personal property tax, both of which are items in the CEX. Since both of these taxes vary substantially between individual households, we found that the method applied to sales taxes resulted in unreasonably large swings from year to year.

We expect that the level of property taxes revealed in these numbers is an acceptable characterization of taxes paid by low-income individuals over time; we smoothed the data from year to year to avoid having variation in property taxes dominate the aggregate picture. For smoothing personal property tax, we used the same methodology as for sales tax already outlined, but took a three-year moving average.

Housing property tax was significantly more volatile, since one or two low-income individuals with a substantial property could significantly affect the results in a given year. To calculate housing property tax, we took the average of property taxes owed by nonelderly households that owned property that is, had property taxes of less than zero) and had incomes within certain bands, regardless of household size. For married couples, we calculated the average property tax for households with incomes between $20,000 and $30,000. For the single mother and the unmarried adult, we took the average for households with incomes between $10,000 and $20,000. Then, to smooth property tax liability, we took the three-year moving average. These sample sizes were fairly large, and the constructed series was less prone to being driven by outliers.

However, since most low-income families rent rather than own their homes, and some part of the rent must go to pay the property taxes of the landlord, it was necessary to also calculate the value of property taxes indirectly paid by renters. We found the median property tax as a percentage of rental receipts from the Census Bureau's Residential Finance Surveys of 1981, 1991, and 2001.

Since the median had decreased over time (from 11.9 percent in 1981 to 7.6 percent in 2001), we took a trend to estimate the percentage in each of the intervening years. We then multiplied this percentage by the average rent paid by the hypothetical families (calculated using the sales tax methodology but selecting only families who paid rent) to find the total amount of rent that was due to property taxes.

After estimating the property tax burden of owners and renters, we calculated the likelihood of each of the hypothetical families owning or renting their home. We found the average annual homeownership percentage for households with characteristics similar to those of our hypothetical families from the CEX. To smooth the homeownership percentage, we then regressed it on a constant and a trend for each family type. Assuming that those who do not own must be renters, we then took the average of the owned housing and rental housing property tax burdens, weighting by the homeownership percentage, in order to find the average housing property tax owed by our hypothetical families.

To find total property taxes, we took the sum of personal and housing property taxes. To predict property taxes for the years missing from the CEX dataset, we regressed property tax on a constant and a trend.

Lottery Expenditures

Lottery expenditures represent a significant fraction of total expenditure for many low-income individuals (Clotfelter and Cook 1989; Clotfelter et al. 1999; Cornwell and Mustard 2001). Because the payout rates of lotteries are relatively low, some fraction of lottery expenditure is conceptually a tax. Moreover, since the lottery payout formulas tend to be highly skewed toward low-probability large payouts, most individuals probably spend more on tickets than they win. Accordingly, we endeavored to estimate net lottery payments for our hypothetical families, and we include these in parts of our analysis.[11]

The CEX includes a question concerning expenditures on gambling activity, but virtually every respondent either refused to answer the question or answered that they did not gamble at all. Therefore, we turned to other sources to acquire a more realistic picture of lottery expenditures.

For survey data—which show that per capita lottery expenditures vary by household income—we used Brinner and Clotfelter (1975), Suits (1977), Clotfelter and Cook (1987), Clotfelter et al. (1999), Cornwell and Mustard (2001), and Kearney (2002). For each of the six sources of data on lottery expenditures by income group, we computed the average per capita (or per household) lottery expenditures by income group, expressed as a multiple of the population average. We then applied these ratios to aggregate lottery expenditures, which we obtained from state lottery commissions.[12] For the families of the single mother and the unmarried adult, per capita and per household figures are equivalent, but for the married-couple family, we multiplied per capita figures by two to obtain per household figures. Multiplying these average expenditure ratios by the average sales per capita, we determined the average annual lottery expenditures for the hypothetical families.

RESULTS

A Skyline Chart of Marginal Income Tax Rates

Figures 9.1 through 9.3 present marginal tax rates for our three hypothetical families in 1980 and 2004, when federal income taxes, the employee and employer share of FICA taxes, and food stamps and AFDC/TANF benefits (and their relevant phase-outs) are included.[13]

For the married couple and the single mother, one of the main factors affecting their federal income marginal tax rate in both years is the Earned Income Tax Credit (EITC). It causes a negative marginal tax rate as it phases in from zero earnings to the level at which it reaches its maximum value, a 0 percent rate after it reaches the maximum value up to the phase-out level, and then a positive rate as it phases out to zero. The phase-in rate for families changed from –10 percent in 1980 to –40 percent in 2004, leading to very low marginal tax rates at the lowest levels of income. Because the EITC is so small for individuals without children, it has little effect on their marginal tax rates.

However, the increase in the phase-out rate from 12.5 percent to 21 percent and the increase in the income eligibility limits of the EITC have led to higher marginal tax rates at moderate income levels.[14] In addition, whereas the marginal federal income tax rates are negative for low incomes, payroll taxes and the phase-out of benefits impose a high enough rate to more than fully offset the low-income tax rates. This is true over both years.

The benefit reduction effect is very large, so a bit more detail is in order. We assume that the single mother is eligible for both AFDC/TANF and food stamps. Because AFDC/TANF recipients are overwhelmingly single mothers, we assume that married couples are eligible for only the Food Stamp Program. AFDC/TANF and food stamp benefits decrease as earnings increase, so these programs dramatically increase the marginal tax rate for the single mother, and the food stamp phase-out increases the rate for the married couple as well. However, different welfare rules in different years caused the marginal tax rate to move around sharply. In 1980 the marginal tax rate for AFDC benefits was around 60 percent. In 2004 the marginal tax rate for TANF benefits was reduced to 50 percent, since half of earnings could be disregarded.[15] The calculation for food stamp benefits did not change much from 1980 to 2004, so they always added twenty-four percentage points to the marginal tax rate when food stamp benefits were received without welfare.[16] However, when welfare benefits were also being received, food stamps phased out more slowly, although the exact phase-out rate depended on the AFDC/TANF benefit calculation.

Notice that, at $10,000 of earnings, the total marginal rate for a married couple was 21 percent in 1980, but that it had fallen to around 0 percent in 2004 because

FIGURE 9.1 / Marginal Tax Rate for a Married Couple with Two Children

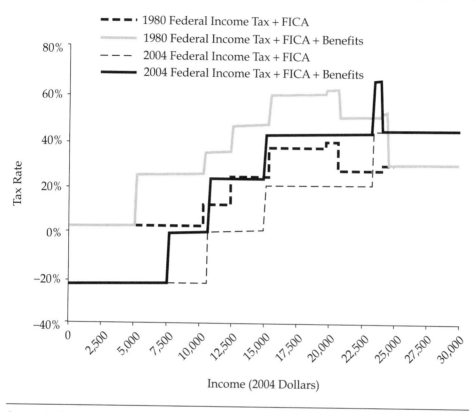

Source: Authors' calculations.

the negative rate of the EITC phase-in had increased. However, at an income of $25,000, the marginal tax rate has since increased from 29 to 43 percent, primarily because the EITC was available at higher incomes in 2004 and so the family faced the high EITC phase-out.

There is a similar pattern for the single mother's skyline in figure 9.2. At $10,000, the total marginal tax rate fell from 62 percent in 1980 to about 0 percent in 2004. The drop was due to the increase in the EITC phase-in rate and the decrease in real income eligibility limits for welfare; at $10,000 of earnings in 2004, the single mother was no longer eligible for TANF, and so she did not face the high phase-out rate of welfare benefits that she did in 1980. At $25,000 of income, the direction of change in the marginal rate is the opposite: the marginal rate in 1980 was 32 percent and increased to 43 percent in 2004 because of the increase in the income eligibility limits of the EITC and the higher phase-out rate.

The unmarried adult (figure 9.3) has very different marginal tax rates than the married couple and single mother. In 1980 the unmarried adult was not eligible

FIGURE 9.2 / Marginal Tax Rate for a Single Mother with Two Children

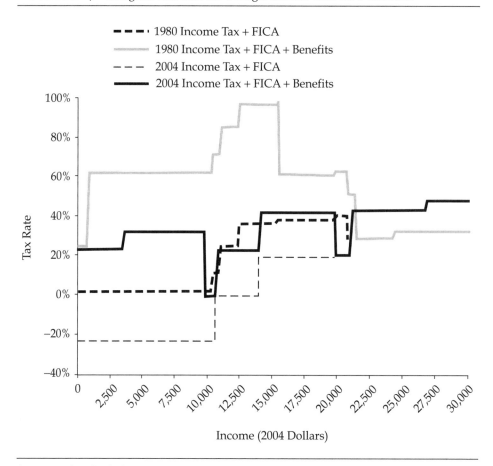

Source: Authors' calculations.

for the EITC because he had no children, so his federal income marginal tax rates were driven only by the standard deduction, his personal exemption, and his tax brackets. In 2004 he was able to receive the EITC, although the phase-in and phase-out rates were much lower than for taxpayers with children and had much less impact on marginal tax rates. The EITC rate for people without children has been set at –7.65 percent, so that it offsets the employee portion payroll tax at the lowest levels on income but does not offset the employer's share.

The unmarried adult never qualifies for welfare since he does not have children who are listed as dependents, and he also is not eligible for food stamps in 2004. In 1980, at the lowest levels of income, food stamps had no effect because they remained at the maximum benefit level, owing to income deductions. As the food stamp benefit phases out, it adds 24 percent to the marginal tax rate.

FIGURE 9.3 / Marginal Tax Rate for an Unmarried Adult with No Dependents

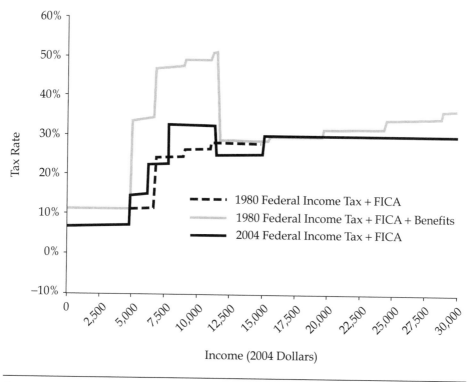

Source: Authors' calculations.

Note that, mainly because there was no food stamp benefit phase-out in 2004, marginal rates fell from 49 percent to 33 percent between 1980 and 2004 at $10,000 of earnings. At $25,000 of income, marginal rates in the two years were almost equal at around 30 percent, which was simply the unmarried adult's tax bracket plus FICA payments.

Marginal tax rates have varied enormously over time for low-income individuals. At the lowest levels of income, marginal rates have decreased tremendously as the EITC phase-in rate has become more negative. The EITC has also enabled families with children to see their average tax rates decrease at low to moderate levels of income, but because the larger EITC requires a higher phase-out rate, they face higher marginal rates as the EITC phases out.

Income Taxes Paid

We now discuss the movement over time in income taxes paid by low-income individuals. Figure 9.4, which we constructed from the IRS Statistics of Income,

FIGURE 9.4   /   Federal Income Tax (Including Refundable Credits) as a Percentage
of AGI for Tax Filers, 1979 to 2002

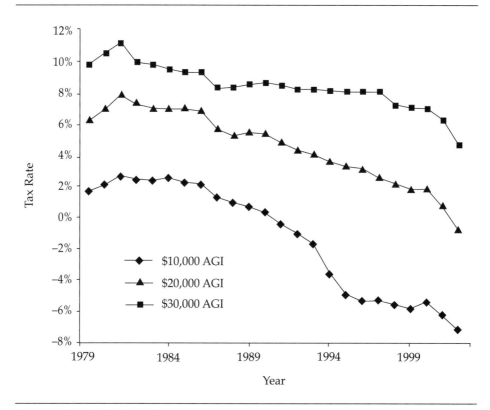

Source: Authors' calculations based on IRS SOI data.
Note: AGIs are in 2004 dollars.

shows the movement in the average federal income tax rate for filers (of all
marital and filing statuses) with income of $10,000, $20,000, and $30,000 for each
year from 1979 to 2002. Each line shows a significant downward trend, with the
average tax rate for filers with $10,000 in income falling from about 2 percent in
1979 to about −8 percent in 2002. This decline is primarily due to the introduction
of the refundable child credit in 2001 and the expansion of the EITC in the early
1990s.[17] For filers at $30,000, the average tax rate fell from about 10 percent in
1979 to about 5 percent in 2002.

The SOI data do not allow us to characterize the movement in taxes for our
hypothetical families. For that, we rely on the NBER TAXSIM calculator.

Figure 9.5 plots the tax bill in each year from 1979 to 2004 for a married couple
with two children and an income of $27,300 (in 2004 inflation-adjusted dollars).
The chart indicates what the family's tax liability was under each year's tax law
for federal income taxes, state income taxes, the employee and employer share

FIGURE 9.5 / Income and Payroll Tax Liability for a Married Couple with Two Children and Total Income of $27,300 (2004 Dollars)

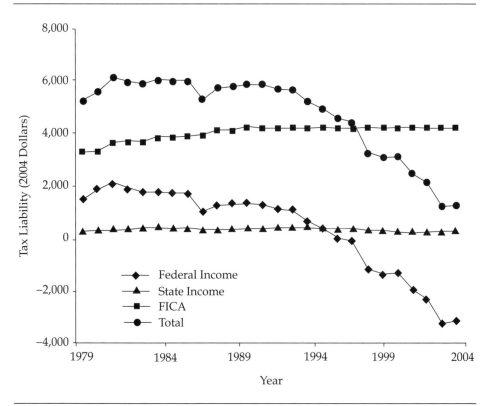

Source: NBER TAXSIM.

of Social Security payroll taxes (FICA), and the sum of these three taxes. Because of the expansion of the EITC and the child credit, in particular, the downward trend that was evident in the early part of the sample had accelerated by the end. In 1979 this family paid about $5,236 in total income and payroll taxes; by 2004 its liability had fallen to $1,208. State income taxes were very small across the years ($230 in 2004), and FICA was $4,176. (The rate has been 7.65 percent each for employer and employee since 1990.)

Figure 9.6 provides a similar chart for a family of three with a single parent earning $14,000 in constant dollars. The tax system provides a net subsidy to work for this family, a subsidy that climbs sharply over time. By 2004, the net subsidy is $2,613, an impressive 19 percent of total income. (The $4,622 federal income tax refund is offset by $2,142 in FICA; state taxes are negative, but negligible.)

Figure 9.7 tells a strikingly different story. It plots the income and payroll tax

FIGURE 9.6 / Income and Payroll Tax Liability for a Single Parent with Two Children and Total Income of $14,000 (2004 Dollars)

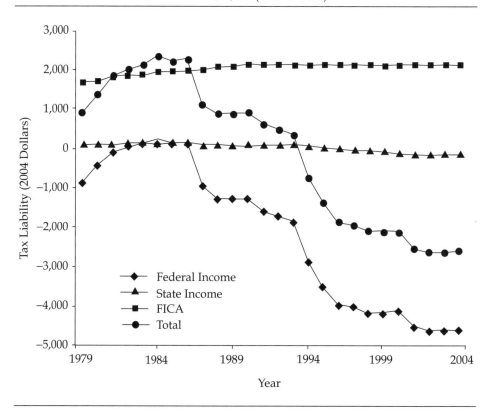

Source: NBER TAXSIM.

liability for a single adult. While the tax code has moved toward subsidizing work for low-income families with children, it has not changed in its treatment of unmarried individuals without children. The total tax liability for an unmarried adult with no children has declined only slightly and was still positive, at about $3,923, in 2004. The average tax rate is roughly the same as that paid by single individuals with incomes almost twice as high.

Thus, the federal and state income tax codes have, on net, moved toward work subsidies only for families with children. There is far less progressivity of the tax code for individuals without children than may be popularly perceived.

Sales Taxes Paid

As mentioned earlier, a key innovation of our analysis is the focus on other taxes paid. Figure 9.8 summarizes in the aggregate what has happened to state sales

FIGURE 9.7 / Income and Payroll Tax Liability for an Unmarried Adult with No Dependents and Total Income of $17,000 (2004 Dollars)

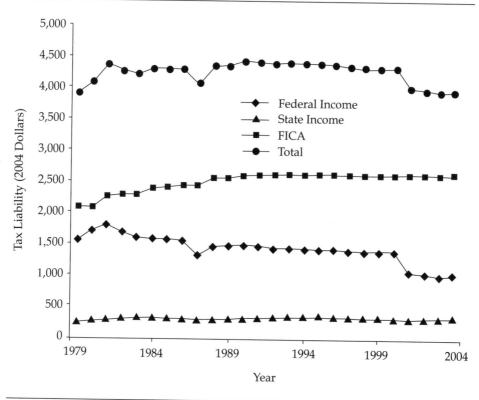

Source: NBER TAXSIM.

taxes over time by plotting a weighted average of the state sales tax rates for each year. Although statutory marginal income tax rates have declined over time, state sales tax rates have increased, climbing from just over 4 percent in 1979 to 5.4 percent in 2004.

Many states exclude numerous items from their state sales tax, and these exclusions have changed over time. To provide intuition for the figures that follow, table 9.1 provides for each year of our CEX database the ratio of taxable consumption to total consumption. The table indicates that the consumption tax base has remained roughly constant over time, with no clear trend. Note how low taxable consumption is relative to the total: it began the sample at 38.22 percentage points and ended at 36.48 percentage points. Key excluded factors include rent, mortgage payments, most food purchases, and most services, depending on the state.

Because the fraction of taxable consumption is low and sales tax rates are

FIGURE 9.8 / Average State Sales Tax Rate (Weighted by State Population)

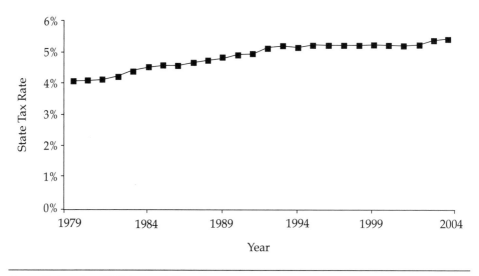

Source: University of Michigan, Office of Tax Policy Research, World Tax Database; Commerce Clearing House *State Tax Reporters.*

about 5 percent, the importance of sales taxes in developing the overall picture is lower than we might have expected.

Figure 9.9 plots our estimate of the evolution of sales and excise taxes for the three hypothetical families. As mentioned earlier, we performed a separate calculation for the tax levied on gasoline, but we show the combined sales and gas taxes in the chart. For the family of four, indicated by the black line, the total sales tax (excluding gasoline taxes) was approximately $411 in 1979; this figure climbed to $530 in 1998, the last year for which we have CEX data. Interestingly, the gasoline tax paid is fairly large relative to the total state sales tax, starting out at $240 in 1979 and climbing to $427 in 1998. The total sales and gas taxes owed by the family climbed from $650 in 1979 to $956 in 1998. The dotted exten-

TABLE 9.1 / Ratio of Taxable Consumption to Total Consumption

1980	38.22%	1987	37.95	1993	37.36
1981	38.18	1988	40.45	1994	37.12
1982	38.27	1989	40.22	1995	36.60
1983	38.01	1990	39.56	1996	36.31
1984	38.55	1991	39.03	1997	36.62
1985	39.94	1992	37.76	1998	36.48
1986	38.61				

Source: Authors' calculations.

FIGURE 9.9 / Sales and Excise Tax Liability

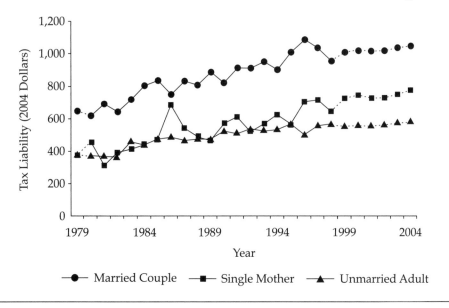

Source: Authors' calculations based on CEX data.

sion of the total sales tax line indicates our estimate of the most likely continued path of the sales tax to approximately $1,050 in 2004.

The two gray lines provide the same data for our other two sample families. Both lines indicate upward-sloping sales and excise taxes over time. Perhaps the most interesting pattern is the much sharper increase in sales tax paid by the single-parent household with earnings of $14,000. This increase clearly reflects the sharp increase in after-tax income (and hence consumption) attributable to the refundable EITC and child credits received by the single mother. Despite her constant earnings, the single mother's income increases each year. In contrast, the unmarried adult—who has a positive federal tax liability—sees no increase in after-tax income and hence has a smaller increase in sales taxes paid.

Figure 9.10 provides our estimates of property tax paid for our three sample families. For each of them, our estimate of average property tax paid is about the same order of magnitude as our estimate of total sales and excise taxes paid. Our estimates in figure 9.10 assume that the homeownership rate is 40 to 50 percent for the married couple, 11 to 16 percent for the single mother, and 24 to 30 percent for the unmarried adult, based on our calculations of the homeownership rate percentage in the CEX. For our family of four, which is much more likely to own a home or, if renting, to pay a higher rent, the average property tax across all households was about $790 in 1979, and it stayed relatively constant over time. The property tax paid by the single mother was slightly more

FIGURE 9.10 / Property Tax

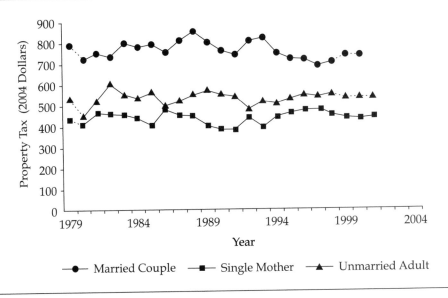

Source: Authors' calculations based on CEX data.

than half that paid by the family of four, and it also stayed roughly steady over time. The property tax paid by the average unmarried adult was slightly higher than that of the single mother.

Figure 9.11 indicates the evolution of lottery spending over time. As has been remarked upon elsewhere (Clotfelter et al. 1999), our estimates show a rapid upward trend in total lottery spending for low-income individuals. A typical family of four, for example, is estimated to spend about the same on the lottery as they do on all state sales taxes (excluding gas taxes), and they spend significantly more on the lottery than they do on gasoline taxes. Although our estimates are imputations, they do suggest that the share of lottery "taxes" in total is likely to be very significant for low-income individuals.

Putting It All Together

In this section, we aggregate the taxes paid calculations we have done for the various components into an estimate of the total taxes paid by each of our sample families.[18]

Figure 9.12 plots the total tax paid across all jurisdictions for each of the sample families from 1979 to 2004. The bottom line in the chart is our estimate of taxes paid for the single mother with two children. These taxes paid actually increased from 1979 until 1986, peaking at $3,435. Since that time, they have

FIGURE 9.11 / Lottery Expenditures (2004 Dollars)

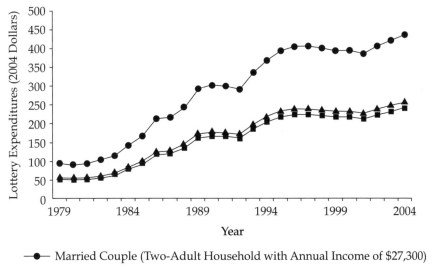

— ● — Married Couple (Two-Adult Household with Annual Income of $27,300)
— ■ — Single Mother (One-Adult Household with Annual Income of $14,000)
— ▲ — Unmarried Adult (One-Adult Household with Annual Income of $17,000)

Source: Authors' calculations based on data from state lottery commissions and published expenditure surveys.

declined steadily. Although the various state and local taxes still impose a burden on single mothers, the total burden across all levels of government had dropped to a net subsidy of about $1,130 by 2004.

The family of four also saw its tax liability drop sharply at the end of the sample. However, for this family, the many taxes faced other than the income tax collected enough revenue that the net tax was positive, despite the large income tax net subsidy. The tax paid by the unmarried adult was remarkably constant over time at around $5,500.

Figure 9.13 provides perspective on the changing relative importance of the various taxes over time. It charts the share of taxes other than income and payroll taxes in total taxes. Since the total tax paid by the single mother with two children is now negative, we omitted that line. For a married couple with two children, the share of non-income taxes rose dramatically over time, beginning the sample at about 25 percent and climbing to more than 60 percent by the end. No such change is evident for the adult without children.

Thus, while concerns about redistribution have clearly motivated a dramatic change in the income tax, changes elsewhere in the code have not kept pace, and the tax system has not increased in progressivity as much as we would think if we focused solely on the income tax.

FIGURE 9.12 / Total Tax Liability for Sample Families, with Employee and Employer FICA Contribution

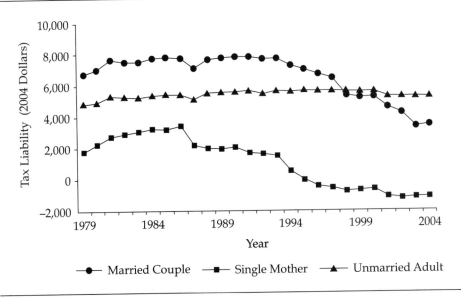

Source: Authors' calculations.

CONCLUSIONS

It is important to caution the reader at this point that direct measures of taxes paid, as reported in this chapter, may be poorly correlated with the actual incidence of the tax. Laurence Kotlikoff and Lawrence Summers (1987) review the literature on tax incidence and find that it is often the case that taxes paid are a poor guide to the actual effect of the tax. Generally speaking, things that are elastically supplied or demanded bear less of the final burden than things that are inelastically supplied. To the extent that labor supply is highly inelastic, it may be the case that workers, as implicitly assumed in this chapter, bear the brunt of the income taxes described here, but a fuller analysis would be required before we could draw firm conclusions. Property taxes, especially to the extent that they are imposed on land, may be capitalized into prices and ultimately borne by whoever owned the property when it was first taxed.

In addition, this study has made no effort to attribute the corporate income tax to low-income individuals, although increasing tax competition over time may have led to this tax increasingly being borne by workers. Suggestive evidence that this may be the case is provided by Young Lee and Roger Gordon (2005), who find a strong negative relationship between corporate tax rates and economic growth, and also by Kevin Hassett and Anne Moore (2005), who find a strong negative relationship between corporate tax rates and both labor income and poverty.

FIGURE 9.13   /   Non-Income and Payroll Tax Liability as a Percentage of Total
Tax Liability

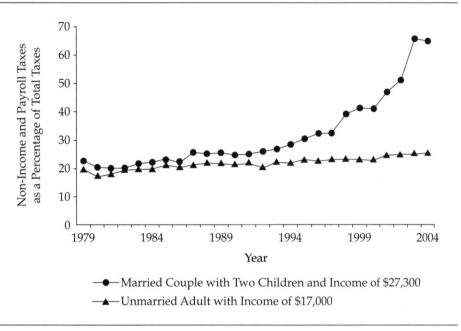

Source: Authors' calculations.

These factors suggest that there is ample room for future research. However,
the data on taxes paid, limited as they are, support three principal findings:

1. The taxes paid by low-income individuals with children have declined over
    the last quarter-century, even in the most comprehensive measure. Low-
    income individuals without children have seen little change in their overall
    tax burden over this period.

2. The proportion of taxes paid that is attributed to non-income taxes has
    climbed sharply over time.

3. Marginal income tax rates have declined in very low income ranges but have
    increased or stayed the same in moderate income ranges.

NOTES

1. We would like to thank Dan Feenberg, John Sabelhaus, Jon Bakija, Therese McGuire,
    and the participants at the National Poverty Center preconference for this book for
    their helpful comments. We would also like to thank Katie Newmark and Gordon
    Gray for their excellent research assistance.

2. In work in progress, we will extend our analysis to individuals with higher incomes.

3. The programs to calculate marginal tax rates are written in Excel and are available from the authors on request. We can also provide individual year skylines on request for any year between 1979 and 2004.

4. Raymond Ring (1999) calculates similar nationwide average sales tax rates using a comparable method, but he does so for only one year, 1989.

5. Our state tax database is now the most complete and comprehensive of any we are aware of. Our data are available on request.

6. This method assumes that local and state sales taxes have the same base, that is, if, for example, the state exempts grocery purchases, then the locality does also. Although this is not always the case, we believe that this assumption is mostly valid and does not significantly affect our results.

7. For the married couple and the single mother, there were not always thirty households of the correct family size with a lower income for each year, but the sample size was always greater than forty.

8. We also checked that the distribution of income around our point of interest was approximately uniform, so that the mean was approximately the same as our point of interest. In each case, the mean and median were close.

9. There is a large literature documenting the underreporting of income in the CEX. Our approach to this issue follows John Rogers and Maureen Gray (1994), who outline the total outlays measure. Bruce Meyer and James Sullivan (2003) and James Poterba (1990) also discuss the merits of using consumption measures.

10. Generally speaking, Americans refer to taxes on commodity units rather than on sales as excise taxes. This usage varies across countries, but is the one relied upon here.

11. It should be noted that the lottery is one of the few taxes that people opt into paying and that people gain utility from the fun of playing the game. Therefore, the tax burdens presented here are overstated to the extent that monetary losses are partially made up for by the lottery's entertainment value.

12. Where possible, data on total lottery sales and net lottery revenues come from state lottery commissions. We filled in missing data using fiscal year 1985 data from Clotfelter and Cook (1987), fiscal year 1989 data from Clotfelter and Cook (1990), fiscal year 1997 data from Clotfelter et al. (1999), and fiscal years 2002 to 2004 data from the North American Association of State and Provincial Lotteries (NASPL). We then used these data points to estimate any remaining missing data. The population figures are Census Bureau estimates of the national population age eighteen or older, since, according to the NASPL, the legal minimum age for buying lottery tickets is eighteen in almost every lottery state. Sales per capita are computed as total national lottery sales divided by the population age eighteen or older.

13. AFDC/TANF benefits are based on the rules and standards of Pennsylvania, which has had average-size benefits over the last twenty-five years. AFDC/TANF benefits were calculated based on the rules for recipients who had been receiving benefits for more than a year rather than on the rules for applicants or for newer recipients.

14. See Hotz and Scholz (2001) and Moffitt (2002) for discussions of how the EITC's impact on marginal tax rates might affect labor supply. Joseph Hotz and John Karl

Scholz (2001) suggest that the EITC encourages participation in the workforce, but that the effect on hours worked might be smaller than the marginal rates imply if recipients have an imperfect understanding of the credit structure.

15. We are using the program rules for Pennsylvania as the representative state. In 2004 income disregards varied substantially by state.

16. This is lower than the 30 percent that food stamps normally decrease by with each increase in income, since one-fifth of earned income is disregarded when calculating the food stamp benefit.

17. The refundable child credit was first introduced in 1998, but it was not available to filers with fewer than three children until 2001.

18. There are a number of other taxes that we investigated but did not include in the final analysis because they were too small to affect our conclusions. For example, average cigarette taxes paid were relatively small given the large share of individuals made up of nonsmokers.

REFERENCES

Auerbach, Alan. 1985. "The Theory of Excess Burden and Optimal Taxation." In *Handbook of Public Economics*, vol. 1, edited by Alan Auerbach and Martin Feldstein. Amsterdam: North Holland.

Brinner, Roger E., and Charles T. Clotfelter. 1975. "An Economic Appraisal of State Lotteries." *National Tax Journal* 28(4): 395–404.

Burman, Leonard E., and Mohammed Adeel Saleem. 2004. "Income Tax Statistics for Sample Families, 2003." *Tax Notes* 102(3): 413–18.

Carasso, Adam, and C. Eugene Steuerle. 2003. "Personal Exemption: Not What It Used to Be." *Tax Notes* 9(4): 563.

Center on Budget and Policy Priorities. 2004. *State Income Tax Burdens on Low-Income Families in 2003*. Washington, D.C.: Center for Budget and Policy Priorities.

Clotfelter, Charles T., and Philip J. Cook. 1987. "Implicit Taxation in Lottery Finance." *National Tax Journal* 40(4): 533–46.

———. 1989. *Selling Hope: State Lotteries in America*. Cambridge, Mass.: Harvard University Press.

———. 1990. "On the Economics of State Lotteries." *Journal of Economic Perspectives* 4(4): 105–19.

Clotfelter, Charles T., Philip J. Cook, Julie A. Edell, and Marian Moore. 1999. "State Lotteries at the Turn of the Century: Report to the National Gambling Impact Study Commission" (April 23). Available at: http://govinfo.library.unt.edu/ngisc/reports/lotfinal.pdf.

Cornwell, Christopher, and David B. Mustard. 2001. "The Distributional Impacts of Lottery-Funded Aid: Evidence from Georgia's HOPE Scholarship." Working paper (August). Athens: University of Georgia. Available at: http://www.terry.uga.edu/hope/hope.lottery.pdf.

Devarajan, Shantayanan, Don Fullerton, and Richard A. Musgrave. 1980. "Estimating the Distribution of Tax Burdens: A Comparison of Different Approaches." *Journal of Public Economics* 13(2): 155–82.

Fullerton, Don, John B. Shoven, and John Whalley. 1978. "General Equilibrium Analysis of U.S. Tax Policy." *1978 Compendium of Tax Research*. Washington: U.S. Treasury Department.

Gale, William G., and Peter R. Orzag. 2004. "Bush Administration Tax Policy: Distributional Effects." *Tax Notes* 104(14): 1559–66.

Harberger, Arnold C. 1962. "The Incidence of the Corporation Income Tax." *Journal of Political Economy* 70(3): 215–40.

Hassett, Kevin A., and Anne Moore. 2005. "Tax Competition and Wages." Working paper. Washington, D.C.: American Enterprise Institute.

Hotz, Joseph V., and John Karl Scholz. 2001. "The Earned Income Tax Credit." Working paper 8078. Cambridge, Mass.: National Bureau of Economic Research.

Institute on Taxation and Economic Policy. 2003. *Who Pays? A Distributional Analysis of the Tax Systems in All Fifty States*. Washington, D.C.: Institute on Taxation and Economic Policy.

Kearney, Melissa Schettini. 2002. "State Lotteries and Consumer Behavior." Working paper 9330. Cambridge, Mass.: National Bureau of Economic Research.

Kotlikoff, Laurence J., and Lawrence H. Summers. 1987. "Tax Incidence." In *Handbook of Public Economics*, vol. 2, edited by Alan Auerbach and Martin Feldstein. Amsterdam: North Holland.

Lee, Young, and Roger H. Gordon. 2005. "Tax Structure and Economic Growth." *Journal of Public Economics* 89(6): 1227–43.

Maag, Elaine, and Diane Lim Rogers. 2000. "The New Federalism and State Tax Policies Toward the Working Poor." Occasional paper 38. Assessing the New Federalism Series. Washington, D.C.: Urban Institute.

Meyer, Bruce D., and James X. Sullivan. 2003. "Measuring the Well-being of the Poor Using Income and Consumption." Working paper 9760. Cambridge, Mass.: National Bureau of Economic Research.

Moffitt, Robert. 2002. "Welfare Programs and Labor Supply." Working paper 9168. Cambridge, Mass.: National Bureau of Economic Research.

Pechman, Joseph A. 1985. *Who Paid the Taxes, 1966–1985*. Washington, D.C.: Brookings Institution.

Pechman, Joseph A., and Benjamin A. Okner. 1974. *Who Bears the Tax Burden?* Washington, D.C.: Brookings Institution.

Poterba, James M. 1990. "Is the Gasoline Tax Regressive?" Working paper 3578. Cambridge, Mass.: National Bureau of Economic Research.

Ring, Raymond J. 1999. "Consumers' Share and Producers' Share of the General Sales Tax." *National Tax Journal* 52(1): 79–90.

Rogers, John M., and Maureen B. Gray. 1994. "CE Data: Quintiles of Income Versus Quintiles of Outlays." *Monthly Labor Review* 117(2): 32–37.

Suits, Daniel B. 1977. "Gambling Taxes: Regressivity and Revenue Potential." *National Tax Journal* 30(1): 19–35.1. 2.

Chapter 10

State Spending on Social Assistance Programs over the Business Cycle

Therese J. McGuire and David F. Merriman

The passage in 1996 of the Personal Responsibility and Work Opportunity Reconciliation Act (PRWORA) brought about a major change in the way the federal government and the states share financial responsibility for cash assistance and related welfare programs.[1] Prior to PRWORA, the federal government provided a matching grant program, Aid to Families with Dependent Children (AFDC), and was responsible for an average of fifty-five cents out of every dollar of AFDC spending. Since the passage of PRWORA, the federal government has given an annual block grant to the states for funding the AFDC replacement program, Temporary Assistance for Needy Families (TANF). Our goals in this chapter are to review the history of federal and state spending on public welfare programs, focusing on the business cycles of the past twenty-five years, and to investigate whether state spending on public welfare programs has been affected by the meaningful change in funding brought about by PRWORA.

We are particularly interested in whether the responsiveness to recessions of state spending on social assistance programs changed after welfare reform. In general, during recessions state spending on social assistance programs can increase or decrease. It might be expected to increase as people become unemployed and experience declines in well-being. On the other hand, states facing fiscal distress might cut discretionary spending, which includes some forms of social assistance. The passage of PRWORA changed the incentives to spend on AFDC/TANF programs, since the act eliminated the significant cost sharing associated with the federal matching grant program. Spending on AFDC/TANF programs at the margin is more expensive since PRWORA. Other financial arrangements under PRWORA, such as the maintenance-of-effort requirements and the ability to carry over surplus funds, might also affect state spending during periods of fiscal distress in unpredictable ways. Ultimately, the responsiveness of state spending on welfare programs to recessions before and after the passage of PRWORA is an empirical question.

As we discuss later, despite the mild drop in national output during the recession of 2001, state revenue systems were put under severe strain. States weathered this first revenue slump post–welfare reform with little assistance from the federal government beyond the nominal-dollar, fixed block grants they were guaranteed as part of the PRWORA legislation. In this chapter, we set out to learn whether states acted as many feared they would and disproportionately cut social assistance spending during the 2001 recession.

Our answer, in short, is that they did not. We think the reasons for this go beyond the simple notion that most state legislators have a charitable nature and reflect the fact that spending for cash assistance—the traditional center of welfare policy—is no longer a large portion of state budgets. The safety net has become multifaceted and considerably more dominated by the federal government despite the fixed block grants introduced by PRWORA. Still, we acknowledge that, because the recession of 2001 was relatively mild and followed a period of unusual revenue gains in the late 1990s, we cannot be sure that states will always maintain spending for low-income populations when faced with fiscal stress. Also, because of the unusual sluggishness in the recovery of state revenues following the 2001 recession, we cannot yet be sure how state spending will adapt in the long run.

THE FISCAL FEDERALISM OF SOCIAL ASSISTANCE SPENDING

The Legislative History of Social Assistance Spending

Over the past four decades, social assistance spending (spending for the basic needs of the indigent population) at the state government level has centered on two interconnected federal-state programs: Aid to Families with Dependent Children (AFDC), created in 1935, and Medicaid, enacted in 1965. Social changes and legislative amendments to the Social Security Act in the early 1960s resulted in major expansions of these and other federal-state social assistance programs. Passed in 1960, the Kerr-Mills Act provided federal matching funds for participating states that made payments to those providing health care to certain low-income elderly individuals. Further legislative amendments created the Medicaid entitlement program in 1965 and linked eligibility for Medicaid to eligibility for AFDC. Both AFDC and Medicaid were designed as intergovernmental partnerships, with the federal government providing 50 to 85 percent of the funding and the states retaining significant control over program design and operation.

By 1969, four years after Medicaid's enactment, (nominal) state and local spending for non-Medicaid welfare (mostly AFDC) had nearly doubled, and by 1974 it had nearly quadrupled. Expenditures for Medicaid continued to grow rapidly over the next two decades as states covered more categories of recipients and found ways to extract federal matching payments for low-income health services they were already providing. States also expanded the services they provided under AFDC by combining work supports with cash assistance. Many states received waivers for both AFDC and Medicaid and developed innovative programs to deliver assistance to their low-income residents.

AFDC underwent a sea change when Congress passed PRWORA in 1996. This act abolished the AFDC program and replaced it with Temporary Assistance for Needy Families (TANF). TANF represented a major practical and philosophical shift in the nation's and the states' approaches to economic assistance for low-income households. Recipients were limited to five years of cash assistance over their lifetime. Federal matches for state assistance were replaced with a block grant equal to the amount of federal aid for AFDC received in 1994 in most cases. States were given a maintenance-of-effort provision that required them to maintain their TANF spending at a minimum of 75 percent of their 1994 contribution to AFDC-related programs. States also were given considerable flexibility in how they directed their efforts. In particular, states could transfer a significant share of their TANF block grant to related programs that aided children from low-income families. A particularly unusual feature of TANF financing arrangements was that states were not required to spend their federal block grant in the year in which it was received. States that did not expend their entire federal TANF grant in a particular year accumulated "surpluses" that could be expended in future years. With rapid caseload declines in the late 1990s, many states accumulated considerable surpluses that they were able to use to supplement TANF spending in later years (see Lazere 2000).

States were required to get welfare recipients into the workforce and faced penalties if they failed to do so. Other facets of the TANF program included comprehensive child support enforcement, various supports—including transitional Medicaid eligibility—for families moving from welfare to work, and performance bonuses to the states that were most successful at getting welfare recipients into the labor market and reducing out-of-wedlock births.

Elimination of the federal match for state expenditures led some analysts to worry that states would be reluctant to increase social welfare spending to meet increased need for assistance during recessionary periods. TANF legislation included a $2 billion federal contingency fund from which states could borrow if they experienced increasing, high, and persistent unemployment rates. A state was eligible to use the fund if its unemployment rate exceeded 6.5 percent or its food stamp caseload increased at least 10 percent over either its 1994 or 1995 level. To gain access to the contingency fund, states had to maintain their own spending at 100 percent of fiscal year 1994 levels (rather than the 75 percent maintenance-of-effort level). However, this fund was widely regarded as providing little benefit to states because of the stringent conditions for gaining access to it and the payback requirements (Holzer 2002; Powers 1999). Despite a two-percentage-point increase in the national unemployment rate between October 2000 and August 2003, no state used the contingency fund (Fremstad and Parrott 2004).

TABLE 10.1 / Total Federal, State, and Local Spending by Program

			Millions of Nominal Dollars			
Year	Medicaid	AFDC/TANF	Food Stamps	SSI	EITC	GA
1980	25,781	13,019	9,576	8,435	2,033	1,386
1990	72,492	21,200	17,686	17,233	5,303	2,924
2000	207,195	14,490	20,341	35,066	25,800	2,649
2002	258,216	13,035	24,054	38,522	27,830	3,251
			Real Dollars Per Capita			
Year	Medicaid	AFDC/TANF	Food Stamps	SSI	EITC	GA
1980	1374	694	510	450	108	74
1990	2217	648	541	527	162	89
2000	4276	299	420	724	532	55
2002	4973	251	463	742	536	63

Source: Authors' compilations from U.S. Census Bureau *Statistical Abstract of the United States* (various years).

PRWORA also contained provisions that directly affected Medicaid: states were required to cover families meeting AFDC eligibility criteria as of July 1996, and legal immigrants who entered the United States prior to August 1996 were barred from Medicaid coverage for a five-year period. Perhaps more importantly, PRWORA severed the link between the receipt of cash assistance and Medicaid eligibility that had been in place since the 1960s.

Spending on and Funding of Social Assistance Programs

Responsibility for the funding of social assistance programs is very much shared among all levels of government in the United States. The funding for Medicaid and AFDC/TANF is shared in roughly equal proportions between the federal government and the states. The Earned Income Tax Credit (EITC) is solely a federal program, while the federal Food Stamp Program involves administrative and minor funding responsibility on the part of the states.[2] Supplemental Security Income (SSI) is largely a federal program, but some states supplement the program. Finally, general assistance programs are completely in the hands of state (and local) governments.

Table 10.1 presents total federal, state, and local spending in current dollars and in real dollars per capita by program over the last few decades. Nominal spending on Medicaid increased tenfold from 1980 to 2002. The only other program to show such a rapid increase in spending over the period was the federal

FIGURE 10.1 / Average Monthly Recipients, by Program

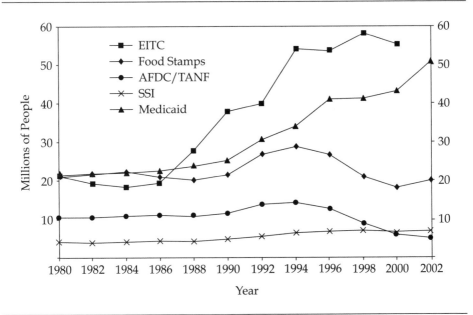

Source: Authors' compilations from U.S. Census Bureau *Statistical Abstract of the United States* (various years).

EITC. Both food stamps and the states' general assistance programs roughly tripled in size over the period, while SSI increased three and a half times. Interestingly, spending on AFDC/TANF (cash assistance only) started and ended the time period at about $13 billion. Real per capita spending actually declined over the period for AFDC/TANF, food stamps, and general assistance programs.

Much of the spending in social assistance programs is driven by caseload. In figure 10.1, we plot the average monthly recipients (AMR) in even years from 1980 to 2002 for five of the six programs.[3] The fairly consistent and strong upward trend in AMR for the EITC and Medicaid mirrors the trends in spending on these two programs. The AMR for food stamps and the AMR for AFDC/TANF are broadly flat over the time period and track one another when they are not flat, with a few exceptions. For example, in the early 1990s, the number of food stamp recipients increased sharply relative to the number of AFDC/TANF recipients. Both figures began to decline in 1994, then fell fairly steeply from 1996 to 2000. From 2000 to 2002, the AMR for food stamps ticked up, while the AMR for AFDC/TANF continued to decline, but at a reduced rate. Throughout the time period, the number of food stamp recipients was two to three times as large as the number of AFDC/TANF recipients, and by 2002, because of the deviations in trends since the early 1990s, the number of food stamp recipients (slightly more than 20 million) was nearly four times the number of AFDC/TANF recipi-

TABLE 10.2 / Allocation of State Spending Across Categories (Percentage of Total)

Major Categories

Year	Public Welfare	Health and Hospitals	Higher Education	Elementary and Secondary Education	Other
1980	19.4%	7.8%	12.3%	21.8%	38.7%
1985	19.5	8.0	13.9	21.0	37.7
1990	20.7	8.4	13.2	20.7	37.1
1995	26.6	8.2	12.2	19.4	33.6
2000	24.8	7.8	12.5	21.0	34.0
2003	26.9	7.6	12.5	20.3	32.7

Source: U.S. Census of Governments.

Public Welfare Subcategories

Year	Medical Vendor Payments	Cash Assistance	Other Public Welfare
1980	8.3%	3.3%	7.8%
1985	9.3	2.8	7.4
1990	11.1	2.4	7.2
1995	16.4	2.1	8.1
2000	15.9	1.2	7.7
2003	18.1	1.0	7.8

Source: Authors' calculations based on data from U.S. Census Bureau, *State Government Finances* (various years).
Note: The "other" category includes spending on highways, police protection, corrections, natural resources, parks and recreation, and government administration.

ents (5.1 million). Unlike spending on SSI, which increased steadily and fairly steeply, the number of SSI recipients exhibited only a slight drift upward during the period.

State spending on social assistance programs makes up a large part of the total state budget. In the top panel of table 10.2, we display the budget shares for four major categories of state spending and a residual "other" category at five-year intervals beginning in 1980 and for the most recent year available, 2003. Spending on public welfare rose from 19.4 percent of total state spending in 1980 to 26.9 percent in 2003. State spending on public welfare was on roughly the same order of magnitude as state spending on elementary and secondary education, although the latter did not experience the increase in budget share that public welfare did. The budget shares for health and hospitals and for higher education were virtually constant over the period, and their shares were relatively low

FIGURE 10.2 / Federal Grants for Medicaid and Income Security

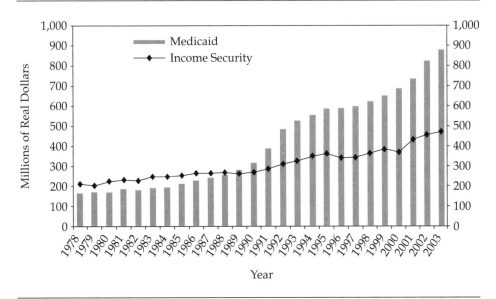

Source: Authors' compilations from U.S. Census Bureau *Statistical Abstract of the United States* (various years).

(about 8 percent for health and hospitals and about 13 percent for higher education).

It is clear from table 10.3, where we break out public welfare into component parts, that the growth in public welfare's spending share was driven by the growth in medical vendor payments (largely Medicaid). Medical vendor payments' share of state spending grew from 8.3 percent in 1980 to 18.1 percent in 2003. Cash assistance, the focus of the most recent welfare reform, accounted for a small and dwindling share of total state spending. In 1980 cash assistance was only 3.3 percent of total state spending. By 2003, that share had declined to a mere 1 percent.

In figure 10.2, we plot real dollar amounts of federal grants-in-aid to state and local governments over the last few decades for Medicaid and for Income Security (public assistance, primarily cash payments to individuals; food stamps administration; child nutrition programs; housing assistance; and other programs). The figure illustrates the phenomenal growth in federal aid for Medicaid. In 1980 federal aid for Income Security exceeded federal aid for Medicaid by about $55 million (in constant dollars), but only ten years later the reverse was true. By 2003, federal grants for Medicaid were nearly twice federal grants for Income Security.

Federal grants for AFDC/TANF increased much more slowly over the last few decades. In constant dollars 2003 federal grants for TANF were just 20 percent greater than 1981 federal grants for AFDC compared with an increase over the same period in federal grants for Medicaid of about 372 percent and for Income Security, which contains AFDC/TANF as one component, of about 103 percent.[4]

STATE FINANCES AND ECONOMIC RECESSIONS

The extent to which economic downturns put states in a fiscal bind depends on the responsiveness of state revenues and expenditures to those downturns. The responsiveness in turn depends on the underlying structure of revenues and expenditures as well as the willingness of state policymakers to make adjustments to spending and revenues. In this section, we review the relevant literature and present some descriptive statistics to shed light on the responsiveness of state revenues and expenditures during times of economic distress.

The Behavior of State Revenues over the Business Cycle

The cyclical properties of state tax revenues have been the focus of a recent series of papers. Russell Sobel and Randall Holcombe (1996) and Richard Dye and Therese McGuire (1998, 1999) examine the short-run elasticity—the variability over the business cycle—of proxies for the major tax bases used by state governments. These studies relate the volatility of tax revenues to the design of the tax. For example, the short-run elasticity of personal consumer services is higher than the value for a typical goods-based tax base, and the short-run elasticity of the income tax rises uniformly with increases in the income range subject to tax. Dye and McGuire (1999) find that state tax policy changes during economic downturns often fully offset revenue declines from slowed economic activity, so that during recessions changes in gross state product (GSP) are inversely correlated with changes in tax revenues.[5]

The behavior of state revenues during the most recent recession has been the focus of several studies. Fred Giertz and Seth Giertz (2004) examine the history of state revenues over the last fifty years, a period that includes nine recessions. They find that the downturn in revenues associated with the 2001 recession was like no other in recent experience and that there was little the states could have done to foresee or forestall the fluctuation in revenues. Brian Knight, Andrea Kusko, and Laura Rubin (2003) and Elaine Maag and David Merriman (2003) compare across time the responses of states to the fiscal difficulties associated with the recessions of the early 1980s, the early 1990s, and 2001. In contrast to Giertz and Giertz, these researchers attribute much of the fiscal crisis of 2001 to the lack of response of state policymakers to the need to make structural adjustments to revenues and expenditures. In all likelihood, the 2001 fiscal crisis resulted from a combination of an unprecedented swing in the income tax base and a general lack of policy response.

In figure 10.3, we examine how total state tax revenues, revenues from the

FIGURE 10.3 / State Tax Revenues Immediately Before, During, and After Recent U.S. Recessions (Billions of Real 1983 Dollars)

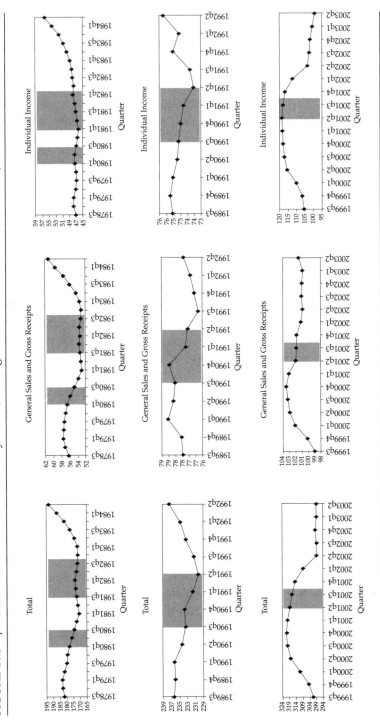

Sources: Authors' compilations based on data from U.S. Census Bureau, Quarterly Summary of State and Local Government Tax Revenue, (various quarters).

Notes:

Recessions: The first was a double-dip recession from January 1980 to July 1980 and from July 1981 to November 1982. The second recession occurred from July 1990 to March 1991. The third recession occurred from March 2001 to November 2001.

general sales and gross receipts tax, and revenues from the individual income tax were affected by the three most recent recessions. We display annualized real revenues for each calendar quarter. In each of the three time periods, we begin with the start of the last full fiscal year prior to the recession and end with one complete fiscal year following the recession.[6] This protocol is complicated somewhat by the fact that the United States was in recession for parts of each fiscal year from fiscal year 1980 through fiscal year 1983, with a recovery from August 1980 to June 1981 (that is, most of fiscal year 1981). We treat this period as a single recession and show data for each fiscal year from 1979 through 1984. The recession that began in July 1990 was confined exclusively to fiscal year 1991, so we display only three years of data. The most recent recession encompassed parts of fiscal year 2001 and fiscal year 2002, and so we exhibit four years of data.

Examining total tax revenues, we see that in both the double-dip recession of the early 1980s and the recession of the early 1990s, revenues began falling prior to the start of the recession. Once the recession began, total revenues fell sharply in both cases but recovered as soon as the recession ended. The most recent recession was clearly different. First, revenues rose very rapidly in the period immediately preceding the recession—growing about 6 percent in fiscal year 2000. Revenues stabilized and then dipped slightly in the last two quarters before the recession began, but the bulk of the fall occurred four to six months after it ended. Furthermore, revenues remained flat at this low level for more than a year.

The story for sales tax revenues differs only slightly from the total revenue story. Sales tax revenues clearly softened prior to all three recessions. Sales tax revenues fell sharply and stayed down in the 1980 recession but rose and then fell in the 1990 to 1991 recession. In the most recent recession, sales tax revenues fell only slightly but continued falling for several quarters after the recession and stayed far below their peak even a full year after the recession was over.

Individual income tax revenues actually rose slightly over the course of the 1980 recession, and they rose dramatically once the recession ended in November 1982. Income tax revenues fell during the 1990 to 1991 recession but again rose rapidly as soon as it ended. As with total revenues, the most recent recession was dramatically different. Growth in income tax revenues slowed going into the recession but did not fall until after the recession began; then income tax revenues plummeted over the course of the next year and a half or so, with no sign of recovery in the displayed data. Clearly, the major revenue impacts of the most recent recession occurred after, not during, the recession.

The dramatic fall in individual income tax revenues is the defining characteristic of the state fiscal crisis of the early 2000s. The depth and persistence of the fall in revenues far beyond the end of the recession are not well understood. Contributing factors probably include the sluggish recovery, a relatively large fall in income in the upper brackets, and, as stated earlier, a lack of policy response.

The Behavior of State Expenditures over the Business Cycle

Very little research has been focused on the cyclical behavior of state expenditures. One study, Dye and McGuire (1999), examines the behavior of various categories of state spending during recessionary years in the period 1977 to 1995. These authors report recession-year elasticities, which they calculate as ratios of recession-year average percentage changes in real expenditures divided by recession-year average percentage changes in real GSP. They find negative recession-year elasticities for many states and for the U.S. average for each category of spending (including public welfare, AFDC, K-12 education, and higher education). These findings indicate that state spending was countercyclical during the recessions analyzed.

The onset of the 2001 recession presents an opportunity to test the theory that major structural changes in welfare policy resulting from the replacement of AFDC with TANF altered state responses to fiscal stress. Although the data necessary to conduct rigorous statistical studies of state responses to the recession are just beginning to be available, several groups of researchers have already conducted detailed case studies in some representative states.

A team of Urban Institute researchers conducted site visits and interviews in seven states in mid-2002 to assess the impact of the fiscal downturn on social assistance spending (Finegold et al. 2003). The study teams found that state revenues were insufficient to maintain real spending at fiscal year 2001 levels in all of the states they visited with budget gaps ranging from 2.5 to 17.2 percent. States used a variety of mechanisms to balance their budgets in fiscal years 2002 and 2003. Every state in the sample closed a significant portion of the budget gap with short-term revenue-enhancement measures, such as drawing down reserve funds, debt refinancing, and securitization of payments from the tobacco industry mandated by a recent court settlement.

A separate team of Urban Institute researchers (Holohan et al. 2003, 7–11) found that

> Medicaid cuts were numerous but small as a share of the budget gaps. . . . Almost all of the states [in the study] . . . sought to increase federal Medicaid matching funds by shifting state-funded programs into Medicaid. . . . For example, California shifted some state-funded services for the developmentally disabled into Medicaid in order to obtain the federal match; the result is that total Medicaid spending went up, but state spending was reduced. . . . Michigan and Mississippi turned to the use of provider taxes or "assessments" to draw down additional federal Medicaid money without having to spend any additional [state] general revenue funds.

Another research team collected qualitative and quantitative data and conducted site visits during late 2003 in six poor states to assess, among other things, how social welfare spending responds to short-term fiscal challenges such as the recent state fiscal crises (Lewin Group 2004). The research team found that the growth in Medicaid spending continued despite budgetary pressures in the states. Among the poor states that were the focus of that study, cash assistance spending had changed little as a result of the 1996 welfare reform, and this was still true as of 2002. The researchers found that states used TANF surpluses from previous years to maintain or increase social welfare spending during the fiscal downturn.

These case studies suggest that, despite rapid drops in tax revenues and daunting budget gaps in the most recent recession, states generally were able to weather the storm without making dramatic cuts in spending for their most vulnerable populations. The lack of cuts in TANF seems to be the combined result of adequate funds, due to dramatic caseload declines in the late 1990s, and the program's maintenance-of-effort requirement. The U.S. Government Accountability Office (2003) estimated that states had accumulated $5.6 billion in TANF surpluses by the end of September 2003. The GAO also found that in the wake of the fiscal crisis the states it examined intended to use unspent TANF funds to supplement spending in fiscal 2004. It is more surprising that most states also were able to avoid drastic cuts in Medicaid. It appears that states made use of temporary revenues and administrative restructuring to avoid severe cuts, at least temporarily.

In figure 10.4, we examine how state spending on two primary subcomponents of public welfare—medical vendor payments (Medicaid) and cash assistance— and, for purposes of comparison, total state spending and state spending on education fared in the three most recent recessions. Since nationally comparable data on state spending are available only on an annual (fiscal year) basis, we have fewer data points than we have for tax revenues, which are reported on a quarterly basis, but we display data covering the same periods. In each case, we show real per capita spending for the last full fiscal year prior to the recession, the fiscal year or years containing the recession, and one complete fiscal year following the recession.

The three bar graphs running down the left-most column of figure 10.4 show a clear difference between the recession of the early 1980s and the two subsequent recessions. Total spending fell and recovered during the course of the early recession, but increased throughout the latter two recessions. Total real per capita state spending increased at a rate of less than .05 percent per year between fiscal years 1979 and 1984 (with declines in fiscal years 1980, 1981, and 1982), but increased at a rate of 3.5 percent per year from fiscal year 1990 to fiscal year 1992, and nearly 7 percent per year from fiscal year 2000 to fiscal year 2003, with no years of decline.

The three bar graphs running down the second column of figure 10.4 display per capita spending on education during the three most recent recessions. Education spending declined fairly dramatically during the recession of the early 1980s before recovering in the year after the recession ended. In the two most recent recessions, education spending grew throughout the cycle.

In our examination of the major subcomponents of public welfare displayed

FIGURE 10.4 / State Expenditures Immediately Before, During, and After Recent U.S. Recessions (Real 1983 Dollars Per Capita)

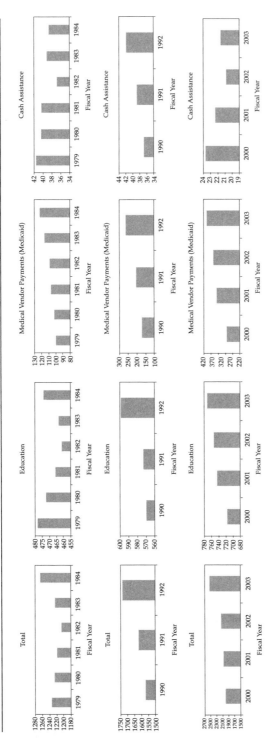

Source: Authors' calculations based on data from U.S. Census Bureau, *State Government Finances* (various years).

Notes:

Recessions: The first was a double-dip recession from January 1980 to July 1980 and from July 1981 to November 1982. The second recession occurred from July 1990 to March 1991. The third recession occurred from March 2001 to November 2001.

Inflation correction uses U.S. Consumer Price Index from the Federal Reserve Bank of Minnesota, State government spending and population from U.S. Census Bureau Annual Series State Government Finances.

in the final two columns, we focus on the two most recent recessions (rows 2 and 3). During the recession of fiscal year 1991, spending on cash assistance increased. In contrast, spending on cash assistance declined in fiscal year 2002. These changes in spending can be explained by the fact that welfare rolls increased in the earlier recession but fell despite the recession of fiscal year 2002. Cash assistance spending rose slightly in fiscal year 2003, but still remained below its level in fiscal year 2000 and far below its level in the early 1990s.

In contrast, medical vendor payments—the payments that states make, generally through Medicaid, to cover the health care of indigent patients—rose steadily in both recessions. These expenditures rose at an astounding 17.1 percent annual rate in the 1990 to 1992 period and rose 6.2 percent a year from fiscal year 2000 to fiscal year 2003.

In summary, states maintained growth in both total spending and its major components in the most recent recession, despite the dramatic declines in revenue documented here. The net result was the fiscal crisis of the early part of the decade.

THE SENSITIVITY TO ECONOMIC CONDITIONS OF STATE SPENDING ON SOCIAL ASSISTANCE

In this section, we study the cyclicality of various categories of state government expenditures by estimating regressions using panel data on the fifty states over the period 1979 to 2003. We are interested in whether states disproportionately cut or expand spending on social welfare during economic downturns. We are particularly interested in whether states changed their behavior in this regard after 1997, when TANF replaced AFDC and the federal government's matching of state welfare expenditures ended.

Table 10.3 displays descriptive data for the most important variables in our analysis for the period before welfare reform was implemented (fiscal years 1979 through 1997) and the period after welfare reform (fiscal years 1998 to 2003). We analyze seven categories of state spending. Total spending, K–12 education spending, and higher education spending are self-explanatory categories. Social assistance spending includes two broad categories: public welfare spending and spending on health and hospitals. Public welfare spending in turn contains medical vendor payments (mostly for Medicaid), cash assistance (both AFDC/TANF and state spending on SSI), and other expenditures. Note that mean spending in each category was higher in the post–welfare reform era, with the exception of cash assistance, which fell 27 percent.[7] Our indicator of economic downturns is the unemployment rate, which was much higher on average and slightly more variable in the early period. (A coefficient of variation of 0.32 in the pre–welfare reform era compared to 0.24 in the post–welfare reform era.)

In table 10.4, we display coefficient estimates for our variables of interest from several regressions, where each regression is defined by its dependent variable being a different category of spending. We include state fixed effects so that the

TABLE 10.3 / Real Per Capita (1983 Dollars) State Spending and State Unemployment Rates, Before and After Welfare Reform

Variable	Obser-vations	Mean	Standard Deviation	Mini-mum	Maxi-mum
FY1979 to FY1997					
Total spending	950	$1,630	$770	$832	$8,215
Elementary and secondary education	947	320	150	3	1,467
Higher education	950	219	69	71	547
Social assistance spending	950	423	170	134	1,151
Public welfare	950	302	140	62	948
Medical vendor payments	950	173	97	2	578
Cash Assistance	871	48	29	0.2	178
Unemployment rate	950	6.42%	2.08%	2.30%	17.40%
FY1998 to FY2003					
Total spending	300	$2,162	$617	$1,441	$5,971
Elementary and secondary education	300	429	118	115	915
Higher education	300	282	69	139	511
Social assistance spending	300	649	176	242	1,347
Public welfare	300	498	153	153	1,102
Medical vendor payments	300	340	105	60	768
Cash assistance	276	35	27	0.1	161
Unemployment rate	300	4.44%	1.09%	2.30%	7.60%

Source: Authors' calculations based on data from U.S. Census Bureau, State Government Finances (various years).
Notes: Inflation correction uses the U.S. consumer price index from the Federal Reserve Bank of Minnesota. Unemployment rates are calendar year averages, not seasonally adjusted.

reported regression coefficients explain within-state deviations. We also include year dummy variables that control for national-level policy changes, including welfare reform as well as national economic conditions. We also include, but do not report, controls for Republican political power in the various branches of state government. The regressions in table 10.4 include an interaction term between the state unemployment rate and the dummy variable for being in the post–welfare reform era. This variable enables us to assess whether spending has become more sensitive to economic downturns since the implementation of PRWORA.

The negative and significant coefficients on the unemployment rate variable in the first three columns of table 10.4 imply that an increase in the unemployment rate is associated with lower total spending and lower education spending. Although these effects are small—prior to 1998 a three-percentage-point increase in the unemployment rate caused per capita total expenditures to decline by only $36—they contrast sharply with the coefficient on social assistance spending,

TABLE 10.4 / Selected Regression Coefficients with Categories of State Spending as the Dependent Variable

	Total Spending	Elementary and Secondary Education	Higher Education	Social Assistance Spending	Public Welfare	Medical Vendor Payments	Cash Assistance
Unemployment rate	−11.90**	−5.00**	−4.23**	0.93	2.97	0.39	3.25**
	(5.07)	(1.79)	(0.60)	(1.65)	(1.63)	(1.39)	(0.49)
Dummy for post-1997 multiplied by unemployment rate	−61.00**	−31.05**	−6.28**	28.13**	20.30**	18.73**	2.57*
	(19.49)	(6.39)	(2.32)	(4.05)	(4.27)	(3.65)	(1.12)
Observations	1,250	1,247	1,250	1,250	1,250	1,250	1,147
R-squared	0.95	0.85	0.89	0.92	0.90	0.86	0.77

Sources: Authors' calculations based on data from U.S. Census Bureau, State Government Finances (various years). Political control variables through 1996 were kindly supplied to us by Rebecca Blank and were updated using various editions of The Book of the States.
Notes: All regressions also include state fixed effects, year fixed effects, and dummy variables indicating Republican control of state governership, state Senate, and state House of Representatives. Standard errors are in parentheses below coefficients.
**(Two-tailed) significant at 1 percent; *(two-tailed) significant at 5 percent.

which is positive though not statistically different from zero. Looking at some of the components of social assistance spending, we find that increases in unemployment are associated with no change in public welfare spending as a whole, but with a small increase in cash assistance. Thus, we find no evidence that states disproportionately cut spending on social welfare during economic downturns.

The inclusion of a variable that interacts a post-1997 dummy variable with the unemployment rate allows us to examine whether welfare reform is associated with a change in the responsiveness of state spending to unemployment. The regression results reported in table 10.4 suggest that there has been a fairly large change in the responsiveness of total spending to the unemployment rate since the implementation of welfare reform. The estimated coefficient suggests that total state spending has become much more procyclical (it falls in recessions) than it was prior to welfare reform. After welfare reform, each 1 percent increase in the unemployment rate was associated with an additional $61 per capita drop in state spending beyond that which would have taken place in the pre–welfare reform period. This finding is surprising given the anecdotal evidence (discussed earlier) that states weathered the 2001 recession with few severe cuts in spending.

We also find evidence that elementary and secondary education and higher education have both become more procyclical. On the other hand, social assistance spending became countercyclical after welfare reform. These results imply that spending on elementary and secondary education is six to seven times as responsive to unemployment in the post-1997 period as it was previously. In the post-1997 period, the quantitative effect is sizable—a three-percentage-point increase in the unemployment rate is associated with a decline of $108 per capita (a 25 percent decrease) in state support for elementary and secondary education. The relationship between unemployment and social assistance spending in the post-1997 period is of a smaller magnitude and in the opposite direction. According to our results, a three-percentage-point increase in the unemployment rate would be associated with an increase of $87 per capita (a 13 percent increase) in social assistance spending. More than two-thirds of the increase in social assistance spending is attributable to increases in public welfare spending, nearly all of which is, in turn, attributable to increases in spending on medical vendor payments. The coefficient on the interaction term in the cash assistance regression is positive (and statistically significant), indicating that cash assistance spending is, if anything, more countercyclical than it was prior to welfare reform. These results emphatically do not support the hypothesis that states disproportionately cut social assistance spending in the last recession despite the change to a block grant for federal support of welfare spending.

One potential explanation for the increased countercyclicality of medical vendor payments in the post–welfare reform era may be the federal government's temporary 3 percent increase in the federal Medicaid match rate as a response to the state fiscal crisis of fiscal year 2002 (Hynes 2004). This legislation was not approved until well after the fiscal crisis from the recession of 2001 had begun, and even then it provided a relatively small share of state spending for Medicaid during state fiscal year 2003. However, the legislation had been discussed as early as October 2001 (Lav 2001), and it is possible that the hope of future Medicaid funds made states more reluctant to cut the program.

We ran a number of variants of our basic regression specification to see whether our qualitative conclusions were sensitive to reasonable changes in assumptions. We display coefficient estimates (and standard errors) for our key variable—the unemployment rate times a post-1997 dummy—for a number of specifications in table 10.5. The first row of the table repeats the coefficients from our base specification reported in table 10.4. The second specification in table 10.5 displays the parameters that we obtain when observations are weighted by population so that large states carry more weight than small states. In the third specification, we use the natural logarithm of real per capita spending rather than its level as the dependent variable. In this case, the coefficients should be interpreted as the percentage—rather than the dollar value per capita—change in spending resulting from a one-percentage-point increase in the unemployment rate after PRWORA. In the fourth specification, we use the lag of the unemployment rate and the lag of the unemployment rate interacted with a post-1997 dummy as independent variables rather than the concurrent unemployment rate. This specification is meant to address the concern that states may be able to maintain social assistance spending temporarily in the face of economic downturns by using the kind of temporary fixes described in recent case studies (see the earlier discussion), but they may significantly reduce spending over the longer term. The fifth specification includes fifty state-specific time trends and a post-1997 dummy variable, but drops year fixed effects while retaining the other independent variables used in the base specification. This specification allows each state to have its own dynamic pattern with regard to spending and is in that sense the most general of our alternative specifications and therefore our most preferred.

None of these specifications leads to a fundamental qualitative change in our conclusion, although some of the details of our analyses are altered. In contrast to the base specification, when we weight observations by population (specification 2), we fail to find that states acted more procyclically with respect to total and elementary and secondary education spending or countercyclically with respect to cash assistance after welfare reform. With this specification, we continue to find evidence of increased procyclicality in higher education spending and countercyclicality in social assistance spending after welfare reform. When we use the log of the dependent variable, our qualitative results are very similar to our base specification, except that cash assistance spending is not more countercyclical after welfare reform. Estimates with a lag of the unemployment rate yield results almost identical to those of the base specification. Finally, in specification 5, our most preferred specification, we allow state-specific time trends on spending and include a post–welfare reform dummy variable while dropping year fixed effects. With this specification, we find no evidence of a post–welfare reform change in the cyclicality of total spending but continue to find an increase in the procyclicality of elementary and secondary education spending and an increase in the countercyclicality of social assistance spending and medical ven-

TABLE 10.5 / Analysis of Robustness of the Results on Key Parameter

Specification	Variable	Total Spending	Elementary and Secondary Education	Higher Education	Social Assistance Spending	Public Welfare	Medical Vendor Payments	Cash Assistance
1. Base specification	Dummy for post-1997 multiplied by unemployment rate	−61.00** (19.49)	−31.05** (6.39)	−6.28** (2.32)	28.13** (4.05)	20.30** (4.27)	18.73** (3.65)	2.57* (1.12)
2. Population weighted	Dummy for post-1997 multiplied by unemployment rate	−5.51 (11.02)	−5.80 (4.48)	−7.16** (1.68)	33.81** (6.66)	20.89** (6.92)	14.91** (6.27)	−1.04 (1.70)
3. Log of dependent variable	Dummy for post-1997 multiplied by unemployment rate	−0.02** (0.01)	−0.08** (0.01)	−0.012 (0.01)	0.03** (0.01)	0.02** (0.01)	0.05** (0.01)	−0.005 (0.04)
4. Lag of unemployment rate	Dummy for post-1997 multiplied by lagged unemployment rate	−60.31** (19.99)	−32.17** (6.27)	−7.46** (2.30)	31.53** (4.13)	23.29** (4.44)	21.61** (3.71)	2.99** (1.14)
5. State specific time trends and post-1997 dummy; no year fixed effects	Dummy for post-1997 multiplied by unemployment rate	0.06 (11.71)	−11.67** (3.32)	4.79** (1.56)	13.69** (3.82)	9.88** (3.54)	10.06** (3.24)	−0.41 (0.88)

Sources: Authors' calculations based on data from U.S. Census Bureau, *State Government Finances* (various years). Political control variables through 1996 were kindly supplied to us by Rebecca Blank and were updated using various editions of *The Book of the States*.
Note: Standard errors are in parentheses below the coefficient.
**(Two-tailed) significant at 1 percent; *(two-tailed) significant at 5 percent.

dor payments. In this specification, we also find that higher education spending was countercyclical after welfare reform.

In summary, we find no evidence that would invalidate our key conclusion: social assistance spending and its components did not become more procyclical after welfare reform. Our analysis suggests that total state government spending was somewhat procyclical over the entire period and may have become significantly more so after welfare reform. Furthermore, we find evidence that social assistance spending and its component public welfare spending were countercyclical and became more so following welfare reform. We find no evidence that states' social welfare spending—including cash assistance—became less generous in response to unemployment increases following welfare reform.

The evidence thus far should be regarded as tentative, for several reasons. First, states were in an unusually strong position to fund social service spending going into the 2001 recession, in part because of the revenue boom of the late 1990s. Also, the unusual carryover provisions of welfare reform, together with rapid caseload declines, allowed states to build up significant surpluses to fund social assistance spending. Second, we have data on state spending only through the end of fiscal 2003, and at that time states were still experiencing diminished government revenues, owing to the sluggish recovery from the 2001 recession. We cannot be sure of the long-term impact of the fiscal crisis on social assistance spending until more years of data become available. Finally, the recession of 2001 was relatively mild, and the nation has not yet experienced a high unemployment rate period in the post–welfare reform era. With these caveats, we interpret the evidence to suggest cautious optimism for the view that states have the ability and resources necessary to maintain social assistance spending in the face of economic downturns.

CONCLUSIONS

When the Personal Responsibility and Work Opportunity Reconciliation Act passed with great fanfare in 1996, much was rightly made of the potential for change in recipient behavior and in the outcomes associated with the legislation's time limits and other new rules and incentives regarding work and family arrangements. From a public finance perspective, an equally radical component of the legislation was the shift from a matching grant, whereby the federal government matched every dollar spent on AFDC by the states with fifty to eighty-five cents in federal monies, to a fixed block grant set at the amount each state had received under the old system in 1994, with no adjustments for inflation, caseload, or state spending. Many observers wondered whether states would have the financial capacity under the new regime to support TANF and related social assistance programs when the economy entered a downturn.

In this chapter, we have attempted to shed light on this question. We are hampered in our study by the good economic fortunes of the country in the post–welfare reform era: only one recession has occurred, and it has been relatively mild. Nevertheless, we have undertaken an analysis of the fiscal behavior of the states over the past twenty-five years, encompassing three recessions (a severe one in the early 1980s, a mild one in the early 1990s, and an even milder one in 2001). Somewhat surprisingly, we find that state spending on cash assistance remained countercyclical and was more responsive to economic distress after welfare reform. One potential explanation is that other social assistance programs—the EITC and SSI in particular—have become much more important components of the social safety net and these programs are not the responsibility of state governments. Given the small role that TANF spending plays in state budgets, the fact that it is funded by a federal block grant rather than a matching grant may have little influence on state spending in (at least mild) recessions.

The effect of recessions on state spending on Medicaid—which is still financed by a matching grant from the federal government and is the largest and fastest-growing social assistance program for the states—may be more important. Our analysis provides evidence that Medicaid spending has become more countercyclical in the post–welfare reform era. We do not have a clear story to explain this phenomenon, but we speculate that it may be the combined effect of the federal government's temporary increase in Medicaid matching rates in fiscal years 2003 and 2004 and opportunistic behavior by states to increase Medicaid funding during times of fiscal distress.

NOTES

1. We are grateful to Melissa Kearney, Rebecca Blank, Julie Cullen, and seminar participants at Northwestern University's Institute for Policy Research for helpful comments. We thank Donald Boyd and Rebecca Blank for sharing data. Finally, we thank Kate Solinger and Jon Gemus for assisting with data collection and creating the figures and tables.
2. Seventeen states have implemented state-level EITC programs in recent years. We do not present information here on the state EITC programs.
3. AMR data on state general assistance programs are spotty and missing altogether for recent years. The 2002 observation for the EITC is not reported because the source switched in 2001 from counting individuals to counting families. For Medicaid, the figure is an "unduplicated annual number" rather than AMR.
4. The data sources for federal grants for AFDC/TANF are various annual editions of the Census Bureau publications *Federal Expenditures by State* (through fiscal year 1997) and *Federal Aid to States* (for fiscal years 1998 through 2003).
5. Dye (2004) provides a thorough review of the literature on state revenue cyclicality.
6. We denote the period from July 1, 1979, to June 30, 1980, as state fiscal year 1980. The vast majority of states use a July 1 to June 30 fiscal year.
7. The state-local division of responsibility for administering cash assistance differs across states. Since the census expenditure data that we use track the level of government at which money is spent, states that have assigned responsibility for cash assistance spending to local governments, such as California and New Jersey, display state

spending on cash assistance as zero in our data. We have dropped these observations from our analysis but retained states that have some spending responsibility for cash assistance (no matter how small).

REFERENCES

Dye, Richard F. 2004. "State Revenue Cyclicality." *National Tax Journal* 57(1, March): 133–45.

Dye, Richard F., and Therese J. McGuire. 1998. "Block Grants and the Sensitivity of State Revenues to Recessions." *Proceedings of the Ninetieth Annual Conference.* Washington, D.C.: National Tax Association.

———. 1999. "State Fiscal Systems and Business Cycles: Implications for State Welfare Spending When the Next Recession Occurs." Discussion paper 99–04. Washington, D.C.: Urban Institute (June).

Finegold, Kenneth, Stephanie Schardin, Elaine Maag, Rebecca Steinbach, David Merriman, and Alan Weil. 2003. "Social Program Spending and State Fiscal Crises." Occasional paper 70. Assessing the New Federalism Series. Washington, D.C.: Urban Institute. Available at: http://www.urban.org/url.cfm?ID=310888.

Fremstad, Shawn, and Sharon Parrott. 2004. "The Senate Finance Committee's TANF Reauthorization Bill." Washington, D.C.: Center on Budget and Policy Priorities. Available at: http://www.cbpp.org/9-9-03tanf.htm.

Giertz, J. Fred, and Seth H. Giertz. 2004. "The 2002 Downturn in State Revenues: A Comparative Review and Analysis." *National Tax Journal* 57(1, March): 111–32.

Holohan, John, Joshua W. Weiner, Randall R. Bovbjerg, et al. 2003. "The State Fiscal Crisis and Medicaid: Will Health Programs Be Major Budget Targets? Overview." Publication 4074. Washington, D.C.: Kaiser Commission on Medicaid and the Uninsured. Available at: http://www.kff.org/medicaid/4074-index.cfm (accessed July 29, 2006).

Holzer, Harry. 2002. "Do We Need a Stronger Welfare Policy for a Weaker Economy?" Short Takes on Welfare Policy Series 1. Washington, D.C.: Urban Institute. Available at: http://www.urban.org/url.cfm?ID=310476.

Hynes, Daniel W. 2004. "State Economic Revenues Show Slight Improvement." *Fiscal Focus.* Springfield, Ill.: Illinois State Comptroller. Available at: http://www.spps.ioc.state.il.us/ioc-pdf/FFWebApril04.pdf.

Knight, Brian, Andrea Kusko, and Laura Rubin. 2003. "Problems and Prospects for State and Local Governments." In *State Fiscal Crises: Causes, Consequences, Solutions*, edited by Therese J. McGuire and C. Eugene Steuerle. Special supplement issue of *State Tax Notes* 30(5, November 3).

Lav, Iris J. 2001. "State Fiscal Problems Could Weaken Federal Stimulus Efforts: Low-income Households Likely to Be Hardest Hit by State Fiscal Actions." Washington, D.C.: Center for Budget and Policy Priorities. Available at: http://www.cbpp.org/10-4-01sfp.htm (accessed May 29, 2005).

Lazere, Ed. 2000. "Welfare Balances After Three Years of TANF Block Grants: Unspent TANF Funds at the End of Federal Fiscal Year 1999." Washington, D.C.: Center on Budget and Policy Priorities (January 12). Available at: http://www.cbpp.org/1-11-00wel.pdf.

Lewin Group and Nelson A. Rockefeller Institute of Government. 2004. "Spending on Social Welfare Programs in Rich and Poor States." Washington: U.S. Department of Health and Human Services, Assistant Secretary for Planning and Evaluation (July). Available at: http://aspe.hhs.gov/hsp/social-welfare-spending04.

Maag, Elaine, and David F. Merriman. 2003. "Tax Policy Responses to Revenue Short-falls." In *State Fiscal Crises: Causes, Consequences, Solutions*, edited by Therese J. McGuire and C. Eugene Steuerle. Special supplement issue of *State Tax Notes* 30(5, November 3).

Powers, Elizabeth T. 1999. "Block Granting Welfare: Fiscal Impact on the States." Occasional paper 23. Washington, D.C.: Urban Institute (May 1). Available at: http://www.urban.org/url.cfm?ID=309040.

Sobel, Russell S., and Randall G. Holcombe. 1996. "Measuring the Growth and Variability of Tax Bases over the Business Cycle." *National Tax Journal* 49(4, December): 535–52.

U.S. Census Bureau. Various years. *State Government Finances*. Washington: U.S. Census Bureau.

———. Various years. *Statistical Abstract of the United States*. Washington: U.S. Census Bureau.

———. Various quarters. *Quarterly Summary of State and Local Government Tax Revenue*. Washington, D.C.: Governments Division, U.S. Census Bureau.

U.S. Government Accountability Office. 2003. "Welfare Reform: Information on TANF Balances, *GAO-03–1094*. September 8. Washington, D.C.: United States Government Accountability Office.

Chapter 11

Temporary Agency Employment: A Way Out of Poverty?

David Autor and Susan Houseman

One in eight Americans and one in five children under the age of six lived in poverty in 2003, according to official U.S. Census Bureau statistics.[1] Poverty is strongly associated with lack of full-time, year-round employment. Government programs such as welfare-to-work and the Workforce Investment Act (WIA) try to help the poor find stable employment and thereby escape poverty. As one strategy to facilitate such transitions, several researchers have recently proposed the use of labor market intermediaries, including temporary help agencies, for the poor (Andersson, Holzer, and Lane 2005; Holzer 2004; Lane et al. 2003). Drawing on a unique policy quasi-experiment from a large welfare-to-work program, we provide new and direct evidence on whether temporary agency jobs help low-skilled workers escape poverty.

A large minority of participants in government employment programs already work in the temporary help sector. In our data on participants in a welfare-to-work program, 21 percent who found jobs worked for temporary agencies. A number of studies have found similarly high levels of temporary help employment—ranging from 15 to 40 percent—in other studies of government employment programs (see Autor and Houseman 2002, on Georgia and Washington state; Cancian et al. 1999, on Wisconsin; Heinrich, Mueser, and Troske 2005, on North Carolina and Missouri; and Pawasarat 1997 on Wisconsin). These figures are especially striking in light of the fact that temporary agency employment accounts for only 2 to 3 percent of daily employment in the United States.

The high incidence of temporary agency employment among participants in government programs has sparked debate about whether temporary agency jobs help the poor transition into stable employment and out of poverty or instead harm their long-term labor market outcomes. Those favoring an expanded role for temporary help agencies cite evidence that some agencies provide valuable skills training, that many employers screen workers for permanent positions through agencies, and that these agencies may provide an important port-of-entry for low-skilled workers (Abraham 1988; Autor 2001, 2003; Houseman 2001; Kalleberg, Reynolds, and Marsden 2003). Those skeptical of an expanded role for temporary agencies tend to view most agency jobs as dead-end jobs that provide little in the way of valuable work experience, training, or opportunity for career advancement.

Both of these scenarios could be correct. In some situations, companies may use temporary agencies to screen individuals for permanent jobs with good pay, benefits, and career ladders. In these circumstances, temporary agencies may provide access for workers to good jobs. In other situations, companies may utilize temporary agencies to staff short-term positions that require few skills and provide few chances for promotion. What matters for policy is which scenario dominates in the low-skilled markets targeted by government programs.

Our study, based on a quasi-experiment in a welfare-to-work program in Detroit, Michigan, provides direct evidence on this policy question. Program participants were, in effect, randomly assigned to service providers (termed "contractors") who provided different degrees of encouragement to take temporary help agency jobs versus direct-hire jobs. Our analysis draws on data from a survey of contractors and on administrative data linked with wage records data on all participants entering the program over a three-and-a-half-year period.

Our survey data provide a detailed picture of how temporary agencies are utilized as labor market intermediaries in poor neighborhoods. They also document considerable variation among contractors in their assessments of the consequences of temporary agency placements. Contractors with more favorable views of temporary agencies provide participants with more contact with temporary agency jobs and have higher placement rates in these positions than do contractors with less favorable views of agencies.

Using Michigan administrative welfare-to-work and wage records data, we exploit variation across contractors in the probability that randomly assigned participants will be placed in a temporary agency job, in a direct-hire job, or in no job at all to identify the labor market consequences of temporary agency placements. We focus on whether, relative to a direct-hire or no job placement, temporary agency placements help participants achieve earnings sufficient to leave welfare and escape poverty.

We find that placing a participant in either a temporary or direct-hire job improves her chances of leaving welfare and escaping poverty in the short term, defined as one quarter following the quarter of program entry. Over a one- to two-year time horizon, however, only direct-hire placements confer any labor market benefit. Over these longer horizons, having been placed in a temporary agency job makes a participant no better off than she would have been not receiving any job placement. Contradicting conclusions drawn by several previous studies, our findings do not support policy recommendations to expand the use of temporary agencies in employment and poverty reduction programs, although they do support a broad role for labor market intermediaries in welfare-to-work transitions.

THE WORK FIRST PROGRAM IN MICHIGAN

A principal objective of the 1996 welfare reform legislation—the Personal Responsibility and Work Opportunity Reconciliation Act (PRWORA)—was to encourage welfare recipients to obtain jobs rapidly. The premise of welfare reform was that recipients could find stable employment and escape poverty and welfare dependency given proper incentives and assistance in finding jobs. Pursuant to federal regulation, states generally require that those on welfare work as a condition of benefits receipt. Most states, including Michigan, have implemented a "Work First" strategy in which applicants for Temporary Assistance for Needy Families (TANF) funds who do not meet mandatory work requirements must participate in programs that help them find employment.

As the name implies, Work First programs emphasize job search assistance and rapid placement into employment. Michigan requires most TANF recipients to work forty hours per week to remain eligible for assistance.[2] Work First participants, likewise, are required to treat the program like a job and to engage in program activities or search for employment for forty hours per week until they are successful. Individuals who fail to comply with program requirements are terminated from Work First and face sanctions and, ultimately, the termination of TANF benefits.

A unique aspect of Detroit's Work First Program is its effective random assignment of Work First participants to Work First providers. The city is divided into geographic districts for the purpose of administering TANF and Work First programs. A state agency determines welfare eligibility and administers TANF benefits. A city agency administers the Work First program, but the provision of services is contracted out. Currently, over thirty contractors, all nonprofit or public-sector entities, provide Work First services. Individuals apply for TANF benefits at a government office that services the district in which they reside. If applicants are deemed eligible for benefits but do not meet work requirements, they must enroll within two weeks in a Work First program run by a contractor operating in their district. In most districts, two or three contractors operate programs. In these districts, contractors take turns enrolling Work First participants. Using multiple comparison tests of participant characteristics across contractors operating in the same districts, we demonstrate that within almost all districts with two or more contractors (and within all districts included in our analysis sample), the assignment of participants to contractors is consistent with random assignment (Autor and Houseman 2005).

The Work First program structure and set of services is largely standardized among contractors. Contractors typically spend one week—forty hours—providing new participants with basic job search skills and strategies, such as skills assessment and employability planning, résumé writing, interviewing and self-presentation skills, and job readiness and life skills training. Except for "tech prep" courses, which quickly review skills that might be tested on an employment application, little in the way of remedial, vocational, or computer skills training is provided. The availability of more intensive training is quite limited, and such courses are provided outside the Work First system to all eligible participants.

After the first week, participants are expected to look for work full-time until they are successful at finding it. At this stage, contractors play an integral role in placing participants into jobs. Virtually all of the contractors provide individual job search assistance, refer participants to jobs with specific employers, accompany participants to job fairs, bring employers on-site to recruit participants, and sponsor group job search assistance programs, such as job clubs.

Once participants find suitable jobs, contractors are required to follow up with participants and their employers on a monthly basis until the participant achieves earnings sufficient to close her TANF case or until the participant is terminated from the program for other reasons.[3] Contractors check on participants' employment status and collect information on their wages and hours worked. This information determines whether they are still eligible for TANF benefits. Work First providers' contracts with the city are written for a one-year period. The city evaluates contractors based on the fraction of participants who get jobs and on the ninety-day retention rate at those jobs.

THE DATA

We draw on two types of evidence to frame and test hypotheses about the effects of temporary agency employment on low-skilled workers. The first is a telephone survey of Work First contractors operating in the city. The second is administrative and earnings data on Work First participants who entered the program over a three-and-a-half-year period from 1999 to 2003. From these data, we utilize a sample that includes over thirty-six thousand Work First spells and covers nine geographic districts in which twenty-five contractors operated programs.

The Telephone Survey

We developed a survey instrument based on extensive in-person interviews with several contractors and then pretested the telephone survey with another contractor. Of the twenty-five contractors in our sample, we completed surveys, lasting about thirty minutes, with twenty-one; we were unable to contact two contractors, and two contractors no longer operated Work First programs. All telephone surveys were conducted between the fall of 2004 and the spring of 2005—a year and a half to two years following the last cohort of Work First participants represented in our administrative data. Because the survey included several open-ended questions, all surveys were tape-recorded and transcribed. We interviewed the person heading the Work First program in each organization.

Part of the survey asked questions about the basic structure of the Work First program and the services provided. These questions were designed to uncover any differences across contractors in resources or program services that might have an impact on participants' outcomes. As noted earlier, we found that the program structure and services provided were virtually identical across contractors.

Most questions focused on temporary agency jobs and the agencies' role in welfare-to-work transitions. We asked a series of questions about the contractor's policies toward working with temporary agencies to place participants in jobs, their assessments of the characteristics of temporary jobs compared to direct-hire jobs, and their views on the long-term consequences of temporary agency employment for Work First clients. We also asked contractors a series of questions designed to help us better understand the types of temporary agencies operating in the labor market and whether and why the contractors worked with particular agencies. Finally, we asked several questions about how participants with low skills and poor work histories fared in temporary agency jobs compared to those with relatively good skills and work histories.[4]

The Administrative Data

We analyzed administrative data on all Work First participants who entered the program from the fourth quarter of 1999 through the second quarter of 2003. These data include the participants' geographic district, the contractor to which each was assigned, and basic demographic information such as race, age, gender, and educational attainment. These administrative data do not include information on family size or age of children. The unit of observation is a Work First spell, and some individuals have repeat spells. The 36,105 Work First spells represented in our data come from 23,746 participants.

Unlike previous studies of welfare-to-work transitions, our data provide detailed information on the jobs obtained through the welfare-to-work program.[5] This information includes hourly wages, weekly hours, job title, and the name of the employer for up to six jobs obtained during a Work First spell. We coded the job titles into occupational classifications and identified the employer as a temporary agency or not by using three comprehensive lists of temporary agencies operating in the city at various points in time represented by our data.[6]

THE ROLE OF TEMPORARY AGENCIES
IN WELFARE-TO-WORK TRANSITIONS:
THE VIEWS OF SERVICE PROVIDERS

The telephone survey served several purposes. The first was to better understand how contractors placed participants into jobs and the mechanisms by which they encouraged or discouraged placement with temporary agencies. The second was to document the range of policies and practices regarding temporary agency placements and any consensus or disagreement about the consequences of agency placements. The third purpose was to solicit opinions about the potentially varying impacts of temporary agency employment.

The Role of Contractors in Job Placements

Contractors played an integral role in placing Work First participants into jobs. In regard to participants who found jobs while in the program, contractors were asked to estimate what fraction of them found jobs on their own and what fraction they directly helped through referrals, on-site employer visits, and the like. Half of all contractors indicated that they were directly involved in 75 percent or more of the job placements, and all but three (15 percent) took credit for more than 50 percent of the jobs obtained in their program. Even if these estimates are inflated, they suggest that a large majority of contractors played a significant role in determining whether participants obtained jobs and, by implication, where they obtained jobs.

Seventeen of the twenty-one contractors provided an estimate of the fraction of employed participants who obtained work through temporary agencies. Although the median response was 15 percent, there was large variation in reported estimates: three contractors reported that 5 percent or fewer of their job placements were with temporary agencies, and three reported that placements with agencies accounted for one-quarter, one-third, and even three-fourths of all placements.[7]

Table 11.1 reports the frequency with which contractors invited temporary help agencies to speak with or recruit participants at their Work First site and the frequency with which contractors referred participants to temporary agencies for jobs. What is most striking is the variation in the amount of contact with temporary help agencies that contractors provided to their participants, especially in regard to referrals for specific jobs. Whereas five contractors (24 percent) reported referring clients to temporary help jobs on a weekly basis, eight (38 percent) reported making such referrals only sporadically or never.

If, as they reported, contractors heavily influenced the jobs that participants took, and if contractors varied substantially in the amount of exposure to temporary agency jobs they gave participants, then we should observe an association between the amount of contact with temporary agencies and the placement rate in such jobs. We computed the correlations between reported placement rates with temporary agencies and frequency of contact with such agencies, coding the frequency on a five-point scale with "never" being the lowest and "weekly" being the highest. The correlations of temporary agency placement rates with frequency of temporary agency visits and frequency of referrals to temporary help agencies are positive, 0.29 and 0.53, respectively; the latter correlation is both large and statistically significant.

TABLE 11.1 / Frequency of Temporary Agency Visits and Referrals to Agencies by Work First Contractors (Percentage)

	Weekly	Monthly	Every Few Months	Sporadically	Never
Invited temporary agencies on-site	4.8%	9.5%	19.1%	38.1%	28.6%
Referred participants to jobs at temporary agencies	23.8	33.3	4.8	28.6	9.5

Source: Authors' compilations.
Note: Tabulations based on survey responses from twenty-one Work First contractors. Reported numbers represent the percent of contractors providing the indicated response.

Contractor Views About Temporary Agencies and Their Jobs

Reflecting these differential rates of temporary agency placement, contractors differed in their assessments of the benefits and drawbacks of temporary agency jobs for participants. Contractors were asked whether their organization encouraged, discouraged, or took a neutral stance toward Work First participants taking such jobs. They were then asked to explain this position. A majority (thirteen of the twenty-one) reported that their organization took a neutral stance toward temporary agency jobs; five contractors reported discouraging temporary agency jobs, and three reported encouraging them.

The reasons contractors gave for these differing stances are informative. All of those who discouraged temporary agency jobs and most of those who took a neutral stance mentioned that such jobs tend to be temporary and generally do not lead to permanent positions. Among this group, two contractors indicated that they used temporary help jobs only as a last resort. Even two of the three contractors who indicated that they encouraged participants to take agency positions qualified their answer by saying that they did so only in cases where the position was explicitly temp-to-hire or when direct-hire job options were poor. Striking a more positive note, four contractors stated that temporary agency positions can provide useful experience and skills to those with little prior work experience.

To obtain more systematic evidence of their views on temporary agencies, we asked contractors to rank temporary agency jobs and direct-hire jobs on a series of characteristics, indicating whether temporary agency jobs are generally better, direct-hire jobs are generally better, or the two are generally about the same. The answers to this set of questions are reported in table 11.2. Not surprisingly, a large majority of contractors (76 percent) viewed direct-hire jobs as superior to temporary agency jobs in terms of job duration or stability. A majority (57 percent) also viewed direct-hire jobs as better or about the same as temporary

TABLE 11.2 / Work First Contractors' Views of Temporary Agency Jobs
and Direct-Hire Jobs (Percentage)

	Direct-Hire Jobs Better	Temporary Jobs Better	Same	Don't Know
Hours per week	57.1%	0.0%	23.8%	19.1%
Hourly pay	57.1	9.5	19.1	14.3
Job stability and duration	76.2	4.8	9.5	9.5
Transportation issues[a]	20.0	15.0	45.0	20.0
Willing to accommodate clients' needs for flexibility, especially in scheduling work hours	19.1	61.9	14.3	4.8
Willing to accommodate participants' special issues	19.1	23.8	42.9	14.3
Participants well treated	23.8	14.3	47.6	14.3

Source: Authors' compilations.
Note: Tabulations based on survey responses from twenty-one Work First contractors. Reported numbers represent the percent of contractors providing the indicated response.
[a]Tabulations based on twenty responses.

agency jobs in terms of pay and hours of work. Sixty-two percent saw temporary agency jobs as better at accommodating clients' needs for flexibility, especially in scheduling work hours. No consensus emerged as to the relative ranking of temporary agency and direct-hire jobs on transportation issues (that is, the ease or difficulty of getting to the job), willingness to accommodate participants' special issues, and treating participants well.

Differentiating Between Temporary Agencies: Are Some Better Than Others?

Many contractors have strong reservations about placing workers in jobs with temporary help agencies, particularly because they believe the assignments typically are short-term and do not lead to longer jobs. Perhaps as a result, contractors that work with agencies in placing participants tend to work with selected agencies. Sixteen of the twenty-one contractors indicated that their job developers worked with particular agencies. Those who did not work with particular temporary help agencies seldom or never worked with such agencies; no contractor reported being open to working with all types of agencies. Most of those that worked with selected agencies explained that they had developed specific relationships or understandings with those agencies, that the agencies regularly provided temp-to-perm opportunities, or that the agencies were honest about the nature and length of assignments. Three contractors stressed that they worked with agencies that had been successful at placing low-skilled, difficult-to-place workers in jobs or at placing large groups of workers in jobs. Those who worked with selected agencies reported that they had specific understandings with these agencies about the duration of job assignments and that, when possible, these assignments were temp-to-perm.

Just as many contractors worked primarily with selected agencies, many avoided working with certain agencies. Eleven of seventeen contractors that worked with agencies reported avoiding particular agencies because of bad experiences, primarily ones involving very short-term assignments. Some contractors discouraged participants from taking assignments with day laborer agencies, which require that participants report to the agency each morning and do not guarantee assignments. Four contractors stated that they avoided all or virtually all agencies.

Differentiating Between Work First Participants: Do Some Participants Do Better in Temporary Help Agency Jobs?

While contractors differentiate between types of temporary help agencies, many also distinguish between types of participants when placing them in agency jobs. Contractors were asked whether temporary agency positions were more or less difficult to obtain than direct-hire positions for those with relatively weak skills or experience and for those with relatively strong skills or experience; whether certain types of workers did better at temporary agency jobs than at direct-hire jobs; and whether temporary agency jobs were the only realistic alternative to unemployment for some.

Few contractors believed that temporary agency jobs are harder than direct-hire jobs for their clients to obtain. Over half viewed them as easier to obtain for those with weak skills or experience, while over one-third viewed them as easier to obtain for those with strong skills or experience. About half of the contractors (twelve of twenty-one) believed that certain participants did better in temporary agency jobs than in direct-hire jobs, and one-third believed that those with weak skills or experience did better working for temporary agencies.[8] A large minority (43 percent) expressed the view that temporary agency jobs are the only realistic alternative to unemployment for some. Contractors holding the view that those with weak skills or experience benefit from temporary agency jobs coincided for the most part with those who believed that temporary agency jobs are easier than direct-hire jobs for these workers to get and, indeed, that such jobs may be the only alternative to unemployment for certain workers.

When asked to elaborate on why they believed that participants with weak skills or experience were better off in agency jobs, several of these contractors expressed the view that some clients simply were not ready to hold a permanent job and that agency jobs gave them work experience and an understanding of employer expectations. Others mentioned the valuable role that agencies could play in allowing these participants to sample different jobs and find a suitable match. Agencies could provide participants with contacts with many different employers and jobs. Moreover, if a participant decided that she did not like a

TABLE 11.3 / Work First Contractors' Views of Long-Term Consequences
of Temporary Help Jobs (Percentage)

	Rarely	Occasionally	Frequently	Most of the Time
Help participants build skills	23.8%	28.6%	38.1%	9.5%
Help participants improve work habits	33.3	23.8	33.3	9.5
Help participants develop confidence	19.1	23.8	42.9	14.3
Generate contacts that may lead to other jobs	19.1	33.3	28.6	19.1
Result in temp-to-hire positions	33.3	42.9	19.1	4.8
Prevent participants from searching for better, possibly direct-hire jobs	47.6	9.5	33.3	9.5
Allow participants to avoid making a serious employment commitment	38.1	19.1	23.8	19.1

Source: Authors' compilations.
Note: Tabulations based on survey responses from twenty-one Work First contractors. Reported numbers represent the percent of contractors providing the indicated response.

particular job, she could request a reassignment and avoid the stigma of a quit, which would be recorded if she were in a direct-hire relationship.

Long-Term Consequences of Temporary Agency Placements

The question that is most relevant for welfare-to-work policy is whether temporary agency placements foster stable longer-term employment, ideally at wages that can support a family. The preceding discussion revealed a division among contractors on this question: some felt that certain groups, particularly low-skilled participants, can benefit from temporary agency placements, and some felt that working with agencies confers no benefits or even harms clients. Contractor assessments of the long-term consequences of temporary agency placements, summarized in table 11.3, reflect this division. The contractors were most likely to feel that temporary agency placements helped participants develop confidence (57 percent answered that such placements did so "frequently" or "most of the time"), and they were least likely to believe that temporary agency jobs resulted in temp-to-hire positions (76 percent answered "rarely" or "occasionally"). However, what is most striking about table 11.3 is the lack of consensus among contractors about these long-term effects.

A majority of contractors (62 percent) believed that temporary agency placements allow participants to avoid making a serious employment commitment, although there was considerable variation in contractors' assessments of the prevalence of this problem. Contractors pointed out that, even when the position is explicitly temporary, agency jobs allow participants to comply with the program's work requirements. Most contractors emphasized that many participants focused only on the short term and hence failed to fully appreciate that when they took a temporary agency job, they were more likely to need to repeat the job search process in the near future.[9]

The Value of Temporary Agency Jobs: A Synthesis of Contractors' Conflicting Views

Contractors varied widely in their policies and practices regarding the use of temporary agencies in welfare-to-work transitions. Some avoided using temporary help agencies altogether. Others used them only in selected instances where the assignments were for reputable employers who were screening for permanent positions. Others relied more extensively on temporary agencies for placing their clientele, especially those with weak skills or experience.

There was little disagreement among contractors about the benefits of using temporary agencies in temp-to-hire situations. When a company screens for permanent employees through an agency, however, it is usually looking for workers whose skill levels will be at the high end of the skill distribution of Work First participants. Contractors noted that workers with some marketable skills were relatively easy to place in either direct-hire or temporary agency positions.

The real challenge facing Work First providers was developing strategies for placing participants with very low skills, little or no work experience, or a poor work ethic. Contractors were under considerable pressure to increase their job placement rates; typically, 40 to 50 percent of Work First participants will leave the program without finding a job. As contractors quickly pointed out, openings in direct-hire jobs for the least job-ready participants were often scant. A majority believed that it was easier for low-skilled workers to find jobs with temporary agencies.

Contractors sharply differed, however, in their views about whether those with weak skills or experience *should* be placed in agency jobs. On the one side, many believed that agency jobs could help these participants develop skills and an improved work ethic and that temporary employment was the only alternative to unemployment for some participants. On the other side, some contractors endorsed an agency job only when it was a temp-to-hire position. As expressed by one contractor, a temporary agency job "allows a person to stay compliant with Work First requirements, so they can't be terminated from the program. But, unless the job is temp-to-hire, they will end up back in the program. It could be in six months, it could be a year later, but they will end up back in the program, in the same place. They won't have made any advances."

These divergent policies and practices were followed by contractors who provided services to the same Work First population and operated in the same labor market. Coupled with the random assignment of participants among contractors, these different practices, which resulted in different placement rates into temporary agency jobs, direct-hire jobs, or no jobs, enable us to identify the labor market effects of temporary agency placements. We turn now to a formal examination of these effects, with a particular focus on whether temporary agency jobs increase the probability that an individual will leave welfare and escape poverty.

DO TEMPORARY AGENCY JOBS HELP PARTICIPANTS ESCAPE WELFARE AND POVERTY? EVIDENCE FROM ADMINISTRATIVE DATA

A Methodology for Identifying the Effects of Temporary Agency Employment

We apply the methodology we developed in Autor and Houseman (2005) to examine whether temporary agency jobs help participants achieve income levels sufficient to leave welfare and escape poverty. A key challenge for any empirical investigation of this sort is establishing causality. Simple comparisons of subsequent employment and earnings outcomes among those who obtained direct-hire jobs, those who were placed in temporary agency jobs, or those who obtained no job while in the Work First program may be misleading because the average characteristics of individuals in these three categories differ. Whereas those placed in both temporary agency and direct-hire jobs earned substantially more over the subsequent two-year period than those not placed in any job, they also had significantly higher education levels and significantly higher employment and earnings levels prior to Work First program entry (Autor and Houseman 2005). If there is significant selection on observable characteristics into job types (direct-hire, temporary, or no job), it is likely that selection on unmeasured characteristics, such as motivation and employment barriers, is also important. These confounding factors make it difficult to disentangle the effects of the type of job taken (temporary help, direct-hire, no job) on subsequent labor market outcomes from the determinants of the jobs taken initially.

Several U.S. studies have endeavored to determine whether temporary agency jobs can facilitate the transition to employment among the low-skilled or low-income unemployed and improve their longer-term employment and earnings outcomes (Andersson et al. 2005; Corcoran and Chen 2004; Ferber and Waldfogel 1998; Heinrich, Mueser, and Troske 2005; Lane et al. 2003). These studies, based on nonexperimental data and methodologies, all find some evidence that temporary agency employment improves longer-term labor market outcomes.[10]

Our study is the first to use a quasi-experimental research design. As described earlier, in most geographic districts in the city we study, two or three contractors alternate in taking on new Work First participants. Contractors that operate within the same district, in turn, may have different policies and contacts that influence the fraction of participants they place in jobs and, among those, the fraction they place in direct-hire or temporary agency jobs. In Autor and Houseman (2005), we demonstrate that within nine geographic districts two critical assumptions that underlie our empirical strategy hold true. First, participants assigned to contractors operating within the same geographic district were insignificantly different across a broad set of demographic characteristics and in their prior employment and earnings history, and thus the assignment of participants to contractors was consistent with random assignment. Second, there were large, persistent, and significant differences across contractors operating in the same district in the fraction of participants they placed in temporary jobs, in direct-hire jobs, or in no jobs.

We exploit these cross-contractor differences in the probabilities of being placed in a direct-hire job, temporary job, or no job among statistically identical populations living in the same neighborhood to identify the effects of a temporary agency placement, relative to a direct-hire or no job placement, on earnings outcomes over a two-year period following program entry. We directly address the policy question of interest: is placing workers in temporary agency jobs a viable strategy for moving additional low-skilled workers out of poverty? It is critical to bear in mind that the effect of a temporary agency job may not be the same for all individuals. Indeed, our survey showed that contractors often distinguished between types of workers when assessing whether agency placements were beneficial. Even if, on average, those who take an agency job derive long-term labor market benefits, it does not mean that a policy to increase placements with temporary help agencies will benefit the individuals affected by this policy change, since the effects of temporary agency placements for the average temporary help worker may differ from the effects for the marginal temporary help worker.[11]

Our quasi-experimental research design allows us to measure the effects of marginal temporary agency placements. That is, we identify whether a temporary agency placement, relative to no job placement or a direct-hire job placement, improves or harms labor market outcomes for those whose job placement status is affected by contractor assignment.

A potential concern about our research design is that other contractor practices may affect participants' labor market outcomes; if these other practices are correlated with contractor placement rates in temporary help and direct-hire jobs, our estimates will be contaminated by the effects of these other practices. For instance, if contractors with high placement rates with temporary help agencies were more likely to adopt other practices that negatively affected participant outcomes, we might misattribute these weaker participant outcomes at these contractors to their temporary help jobs. Our earlier discussion, however, suggests that contractors had little time and few resources for providing other services; hence, it is reasonable to assume that contractors' impact on participant outcomes would have come almost exclusively through job placements. In Autor and Houseman (2005), we present formal tests showing that, indeed, contractors had no measurable impact on participant outcomes beyond their placement rates into temporary help and direct-hire jobs.[12]

FIGURE 11.1 / Occupational Distribution of Temporary Help Agency Jobs
and Direct-Hire Jobs

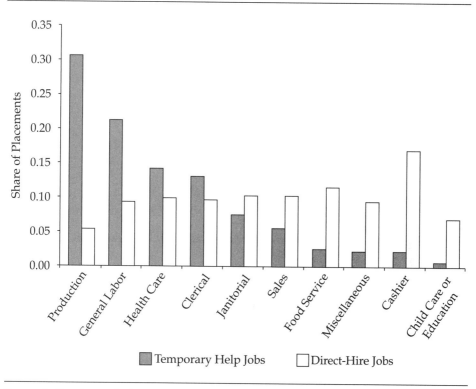

Source: Authors' compilations.

Descriptive Statistics on the Characteristics of Temporary Help Agency Jobs and Direct-Hire Jobs

In our sample of Work First spells, 47 percent resulted in some job placement. Among spells resulting in jobs, 21 percent were with temporary help agencies. Figure 11.1 compares the occupational distribution of temporary agency jobs and direct-hire jobs. Temporary agency jobs were heavily concentrated in a subset of occupations. Almost one-third of the agency jobs were in production occupations, and 23 percent were in manual, general laborer positions. Health care and clerical occupations each accounted for about 14 percent of agency jobs. Direct-hire jobs were more dispersed across occupational categories. The large differential between the fraction of temporary agency jobs and direct-hire jobs in production occupations reflects the extensive use of temporary help agencies by manufacturers to staff low-skilled positions.[13]

Many contractors ranked temporary agency jobs less favorably than direct-hire jobs in terms of their wage levels and weekly hours. Our administrative

TABLE 11.4 / Distribution of Hourly Wages, Weekly Hours, and Weekly Earnings
in Temporary Help Agency Jobs and Direct-Hire Jobs

	Mean (Standard error)	Tenth Percentile	Fiftieth Percentile	Ninetieth Percentile	Number of Observations
Hourly wages					
Temporary help	$7.96	$6.07	$7.37	$10.33	3,286
	(0.03)				
Direct-hire	7.74	5.45	7.18	9.79	13,709
	(0.02)				
Weekly hours					
Temporary help	37.01	30	40	40	3,286
	(0.10)				
Direct-hire	33.54	20	35	40	13,709
	(0.06)				
Weekly earnings					
Temporary help	$294.17	$208	$284	$405	3,286
	(1.47)				
Direct-hire	253.73	147	244	371	13,709
	(0.82)				

Source: Authors' compilations.
Note: Wages and earnings data were inflated to 2003 dollars using the consumer price index
(CPI).

data, however, show that the mean hourly wage ($7.96 versus $7.47) and weekly
hours (thirty-seven versus thirty-four)—and in fact the entire distribution of
wages and hours—are uniformly higher for temporary agency jobs than for direct-hire jobs (table 11.4). This fact reflects, in part, the different occupational
distribution of temporary agency jobs and direct-hire jobs displayed in figure
11.1.

Econometric Evidence on the Effects of Temporary
Agency Employment on Welfare Dependency and Poverty

Descriptive evidence on the wages and hours of temporary agency jobs compared to direct-hire jobs suggests that the former are no worse—and possibly
better—than the direct-hire jobs that participants obtain. Though we caution that
these simple comparisons should not be taken as causal, the evidence in table
11.4 underscores that temporary agency positions may confer benefits, at least in
the short run. Whether over the longer term temporary agency jobs help the low-
skilled end welfare dependence and escape poverty depends on whether these
jobs help workers transition to stable employment.

To formally examine this issue, we estimate the following econometric model:

$$y_{icdt} = \alpha + \beta_1 T_i + \beta_2 D_i + X'_i \lambda + \gamma_d + \theta_t + (\gamma_d \times \theta_t) + \varepsilon_{idtc},\qquad(11.1)$$

where y_{icdt} is the outcome of interest for a participant in Work First spell i, with contractor c, in district d, and in program year t; D_i and T_i are dummy variables indicating that the participant was placed in a direct-hire job or temporary agency job, respectively; X_i is a vector of characteristics including gender, race, age, and age-squared, highest level of education achieved, and earnings in the four quarters prior to the quarter of Work First entry; γ is a vector of district dummy variables, and θ is a vector of calendar-year-by-calendar-quarter dummy variables.

We first estimate this model using ordinary least squares (OLS) and then follow with two-stage least squares (2SLS) estimates. In the two-stage least squares model, we instrument for the indicator variables D_i and T_i—that is, whether the participant obtained a direct-hire job or a temporary agency job—using contractor and contractor-program year dummy variables. We report robust standard errors, allowing for clustering of the error term on contractor assignment by program year.[14]

As noted earlier, the effects of temporary agency or direct-hire jobs on the outcome of interest are estimated for individuals whose job placement type was changed by contractor assignment. In Autor and Houseman (2005), we show that, on the margin, those placed into temporary agency and direct-hire jobs had significantly weaker prior work histories than did average workers placed in temporary agency and direct-hire positions. This finding makes sense: when contractors increase job placements, whether with direct-hire or temporary agency employers, they place participants who, on average, have weaker skills and experience than those initially placed.[15] Conceptually, then, our 2SLS estimates of β_1 and β_2 in equation 11.1 indicate how a "marginal" worker among the Work First population—that is, an individual with relatively weak skills or experience— would fare over time if she were placed in a direct-hire job or a temporary agency job relative to no job at all.

Estimating equation 11.1, we show in earlier work that both direct-hire and temporary agency placements significantly increase participants' employment and earnings relative to no job placement over the short term—one quarter following the quarter of program entry. However, whereas direct-hire placements significantly increase participants' employment and earnings for up to two years following program entry relative to no job placement, the positive labor market effects of temporary agency job placements are short-lived. Two to eight quarters following program entry, temporary agency placements result in no increase in employment and earnings relative to no job placement; they also result in lower employment rates and labor earnings relative to direct-hire job placements.

We extend the analysis here to consider whether temporary agency placements help participants leave welfare and escape poverty—which is the ultimate goal of welfare policy and the Work First program in particular. We use several measures of welfare dependency and poverty to study this issue. The first comes from the Work First administrative data. When individuals leave the Work First program, the reason for program termination is coded. One code indicates that the participant has obtained a job providing a stream of income sufficient to close her TANF case ("terminated because of earnings"). This is the immediate and explicit goal of the program, so a case closed because of earnings is an indicator of program success. About 18 percent of Work First spells in our sample were terminated because of earnings. Those who fail to find a job while in the program are terminated for other reasons, mostly because they fail to comply with program rules or refuse to continue. Among those finding a job in the Work First program, about 38 percent with a direct-hire job and 33 percent with a temporary agency job achieved earnings levels sufficient to close their TANF case during their Work First spell.

We estimate equation 11.1 with a dummy dependent variable indicating whether the participant achieved sufficient earnings during the spell to close her welfare case.[16] Selected coefficients from the OLS and instrumental variables (IV) models are reported in table 11.5. In the OLS models, the coefficients on the variables indicating the participant held a temporary agency job (33.0) or direct-hire job (37.6) while in Work First reflect the percentage in each category whose case was closed because of earnings. We stress that although these OLS models include controls for demographic characteristics and prior earnings, the results are purely descriptive.

By contrast, the 2SLS models have a causal interpretation. Notably, the coefficient estimates in column 2 of table 11.5 are both smaller than the OLS coefficients in column 1. The coefficient on the direct-hire variable remains highly significant, however, and indicates that direct-hire placements increase the probability of successful program termination by 24.6 percentage points. The coefficient estimate on the temporary agency variable (11.5), while still positive, is insignificantly different from zero. The 2SLS models do not support the inference that temporary agency jobs significantly increase the probability of successful earnings-based case closure, though they do demonstrate that direct-hire job placements substantially increase this probability.

Termination of TANF benefits as a result of a job obtained in the Work First program is highly relevant to contractors because they are evaluated on this measure. From a broader policy perspective, however, this measure has potential flaws. First, those who do not find a job while in the Work First program may find employment on their own and leave welfare, yet they are not counted as "successes" by this measure. Second, individuals who are terminated because of earnings may lose their job and end up back on welfare and in Work First in a relatively short period of time.

To surmount these limitations, we examine measures that indicate whether, over longer time horizons, participants achieved earnings sufficient to end welfare dependency and escape poverty. Because we cannot compute individual-level welfare and poverty thresholds with our data (since the data do not include information on family composition), we select a variety of welfare and poverty

TABLE 11.5 / The Effect of Work First Job Placements on the Probability of a Participant's Welfare Case Being Closed Because of Earnings

	Cases Closed Because of Earnings	OLS	2SLS
Temporary agency job	32.9%	33.0**	11.5
		(1.8)	(11.1)
Direct-hire job	37.6	37.6**	24.6**
		(1.4)	(7.1)
R-squared		0.24	0.20
H_0: Temporary = Direct-hire		0.00	0.41

Source: Authors' compilations.
Notes: Number of observations: 34,510. Robust standard errors in parentheses are clustered on Work First contractor assignment times year. All models include year times quarter of assignment and randomization-district times year of assignment dummy variables, controls for age and its square, race, sum of UI earnings in the four quarters prior to Work First assignment, and four education dummies (elementary education, less than high school, greater than high school, and education unknown). Coefficient estimates and standard errors are multiplied by 100.
**Significant at the 0.05 percent level; *significant at the 0.10 percent level.

thresholds as outcome measures: earnings needed to terminate welfare benefits for a family of three and for a family of four (typically a mother with two or three dependent children) and earnings exceeding the poverty level for a family of three with two dependent children or a family of four with three dependent children.[17]

Table 11.6 reports descriptive statistics for the percentage of Work First participants with earnings above these thresholds over various time horizons for those obtaining a direct-hire job, a temporary agency job, or no job while in the program. The income threshold for welfare benefits is considerably below the poverty level for any given family size. In 2003 the income level above which a family's welfare benefits would be cut was 64 percent of the poverty level for a family of three with two dependent children and 59 percent for a family of four with three dependent children.[18]

Relatively few participants attained earnings even above the lowest threshold. For instance, in the first four quarters following program entry, the percentage with earnings exceeding the welfare threshold level for a family of three, $9,504 in annual earnings, was 9.1 percent for those with no job in Work First, 22.1 percent for those with a direct-hire job, and 21.3 percent for those with a temporary agency job. The fraction earning above the poverty threshold for a family of four with three dependent children in the first year following the quarter of program entry was 5 percent or less for all groups.

Paralleling the analysis reported in table 11.5, we use equation 11.1 to estimate a series of models with dummy-dependent variables indicating earnings above each of the four thresholds over the various time horizons. The first panel of

TABLE 11.6 / Work First Participants Who Achieved Earnings Sufficient to Escape Welfare or Poverty, by Time from Work First Orientation and by Job Type, Various Thresholds

	Welfare Threshold, Family of Three	Welfare Threshold, Family of Four	Poverty Threshold, Family of Three	Poverty Threshold, Family of Four
Quarter 1				
No job	6.7%	5.4%	3.4%	2.1%
Direct-hire job	21.3	17.0	9.9	5.2
Temporary job	21.1	16.4	9.7	5.2
Quarters 1 to 4				
No job	9.1	7.1	4.2	2.2
Direct-hire job	22.1	17.5	10.0	5.3
Temporary job	21.3	17.1	9.5	5.4
Quarters 5 to 8				
No job	15.4	13.0	8.8	5.1
Direct-hire job	26.0	22.1	15.0	8.5
Temporary job	25.1	21.3	14.5	8.9

Source: Authors' compilations.
Notes: Number of observations in quarter 1 and in quarters 1 to 4: 36,105, representing participants entering from the third quarter of 1999 through the second quarter of 2003. Number of observations in quarters 5 to 8: 25,118, representing participants entering from the third quarter of 1999 through the second quarter of 2002.

table 11.7 reports coefficient estimates pertaining to the welfare and poverty thresholds for the first quarter following program entry; the second panel covers the combined first through fourth quarters; and the last panel covers the fifth through eighth quarters following the quarter of program entry.

Our 2SLS estimates of the effects of job placement on *short-term* earnings are generally similar to the OLS estimates. The 2SLS models indicate that for three out of the four thresholds, temporary agency placements significantly raised the probability (relative to no job placement) that participants' earnings would exceed the welfare or poverty threshold in the near term—that is, the first quarter following program entry.

The IV models also indicate that, relative to no job placement, direct-hire placements significantly increased the probability that participants' earnings in the first quarter would exceed the two welfare thresholds. From table 11.7, column 4, for instance, we estimate that a temporary agency placement increased by 14.8 percentage points the probability that a participant's earnings in the first quarter following the quarter of entry would exceed the welfare threshold for a family of four, whereas a direct-hire placement increased that probability by 9.6 percentage points.

TABLE 11.7 / The Effect of Work First Job Placements on the Probability of Escaping Poverty One to Eight Quarters Following Work First Assignment

	Welfare Threshold, Family of Three		Welfare Threshold, Family of Four		Poverty Threshold, Family of Three		Poverty Threshold, Family of Four	
	OLS (1)	2SLS (2)	OLS (3)	2SLS (4)	OLS (5)	2SLS (6)	OLS (7)	2SLS (8)
Quarter 1								
Temporary	12.4**	17.6**	9.2**	14.8**	5.0**	8.8**	2.2**	2.9
agency job	(0.9)	(4.3)	(0.8)	(3.6)	(0.6)	(2.2)	(0.4)	(1.9)
Direct-hire job	13.3**	12.2**	10.3**	9.6**	5.5**	0.7	2.4**	−0.6
	(0.5)	(2.1)	(0.4)	(2.1)	(0.3)	(1.4)	(0.2)	(1.1)
R-squared	0.11		0.11)		0.09		0.07	
H_0: Tempo-rary = Direct-hire	0.41	0.26	0.22	0.26	0.42	0.01	0.67	0.17
Quarters 1 to 4								
Temporary	9.8**	−0.3	7.8**	−0.9	3.7**	−1.0	2.3**	−4.1*
agency job	(0.9)	(5.8)	(0.8)	(4.4)	(0.5)	(3.0)	(0.4)	(2.1)
Direct-hire job	11.1**	6.7**	8.7**	5.9**	4.6**	0.7	2.3**	2.5*
	(0.4)	(3.2)	(0.4)	(2.6)	(0.3)	(1.3)	(0.2)	(1.3)
R-squared	0.14		0.13		0.10		0.08	
H_0: Tempo-rary = Direct-hire	0.16	0.35	0.30	0.24	0.16	0.61	0.88	0.01
Quarters 5 to 8								
Temporary	6.8**	−4.5	5.6**	−2.77	3.7**	−5.8	2.2**	−3.5
agency job	(1.0)	(6.7)	(0.9)	(6.7)	(0.7)	(5.5)	(0.5)	(4.5)
Direct-hire job	8.3**	15.1**	7.0**	10.8**	4.5**	6.3	2.2**	3.4
	(0.6)	(4.9)	(0.5)	(4.8)	(0.4)	(4.4)	(0.3)	(3.2)
R-squared	0.12		0.12		0.11		0.09	
H_0: Tempo-rary = Direct-hire	0.20	0.05	0.17	0.17	0.36	0.11	0.92	0.25

Source: Authors' compilations.
Notes: Number of observations for quarter 1 and quarters 1 to 4: 36,105, representing participants entering from the third quarter of 1999 through the second quarter of 2003. Number of observations for quarters 5 to 8: 25,118, representing participants entering from the third quarter of 1999 through the second quarter of 2002. Robust standard errors in parentheses are clustered on Work First contractor assignment times year. All models include year times quarter of assignment and randomization-district times year of assignment dummy variables, controls for age and its square, race, sum of UI earnings in the four quarters prior to Work First assignment, and four education dummies (elementary education, less than high school, greater than high school, and education unknown). Coefficient estimates and standard errors are multiplied by 100.
**Significant at the 0.05 percent level; *significant at the 0.10 perrcent level.

Results from our IV models portray a distinctly different picture when we evaluate the effects of job placements on earnings over a longer time horizon. Direct-hire placements significantly raised the probability that participant earnings would exceed the income level necessary for a family of three or four to remain off of welfare for up to two years following the quarter of program entry. Relative to no job placement, placing an individual in a direct-hire job increased the likelihood that her earnings would exceed the welfare threshold for a family of four by 5.9 percentage points over the first year following the quarter of program entry and by 10.8 percentage points for the second year following the quarter of program entry.

In contrast, the initial positive effects of temporary agency placements disappeared over longer time horizons. Over the first and second years following program entry, the IV estimates of the effects of temporary agency placements on the probability of earning above welfare thresholds are negative, though small and insignificantly different from zero. Thus, marginal temporary agency placements do not appear to help participants stay off of welfare.

For higher thresholds, as represented by the poverty threshold for a family of three and for a family of four, we find that neither temporary agency nor direct-hire placements helped participants escape poverty over a one- to two-year period following program entry. In fact, relative to no job placement and to a direct-hire job placement, placements into temporary agency jobs actually have modest but significant negative effects on the probability that participants would earn above the poverty threshold for a family of four over the four quarters following program entry.

In summary, we find that placements in temporary agency jobs helped Work First participants escape welfare and poverty only in the short term. Over longer horizons, these placements did not increase, and may even have reduced, participants' chances of attaining earnings levels sufficient to leave welfare and escape poverty. In contrast, placements in direct-hire jobs modestly increased the chances that participants would earn enough to leave welfare, though we find no significant effects of marginal direct-hire jobs on the probability of exceeding poverty thresholds.

CONCLUSIONS AND POLICY IMPLICATIONS

In contrast to previous studies, we find no evidence that would support a policy recommendation that employment programs should increase the use of temporary agencies as labor market intermediaries for low-skilled workers. Although temporary agency job placements raise the probability that Work First participants will earn above welfare and poverty thresholds over very short time horizons, these positive effects quickly dissipate. Over horizons of one to two years, placements in temporary agency jobs (relative to no job placement) do not increase the chances that participants will earn enough to leave welfare and escape poverty. Moreover, by some measures these placements reduce the chances that earnings will exceed poverty thresholds. Our results suggest that raising direct-hire placements is probably a much more effective means for job assistance programs to reduce welfare dependency over both the short and long term. Even marginal direct-hire placements, however, do not appear to improve participants' chances of escaping poverty over longer time horizons.

In summary, we do find that Work First programs improve labor market outcomes for participants. Our findings therefore lend support to some role for labor market intermediaries in low-skilled labor markets, as is generally advocated in Andersson et al. (2005) and Holzer (2004). However, our results do not support the conclusion that temporary agencies are effective labor market intermediaries for the poor.

It must be emphasized that our results do not imply that temporary agency jobs never improve long-term participant outcomes. Our estimates pertain only to "marginal" workers—that is, to participants whose job placement is affected by random assignment among contractors. As we show in Autor and Houseman (2005), these marginal temporary help and direct-hire workers have weaker skills and experience than the average participant placed in a job. To the degree that there is heterogeneity among temporary agency jobs or workers, the effects of temporary agency placements may differ between marginal and infra-marginal placements.[19] Our survey evidence, for instance, revealed some consensus among contractors that temp-to-perm jobs, which tend to be taken by relatively high-skilled participants, are often beneficial, but we cannot formally test this proposition with our data. Nevertheless, our findings are particularly germane to the design of welfare programs. The operative question for program design is whether job programs assisting welfare clients and low-wage workers can improve participants' labor market outcomes by placing more of them with temporary agency positions. Our analysis suggests not.

Among marginal temporary help workers (that is, those with relatively weak skills and experience), why do temporary agency jobs fail to provide lasting benefits and sometimes even harm their long-term labor market outcomes? Although we cannot provide definitive answers to this critical question, our survey evidence and statistical analysis suggest some plausible explanations. Work First contractors reported that temporary agency jobs were relatively more plentiful than direct-hire jobs for those with weak skills and experience, but that these agency jobs generally did not lead to permanent positions. These perceptions are reinforced in Autor and Houseman (2005), where we find no evidence that temporary agency placements help participants transition into stable, direct-hire jobs. Over short time horizons, increased earnings in the temporary help sector are more than offset by reduced earnings in direct-hire jobs. Over longer time horizons, temporary help placements lead to lower employment rates, lower earnings in direct-hire jobs, more frequent job changes, and greater risk of welfare recidivism.

One perspective expressed in our contractor survey was that a certain segment of the temporary agency market accommodates individuals with very weak skills, experience, and work ethic by providing them with jobs that require few skills and no long-term commitment. Yet it is the lack of skills, experience, and work ethic that keeps these individuals in poverty. Although temporary agency positions may help them fulfill program work requirements in the short term, these jobs appear ineffective at reducing their dependency on welfare. Job placements that might help participants overcome, rather than accommodate, their employment barriers may be more beneficial.

We conclude that in some circumstances it would be better for individuals to pass up an opportunity to work for a temporary agency and to continue to search for direct-hire employment. Yet the incentives built into the Work First program for both participants and contractors may not support such a decision. Participants are encouraged to obtain work quickly and officially are required to accept any employment offering the minimum wage and sufficient hours. Contractors are primarily evaluated on job placement rates and ninety-day retention rates, and over such short time horizons temporary agency placements do yield benefits. Moving to an incentive structure that places greater weight on longer-term outcomes may reduce welfare dependence and poverty levels by mitigating short-term pressures on program providers to place participants in any job available, including potentially counterproductive ones.

NOTES

1. We thank Mary Corcoran and the editors of this volume for excellent comments, Lillian Vesic-Petrovic for excellent research assistance throughout the project, Erica Pavao and Lauren Fahey for assistance in conducting interviews, and Claire Black for transcribing interviews. The Russell Sage Foundation and the Rockefeller Foundation provided support for this research.

2. An individual may work forty hours per week and still be eligible for TANF if her earnings are lower than a specified threshold, as determined by her family size.

3. Even if a participant's earnings are high enough to require closing her TANF case, the contractor must conduct a ninety-day follow-up. Typically, if earnings do not lead to the closure of a participant's case, her Work First spell is terminated because of noncompliance with the program. The median Work First spell in our sample is slightly under three months. Ninety-six percent of participants are terminated from the program in less than a year.

4. A copy of the survey instrument is available from the authors.

5. An exception is Corcoran and Chen (2004), in which data on jobs come from interviews with welfare recipients.

6. Particularly helpful was a list supplied by David Fasenfest and Heidi Gottfried from their study mapping the location of all temporary agencies in this metropolitan area. In a few cases, the name alone was insufficient to classify an employer correctly, but we generally were able to determine the nature of an employer's operation through an Internet search or by contacting the employer by phone.

7. Although contractors do not formally track temporary agency placements, their estimates are consistent with administrative data from earlier years. The median survey

response, 15 percent, compares with a mean of 21 percent from the administrative data across all years and all contractors; rates of temporary employment were somewhat lower in more recent years in our data.

8. The contractors who cited others as benefiting from temporary agency positions were referring to those with particular skills, such as clerical or health care; agencies could place these workers in temp-to-hire positions with good companies.

9. A couple of contractors noted that it is more difficult to monitor employment status in temporary agencies and that some Work First participants who do not want permanent employment use these jobs to give the appearance of complying with work requirements, hence gaming the system.

10. A number of studies examine the role of temporary employment (temporary agency and fixed-term contract employment) in labor market transitions in Europe. For a description and critique of methods used in these U.S. and European studies, see Autor and Houseman (2005).

11. There is a large and growing literature on the heterogeneity of treatment effects. See, for example, Angrist (2004) and Heckman and Vytlacil (2005).

12. See Autor and Houseman (2005) for a much more extensive discussion of this issue and a presentation of evidence that our estimates are not biased by the effects of other contractor practices.

13. The occupational distribution of temporary agency jobs in our sample is broadly consistent with available national data from the Occupational Employment Survey (OES). According to the OES, production and clerical occupations accounted for the greatest concentration of temporary agency jobs in 2000, each accounting for about one-third of employment. The relatively low concentration of clerical occupations in our sample no doubt reflects the low skill level of our population. According to the contractors surveyed, temporary clerical positions tend to require higher skill levels than most of their clientele have.

14. The unit of observation is the Work First spell. We do not correct for potential clustering of the error term for individuals with multiple spells in our data since we cannot simultaneously correct for clustering at the contractor-by-year and at the level participant level. However, limiting the sample to the first spell yields virtually identical results to those reported here.

15. This finding is also consistent with our survey results, which show that the debate among contractors over temporary help agencies pertains primarily to whether agency placements benefit or harm those with weaker skills or experience. Thus, we would expect that the contractors with relatively high temporary agency placement rates would be placing relatively more participants with weak skills or experience into those agency jobs. In turn, for the whole sample, we would expect marginal temporary agency workers to have, on average, weaker skills or experience.

16. Information on the reason for case closure was missing for 1,595 spells, and these observations were dropped from the sample.

17. Welfare thresholds change infrequently. Therefore, to assess whether a participant's earnings exceeded a threshold, we compared unadjusted earnings to the welfare threshold that applied during the time period. For poverty thresholds, we used 2003 Census Bureau definitions, which are defined only at the national level, and adjusted

both earnings and poverty thresholds for inflation to 2003 levels using the consumer price index.

18. Those not eligible for TANF may still be eligible for food stamps, other assistance, and the EITC, and thus the discrepancy between welfare and poverty thresholds may be smaller once these benefits are taken into account.

19. Heterogeneity of effects between marginal and infra-marginal workers may partly explain the differences between our results and those from previous studies. For an extensive discussion of this issue, see Autor and Houseman (2005).

REFERENCES

Abraham, Katharine G. 1988. "Flexible Staffing Arrangements and Employers' Short-Term Adjustment Strategies." In *Employment, Unemployment, and Labor Utilization*, edited by Robert A. Hart. Boston: Unwin Hyman.

Andersson, Frederik, Harry J. Holzer, and Julia I. Lane. 2005. *Moving Up or Moving On: Who Advances in the Labor Market?* New York: Russell Sage Foundation.

Angrist, Joshua D. 2004. "Treatment Effect Heterogeneity in Theory and Practice." *Economic Journal* 114(494): C52–83.

Autor, David H. 2001. "Why Do Temporary Help Firms Provide Free General Skills Training?" *Quarterly Journal of Economics* 116(4): 1409–48.

———. 2003. "Outsourcing at Will: The Contribution of Unjust Dismissal Doctrine to the Growth of Employment Outsourcing." *Journal of Labor Economics* 21(1): 1–42.

Autor, David H., and Susan N. Houseman. 2002. "The Role of Temporary Employment Agencies in Welfare to Work: Part of the Problem or Part of the Solution?" *Focus* 22(1): 63–70.

———. 2005. "Do Temporary Help Jobs Improve Labor Market Outcomes for Low-Skilled Workers? Evidence from Random Assignments." Working paper 11743. Cambridge, Mass.: National Bureau of Economic Research.

Cancian, Maria, Robert Haveman, Thomas Kaplan, and Barbara Wolfe. 1999. "Post-Exit Earnings and Benefit Receipt among Those Who Left AFDC in Wisconsin." Special Report no. 75. Institute for Research on Poverty, University of Wisconsin, Madison.

Corcoran, Mary, and Juan Chen. 2004. "Temporary Employment and Welfare-to-Work." Unpublished paper. Ann Arbor: University of Michigan.

Ferber, Marianne A., and Jane Waldfogel. 1998. "The Long-Term Consequences of Non-traditional Employment." *Monthly Labor Review* 121(5): 3–12.

Heckman, James J., and Edward Vytlacil. 2005. "Structural Equations, Treatment Effects, and Econometric Policy Evaluation." Working paper 11259. Cambridge, Mass.: National Bureau of Economic Research.

Heinrich, Carolyn J., Peter R. Mueser, and Kenneth R. Troske. 2005. "Welfare to Temporary Work: Implications for Labor Market Outcomes." *Review of Economics and Statistics* 87(1): 154–73.

Holzer, Harry J. 2004. "Encouraging Job Advancement Among Low-Wage Workers: A New Approach." "Welfare Reform and Beyond" policy brief 30 (May). Washington, D.C.: Brookings Institution.

Houseman, Susan N. 2001. "Why Employers Use Flexible Staffing Arrangements: Evidence from an Establishment Survey." *Industrial and Labor Relations Review* 55(1): 149–70.

Kalleberg, Arne L., Jeremy Reynolds, and Peter V. Marsden. 2003. "Externalizing Employment: Flexible Staffing Arrangements in U.S. Organizations." *Social Science Research* 32(December): 525–52.

Lane, Julia, Kelly S. Mikelson, Pat Sharkey, and Doug Wissoker. 2003. "Pathways to Work for Low-Income Workers: The Effect of Work in the Temporary Help Industry." *Journal of Policy Analysis and Management* 22(4): 581–98.

Pawasarat, John. 1997. "The Employer Perspective: Jobs Held by the Milwaukee County AFDC Single Parent Population (January 1996–March 1997)." Employment and Training Institute, University of Wisconsin, Milwaukee.

Chapter 12

Child Support and the Economy

Maria Cancian and Daniel R. Meyer

As the proportion of children living with both parents has fallen and as public support for sole-parent families has been reduced, child support has become a crucial source of income for single-parent families.[1] In this chapter, we describe the logic and outcomes of the child support system and consider the relationship between economic conditions, child support, and poverty.

We show that child support is an important, if often unreliable, source of income for the poor single-mother families who receive it. But mothers with limited earnings potential often have had children with men who also have limited economic resources. This constrains the potential for child support to lift families out of poverty, since child support payments may constitute a transfer from one poor household to another. Moreover, parents who live in separate households lose the economies of scale associated with shared housing and other resources and therefore are at an economic disadvantage relative to two-parent households, regardless of their individual incomes. Finally, child support policies themselves have been formulated with sometime contradictory objectives—supporting families, but also offsetting the costs to government of public supports. This has contributed to a system with complex incentives that may have unintended consequences for economically vulnerable and otherwise fragile families, many of whom may have difficulty managing the system to the best advantage of their children.

This volume highlights the interactions between the economy, policy, and outcomes for the poor. In this chapter, we explain why child support payments from nonresident to resident parents do not vary substantially with the economic cycle and explore the implications of this invariance for the economic vulnerability of both resident and nonresident parents. Official child support payments may vary because the child support order (the obligation) changes or because the proportion of the ordered support that is actually paid (compliance) changes. As we show, orders are often not responsive to income changes, leaving the nonresident parent vulnerable to changes in earnings associated with the economic cycle. A fixed child support obligation is more financially burdensome for nonresident parents who experience earnings losses and less financially burdensome for those whose earnings increase. In this sense, a fixed child support obligation functions as a procyclical tax on earnings for nonresident parents. The corollary is the potentially countercyclical nature of child support *payments* received by resident parents. Stable child support orders and payments could provide insurance against cyclical variations in the resident parent's earnings.

In this chapter, we consider how child support policy affects the relationship between work and poverty for the families of both resident and nonresident parents. The relationship is complex, and differences over time and across families have been mediated by a diverse set of policy and demographic factors. The role of child support for poor resident-mother families depends on whether they have a child support order, the amount of support ordered, and, ultimately, how much support is paid and received. For each of these outcomes, we review recent national estimates, briefly discuss the related policies, review the research on the characteristics associated with the outcome, and discuss the relationship between the outcome and economic conditions. Second, we turn our attention to the economic impact of child support on payers and recipients. We review research on the impact of paying support on the economic well-being of nonresident fathers and the role of child support in the income packages of resident mothers. We close with a discussion of implications for policy and future research.

Our analysis focuses on separated parents—we do not review the effects of the economy on union formation, dissolution, or fertility (see London and Fairlie, this volume). We focus on fathers as nonresident parents and mothers as resident parents, since this is the typical child support case (Grall 2003). Other chapters in this volume address the relationship between economic cycles and employment or income; here our focus is on how employment and income, which are affected by economic cycles, are related to child support. There are substantial limitations in the national data, so we supplement national information with more detailed information from Wisconsin.

THE CURRENT CHILD SUPPORT SYSTEM

The Existence of Child Support Orders

WHAT POLICIES AFFECT WHETHER MOTHERS HAVE CHILD SUPPORT ORDERS? Child support orders are legal obligations that are generally set through the legal system. Parents enter the child support system through several paths. For a divorce to be final in most states, parents must go before a judge or a family court commissioner. Decisions are made about how property will be distributed, where a child will live, how often the other parent will be able to visit, whether child support (or alimony) is due, and how much is owed. Each state must have a numerical guideline that indicates the level of a child support order. The guidelines almost always imply that child support should be ordered, even if the amount is minimal, regardless of the income and employment of the parents.[2]

When married parents separate, they may or may not have an informal agreement on where the children will live and whether the nonresident parent will contribute toward their support. If a resident parent applies for cash assistance (welfare), a condition of eligibility is cooperation with the child support office in pursuing formal child support. If no support order exists, the agency will bring the case to the legal system to establish an order. Even a mother not receiving welfare can receive assistance from the child support office if she is not satisfied with an informal arrangement.

Mothers who have children outside marriage must cooperate with the child support system if they apply for cash assistance; they can also request help from the child support office even if they are not receiving cash assistance. However, a child support order cannot be issued without a formal finding of paternity. In the last fifteen years there have been substantial changes in the paternity establishment process, including efforts to increase voluntary paternity acknowledgment (especially in hospitals at the time of birth), payment by the federal government for genetic testing to determine paternity, and the establishment of paternity "in default" if a putative father does not appear at a court hearing.

HOW LIKELY ARE MOTHERS TO HAVE CHILD SUPPORT ORDERS?   Figure 12.1 shows the percentage of resident mothers who were owed child support from 1978 to 2001.[3] The middle line shows that the overall rate is fairly stable, masking a substantial change within marital status groups. Among divorced mothers (top line) 64 to 72 percent had an order, with slight declines since 1985. In contrast, the proportion of never-married mothers with orders increased dramatically over this period, from 8 to 45 percent. The overall rate changed little despite this increase because never-married mothers accounted for a greater proportion of the total, increasing from 20 to 30 percent of all mothers between 1978 and 2001. The proportion of poor mothers with orders rose from about 30 percent to close to 50 percent over the same period (not shown). This increase is consistent with the increase in orders for never-married mothers, who are disproportionately poor.

WHAT CHARACTERISTICS ARE ASSOCIATED WITH HAVING AN ORDER? Marital status is very important, since divorced and remarried mothers are substantially more likely to have orders than never-married mothers. Custody type is also important: many cases with joint custody have no child support order, and resident fathers are less likely to have an order (34 percent) than resident mothers (55 percent). More-educated resident mothers are also more likely to have orders: only about 40 percent of mothers without a high school degree have a child support order, compared to about 60 percent of college-educated resident mothers.

Multivariate analysis generally confirms these descriptive relationships. Those

FIGURE 12.1 / Custodial Mothers with a Child Support Order

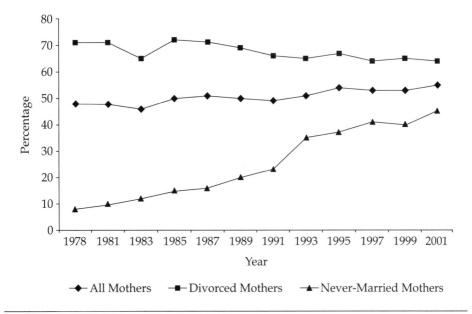

Source: Authors' compilations based on Current Population Survey, Child Support Supplements.

more likely to have an order are those who have been divorced (Hanson et al. 1996), who are older (Hanson et al. 1996), who are white (Argys, Peters, and Waldman 2001; Hanson et al. 1996), who have more education (Hanson et al. 1996), and who have more children (Argys et al. 2001; Hanson et al. 1996). Mothers' income is not related to having an order (Argys et al. 2001; Hanson et al. 1996).

There are conflicting findings on the relationship between orders and fathers' income. Thomas Hanson and his colleagues (1996) find that mothers are more likely to have an order if the father's estimated income is higher, but Laura Argys and her colleagues (2001) and Cynthia Miller and Irwin Garfinkel (1999) find no effect. There are also conflicting results on the time trend: once other characteristics are controlled, Argys and her colleagues (2001) find an increasing likelihood that there will be an order for divorce cases, but in a finding similar to that of the Argys team's for nonmarital births, Hanson and his colleagues (1996) find no clear time trend and show that most of the change in order rates is due to changes in the marital status of the caseload.

HOW DOES THE ECONOMY AFFECT WHETHER MOTHERS HAVE ORDERS?   Because divorces require court action, they nearly always include child support orders. A child support order is typically set even if the nonresident parent is unemployed and is often based on anticipated or imputed income.

Economic conditions affect employment and earnings, which may have some effect on the likelihood of orders, but the effect is not large. According to the policy guidelines in Wisconsin and in many other states, whether there is an order (and often the size of the order) is independent of the employment or earnings of the mother. Thus, in general there is little direct way in which the economy could affect whether there is an order among cases coming to court.

If informal separations and nonmarital births come to court, child support is typically considered and an order established. If these situations do not come to court, there may be informal child support arrangements. A difficult economic period could be associated with a chain of events that lead to a child support order. For example, if difficult economic conditions led to a decline in informal support, the resident parent might be motivated to go to the child support agency to try to gain a formal child support order. Similarly, a decline in the resident parent's earnings might inspire an attempt to gain a formal child support order. An alternative link between economic conditions and child support orders is through welfare (Temporary Assistance for Needy Families, or TANF). If a difficult economic period leads a mother to apply for such assistance, she is required to cooperate with the child support agency as a condition of eligibility. The agency then tries to establish a child support order.

There is little observable relationship in the CPS data between economic conditions and the existence of child support orders, especially among those who have gone through a court process. Neither policy nor the research described earlier suggests that mothers' and fathers' earnings have consistent effects on the existence of orders. However, the impact of economic conditions on the earnings and income of the parents could lead to a desire to formalize financial relationships through an order; more contact with the formal child support system and/or applications for public assistance could also result in more orders.

The Amount of Child Support Orders

WHICH POLICIES AFFECT THE AMOUNT OF CHILD SUPPORT ORDERS? In 1984 each state was required to develop child support guidelines—numerical formulas to be used as advice in determining order levels. In 1988 these guidelines were made presumptive—that is, they were assumed to apply unless evidence to the contrary was forthcoming. States developed different guidelines, but there are two constants. In each state, the order amount increases with the nonresident parent's income and with the number of children.

In nearly all states, the guidelines are based on a principle of "continuity of expenditures" (Garrison 1999), which tries to ensure that children receive the same level of resources they would have had if their parents still lived together. The most common guideline within this principle, "income shares," begins by summing the two parents' incomes. This total is multiplied by a percentage typically spent on children by parents in this income range. The resulting amount is then divided between the two parents on the basis of their relative incomes. In these guidelines, typically the amount ordered is a smaller percentage of income for higher-income nonresident parents.

In the other common guideline type within this principle, "percentage of income," the percentage spent on children is thought to be constant across income levels. This simplifies the formula so that amounts are based only on the number of children and the nonresident parent's income. Wisconsin's guidelines, for example, require the expenditure of 17 percent of income for one child, 25 percent for two, 29 percent for three, 31 percent for four, and 34 percent for five or more.

Many states have special rules for upper-income and lower-income nonresident parents. The rules generally decrease the percentage of income ordered for those with higher incomes. Those with lower incomes are sometimes required to pay a higher share (because minimum order levels are a higher proportion of income for very low-income fathers) and sometimes to pay a lower share (as provisions protecting minimum income to cover the father's own needs may leave very low-income fathers with less to contribute in child support). Many states also have special rules when children live with both parents a portion of the time or when nonresident parents owe support to multiple families (for a history of child support guidelines and the issues associated with them, see Rothe and Meyer 2000).

The Family Support Act of 1988 required that states regularly examine the orders of AFDC recipients to see whether they should be updated, and it required states to review orders, and update them if appropriate, at the request of either parent for those not receiving AFDC. Few individuals request a review, even those whose orders would rise substantially, perhaps because they do not want to upset a delicate balance between the parents (Kost et al. 1996). States have experimented with different strategies to keep orders current, including automatic cost-of-living adjustments and percentage-expressed orders (ordering, for example, a father to pay "17 percent of income").

WHAT IS THE LEVEL OF CHILD SUPPORT ORDERS? WHAT CHARACTERISTICS ARE ASSOCIATED WITH THE AMOUNT ORDERED?   In 2001, among mothers due support, the mean annual amount due was about $5,100; about one in five were due $1 to $2,000, and about one-third were due $5,000 or more.[4] Among poor mothers, amounts due were somewhat lower: the mean was $3,950, with about 30 percent due $2,000 or less and one-fourth due $5,000 or more. There were small decreases in the amounts due over the 1980s; looking only at recently established orders, Hanson and his colleagues (1996) report a decline of over $1,200 in annual support between 1978 and 1989 (2000 dollars). This decline is associated with changes in the population of mothers due support: increasingly, it included never-married mothers. The trend changed in the 1990s: average amounts increased from about $4,300 in 1993 to $5,100 in 2001.

Hanson and his colleagues (1996) find that many of the characteristics of women who are less likely to have an order are also associated with lower order amounts. Mothers who have never been married, are African American or Latina, have lower educational levels, and have fewer children have lower orders. They also find that fathers' estimated income is an important predictor of order amounts. Argys and her colleagues (2001) also find that fathers' income is strongly related to order amounts and that once fathers' actual income is controlled, few demographic variables are related to order levels in divorce cases. The Hanson team's analysis suggests that the main explanation for changes in order amounts over time is the lack of orders to keep up with inflation. Argys and her colleagues (2001) find that, over time, order levels decline among formerly married women, but not among those who have children outside marriage; for the latter, the presence of child support guidelines may be associated with higher orders.[5]

One effect of the guidelines was to increase consistency in order amounts among cases at a given income level rather than to change the overall mean amount due (Argys et al. 2001). Daniel Meyer and his colleagues (1996) have reported that the percentage of cases in Wisconsin that were consistent with the guideline doubled in the first year after the guidelines were published and continued to increase until it was around half of all cases after the guidelines were made presumptive. More recent analysis, however, shows that the percentage of cases consistent with the guidelines may have peaked in the early 1990s and that it has either held level or declined since that time.

Policy has strong effects on the amounts of initial orders. The most important factors associated with order amounts are the nonresident parent's income and the number of children (Argys et al. 2001; Hanson et al. 1996), as would be expected from policy.

Order amounts generally do not change once they are instituted, and if they change, the changes are not necessarily consistent with observed earnings changes. No national data exist to address this question, but there is evidence from Wisconsin. For a sample of fathers who first owed child support in Wisconsin in 2000, we examined orders and income through 2003 and found that fewer than one-quarter of the orders changed by 5 percent in either direction. Among fathers whose formal earnings increased by 25 percent or more, orders increased for only 15 percent; perhaps more surprisingly, orders decreased for 11 percent of these fathers. Among fathers whose formal earnings decreased by 25 percent or more, orders decreased for only 16 percent, and they increased for 8 percent.

HOW DOES THE ECONOMY AFFECT THE LEVEL OF ORDERS? The economy primarily affects order levels through the nonresident parent's employment and income at the time of the order. But the relationship is not as strong as we might expect, in part because in most states orders can be based on imputed income rather than actual income. For example, an order could assume full-time, minimum-wage work even if the parent has no known income. In most states, the resident parent's employment and income are designed to have minimal effects on order levels. Thus, changes in the economy may or may not be reflected in initial orders. Moreover, even when earnings change by a large amount, orders are not routinely changed as a result.

Child Support Payments

WHAT POLICIES AFFECT CHILD SUPPORT PAYMENTS AND RECEIPTS? The child support payment system is generally routine for those with formal employment. When a child support order is instituted, a payment mechanism is set. If the nonresident parent is employed at that time, an automatic wage withholding order is supposed to be issued. The employer sends the amount withheld to a child support central processing office (one in each state), which then forwards an amount to the resident parent. Employers are required to report the Social Security number of all new employees, and the child support agency matches the number against a database containing lists of those who owe child support. If there is a match, the system issues a new withholding order to the employer.

Nevertheless, some nonresident parents get behind in their payments, especially those who are not working in formal employment. Penalties for noncompliance can be severe: driver's, recreational, and professional licenses may be rescinded, liens imposed on personal property, and tax refunds intercepted. Ultimately, a defaulter may be jailed.

The amount collected is not necessarily the amount distributed to the resident parent, since some states charge a processing fee. A large disjunction between payments and receipts is common among families receiving TANF. As a condition of TANF eligibility, resident parents sign away their rights to child support. Since 1996, states have set their own policies on how much child support they "pass through" to the parent and "disregard" in calculating the level of TANF benefits. About two-thirds of states now keep all child support paid on behalf of TANF recipients, using it to offset state expenditures; most of the remaining states pass through the first $50 each month and then disregard this amount in the calculation of benefits (Roberts and Vinson 2004). Two states have notable policies. Minnesota passes through all child support to the family, but then counts it dollar for dollar against benefits (a full pass-through without a disregard). Wisconsin is the most generous: all child support goes to the family, and it is ignored in the calculation of TANF benefits (a full pass-through and full disregard).

HOW MUCH CHILD SUPPORT IS PAID AND RECEIVED? WHAT CHARACTERISTICS ARE ASSOCIATED WITH PAYMENTS? In 2001, 75 *percent* of all mothers, and 66 *percent* of poor mothers, who were due child support reported receiving some amount. Among all mothers, this percentage has been relatively constant since 1978 but has shown slight increases since 1993. Figure 12.2 shows the time trend in the average amount of child support received among mothers

FIGURE 12.2 / Average Child Support Received and Unemployment Rate

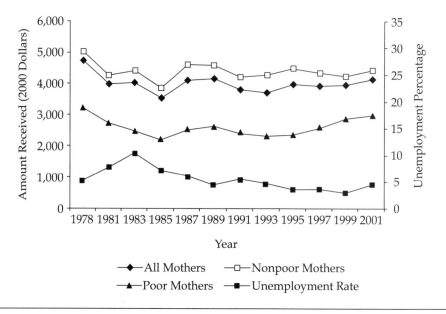

Source: Authors' compilations based on Current Population Survey, Child Support Supplements.

receiving some support. The unemployment rate is also shown, for reference. Amounts received have remained fairly stable. In 2001 the average amount received among all mothers with orders was $4,150. The average among poor mothers was $3,000.

Compliance (the percentage of the amount due that is paid) shows a somewhat different pattern. Between 1978 and 1991, about 50 percent of mothers reported receiving the full amount due; the percentage declined sharply in 1993 to 37 percent,[6] and for the last several years has been about 45 percent. In contrast, in 2001 only 32 percent of poor mothers received all the child support they were due.

Economic theory suggests that payments would be affected by at least three factors: the nonresident father's ability to pay support; his willingness to pay support, which may be affected by the economic need of the resident-parent family; and the policy environment (see, for example, Bartfeld and Meyer 1994; Beller and Graham 1993). There is a clear link between a nonresident father's economic status and his payments. For example, national data show that the median child support payment for fathers with incomes below $22,500 was zero (fewer than half of these fathers made payments), compared to a median payment of about $3,800 for those with incomes over $45,000 (Meyer 1998). Elaine Sorensen and Chava Zibman (2001) report that more than 40 percent of fathers with incomes above the poverty level paid support in 1997, compared to fewer than 15 percent of poor fathers.

Studies have also examined whether compliance is related to the "burden" of the child support order. Orders that are a high percentage of the nonresident parent's income have been associated with lower compliance rates (Bartfeld and Meyer 2003; Meyer 1999). Anne Case, I.-Fen Lin, and Sara McLanahan (2003) report that declines in men's earnings over time are a key explanation for declines in child support payments.

As the child support system has become more routinized (especially for those in formal employment), there is less room for a father's willingness to pay to affect payments (see, for example, Bartfeld and Meyer 2003). There is little evidence that the economic circumstances of the resident parent are related to payments (see, for example, Smock and Manning 1997).

In contrast, there is strong evidence suggesting that the enforcement system has important effects. Sorensen and Ariel Hill (2004) find substantial improvements in child support receipts as a result of child support policies once other characteristics are controlled. Richard Freeman and Jane Waldfogel (2001) find that receipts are related to policy reforms; their results are strongest when policy reforms are combined with expenditures on enforcement. Policies associated with payments (or compliance) include income withholding (Beller and Graham 1993; Garfinkel and Klawitter 1990; Lin 2000; Sorensen and Hill 2004), presumptive guidelines (Sorensen and Hill 2004), income tax intercepts (Sorensen and Hill 2004), in-hospital paternity establishment (Sorensen and Hill 2004), new-hire reporting (Cassetty, Cancian, and Meyer 2002), and a fully automated system (Cassetty et al. 2002).

In an experimental evaluation, the Wisconsin policy of fully disregarding child support payments for TANF recipients was associated with increased payments (Meyer and Cancian 2001). Nonexperimental results also find a positive relationship between payments and the level of child support disregarded (Meyer and Cancian 2002a; Sorensen and Hill 2004). Some policies have been associated with declines in child support payments: Case and her colleagues (2003) find that mothers in states and time periods where there is no-fault divorce have lower receipts.

Consider the steps in the child support process. Because marital status is linked to the likelihood of orders, divorced mothers generally have higher child support than never-married mothers. Because order levels are generally tied to the nonresident parent's income, child support is higher among those connected to higher-earning fathers (mothers with higher levels of education, for example, or those who are older). Because order levels are connected to the number of children, child support may be higher among those with more children; however, if those with more children are less likely to be connected to higher-earning men, these factors could offset each other. Finally, child support orders vary with state guidelines.

Putting all these factors together, in 2001 the average amount received among all resident mothers was about $1,700. Among poor mothers, the average was just $950. Amounts were substantially higher for divorced mothers ($2,500) than for never-married mothers ($800) and for non-Hispanic white mothers ($2,250) than for African Americans ($900) or Hispanics ($1,250). Younger women received less ($800 for those age eighteen to twenty-nine, compared to $2,350 for those forty and over). Educational level was also quite important: only $700 was received by those with less than a high school diploma, compared to $3,100 for those with a bachelor's degree. Finally, those with two children did receive more than those with one child ($2,400 versus $1,350), but they also received more than those with three or more children ($1,700).

HOW DOES THE ECONOMY AFFECT CHILD SUPPORT PAYMENTS?   Fathers who are in the formal economy generally pay what they are ordered to pay because of the automated system (Bartfeld and Meyer 2003). As a result, the main effect of the economic cycle on compliance should be due to effects on the extent to which nonresident parents are in formal employment.

CHILD SUPPORT AND THE ECONOMIC WELL-BEING OF NONRESIDENT FATHERS

We now turn to some issues regarding the impact of the child support system on resident and nonresident parents. We first focus on nonresident fathers, looking at how fathers' economic status is tied to child support outcomes and discussing the impacts of the child support system on fathers' poverty status. We then consider related issues for resident mothers.

The economic resources of nonresident fathers are difficult to estimate because of data limitations. Survey reports substantially underreport nonresident fatherhood (Garfinkel, McLanahan, and Hanson 1998; Sorensen 1997). Respondents may be unaware that they are fathers, or they may choose not to report fatherhood. These underreports are likely to be greatest for fathers of children born outside of marriage (or other stable long-term relationships) and for fathers who do not have regular contact with their children. Nonresident fathers may have less stable residential patterns or otherwise be more difficult to survey. And many surveys do not include incarcerated fathers. An alternative source of survey information is a proxy report on the father by the resident mother, but mothers often have limited information on the economic resources of nonresident fathers.

An alternative to relying on surveys is to analyze administrative records. State administrative data systems have improved in quality and scope in recent years. These systems generally provide accurate and detailed data on fathers who pay through the formal system, though they do not include fathers with informal arrangements or those for whom paternity has not been legally established.

We review estimates based on both survey and administrative data. We largely rely on new data on orders and payments for 10,771 fathers in Wisconsin who were given their first child support order in 2000.[7] For many questions, the sample of fathers with new orders is of more interest than a sample of the stock of existing cases, which may reflect orders and related payment patterns set under very different policy regimes. Administrative data, however, include limited information on fathers' characteristics and economic resources.

The Economic Status of Nonresident Fathers

Garfinkel, McLanahan, and Hanson (1998) find that mean incomes for all nonresident fathers are about $30,000 to $34,000. Sorensen (1997) reports average personal income of $25,000 to $26,000 and poverty rates of 15 to 25 percent. Meyer (1998) reports substantial diversity in personal income, with one-quarter of fathers having incomes below $7,600 and one-quarter with incomes above $42,000. Sorensen and Zibman (2001) find that in 1997, 26 percent of nonresident fathers were poor. The incomes of fathers of children receiving public assistance are substantially lower, though there is considerable variation in the economic status of nonresident fathers of children on welfare (see Cancian and Meyer 2004).

Using administrative measures for Wisconsin nonresident fathers with new child support orders in 2000, we measure only formal earnings, not total income. In the year after the order, 23 percent of fathers had no reported earnings, perhaps because they had earnings in another state or perhaps because they actually had no reported earnings (including men in prison, men with self-employment income, and men with informal income). Mean earnings ($25,200) in the first year after the order were quite similar to the national estimates of income, though medians were lower ($21,100, compared to $25,000). Similar to the national results, there was substantial diversity: in the first year, 22 percent of fathers had earnings between $1 and $10,000, while 15 percent had earnings over $40,000.

Men with new child support orders are younger than all nonresident fathers, and the earnings of young fathers may increase over time.[8] Finally, some data suggest that Wisconsin's system is particularly effective: more men who have children born outside marriage may have paternity established and be ordered to pay support than in other states.

Fathers' Economic Status and Child Support Outcomes

In every state the amount of child support a father is ordered to pay is higher if his income is higher. In addition, fathers are more likely to pay what is ordered when their income is higher. As a result, we expect fathers with higher incomes to pay more. For our sample of Wisconsin fathers with new orders, figure 12.3 shows the relationship between nonresident fathers' income and the amount of child support they owed and paid. We show both the actual amounts ordered and paid and our calculation of the amount that should have been ordered according to the Wisconsin standards, given each father's income and number of children.

By definition, the expected amount ordered rises with income.[9] For fathers in

FIGURE 12.3 / Median Amount of Expected and Actual Orders and Payments for
Fathers, 2001

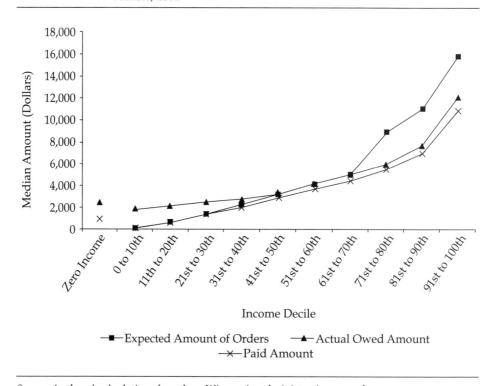

Income Decile

──■── Expected Amount of Orders ──▲── Actual Owed Amount
──✕── Paid Amount

Source: Authors' calculations based on Wisconsin administrative records.

the middle range, the actual order and expected order are quite similar. Median actual orders are set above the median expected order for those with the lowest incomes and below the median expected order for those with the highest incomes. The amount paid rises with income and orders. If we exclude the poorest and richest 30 percent of fathers, median payments are generally slightly below the amount ordered. For those in the lowest two deciles, the amount paid is quite close to the expected order (based on earnings and the Wisconsin guidelines), but well below the actual order. In contrast, for those in the top two deciles, actual orders and payments are close, but both are well below the expected order.

Does Paying Child Support Impoverish Fathers?

Several authors who have examined whether paying child support is impoverishing fathers find that few fall below the poverty line because of their payments (see, for example, Bartfeld 2000; Meyer 1998; Nichols-Casebolt 1986; Sorensen 1997). These studies generally assume that paying support has no behavioral effect on a father's sources of income.[10] Contributing fathers with low incomes pay a higher proportion of their income in child support than do fathers with moderate or high incomes (Meyer 1998; Sorensen and Oliver 2002).

If we consider only formal earnings recorded in our Wisconsin administrative data, 44 percent of nonresident fathers had earnings below the poverty line in 2001. Of those above poverty, 6 percent had incomes below the poverty line after subtracting their child support payments; paying child support increased the poverty gap for poor fathers paying support by about 22 percent ($2,200).

We find little relationship between changes in child support and changes in poverty status. For example, 15 percent of those whose post–child support earnings were above the poverty line in the first year had post-payment earnings below the poverty line in the second year, but in nearly all cases (97 percent), this change in economic status resulted from changes in earnings and not from increases in child support.

In summary, estimates generally suggest that few fathers become impoverished by the support they pay. But when fathers with lower incomes do pay, they tend to pay a higher proportion of their earnings or income and thus face larger burdens.

CHILD SUPPORT AND THE ECONOMIC WELL-BEING OF RESIDENT MOTHERS

Although average child support outcomes have been improving over time, understanding the contribution of child support to the economic well-being of resident-mother families requires consideration of factors beyond the average amount of child support received. We focus here on several issues. First, we analyze the regularity and dependability of child support income. We document the extent to which economically vulnerable mothers benefit from child support and the extent to which child support reduces poverty among single-mother families.[11] For most of this analysis, we use administrative records from Wisconsin.[12]

Table 12.1 shows the distribution of child support received from 2001 to 2003 by 14,729 resident mothers in Wisconsin with new child support orders in 2000. Most mothers with new orders received some child support in 2001—only 11 percent of all mothers and 14 percent of pre–child support poor mothers received none. Median amounts received were about $2,800 for all mothers and $2,200 among those who were pre–child support poor. The remaining columns show substantial stability in the distribution from year to year, though there is some increase in the proportion who received no support.

Regularity of Child Support Income

The contribution of child support to family economic well-being depends on both the level and regularity of support. A given level of child support may

TABLE 12.1 / Distribution of Child Support Received

Child Support Amount	2001		2002		2003	
	All Mothers	Poor Mothers	All Mothers	Poor Mothers	All Mothers	Poor Mothers
$0	11.3	13.6	12.5	14.9	12.9	15.2
$1 to $1,200	19.6	22.5	17.5	20.4	18.1	20.9
$1,201 to $2,400	14.7	15.8	14.2	14.7	13.5	14.2
$2,401 to $3,600	13.5	13.5	14.4	14.1	13.9	13.3
$3,601 to $4,800	10.5	9.4	11.3	10.4	11.2	10.7
Above $4,800	30.3	25.2	30.2	25.5	30.4	25.8
Median	$2,794	$2,240	$2,883	$2,398	$2,883	$2,377
Mean	$4,063	$3,601	$4,031	$3,610	$3,993	$3,593

Source: Authors' calculations based on Wisconsin administrative records.
Note: N = 14,729.

make a smaller contribution to well-being if receipt is unpredictable—especially for lower-income families who face credit constraints.

Table 12.1 suggests fairly small changes in the overall distribution of child support over a three-year period, but it does not capture year-to-year changes for a given mother. When we compare amounts received in 2001 and 2002 by families who were pre–child support poor in 2001, we find that only about 30 percent of mothers experienced little year-to-year change—either receiving no child support in either year or receiving amounts within $200 of the previous year's receipt. Child support declined for about one-third of mothers, with 15 percent receiving at least $1,000 less in child support in 2002 than in 2001. Child support grew for the remaining third, with 17 percent of mothers receiving at least $1,000 more in the later year. In sum, the stability in the overall distribution of child support amounts over time obscures substantial changes over time at the individual level.

Using our detailed administrative data, we are also able to consider the pattern of child support receipt on a monthly basis. We consider child support income to be "regular" when child support payments come at consistent intervals (over time) and are for a stable amount. Figure 12.4 shows the distribution of the number of months in which pre–child support poor families received child support. The first bar shows the distribution of months of support in 2001. Fifty-one percent of these families received support in at least ten months of the year; 14 percent received no support in 2001; the remaining 35 percent received irregular support. The characteristics associated with a higher probability of receiving regular support are quite similar to those associated with receipt of any support.

The first bar in figure 12.4 shows only whether any child support was received in a given month. When our measure of regularity also accounts for the amount received, we find lower levels of regularity. In the second bar, we count a family as receiving a regular payment in a given month only if the family received

FIGURE 12.4   /   Months Poor Mothers with Orders Received Child Support, 2001

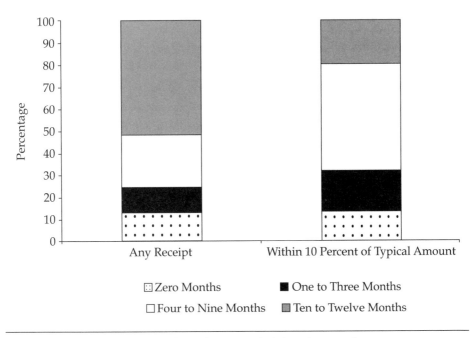

Source: Authors' calculations based on Wisconsin administrative records.

some child support *and* the amount received was within 10 percent of the typical payment.[13] Using this measure reduces the percentage of families with regular receipts in at least ten of twelve months in 2001 from 51 percent to 20 percent.

When we consider payments over thirty-six months, only 7 percent of pre–child support poor mothers with orders received no support, and an additional 14 percent received support in fewer than ten of the thirty-six months; 47 percent received support in at least thirty of the thirty-six months. But when we require amounts received to be within 10 percent of the typical amount, only 10 percent of families received regular support in at least thirty of thirty-six months.

The regularity of support is related positively to the amount received. In 2001, 25 percent of pre–child support poor families received more than $4,800 in support. Of these, 43 percent received regular amounts in at least ten months. In contrast, among families receiving some support but less than $4,800, 15 percent received regular payments in at least ten months.

In summary, child support is not a stable source of income for most families; although 86 percent of pre–child support poor families received some child support in 2001, only one in five received a regular amount (within 10 percent of the typical payment) in at least ten months. The importance of this instability depends in part on the proportion of total income accounted for by child support. In 2001 the mean total personal income of pre–child support poor resident mothers was $9,743; median income was $8,880. (We note that our measure of personal income is based on administrative data and includes only mothers' earnings in employment covered by the UI system, TANF cash benefits, food stamps, and formal child support and excludes, for example, earnings from a new spouse or partner.) Mothers' own earnings were the largest component of total personal income, averaging over $4,500 per year. As shown in the final row of table 12.1, child support averaged $3,601 per year for these families. For 38 percent of all pre–child support poor families, child support accounted for less than 20 percent of family income. But for about one-third of these families, child support contributed more than half of income. Thus, for many pre–child support poor families, child support is a crucial part of the income package, suggesting that irregular receipt has important implications.

The Role of Child Support Across the Income Distribution

Do child support outcomes vary by the resident mother's income? Given positive assortative mating on labor market characteristics, we might expect mothers with higher earnings potential to have had children with men with higher earnings (Mare 1991; Oppenheimer 1988; Sweeney and Cancian 2004). On the other hand, women who receive more child support may have less need to work. (In principle, in Wisconsin the child support order should not vary with the mother's earnings; for related analysis, see Cancian and Meyer 1996.)

Sorensen and Zibman (2000) find that although lower-income mothers receive less than higher-income mothers, the child support they receive is a more important part of their income package. Hwa-Ok Park, Cancian, and Meyer (2005) examine the importance of child support income across the income distribution.[14] They find that mothers with pre–child support incomes below the poverty level are less likely to receive support and more likely to receive lower amounts. However, the proportion of income from child support is higher among mothers whose pre–child support income was below poverty, averaging 11 percent of their income, compared to around 7 percent for near-poor families and less than 5 percent for those with incomes more than three times the poverty line. Results for TANF participants generally show even lower child support outcomes than is found for all poor mothers (see, for example, Acs and Loprest 2001; Bartfeld 2003; Meyer and Cancian 1996, 2002b; Miller et al. 2004).

Using administrative data from new orders in Wisconsin, we find that the proportion of mothers with a child support order who received some child support does not vary greatly across income deciles. In 2001, 89 percent of mothers in the bottom decile and 95 percent of mothers in the top decile received support. Figure 12.5 shows the distribution of child support amounts received by decile of pre–child support personal income in 2001, where income is adjusted by the poverty line. The middle line shows the median amount received—the point at which half of all families in the decile received more child support and half received less. Median child support amounts declined slightly over the first four

FIGURE 12.5 / Amount of Child Support Received, by Income to Needs, 2001

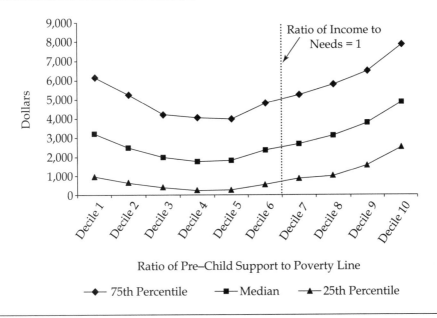

Ratio of Pre–Child Support to Poverty Line

—◆— 75th Percentile   —■—Median   —▲—25th Percentile

Source: Authors' calculations based on Wisconsin administrative records.

deciles and then increased monotonically with other income from the fourth dec-ile onward. The U-shaped pattern is more pronounced when we consider the seventy-fifth percentile of child support for each decile—the point at which one-quarter of all families in the decile received more child support and three-quar-ters received less. Amounts declined from about $6,200 in the first decile to about $4,000 in the fourth, before rising to over $7,800 in the top decile. The relatively high levels of support for those in the lowest deciles may reflect the less compel-ling need to work felt by women with higher levels of child support income.

Finally, we examine differences in regularity across the distribution of moth-ers' pre–child support income. We find that payments are more regular among higher-income families. Families in the highest deciles are about twice as likely to receive regular support as those at the median. Although there is substantial variation in the regularity of support by income level, there is no apparent rela-tionship between year-to-year *changes* in child support and *changes* in non–child support income. Between 2001 and 2002, for example, mothers with large in-creases (over $5,000) or large declines (over $5,000) in non–child support income were equally likely to experience a large decline in child support (over $2,000). We also find little relationship between non–child support income changes and large increases in child support.

TABLE 12.2 / Poverty Status and Child Support

	2001	
	N	Percentage
Total sample	14,729	
Pre–child support poverty	9,059	61.6
Pre–child support poor	9,059	100
With any child support	7,828	86.4
With ten months of child support	4,660	51.4
With ten months of child support within 10 percent of typical amount	1,795	19.8
Cases removed from poverty by child support		
Among all poor mothers	1,462	16.1
Among poor mothers with child support	1,462	18.7
Among poor mothers with ten months of child support	1,256	27.0
Among poor mothers with ten months of child support within 10 percentage of typical amount	582	32.4

Source: Authors' calculations based on Wisconsin administrative records.
Note: N = 14,729.

Poverty

As shown in the first row of table 12.2, among mothers with new child support orders in Wisconsin in 2000, 62 percent had pre–child support personal incomes below the poverty line.[15] About half of them received child support in at least ten months in 2001, but only 20 percent received regular support in at least ten months. The final panel of the table shows that 16 percent of the pre–child support poor families had post–child support incomes above the poverty line. Among those pre–child support poor families that did receive regular support (using the 10 percent rule), nearly one-third had post–child support incomes above the poverty line in 2001.

Even when child support did not add enough to other personal income to bring it above the poverty line, the support reduced the poverty gap (not shown in table). The average poverty gap was $9,434 in 2001; child support filled an average of 44 percent of the gap.

We are also interested in the extent to which changes in child support from year to year are associated with changes in poverty status. Most families have the same poverty status from one year to the next. For example, 56 percent of families were poor in both 2001 and 2002, and 32 percent were not poor in either year. About 6 percent were poor in the first year but not the second, and another 6 percent were poor in the second but not the first. How many families who were not poor in 2001 but were poor in 2002 would have avoided poverty if their child support payments had remained at their 2001 level in 2002? We calculate that 33 percent of these families would have had incomes above the poverty line in 2002 if they had received child support in 2002 equal to the 2001 payment. The figures are virtually identical if we consider changes in poverty status between 2002 and 2003. Again, about 6 percent of all families moved from not poor to poor, and 34 percent of these would have avoided poverty had their child support not declined.

CONCLUSIONS AND IMPLICATIONS FOR RESEARCH AND POLICY

What are the implications of the current child support system for those who are working and poor? We have documented that child support has become an increasingly important source of income as an improved child support enforcement system has increased the potential adequacy and reliability of child support income. However, the growing proportion of never-married families presents the system with a number of challenges. In addition, recent welfare reform, which reduced the availability of cash welfare, makes child support outcomes more critical for many low-income families.

We find that the child support system is not particularly responsive to shorter-term macroeconomic changes because child support orders are not regularly adjusted for changes in parents' economic resources. Although fathers with lower incomes are somewhat less likely to fully comply with child support orders, an increasingly effective child support enforcement system has reduced fathers' ability to avoid paying support if they have earnings in the formal labor market. Despite improvements in the enforcement system, many mothers—especially never-married and poor mothers—do not regularly receive all the support they are due.

These results highlight a number of challenging issues for policy and research. First, not enough attention has been paid to the responsiveness of child support to changes in parents' economic resources, whether these changes are associated with macroeconomic conditions or individual factors. The underlying logic of the system is that child support should maintain a flow of resources comparable to those available in an intact family. Given this logic, it could be argued that as a father's income varies, so should his obligation. At least in principle, a "percentage-expressed" child support order, which obliges a father to pay a set percentage of earnings, would be a sufficient solution: it would reduce the burden for fathers facing large income declines and capture the benefits of income gains. However, there are substantial administrative challenges to implementing such a system, and this type of order increases the vulnerability of resident-mother families to instability in fathers' earnings. Stable child support receipts for mothers require inflexible obligations for fathers. This tension deserves more explicit attention from both policymakers and researchers. As we discuss later in this section, a system of child support assurance is one possible policy response.

A related issue concerns the adequacy of child support for low-income mothers and the burdens of child support for low-income fathers. Given the tendency for positive assortative mating based on education and other characteristics associated with earnings, many mothers with low incomes (and a greater need for child support) have children with low-income fathers (who have less ability to pay support). This conflict is increasingly important given time-limited welfare and the absence of an entitlement to cash assistance for poor resident mothers.

With guaranteed welfare benefits, mothers and their children could count on a minimum level of income. Under those conditions, some argued that poor fathers who did not have sufficient resources for their own provision should not be required to pay substantial child support.[16] Now that poor resident mothers' access to public assistance has been reduced, expectations for poor fathers might appropriately be revised. These policy changes also draw attention to a need to extend employment and related services to nonresident fathers (see, for example, Mincy and Sorensen 1998; Pate 2002; Sorensen and Zibman 2001).

In our review of the child support system, we focused exclusively on resident mothers and nonresident fathers. Mothers with sole custody remain the predominant arrangement, especially for low-income families. However, a growing proportion of children live with their fathers (see, for example, Cancian and Meyer 1998; Cancian and Reed 2001; Garasky and Meyer 1996). Shared physical placement, in which children spend a substantial portion of time living with each parent, is also growing, though it is more common among higher-income families (Cancian et al. 2002). These changes have important implications for both research and policy.

Our discussion has also largely ignored the family complexity that results from multiple-partner fertility. This area of research is in a formative stage—we are just beginning to document the extent of complex family arrangements and to consider their implications for research design and policy—but especially for low-income families, complexity is common. For example, recent estimates based on TANF-participating families in Wisconsin suggest that about two-thirds of families are "complex" in the sense that the resident mother has children with multiple fathers, the nonresident father has children with multiple mothers, or both (Meyer, Cancian, and Cook 2005). Other research also documents substantial levels of complexity (Carlson and Furstenberg 2003; Mincy 2002). Child support policy and family law have not yet adequately responded to this challenge (Brito 2005).

In light of the issues outlined here, we would argue for a number of policy reforms and related research efforts. First, the structure of the child support enforcement system should be reconsidered, given the high proportion of children living apart from one of their parents, their vulnerability to poverty, and the declining availability of public assistance. The enforcement system was originally designed to recover the costs of public welfare from absent parents; thus, child support paid on behalf of families receiving benefits was generally kept by the government. But there is substantial evidence, from both qualitative research and experimental and nonexperimental evaluations, that fathers are less likely to pay support if their children do not benefit, and so the current system reduces the long-term effectiveness of the formal child support system (Edin 1995; Meyer and Cancian 2001, 2002a; Pate 2002; Waller and Plotnick 2001). We believe that a full pass-through and disregard of child support for TANF participants, currently the policy in Wisconsin, should be expanded nationally. The TANF reauthorization in 2006 included a provision that moves in this direction and will make an expanded pass-through and disregard more feasible for states in the future.

Changes in pass-through and disregard policy are part of the current policy debate. In contrast, our second proposal, a system of child support assurance, is a longer-term policy goal. Child support assurance—government-guaranteed child support payments—would respond to many of the inadequacies of the current system. As a first step, if orders were set as they are now but regular child support were paid to mothers by the government independent of whether the father had made the requisite payments to the government, resident mothers would no longer be vulnerable to the consequences of uneven compliance. Of course, any policy that guaranteed that children would receive support regardless of whether payments were made would decrease the incentive for fathers to pay. This policy would have to be constructed with careful attention to enforcement and incentives to pay.

To address the problem of parents who both have low incomes, a minimum level of assured support should also be considered so that mothers would receive a guaranteed level of support even when the income level of their children's father resulted in an inadequate child support order amount. There is a long history of child support assurance proposals (see, for example, Ellwood 1988; Garfinkel 1992), but the topic is worth reconsidering in the context of current income support policy.

The appropriate level of assured benefits is far from clear. Potential points of comparison include TANF benefits, the poverty line, median child support orders, the amount of child support that would be ordered for a person with median earnings, and the estimated cost of raising children (for a discussion of various options, see Meyer, Kaplan, and Corbett 1995). A variety of simulation estimates of different levels of assured benefits have been conducted (see, for example, Lerman 1989; Meyer and Kim 1998), but these estimates predate welfare reform and generally do not incorporate the possibility that assured benefits could affect the incentives for fathers to pay support. These estimates also do not take into account issues related to the regularity of support. Regardless of the level of assurance, the fiscal implications are complex. The increased income provided by assured child support would affect eligibility for other benefits. But perhaps even more important, assured child support would change the incentives for resident parents to pursue child support and for nonresident parents to pay.

There have been remarkable recent changes in the configurations of families and the relationships and obligations to children of parents and government. More adults are parenting children outside of marriage or ending marriages after children are born. As marriage and coparenting ties have become less permanent, complex family arrangements associated with multiple-partner fertility have become more common. At the same time, government has moved to redefine the nature and extent of its obligation to parents and their children, as is evident in welfare reform and in tax policy tied to children, including the Earned Income Tax Credit (EITC). These changes raise a host of challenges for the appropriate design of child support policy at the same time that they make more urgent the need to meet those challenges.

NOTES

1. We would like to thank Rebecca Blank, Sheldon Danziger, Robert Schoeni, participants at the "Working and Poor" preconference in Ann Arbor, Michigan, the volume reviewers, and Ingrid Rothe for valuable input on earlier drafts. Steven Cook and Hwa-Ok Park collaborated on related research. Yoonsook Ha, Jeungkun Kim, and Kisun Nam provided excellent research assistance. We thank Jan Blakeslee for editorial assistance and Dawn Duren for assistance in preparing the manuscript.

2. For information on how states handle orders for low-income nonresident parents, see U.S. Department of Health and Human Services (2000).

3. Our data source, the Current Population Survey (CPS)—Child Support Supplement (CSS), has the longest national time trend of child support owed and paid. The most recent report in this series includes data from 2001 (Grall 2003). The CSS is administered in April of even-numbered years. The data include two measures of child support orders. One question asks whether the mother had a child support order at the time of the survey. The other asks whether something was due to her in the previous calendar year. In every year there are women who respond that they have an order but are not due any money. This could be because the order covered visitation or the distribution of property but did not include an amount of child support. Or it could be that these mothers gained their orders between January 1 and the April survey. We use the second measure because it is only these mothers who we know are due something. In this section, we rely on published figures, which distinguish poor mothers by their post–child support income.

4. All dollar amounts were converted to 2000 dollars using the CPI-U.

5. Philip Robins (1992) found that one factor in the decline of order amounts was the increase in the relative earnings of women compared to men. However, the more recent analysis by Hanson and his colleagues (1996) does not corroborate this finding.

6. A major change in the questionnaire in 1993 may be associated with the sharp decline.

7. In this sample, we excluded those who owed support to multiple families.

8. For example, Sorensen (1997) reports that 25 to 29 percent of all nonresident fathers are younger than thirty and 24 to 30 percent are at least forty, compared to 47 percent and 19 percent, respectively, for the new-order sample.

9. The increase in expected orders as income rises reflects both the increase in income (since guidelines suggest orders as a fixed percentage of income) and increases in average family size. The mean number of children rises from about 1.2 in the lowest deciles to about 1.9 in the highest deciles. This reflects the tendency for older fathers and divorced fathers to have both higher incomes and more children.

10. In general, child support orders and payments have been found to have few effects on fathers' labor supply (Freeman and Waldfogel 1998; Klawitter 1994).

11. This section is drawn primarily from Cancian and Meyer (2005).

12. We exploit a unique set of linked administrative data for the population of mothers with new child support orders in Wisconsin. Because these longitudinal data include detailed records of child support received, we can analyze fluctuations in child support receipts from month to month as well as from year to year. Our data are derived from linked administrative data on child support taken from the Wisconsin state child support registry, KIDS. We also include data on earnings (from unemployment insurance [UI] records) and public benefits, including TANF cash welfare benefits and food stamps (also from the state's administrative records). We begin with all 17,896 resident mothers in Wisconsin who received their first child support order from a particular partner in 2000. Our base sample includes 14,729 mothers who were owed child support during every year from 2001 to 2003; much of our analysis includes only the 9,059 mothers whose pre–child support income was below the poverty line in 2001. See Cancian and Meyer (2005) for further details on the data and analysis.

13. In particular, we use detailed data on the history of child support receipt to determine the most common monthly amounts received by each family. We then calculate the number of months with receipts close to this typical amount, averaging across adjoining months to smooth receipt amounts. See Cancian and Meyer (2005) for more details and a discussion of the sensitivity of these calculations to alternative definitions of regularity.

14. There are two important differences between the National Survey of America's Families (NSAF) analyses of Park, Cancian, and Meyer (2005) and the analyses based on Wisconsin data that we use in this section. First, the Wisconsin data are for mothers with new child support orders only (the flow of new orders), while the NSAF analysis includes all child support–eligible mothers (the stock of cases, regardless of the existence of an order). Second, our measure of child support includes formal support taken from the administrative record, whereas the NSAF data include all economic contributions (both formal and informal) from a nonresident father, as reported by the resident mother.

15. The high poverty rate relative to estimates for all single-mother families reflects in part the exclusion of child support (as demonstrated by the table) and also the inclusion in our sample of only mothers with new orders. Mothers are particularly vulnerable to poverty in the years immediately following a divorce or nonmarital birth (Bartfeld 2000). Finally, our measure of income includes only public benefits and earnings.

16. This is particularly the case when child support is retained by the government to

offset welfare costs. Under those conditions, which currently exist in most states, payments from fathers to mothers receiving welfare do not increase the resources available to the mothers and their children.

REFERENCES

Acs, Gregory, and Pamela Loprest, with Tracy Roberts. 2001. *Final Synthesis Report of Findings from ASPE Leavers Grants.* Washington: U.S. Department of Health and Human Services.

Argys, Laura M., H. Elizabeth Peters, and Donald M. Waldman. 2001. "Can the Family Support Act Put Some Life Back into Deadbeat Dads? An Analysis of Child Support Guidelines, Award Rates, and Levels." *Journal of Human Resources* 36(2): 226–52.

Bartfeld, Judi. 2000. "Child Support and the Post-Divorce Economic Well-being of Mothers, Fathers, and Children." *Demography* 37(2): 203–13.

———. 2003. "Falling Through the Cracks: Gaps in Child Support Among Welfare Recipients." *Journal of Marriage and the Family* 65(1): 72–89.

Bartfeld, Judi, and Daniel R. Meyer. 1994. "Are There Really Deadbeat Dads? The Relationship Between Ability to Pay, Enforcement, and Compliance in Nonmarital Child Support Cases." *Social Service Review* 68(2): 219–35.

———. 2003. "Child Support Compliance in the Welfare Reform Era." *Social Service Review* 77: 347–72.

Beller, Andrea H., and John W. Graham. 1993. *Small Change: The Economics of Child Support.* New Haven, Conn.: Yale University Press.

Brito, Tonya. 2005. "Child Support Guidelines and Complicated Families: An Analysis of Cross-State Variation in Legal Treatment of Multiple-Partner Fertility." Report to the Wisconsin Department of Workforce Development. Madison: Institute for Research on Poverty.

Cancian, Maria, Judith Cassetty, Steven T. Cook, and Daniel R. Meyer. 2002. "Placement Outcomes for Children of Divorce in Wisconsin." Report to the Wisconsin Department of Workforce Development. Madison: Institute for Research on Poverty.

Cancian, Maria, and Daniel R. Meyer. 1996. "Changing Policy, Changing Practice: Mothers' Incomes and Child Support Orders." *Journal of Marriage and the Family* 58: 618–27.

———. 1998. "Who Gets Custody?" *Demography* 35: 147–57.

———. 2004. "Fathers of Children Receiving Welfare: Can They Provide More Child Support?" *Social Service Review* 78(2): 179–206.

———. 2005. "Child Support: An Uncertain and Irregular Income Source?" Revised report to the Wisconsin Department of Workforce Development. Discussion paper 1298–05. Madison: Institute for Research on Poverty.

Cancian, Maria, and Deborah Reed. 2001. "Changes in Family Structure: Implications for Poverty and Related Policy." In *Understanding Poverty,* edited by Sheldon H. Danziger and Robert H. Haveman. New York: Russell Sage Foundation.

Carlson, Marcia, and Frank Furstenberg Jr. 2003. "Complex Families: Documenting the Prevalence and Correlates of Multi-Partnered Fertility in the United States." Working paper 2003–14-FF. Princeton, N.J.: Center for Research on Child–Well-being (October).

Case, Anne C., I.-Fen Lin, and Sara S. McLanahan. 2003. "Explaining Trends in Child Support, Economic, Demographic, and Policy Effects." *Demography* 40(1): 171–89.

Cassetty, Judith, Maria Cancian, and Daniel R. Meyer. 2002. "Child Support Disregard Policies and Program Outcomes: An Analysis of Data from the OCSE." In *Nonexperimental Analyses of the Full Disregard and Pass-Through*, vol. 3, edited by Daniel R. Meyer and Maria Cancian. Report to the Wisconsin Department of Workforce Development. Madison: Institute for Research on Poverty (March).

Edin, Katherine. 1995. "Single Mothers and Child Support: The Possibilities and Limits of Child Support Policy." *Children and Youth Services Review* 17: 203–30.

Ellwood, David T. 1988. *Poor Support*. New York: Basic Books.

Freeman, Richard B., and Jane Waldfogel. 1998. "Does Child Support Enforcement Policy Affect Male Labor Supply?" In *Fathers Under Fire: The Revolution in Child Support Enforcement*, edited by Irwin Garfinkel, Sara S. McLanahan, Daniel R. Meyer, and Judith A. Seltzer. New York: Russell Sage Foundation.

———. 2001. "Dunning Delinquent Dads: The Effect of Child Support Enforcement Policy on Child Support Receipt by Never-Married Women." *Journal of Human Resources* 36: 207–25.

Garasky, Steven, and Daniel R. Meyer. 1996. "Reconsidering the Increase in Father-Only Families." *Demography* 33: 385–93.

Garfinkel, Irwin. 1992. *Assuring Child Support: An Extension of Social Security*. New York: Russell Sage Foundation.

Garfinkel, Irwin, and Marieka M. Klawitter. 1990. "The Effect of Routine Income Withholding on Child Support Collections." *Journal of Policy Analysis and Management* 9: 155–77.

Garfinkel, Irwin, Sara S. McLanahan, and Thomas Hanson. 1998. "A Patchwork Portrait of Nonresident Fathers." In *Fathers Under Fire: The Revolution in Child Support Enforcement*, edited by Irwin Garfinkel, Sara S. McLanahan, Daniel R. Meyer, and Judith A. Seltzer. New York: Russell Sage Foundation.

Garrison, Marsha. 1999. "Child Support Policy: Guidelines and Goals." *Family Law Quarterly* 33(1): 157–89.

Grall, Timothy, S. 2003. "Custodial Mothers and Fathers and Their Child Support: 2001." *Current Population Reports* P60–225. Washington: U.S. Bureau of the Census.

Hanson, Thomas L., Irwin Garfinkel, Sara S. McLanahan, and Cynthia K. Miller. 1996. "Trends in Child Support Outcomes." *Demography* 33(4): 483–96.

Klawitter, Marieka M. 1994. "Child Support Awards and the Earnings of Divorced Noncustodial Fathers." *Social Service Review* 68(3): 351–68.

Kost, Kathleen A., Daniel R. Meyer, Tom Corbett, and Patricia R. Brown. 1996. "Revising Old Child Support Orders: The Wisconsin Experience." *Family Relations* 45: 19–26.

Lerman, Robert I. 1989. "Child Support Policies." In *Welfare Policy for the 1990s*, edited by Phoebe H. Cottingham and David T. Ellwood. Cambridge, Mass.: Harvard University Press.

Lin, I.-Fen. 2000. "Perceived Fairness and Compliance with Child Support Obligations." *Journal of Marriage and the Family* 62(2): 388–99.

Mare, Robert D. 1991. "Five Decades of Educational Assortative Mating." *American Sociological Review* 56: 15–32.

Meyer, Daniel R. 1998. "The Effect of Child Support on the Economic Status of Nonresident Fathers." In *Fathers Under Fire: The Revolution in Child Support Enforcement*, edited by Irwin Garfinkel, Sara S. McLanahan, Daniel R. Meyer, and Judith A. Seltzer. New York: Russell Sage Foundation.

———. 1999. "Compliance with Child Support Orders in Paternity and Divorce Cases." In *The Postdivorce Family*, edited by Ross A. Thompson and Paul R. Amato. Thousand Oaks, Calif.: Sage Publications.

Meyer, Daniel R., Judi Bartfeld, Irwin Garfinkel, and Pat Brown. 1996. "Child Support Reform: Lessons from Wisconsin." *Family Relations* 46: 11–18. (Orig. pub. under the title "An Evolving Child Support System.")

Meyer, Daniel R., and Maria Cancian. 1996. "Life After Welfare: The Economic Well-being of Women and Children Following an Exit from AFDC." *Public Welfare* 54(4): 25–29.

———. 2001. *W-2 Child Support Demonstration Evaluation, Phase 1: Final Report*, vol. 1, *Effects of the Experiment*. Report to the Wisconsin Department of Workforce Development. Madison: Institute for Research on Poverty.

———. 2002a. *Summary of Nonexperimental and Experimental Impact Analyses of the Full Disregard and Pass-Through*, vol. 1, *Nonexperimental Analyses of the Full Disregard and Pass-Through*. Report to the Wisconsin Department of Workforce Development. Madison: Institute for Research on Poverty (March).

———. 2002b. "Ten Years Later: Economic Well-being Among Those Who Left Welfare." *Journal of Applied Social Sciences* 25: 13–30.

Meyer, Daniel R., Maria Cancian, and Steven Cook. 2005. "Multiple-Partner Fertility: Incidence and Implications for Child Support Policy." *Social Service Review* 79: 577–601.

Meyer, Daniel R., Thomas Kaplan, and Thomas Corbett. 1995. "Developing a Child Support Assurance Program for Minnesota: Report to the Minnesota Legislature." Special report 66: final report submitted to the Minnesota Department of Human Services. Madison: Institute for Research on Poverty.

Meyer, Daniel R., and Rebecca Yeun-Hee Kim. 1998. "Incorporating Labor Supply Responses into the Estimated Effects of an Assured Child Support Benefit." *Journal of Family Issues* 19: 534–55.

Miller, Cynthia, Mary Farrell, Maria Cancian, and Daniel R. Meyer. 2004. "The Interaction of Child Support and TANF: Evidence from Samples of Current and Former Welfare Recipients." Report to the U.S. Department of Health and Human Services. New York: Manpower Demonstration Research Corporation.

Miller, Cynthia, and Irwin Garfinkel. 1999. "The Determinants of Paternity Establishment and Child Support Award Rates Among Unmarried Women." *Population Research and Policy Review* 18(3): 237–60.

Mincy, Ronald B. 2002. "Who Should Marry Whom? Multiple-Partner Fertility Among New Parents." Working paper 02–03-FF. Princeton, N.J.: Center for Research on Child Well-being.

Mincy, Ronald B., and Elaine J. Sorensen. 1998. "Deadbeats and Turnips in Child Support Reform." *Journal of Policy Analysis and Management* 17(1): 44–51.

Nichols-Casebolt, Ann. 1986. "The Economic Impact of Child Support Reform on the Poverty Status of Custodial and Noncustodial Families." *Journal of Marriage and the Family* 48(4): 875–80.

Oppenheimer, Valerie K. 1988. "A Theory of Marriage Timing." *American Journal of Sociology* 94: 563–91.

Park, Hwa-Ok, Maria Cancian, and Daniel R. Meyer. 2005. "The Role of Child Support in the Economic Well-being of Custodial Mothers." Report to the Wisconsin Department of Workforce Development. Madison: Institute for Research on Poverty.

Pate, David J., Jr. 2002. "An Ethnographic Inquiry into the Life Experiences of African American Fathers with Children on W-2." In *Nonexperimental Analyses of the Full Disregard and Pass-Through*, vol. 2, *Fathers of Children in W-2 Families*, edited by Daniel R. Meyer and Maria Cancian. Report to the Wisconsin Department of Workforce Development. Madison: Institute for Research on Poverty.

Roberts, Paula, and Michelle Vinson. 2004. *State Policy Regarding Pass-Through and Disregard of Current Month's Child Support Collected for Families Receiving TANF-Funded Cash Assistance*. Washington, D.C.: Center for Law and Social Policy.

Robins, Philip K. 1992. "Why Did Child Support Award Levels Decline from 1978 to 1985?" *Journal of Human Resources* 27: 362–79.

Rothe, Ingrid, and Daniel R. Meyer. 2000. "Setting Child Support Orders: Historical Approaches and Ongoing Struggles." *Focus* (newsletter of the Institute for Research on Poverty) 21(1): 58–63.

Smock, Pamela J., and Wendy D. Manning. 1997. "Nonresident Parents' Characteristics and Child Support." *Journal of Marriage and the Family* 59(4): 798–808.

Sorensen, Elaine. 1997. "A National Profile of Nonresident Fathers and Their Ability to Pay Child Support." *Journal of Marriage and the Family* 59(4): 785–97.

Sorensen, Elaine, and Ariel Hill. 2004. "Single Mothers and Their Child Support Receipt: How Well Is Child Support Enforcement Doing?" *Journal of Human Resources* 39(1): 135–54.

Sorensen, Elaine, and Helen Oliver. 2002. "Policy Reforms Are Needed to Increase Child Support from Poor Fathers." Research report (April). Washington, D.C.: Urban Institute. Available at: http://www.urban.org/UploadedPDF/410477.pdf.

Sorensen, Elaine, and Chava Zibman. 2000. "Child Support Offers Some Protection Against Poverty." Policy brief B-10. Assessing the New Federalism Series. Washington, D.C.: Urban Institute.

———. 2001. "Getting to Know Poor Fathers Who Do Not Pay Child Support." *Social Service Review* 75(3): 420–34.

Sweeney, Megan, and Maria Cancian. 2004. "The Changing Importance of Economic Prospects for Assortative Mating." *Journal of Marriage and the Family* 66: 1015–28.

U.S. Department of Health and Human Services. Office of the Inspector General. 2000. *The Establishment of Child Support Orders for Low-Income Noncustodial Parents*. OEI-05-99-00390. Washington: USDHHS.

Waller, Maureen R., and Robert Plotnick. 2001. "Effective Child Support Policy for Low-Income Families: Evidence from Street-Level Research." *Journal of Policy Analysis and Management* 20(1): 89–110.1.

Chapter 13

Unemployment Insurance over the Business Cycle: Does It Meet the Needs of Less-Skilled Workers?

Phillip B. Levine

The unemployment insurance (UI) system is one of the primary ways that the government seeks to alleviate the hardship associated with an economic downturn.[1] It was first introduced in the United States at the national level as part of the 1935 Social Security Act to provide financial support for the millions of workers who lost their jobs during the Great Depression.

The system is still designed to provide greater relief at times of economic hardship. Workers are more likely to receive benefits in a recession, since benefits are paid only to those who lose their jobs through no fault of their own and these circumstances are much more common at such times. But the system of UI financing also helps offset the hardship associated with a downturn. Firms pay a tax to fund benefits that is at least partially "experience-rated" in that those firms that lay off more workers often have to pay a higher tax. This higher tax provides them with an incentive to lay off fewer workers. Since layoffs are more common during a recession, experience rating can reduce layoffs the most during those periods.

On the other hand, the insurance aspect of unemployment insurance serves to lessen the ability of the system to help out during hard times. Benefits are not paid out according to need but according to the loss incurred. In fact, eligibility rules make it more difficult for those with the greatest need to qualify for benefits. To satisfy those rules, workers cannot have left a job voluntarily, although this serves as less of a constraint during a recession. But more importantly, workers must have had a sufficient work history prior to the job loss, typically measured as minimum earnings requirements, to qualify for benefits. Lower-wage workers and those who have difficulty maintaining steady employment because of lack of skills may have a tougher time satisfying these requirements, particularly during periods when jobs are scarce.

The insurance aspect of the system also contributes to the way in which it is financed, and that structure may limit its benefits during a recession. The taxes paid in can be thought of as an insurance premium that covers the costs of benefits paid out. In this way, the system is self-financing. But benefits must be limited in duration to prevent an excessive drain on fund reserves, even when it is difficult for a worker to find a job. Moreover, if the system's reserves become too low during a recession, taxes may need to rise to cover the greater benefit payments. This raises the cost of labor at precisely the time when firms are more likely to be struggling and may result in additional layoffs.

These conflicting provisions of the system make it unclear to what extent UI helps out during a recession. The purpose of this chapter is to explore this issue, especially UI's impact on less-skilled workers over the course of the business cycle and changes in this effect over the last quarter-century. I also briefly explore whether this impact differs by race-ethnicity and gender. Throughout the chapter, I separately examine both the benefit and tax sides of the program, since both may affect workers' outcomes. I partly rely on a review of past empirical work and partly provide original data analysis to draw conclusions. I also provide policy recommendations directed at improving the system's ability to help out less-skilled workers without sacrificing the insurance nature of the UI system.

INSTITUTIONAL DETAILS

The UI system is administered at the state level, although the federal government establishes certain minimum guidelines. Each state system has different rules, but the general organization of the programs is similar. In this section, I describe the benefit and tax sides of the system separately.

UI Eligibility and Benefits

Before an unemployed worker can collect UI benefits, she or he must first satisfy two different sets of eligibility requirements. The first, labeled "nonmonetary eligibility," involves the circumstances under which the individual has become unemployed (for a detailed discussion of nonmonetary eligibility and related issues, see Fishman, Farrell, and Gardiner 2003). To qualify for UI benefits, an individual generally has to lose a job through no fault of his or her own.[2] Workers who satisfy this requirement must also demonstrate that they are actively looking for work and willing to accept suitable employment. This is typically done through an automated phone-in system (or, more recently, by the Internet) in which UI recipients provide weekly reports that they have been actively looking for work but did not accept a new job. Workers are required to appear in person if a question arises regarding their activities (potentially including the weeks of benefits received).

Workers who lose their jobs through no fault of their own must also prove that they had a sufficient work history prior to job loss to qualify for benefits. This provision is called "monetary eligibility." Each state has a different definition of a sufficient work history, but in virtually all states the definition is based on earnings received in the worker's "base period."[3] The base period is defined as the first four of the last five calendar quarters prior to job loss. For example, if a worker lost his or her job in May 2005, then the relevant base period was January through December 2004. The reason for the delay is historical in nature and is based on the time it takes for employers' wage reports to be processed with the UI agency so that monetary eligibility can be assessed.

Technological advances have now speeded up this process. Recently, some states have adopted an "alternative base period," typically based on earnings in the past four calendar quarters. I discuss later the impact of using an alternative base period.

Although specific monetary eligibility rules are complex, they can be simplified for the purposes of presentation into the "annual" (base period) earnings required to satisfy them. I have done so for the 2004 calendar year and report the results in table 13.1. First, notice the extent of variability across the states in the level of earnings prior to job loss required to be eligible to collect UI. In Nevada and Connecticut, annual earnings of $600 prior to job loss are sufficient to qualify (and the figure is only $130 in Hawaii), whereas North Carolina requires $3,749. The simple average across the states is $1,879. To provide some perspective on how difficult it is for a less-skilled worker to become monetarily eligible, suppose that a worker earns the federal minimum wage of $5.15 per hour and works thirty hours per week. This worker would qualify for UI benefits based on the national average earnings requirement if she or he worked twelve weeks during the calendar year.

The benefit available to those satisfying the eligibility requirements also differs dramatically because the states have different benefit formulas. As a broad characterization, individuals typically receive an amount equal to roughly half of their pre-unemployment weekly wage, subject to a minimum and maximum benefit. In virtually all states, the minimum benefit is a small amount and is rarely relevant in the benefit computation. Therefore, the major source of state variability in the generosity of UI benefits is the maximum weekly benefit. These values are reported for each state in table 13.1 as well. Some states' benefits are considerably more generous than others. For instance, the maximums in Mississippi and Alabama are the lowest available at $210 per week, whereas Massachusetts offers up to $580. Based on a 50 percent replacement rate, workers in the lowest-benefit states hit the maximum at a weekly earnings rate of $420, which means that the maximum benefit is binding for a large proportion of earners.[4]

Weekly benefits are available for a limited duration, typically twenty-six weeks. During a recession, however, this maximum benefit duration is often extended to a longer time period. In theory, a federal extended benefits program exists that triggers the extension in a state whenever local labor market conditions deteriorate significantly, but in practice this system has structural limita-

TABLE 13.1 / Annual Earnings Required for UI Eligibility and Maximum Weekly Benefits, 2004

State	Annual Earnings Required for Eligibility	Maximum Benefit
Alabama	$2,136	$210
Alaska	1,000	248
Arizona	1,500	240
Arkansas	1,701	345
California	1,125	410
Colorado	2,500	398
Connecticut	600[a]	429
Delaware	720	330
District of Columbia	1,950	309
Florida	3,400	275
Georgia	1,600[a]	300
Hawaii	130[a]	417
Idaho	1,657	320
Illinois	1,600	326
Indiana	2,750	348
Iowa	1,500	300
Kansas	2,610	351
Kentucky	1,500	365
Louisiana	1,200	258
Maine	3,376[a]	292
Maryland	864	310
Massachusetts	3,000[a]	508
Michigan	2,997[a]	362
Minnesota	1,250	478
Mississippi	1,200	210
Missouri	1,500	250
Montana	1,773	323
Nebraska	1,600	280
Nevada	600	317
New Hampshire	2,800[a]	372
New Jersey	2,060[a]	490
New Mexico	1,799[a]	290
New York	2,400[a]	405
North Carolina	3,749[a]	416
North Dakota	2,795	312
Ohio	3,520[a]	323
Oklahoma	1,500	275
Oregon	1,000	410
Pennsylvania	1,320	461
Rhode Island	2,700[a]	441
South Carolina	900	285

(*continued on p. 370.*)

TABLE 13.1 / Continued

State	Annual Earnings Required for Eligibility	Maximum Benefit
South Dakota	1,288	248
Tennessee	1,560	275
Texas	1,961	330
Utah	2,500	362
Vermont	2,390[a]	359
Virginia	2,500[a]	326
Washington	680 hours[a]	496
West Virginia	2,200	358
Wisconsin	1,470[a]	329
Wyoming	2,200	306

Sources: U.S. Department of Labor (various issues [A] and [B]) and National Foundation for Unemployment Compensation and Workers' Compensation (various issues).
Notes: Annual earnings reflect those in the worker's "base period," which represents the first four of the last five calendar quarters.
[a]An alternative base period is available, which typically represents the last four completed calendar quarters.

tions that rarely allow the built-in trigger to be fired.[5] When a recession occurs, a formal act of Congress is usually required to extend benefits; this has happened in every recession since 1957.

Although these congressional acts provide some relief to unemployed workers having difficulty finding jobs when few are available, the ad hoc procedure has some limitations. In particular, the timing of the extensions is not well coordinated with the period of greatest economic need. Figure 13.1 presents the national unemployment rate and the periods in which extended benefits have been available. When legislation is enacted, it usually provides additional benefits for future UI beneficiaries as well as for those who may have already exhausted their benefits. This feature is called "reach-back." In figure 13.1, the dark gray shaded regions reflect the prospective extended benefit period following enactment, and the light gray shaded regions reflect reach-back. As the figure illustrates, the extensions always occur around the peak of the recession. Reach-back sometimes occurs earlier in the recession, but not always.

Furthermore, the reach-back provisions do not provide the same level of protection from income loss. First, some workers have hit their maximum benefit duration and experienced some income loss prior to reach-back. Second, unnecessary anxiety may be associated with the expectation of hitting the limit for those receiving UI at the time of reach-back. Providing better automated triggers that kick in extended benefits at the beginning of a recession would be preferable. Although this problem is not limited to less-skilled workers, to the extent

FIGURE 13.1 / The Timing of Benefits Extensions

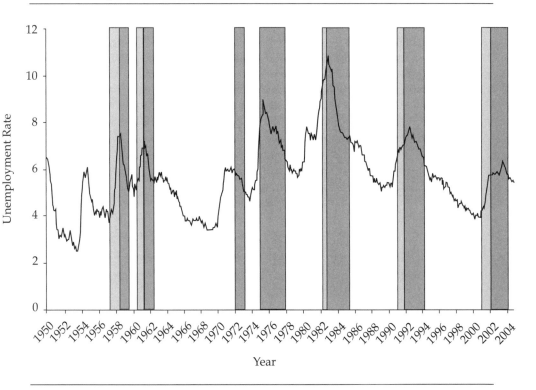

Source: U.S. Department of Labor (2004).
Notes: Light gray areas reflect periods in which extended benefits were enacted retrospectively, and dark gray areas reflect periods in which extended benefits were available prospectively.

that they are in a more precarious financial position, these workers would benefit the most from such a change.

UI Financing and Taxes

Different states have different tax provisions that must satisfy federal guidelines (for a more complete description of UI financing and relevant related issues, see Levine 1997). Most states use the reserve ratio system. Although the provisions of the other systems are somewhat different, similar basic principles are present in all of them.

The UI system is financed by a payroll tax typically levied just on firms. Firms in reserve ratio states have separate accounts to which their tax payments are credited. Benefits paid out to the workers laid off by that firm are charged against that account. The account balance depends on the firm's entire history of taxes paid in and benefits paid out. A firm's tax rate is assigned according to its "reserve ratio," which reflects the ratio of the trust fund balance to the size of its taxable payroll. Firms are rewarded for having a higher reserve ratio by being charged a lower tax rate. Firms with lower reserve ratios, and especially those with negative ratios (reflecting less taxes paid than benefits paid out), are charged a higher rate. This system of charging tax rates according to a firm's layoff history is called "experience rating." The tax is experience-rated in much the same way that insurance companies charge premiums linked to the risk of coverage; since high-layoff firms run a higher risk of incurring a "loss" (a layoff), they pay higher premiums (higher taxes).

However, experience rating is not complete in the sense that the cost of an additional layoff in the form of UI benefits paid is not entirely borne by the firm that instigated the layoff. The main reason for this is that states cap the tax at both ends with minimum and maximum rates. Thus, once a firm has laid off enough workers and hit the maximum rate, it can lay off additional workers without having its tax rate raised. Similarly, firms that lay off very infrequently and have high reserve ratios cannot save any more on taxes by continuing that behavior.

Once a tax rate is assigned to a firm, it is levied on the wages of each worker, but taxable wages are typically capped at a level far below what the worker actually makes. This "taxable wage base" is set by the federal government to be no less than $7,000 per year per worker. Most states, particularly larger ones, set their taxable wage base to be at or slightly higher than the federal level; in thirty states (including the District of Columbia) it is $10,000 or under. Only in ten states (mostly smaller ones) is the base above $20,000. As I discuss later, this has implications for less-skilled workers.

The financial well-being of the entire state and federal UI system is also tracked by the reserve ratio, which reflects the balance in the accumulated accounts of every firm in the state and the nation and is determined by dividing this figure by the total taxable payroll of all firms. Figure 13.2 presents the trend in the national reserve ratio between 1973 and 2003. It shows a strong cyclical pattern: the trust fund shrinks during recessions and grows during expansions. In the mid-1970s, national reserves were nearly exhausted, and in the early 1980s the fund actually went into deficit.

When its trust fund becomes insolvent, a state must borrow from the federal government to help pay its continuing benefit obligations. Up until the early 1980s, these loans were provided interest-free, which may explain the willingness of states to allow their funds to become insolvent. Since then, however, market rates of interest are charged on the loans; coupled with the economic expansions of the rest of the 1980s and much of the 1990s, this incentive has led states to place their systems on more solid financial footing. Nevertheless, at present the trust fund is at its lowest level since the early 1980s: the ratio was 0.64 in 2003, despite the two long expansions with only two relatively short and mild recessions. The implications of the risk of insolvency for the financing sys-

FIGURE 13.2 / Trust Fund Balances over Time

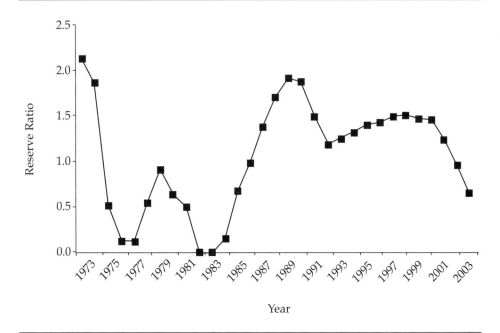

Source: Author's compilations.

tem and for the well-being of workers, particularly those with lower levels of skill, will be explored later in the chapter.

UI RECIPIENCY AND THE BUSINESS CYCLE

How well does the UI system respond to the increased need that workers face during a recession? How does that response differ by workers' skill levels? Has this responsiveness changed over time? This section answers these questions, focusing separately on the elements that affect the receipt of benefits, including monetary and nonmonetary eligibility, the take-up of benefits among eligible workers, and indicators of UI receipt. I also address the generosity of benefits among individual UI recipients.

Previous Research

I begin by reviewing relevant previous research. The first strand of this literature addresses a dramatic decline in UI receipt that took place in the early 1980s. At that time, the fraction of unemployed workers who were collecting UI benefits (a statistic known as the "standard recipiency rate") fell dramatically, from about 44 percent in 1980 to 29 percent in 1984. A number of analysts have explored the reasons behind the decline (Anderson and Meyer 1997; Blank and Card 1991; Corson and Nicholson 1988; Vroman 1991) and find that a number of factors are relevant, including the decline in unionization and manufacturing employment, the shifting of the population from traditional high-recipiency-rate states to low-recipiency-rate states, policy changes that tightened eligibility standards, and the introduction of taxation of UI benefits, phased in between 1978 and 1986.[6]

None of this research, however, distinguishes workers by skill level. One related strand of the literature that does address UI recipiency for less-skilled workers is the impact of welfare reform on UI receipt. At the time it was enacted, analysts conjectured that potential welfare recipients would respond to the strong labor supply incentives incorporated into the law, but might have unstable work patterns. If so, the UI system could help fill in part of the safety net taken away by welfare reform, particularly during recessions. Early studies on this topic, relying on pre–welfare reform data in their estimations, suggested that UI receipt among potential welfare recipients would be very low (on the order of 10 percent) based on the fact that these workers would be unlikely to satisfy UI eligibility requirements (Kaye 1997; Decker and Levine 2001; Vroman 1998). More recent studies that have taken advantage of data in a post–welfare reform environment have provided more optimistic findings: potential welfare recipients are more likely (perhaps by 20 to 30 percent) to be eligible and to receive UI than would have been expected based on the experiences of similar workers prior to welfare reform (Holzer 2000; Isaacs 2005; Kaye 2001). Nevertheless, most workers in this group still do not receive UI when they are unemployed. Because welfare recipients represent just a small slice of all less-skilled workers, this research does not fully inform the questions I address.

The importance of UI receipt for unemployed workers has also been documented. UI helps families smooth income during spells of unemployment (Congressional Budget Office 2004; Gruber 1997). Although this research does not distinguish between workers with different levels of skill, presumably the income-smoothing component of UI is more important for less-skilled workers, who command fewer resources in the first place. This emphasizes the need for evidence regarding UI receipt and its determinants by skill level; next I turn my attention to providing such evidence.

The Data Used to Estimate UI Eligibility and Receipt

The data requirements necessary to estimate whether unemployed workers are eligible to receive UI are daunting. Information is required on an individual's current labor force status, the components of his or her income, his or her work history going back up to one and a half years (the definition of the base period), the reasons for his or her exit from employment, and the individual's search activities in the subsequent period. Beyond that, information is required on an individual's state of residence, since there is so much variation in program rules across the states.

Large samples of such data are needed to generate precise estimates. Administrative data could be used, but their main limitation for this analysis is that they do not identify a worker's skill level. Therefore, I am restricted to using survey data and must make some simplifying assumptions.[7]

I rely primarily on data from the March Current Population Survey (CPS) from 1979 to 2004, focusing on workers between the ages of eighteen and fifty-four. To measure UI recipiency, I take advantage of retrospective information on household income in the preceding calendar year, which includes receipt of UI.[8] I do not know at what point in the year benefits were received, however, or for how many weeks. The CPS provides information on labor market activity in the preceding calendar year, including whether the worker experienced any unemployment. I combine this information to estimate a UI recipiency rate, which is defined as the fraction of workers who experienced some unemployment in the past calendar year and also reported some UI receipt during that year.

To estimate both monetary and nonmonetary UI eligibility from the CPS requires a number of compromises. To determine nonmonetary eligibility, I need the exact cause of a worker's job separation, including whether a quit was warranted, and an account of his or her job search efforts. To simplify, I rely on those workers who have been determined to be unemployed by the official CPS definition (used to construct the national unemployment rate) on the date of the survey. Workers thus classified meet the CPS standard of job search, so I assume that those workers also satisfy UI requirements. I also base a nonmonetary eligibility determination on the reason the worker gave for the start of his or her unemployment spell. If the worker reported that the spell began because she or he lost a job or was laid off, then I judge the worker to be nonmonetarily eligible. This misses those who quit for cause or who quit voluntarily but satisfied some other lengthy waiting period established for quitters.

To estimate monetary eligibility, I have to use a simulation program that runs an individual's work history through the different state-specific eligibility rules. To that end, I use those workers unemployed on the survey date; they provided retrospective information for the past calendar year on their labor market activity and earnings that can be used in the simulation. I restrict the sample to those who have been unemployed for at least one week and no more than twenty-six weeks, for two reasons.[9] First, other unemployed workers would be ineligible for UI either because they had not satisfied the one-week waiting period required before one can collect benefits or because they exhausted their benefits. Second, it is unfair to determine their monetary eligibility with so little of their prior work experience available (for those unemployed longer than twenty-six weeks); their current unemployment spell would have occupied much of the preceding year. Monetary eligibility calculations are conducted for the sample of workers who meet nonmonetary eligibility requirements, since having a sufficient work history is irrelevant for workers who are new entrants to the labor force or who quit their jobs.

This method of computing monetary eligibility is far from perfect. Among other things, labor market information provided in the past calendar year for a worker unemployed in March does not represent the actual base period. If that worker just lost a job in March, his or her base period would have ended in the preceding September and extended backwards to the September before that. For workers unemployed for longer periods (up to the twenty-six-week limit I have imposed), the past calendar year represents an even poorer approximation of the base period. Nevertheless, this is the only work experience information available; perhaps it provides a sufficient representation of the work record the individual established during his or her actual base period.

The one determinant of UI receipt that I cannot adequately capture in the CPS data is take-up. Some unemployed workers who are eligible for UI do not claim their benefits. Since I cannot determine UI eligibility and UI receipt for the same group of workers, I cannot compare them to see which ones have taken up their benefits.[10] Because I want to make comparisons by skill level (defined by educational attainment), I have to rely on microdata to estimate take-up rates rather than infer them from aggregated statistics, as Blank and Card (1991) do.

To provide some information in this regard, I have also conducted a similar analysis using panel data from the 1979 National Longitudinal Survey of Youth (NLSY79). These data track the lives of over twelve thousand individuals who were between the ages of fourteen and twenty-one in 1979, when the panel commenced; they continue to be followed today. Virtually complete labor market histories and income receipt are available for these individuals, so all dimensions of UI eligibility and receipt can be determined for each job separation that occurs. Because eligibility and receipt can be directly compared in these data, take-up can also be measured. The obvious weakness of the NLSY data is that these individuals were very young early in the survey and have aged to become prime-age workers now. All changes over time in their outcomes represent a mixture of aging effects and changes in the environment. Therefore, I present the NLSY analysis in a regression context that partially controls for aging effects.

Estimated UI Eligibility and Receipt by Skill Level

Figures 13.3 through 13.6 provide a descriptive analysis of UI recipiency and its components (including benefit generosity) for workers who differ according to their level of skill. I have examined differences in outcomes for skill levels defined by four educational attainment groups: high school dropouts, high school graduates, workers who attended some college, and college graduates. In terms of UI recipiency and eligibility, high school dropouts looked very different from the other three groups, but those with higher educational attainment levels all

FIGURE 13.3 / UI Recipiency Rate, by Educational Attainment

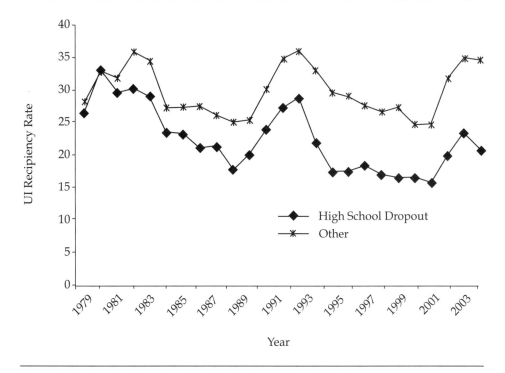

Source: Author's calculations based on March Current Population Surveys.

looked similar. Therefore, in figures 13.3 through 13.5 I only distinguish high school dropouts from workers with more education.

Figure 13.3 displays the overall UI recipiency rate estimated from the CPS. The primary pattern that we observe in the figure is the countercyclical nature of UI receipt. Regardless of skill level, UI receipt peaked in the early 1980s, the early 1990s, and the early part of this decade; each of these periods represents a time of economic downturn. For example, for high school dropouts, the rate was 30.4 percent in 1982, 28.9 percent in 1992, and 23.5 percent in 2002. This pattern is well established and has recently been noted by Wayne Vroman (2002); as we see later in this chapter, the pattern is largely driven by the fact that unemployed workers are much more likely to have lost their jobs than to have quit during a recession.

Beyond the cyclical pattern, the next noticeable feature in this figure is the growing divergence between the rates of UI recipiency observed among less-skilled and other unemployed workers over time. Over the 1979 through 1981 period, roughly 30 percent of both groups of unemployed workers collected benefits, according to this CPS-based measure. But over the next two decades or so, a gap between them emerged and has grown considerably. By 2003, only about

FIGURE 13.4 / Rate of "Nonmonetary Eligibility" Among the Unemployed

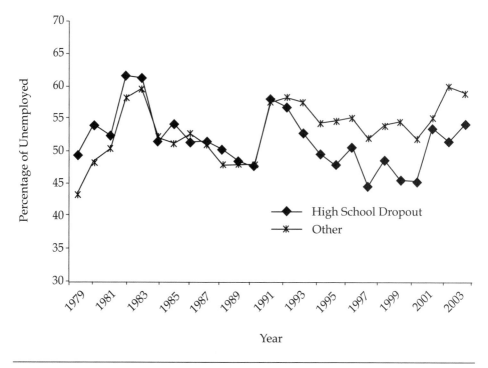

Source: Author's calculations based on March Current Population Surveys.

21 percent of unemployed high school dropouts collected UI compared to almost 35 percent of unemployed workers with more education. Although this growing gap appears to be independent of the business cycle, the need for benefits may be greatest during recessions, and less-skilled workers appear increasingly likely to be left behind by the UI system at those times compared to others.

Figures 13.4 and 13.5 present trends in nonmonetary eligibility among the unemployed and monetary eligibility among job-losers, respectively, by skill level. The results suggest that the growing gap in recipiency between the two skill groups can be distinguished by two separate periods. Through the 1980s, little difference existed between the groups in the fraction of unemployment attributable to job loss, but in the early 1990s that changed. For example, in 1992, 57.1 percent of unemployed high school dropouts and 58.6 percent of other unemployed workers were job-losers. Over the past decade or so, less-skilled unemployed workers appear to have been less likely to enter that state through a job loss. In 2002, 51.8 percent of unemployed dropouts, but 60.2 percent of other unemployed workers, were job-losers. No obvious explanation is available for this pattern.[11] In the 1980s, the emergence of the gap in UI receipt between the groups appears to have been attributable to changes in monetary eligibility. That

FIGURE 13.5 / Rate of "Monetary Eligibility" Among Job-Losers

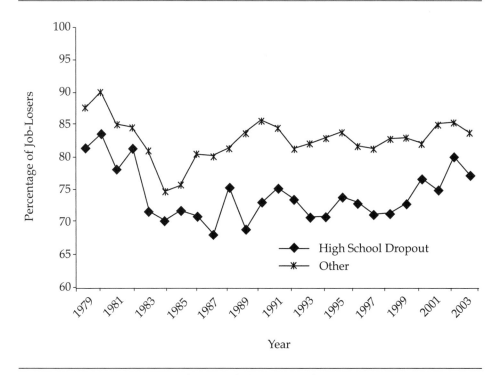

Source: Author's calculations based on March Current Population Surveys.

pattern may be attributable to the stricter eligibility rules that were enacted in the early 1980s in response to the financial troubles that many state trust funds experienced at that time. Note that the overall trends across both groups over the business cycle suggest that the cyclical pattern in UI receipt is dictated by nonmonetary eligibility (quit behavior), not monetary eligibility.

One final indicator of the ability of UI to help out in tough times is the value of the benefits paid out. Figure 13.6 displays the rate at which UI benefits "replace" pre-unemployment wages over time by skill level. Less-skilled workers are not the interesting group when it comes to benefit generosity. Since the patterns in replacement rates are comparable across all workers with less than a college degree, I have aggregated these groups. Among these workers, average replacement rates have hovered in the vicinity just below 40 percent, with perhaps a slight upward trend over time. But for those with a college degree, the value of UI benefits has slowly eroded, with the replacement rate falling to about 32 percent by the end of the period despite starting out at levels comparable to the other groups (about 40 percent in 1979). The likely explanation for this is that this group is the most likely to be constrained by the maximum weekly benefit amount that each state sets. These constraints are generally fixed in nominal

FIGURE 13.6 / Benefit Replacement Rate Among the UI Eligible

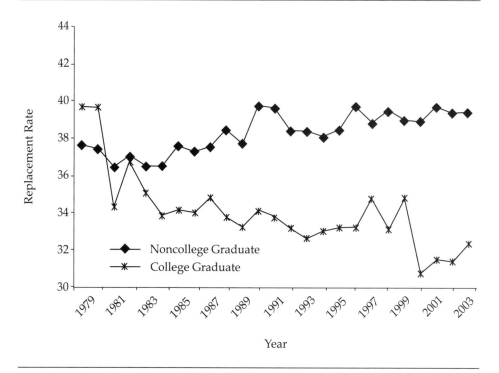

Source: Author's calculations based on March Current Population Surveys.

dollars and are increased in an ad hoc manner, and they have typically not kept up with inflation over time. In this dimension, more-skilled workers appear to be increasingly disadvantaged over time.

To summarize the differences in the cyclical responsiveness of UI eligibility and receipt, I have estimated regression models that relate each of these outcomes at the individual level to the unemployment rate in their state of residence, along with a standard array of personal characteristics (race-ethnicity, gender, age, marital status, and number of children) and state and year fixed effects. I estimated these models separately by level of education, continuing to focus on the difference between high school dropouts and workers with higher levels of education.

The results of this analysis using the CPS data are presented in the top panel of table 13.2. As displayed in the figures, the cyclical responsiveness of UI receipt does not appear to differ dramatically across skill levels. Regardless of skill, UI receipt increases by about the same amount during a recession. For each group, a one-percentage-point increase in the unemployment rate increases the number of unemployed individuals who receive UI by about one percentage point. The

TABLE 13.2 / Cyclical Responsiveness of UI Eligibility and Receipt, by Skill Level

	Received UI	Nonmonetary Eligibility	Monetary Eligibility	Overall Eligibility	Take-Up Rate
CPS data					
All workers	1.115	0.816	−1.390	0.013	
	(0.154)	(0.284)	(0.281)	(0.344)	
High school dropouts	0.941	−0.035	−1.391	−0.589	
	(0.237)	(0.401)	(0.431)	(0.410)	
High school graduates and beyond	1.204	1.222	−1.590	0.303	
	(0.153)	(0.267)	(0.319)	(0.359)	
NLSY data					
All workers	0.818	1.125	−0.728	0.573	1.253
	(0.104)	(0.108)	(0.126)	(0.124)	(0.288)
High school dropouts	0.902	1.848	−0.649	0.758	1.163
	(0.225)	(0.196)	(0.246)	(0.257)	(0.452)
High school graduates and beyond	0.783	0.955	−0.787	0.511	1.206
	(0.122)	(0.131)	(0.113)	(0.131)	(0.291)

Source: Author's compilations.
CPS notes: A unit of observation in the eligibility regressions reflects workers unemployed on the survey date for twenty-six weeks or less and in the UI receipt regression reflects all workers unemployed in the preceding calendar year. Estimates reflect the coefficient on the local area unemployment rate in a regression that includes controls for race-ethnicity, gender, age, marital status, number of children, and state and year fixed effects. Monetary eligibility regressions are estimated on the sample of individuals who meet nonmonetary eligibility requirements. Reported standard errors correct for heteroskedasticity and for arbitrary forms of covariance between residuals over time within states.
NLSY notes: A unit of observation reflects a job separation that led to at least one week of unemployment. Estimates reflect the coefficient on the local area unemployment rate in a regression that includes controls for race-ethnicity, gender, age, marital status, number of children, AFQT score, and state and year fixed effects. Reported standard errors correct for heteroskedasticity and for arbitrary forms of covariance beween residuals over time within states.

growing gap in UI receipt between more- and less-skilled workers appears to be related to a secular trend rather than a cyclical one.

These results also indicate that the cyclicality of UI receipt for each group must be attributable to trends in the UI take-up rate rather than eligibility. Nonmonetary eligibility tends to rise as the unemployment rate rises (particularly for more-skilled workers) and the composition of the unemployed who either lost their job or were laid off rises. But monetary eligibility tends to fall as the difficulty that workers face in finding work is reflected in the weaker labor force histories of newly unemployed workers. On net, these two effects roughly balance each other out and leave UI eligibility largely insensitive to labor market conditions. If so, then take-up rates must be responsible for driving the overall cyclical sensitivity in UI receipt.

To address the issue of take-up further, I have also estimated comparable models using data from the NLSY79. In these data, I have identified every job separation that took place for each individual at age eighteen or over in the sample between 1982 and 2001. For each separation, I have calculated UI receipt and eligibility along with UI take-up. Using these data, I have estimated regression models for each outcome as a function of the local unemployment rate, an array of personal characteristics (the same characteristics as in the CPS along with the AFQT (Armed Forces Qualification Test) score, which represents the results of an aptitude/achievement test), and a complete array of individual age dummy variables to control for underlying aging patterns in each outcome that are correlated with time in these data.[12] The chief benefit of using these data is that I can observe UI take-up and draw conclusions based on the data for this outcome rather than by inference.

The results of this analysis of the NLSY79 data are presented in the lower panel of table 13.2. Most of the findings reported here are quite consistent with those obtained using the CPS. UI receipt is countercyclical, and roughly equally so for more- and less-skilled workers. In these data, a one-percentage-point rise in the unemployment rate increases the likelihood that a worker separated from his or her job will receive UI by just under one percentage point. Nonmonetary eligibility rises when the unemployment rate rises (by about one percentage point for high school graduates and beyond and by almost twice that for high school dropouts in response to a one-percentage-point increase in the unemployment rate), but monetary eligibility tends to fall (by about 0.7 percentage points for both groups in response to a one-percentage-point increase in the unemployment rate).

In these data, however, overall eligibility tends to increase when labor market conditions deteriorate, and perhaps more so for less-skilled workers. For the less-skilled, a one-percentage-point increase in the unemployment rate increases the rate of UI eligibility by about three-quarters of a percentage point; the effect for more-skilled workers is about half a percentage point. As suspected, take-up rates are also found to increase with the unemployment rate, rising by over a full percentage point in response to a one-percentage-point increase in the unemployment rate. Despite the general similarity in cyclical responsiveness of UI receipt across skill groups in these data, results in the NLSY also confirm the findings in the CPS indicating a secular trend toward less UI receipt among high school dropouts relative to more-educated workers. This conclusion is based on patterns in the year fixed effects in these regressions across skill groups, which are not reported here.

Estimated UI Eligibility and Receipt by Race-Ethnicity and Gender

The contribution of the analysis reported so far is to distinguish workers by their skill level, but within each level to group together all workers. Yet there may be important differences by race-ethnicity and gender within skill groups that are relevant as well. For instance, the Hispanic population is more likely to include immigrants, and these workers may have more difficulty in the labor market than other workers over the business cycle.[13]

To examine this issue, I have replicated the analysis reported earlier, but with the sample separated into women and men and into non-Hispanic whites, non-Hispanic nonwhites (African American and other races), and Hispanics. The main findings suggest that the cyclical sensitivity of UI eligibility and receipt is similar across gender and racial-ethnic groups. The level of these outcomes, however, often differs considerably. For instance, women are about 10 percent less likely to receive UI than men, largely because they are about 25 percent less likely to satisfy nonmonetary eligibility requirements.[14] Those who are non-Hispanic nonwhites are about 7 percent less likely to receive UI than whites; they are roughly 10 percent less likely to satisfy monetary eligibility requirements and 5 percent less likely to meet the nonmonetary guidelines. Although Hispanics are slightly less likely (about 3 percent) to satisfy monetary eligibility requirements than whites, they are also slightly more likely (about 5 percent) to have lost their job or to have been laid off. Although they are about equally likely to be eligible for UI benefits compared to whites, they still are slightly less likely (about 3 percent) to collect benefits, suggesting that their take-up rates are a little lower. These differences by demographic status are independent of skill level.

UI FINANCING AND THE LESS-SKILLED

Although the relationship between UI receipt and well-being is more direct, the system of financing UI payments also affects the well-being of unemployed workers. This is partly attributable to the stress that a recession places on the UI financing system and the policy responses that result. But the broader impact of the tax structure on a firm's willingness to hire and fire workers is also an important component. In this section, I review the evidence on the system of financing UI benefits and its impact on layoffs. I then turn to an empirical analysis of the policy responses that states are likely to make when trust funds run low.

Experience Rating and Layoffs

The UI system is financed by a tax that is experience-rated in the sense that a firm that lays off more workers faces a higher UI tax rate in subsequent periods. In essence, the firm has to pay for the UI benefits paid out to the workers it lays off in the form of higher future taxes. This system of experience rating is not perfect, however, because many firms either lay off so infrequently or so often that they face a minimum or a maximum tax rate, respectively. For firms facing constant tax rates, there is no cost associated with laying off additional workers.

Researchers have recognized the incentives created by this imperfectly experience-rated system relative to one in which experience rating is perfect. The early literature described an implicit contract model in which firms and workers establish agreements that allow for layoffs, since a surplus is created when workers receive benefits that are not paid for by the firm (Feldstein 1978; Topel 1983). Recent work has incorporated a different theoretical framework that treats the UI tax as an adjustment cost. By making it cheaper to fire a worker when times are bad, imperfect experience rating also makes it easier to hire a worker when times are good (Anderson 1993; Card and Levine 1994). Regardless of the models employed, past work has found that a greater degree of experience rating reduces layoffs (see Anderson and Meyer 1994). In addition, the impact of imperfect experience rating on layoffs is greatest when labor market conditions are weakest (Card and Levine 1994), since firms are more likely to want to lay off workers at those times and any financial incentive then may be more valuable.

This discussion has not made the distinction between workers with different levels of skill in determining the layoff impact of imperfect experience rating. Nevertheless, it seems likely that this is an issue that is more likely to target less-skilled workers. First, the likelihood of layoff is much greater for less-skilled workers in the first place, so it would not be surprising if incentives to lay off hit this group the hardest. Second, construction is the industry in which the most firms face the maximum tax rate, and hence no experience rating. To the extent that workers in these industries are more likely to be less-educated, the incentive to lay off is greatest for them. Thus, the system of financing UI benefits probably encourages firms to lay off more workers during recessions than they would if taxes were perfectly experience-rated, and this effect is likely to be larger for less-skilled workers. One way that the UI system could better meet workers' needs during a recession would be to introduce more (or even perfect) experience rating.

Policy Responses to Financial Stress

The taxes that firms pay go into their own separate UI accounts and determine their own tax rates. Then all the accounts are accumulated into state- and federal-level aggregates to determine the financial well-being of the system. Figure 13.2 showed that the ratio of fund reserves to taxable payroll (called the reserve ratio) was quite low between the mid-1970s and the mid-1980s. But even in the most recent period, trust fund levels have been relatively low despite two decades in which economic expansion was largely the norm.

If another recession occurs in the near future, a number of state funds are likely to become insolvent. Estimates provided in Levine (1999) indicate that a relatively mild recession like that in the early 1990s would lower a state's reserve ratio by 0.75. This is more than the current fund levels in twenty-four states (as of the fourth quarter of 2004), including many large states like New York (currently insolvent), Illinois (0.08), Massachusetts (0.09), California (0.13), and Texas (0.27).

If the economy suddenly slips, each of these states could easily run out of funds.

This raises the question of how financial instability affects the UI system. How does a state respond when the funds it has available to pay UI benefits are low? There are several potential responses, and each has different implications for workers more generally and for less-skilled workers in particular. On the one hand, states could reduce benefit payments in one of two ways. First, states could leave eligibility rules unchanged and simply reduce the level of benefits. In general, states pay workers a weekly benefit that is around 50 percent of their pre-unemployment earnings subject to a minimum and maximum value. The minimum value is very low in virtually every state and is rarely binding. The maximum benefit, however, does represent a constraint for many workers. The typical policy change that is implemented when a state wants to alter benefit generosity is to change the maximum weekly benefit. The replacement rate for workers below the minimum is rarely changed, and the minimum benefit is binding on too few workers to matter (and is less frequently changed anyway). But changes in the maximum weekly benefit generally do not affect the well-being of less-skilled workers, since they are less likely to earn enough to qualify for that maximum. The workers whose benefits would be affected are more likely to be middle-income workers.

The second potential policy response is to reduce benefits by restricting UI eligibility. In this dimension, altering the monetary eligibility rules is easier to do, since it involves a simple formula change. When monetary eligibility rules are tightened, workers must have earned more in their base period to qualify for UI. But monetary eligibility requirements are not that high. The types of workers who would be more likely to be constrained by changes in monetary eligibility requirements are less-skilled workers who make a lower wage (since more weeks of work are required at a lower wage to surpass the threshold).

A state can also circumvent UI financial problems by generating more revenue via several options. The first is to raise tax rates. But the way in which a state institutes higher rates determines which workers are affected. One way to raise revenue is to shift the entire tax schedule upward. This raises the tax rate for all firms, but firms that face no experience rating (those at the maximum tax rate) continue to be able to lay off additional workers without paying any additional cost. A policy shift like this amounts to something like a lump sum tax that affects all workers equally. To the extent that firms respond to higher labor costs (including the tax) by reducing employment, workers at any point in the distribution may be affected.

Alternatively, states can extend the sloped portion of the tax schedule by increasing the maximum tax rate only. This generates more revenue from firms that otherwise would face no experience rating. To the extent that such a policy shift provides these firms with less of an incentive to lay off workers, it could actually improve the well-being of less-skilled workers, assuming that these workers are more likely to work in firms like this. (I am basing this assumption on the likelihood that construction firms are at the maximum tax rate.) On the other hand, if these firms have laid off so many workers in the past because they are struggling, then the imposition of greater UI taxes may put them over the edge and lead them to shut down, resulting in more layoffs for these workers.

The final way in which states can raise additional revenue does not require changing tax rates but increasing the taxable wage base. Recall that the federal taxable wage base is set at $7,000 per employee per year, although it is somewhat higher than that in a number of states. An increase in the wage base generates additional revenue even if tax rates are held constant. Since firms would face a greater tax liability for workers between the old level of the base and the new level of the base, the cost of employing less-skilled workers is likely to rise. If, for example, the base was increased from $7,000 to $10,000, then all workers with annual earnings over $7,000 would be affected, but the percentage increase that would be felt by firms employing workers earning not much more than $7,000 would be greater. To the extent that firms respond to the increase in labor costs by reducing labor demand, more less-skilled workers may find themselves without jobs.

Since there are multiple ways in which states might respond when their trust fund balances fall, each with its own implications for less-skilled workers, I have conducted an empirical exercise to determine what actually happens. I collected data on maximum weekly UI benefits, the annual earnings required to satisfy monetary eligibility requirements, minimum and maximum tax rates, and the taxable wage base in each state (including the District of Columbia) for the years 1979 through 2004. I estimated regression models that relate each of these outcomes to the level of trust fund reserves in each state/year in specifications that include a full vector of state and year fixed effects. This process is complicated by the fact that each of these outcomes is jointly determined with the UI provisions, since, for instance, a state that raises its maximum tax rate will have higher trust fund reserves. To circumvent this problem, I implemented an instrumental variables approach in which I use three lagged values of the state/year unemployment rate to instrument for the reserve ratio. This procedure provides variation in the reserve ratio that is attributable to lagged labor market characteristics, not concurrent changes in UI policy.

The results, presented in table 13.3, indicate that states tend to respond to financial shortfalls by changing tax provisions, not benefit generosity. Neither the maximum weekly benefit amount nor the minimum earnings necessary to satisfy monetary eligibility requirements are statistically significantly different from zero.[15] On the other hand, firms' tax liabilities increase when reserve ratios fall. Both the minimum and maximum tax rates shift up by roughly comparable amounts—about half a percent for every one-point reduction in the reserve ratio. This suggests that the entire tax schedule increases, rather than that the degree of experience rating is extended, so this could be thought of as an increase in a lump sum tax. It has no differential impact on workers who vary by skill level. States also appear to increase their taxable wage base when their trust fund balance gets low, raising it by nearly $1,000 for every one-point reduction in the reserve ratio. This increase may have more of an impact on the labor demand of

TABLE 13.3 / Responsiveness of UI Program Parameters to the Financial Condition of the Trust Fund

	Maximum Weekly Benefit	Required Annual Earnings	Minimum Tax Rate	Maximum Tax Rate	Taxable Wage Base
Reserve ratio	−2.91	−133.01	−0.668	−0.423	−929.08
	(5.48)	(120.74)	(0.190)	(0.077)	(400.16)

Source: Author's compilations.
Notes: Estimates reflect the coefficient on the reserve ratio in a two-stage least squares regression where the instruments represent three lagged values of the state-specific annual unemployment rate. Each specification also includes a full set of state and year fixed effects. All dollar values have been indexed to inflation and represent 2004 dollars. Reported standard errors are corrected for heteroskedasticity and for arbitrary forms of covariance between residuals over time within states.

those workers who have earnings just above the existing wage base, who are likely to be the less-skilled.

POLICY IMPLICATIONS

Based on the earlier discussion, we can now ask: how can the UI system better meet the needs of less-skilled workers, particularly during periods of economic downturn? The issues I discuss are not new ones; they were raised by the Advisory Council on Unemployment Compensation (ACUC), which made its final recommendations in 1996. For proposals that fit within the scope of this chapter, I discuss their potential impact on the well-being of less-skilled workers.[16]

1. Fixing the System for Extending Benefits Reform

The system by which the maximum benefit duration is extended during recessions is broken—emergency legislation has been required in every recession since the 1950s to provide the extension. This is troubling because federal legislation was enacted in 1970 that was designed to trigger those benefits automatically as labor market conditions deteriorate. That trigger is clearly broken. The current ad hoc system is poorly timed to the period in which unemployed workers are most at risk of exhausting their regular UI benefits, posing a risk to their well-being precisely when their need may be greatest.

Research suggests that benefit exhaustion is not a phenomenon that is more likely to occur among the less-skilled (Corson and Dynarski 1990). Nevertheless, these workers may be more likely to live in lower-income households in which the lack of benefits may have a greater impact on well-being. Fixing the trigger that automatically starts a benefit extension when a recession is beginning (by pegging the benefit extension to the overall unemployment rate, for instance) will help less-skilled workers better weather a downturn.

2. Relaxing Monetary Eligibility Requirements

The threshold that workers must satisfy to become monetarily eligible for UI benefits is typically set in dollar amounts; less-skilled workers thus face a higher hurdle because they need to work more hours to surpass it. On the basis of equity, one could easily argue that this should be changed if the goal is to increase UI receipt among less-skilled workers, particularly in light of welfare reform legislation that strongly encourages a subgroup of these workers to enter the labor force. This could also help reverse the differential in monetary eligibility that emerged in the mid-1980s between more- and less-skilled workers, which I documented earlier.

Although such a change would benefit less-skilled workers somewhat, I believe reasonable arguments could be made to the contrary. First, a very high percentage of workers satisfy monetary eligibility requirements already, even among the less-skilled. As figure 13.5 highlighted, roughly three-quarters of less-skilled job-losers already satisfy monetary eligibility requirements; marginal reductions in these requirements are likely to help some, but probably not a lot, of them qualify for benefits. In addition, the gap in monetary eligibility between more- and less-skilled workers that grew starting in the mid-1980s appears to be closing more recently, probably because eligibility thresholds, which are often set in nominal dollars, have not kept pace with inflation.

Nonmonetary requirements that unemployed workers need to have lost their job to get benefits turns out to be the more common obstacle. As the regulation now stands in the average state, a minimum-wage worker needs to have worked only about twelve weeks in their one-year base period to be monetarily eligible. Reducing the limit much below that may threaten the delicate balance between insurance and welfare that has largely maintained the political support for UI; the welfare system has not been so fortunate.

3. Introducing an Alternative Base Period

Basing monetary eligibility rules on lagged earnings histories is a vestige of a system in which earnings reports were recorded with a significant lag. There is no reason for this to occur today—eligibility should be determined by a worker's earnings record in the past year. Although such a move makes sense, it would probably increase only marginally the likelihood that a less-skilled worker will satisfy monetary eligibility requirements. Cynthia Decker and Phillip Levine (2001) simulate the impact of moving to an alternative base period on UI eligibility for more- and less-skilled workers separately. They find that considerably more individuals who leave their jobs would satisfy monetary eligibility require-

ments with an alternative base period, but when nonmonetary eligibility requirements are also imposed on those job separators, the increased likelihood of quali-
fying for UI is relatively small (for similar conclusions, see Vroman 1995). They
report that the alternative base period may provide benefits to an additional 10
percent of workers deemed ineligible by the traditional method. This figure is
slightly higher for less-skilled workers. Introducing an alternative base period
makes sense but is unlikely to have a large impact.

4. Extending Benefits to Seasonal Workers and Those Seeking Part-time Work

The ACUC identified two groups of workers for whom policy changes could
increase their ability to collect UI benefits. Currently, twenty-five states have
rules in place that deem those seeking part-time work ineligible for benefits because they do not satisfy nonmonetary eligibility requirements, despite meeting
those for monetary eligibility (National Employment Law Project 2004). Seasonal
workers face similar constraints in collecting benefits in sixteen states (U.S. Department of Labor 2005). Presumably these workers are more likely to be less-
skilled workers, so changes to these provisions would provide greater benefits
to them. The rationales for and against this proposal are somewhat philosophical
in nature. For instance, insurance principles suggest that seasonal workers
should not receive benefits since they are not suffering a loss—the job was supposed to end anyway. On the other hand, if those workers take seasonal jobs
because they cannot find regular employment, then they may find themselves in
need of those benefits. Unfortunately, I cannot say much about the merits of
proposals of this type based on my research; a complete analysis of this issue is
beyond the scope of this chapter.

5. Increasing Benefit Generosity

The ACUC proposed a system in which all states would replace at least 50 percent of lost earnings with a maximum weekly benefit amount equal to two-thirds
of the state's average weekly wage. The proposal is based on the adequacy of
benefits and the ability of UI to smooth consumption during difficult financial
times. Such a proposal provides little additional benefit to less-skilled workers.
For the most part, state benefit formulas satisfy the 50 percent replacement rate
component for most less-skilled workers.

6. Promoting the Forward Funding of the UI System

The remainder of the proposals involve the system of financing UI benefits. The
ACUC advocated proposals that provide incentives to states to accumulate

greater reserves during economic expansions (called "forward funding"). As we saw in figure 13.2, trust fund reserve levels are not very high considering the strong economic conditions that have prevailed for most of the last two decades. Particularly during the boom of the 1990s, states adopted policies that led to very little growth in the UI trust fund. Many state systems do not now have sufficient reserves to weather even a moderate recession.

As discussed earlier, the implications for less-skilled workers depend on states' policy responses when their reserves run low. According to my results, states do not appear to reduce maximum weekly benefits amounts, which would hurt more-skilled workers, or to increase monetary eligibility requirements, which would hurt less-skilled workers. States generally respond on the tax side by shifting their tax schedules upwards for all firms, regardless of their layoff history. This acts something like a lump sum tax, which is unlikely to have much of a differential impact on less-skilled workers. On the other hand, states also appear to be more likely to increase the taxable wage base.

7. Increasing the Taxable Wage Base

The ACUC also recommended increasing the federal taxable wage base to $9,000. The impact on workers of such a change depends on firms' responses to changes in the cost of employment for workers at various points in the earnings distribution. For very low-wage workers (or those who only work part-time or part-year) whose earnings are below the current taxable wage base, there would be no change in the cost of their compensation. Firms would pay higher taxes on all workers above that level. However, the percentage increase in the level of compensation (including the tax) is greatest for those workers with earnings in the range just above the current taxable wage base. Less-skilled workers, who are more likely to earn just above the taxable earnings threshold, are more likely to be negatively affected to the extent that a firm's labor demand falls when these costs increase. Unfortunately, the magnitude of this response is unknown.[17] As a policy alternative, the impact on less-skilled workers would be minimized if the taxable wage base were raised to a much higher level (or even eliminated), reducing the targeted impact on those with lower earnings. Interestingly, the UI taxable wage base was initially set at the same level as the Social Security taxable wage base, at $3,000 in 1940, which was equal to average annual earnings at that time. Average annual earnings have since increased to about $37,000 in 2003. Moreover, the Social Security taxable wage base stood at $90,000 in 2005. On that basis, I would view the ACUC proposal as modest.[18]

8. Increasing the Degree of Experience Rating

Past research shows that imperfect experience rating leads firms to lay off more workers than they otherwise would if experience rating were perfect. The impact on layoffs is greatest during a recession, when firms' desire to lay off is greatest. Although I have no direct evidence, it appears that workers in firms likely to face no experience rating, like those in the construction industry, are more likely to be less-skilled workers and therefore are at greatest risk. As a result, increasing the degree of experience rating would differentially assist less-skilled workers in maintaining employment over the course of the business cycle. The easiest way to accomplish this would be to raise or eliminate the maximum tax rate (and perhaps lower the minimum rate) without altering the remainder of the tax schedule.

SUMMARY AND CONCLUSIONS

This chapter has examined the cyclical sensitivity of UI eligibility and receipt, paying particular attention to differences by skill level. I began by describing the sometimes intricate institutional features of the UI system that may contribute to differences in these outcomes for workers with different levels of skill. For instance, minimum earnings requirements to qualify for UI are tilted against the less-skilled, but these requirements are typically so low as to be within the reach of all but those with very limited labor market attachment. On the other hand, I argued that the failed system by which benefits are extended during a recession hurts the less-skilled more since they need the support more. Similarly, the impact of imperfect experience rating on layoffs hurts the less-skilled more since they are more likely to have employers that are facing the maximum tax rate.

After a brief review of past research, I embarked on an empirical investigation designed to determine the sensitivity of UI eligibility and receipt to business cycle conditions and to determine whether this differs by skill level. In that analysis, I found substantial evidence of cyclical variation in UI eligibility and receipt, but little evidence of a difference between skill groups. What did emerge as an important distinction between skill groups is an unexplained secular trend toward less UI receipt among the less-skilled. Then I turned to a discussion of state policy responses to the financial difficulties encountered by a UI system after the strain of a recession. This is relevant since some responses, like increasing monetary eligibility requirements, may affect less-skilled workers more than others. My results indicate that states typically respond to decreases in their trust fund balance by increasing the taxable wage base and increasing tax rates. Since an increase in the taxable wage base affects those with earnings just above that level and the wage base is typically low, this response would tend to have a differential impact on less-skilled workers.

I concluded the analysis with a discussion of the policy implications of my findings. I identified two reforms that may provide the greatest benefit to less-skilled workers during a recession without compromising the insurance nature of the UI system: fixing the system so that the trigger to extend benefits occurs at the beginning of a recession rather than relying on poorly timed ad hoc legislation, and improving experience rating to reduce the incidence of job loss in the first place, particularly during a recession. I would also encourage the adoption of an alternative base period in all states. Although it is not clear that many workers would benefit from this change, it would replace the currently anachronistic system of determining monetary eligibility. Other proposals may be meritorious from a broader perspective (such as greater incentives for forward funding), but it is less clear that they would provide targeted benefits for the less-skilled.

NOTES

1. I would like to thank Becky Blank, Sheldon Danziger, and Bob Schoeni for their comments, as well as those of other participants attending the conference and the reviewers of this book.
2. Of course, the implementation of these criteria is more complicated. For instance, a worker who quits a job for "good cause" (like sexual harassment) would still be eligible for benefits. In some states, those who quit a job without good cause can eventually receive UI benefits after a lengthy waiting period.
3. The state of Washington establishes monetary eligibility on the basis of hours worked in the base period.
4. Median weekly earnings in Alabama and Mississippi were $588 and $517, respectively, in 2003.
5. For a brief history of emergency extended benefits legislation and a detailed discussion of the early 1990s experience, see Corson, Needels, and Nicholson (1999). Ten states have instituted alternative triggers that extend benefits if the state's unemployment rate rises above 6.5 percent.
6. For reviews of this research, see Advisory Council on Unemployment Compensation (1994) and Wittenberg et al. (1999). Robert Hall (this volume) and David Card and John DiNardo (this volume) discuss trends in the industrial composition and rate of unionization of the workforce in more detail.
7. The procedures I have undertaken are similar, but not identical, to those implemented by Rebecca Blank and David Card (1991), who also use the CPS to measure UI receipt and eligibility. The differences are partly attributable to our different concerns: their analysis is focused on explaining the diverging rates of total unemployment and insured unemployment that occurred in the early 1980s, and this is less of a concern for me.
8. Marc Roemer (2000) reports that the CPS captured about 82 percent of actual UI receipt based on administrative records over the 1990 to 1996 period.
9. To make the calculations of nonmonetary eligibility comparable, I impose the same restrictions on unemployment spell length there as well.
10. Note that the data I have used to estimate UI recipiency (retrospective data) are different from those used to estimate eligibility (contemporaneous data), so direct comparisons of the results are not appropriate.
11. Although I do not have evidence to support any of these hypotheses, possible explanations include: (1) policy changes designed to encourage labor market activity

among potential welfare recipients have led many individuals to be reclassified from "out of the labor force" to "unemployed." These individuals are unemployed, but not job-losers; (2) these same policy changes increased employment levels for less-skilled workers, but the match quality of these jobs may not be very high, resulting in a high quit rate; and (3) the growth in the temporary employment industry may have increased the number of individuals whose jobs ended, so there are more people in this category compared with job-losers. Other explanations certainly may exist, but further research would be necessary to determine the extent to which any of them actually explain the observed phenomenon.

12. Including these individual age dummy variables completely corrects for the deficiencies of the nature of this sample so long as age effects are constant over time.

13. Immigrant status was not separately identified in the Current Population Survey until 1994, so I cannot distinguish this group directly for this analysis.

14. These results are obtained from the coefficients on race-ethnicity and gender dummy variables in the same regressions used to generate table 13.2. I have also estimated these regressions separately by race-ethnicity and gender to determine that the unemployment rate coefficients in models of that form are roughly similar across groups.

15. It is relevant to note, however, that similar regressions using data from the 1980s find a significant negative relationship between the reserve ratio and required annual earnings. This is because many states strengthened their monetary eligibility requirements in the early 1980s in response to the funding crises that they were experiencing at that time. The introduction of interest charged on loans from the federal government made them take more drastic actions to get their finances in order. Since then, however, no such relationship is apparent, so that the effect over the entire twenty-five-year period turns out not to be statistically significant.

16. The ACUC made several additional recommendations beyond those that I discuss here, including changes to rules for nonprofit employers and agricultural workers, obscure provisions of the Internal Revenue Code, data reporting requirements, administrative federal-state interactions, and the like. Without disputing the importance of topics like these, none of the analysis provided here sheds light on any of them.

17. Robert Cook and his colleagues (1995) simulate the impact of increasing or eliminating the taxable wage base and report small employment effects, although their analysis does not distinguish workers by level of skill.

18. If we do increase the wage base substantially, tax rates could be significantly reduced to maintain revenue neutrality, if such an outcome were desired.

REFERENCES

Advisory Council on Unemployment Compensation. 1994. *1994 Report and Recommendations*. Washington, D.C.: Advisory Council on Unemployment Compensation.
———. 1996. *Collected Findings and Recommendations: 1994–1996*. Washington, D.C.: Advisory Council on Unemployment Compensation.

Anderson, Patricia M. 1993. "Linear Adjustment Costs and Seasonal Labor Demand: Evidence from Retail Trade Firms." *Quarterly Journal of Economics* 108(4): 1015–42.

Anderson, Patricia M., and Bruce D. Meyer. 1994. "The Effects of Unemployment Insurance Taxes and Benefits on Layoffs Using Firm and Individual Data." Working paper 4960. Cambridge, Mass.: National Bureau of Economic Research.

———. 1997. "Unemployment Insurance Take-up Rates and the After-Tax Value of Benefits." *Quarterly Journal of Economics* 112(3): 913–37.

Blank, Rebecca M., and David Card. 1991. "Recent Trends in Insured and Uninsured Unemployment: Is There an Explanation?" *Quarterly Journal of Economics* 106(4): 1157–89.

Card, David, and Phillip B. Levine. 1994. "Unemployment Insurance Taxes and the Cyclical and Seasonal Properties of Unemployment." *Journal of Public Economics* 53(1): 1–30.

Congressional Budget Office. 2004. *Family Income of Unemployment Insurance Recipients.* Washington: Congressional Budget Office.

Cook, Robert F., Wayne Vroman, Joseph Kirchner, Anthony Brinsko, and Alexandra Tan. 1995. "The Effects of Increasing the Federal Taxable Wage Base for Unemployment Insurance." Unemployment Insurance Occasional Paper 95–1. Washington, D.C.: U.S. Department of Labor, Employment and Training Administration.

Corson, Walter, and Mark Dynarski. 1990. *A Study of Unemployment Insurance Recipients and Exhaustees: Findings from a National Survey.* Unemployment Insurance Occasional Paper 90–3. Washington: U.S. Department of Labor, Employment and Training Administration.

Corson, Walter, Karen Needels, and Walter Nicholson. 1999. *Emergency Unemployment Compensation: The 1990s Experience,* rev. ed. Unemployment Insurance Occasional Paper 99–4. Washington: U.S. Department of Labor, Employment and Training Administration.

Corson, Walter, and Walter Nicholson. 1988. *An Examination of Declining UI Claims During the 1980s.* Unemployment Insurance Occasional Paper 88–3. Washington: U.S. Department of Labor, Employment and Training Administration.

Decker, Cynthia K. Gustafson, and Phillip B. Levine. 2001. "Less-Skilled Workers, Welfare Reform, and the Unemployment Insurance System." *Research in Labor Economics* 20: 395–432.

Feldstein, Martin S. 1978. "The Effect of Unemployment Insurance on Temporary Layoff Unemployment." *American Economic Review* 68(5): 834–46.

Fishman, Michael E., Mary Farrell, and Karen N. Gardiner. 2003. *Unemployment Insurance Nonmonetary Policies and Practices: How Do They Affect Program Participation? A Study of Eight States.* Unemployment Insurance Occasional Paper 2003–01. Washington: U.S. Department of Labor, Employment and Training Administration.

Gruber, Jonathan. 1997. "The Consumption Smoothing Benefits of Unemployment Insurance." *American Economic Review* 87(1): 192–205.

Holzer, Harry. 2000. "Welfare Reform and the Unemployment Insurance: What Happens When the Recession Comes?" Assessing the New Federalism Series. Policy brief. Washington, D.C.: Urban Institute.

Isaacs, Julia B. 2005. "Receipt of Unemployment Insurance Among Low-Income Single

Mothers." Issue brief. Washington: U.S. Department of Health and Human Services, Office of the Assistant Secretary for Planning and Evaluation.

Kaye, Kelleen. 1997. "Unemployment Insurance as a Potential Safety Net for Former Welfare Recipients." Unpublished paper. Washington: U.S. Department of Health and Human Services, Office of the Assistant Secretary for Planning and Evaluation.

———. 2001. "Reexamining Unemployment Insurance as a Potential Safety Net for Workers at Risk of Public Assistance Receipt." Unpublished paper. Washington: U.S. Department of Health and Human Services, Office of the Assistant Secretary for Planning and Evaluation.

Levine, Phillip B. 1997. "Financing Benefit Payments." In *Unemployment Insurance in the United States: Analysis of Policy Issues*, edited by Christopher J. O'Leary and Steven A. Wandner. Kalamazoo, Mich.: W. E. Upjohn Institute for Employment Research.

———. 1999. "Cyclical Welfare Costs in the Post-Reform Era: Will There Be Enough Money?" In *Economic Conditions and Welfare Reform*, edited by Sheldon Danziger. Kalamazoo, Mich.: W. E. Upjohn Institute for Economic Research.

National Employment Law Project. 2004. *Part-time Workers and Unemployment Insurance*. Washington, D.C.: National Employment Law Project.

Roemer, Marc I. 2000. "Assessing the Quality of the March Current Population Survey and the Survey of Income and Program Participation Income Estimates, 1990–1996." Unpublished paper. Washington: U.S. Bureau of the Census.

Topel, Robert H. 1983. "On Layoffs and Unemployment Insurance." *American Economic Review* 73(4): 541–59.

U.S. Department of Labor, Employment and Training Administration. 2004. "Special Extended Benefit Programs" (last modified July 19). Available at: http://workforcesecurity. doleta.gov/unemploy/pdf/spec_ext_ben_table.pdf.

———. 2005. *Comparison of State Unemployment Insurance Laws*. Washington: U.S. Department of Labor.

Vroman, Wayne. 1991. *The Decline in Unemployment Insurance Claims Activity in the 1980s*. Unemployment Insurance Occasional Paper 91–2. Washington: U.S. Department of Labor, Employment and Training Administration.

———. 1995. "The Alternative Base Period in Unemployment Insurance: Final Report." Unemployment Insurance Occasional Paper 95–3. Washington: U.S. Department of Labor, Employment and Training Administration.

———. 1998. "Effects of Welfare Reform on Unemployment Insurance." Assessing the New Federalism Series. Policy brief. Washington, D.C.: Urban Institute.

———. 2002. *Low Benefit Recipiency in State Unemployment Insurance Programs*. Unemployment Insurance Occasional Paper 2002–2. Washington: U.S. Department of Labor, Employment and Training Administration.

Wittenburg, David C., Michael Fishman, David Stapleton, Scott Scrivner, and Adam Tucker. 1999. *Analysis of Unemployment Insurance Recipiency Rates*. Unemployment Insurance Occasional Paper 99–7. Washington: U.S. Department of Labor, Employment and Training Administration.

Chapter 14

How Is Health Insurance Affected by the Economy? Public and Private Coverage Among Low-Skilled Adults in the 1990s

Helen Levy

In 1992, 38.6 million Americans were uninsured (DeNavas-Walt, Proctor, and Mills 2004). Eight years later, at the end of the longest economic expansion in the United States since World War II, the number of uninsured had increased to nearly 40 million (DeNavas-Walt et al. 2004). Why did the booming economy not translate into gains in insurance coverage? This puzzle is even more pronounced when we look at trends by education level, since low-skilled individuals experienced both the largest gains in employment and the largest declines in insurance coverage. Among high school dropouts between the ages of twenty-five and fifty-four, the fraction employed increased from 67 percent to 71 percent, and mean real family income increased by more than 15 percent. But the fraction of dropouts who were uninsured increased from 36 percent to 40 percent. What happened?

This chapter analyzes the puzzle of declining coverage in the booming 1990s. Using data from the Current Population Survey (CPS) describing the years 1988 through 2003, I look at trends in income, employment, and insurance coverage by education and sex. I analyze the relationship at a point in time between health insurance coverage and a variety of economic indicators that reflect the health of the economy and the economic well-being of an individual's own family: the employment of an individual and his or her spouse, family income, and the unemployment rate in the individual's state of residence. Once these static relationships have been established, I analyze the trends in coverage during the boom and the downturn that followed it. Was the decline driven by public or private coverage? How much of the decline in coverage can be explained by observable factors such as income and employment?

The story that emerges suggests that, during the boom, gains in employment and income increased private coverage for men and women at all levels of education, including the least-skilled. For low-skilled men and high-skilled women, who do not rely heavily on public coverage, these employment and income gains triggered small declines in public coverage that only partially offset the gains in private coverage. But for low-skilled women, who have much higher baseline rates of public coverage, these employment and income gains triggered losses of public coverage that offset the gains in private coverage. The loss of public coverage is even larger than can be explained by the employment and income gains, so that the net effect is an increase in the fraction of low-skilled women who are uninsured. It is unclear why the declines in public coverage are so much larger than what the employment and income gains would have predicted. Welfare reform may have played a role in reducing take-up of public insurance, although the evidence on this point is not conclusive.

During the downturn that followed the boom, private coverage declined for men and women at all education levels; public coverage increased, but by much less than private coverage declined, so that uninsurance increased for all groups. Between one-quarter and one-half of the decline in private coverage and the increase in public coverage is explained by changes in the joint distribution of income and employment that occurred during the downturn.

THE DATA

The data for the analysis come from the Current Population Survey Annual Social and Economic Supplement (the "March supplement") for the years 1989 through 2004. I restrict the sample to adults age twenty-five to fifty-four, yielding a sample of between 70,000 and 112,000 observations in each year, for a total of 1.3 million observations. Based on responses to questions about health insurance coverage in the calendar year prior to the survey date, I code each individual as having private insurance, public insurance, or no insurance. Each individual is assigned to one of three education categories: less than a high school education ("dropouts"), education exactly equal to high school graduation, and education greater than high school. I also use demographic information (age, race, ethnicity), labor force participation variables, and information on family income. All income data presented in this chapter have been adjusted to 2000 dollars using the consumer price index (CPI) for all urban consumers. These data are supplemented with information on aggregate unemployment rates by state and year from the Bureau of Labor Statistics (BLS) and on Medicaid eligibility levels for infants and pregnant women from the National Governors' Association (various years).

FIGURE 14.1 / Trends in Employment of Adults Age Twenty-Five to Fifty-Four,
by Education and Sex, 1988 to 2003

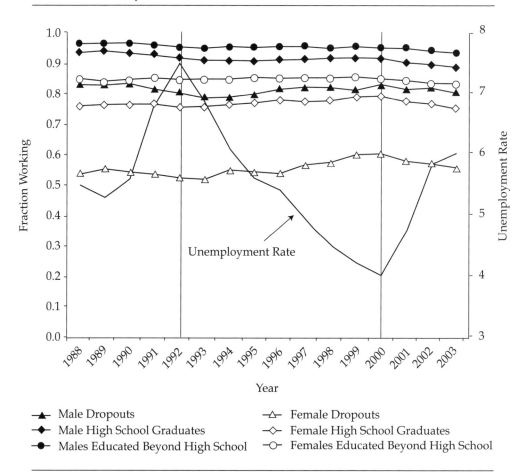

Source: Author's compilations from Current Population Survey.

DESCRIPTIVE TRENDS IN EMPLOYMENT, INCOME, AND HEALTH INSURANCE FOR LOW-SKILLED ADULTS

Figure 14.1 documents trends in employment during the 1990s using the CPS data. The figure plots the fraction of adults who were working by education and sex and, on the right axis, the national unemployment rate. The vertical lines highlight 1992 and 2000 as the beginning and the end of the boom, as measured by the maximum and minimum levels of overall unemployment. Female high school dropouts experienced a large increase in labor force participation during

FIGURE 14.2 / Trends in Mean Real (2000 dollars) Family Income of Adults Age
Twenty-Five to Fifty-Four, by Education and Sex, 1988 to 2003

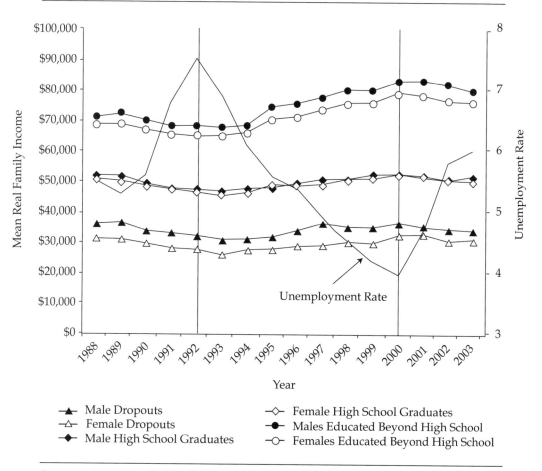

Source: Author's compilations from Current Population Survey.

this period; the fraction of this group who did at least some work during the
calendar year increased from 52.3 percent in 1992 to 59.9 percent in 2000, falling
back down to 53.7 percent in 2003. Women with exactly a high school education
also experienced a small increase in employment during the 1990s (3.2 percentage points); that increase was followed by a decline to just below the 1992 level
by 2003. For other groups—men at all levels of education and women with education beyond high school—employment was flat during the 1990s and declined
between 2000 and 2003.

Average real family income in 2000 dollars (figure 14.2) rose or remained constant for all groups during the 1990s and then declined after 2000. For female
high school dropouts, average real family income rose from $27,977 in 1992 to

FIGURE 14.3 / Trends in Uninsured Adults Age Twenty-Five to Fifty-Four,
by Education and Sex, 1988 to 2003

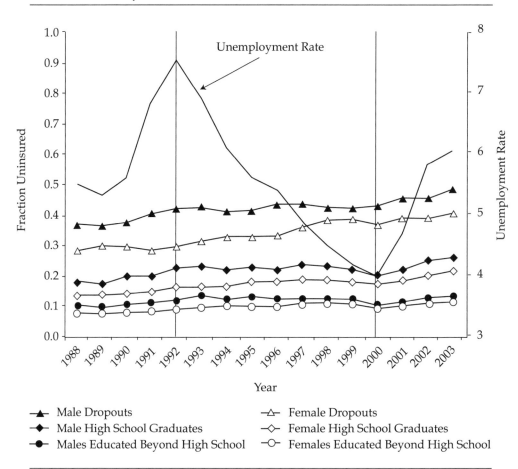

Year

—▲— Male Dropouts   —△— Female Dropouts
—◆— Male High School Graduates   —◇— Female High School Graduates
—●— Males Educated Beyond High School   —○— Females Educated Beyond High School

Source: Author's compilations from Current Population Survey.

$32,544 in 2000, an increase of 16 percent. Male dropouts also experienced a proportional increase of almost the same size. Real family incomes increased by about 11 percent for male and female high school graduates and by about 21 percent for men and women with higher levels of education.

What about health insurance? Did the rising economic tide lift all boats? Figure 14.3 shows that it did not. Figure 14.3 plots the fraction of each sex and education group who did not have insurance and (using the scale on the right axis) the national unemployment rate, from 1988 to 2003. During the period when the unemployment rate was falling, between 1992 and 2000, the fraction uninsured *increased* for low-skilled women. This increase was particularly large for female high school dropouts: the fraction of this group who were uninsured increased

FIGURE 14.4 / Trends in Private Health Insurance Coverage for Adults Age
Twenty-Five to Fifty-Four, by Education and Sex, 1988 to 2003

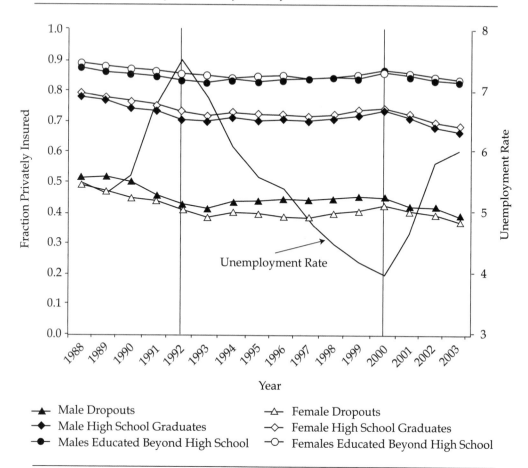

Source: Author's compilations from Current Population Survey.

by seven percentage points, from 30 percent to 37 percent, over the same period
that their employment rate increased by 7.6 percentage points.

Figures 14.4 and 14.5 present separate trends for private and public health
insurance coverage, respectively. All groups had at least some increase in private
coverage over this period, ranging in magnitude from less than a percentage
point for women with more than a high school education to 2.9 percentage points
for men with education exactly equal to high school (figure 14.4). All groups also
experienced declines in public coverage; for low-skilled women (both dropouts
and high school graduates), these declines were larger than the increases in private coverage (figure 14.5).

These trends are even more striking among low-skilled single mothers, who

FIGURE 14.5 / Trends in Public Health Insurance Coverage for Adults Age
Twenty-Five to Fifty-Four, by Education and Sex, 1988 to 2003

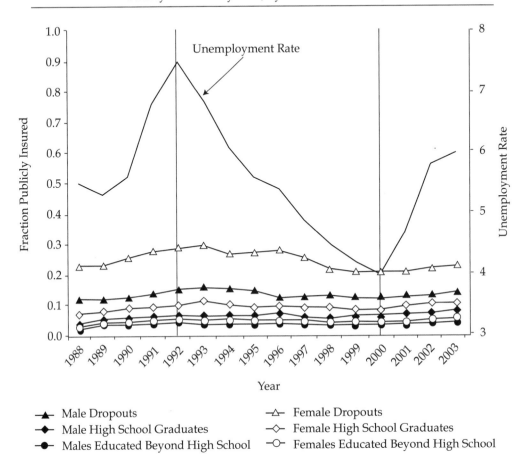

Source: Author's compilations from Current Population Survey.

were the most likely to have been affected by the changes in welfare policies that
occurred during the 1990s. Figure 14.6 shows a striking increase in the fraction
of high school dropout single mothers who were uninsured, from 24 percent in
1992 to 35 percent in 2000. Although this group did experience a gain in private
coverage, from 23 percent in 1992 to 32 percent in 2000 (a remarkable increase—
nearly 40 percent!—in proportional terms), this gain was overwhelmed by a precipitous drop in public coverage over the same period, from 53 percent to 33
percent, as shown in figures 14.7 and 14.8.

These simple figures are consistent with a story in which employment and
income gains lead to increases in private coverage, but for low-skilled women
who have relatively high rates of public coverage to begin with, declines in pub-

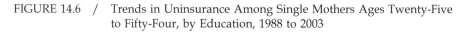

FIGURE 14.6 / Trends in Uninsurance Among Single Mothers Ages Twenty-Five
to Fifty-Four, by Education, 1988 to 2003

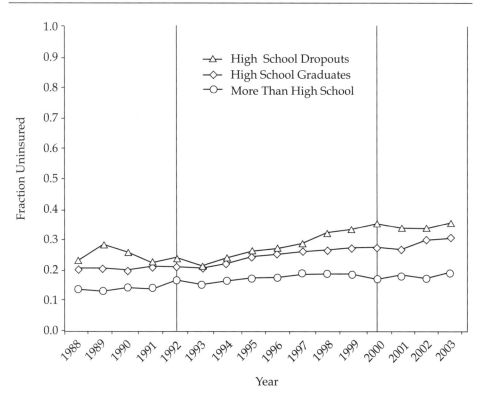

Source: Author's compilations from Current Population Survey.

lic coverage overwhelmed these increases.[1] Later in the chapter, I analyze more
precisely the extent to which income and employment gains for each group were
responsible for these increases in private coverage and decreases in public coverage.

THE IMPACT OF THE MACROECONOMY
ON HEALTH INSURANCE COVERAGE

Before attempting to unravel further the puzzle of declining coverage in the
booming 1990s, it is worth reviewing what theory predicts and what previous
empirical research has shown about the relationships between health insurance,
employment, and the macroeconomy. That is, how would we expect health insurance coverage to respond to economic fluctuations? Common sense predicts

FIGURE 14.7 / Trends in Private Insurance Among Single Mothers Age Twenty-Five to Fifty-Four, by Education, 1988 to 2003

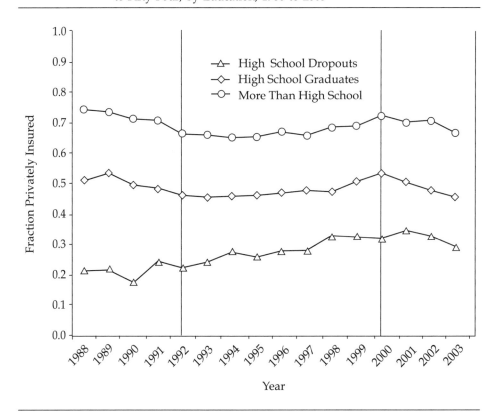

Source: Author's compilations from Current Population Survey.

that the main effect of the economy on insurance coverage would be through the probability of employment, which affects both income and the price of health insurance; these factors would in turn affect the likelihood of either private or public coverage. There might also be secondary effects through changes in the employment of family members or changes in the nature of employment, conditional on remaining employed.

More specifically, economic fluctuations might affect insurance coverage through the following mechanisms:

1. *One's own employment*: In a recession, the risk of job loss rises, particularly for low-skilled workers. As a result, income goes down and the effective price of private insurance goes up, for two reasons. First, even if an unemployed worker continues to purchase health insurance at a group rate through COBRA, the implicit tax subsidy to employer-provided benefits is

FIGURE 14.8 / Trends in Public Insurance Among Single Mothers Age Twenty-Five to Fifty-Four, by Education, 1988 to 2003

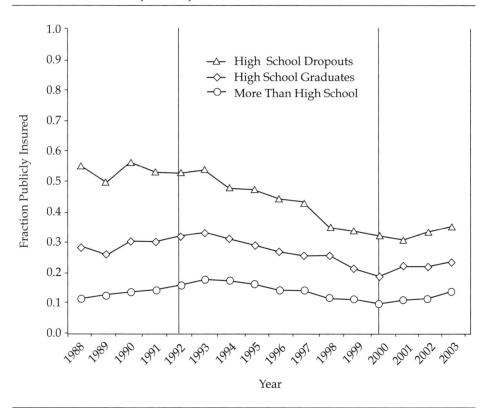

Source: Author's compilations from Current Population Survey.

no longer available. Second, at the end of eighteen months, COBRA eligibility runs out and the worker may lose access to health insurance at a group rate.[2] Both the income decrease and the price increase should reduce the probability of having private insurance and increase the probability of having public coverage. Empirical work by Jonathan Gruber and Brigitte Madrian (1997) has shown that in a sample of working men, job separation is associated with a twenty-percentage-point drop in the probability of having health insurance coverage. John Cawley and Kosali Simon (2005) also find that employment status mediates the relationship between insurance coverage and state-level unemployment rates, implying a significant effect of an individual's own employment on coverage, although the magnitude of this effect is not reported.

2. *Employment of other family members*: When a family member loses a job, not only is family income reduced, but the effective price of private insurance

may increase if the job was one that offered insurance coverage. Like an individual's own job loss, the job loss of a family member should reduce the probability of having private insurance and increase the probability of having public coverage.

3. *Changes in type of job*: Even conditional on remaining employed, the nature of a job may change in a recession—going from full-time to part-time, for example, or shifting from the wage and salary sector to self-employment. These changes may affect the probability of having private insurance. That is, the mix of jobs changes in a recession and may shift toward jobs that are less likely to provide benefits.[3] In addition, even holding constant the observable job characteristics that affect the probability that a job provides benefits—for example, part-time versus full-time—the probability of insurance may vary over the business cycle as wages do, for the same reasons.[4] Even absent any cyclical behavior by employers with regard to the provision of insurance, cyclicality in earnings would itself be sufficient to cause cyclicality in health insurance coverage, conditional on employment, because of an income effect.

4. *Changes in the mix of jobs*: An additional indirect effect of the macroeconomy arises because private health insurance is typically provided to *groups* of workers, and an employer's willingness to provide insurance depends on the distribution of demand for coverage of all workers at the firm. As a result, whether your coworkers want insurance may affect whether or not you are offered it. If the changing composition of the workforce combines with a drop in demand for insurance, owing to lower family incomes, to change the distribution of worker demand for health insurance, firms may add or drop benefits. Two examples illustrate the extremes. First, suppose that all low-skilled workers prefer not to get insurance as a fringe benefit but opt instead for charity care at the emergency room or Medicaid coverage. Suppose also that in a recession all low-skilled workers are laid off. Then everyone in the labor force in a recession wants health insurance, and firms should all offer it. Second, and in contrast, suppose that in a recession some of your coworkers' spouses lose their jobs and as a result of the drop in family income they decide to stop buying health insurance. Suddenly, you are the only one in your firm who wants insurance, and your firm stops offering insurance. In short, since health insurance has some of the attributes of a local public good, the demand of your coworkers affects whether or not you will get it (see Bundorf 2002; Goldstein and Pauly 1976). This mechanism suggests that aggregate unemployment rates may affect the probability of insurance coverage, even controlling for one's own employment and income and the employment and income of other family members.

5. *Changes in public programs*: During a recession, states may respond to declining revenues by reducing eligibility for public programs like Medicaid. Conditional on income, public coverage rates may therefore be lower in a recession. This effect may be swamped by the changes in the income distribution

FIGURE 14.9 / Potential Effects of the Macroeconomy on Health Insurance Coverage

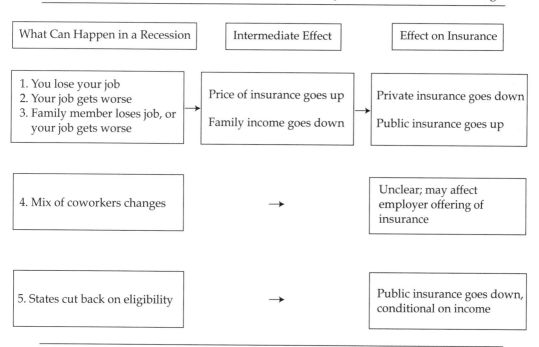

Source: Author's compilations.

that occur during a recession. That is, public coverage could go up or down in a recession because, while there are more poor people, there may also be cutbacks in eligibility.

The first three of these factors suggest that in a recession private coverage should decline and public coverage should increase; during an expansion, we would expect the opposite. In either case, it is not clear whether the change in public coverage would be large enough to offset any change in private coverage. The last two factors have an ambiguous effect on coverage. As a result, there is no clear prediction about the effect of economic fluctuations on the fraction uninsured. Figure 14.9 summarizes these factors and their likely effects on private and public insurance coverage.

THE IMPACT OF THE MACROECONOMY ON INSURANCE COVERAGE AT A POINT IN TIME

The first step in solving the puzzle of what happened in the 1990s is to establish a clearer understanding of the static relationship between health insurance and the macroeconomy. I begin by estimating a set of regressions that summarize the relationship between the macroeconomy and individual health insurance coverage, using the following specification:

$$P(HI) = a_0 + a_1 \cdot \text{(state unemployment rate)} + a_2 \cdot \text{(demographic controls)}$$
$$+ a_3 \cdot \text{(Medicaid generosity)} + \text{(year dummies)}$$
$$+ \text{(state dummies)} \tag{14.1}$$

Where

- $P(HI)$ is the insurance outcome (private insurance, public insurance, uninsured);
- *State unemployment rate* is the annual average unemployment rate in each state from the Bureau of Labor Statistics data;
- *Demographic controls* include race (black and other nonwhite; white is the omitted category) and Hispanic ethnicity dummies, age and age-squared, and a marital status dummy;
- *Medicaid generosity* is measured using two variables containing the state-year specific Medicaid income eligibility cutoffs for infants and for pregnant women, respectively.

This specification omits employment characteristics of the individual and his or her spouse, as well as family income, so it does not shed light on which of the mechanisms discussed earlier may be responsible for any relationship between health insurance and the macroeconomy. Rather, it is a starting point for the discussion of how the macroeconomy affects health insurance. I discuss the effect of including additional controls shortly.

Table 14.1 presents a_1, the coefficient on the state unemployment rate, for eighteen separate regressions corresponding to three different outcome variables (private insurance, public insurance, no insurance), estimated separately for men and women by education (less than high school, equal to high school, more than high school). The other coefficients from these regressions are not reported, but in general they yield results consistent with the existing literature. For example, Hispanics and nonwhites are less likely than non-Hispanic whites to have private insurance and more likely to be uninsured; marriage increases the probability of private coverage for men and decreases it for women.

The results for men (columns 1 through 3 of table 14.1) suggest that macroeconomic fluctuations affect coverage for men at all levels of education. The coefficient on the state unemployment rate suggests that a one-percentage-point increase in the unemployment rate reduces private coverage for men significantly, by about one percentage point for high school dropouts and by half a percentage point for men with more education. Public coverage does not vary with the state unemployment rate for men with a high school education or more, but it does

TABLE 14.1 / The Effect of Macroeconomic Conditions on Health Insurance Coverage, by Education and Sex, 1988 to 2003

	Men (1) Private	Men (2) Public	Men (3) Uninsured	Women (4) Private	Women (5) Public	Women (6) Uninsured
Education less than high school Coefficient on state unemployment rate	−0.010	0.003	0.006	−0.003	0.001	0.002
Standard error	(0.002)**	(0.002)*	(0.002)**	(0.002)	(0.002)	(0.002)
R-squared	0.12	0.05	0.12	0.14	0.14	0.06
Observations	69,483	69,483	69,483	69,772	69,772	69,772
Education equal to high school Coefficient on state unemployment rate	−0.004	0.001	0.004	−0.001	<0.001	0.001
Standard error	(0.001)**	(0.001)	(0.001)**	(0.001)	(0.001)	(0.001)
R-squared	0.12	0.02	0.10	0.13	0.07	0.06
Observations	170,294	170,294	170,294	189,415	189,415	189,415
Education greater than high school Coefficient on state unemployment rate	−0.004	<0.001	0.004	−0.003	0.001	0.002
Standard error	(0.001)**	(0.001)	(0.001)**	(0.001)**	(0.001)	(0.001)**
R-squared	0.08	0.01	0.08	0.07	0.03	0.04
Observations	277,493	277,493	277,493	297,709	297,709	297,709

Source: Author's compilations from March Current Population Survey.
Notes: Regressions also include race, ethnicity, age, age-squared, marital status, state dummies, and year dummies.
*p ≤ 0.05; **p ≤ 0.01

increase slightly with unemployment among high school dropouts: an increase of about one-third of a percentage point in the public coverage rate for each percentage-point-increase in the unemployment rate.[5] The overall effect of the macroeconomy on men's health insurance coverage, then, is to decrease private coverage and increase the fraction uninsured.[6]

The results for women (columns 4 through 6 of table 14.1) with a high school education or less do not show a significant relationship between the macroeconomy and women's health insurance coverage. For women with more than a high school education (who make up just over half the sample of women), a one-percentage-point increase in the state unemployment rate is associated with about a 0.3-percentage-point reduction in private coverage and a 0.2-percentage-point increase in the fraction uninsured.[7] The overall picture, then, is one in which macroeconomic downturns increase uninsurance for men and more highly skilled women, while not significantly affecting lower-skilled women's overall rate of coverage.

The results in table 14.1 are useful as a summary measure of how the macroeconomy affects health insurance coverage. We can target the mechanisms through which these effects occur more precisely by augmenting the regression described earlier with individual- and family-level controls for employment and income. Tables 14.2 and 14.3 present selected coefficients from these augmented regressions for high school dropouts and for those with education exactly equal to high school, respectively. Several things are evident from these two tables. First, including the additional individual and family controls reduces the magnitude of the coefficient on the state unemployment rate. This is true for both men and women and for all three outcomes. In many cases, the inclusion of individual- and family-level employment and income controls renders the coefficient on the aggregate macroeconomic variable statistically insignificant. That is, the macroeconomy affects individual health insurance mainly because it affects own employment, spouse's employment, and family income. Moreover, all three sets of variables are highly significant determinants of coverage. For high school dropouts, an individual's own employment status is a significant predictor of insurance coverage, increasing the probability of private coverage and reducing the probability of public coverage, with a net increase in the probability of being uninsured.[8] For high school graduates, the effect of employment is similar, except that full-time, full-year employment has a sufficiently positive effect on the probability of private coverage that it outweighs the negative effect on public coverage and results in a net decrease in the probability of being uninsured for both men and women.

A spouse's employment has different effects for women than for men. For female dropouts, having a husband who works full-time year-round has no effect on the probability of being uninsured; the gain in private coverage associated with a working husband is exactly offset by the loss of public coverage. A husband who works part-time or part of the year costs a woman more, in terms of public coverage, than he provides in private coverage: a husband's weak attachment to the labor force increases the probability that a female high school dropout is uninsured by six to eleven percentage points. For female high school graduates, the effect of a husband's employment is similar, except that for this group having a husband who works full-time year-round significantly reduces the probability that a woman is uninsured, by 6.2 percentage points. Part-time or part-year work by the husbands of female high school graduates increases significantly the probability that the woman is uninsured, by reducing public

TABLE 14.2 / Selected Determinants of Insurance Coverage for High School Dropouts Age Twenty-Five to Fifty-Four, 1988 to 2003

Source of Coverage	Men: Private (1)	Men: Public (2)	Men: Uninsured (3)	Women: Private (4)	Women: Public (5)	Women: Uninsured (6)
State unemployment rate	-0.004 (0.002)	-0.001 (0.001)	0.004 (0.002)*	0.002 (0.002)	-0.002 (0.002)	-0.000 (0.002)
Individual works:						
Full-time, full-year	0.349 (0.005)**	-0.452 (0.003)**	0.103 (0.005)**	0.277 (0.004)**	-0.323 (0.004)**	0.046 (0.004)**
Part-time, full-year	0.110 (0.010)**	-0.324 (0.007)**	0.215 (0.011)**	0.116 (0.006)**	-0.232 (0.006)**	0.116 (0.007)**
Full-time, part-year	0.182 (0.005)**	-0.405 (0.004)**	0.222 (0.006)**	0.131 (0.005)**	-0.208 (0.004)**	0.076 (0.006)**
Part-time, part-year	0.050 (0.009)**	-0.329 (0.006)**	0.279 (0.009)**	0.074 (0.006)**	-0.160 (0.005)**	0.086 (0.007)**
Spouse works:						
Full-time, full-year	0.161 (0.005)**	-0.104 (0.004)**	-0.057 (0.006)**	0.235 (0.007)**	-0.234 (0.006)**	-0.002 (0.007)
Part-time, full-year	0.083 (0.009)**	-0.080 (0.006)**	-0.004 (0.009)	0.047 (0.015)**	-0.157 (0.013)**	0.110 (0.016)**
Full-time, part-year	0.082 (0.007)**	-0.057 (0.005)**	-0.025 (0.007)**	0.108 (0.008)**	-0.172 (0.007)**	0.064 (0.009)**
Part-time, part-year	0.060 (0.008)**	-0.039 (0.006)**	-0.021 (0.009)*	0.003 (0.014)	-0.100 (0.012)**	0.097 (0.015)**
Real family income (divided by 10,000)	0.045 (0.001)**	-0.008 (0.001)**	-0.037 (0.001)**	0.059 (0.001)**	-0.017 (0.001)**	-0.042 (0.001)**
Real family income-squared	-0.001 (0.000)**	0.000 (0.000)**	0.001 (0.000)**	-0.001 (0.000)**	0.000 (0.000)**	0.001 (0.000)**
Observations	69,483	69,483	69,483	69,772	69,772	69,772
R-squared	0.29	0.31	0.17	0.31	0.29	0.09

Source: Author's compilations from March Current Population Survey.
Notes: Regressions also include race, ethnicity, age, age-squared, marital status, state dummies, and year dummies.
*p ≤ 0.05; **p ≤ 0.01

coverage more than it increases private coverage. On the other hand, a wife's work gains a man more in private coverage than it costs in public coverage, even if that work is only part-time or part-year. This effect is significant for both male dropouts and male high school graduates (except for male dropouts whose wives work part-time year-round: the effect of this work on the probability that these men are uninsured is negative, but not significant).

The inclusion of family income in the regression reduces the effect of the em-

TABLE 14.3 / Selected Determinants of Insurance Coverage for High School Graduates Age Eighteen to Fifty-Four, 1988 to 2003

Source of Coverage	Men: Private (1)	Men: Public (2)	Men: Uninsured (3)	Women: Private (4)	Women: Public (5)	Women: Uninsured (6)
State unemployment	0.001	−0.002	0.001	0.002	−0.001	−0.001
rate	(0.001)	(0.001)**	(0.001)	(0.001)	(0.001)	(0.001)
Individual works:						
Full-time, full-	0.432	−0.371	−0.062	0.261	−0.210	−0.051
year	(0.004)**	(0.002)**	(0.004)**	(0.002)**	(0.002)**	(0.002)**
Part-time, full-	0.147	−0.287	0.140	0.121	−0.150	0.028
year	(0.007)**	(0.004)**	(0.007)**	(0.003)**	(0.002)**	(0.003)**
Full-time, part-	0.255	−0.346	0.091	0.128	−0.144	0.015
year	(0.004)**	(0.002)**	(0.004)**	(0.003)**	(0.002)**	(0.003)**
Part-time, part-	0.067	−0.258	0.191	0.082	−0.098	0.016
year	(0.007)**	(0.004)**	(0.007)**	(0.004)**	(0.002)**	(0.003)**
Spouse works:						
Full-time, full-	0.086	−0.046	−0.040	0.173	−0.111	−0.062
year	(0.003)**	(0.002)**	(0.003)**	(0.004)**	(0.003)**	(0.004)**
Part-time, full-	0.055	−0.035	−0.020	0.037	−0.064	0.027
year	(0.005)**	(0.003)**	(0.004)**	(0.009)**	(0.006)**	(0.009)**
Full-time, part-	0.045	−0.022	−0.022	0.087	−0.094	0.007
year	(0.004)**	(0.002)**	(0.004)**	(0.005)**	(0.004)**	(0.005)
Part-time, part-	0.039	−0.016	−0.023	−0.007	−0.048	0.055
year	(0.005)**	(0.003)**	(0.005)**	(0.009)	(0.006)**	(0.009)**
Family income	0.038	−0.008	−0.029	0.041	−0.013	−0.028
(divided by 10,000)	(0.001)**	(0.000)**	(0.001)**	(0.000)**	(0.000)**	(0.000)**
Family income-	−0.001	0.000	0.001	−0.001	0.000	0.001
squared	(0.000)**	(0.000)**	(0.000)**	(0.000)**	(0.000)**	(0.000)**
Observations	170,294	170,294	170,294	189,415	189,415	189,415
R-squared	0.28	0.22	0.17	0.27	0.19	0.10

Source: Author's compilations from March Current Population Survey.
Notes: Regressions also include race, ethnicity, age, age-squared, marital status, state dummies, and year dummies.
*$p \leq 0.05$; **$p \leq 0.01$

ployment variables but does not render them insignificant, suggesting that employment (both one's own and that of a spouse) does have both price and income effects, as hypothesized earlier. To summarize, there seems to be support for the first three mechanisms by which the macroeconomy might affect health insurance coverage.

The general pattern that emerges from these cross-sectional results is that for higher-skilled workers of both sexes, employment translates into higher rates of insurance coverage, while for lower-skilled workers, the gains in private coverage are offset or even overwhelmed by the losses in public coverage. These results begin to suggest a solution to the apparent puzzle of declining coverage among the low-skilled in the booming 1990s.

WHAT EXPLAINS TRENDS IN INSURANCE COVERAGE OVER TIME?

My analysis of trends over time begins with a simple tabulation that answers the question: what were women doing in terms of employment and health insurance in 1992 and 2000? Table 14.4 shows how different groups of potentially vulnerable women (low-skilled and/or single mothers) were distributed across employment and health insurance categories in 1992, 2000, and 2003. Figure 14.10 shows the distribution of female high school dropouts by employment and insurance status in both years based on data from table 14.4. The category with the largest decline between the two periods is "not working, public insurance," which dropped by 8.7 percentage points; the category with the largest increase is "working, no insurance," which increased by 5.3 percentage points. Of course, this does not mean that there was movement from the former cell directly to the latter; these are not the same individuals. But as a simple way of describing what seems to have happened for this group, this chart is compelling. Table 14.4 shows that in the economic downturn that followed, there was an increase of a few percentage points in the category "not working, public insurance," but it does not even come close to its 1992 level.

A similar analysis of the work and health insurance coverage of single mothers who did not complete high school shows similar trends that are even more pronounced. In 1992, 45.6 percent of this group was not working and had public health insurance; in 2000 this figure had fallen to 18.7 percent (figure 14.11). The fraction working and with no health insurance almost doubled, from 16.7 percent in 1992 to 29.2 percent in 2000.

For a more detailed analysis of the factors underlying these changes, I calculate two sets of Blinder-Oaxaca decompositions for coverage rates, one set for the period 1992 to 2000 and another for the period 2000 to 2003. The regression on which the decompositions are based is specified parsimoniously, but with sufficient detail to capture the complex relationships established in the previous section:

$$P(HI) = b_0 + b_1 \cdot \text{(income/employment dummies)} + b_2 \cdot \text{(married)}$$
$$+ b_3 \cdot \text{(Hispanic)} + b_4 \cdot \text{(other demographics)}$$
$$+ \text{(state dummies)} \tag{14.2}$$

As before, $P(HI)$ represents the three different insurance outcomes (private insurance, public insurance, uninsured). The income and employment dummies in-

TABLE 14.4 / Work and Health Insurance Characteristics of Low-Skilled Women, 1992, 2000, and 2003

	1992	2000	2003
All women with education less than high school			
Not working, private health insurance	0.120	0.117	0.106
Not working, public health insurance	0.226	0.139	0.154
Not working, no health insurance	0.132	0.146	0.191
Working, private health insurance	0.293	0.310	0.268
Working, public health insurance	0.063	0.069	0.072
Working, no health insurance	0.167	0.220	0.210
All single mothers			
Not working, private health insurance	0.024	0.020	0.025
Not working, public health insurance	0.212	0.083	0.107
Not working, no health insurance	0.052	0.046	0.064
Working, private health insurance	0.450	0.556	0.493
Working, public health insurance	0.112	0.099	0.109
Working, no health insurance	0.151	0.196	0.203
Single mothers with education less than high school			
Not working, private health insurance	0.029	0.024	0.023
Not working, public health insurance	0.456	0.187	0.213
Not working, no health insurance	0.077	0.112	0.132
Working, private health insurance	0.137	0.197	0.192
Working, public health insurance	0.135	0.189	0.179
Working, no health insurance	0.167	0.292	0.261
Single mothers with education equal to high school			
Not working, private health insurance	0.015	0.019	0.017
Not working, public health insurance	0.191	0.084	0.121
Not working, no health insurance	0.052	0.039	0.066
Working, private health insurance	0.460	0.534	0.443
Working, public health insurance	0.117	0.103	0.106
Working, no health insurance	0.167	0.221	0.246
Single mothers with education greater than high school			
Not working, private health insurance	0.030	0.020	0.031
Not working, public health insurance	0.097	0.044	0.062
Not working, no health insurance	0.037	0.028	0.039
Working, private health insurance	0.615	0.704	0.627
Working, public health insurance	0.095	0.062	0.087
Working, no health insurance	0.126	0.142	0.154

Source: Author's compilations from March Current Population Survey.

FIGURE 14.10 / Trends in Work and Insurance for Women Age Twenty-Five to Fifty-Four and with Less Than a High School Education, 1992 and 2000

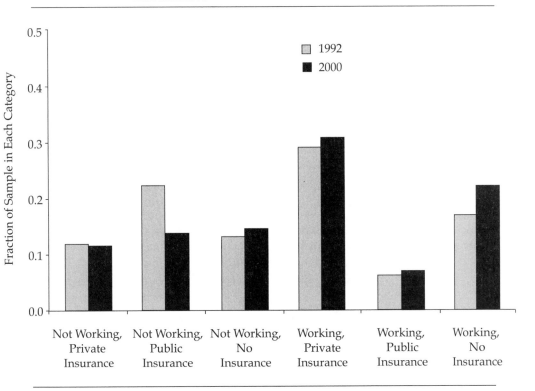

Source: Author's compilations from Current Population Survey.

clude fourteen categories of family income relative to poverty level, interacted fully with an indicator for whether the individual or his or her spouse is working. Married and Hispanic are simply dummy variables. "Other demographics" include race dummies (black, other nonwhite), age, and age-squared.

The results are presented in table 14.5 (for the period 1992 to 2000) and table 14.6 (for the period 2000 to 2003).[9] Table 14.5 tells the following story: between 1992 and 2000, men and women at all education levels experienced increases in private coverage. For low-skilled women, these increases are entirely explained by increases in employment and income that were slightly offset by increases in the fraction Hispanic and declines in the probability of being married.[10] These same gains in income and employment triggered reductions in public coverage for low-skilled women that exactly offset the gains in private coverage. There were, in addition, large unexplained declines in public coverage for low-skilled

FIGURE 14.11   /   Trends in Work and Insurance for Single Mothers Age Twenty-five
to Fifty-four and with Less Than a High School Education, 1992
and 2000

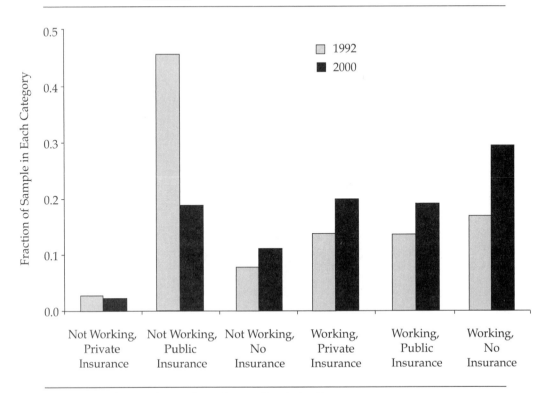

Source: Author's compilations from Current Population Survey.

women (more on these later). As a result, the fraction of low-skilled women who
were uninsured went up.

Looking next at what happened during the subsequent economic downturn,
the decompositions for 2000 to 2003 analyze across-the-board increases in the
fraction uninsured (table 14.6). Here the story is more predictable than what
happened during the boom: for all groups, private insurance declined, and about
half of the decline is explained by changes in the joint distribution of income and
employment. Public coverage increased, but not enough to offset the declines in
private coverage; as a result, the fraction uninsured went up. An important difference between the 1992 to 2000 changes and those in 2000 to 2003 is the nature
of the unexplained changes in private coverage. During the expansion, the unexplained changes in private coverage were positive for all groups except low-
skilled women. During the downturn, on the other hand, a substantial portion
of the change in private coverage for each group was due to an unexplained

TABLE 14.5 / Changes in Health Insurance between 1992 and 2000: Blinder-Oaxaca Decomposition

	Men			Women		
Coverage type:	Private	Public	Unin-sured	Private	Public	Unin-sured
Education less than high school						
Change, 1992 to 2000	0.024	−0.029	0.005	0.014	−0.081	0.067
Due to coefficients	0.008	−0.003	−0.005	−0.014	−0.029	0.042
Due to characteristics	0.016	−0.026	0.010	0.028	−0.052	0.025
Income or employment	0.028	−0.018	−0.009	0.041	−0.048	0.006
Marriage	−0.001	0.000	0.002	−0.001	0.001	0.000
Hispanic	−0.009	−0.006	0.015	−0.009	−0.001	0.010
Other demographics	0.002	−0.001	0.000	0.000	−0.002	0.002
State-level factors	−0.003	0.000	0.003	−0.003	−0.003	0.006
Education equal to high school						
Change	0.029	−0.004	−0.025	0.009	−0.017	0.008
Due to coefficients	0.023	0.000	−0.023	−0.004	−0.007	0.011
Due to characteristics	0.006	−0.005	−0.002	0.013	−0.011	−0.002
Income or employment	0.015	−0.002	−0.013	0.016	−0.008	−0.008
Marriage	−0.009	−0.001	0.010	−0.002	0.000	0.002
Hispanic	−0.001	0.000	0.002	−0.001	0.000	0.001
Other demographics	0.004	−0.001	−0.003	0.003	−0.004	0.001
State-level factors	−0.002	0.000	0.002	−0.003	0.000	0.003
Education greater than high school						
Change	0.027	−0.010	−0.017	0.007	−0.011	0.004
Due to coefficients	0.022	−0.007	−0.014	0.000	−0.006	0.006
Due to characteristics	0.005	−0.003	−0.003	0.007	−0.005	−0.002
Income or employment	0.010	−0.002	−0.008	0.009	−0.005	−0.004
Marriage	−0.002	0.000	0.002	0.000	0.000	0.000
Hispanic	−0.001	0.000	0.001	−0.001	0.000	0.001
Other demographics	−0.002	0.000	0.002	0.000	−0.001	0.001
State-level factors	−0.001	0.000	0.000	0.000	0.000	0.000

Source: Author's compilations from March Current Population Survey.

negative shift. Therefore, the main puzzles that remain to be solved are the unexplained decrease in public coverage among low-skilled women during the boom and the unexplained decrease in private coverage during the subsequent bust.

DISCUSSION

The analysis so far has established a number of useful facts that help explain what happened to health insurance coverage during the expansion of the 1990s

TABLE 14.6 / Changes in Health Insurance Between 2000 and 2003: Blinder-Oaxaca
Decomposition

	Men			Women		
Coverage Type	Private	Public	Unin-sured	Private	Public	Unin-sured
Education less than high school						
Change, 2000 to 2003	−0.067	0.017	0.050	−0.053	0.018	0.035
Due to coefficients	−0.033	0.006	0.027	−0.031	0.011	0.020
Due to characteristics	−0.033	0.011	0.023	−0.022	0.007	0.015
Income or employment	−0.017	0.016	0.001	−0.017	0.010	0.007
Marriage	−0.009	0.000	0.010	0.001	−0.001	−0.001
Hispanic	−0.005	−0.003	0.008	−0.005	−0.004	0.008
Other demographics	−0.003	−0.001	0.004	−0.003	0.001	0.001
State-level factors	0.001	−0.001	0.000	0.001	0.000	−0.001
Education equal to high school						
Change	−0.071	0.017	0.055	−0.061	0.021	0.040
Due to coefficients	−0.044	0.003	0.041	−0.037	0.009	0.028
Due to characteristics	−0.028	0.014	0.014	−0.024	0.012	0.012
Income or employment	−0.017	0.013	0.004	−0.020	0.012	0.008
Marriage	−0.005	0.000	0.005	−0.001	0.000	0.001
Hispanic	−0.003	−0.001	0.004	−0.002	0.000	0.002
Other demographics	−0.001	0.001	0.000	−0.001	0.000	0.001
State-level factors	−0.001	0.000	0.001	0.000	0.000	0.000
Education greater than high school						
Change	−0.036	0.008	0.029	−0.032	0.014	0.018
Due to coefficients	−0.022	0.002	0.020	−0.019	0.007	0.012
Due to characteristics	−0.014	0.006	0.009	−0.013	0.007	0.006
Income or employment	−0.011	0.006	0.005	−0.012	0.007	0.004
Marriage	−0.001	0.000	0.001	0.000	0.000	0.000
Hispanic	−0.001	0.000	0.002	−0.001	0.000	0.001
Other demographics	−0.001	0.000	0.001	0.000	0.000	0.001
State-level factors	0.000	0.000	0.000	0.000	0.000	0.000

Source: Author's compilations from March Current Population Survey.

and the subsequent downturn. As noted, two residual puzzles about this period
remain.

Why Did Public Coverage Decline So Much Between 1992 and 2000?

As the data presented here have shown, the decline in public coverage between
1992 and 2000 went well beyond what increases in incomes and employment
can explain. There are a number of possible explanations:

WELFARE REFORM   The Personal Responsibility and Work Opportunity Reconciliation Act (PRWORA) of 1996 and the demonstration waivers that preceded it may have reduced take-up of Medicaid among the target population for these programs, even though eligibility for Medicaid actually expanded as welfare was contracting. There is much concern and speculation in the welfare reform literature that this is true and that Medicaid was in some sense an unintended casualty of welfare reform (see, for example, Ellwood and Ku 1998; Garrett and Holohan 2000). It is difficult to isolate the effects of welfare reform—as opposed to the effects of the economic expansion that occurred at the same time—on Medicaid. Perhaps surprisingly, the two studies that have attempted to do this both conclude that welfare reform did *not* have a large negative effect on Medicaid coverage.[11] Robert Kaestner and Neeraj Kaushal (2003) find that reductions in welfare caseloads are correlated with reductions in Medicaid caseloads. They note, however, that welfare caseloads declined both because of welfare reform and because of the booming economy and that the welfare caseload declines that resulted from welfare reform had a smaller effect on Medicaid caseloads than did those resulting from other factors. That is, they conclude that welfare reform may not have had the negative effect on public health insurance coverage that earlier studies had hypothesized. Similarly, Thomas DeLeire, Judith Levine, and I (DeLeire, Levine, and Levy 2006) find that neither the welfare waivers that preceded welfare reform nor the implementation of Temporary Assistance for Needy Families (TANF) is associated with significant reductions in Medicaid coverage among low-skilled women.[12]

These results are surprising in light of the widespread presumption that welfare reform must have pushed many Medicaid-eligibles off the rolls. It seems that the jury must remain out on whether welfare reform was directly responsible for reductions in Medicaid caseloads. It is worth noting, however, that the hypothesized declines in Medicaid because of welfare reform are due to lower take-up among eligibles rather than declines in eligibility. This may or may not warrant the same degree of policy concern that actual declines in eligibility would. Unlike, for example, food stamps, Medicaid is an insurance program, the value of which is realized primarily in the event of an accident or illness—regardless of whether or not the recipient was enrolled before the event occurs. To the extent that declines in rates of public coverage are driven by these changes in take-up rather than eligibility, policy concern should focus on improving access to care among unenrolled populations who are likely to get a health benefit from improved access, such as the chronically ill. Further research is necessary on how actual enrollment—as opposed to eligibility—affects access to medical care. Expansions of the medical care safety net may also have reduced enrollment in Medicaid among eligible individuals (Lo Sasso and Meyer 2003), again, with unclear effects on access to medical care.

DECLINES IN ELIGIBILITY FOR PUBLIC INSURANCE   While declines in eligibility for public insurance may, in theory, explain declining public coverage, all the available evidence suggests that this did not happen during the 1990s.

PRWORA specifically required that Medicaid eligibility levels remain at or above the income eligibility thresholds in effect for AFDC at the time AFDC was replaced by TANF. In addition, many states *expanded* coverage of adults through their SCHIP programs (see Aizer and Grogger 2002). In the economic downturn that followed the boom, states generally seem to have maintained Medicaid eligibility levels (National Governors' Association 2003, 2005), although some employed other strategies to reduce Medicaid spending—such as freezing reimbursements to providers (Coughlin and Zuckerman 2005)—that may have reduced Medicaid recipients' access to medical care.

MEASURES OF MEDICAID COVERAGE IN THE CPS   Measures of Medicaid coverage in the Current Population Survey may have become less accurate following welfare reform. It is well known that household surveys result in underestimates of Medicaid coverage (see Card, Hildreth, and Shore-Sheppard 2004; Klerman, Ringel, and Roth 2005). In an attempt to correct for underreporting of Medicaid, the Census Bureau imputes Medicaid coverage to welfare recipients. Prior to welfare reform, this imputation presumably captured a large fraction of adults who were eligible for Medicaid as a result of AFDC receipt but may not have reported Medicaid coverage. Following welfare reform, when a larger number of adults not receiving cash transfers were in fact eligible for Medicaid, this imputation would capture a smaller fraction of the truly Medicaid-eligible population. It is unclear how much these changes in measurement error over time—which are, by definition, correlated with welfare reform—may have contributed to the apparent declines in Medicaid coverage measured in the CPS. To the extent that the declines in rates of public coverage are driven by these changes in the accuracy of measurement, policy concern should be directed not toward the uninsured but toward the designers of large-scale government surveys.

These possible explanations for the unexplained declines in Medicaid coverage—lower take-up among eligibles, declines in eligibility, and changes in measurement error in data collection—have very different policy implications, and distinguishing among them should be a high priority for future research.

What Explains the Changes in Private Coverage Between 1992 and 2000?

The unexplained changes in private coverage between 1992 and 2000 constitute the other residual puzzle about this period. Such changes during the downturn of 2000 to 2003 are uniformly negative and therefore consistent with the popular notion that increasing health insurance premiums were responsible for declining coverage. Interestingly, however, this popular notion is *not* consistent with what the data show during the 1992 to 2000 expansion. The unexplained changes in private coverage (controlling for income and employment) during that period were generally positive. That is, unobserved factors affecting private coverage *increased* private coverage rather than decreased it. The increase in health insurance premiums may have been one unobserved factor that affected coverage, but if so, it was overwhelmed by the contribution of other unobserved factors. Reconciling this result with other research that attributes declining coverage during the 1990s to rising health insurance costs (see, for example, Chernew, Cutler, and Keenan 2004; Cutler 2002) is a high priority for future research.

CONCLUSIONS

Health insurance was the proverbial boat not lifted by the rising tide of the 1990s. The analysis of this chapter has shown that the main reason for this was that another current—unexplained declines in public coverage—swamped the rising tide for low-skilled women.

Whether these declines in public coverage are reason for concern awaits further information on their causes and consequences. Good evidence on the impact of health insurance on health outcomes is surprisingly rare (Levy and Meltzer 2004). The health of the economy may also affect health directly, though not necessarily in predictable ways. Christopher Ruhm (2004) reviews a growing body of evidence suggesting that economic bad times are good for your health; morbidity and mortality decline and health behaviors improve during a recession. As Ruhm points out, however, these results describe the relationship between transitory output fluctuations and health. The long-term relationship between economic status and health is likely to be the opposite (see, for example, Deaton 2002). We remain far from understanding the role of economic resources—including but not limited to health insurance and access to medical care—in producing health, and perhaps equally far from understanding the importance of health insurance to economic security.

NOTES

1. John Holohan and Mary Beth Pohl (2002) report a similar result for adults in families with incomes below 200 percent of the federal poverty level.
2. It is also true that a worker with COBRA coverage must typically pay the full premium (employer share plus employee share), which sounds like a price change. Under the assumption that the full incidence of the cost of benefits is on workers, this apparent increase in price is more appropriately modeled as a decrease in income.
3. Or it could shift toward jobs that are *more* likely to provide benefits; Henry Farber and I (Farber and Levy 2000) find that the part-time rate is (insignificantly) lower in slack labor markets. Low-tenure jobs are also less prevalent in slack labor markets.
4. The question of exactly *how* wages vary over the business cycle is unsettled; for more on this debate, see Solon, Barsky, and Parker (1994), Abraham and Haltiwanger (1995), Devereux (2001), and Shin and Solon (2004). Whatever the cyclicality of wages, benefits may experience the same pattern as wages, a different pattern, or no cyclicality.

5. It is reasonable to ask which public health insurance programs serve nonelderly men, and for what reasons. Just over half (55 percent) of publicly insured men in 1992 were disabled, and they were about equally likely to have Medicare or Medicaid. Another 9 percent received some form of cash assistance (Social Security, supplemental security income, or other public assistance) that may have qualified them for public insurance. Very few (2 percent) were veterans. Another 8 percent lived in poverty, and another 7 percent had children and families with income between 100 and 200 percent of the poverty level and therefore may have been eligible for programs targeting the parents of children eligible for the State Child Health Insurance Program (SCHIP). The remaining 19 percent had no characteristics reported in the CPS that might explain their eligibility for public coverage. The increase in public coverage among men between 2000 and 2003 is entirely in this unexplained group, so the data do not suggest an obvious mechanism through which men gain public coverage during an economic downturn.

6. Estimating a pooled regression for men at all three education levels yields results that are generally similar to those reported in Cawley and Simon (2005), in spite of the differences in data (they use the SIPP) and specification (they estimate fixed-effect conditional logit models). The coefficient on the state unemployment rate in my pooled specification for men is –0.006 for private coverage (significant with $p < 0.01$), 0.001 for public coverage (not significant), and 0.005 for uninsured (significant with $p < 0.01$). Comparable results from Cawley and Simon (2005) would be an effect of –0.013 for employer coverage ($p < 0.05$), –0.006 (not significant) for public coverage, and 0.007 ($p < 0.01$) for uninsured.

7. My results for women on average (not reported in table 14.1) are slightly different from those of Cawley and Simon (2005). Like them, I find that the unemployment rate has a significant negative effect on private coverage for women and an insignificant effect on public coverage. But I find a significant increase of one-fifth of a percentage point in the probability of being uninsured associated with each percentage-point increase in the unemployment rate, while they find exactly zero effect on the probability of any insurance overall.

8. If income is not included in the regression, the effect of own full-time, full-year employment on the probability of being uninsured is smaller but still positive and significant for male dropouts (0.042 with a standard error of 0.005); for female dropouts, the coefficient on own full-time, full-year employment becomes negative and weakly significant when income is omitted (–0.009 with a standard error of 0.004).

9. The decomposition is not particularly sensitive to the choice of endpoints. Changes in private health insurance are smaller (and in some cases negative) for all groups when the starting point is 1991; otherwise, varying the starting and/or ending point by one year does not change the basic story.

10. Citizenship information is not available in the CPS before survey year 1994 (corresponding in this analysis to calendar year 1993). To test how much of the estimated effect of Hispanic ethnicity among high school dropouts is actually due to changes in citizenship, I reestimated the decompositions both with and without citizenship information for the periods 1993 to 2000 and 2000 to 2003. The majority of the His-

panic effect for both male and female dropouts is explained by citizenship when both are included in the model, in both periods.

11. Marianne Bitler, Jonah Gelbach, and Hilary Hoynes (2005) analyze the impact of welfare reform on health insurance coverage, but the data they use in their analysis do not distinguish between private and public health insurance coverage and therefore cannot be used to isolate the independent effect of welfare reform on Medicaid coverage.

12. DeLeire, Levine, and I (DeLeire, Levine, and Levy 2006) find a large but not statistically significant effect of TANF on public coverage among single mothers with less than a high school education: a 3.6-percentage-point reduction with a standard error of 2.2 percentage points. Negative effects are therefore not ruled out, but the evidence remains inconclusive.

REFERENCES

Abraham, Katherine G., and John C. Haltiwanger. 1995. "Real Wages and the Business Cycle." *Journal of Economic Literature* 33(3, September): 1215–64.

Aizer, Anna, and Jeff Grogger. 2002. "Parental Medicaid Expansions and Health Insurance Coverage." Working paper 9036. Cambridge, Mass.: National Bureau of Economic Research (July).

Bitler, Marianne, Jonah Gelbach, and Hilary Hoynes. 2005. "Welfare Reform and Health." *Journal of Human Resources* 40(2): 309–34.

Bundorf, Kate. 2002. "Employee Demand for Health Insurance and Employer Health Plan Choices." *Journal of Health Economics* 21: 65–88.

Card, David, Andrew Hildreth, and Lara Shore-Sheppard. 2004. *"The Measurement of Medicaid Coverage in the SIPP: Evidence from a Comparison of Matched Records."* *Journal of Business and Economic Statistics* 22(4): 410–20.

Cawley, John, and Kosali I. Simon. 2005. "Health Insurance Coverage and the Macroeconomy." *Journal of Health Economics* 24(2, March): 299–315.

Chernew, Michael, David Cutler, and Patricia Keenan. 2004. *"Increasing Health Insurance Costs and the Decline in Insurance Coverage."* Working paper 8. Ann Arbor: University of Michigan, Economic Research Initiative on the Uninsured (April). Available at: http://www.umich.edu/~eriu/pdf/wp8.pdf.

Coughlin, Theresa A., and Stephen Zuckerman. 2005. "Three Years of State Fiscal Struggles: How Did Medicaid and SCHIP Fare?" *Health Affairs* web exclusive (August 16). See http://www.healthaffairs.org.

Cutler, David. 2002. "Employee Costs and the Decline in Health Insurance Coverage." Working paper 9036. Cambridge, Mass.: National Bureau of Economic Research (July).

Deaton, Angus. 2002. "Policy Implications of the Gradient of Health and Wealth." *Health Affairs* 21(2, March–April): 13–30.

DeLeire, Thomas, Judith Levine, and Helen Levy. 2006. "Is Welfare Reform Responsible for Low-Skilled Women's Declining Health Insurance Coverage?" *Journal of Human Resources* XLI(3): 467–94.

DeNavas-Walt, Carmen, Bernadette D. Proctor, and Robert J. Mills. 2004. "Income, Poverty, and Health Insurance Coverage in the United States: 2003." *Current Population Reports* P60–226. Washington: U.S. Bureau of the Census (August).

Devereux, Paul J. 2001. "The Cyclicality of Real Wages Within Employer-Employee Matches." *Industrial and Labor Relations Review* 54(4, July): 835–50.

Ellwood, Marilyn R., and Leighton Ku. 1998. "Welfare and Immigration Reforms: Unintended Side Effects for Medicaid." *Health Affairs* 17(3, May–June): 137–51.

Farber, Henry S., and Helen Levy. 2000. "Recent Trends in Employer-Sponsored Health Insurance Coverage: Are Bad Jobs Getting Worse?" *Journal of Health Economics* 19(1, January): 93–119.

Garrett, Bowen, and John Holohan. 2000. "Health Insurance Coverage After Welfare." *Health Affairs* (January–February): 175–84.

Goldstein, Gerald S., and Mark V. Pauly. 1976. "Group Health Insurance as a Local Public Good." In *The Role of Health Insurance in the Health Services Sector*, edited by Richard N. Rosett. New York: National Bureau of Economic Research.

Gruber, Jonathan, and Brigitte C. Madrian. 1997. "Employment Separation and Health Insurance Coverage." *Journal of Public Economics* 66(3, December): 349–82.

Holohan, John, and Mary Beth Pohl. 2002. "Changes in Insurance Coverage: 1994–2000 and Beyond." *Health Affairs* web exclusive (April). See *http://www.healthaffairs.org*.

Kaestner, Robert, and Neeraj Kaushal. 2003. "Welfare Reform and the Health Insurance Coverage of Low-Income Families." *Journal of Health Economics* 22: 959–81.

Klerman, Jacob Alex, Jeanne S. Ringel, and Beth Roth. 2005. "Underreporting of Medicaid and Welfare in the Current Population Survey." Working paper WR-169–3. Santa Monica, Calif.: RAND Corporation (March).

Levy, Helen, and David Meltzer. 2004. "What Do We Really Know About Whether Health Insurance Affects Health?" In *Health Policy and the Uninsured: Setting the Agenda*, edited by Catherine McLaughlin. Washington, D.C.: Urban Institute Press.

Lo Sasso, Anthony T., and Bruce Meyer. 2003. "The Health Care Safety Net and Crowd-Out of Private Health Insurance." Working paper. Evanston, Ill.: Northwestern University, Institute for Policy Research (May).

National Governors' Association. Various issues, January 1990 to September 1997. "MCH Update: State Coverage of Pregnant Women and Children." Available at: www.nga.org.

———. 1998. "MCH Update: Early State Trends in Setting Eligibility Levels for Children and Pregnant Women" (September). Available at: www.nga.org.

———. 2000. "Income Eligibility for Pregnant Women and Children" (January). Available at: www.nga.org.

———. 2001. "Maternal and Child Health (MCH) Update: States Have Expanded Eligibility and Increased Access to Health Care for Pregnant Women and Children" (February). Available at: www.nga.org.

———. 2002. "MCH Update 2001: Trends in State Health Insurance Coverage of Pregnant Women, Children, and Parents" (May). Available at: www.nga.org.

———. 2003. "MCH Update 2002: State Health Coverage for Low-Income Pregnant Women, Children, and Parents" (June). Available at: www.nga.org.

———. 2005. "MCH Update: States Protect Health Care Coverage During Recent Fiscal Downturn" (August). Available at: www.nga.org.

Ruhm, Christopher. 2004. "Macroeconomic Conditions, Health, and Mortality." Working paper 11007. Cambridge, Mass.: National Bureau of Economic Research (December).

Shin, Donggyun, and Gary Solon. 2004. "New Evidence on Real Wage Cyclicality Using Employer-Employee Matches." Unpublished paper. Ann Arbor: University of Michigan.

Solon, Gary, Robert Barsky, and Jonathan A. Parker. 1994. "Measuring the Cyclicality of Real Wages: How Important Is Composition Bias?" *Quarterly Journal of Economics* 109(1, February): 1–25.

Index

Boldface numbers refer to figures and tables.